TEOKRATIA

"Part travelogue, part history, and part theological reflection, Matthew Dal Santo's new book not only tells a gripping story, but makes a bold and profound argument that demands attention from anyone moved to ponder the big-picture political questions. Dal Santo brilliantly connects themes of contemporary relevance with 'old Russia' by unfolding a journey in which he explores the rise and fall of the Romanov family, who were brutally executed a century ago, and investigates how the family is perceived now, in light of their recent canonization. At the heart of his reflections stand two figures, Nicholas II and the theologian Sergei Bulgakov: the tsar represents the fate of *Teokratia* in Russia, the idea that political rule is a sacred office, and the theologian provides the occasion to grapple with the theological significance of authority and the question whether theocracy in some form can still have meaning today. Dal Santo makes a convincing case that the notion of a 'theology of history,' far from being an arcane remnant from the long-gone middle ages, is desperately needed today to make sense of our current global-political condition."

—**DAVID C. SCHINDLER**, Professor of Metaphysics and Anthropology at The John Paul II Institute in Washington DC, author of *The Politics of the Real*

"This extraordinary book is several things at once. It is a scholarly life of Nicholas II set against its background in the history of Imperial Russia. It is a journalist's investigation of attitudes to the martyrs of the Romanov family among ordinary Russians today. It is a travelogue of descriptions, often astonishingly beautiful, of the scenes where the final drama of the dynasty unfolded. It is also — and this will not easily be found among other accounts of the coming of the revolutions of 1917 — a plea to re-examine the significance of 'sacral' monarchy, understood as the symbolization of a Christ-centered cosmic order in which ultimate norms and values are raised above the simple adjudication, whether democratic or bureaucratic, of practical affairs. And finally, it is a retrieval of the thinking in this regard of that audacious Orthodox intellectual, Sergei Bulgakov, for whom the political transformations of the modern era issue ineluctably from the collapse of the metaphysical tradition of the West. Hence the fragility, bordering potentially on nihilism, of shared meaning in our public space. Readers are invited to draw from the author's fast-moving yet deeply reflective narrative their own 'theo-political' conclusions."

—**AIDAN NICHOLS OP**, author of *The Thought of Pope Benedict XVI* and *The Shape of Catholic Theology*

"In the pages of *Teokratia*, Matthew Dal Santo masterfully blends political theology and historiography to offer a unique account of the Russian Revolution as a paradigm of modern secularism. Dal Santo's genius for reading history in light of theology, and theology in light of history, recalls Christopher Dawson and Reinhold Schneider; it has no equal on the contemporary scene. Anyone wishing to understand the Russian experience from within, to plumb the meaning of modernity, or to grasp the cosmo-political implications of Christianity should carefully study this book."

—**ADRIAN WALKER**, Professor of Philosophy and Dogmatics, Saint Patrick's Seminary and University

"Inspired by the writings of Russian polymath Fr. Sergei Bulgakov, Dal Santo has written an engaging, provocative, and highly original interpretation of the meaning of Russian history which takes as its premise Bulgakov's view that all authority, including all political authority, derives from God. Writing at the beginning of the 20th century, Bulgakov argued that this connection had been lost, 'condemned by history' as he put it—but a hundred years later Dal Santo traces its re-emergence in Russian culture. In so doing he opens up for Western readers a modern Byzantine view of politics, in which true political authority does not emerge from self-anointed masses, but is received as a gift from above. Much of our mutual antagonism, he argues, can be traced back to this profound difference between the Russian and Western political imaginations."

—**NICOLAI N. PETRO**, Professor of Political Science, University of Rhode Island

"In *Teokratia: The Theocratic Principle in Russia, 1917 and Today*, Matthew Dal Santo skillfully brings forward and updates—and I would add *deepens*—the analysis of Russia's political order first brought to our attention by the Italian philosopher Augusto Del Noce. He does so by means of a sustained meditation on the political-philosophical and theological writings of Fr. Sergei Bulgakov, Russia's greatest 20th-century theologian, coupled with a sympathetic and yet realistic and never romanticized close observation of Russian realities. The result is one of the most important works yet in existence on Russia. *Teokratia* is absolutely essential reading for all those who want to understand Russia—as opposed to wanting to impose onto it the West's own self-image."

—**PAUL GRENIER**, president of the Simone Weil Center for Political Philosophy

ΤϵΟΗΚΑΤΙΑ

The Theocratic Principle
in Russia, 1917 and Today

MATTHEW J. DAL SANTO

Angelico Press

For information, address:
Angelico Press, Ltd.
169 Monitor St.
Brooklyn, NY 11222
www.angelicopress.com

ppr   979-8-89280-117-1
cloth   979-8-89280-118-8

Book and cover design
by Michael Schrauzer

For the Russian people

. . . everything, everything was predetermined in those days when the inner link of Russia, its historical tie, its determining form of life was broken. Isn't that what philosophers call entelechy? Well, Russia lost its State entelechy. Russia is a tsardom, or in general it is nothing.

"The General," *At the Feast of the Gods*

All the events of our revolution are known in Europe in the minutest detail, but their underlying meaning remains a mystery. Europe sees the body but not the soul of the Russian revolution . . . the Russian revolution is not only a political phenomenon; it is a religious one. This is what Europe understands only with difficulty.

Dmitri Merezhkovsky, *Le Tsar et la Révolution*

God has always willed that there should be a ruling authority, and that they who are invested with it should reflect the divine power and providence in some measure over the human race.

Pope Leo XIII, *Immortale Dei*

CONTENTS

FOREWORD

HE RELEASE OF *TEOKRATIA: THE THEOCRATIC Principle in Russia, 1917 and Today* by Matthew J. Dal Santo amid yet another peak of Russophobia—a sentiment that has, to varying degrees, shaped Anglophone discourse for centuries—is a significant achievement. It provides a much-needed alternative to the reductive narratives propagated by Western media and much of academia, which so often depict Putin as the embodiment of evil and his actions as a militant campaign to restore either the Soviet or Imperial Russian empire. This remarkable book challenges these oversimplified portrayals, aspiring instead to foster a deeper understanding of Russia's cultural and historical matrix. Inviting readers to move beyond narratives that reduce a thousand-year-old civilization to a simplistic dichotomy between "good" and "evil" (often packaged for passive consumption in the style of a Hollywood western), it addresses the concept of the true *Imperium*—a dominion either dedicated to the glory of God or constructed in defiance of Him. This exploration of the sacred and the political, intertwined in the theocratic mystery of power, elevates the discussion beyond contemporary political debates. Against this broad and profound backdrop, many accounts of Putin's Russia that misunderstand or superficially engage with this theocratic dimension are diminished to little more than lightweight, "pleasant Sunday-afternoon" literature. Ultimately, this book serves as both a critique of prevailing Western narratives and an invitation to explore Russia's complex cultural, religious, and historical landscape on its own terms. It offers readers an opportunity to reframe their understanding, free from propaganda and oversimplification, fostering a spring of intellectual and cultural insight.

The book weaves together three interconnected narratives: the *first* examines the fate of the last Russian Tsar, Nicholas II, and his family, along with his imperial predecessors, reflecting on the history of the theocratic principle within Orthodox Christianity; the *second* explores the personal journey of Sergei Bulgakov, a leading figure in Russian religious philosophy, offering a theological interpretation of history, enriched by other influential thinkers of Christian Hellenism and Russian Orthodoxy spanning from the Church Fathers to 20th-century scholars; the *third* recounts the author's personal journey (he describes himself as a "spiritual voyeur") through the Russian homeland, delving deeper into Orthodox Christianity and its theocratic traditions.

The first narrative, centered on Tsar Nicholas II, initially appears to recount the political and social history of that era, but the author then shifts focus to the Tsar's religious life and relationship with God, framing his actions as a profound alignment with the moral-religious ideal of Orthodox Christian *teokratia*. This is the perspective that provides justification for imperial decisions and political events that Western historians too often dismiss as failures to adapt to modern realities. Rather than attributing these actions solely to the personal faith of Nicholas II, the author highlights their grounding in a centuries-old theological vision.

As the second narrative unfolds, the history of Imperial Russia—in particular, the story of the last Tsar—becomes an illustration of Bulgakov's theological interpretation of history, where the sacred and the political converge in the ideal of *teokratia*. This principle, established by St. Constantine the Great and nurtured by Byzantine and Russian emperors, is central to the mystical experience of universal Orthodoxy. For Nicholas II, *teokratia* was not a peripheral element but deeply embedded in the Eucharistic liturgy. The author does not however depict Bulgakov as a defender of Tsarism or autocracy cloaked in mystical ideals; instead, he points out Bulgakov's critiques of the misuse of *teokratia* through the fetishization of dogma, the substitution of sacrament with ecstasy, and the transformation of religion into mysticism (a tendency to which Nicholas II and the Empress were particularly susceptible).

The third narrative presents the author's personal testimony from key sites linked to the life of the last Tsar from his coronation to his murder and subsequent canonization. This journey—spanning Moscow, St. Petersburg, Tsarskoye Selo, Crimea, Belarus, Pskov, Tobolsk, Tyumen, and Ekaterinburg—offers vivid descriptions of significant locations, conversations with locals, and reflections on Orthodox spirituality. This blend of historical analysis and personal experience lends the book its unique depth and resonance.

Matthew J. Dal Santo's *Teokratia: The Theocratic Principle in Russia, 1917 and Today* masterfully blends meticulous historical research with profound insights from Russian religious philosophers, while also serving as a deeply personal introduction to Orthodoxy. On first reading, the book will captivate attentive readers, compelling them to uncover its intertwined narratives; and yet it also invites revisiting—whether to explore its sources or reflect on its nuanced passages. Accessible to both newcomers and experts, it offers a vivid exploration of *teokratia*, Russia, and Orthodoxy. Ultimately, the book carries us beyond solely intellectual depth into profoundly lived experience—proof that life itself writes the most compelling stories.

Vladimir Cvetković, Principal Research Fellow,
Institute for Philosophy and Social Theory,
University of Belgrade

ACKNOWLEDGMENTS

AS ANYONE WHO HAS WORKED ON ANYTHING for a long time will know, coming to the end of a project like this is attended with a sense of unreality. It scarcely seems believable that, almost ten years since the visit to the Danilov Monastery described in Chapter One, the odyssey—for an odyssey it was, which took me from one end of Russia to the other, including to many places (the reader will be relieved to hear) *not* described in this book—that that experience set in motion should now, at last, be over. In many ways, it has often felt like a very lonely path to tread, and there have been not a few occasions when I have wondered whether it would not be healthier to set it aside. The project began in 2014 with a research grant from the Danish Council for Independent Research, and the initial travel in Russia, during which I observed what I later came to describe as the "revival" or "regeneration" of the theocratic principle in Russian culture, was made possible through that grant and a research fellowship at the University of Copenhagen's Saxo Institute. Unfortunately, however, when after two years that grant and the associated fellowship expired, no other body in Denmark or Scandinavia could be found as sponsor, and the project continued for a long time under my own resources. In 2019, however, a residential fellowship at the Wilson Center's Kennan Institute for Russian and Eastern European Affairs, as well as a visiting fellowship at the Catholic University of America's (now unfortunately disbanded) Center for the Study of Statesmanship—both in Washington, DC—allowed the project to continue and, indeed, to develop. It was in the Kennan Institute's wonderful library that I first read Bulgakov's *Autobiographical Fragments*, and the properly theological shape and nature of the project became clear to me. I thank all the organizations named in this paragraph for their generous support.

Among the private individuals I would thank, first and foremost must be my dear friend and colleague at the Simone Weil Center for Political Philosophy Paul Grenier, who, to my mind, knows Russia, Russian culture, and especially Russian philosophy and Russia's contemporary intellectual scene better than anyone else currently living outside Russia and from whom I have learnt more than it is possible to record here. In relation to the Simone Weil Center, I also thank Professor Nicolai Petro of the University of Rhode Island for so generously reading an earlier (and much longer) version of this manuscript and commenting on it so encouragingly. I also thank him for supporting the application that took me to the Kennan Institute, as I also thank Dr Andrew Monaghan of the Royal Institute for International Affairs (Chatham House) for doing the same. I also thank Professor Claes Ryn and Dr Bill Smith for their support at the former Center for the Study of Statesmanship. I also thank Professor Marlene Laruelle of George Washington University for generously sharing copies of her work with me: the footnotes do not do justice to the place her work has had in helping me form a view of contemporary Russia. Of course, this by no means implies that any of those named should be tarred with the brush of my conclusions.

Among my friends and colleagues today at St Patrick's, I thank especially Professor Margaret Turek for her example as a theologian, and Professor Adrian Walker for the innumerable discussions about theology, philosophy, and politics without which this book would simply never have attained such depth as it has succeeded in attaining. I also thank my students in Church History and Patristics for helping me think through these questions even without their really knowing it. I also thank the editors of the *Communio*, *Telos*, *First Things*, and *New Polity* journals for publishing my recent work. I thank Tatiana Wilde for reading a first draft of the manuscript twice as long as the published book, catching many errors and helping me clarify my thoughts. Again, this should not be taken to mean that any of the people here named agree with the conclusions I have reached or the book I have written.

Among my friends I thank especially Academy Travel's Paula Booth for shared delight in all things Russian (and for her example in the courage, in today's unfortunate conditions, to continue to declare it) as well as all those who have traveled with us in Russia over the years. I thank Ben Tate for crucial encouragement over several years with the writing of this manuscript, even if our original plans for it did not work out. I also thank my dear friend, Dr Diana Adis-Tahhan, for sharing the agony and ecstasy of writing (as well as for my first acquaintance with the faith — and Easter customs! — of the Eastern Church), and another dear friend, Alexander Søndergaard, for listening politely while always remaining, I think, unconvinced!

And then, of course, there is my family. As always, I thank my mother and father for their unstinting support in all things — and especially in relation to this book to Dad for joining me the very first time I traveled to Russia, at the age of 21, in 2002 as well as to Mum for letting him go both that time and again in 2018 when we "conquered" Kamchatka. I am also very grateful to my mother-in-law, Bente Lønstrup, for making it possible for me to travel so often and so widely in Russia when my and my wife's daughter was still so small — and for putting us up for two long stretches during the so-called Covid-19 pandemic — and I thank my daughter, Elena, for always being such a good girl both while Daddy was traveling (even on his birthday) and when he was writing at home. Above all, however, I thank my wife, Gitte Maria, without whom I would never have embarked on this project like so many others — and who, as only she could, brought me to think about what my experiences in Russia really meant and how they called for action. *Fino alla fine del mondo.*

Of course, these acknowledgments would be incomplete if I did not thank the Russian people themselves, to whom this book is dedicated. For five years I was met — not always, it is true, with a smile! — but invariably with kindness, willingness to talk, and, often, quite extraordinary acts of humble generosity. Without *them*, the Russians, individually and collectively, both friends I can name and the nameless whom I encountered from St Petersburg to Vladivostok in one direction and to Stavropol in another, there would have been simply nothing to write about. I have changed the names and occasionally altered other details to protect the identity of all the non-historical characters in this book.

Finally, if I may address an appeal to Eastern Orthodox readers, it would be not to take offense at what has been here written about the faith of the Eastern Church, for it is meant not as a criticism but as an act of love from a Catholic addressed to a Church that taught me the meaning of Christian realism. "What man if his son asks him for bread, will give him a stone?" (Matt. 7:9). The truth of that statement, in relation, supremely, to the Bread of Heaven, I, at that time still a Protestant, learnt from the Eastern Church, in Russia. Indeed, if, for all my misunderstandings and bungled renderings of Eastern Christian belief and experience, I may be permitted to justify what I have done, it would be by reference to the words of the Psalmist.

> Walk about Zion, go round about her,
> Number her towers,
> Consider well her ramparts,
> Go through her citadels;
> That you may tell the next generation that this is God,
> Our God, for ever and ever.
> (Ps. 48:12–14, NRSV, Catholic edition)

This, and only this, to the best of my limited ability, I have done.

In conclusion, I thank Angelico Press for taking on this decidedly too large and somewhat unusual manuscript. I can only hope that you will conclude that it was worth it.

PART ONE

FOUNDATIONS

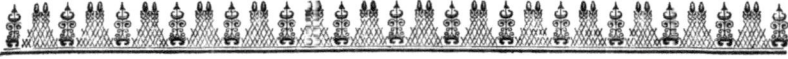

The Vision on the Yalta Embankment

I N THE SPRING OF 1909, THE RUSSIAN ECONO-
mist, philosopher and later Orthodox priest and theologian, Sergei
Bulgakov, went for a walk along the Yalta Embankment, a broad
seaside promenade at the heart of the Russian Empire's most fashionable holiday resort on the Crimean Peninsula. On a coastal bluff a
few miles outside of town stood the Livadia Palace, the imperial family's
summer retreat. Russia's reigning emperor, Nicholas II, his wife, the
Empress Alexandra, and their five children (Tsarevich Alexei and Grand
Duchesses Olga, Tatiana, Maria, and Anastasia) treated Yalta as a second
home. This was significant because, on that day on the Embankment,
for the first time in his life, Bulgakov, who had spent much of his earlier life as a Marxist hoping for the downfall of Nicholas II's autocracy,
saw the tsar and, on seeing him, and in his own words, "fell in love."[1]

It was an "apocalypse," an epiphany, Bulgakov said, that caught him
totally by surprise. "This love was born in my soul suddenly, silently,"
he said. " ... I sensed that the Tsar, too, bore his authority like the
Cross of Christ, and that obedience to him could also be the Cross
of Christ and [carried out] in His name. In my soul, the idea of holy
tsarist authority lit up like a bright star, and in the light of this idea,
the characteristics of Russian history also lit up and glittered like gems.
Where I formerly saw emptiness, lies, Orientalism, there now glittered
the divinely-inspired idea of authority 'by the grace of God' and not
by popular dispensation."[2]

Recording all this thirty years later in an unpublished work entitled
Autobiographical Fragments, Bulgakov could recognize that it was a radical
turning point in his life. Having been born the son of a provincial priest,
Bulgakov rejected Christianity in seminary school in favor of radical
Marxism.[3] His reason for doing so was Orthodoxy's complicity with

---

[1] Sergii Bulgakov, *Avtobiograficheskie Zametki*, 2nd ed. (Paris: YMCA Press, 1991), 29.
The text, which was published posthumously by Bulgakov's friend, Lev Zander, is often
passed over by Bulgakov scholars. For commentary, see Rowan Williams, *Sergii Bulgakov:
Towards a Russian Political Theology* (Edinburgh: T & T Clark, 2001).
[2] Bulgakov, *Avtobiograficheskie*, 82. Note that Bulgakov always capitalizes "Tsar." I have
kept this rendering in quotations since the capital "T" seems to denote that Bulgakov,
properly speaking, is speaking of an idea, an asynchronous symbol, rather than the
historically reigning emperor.
[3] For Bulgakov's biography, see Catherine Evtuhov, *The Cross and the Sickle: Sergei
Bulgakov and the Fate of Russian Religious Philosophy, 1890–1920* (Ithaca, NY: Cornell
University Press, 1997); Paul Valliere, *Modern Russian Theology: Bukharev, Soloviev,
Bulgakov: Orthodox Theology in a New Key* (Grand Rapids, MI: Eerdmans, 2001); and

the autocracy. Bulgakov was eleven years old — a formative age — when the assassination of the "liberal" Tsar Alexander II brought his son, the "reactionary" Alexander III, to the throne in 1881.

On this period in his life, Bulgakov wrote: "From the days of my youth, I experienced this regime [of Alexander III] with all its intransigence and its bond of 'Orthodoxy and Autocracy' as ... a great and overwhelming temptation, not only of a political nature but also of a religious one. I met the accession of his successor [Nicholas II] to the Throne in the same spirit...."[4]

In this spirit Bulgakov lived and thought from the age of fifteen until his early thirties, a stage in his life he called his period of "godlessness" (*bezbozhie*). Exceptionally gifted, he studied economics at Moscow University, became convinced of the materialist theories of Marx, and as a professor at Kiev Polytechnic Institute, founded, with fellow economist Peter Struve, the so-called "Union of Liberation" (forerunner of the Constitutional Democrats or "Kadet" Party), which sought the downfall of Russia's tsarist autocracy. Bulgakov said, "I joined the intelligentsia ... the intelligentsia in all its unquestioned unity with nihilism."[5] And regarding the sacred pretensions of tsarist authority, he "immediately and wholeheartedly stood on the side of the Revolution in the struggle against 'tsarism' and 'autocracy.'" As he put it, "It seemed completely natural to me that the idea of the sacredness of tsarist authority, and especially the veneration of the Tsar as 'God's Anointed,' simply evaporated with the loss of my religious faith.... In unanimity with the whole Russian Revolution, I loathed [the idea of the Tsar's sacred authority] and to this extent share with [the Revolution] all its sin against Russia."[6]

But since then Bulgakov had found Orthodoxy. First, under the influence of Tolstoy (whom he met on several occasions at Tolstoy's home in Moscow), and Dostoevsky, whose novels he had read, Bulgakov left atheism and Marxism behind. Then, an encounter with the works of the great Russian philosopher of religion, Vladimir Solovyov, and a budding friendship with a pious young polymath, Pavel Florensky (with whom he founded the Religious-Philosophical Society in 1904) saw him embrace a theosophically oriented kind of philosophical idealism that in turn gave way to a "radical" interpretation of Orthodoxy that allowed him to reconcile a return to the Church with his political commitments to democracy, freedom of conscience, and social justice.

For above all, Bulgakov believed in freedom. Freedom of conscience seemed to him essential to human dignity. It was a freedom that Christianity itself hallowed. At heart, he thought of himself as a liberal and a democrat not *in spite of* his Orthodox faith, but *because* of it. And yet,

---

Andrew Louth, *Modern Orthodox Thinkers: From the Philokalia to the present* (Downers Grove, IL: IVP Academic, 2015), 42–59.
[4] Bulgakov, *Avtobiograficheskie*, 28.   [5] Ibid., 27.   [6] Ibid., 27–28.

from this time, a rule set in: the more "orthodox" Bulgakov became, the more deeply he became reacquainted with its beliefs and liturgical life, the more he also came to repudiate, not freedom, which was an ideal he never let go, but Russia's revolutionary movement and the nihilistic spirit that animated it. And the more, in a way that shocked even his earlier self, he came to love the tsar and to consider himself a "tsarist." As he put it himself in the wake of his encounter with Nicholas II on the Yalta Embankment, "From that time on I carried him [Nicholas II] with me in my heart. But it was — alas! — a tragic love."[7]

Bulgakov described the moment he ceased to be a revolutionary. Ironically, it was the very day (October 17/30, 1905) when, under great pressure, and after much internal anguish, Nicholas II issued the October Manifesto granting Russians sweeping and previously unheard-of civil and political rights.[8] The revolution appeared to have triumphed. Bulgakov, who in those years held a teaching post in economics at Kiev University's Polytechnic Institute, knew he should have been thrilled. In fact, he was struck with a sense of evil portent.

> On October 18, I left the Polytechnic Institute with a crowd of students to celebrate the triumph of freedom. Like so many others, I was wearing a red ribbon on my lapel. But seeing and feeling what was going on around me, I threw it away into a latrine. Unbidden the words of the Gospel came to my ears: "This kind [of demon] is banished by prayer and fasting" (Matt. 17:21).[9]

From this moment of apparent triumph in 1905 began not only what historians would call the greater Russian Revolution, encompassing the events of the so-called "first" Russian Revolution of 1905 with those of the "second" and more famous Russian Revolution of 1917 and beyond, but what Bulgakov called "the whole Russian catastrophe." Having made this realization, Bulgakov says he "freed himself" of "revolutionary seductions" and, while he never let go of the ideal of freedom ("which I cannot and do not wish to exchange for anything"), one of the conditions necessary for a change in his attitude towards the idea of tsarist authority had been met.[10] The other necessary condition was furnished by Bulgakov's personal experience of Russia's first experiment in parliamentary politics.

After Russia's first-ever national election in 1906 produced a Duma (as the national representative and legislative assembly established by the October Manifesto of 1905 was called) incapable of working pragmatically with the government, Nicholas II, and his new prime minister

---

[7] Ibid., 29.
[8] The literature on the Russian Revolution is obviously vast. I have primarily followed Richard Pipes, *The Russian Revolution* (New York: Vintage Books, 1991); and Sean McMeekin, *The Russian Revolution: A new history* (New York: Profile Books, 2021). Note that the Julian calendar in use in Russia at the time was thirteen days behind the Gregorian calendar. I endeavor to give dates in both calendars throughout.
[9] Bulgakov, *Avtobiograficheskie*, 28, n. 1.   [10] Ibid., 28.

Petr Stolypin, dissolved it and ordered fresh elections. This produced a "Second Duma" in which, in 1907, Bulgakov himself took a seat as an independent Christian Socialist. Quickly, however, the low caliber of Bulgakov's fellow deputies disabused him, apparently forever, of the ideal of the Revolution, which his fellow deputies had no intention of abandoning merely because they now occupied seats in the country's long-awaited legislative chamber.

> Words strong enough do not exist to describe the anger, disappointment, sadness, that I would need to express my feelings [towards the Second Duma]. . . . Go out into the street and take the first hundred people you find, add to their number a handful of powerless but well-meaning people, inspire them with the idea that they're the salvation of Russia, and that their every word instantly becomes the subject of general applause to which all Russia listens, and you've got the Second Duma.[11]

Indeed, the Second Duma was such a "refutation of the lies of the Revolution," said Bulgakov, that he was forever healed of its political seductions. But he was not yet a monarchist. "The question of the monarchy is, in essence, a question of love or un-love," said Bulgakov and, as a member of the Second Duma in 1907 and 1908, "I did not love the Tsar."[12] All this, however, was about to change. "At that time, by some interior act . . . the force of which Orthodoxy gave me my relationship to tsarist authority changed . . . I became, in the dirty expression of the street, a tsarist. I realized that in its essence tsarist authority is the highest kind of authority there is, not on account of its own name, but on account of God's."[13]

The cause of this change in attitude was Bulgakov's vision of Nicholas II on the Embankment at Yalta in 1909. Suddenly, what remained of his prior faith in a revolutionary Russian democracy was swept away. In that moment of "unmasking," he "spat out" the "religious idea of democracy," replacing it with "theocracy in the form of tsarist authority." What Bulgakov suddenly understood was that the two conceptions of Russian politics — theocracy and democracy, of power coming "down" from God or, alternatively, "up" from the people — were incompatible. One was Christian; the other was not. As he put it,

> The godless democracy with which the Revolution was identical is incompatible with the [true] theocratic nature of authority. A watershed separates them: either, or. For and with the Tsar, or without the Tsar and against the Tsar. But the whole Russian Revolution — as I knew by personal experience — had always been against the Tsar and for democracy.[14]

As Rowan Williams observes, when commenting on this episode in

---

[11] Ibid., 80–81.   [12] Ibid., 81.   [13] Ibid., 81–82.   [14] Ibid., 82.

Bulgakov's life, "the tsarist ideal for a moment wholly overshadowed any commitment to democracy as a self-evident good: without the sacramental anchorage of political power in the Christian monarch, democracy was simply the perpetuation of the competing self-interests that had paralyzed the Duma."[15]

Without ceasing to identify with the left, Bulgakov says, and while always rejecting the thuggery of the so-called Black Hundreds (right-wing vigilante groups formed during the "first"' Russian Revolution of 1905, who in the name of "God, Tsar and Fatherland" met the violence of the revolutionaries with counter-revolutionary violence of their own) and their notorious anti-Semitism, Bulgakov became partisan to a principle — *teokratia*, "theocracy," the rule of God over human affairs through the office of a consecrated Christian monarch — that stood in implicit conflict with his prior and unchanged commitment to human freedom and, above all, to the freedom of private conscience, without which religious faith was impossible. But how could two principles, both hallowed by the same Christian faith, be reconciled?

"Before me," says Bulgakov, completing the description of his "apocalypse" on the Yalta Embankment, "arose the whole tragic question of the monarch, of the bearer of tsarist authority, in the era of its decisive collapse." In Nicholas II's very faithfulness to the idea of theocracy, he was "committing the suicide of the autocracy." But what was the alternative? And what was he, Bulgakov, as Nicholas's new-found "lover," to do? "From that very day I foresaw all the tragic fate of the Emperor and his family. For a long time I nurtured the thought of a personal meeting with the Emperor, during which I would express all the 'Tsar-love' and all the 'freedom-love' of my ideas and beg him for the salvation of Russia. But it was only a dream. History had already rendered its verdict."[16]

What Bulgakov apprehended with stunning acuity on the Yalta Embankment, then, was the greater philosophical, and, indeed, theological, significance of the events through which he and his generation were living. Like the elves who in J. R. R. Tolkien's *Lord of the Rings* leave Middle Earth for the distant West, the ideal of "tsarist authority" was now, at the beginning of the twentieth century, "leaving the world." In this sense, Bulgakov realized, the Russian Revolution was at bottom the outworking of a sociological process of demythologization or secularization that deprived the theocratic ideal at the heart of the Russian State of its legitimating rationale. Whereas Bulgakov believed that *teokratia* — the tsarist ideal — was the "spontaneous feeling of the Russian people, on which the Russian Statehood had been built," at the beginning of the twentieth century the historical, social context that made its operation possible was disappearing, and the Russian

---

[15] Williams, *Sergii Bulgakov*, 60.   [16] Bulgakov, *Avtobiograficheskie*, 29.

Revolution, writ on its largest scale, was the unfolding of that demythologization, with all its conflicting hopes (some — like democracy — false, others — like freedom — real) and tragic consequences (for the Tsar and his family personally, but also for the Russian people).

Bulgakov described the internal conflict this gave rise to in him.

> Having become a "Tsar-lover" at a time when tsarist authority was itself leaving the world, I was doomed to suffer a slow agony along with it. From that moment...I, too, was responsible for all the madness and felonies committed by tsarist authority and, indeed, even by this "monarch-suicide." But at the same time, in my love for the Tsar, I exonerated him...of the guilt for which he was himself not responsible as well as of all the evil that did not belong to him, and, in that moment, I loved him with that love unto the grave that a bride and bridegroom share before the altar.[17]

That love unto the grave that a bride and bridegroom share before the altar: these are strong words, and we should not miss their intensity. But we must not misunderstand their object either. To Bulgakov, it was not the man, Nicholas II, that he loved; it was the ideal of *teokratia*, the theocratic principle, which he suddenly understood as something inherent in his Orthodox faith. Or, rather, it was because of his God-inflamed love for the ideal of *teokratia* that he loved Nicholas II. He also understood the nature of Nicholas's passion.

> Having attained this disposition of the heart, I loved the Tsar and, as a result, could not but love the ruling Emperor. That is, I could not but love in him that which was worthy of love and, above all, I could not but love him as a Cross-bearer.[18]

Theocracy, then, demanded a faith in God that Russians no longer had. But this fact did not discharge the theocrat, Nicholas II, from his office; the essence of his vocation as an Orthodox Christian was, it seemed to Bulgakov, to suffer for an ideal — a theocratic conception of politics, a self-consciously Christian political regime that united the political and the sacred and in so doing imaged the eschatological Kingdom of Heaven that Christ preached and revealed — that God had commanded but history rejected. For Bulgakov, the only thing that made the resulting agony bearable was love. This book is the story of the agony of the theocratic principle in Russian culture, its apparent demise as both the highest meaning and primary ideal causality of the Russian Revolution of 1917 and its ambiguous regeneration in Russian culture today, a generation after the collapse of the officially atheist regime of the Soviet Union.

---

[17] Ibid., 82.   [18] Ibid., 83.

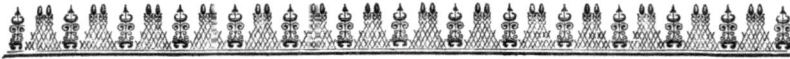

CHAPTER ONE
Moscow
THE WAY TO THE TEMPLE[1]

I N A GREY-BEIGE STREETSCAPE OF CONCRETE
Soviet tower blocks, cut by six lanes of snarling Moscow traffic, I
was lost, and it seemed no one could help me find the church, or
rather the monastery, I was looking for. Across the road, outside a
large, 1990s glass-and-steel shopping center a cluster of young people
selling sandwiches, costume jewelry, and mobile phones shook their heads,
disclaiming any knowledge of what I was talking about. It was left (not
for the last time) to a grey-haired woman in a vinyl jacket and floral
headscarf to show me the way. I was looking for the Danilov Monastery
(founded in 1303 by Prince Daniel of Moscow, youngest son of the famous
Russian great prince or "grand duke" Alexander Nevsky and progenitor
of the Moscow line of princes who would become tsars of all Russia)
which I was looking for, barely three hundred yards away. Lying about
five miles south of the Kremlin, is now the seat of His Holiness Kirill,
Patriarch of Moscow and All Rus', head of the Russian Orthodox Church.

Entering the church as I did from the late autumn half-light outside,
it took a moment for my eyes to adjust to the darker interior. Candles
flickered before scores of icons. A hundred holy eyes gazed down from
the iconostasis on the mainly female supplicants below. To the left, a shaft
of electric light penetrating the nave illuminated the icon shop. Three
middle-aged women in grey-blue jackets and long skirts, with scarves tied
under their chins, loosely covering their greying hair, haggled with the
younger woman in black glasses behind the counter. The disagreement
seemed to center on the prayer slips used to record the names of those
in need of God's assistance. One was for the living, the other for the
deceased. For a small fee, a bearded, black-robed priest would remember
the names the older women recorded on them at the conclusion of the
next Divine Liturgy. One of the women, it seemed, had irritated the
shop assistant by mixing her slips up. But a measure of Christian charity
sufficient to overcome the dispute supervened, the row came to an end,
and one by one the old women set off, slender beeswax candles in hand,
into the candle-lit gloom to make their devotions.

---

[1] The "way to the temple" is a reference to a film of the same name, about an old
woman desperate to recall the path to her local church in Soviet-era Moscow. See Leon
Aron, *Roads to the Temple: Truth, memory, ideas and ideals in the making of the Russian
Revolution, 1987–1991* (New Haven, CT: Yale University Press, 2012).

The revival of Orthodoxy is a defining feature of contemporary Russia.[2] Though the particulars of religious policy differed during the Soviet Union's history, for more than seventy years, it was an officially atheist state.[3] During the first two decades of Soviet rule, especially, the Church — perceived by Russia's new Bolshevik authorities as a reservoir of monarchism, obscurantism, and counter-revolutionary sentiment — suffered intense persecution: its properties were seized, precious objects were melted down to fund the Revolution, the relics of saints destroyed. Bishops were arrested, interrogated, killed. In a bid to split the Church, the Bolsheviks created a parallel hierarchy, loyal to themselves and known as the "Living Church," more liberal in doctrine and practice than the canonical Orthodox Church. When that failed, an Anti-Religion Campaign was proclaimed in 1926 in the course of which the newly founded League of Militant Godless (a kind of anti-Orthodox youth organization) seized, looted, and destroyed churches.[4] Thousands of other church buildings were converted into warehouses, cinemas, and skating rinks. Between 1917 and 1943 (when Stalin, seeking to recruit Orthodoxy in the struggle against the Nazi invaders, authorized a limited revival of Church life) as many as eighty thousand Orthodox clergy, monks, and nuns — about half the pre-revolutionary total — were shot, most of them in the Anti-Religion Campaigns of the 1930s.[5] Meanwhile, of the eighty thousand churches, chapels and other Orthodox places of worship that existed in the empire of Nicholas II, only two to three hundred remained in 1939.[6] While severe restrictions on religious life remained in place until Stalin's death in 1953, a certain reprieve was granted during the later stages of the Second World War.[7] The League of the Militant Godless was disbanded, and the Patriarch had a recognized residence in the Sergei-Trinity Lavra, north of Moscow.

The reprieve ended in 1956. When Nikita Khrushchev, the new Soviet leader, denounced Stalin's cult of personality and established a policy of de-Stalinization, a renewed period of state harassment towards

---

[2] See, for example, John P. Burgess, *Holy Rus': The rebirth of Orthodoxy in the New Russia* (New Haven, CT: Yale University Press, 2017).
[3] For the history of the Russian Church during Soviet times, see Dmitry Pospielovsky, *The Russian Church Under the Soviet Regime, 1917–1982*, 2 vols. (Crestwood, NY: St Vladimir's Seminary Press, 1984); Nathaniel Davis, *A Long Walk to Church: A contemporary history of Russian Orthodoxy* (Boulder, CO: Westview Press, 2003); and on the persecution of the Church by Soviet authorities specifically, Anna Dickinson, "Quantifying religious oppression: Russian Orthodox Church closures and repression of priests, 1917–41," *Religion, State & Society* 28:4 (2000): 327–35.
[4] Pospielovsky, *Russian Church*, 1:163–79.
[5] Davis, *A Long Walk*, 11; Dickinson, "Quantifying," 329–31, whose figures, while not identical, are very close.
[6] Davis, *A Long Walk*, 12–13; Dickinson, "Quantifying," 331–33, with useful graphs and tables.
[7] Pospielovsky, *Russian Church*, 1:193–203.

the Church began. Khrushchev did not resort to the bloody repressions of the 1920s and 1930s, but, seeking to return to the authentic Leninist tradition of Soviet Marxism, he reasserted the atheist character of mainstream Soviet culture and repressed much religious practice.[8] Monasteries, seminaries, and parishes were again closed. Baptism, the veneration of icons, or attendance at the Liturgy, if discovered by the KGB, meant expulsion from the Party. If a Soviet citizen was not a Party member, association with the Church could become the pretext for dismissal (for "anti-Soviet activities") or an impediment to promotion. Priests went underground, and thousands of children were hastily and secretly baptized in the home by disguised clergy. The aim was to marginalize the Church and let the course of history do the rest.

The policy continued under Khrushchev's successor, Brezhnev. The result, by the late 1970s, was a society from which, to all intents and purposes, God had been banished, and so it remained, outwardly, at least, one of the most secular societies in human history. Yet, so long as the Church was still around, Brezhnev's attitude was that it could also be put to good use. In return for permission to continue even a truncated public ministry Soviet authorities co-opted the Church's higher leadership to carry out surveillance of Soviet society domestically and parrot Soviet propaganda overseas.[9]

The Soviet Union fell in 1991. Since then, the Church's astonishingly swift post-Soviet revival has helped transform a secular country into a visibly Orthodox one.[10] In 1991, just 31% of Russians identified as Orthodox when asked about their religious affiliation. In 2008, this number had risen to 72%. Fewer, only 56%, declared a belief in God and figures for church attendance are much lower than for religious identification, with 7% going to church "at least once a month." Far fewer do so every Sunday. Until relatively recently, these figures would have been comparable with those from Western Europe.[11] And yet the difference is that, whereas Western Europe seems stuck in a process of terminal secularization, in Russia the trend for more than a generation now has been towards rising religious attendance and identification.[12] Since the collapse of communism, the number of Orthodox parishes has increased almost fivefold; of necessity, thousands of churches have

---

[8] Pospielovsky, *Russian Church*, 2:330–35.
[9] Ibid., 2:469–71.
[10] See "Russians Return to Religion, But Not to Church," Pew Research Center, February 10, 2014: https://www.pewresearch.org/religion/2014/02/10/russians-return-to-religion-but-not-to-church/. For further statistics, see also Burgess, *Holy Rus'*, 186–87.
[11] For some introductory statistics on the situation in Europe, see "Being Christian in Western Europe," Pew Research Center, May 29, 2018: https://www.pewresearch.org/religion/2018/05/29/being-christian-in-western-europe/.
[12] On this long story, see Charles Taylor, *A Secular Age* (Cambridge, MA: Harvard University Press, 2007).

been reconstructed or built from scratch—at a rate of *three a day*, according to Patriarch Kirill.[13]

As a result, the Russian Church today is both vocal and confident, and the numbers joining both the clergy and monastic life astonishingly healthy. Its program for church construction, and the cultural "in-churching" of Russian society is ambitious. And even if knowledge of doctrine is weak and regular attendance patchy, the signs pointing to an upsurge of popular religion are ubiquitous. Icons again hang on the walls of people's homes and, like talismans, can be found stuck to the dashboards and windscreens of people's cars. During Lent, restaurants in Moscow now commonly offer special Lenten menus, purged of the meat, dairy products and even oil and fish that believers are forbidden in the forty days before Easter. Barely a month before an estimated sixty thousand Muscovites took to the streets to oppose Putin's return to the presidency at the start of the so-called Bolotnaya Protests, two hundred thousand more had stood patiently for hours in the cold for a chance to venerate the Virgin Mary's girdle in Moscow's enormous Cathedral of Christ the Savior, a short distance from the Kremlin; across Russia, 1.8 million people had already done the same.[14] Former Russian President Dmitri Medvedev has called the Russian Orthodox Church "the largest and most authoritative social institution in contemporary Russia."[15] But what does this resurgent "Holy Rus" look and feel like from inside?

My eyes adjusted to the dark and I took a seat on a bench at the end of the church closest to the door. Typically, Orthodox believers stand rather than sit to worship. But towards the back, a bench can usually be found for the aged or infirm. From my vantage point, I surveyed the interior of the church. Unencumbered with clunky pews and creaking wooden kneelers, Orthodox churches are open spaces for believers to circulate around, and my eyes followed several blue-jacketed ladies as they perambulated from icon to icon beneath the penetrating gaze of Christ, the *Pantokrator*, Ruler of the Universe, painted, as a rule, on the underside of the central dome.[16] In Orthodoxy, a church is not merely a place to worship but a "window" onto heaven.

---

[13] Burgess, *Holy Rus'*, 185; "Russia Builds 3 New Churches a Day, Orthodox Leader Says," *Moscow Times*, May 27, 2019: https://www.themoscowtimes.com/2019/05/27/russia-builds-3-new-churches-a-day-orthodox-leader-says-a65755. Accessed September 30, 2024.
[14] For the figures quoted here, see "10 Years Since Bolotnaya, the Biggest Protests of the Putin Era," *Moscow Times*, December 9, 2021: https://www.themoscowtimes.com/2021/12/09/10-years-since-bolotnaya-the-biggest-protests-of-the-putin-era-a75739; and Sophia Kishkovsky, "In Russian Chill, Waiting Hours for Touch of the Holy," *New York Times*, November 23, 2011: https://www.nytimes.com/2011/11/24/world/europe/virgin-mary-belt-relic-draws-crowds-in-moscow.html.
[15] Quoted in Nicolai Petro, "The Russian Orthodox Church," in Andrei Tsygankov, ed., *The Routledge Handbook of Russian Foreign Policy* (London: Routledge, 2018), 219.
[16] According to one authority, the Pantokrator icon "leads us to the very heart of Byzantine [i.e. Eastern Orthodox] piety... the worship of the transcendent Almighty God whom the sinful man can approach only in awe and terror": G. P. Fedotov, *The Russian*

Russia's Orthodox Church has its roots in the Eastern Roman Empire of Byzantium, whose leading religious center was the See of Constantinople, the "New Rome," founded by (St) Constantine (whom the Orthodox number among the saints), the first Christian Roman Emperor in AD 323.[17] Communion between the Orthodox and the See of Rome was broken in 1054, when the Patriarch of Constantinople and the Pope excommunicated each other. In its Orthodox form, Christianity reached Russia from Byzantium shortly before this breach between the two principal foyers of Christendom. In 988, Vladimir, Grand Prince of Kiev, was baptized by a Greek bishop in a Byzantine outpost in Crimea; the forced baptism of his people (the "Baptism of Rus") in the waters of the Dnieper followed upon Vladimir's return home to Kiev. Thereafter, the Russian Church was governed by an archbishop or metropolitan (of Kiev "and all Rus"), generally a Greek appointed by the Byzantine emperor in Constantinople, who was subordinate in ecclesiastical matters to the patriarch of Constantinople. Until the thirteenth century, the seat of this metropolitan was at Kiev. Thereafter, it moved to Moscow. In the fifteenth century, the metropolitan was raised to the rank of a patriarch and, with the fall of Constantinople to the Turks in 1453, the Russian Church became self-governing under the leadership of a Patriarch of Moscow ("and All Rus") appointed by the tsar. In 1722, Emperor Peter the Great abolished the patriarchate and appointed himself and his successors head of the Russian Church directly. The patriarchate was restored with the fall of the monarchy in 1917.

While connections with the Western Church survived for a time (as seen, for example, in the marriage of Western princesses to Vladimir's heirs at Kiev, and in the Romanesque stonework that beautifies the white limestone churches of Suzdalia), they were sundered in the thirteenth century by the rise of Catholic crusading orders in the Baltic, such as the Livonian and Teutonic Knights (which saw the Orthodox as infidel, to

---

Religious Mind. Kievan Christianity: the 10th to the 13th centuries (New York: Harper and Row, 1960), 30. But while his account is considered a classic, Fedotov exaggerates Eastern Christianity's alleged diminishing of Christ's humanity.

[17] For the history of the Orthodox Church generally, see Alexander Schmemann, *The Historical Road of Eastern Orthodoxy* (New York: Holt, Rinehart and Winston, 1963); Timothy Ware, *The Orthodox Church*, rev. ed. (Harmondsworth: Penguin Books, 1997); and, in Russia specifically, Nicholas Zernov, *The Russians and Their Church*, 3rd ed. (Crestwood, NY: St Vladimir's Seminary Press, 1978), and John Fennell, *A History of the Russian Church* (London: Longman, 1995). For Orthodox doctrine, I have relied primarily on John Meyendorff, *Byzantine Theology: Historical trends and doctrinal themes* (New York: Fordham University Press, 1979); Vladimir Lossky, *In the Image and Likeness of God*, John H. Erickson and Thomas E. Bird, eds. (Crestwood, NY: St Vladimir's Seminary Press, 1974); Vladimir Lossky, *The Mystical Theology of the Eastern Church* (Crestwood, NY: St Vladimir's Seminary Press, 1976); Georges Florovsky, *Ways of Russian Theology* = vols. 5 and 6 in idem, *Collected Works of Georges Florovsky*, ed. Richard S. Haugh, trans. Robert L. Nichols (Belmont, CA: Nordland Publishing Co., 1979); and Kallistos Ware, *The Orthodox Way*, rev. ed. (Crestwood, NY: St Vladimir's Seminary Press, 1995).

be slain or converted), and near-contemporaneous invasions by Genghis Khan's Mongols (with whom some local Russian princes, such as the famous Alexander Nevsky, allied themselves for protection against the Knights).[18] Thus, for the Russian Church, the Catholic Church has long been identified as the source of threat and heresy. Indeed, in the fifteenth century, the Russian Church broke even with the "Mother Church" at Constantinople rather than agree to reunion with Rome. The Russian Church thus participated in neither the Renaissance nor the Reformation. In the nineteenth century, the identification of Western Christianity with heresy was extended to Western civilization as a whole. For this reason, today's warmer relations between Russian Orthodoxy and the Holy See in Rome reflect a significant new departure. When Patriarch Kirill of Moscow held talks with Pope Francis in Cuba in 2016, it was the first meeting between a Patriarch of Moscow and the Bishop of Rome in history.[19] By contrast, part of the fallout of the Ukraine War has been that Moscow has itself recently broken off communion *again* with Constantinople, whose patriarch now recognizes the existence of a Ukrainian church hierarchy separate from the Russian.[20]

In the eyes of the non-Orthodox, probably the most distinctive feature of Orthodoxy is the holy image or icons, which cover the walls and ceiling of every Orthodox church.[21] Between the sanctuary and the nave, icons also form an imposing wall called the iconostasis or "icon stand" of haloed faces so tall that not only the altar but the entire apse of the church is invisible to the congregation. The opening at the center of this wall of pictures is called the Beautiful Gates and Holy or Royal (lit. "tsarist," *tsarskie*) Doors. To its right, as the worshiper faces it, is another image of Christ as *Pantokrator*; to its left, an image of His Mother, the "God-bearer," to whom the Orthodox faithful (like their Catholic counterparts) offer a special degree of veneration.

Over the centuries, the Russian Orthodox Church developed its own style of icon-painting, more vigorous and powerful, perhaps, than the

---

[18] For a general introduction to Russian history, see Geoffrey Hosking, *Russia and the Russians: A history*, 2nd ed. (Harmondsworth: Penguin, 2012); and Gregory L. Freeze, ed., *Russia: A history*, 3rd ed. (Oxford: Oxford University Press, 2009).

[19] Alec Luhn, "'Finally!': pope and Russian patriarch meet for first time in 1,000 years," *The Guardian*, February 13, 2016: https://www.theguardian.com/world/2016/feb/12/pope-francis-russian-orthodox-patriarch-kirill-make-history-cuba-first-meeting-in-1000-years. The Pope and Patriarch issued this joint declaration on the occasion: https://www.vatican.va/content/francesco/en/speeches/2016/february/documents/papa-francesco_20160212_dichiarazione-comune-kirill.html.

[20] See Nicolai Petro, "The Gospel According to Poroshenko: Politics, Religion, and the New Church of Ukraine," *Yale Journal of International Affairs*, April 4, 2019: https://www.yalejournal.org/publications/the-gospel-according-to-poroshenko-politics-religion-and-the-new-church-of-ukraine.

[21] On icons, see the classic studies by Leonid Ouspensky, *The Theology of the Icon*, trans. Anthony Gythiel, 2 vols. (Crestwood, NY: St Vladimir's Seminary Press, 1992); and Vladimir Lossky, "The theology of the image," in id., *In the Image*, 125–40.

Greek models that inspired it. All the same, the faces represented in the icons on the walls around me would be recognizable to anyone familiar with Eastern Orthodoxy: the Mother of God in a multiplicity of poses; the fifth-century Greek bishop, St Nicholas the Wonderworker (the ultimate inspiration, in the West, for Santa Claus); the great hierarchs and teachers of the faith, Saints Athanasius, Basil the Great, and Gregory the Theologian; soldier saints such as St George, slaying the dragon on horseback, as well as St Theodore, and St Dmitri; St Panteleimon and Sts Cosmas and Damian, the healers. Others portrayed quintessentially Russian saints: thirteenth-century St Sergei of Radonezh, Russia's patron saint, with his stern, adamantine eyes; and the nineteenth-century hermit St Serafim of Sarov, a stooped figure with long white beard.

To those brought up on the Second Commandment of the Decalogue — "Thou shalt not bow down to graven images" — Orthodox ecclesial space can thus seem jarring, and at various points in history Orthodox theologians have had to defend their Church against the charge of idolatry.[22] But the theological apology for icons stems from the Incarnation. Because God Himself, Who before the Incarnation was invisible and unrepresentable, has become, in the human flesh that He personally took from the Virgin Mary, both visible and representable, so images of Christ, the incarnate God, are, when used properly, neither idols nor mere decorations. Nor are they simply mnemonic devices for remembering events from the life of Christ or sacred history. Rather, they are witnesses to the meaning of the Incarnation itself, the union of the divine and human in Jesus Christ. Because of this union of the divine and human, moreover, which will never be broken, not only Christ but also His Mother and all the saints may be depicted and venerated. For just as the Incarnation made the invisible visible, so it also made the unworthy but deified human nature worthy of veneration. To the Orthodox, icons are a witness to the whole purpose of the Christian life: man's "becoming God," *theosis*.[23] So the Orthodox do not "worship pictures," but they *do* venerate images as a matter of theological urgency. Or, more correctly, they venerate not the board itself on which the image is depicted, but the divine, human, or angelic subject depicted *by means of the image* on the two-dimensional surface of the icon board. Hence, in the famous words of St Basil the Great, the great, fourth-century Church Father cited as the traditional authority in this connection, "the honor paid to the image passes over to the archetype"

---

[22] On Iconoclasm and the Orthodox response, see Ouspensky, *Theology of the Icon*, 1:107–50.

[23] On this last theme, see especially Andrew Louth, "The place of *theosis* in Orthodox theology," in Michael J. Christensen and Jeffrey A. Wittung, eds., *Partakers of the Divine Nature: The history and development of deification in the Christian traditions* (Grand Rapids, MI: Baker Academic, 2007), 23–31.

(a formula in which, to those familiar with Plato's theory of the Forms, something of the fundamentally Platonic structure of the Orthodox worldview, purified and reconfigured in the light of Christian revelation, is immediately apparent).[24]

An essential element not only of Orthodox piety, therefore, icons are approached reverently in a way that reflects their sacred status, and I watched as one of the women whom my eyes had been following waited her turn to venerate an image of Mary. When it arrived, she crossed herself (right to left with her left hand) three times and then bowed, performing a symbolic prostration by brushing the ground with her hand. Only now, having made this act of reverence, did the woman presume to join her own body to the holy image: pressing her forehead to the icon, she whispered a prayer and sealed her act of devotion with a reverential kiss. Before departing in search of other icons to venerate, she lit a thin beeswax candle and placed it in front of the icon she had just venerated, at once an offering to God in itself and a physical symbol of Christ, "Light of the World."[25]

As I continued to sit and watch, I noticed that the woman I was watching had now stopped in front of a newer-looking icon. Larger than many of the others, it had not been blackened through many decades of exposure to candle smoke, and rather than a single figure, it presents a cluster of several, distinctly drawn, people. The woman peered intently at the faces in front of her, as if not sure who they were. Then, a few moments later, having answered her unspoken question, she crossed herself three times, bowed, and then pressed her face hard up against the glass covering over the icon, as if both kissing and speaking to the sainted figures represented in it. Crossing herself again, she bowed deeply, almost to the floor, then turned, and continued her circumambulation.

My curiosity aroused, I walked over to the icon to see whether I, too, could identify the figures. Clad in flowing, medieval robes, their bodies were, as tradition dictates, disproportionately long and otherworldly. But, even at first glance, the faces were strangely familiar — the eyes and beard of the central male figure, especially. Not a face from the Bible, Roman antiquity or the Middle Ages, its features came from somewhere else entirely, somewhere closer to my own time. Then, it dawned on me that I was looking at the face of Russia's last tsar, Nicholas II. As I

---

[24] Thus, St John of Damascus (fl. c. AD 680–750), the great defender of icon veneration, quoted St Basil in his *First Treatise on the Divine Images*, ch. 21 = idem, *Three Treatises on the Divine Images*, trans. Andrew Louth (Crestwood, NY: St Vladimir's Seminary Press, 2003) 35; on the Platonic structure of Basil's thought on this subject, see Norman H. Baynes, "The Hellenistic civilization of East Rome," in Baynes, *Byzantine Studies and Other Essays* (London: Athlone Press, 1955), 19.

[25] Archimandrite Tikhon (Agrikov), "A Sermon on a church candle," *Pravmir*, August 25, 2012: http://www.pravmir.com/a-sermon-on-a-church-candle/.

continued to study the image, the identities of the other figures around the image of Nicholas II also revealed themselves: Empress Alexandra, the Tsarevich Alexei, the Grand Duchesses Olga, Tatiana, Maria and Anastasia—a family extracted from time, shimmering on an incandescent background of candlelit gold leaf, assumed into the timeless realm of the sacred.

As a teenager in Australia in the 1990s, I devoured Russian playwright Edvard Radzinsky's idiosyncratic 1993 edition of Nicholas's diary, *The Last Tsar*, on the beach one summer.[26] But this was my first encounter with Nicholas as a saint, and it perplexed me. To the Orthodox, the veneration of saints is like the veneration of icons: intrinsic to the logic of Christianity as a consequence, as we have seen, of the Incarnation. "You are not struggling against icons," St John of Damascus, the famous eighth-century defender of icons stated in a letter to the iconoclastic emperor Leo III (717–41), "but against the saints."[27] But was Nicholas in fact a saint? And if so, what for?

In counterpoint, a black and white movie reel of historical photographs flickered involuntarily through my mind, recalled after a lapse of almost two decades, from the illustrated pages of Radzinsky's *The Last Tsar*. Nicholas and Alexandra, shy and youthful on their engagement day in Coburg, 1892. Standing together on the roof of the Kremlin Great Palace, Emperor and Empress of Russia, half a decade later. The birth of their children—four daughters and then, finally, a boy, an heir. The revelation of the heir Alexei's illness and the unsettling profile of the long-haired figure with hypnotic eyes whom Nicholas and Alexandra had called on in their desperation to heal him: the mysterious and off-putting Rasputin. Playing lawn tennis at the Imperial Palace at Livadia in the Crimea in the gilded years before the Great War or relaxing on the spotless decks of *Standart*, the Imperial yacht, in the Gulf of Finland. Massed crowds in Moscow for the Romanov tercentenary in 1913. Alexandra knitting in bed to keep Alexei company during an attack of his illness. The War. Revolution. The whole family, except the former Empress, seated together on the roof of the Tobolsk mansion, looking like the exiles they were in 1917. The ominously-named "House of Special Purpose" surrounded by its high fence in Ekaterinburg. The basement room with the plaster torn from the walls by rifle fire. Workers by the forest pit...

Since the Romanovs' gruesome deaths at the hands of a Bolshevik firing squad in 1918, books about them have become a cottage industry

---

[26] Edvard Radzinsky, *The Last Tsar: The Life and Death of Nicholas II*, trans. Marian Schwartz (New York: Anchor Books, 1993).
[27] John of Damascus, *First Treatise on the Divine Images*, ch. 19 = idem, *Three Treatises*, 33.

in the West. Beginning with the publication in the 1920s and 1930s
of the memoirs of many of those (relatives, friends, courtiers, government ministers) who knew them, their story has been told and retold
a hundred times. Abundantly published photographs have made their
eyes, faces, clothes, and homes familiar. But on that grey, late autumn
day in Moscow, I wondered whether, in her silent communion with
Russia's last tsar and his stricken family, the woman who had kissed
their icon a few minutes before recalled the same photographs I did.
Or, for her, had the Romanovs already receded beyond time, beyond
space, beyond history?

Stopping at the icon shop on my way out, I asked the irritated young
shop assistant whether an icon of the family was available for sale. *Nyet*,
she snapped in reply. But in a basement shop built into the external wall
of the monastery compound I found what I was looking for: an icon of
Russia's "Holy Royal Passion-Bearers" as they are properly known. On
its surface, seven figures all wearing crowns, with the same elongated
bodies that I had seen in the original icon in the church, dressed in the
flowing white robes of ancient Roman martyrs that were so intriguingly
unlike the early twentieth-century dress and settings I had seen them
wear in history books. As I put it into my backpack, I felt for the first
time what would become a familiar feeling over the next several years:
that of being a spiritual voyeur, glimpsing one particularly painful side
of a tormented nation's tortured soul, one that it didn't feel quite decent
for an "unbelieving" foreigner to see.

And, yet . . . I was a foreigner, yes, but not unbelieving. Indeed, as (at
the time) an Anglican, I was additionally aware that turning murdered
monarchs into saints wasn't a Russian monopoly. England's Charles I,
beheaded in 1649 during the final phase of the English Civil War, was
declared a saint in the Protestant Church of England after the monarchy's restoration in 1661. But, by comparison to the vigorous afterlives
of the saints in Orthodoxy, saints in the Church of England are often
vague figures, existing, it seems, only to provide names for churches and
to be airily invoked on their feast days. For the Orthodox, however, as
for Catholics, saints are an essential element of the faith, whose place in
the Church flows from fundamental premises about the meaning of the
Incarnation of God and who are, or *can* be, active participants in the
lives of many of the faithful: holy personalities prayed to in some cases
for a lifetime, a source of comfort, companionship, and consolation. In
the setting of *that* kind of religion, making Nicholas II a saint was quite
a different proposition from the sainthood of Charles I. Either Nicholas
II was a heady, full-blooded saint, to be approached and venerated in
the light of the central Christian mystery of the Incarnation, which all
the saints refract, or he was a source of scandal.

What, then, did it say about *Orthodoxy* that it had risked launching Nicholas II on this kind of posthumous career? Certainly, outside Russia, at least, simply being a murdered monarch wasn't enough in itself: the Roman Catholic Church had not, after all, canonized Louis XVI.[28] Why, in the twenty-first century, would a church make a ruler deposed and murdered a hundred years ago, a *saint*? And what did the fact that it had say about Russia?

In answering these questions, the approach adopted by this book is broadly geographical and ethnographic (in that it aims to describe the lay of a land and the habits of a people), while the thesis it explores is alternately historical-philosophical and political-theological. That is to say, tsarism was never, as Bulgakov came to realize on the Yalta Embankment, merely one form of government among many that could be exchanged without loss for "democracy"; rather, it was a form of government that expressed the Orthodox or Eastern Christian ideal of *teokratia*, whereby the tsar, like a living icon, served as an image of the God Who, having created the world, continues to order and govern it (and does so notwithstanding having also later become Incarnate): not merely a "Man of Sorrows" or propitiatory sacrifice, which He sometimes becomes in Western Christianity, the Eastern Orthodox Christ is always the Incarnate Word or Logos, the ordering principle of the cosmos and its source of unity. And although he does not advert to it expressly, what Bulgakov saw on the Yalta Embankment was of a piece with the witness of the Eastern Church's most ancient Fathers: what the Logos is in the cosmos, the emperor (in Greek: *basileus*, "king" or "tsar") is in the *oikumene*, His natural representative or, better still, His icon and image.[29] As St Gregory of Nazianzen, addressing the emperor, put it in

---

[28] But note the sentiments of this kind expressed by Pope Pius VI in his address, *Quare Lacrymae*, delivered on news of Louis's execution, at a meeting of the cardinals on June 17, 1793: https://thejosias.com/2015/01/29/pius-vi-quare-lacrymae/.

[29] On this subject, see, especially, Norman H. Baynes, "Eusebius and the Christian Empire," in Baynes, *Byzantine and Other Studies*, 168–72; Francis Dvornik, *Early Christian and Byzantine Political Philosophy*, 2 vols. (Washington, DC: Dumbarton Oaks Center for Byzantine Studies, 1966); Harry J. Magoulias, *Byzantine Christianity: Emperor, Church, and the West* (Chicago: Rand McNally and Co., 1970), especially 1–16; Meyendorff, *Byzantine Theology*, 212–16; John McGuckin, "The legacy of the 13th apostle: origins of the East Christian conceptions of Church and State relation," *St Vladimir's Theological Quarterly* 47. 3–4 (2003): 251–88; and Vigen Guroian, "Constantine and Christendom," in idem, *The Orthodox Reality: Culture, theology and ethics in the modern world* (Grand Rapids, MI: Baker Academic, 2018), 23–35. Note: Of the works listed above, the two most important (after the founding work of Baynes) are those by Dvornik and McGuckin. McGuckin conceives his account as a refutation of Dvornik, and yet he seems to have reduced Dvornik's own account to a claim that Dvornik did not himself make, namely, that East Christian/Byzantine political theology is *nothing more* than the continuation of the Hellenistic theory of kingship — as if Christianity did not reconfigure some of its essential premises. Taken together, Dvornik and McGuckin point, it seems to me, to a unity of thought, not an opposition (as is in fact brought out quite well by Magoulias). Indeed, rather than playing Hellenistic and Christian accounts of political authority off against each other, the approach to ancient Greek culture as a *praeparatio*

a statement typical of the Cappadocians generally: "You share powers with Christ and with Christ you carry out your functions. From Him you received the sword, not so much to kill as to threaten and caution. Hence, you must see to it that you keep it for Him, Who gave it to you as a gift...You are the image of God...Therefore, imitate God's benevolence and mercy."[30] "It is the Lord who makes and breaks kings, and there is no power on earth but what is set up by God...The king's power does not rest on his might, but on the divine favor," affirmed his friend, St Basil the Great.[31] This complex of ideas this book calls the "theocratic principle."

More than anything else, then, this book is a study in the theocratic principle in Russian culture, from its apparent discreditation and demise in 1917 to its resurgence and regeneration in the first quarter of the twenty-first century. For this reason, as the narrative proceeds, this book will turn its gaze both back towards the Russian past and forward towards the Russian present. In doing so, I will argue that Bulgakov was right. Because tsarism was not merely, at its worst, an arbitrary and despotic form of human government, but, at its best, a certain manifestation of God's governance of the world (and, therefore, even a *theophany*, a revelation of God's existence and character), so the fundamental meaning — and even the higher, ideal causation — of the Russian Revolution was theological and religious: a willed act of secularization that, to borrow the terms of the twentieth-century Italian Catholic philosopher of religion, Augusto Del Noce, translated the atheistic conclusions of nineteenth-century European philosophy into history.[32] And yet, while Bulgakov believed the theocratic principle had vanished definitively from Russia with the Revolution (after all, this was why the Revolution had occurred), I will also argue that the subsequent collapse in 1991 of the revolutionary order established in 1917, together with the canonization as a saint of the tsar on whose body that revolutionary order had been established, can be regarded as signifying, symbolically, not only a certain repudiation (and even repentance) by Russian society of the Revolution, but the reversal in Russia of the atheist logic of secularization more broadly. In short, the

---

evangeliae of the earliest Fathers (Saints Justin Martyr, Clement of Alexandria) would seem to be called for here as much as anywhere else in the Church's relationship with Greco-Roman antiquity. The works of Archimandrite Vasileios of Iveron Monastery, Mount Athos, offer perhaps a model of what ultimately must be done here, an account of the Eastern Christian conception of politics that would run "from Plato and Diotogenes to Sts Constantine and Justinian."

[30] Cited in Dvornik, *Early Christian*, 2:685–86.
[31] Cited in Dvornik, *Early Christian*, 2:690.
[32] See, for example, Augusto Del Noce, "Secularization and the crisis of modernity," in Del Noce, *The Crisis of Modernity*, ed. and trans. Carlo Lancelotti (Montreal: McGill-Queen's University, 2014), 73–84.

theocratic principle has returned.

What emerges, I hope, is a theological reading of history or a certain effort at applying a Christian theology of history to the data of history itself. This imitates Bulgakov's approach, where history is not merely the catalogue of material events that mark the passage of time but the place where both time and the timeless — the ideal or metaphysical world (the so-called "sacred city") not of matter but of the spirit — meet.[33] And because the spirit (and not matter alone, as Marx would have it) is real, history is capable of being driven not only by immediate, material causes but also by a higher, spiritual or ideal logic that in turn explains and lends moral and even metaphysical meaning to it: *pace* some readers of the Western Church Father St Augustine, history is not, or not always or only, the story of a (human) world autonomous of either God or the spirit but an integral part of an integral cosmos of *matter and spirit* bound together by the spiritual (but incarnate) Logos Himself, in which, from the Old Testament patriarchs to the saints of the Church, and supremely in the Incarnation, the eternal and the spiritual are (always) revealed by God, and either received or rejected by man.

If all this is additionally important, it is because the final argument of this book is that we in the West will never understand Russia until we have understood the fate in Russian culture, this past century, of the theocratic principle and the logic of secularization (and its reversal) associated with it. This is because, as one of the most compelling analysts of the twentieth century, the Italian Catholic philosopher of history Augusto del Noce, has it, the reach of the Russian Revolution, as the historical realization of the atheistic conclusions of nineteenth-century European philosophy, extended far beyond the borders of Russia and the Soviet Union. Indeed, according to Del Noce, the logic of secularization was fulfilled not in the Soviet Union at all but among the formerly Christian peoples of the West, which, for reasons of geopolitical necessity in the Cold War, sought from the 1960s to out-compete the Soviet Union on the grounds of the latter's own claims to superiority by demonstrating that the liberal, sexually permissive West was more perfectly emancipated from the claims of God and tradition — and therefore more perfectly *rational* and *modern* in terms of the philosophical conclusions of the nineteenth century — than the Soviet Union.[34]

---

[33] See Jean Daniélou, "The conception of history in the Christian Tradition," *Journal of Religion* 30 (1950): 171–9. Daniélou notes that the "scandal" for classical Greek thought presented by Christianity was precisely the Christian claim that the timeless and metaphysically true could be manifested in time and history, which was manifestly in flux. Daniélou notes that Christian writers developed the type or the symbol to meet this challenge. On symbols, see also Jean Daniélou, *The Lord of History: Reflections on the inner meaning of history*, trans. Nigel Abercrombie (London: Longmans, 1958), especially 130–48.

[34] See, for example, Augusto Del Noce, "The Latent Metaphysics within Contemporary Politics," "The Death of the Sacred," and "The Roots of the Crisis," in Del Noce,

Apparently vindicated by the West's subsequent "victory" in 1989–91, this fundamentally *revolutionary* logic of secularization has in no way been reversed or mitigated since then. (On the contrary, its reach has only been ever more relentlessly extended, such that the very biology of sexual differentiation is something from which Western man demands emancipation.) In Russia, by contrast, where this logic was never so radically applied, it would now (if this book's argument regarding the symbolical significance of the canonization of Nicholas II as a certain sign of the regeneration in Russian culture of the theocratic principle, is accepted) be in reverse. As it stands, the relative ascendancy of a logic of secularization — the antithesis of the Russian, and Eastern Orthodox, ideal of *teokratia* — is the measure of the distance between us, as well as an avoidable element (however uncomfortable) of debates among us about the merits or otherwise of the extension of the West's power, influence and way of life ("Westernization").[35]

All this leaves only the book's primary protagonist: Russia's last tsar, Nicholas II. Encountering Nicholas II only from a distance, Bulgakov could only guess at Nicholas II's true spiritual disposition. A hundred years later, however, Nicholas II's letters and diaries stand open to us in a way they did not to Bulgakov. Can we trace the demise of Russia's *teokratia* from the inside? In this sense, the final thing this book will attempt to offer is a spiritual biography of Nicholas II, the conscientious theocrat, that takes his religion seriously.

Crisis of Modernity, 59–72, 118–36, and 137–56, respectively.
[35] Matthew J. Dal Santo, "Russia, the Ukraine War, and the West's Empire of Secularization," *Telos* 201 (Winter 2022): 146–64; id., "Theopolitics of Ukraine," *First Things*, August 2023.

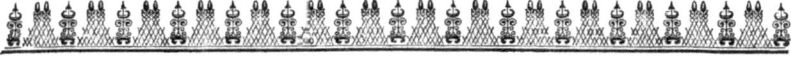

CHAPTER TWO

Petersburg

STAGE-SET OF A DYNASTY

§T PETERSBURG—TO RUSSIANS SANKT-PETER-burg, or more simply "Piter"—remains Russia's other capital, a city of six million people, and the only Russian city that can remotely compete with Moscow as a source of the ideas, fashions, and movements that define national life. Vladimir Putin was born here, in the devastation left behind by the Second World War, and so was the reigning patriarch of Moscow, Kirill. Indeed, since the end of Communism, Russia has been largely ruled by men with roots not in Moscow but in Petersburg, economists and lawyers for the most part, who oversaw first the country's economic liberalization and then, a few years later, its consolidation as a capitalist, semi-authoritarian state under Putin.[1] Contemporary Russia is inconceivable without them. But perhaps the most obvious feature of twenty-first-century Petersburg is that it is a city built as a capital for a dynasty that no longer exists. St Petersburg was the Romanovs' stage set. The props are still in place, and the city still stands on the same patch of boggy ground at the mouth of the Neva, but without the imperial court, the city seems strangely deserted. The old Imperial-era financial district between Nevsky, with the great bronze dome of St Isaac's, especially, appears to rebel against the travel agents, Chinese restaurants, and English-language schools installed behind its granite facades. And without a ruling emperor to appear periodically on the balcony or ride by horse-drawn carriage down the city's ceremonial boulevards, what exactly is the point today of Rastrelli's masterpiece, the Winter Palace? Even in its current iteration as one of the world's great encyclopedic museums, the old Palace, now known as the Hermitage, seems to miss its original calling.

Petersburg's people, too, have suffered more than most. Twice in the twentieth century the city itself was all but deserted and resettled with new inhabitants, first after the Civil War (1918–21) had brought about the collapse of the food supply system on which northern, artificial Petrograd (as Petersburg was known at the time) depended, and again after the Second World (or "Great Patriotic") War (1941–45), when the famine induced by the nine-hundred-day German blockade sent some

---

[1] Mikhail Zygar, *All the Kremlin's Men: Inside the court of Vladimir Putin* (New York: Public Affairs, 2016), 51–53.

700,000 Leningraders to an early grave.[2] And then, like everywhere else in
Russia, there was the disastrous 1990s. From the time of the perestroika
reforms introduced by Mikhail Gorbachev, the last Communist Party
General-Secretary, Russians, like most of the peoples of Eastern Europe,
welcomed with relief and even moments of euphoria the dismantling of
totalitarianism. But the collapse of Communism itself, as an economic
system, Russians especially experienced as a trauma. When price controls
were lifted under Boris Yeltsin in January 1993, inflation rose 245 percent
in a single month.[3] By 1999, GDP had shrunk 65 percent and two fifths
of the population of what had recently been an industrial and military
superpower lived below the poverty line.[4] Even those with jobs were
often seldom or only irregularly paid, in a currency that had lost almost
all its value. Savings, accumulated over years if not decades under the
Soviet system, were almost overnight rendered worthless. To get by, people
tended garden plots and hawked what they could on street corners. But
this was how it had to be, said the Petersburg set, who advised Russia's
first democratic president, Boris Yeltsin. Such immiseration was the only
way Russia could turn its back on Communism. Russians went along
with it because they had to. And when they objected, and were minded
to support a return to the certainties of Communism, or a system like it,
both their own democratic rulers and the world's self-appointed observers
and guarantors of what was being sold to Russians as democracy worked
together to ensure that they were overruled and ignored.

Today, the legacy of all this is that, to the visitor, Petersburg's modern inhabitants can seem to squat in a streetscape their ancestors did not
build, and to whose history they can often seem indifferent. Like almost
every other urban agglomeration of a certain size in the era of global-
ization, modern Petersburg (until 1992, Leningrad) is a city of twenty-
four-hour kiosks, mobile phone accessories shops, MacDonald's and
Subway sandwich franchises. Rather than elegant or "imperial," then,
the feel is often jarringly gritty, unshaven, hipster. Just doors down
from the grandest establishments of the old imperial capital, students
chew gum or smoke cheap cigarettes bought from one of St Petersburg's
ubiquitous all-night kiosks, while street vendors hawk T-shirts featuring
the stubbled, scruffy face of Sergei Shchnurov ("Shchnur"), the lead

---

[2] As the urban historian Blair Ruble points out, in the 1950s and 1960s "a large number, perhaps even a majority, of the city's residents, had not lived in the city before
the outbreak of hostilities" and "had only limited personal or familial ties to the city":
Blair A. Ruble, *Leningrad: Shaping a Soviet City* (Berkeley: University of California
Press, 1990), 51.
[3] Robert Service, *Penguin Modern History of Russia: From tsarism to the twenty-first
century*, 3rd ed. (Harmondsworth: Penguin Books, 2009), 516.
[4] World Bank, National Accounts Data: https://data.worldbank.org/indicator/
NY.GDP.MKTP.CD?locations=RU (accessed January 3, 2025); Service, *Penguin Modern History*, 541.

singer of Russia's most famous punk band, *Leningrad*, a half-smoked cigarette dangling from his lips.[5] Despite the apparent solidity of its elegant façades, then, the exotic, European cultivar that the Romanovs had planted on the edge of the permafrost was always more fragile than it looked. Indeed, what visitors see today often seems less the descendant of a great world capital than it does a botanical graft — a new plant on an old stem.

Yet such a picture, while not itself incorrect, is also incomplete. At turns and unexpectedly, the mood of old imperial St Petersburg can still descend like a veil, covering for a sacred moment the blemishes on the face of the modern city. Dawn on an autumn morning when the sky behind the great bronze, neo-Byzantine dome of St Isaac's turns first soft pink and then white-gold, before giving way to one of the last days of sunshine. Or on a dark evening with autumn fast yielding to winter, when the streets of the rain-sodden, leaf-blown square in front of the cathedral's phalanx of red granite columns seem to wait at attention for the passage of an imperial carriage ferrying a grandee past the rearing equestrian statue of Nicholas I to a meeting in the cold and imposing Mariinsky Palace. For nostalgists of the days of empire, evenings such as these are best savored through the windows of the Astoria Hotel, immediately opposite. Opened in 1911, it was here that St Petersburg's officers made their last futile stand against the insurrectionary lower ranks in 1917, who dragged their officers out of the building and shot them in the street. Today, privileged patrons once again enjoy tea, champagne, and blinis from crystal and imperial porcelain among the liveried staff, Gobelins tapestries, and elegant Karelian birch lounges of the piano bar.

Nearby, on the morning after such an evening, the wind-whipped waters of the Neva are a reminder that St Petersburg was built as a saltwater port — Russia's first — designed to take advantage of the Neva, which drains the cold, fresh waters of Lake Ladoga into the brackish Gulf of Finland. But there is no longer any evidence of its being a working port in the monumental heart of the city, and the Winter Palace seems as distant from the salt and grime of the docks as it's possible to be. Only on a clear day, from the dome of St Isaac's, do you realize that Peter the Great's city sits sidesaddle. The Neva's chute is short. Barely half a mile from the Winter Palace, it makes a sharp dog-leg and meets the Baltic, and in the afternoon sun-silhouetted cranes and container ships testify to its continued activity. Having been born in land-locked Muscovy, Peter the Great would rejoice that

---

[5] Formed in post-Soviet St Petersburg, and playing essentially American-inspired music, the band's nostalgic Soviet-era name seems to capture a lingering ambivalence about the city's identity, even among those too young to remember communism.

his foundation remains Russia's busiest commercial harbor and that, even today, shipbuilding remains one of St Petersburg's main industries. Fittingly, in the gardens between St Isaac's and the Neva, the famous Bronze Horseman, Catherine the Great's monumental tribute to Peter, looks towards the river.

But what of the symbol I have come in search of, the sainted Nicholas II and his family, the last Romanovs, the Royal Passion-bearers? If the Russian Church's canonization of Nicholas II as a saint can be interpreted as a sign of the regeneration in Russian culture of the theocratic principle, does this resurgence spring spontaneously from the heart of the Russian people themselves, or has it been manufactured by Church and State authorities? Is the veneration of Russia's last tsar a popular cult, with a genuine footing in popular piety, or is it something artificial sponsored and imposed from the top? I could only answer such questions by going to the people themselves, and for that reason, after my first encounter with the veneration of Nicholas II in Moscow, I set out on a journey across Russia to observe the treatment of Nicholas and his family's memory by modern Russians in situ. My first destination was that place where Nicholas's bones are now to be found: the Romanov mausoleum in Petersburg's Peter and Paul Fortress.

                    ෴   ෴   ෴

For the resting place of one of Europe's greatest dynasties, St Petersburg's Romanov mausoleum is a modest affair. Housed in a quaint, Dutch-style cathedral, painted in a chaste combination of white and yellow, at the heart of St Petersburg's diamond-shaped Peter and Paul Fortress, it's outwardly not very Russian either. The original kernel of Peter the Great's new, westward-looking capital, the fortress on the banks of the Neva bears witness to his hope that the city would become, not the cliched "Venice of the North," but a "new Amsterdam," a city, unlike Venice, that Peter actually visited, and a center, in Peter's day, of the early European Enlightenment, where, in striking contrast to the integral Orthodox society of Peter's own Moscow, the French rationalist Catholic Descartes and the skeptical Jew Spinoza had in recent memory found home and refuge. If Peter had his way, the spirit of his city, too, would be tolerant, rational, enlightened.

Perhaps that is why the cathedral that houses the mausoleum is so small. On a bright, sunny day, I enter it. In serried rows on the floor-space before me, the church's marble tombs provide a potted history of Romanov Russia.[6] To the right, facing the gilded baroque icon

---

[6] In what follows, I draw especially on James H. Billington, *The Icon and the Axe: An interpretive history of Russian culture* (New York: Vintage Books, 1970); Richard Pipes, *Russia under the Old Regime*, 2nd ed. (Harmondsworth: Penguin Books, 1995); and Geoffrey Hosking, *Russia: People and empire, 1552–1917* (London: Fontana Press, 1998).

stand, lie Peter the Great (*r.* 1682–1725) and his consort and successor, Catherine I (*r.* 1725–27). Born in the Moscow Kremlin in 1672, the only son of the second Romanov tsar, Alexei (1645–76), Peter is the figure all modern Russian history proceeds from, and whose legacy it grapples with. Impatient, as a young tsar, with the traditional, Orthodox Church-dominated culture and outlook of early modern Moscow, Peter at the age of twenty-six went to Western Europe, where for almost two years he worked in the shipyards of Amsterdam and London and immersed himself in European ways and culture. Returning to Moscow in 1699 to crush a revolt that had broken out in his absence, Peter resolved to plant the early modern Muscovite State and society on a new European footing. Men's beards were shaved; women shed their veils. Cards and dances, the poll tax and a standing army were introduced. Time itself bowed at Peter's command as the old Byzantine calendar counting the years from creation was replaced overnight with the Julian calendar then in use in Europe. In 1702, a new capital — Petersburg — was proclaimed on an unhealthy toehold of marshy land that Peter had captured from the Swedes on the Baltic.

Petersburg's foundation was the signal for, and later the enduring symbol of, a profound cultural revolution. Peter was a phenomenon. In short time, the government was restructured, the ancient medieval offices staffed by monks replaced by an up-to-date college system imported from Sweden. In 1721, the State itself was founded anew: at Peter's command, the old theocratic tsardom of Moscow, where the God-given authority of the tsar had always been in principle but one aspect of the all-encompassing authority of the Church, was replaced with the thoroughly secular Russian Empire where Peter alone as, officially, emperor and no longer as tsar, reigned supreme and unchallenged by anyone or anything, according to the principles, then in fashion, of Western European "enlightened absolutism." The same year, by a stroke of the pen, Peter abolished the patriarchate and made a committee of civil servants administrators in the emperor's name of the Russian Church.

But change as profound as the one initiated by Peter cannot but elicit opposition. And for half a century after Peter's death in 1725, the great question in Russian history was whether Peter's revolution would survive. Peter himself had ensured that this was a genuinely open question: in 1718, Peter's only heir died from the torture wounds inflicted on him following a conviction for treason, and none of the boys by Peter's second marriage survived their father. In any case, Peter had declared the dynastic principle irrational and void. He would name his own successor on the basis not of blood but of shared vision and merit. Only he never got round to it; and beside him now in the Peter and Paul fortress cathedral lies the tomb of his second wife, an illiterate

Lithuanian servant girl known to history as Catherine I (1725–27), who fell into Peter's baggage train during his wars with Sweden and caught the young warrior-tsar's attention. Catherine was a useful cypher for the men whose fortunes depended on maintaining Peter's revolution, and when Peter died, she was rushed to the throne to prevent any return to the old ways and Moscow.

Unfortunately for these men, Catherine reigned only two years before going the way of her husband, and also entombed here in the cathedral are Peter II (r. 1727–30), Peter the Great's grandson and only legitimate heir, who wanted to return the seat of government to Moscow, but who died of smallpox at the age of fourteen, after less than three years on the throne; Anna (r. 1730–40), the corpulent, coal-haired daughter of Peter's dim-witted half-brother, Ivan, who notoriously turned the running of her empire over to her lover; Elizabeth I (r. 1740–61), the profligate offspring of Peter the Great and Catherine I, who, proverbially, never wore the same dress twice and whose chief architect, Bartolomeo Rastrelli, left St Petersburg and its environs with some of Europe's most splendid high rococo buildings; the mean and unattractive Peter III (r. 1761–62), Elizabeth's nephew, who despite having been born in Germany, succeeded his aunt, briefly, to the throne; and next to this limited and ill-fated man, his extraordinary wife, the German princess Sophie Friederike Auguste von Anhalt-Zerbst-Dornburg, who arrived in Russia at the age of fifteen and who (having driven her husband from the throne in 1762) died there, fifty-two years later, as Catherine II "the Great" (r. 1762–96), Russia's ablest ruler since Peter the Great himself, despite not possessing a drop of Romanov (or Russian) blood. By the end of the second decade of Catherine's reign, the permanence of Peter's revolution was assured. Having annexed half of Poland and the northern Black Sea coast, Russia was indisputably one of Europe's Great Powers and Catherine's extravagant court a byword, with its deep debt to Voltaire, the contemporary skeptical French satirist of religion, for moral (and sexual) libertinage.

To continue the stroll among the Romanov dead, I cross to the other side of the nave. Here, in identical black marble tombs with gold lettering, lie Paul I (r. 1796–1801), Catherine's estranged son (and, according to rumor, the product of an affair between her and a dashing guardsman), murdered in 1801; Alexander I (r. 1801–25), Catherine the Great's favorite grandson, who led Russia's armies to victory over Napoleon in 1812–1814, and died without legitimate issue in mysterious circumstances eleven years later. Next come Alexander's two younger brothers: Constantine, named to fulfil the role mapped out for him by his grandmother Catherine the Great's unrealized plan to revive the Byzantine Empire; and Nicholas I (r. 1825–55) who suppressed the 1825 Decembrist uprising in favor of a constitution limiting the tsar's power, and led autocratic Russia to defeat at the hands of "liberal" Britain and France in the Crimean War (1853–56). From here, I perform an about-face. On the right-hand side of the nave (behind a baroque pulpit as foreign to traditional Orthodox church décor as the iconostasis's gilded crucifix and the church's needle-like steeple), sits a heavy tomb carved out of a solid piece of deep, blood red marble, surrounded by a brass grate. This is the resting place of Nicholas I's son and successor Alexander II (*r.* 1856–81), the "Tsar-Liberator," who emancipated the serfs and presided over an era of reform that seemed to herald Russia's transformation into a liberal-bureaucratic (if not exactly a liberal-parliamentary) monarchy, and whose 1881 assassination heralded the coming internal theological crisis of the Russian *teokratia*.[7] Alexander II was also the last Romanov emperor to model his public image in accordance with Peter the Great's "Europeanizing" mission, as a European prince.[8] Buried in the tomb alongside him is his son and successor, the bearded, heavy-set Alexander III (1881–94), who broke with the dynasty's Europeanizing ideology, and chose instead to identify Russia's future with a return to its own distinctive, Orthodox-Slavophile civilization (hence both his invitation to Dostoevsky, in 1880, to have tea at Alexander's home in St Petersburg's Anichkov Palace, as well as Alexander's low reputation in the eyes of most Western historians). Guided by the able Sergei Witte, Alexander III also set in motion the decade-long spurt of breakneck industrial expansion that saw Russia's economy grow faster than almost any other in the world, and St Petersburg become an industrial city almost overnight. Sadly, he died too early to see many of its fruits — or to appreciate many of its dangers to the dynasty.

Until 1998, this roll-call ended here. Officially, the Soviet public did not know what had happened to Nicholas II's body after his and

---

[7] As seen acutely if idiosyncratically by Vladimir Solovyov, the "first" Russian philosopher, who played such an important role not only in Bulgakov's but a whole generation's return to Orthodoxy: Andrei Walicki, *A History of Russian Thought: From the Enlightenment to Marxism*, trans. Hilda Andrews-Rusiecka (Stanford, CA: Stanford University Press, 1979), 382–87. According to Solovyov, who was at only the beginning of his career in 1881, Alexander III's insistence on having the perpetrators of his father's assassination executed betrayed the Christian principles that should have underlain the tsarist regime as — Solovyov took the regime at its word — an Eastern Orthodox *teokratia*. For an account of events and Solovyov's reaction to them, see K. V. Mochul'skii, *Vladimir Solov'ev* (Paris: YMCA Press, 1951), 222–30. Returning for the next two decades to the theocratic ideal again and again in his works, Solovyov was doubtless the thinker who placed the notion in Bulgakov's mind. See, for example, Greg Gaut, "Christian politics: Vladimir Solovyov's Social Gospel theology," *Modern Greek Studies Yearbook* 10/11 (1994/1995): 653–74; and V. K. Kantor, "Vladimir Solov'ev: The imperial problems of world theocracy," *Russian Studies in Philosophy* 46 (2007): 76–102.
[8] The aesthetics of this shift are well evoked by Richard S. Wortman, *Scenarios of Power: Myth and ceremony in Russian Monarchy from Peter the Great to the abdication of Nicholas II*, rev. ed. (Princeton, NJ: Princeton University Press, 2006).

his family's murder. Everybody knew that it wasn't in the mausoleum and that the rest was a closely guarded state secret.[9] Today, however, behind a pair of double oak doors, a single slab of white marble lies bathed — on sunny days — in the light that streams in from a large window behind, illuminating the surface of an icon of the Royal Passion-bearers. Large marble plaques with gold lettering identify this as the last resting place of Nicholas II, his wife Alexandra, and their five children, Olga, Tatiana, Maria, Anastasia, and Alexei. Discovered in a waterlogged trunk buried in a depression in a muddy loggers' track in a conifer forest outside the Urals city of Sverdlovsk (formerly, and now, once again, Ekaterinburg) at the beginning of the last decade of Communism, Nicholas and his family's broken, decomposed and incomplete remains were DNA-tested when the technology became available in the early 1990s and declared in the eyes of science to be theirs.[10] With Russian President Boris Yeltsin, Romanov descendants and other European royals in attendance they were buried in the mausoleum in a nationally televised ceremony in 1998. And here the paradox arises. For while, two years later, the Russian Orthodox Church declared Russia's last tsar and his family saints, this simple but poignant chapel in the imperial mausoleum is *not* a shrine or a place of pilgrimage: despite the evidence of the DNA-testing, the Russian Church, holding fast to the earliest forensic investigation into the Romanovs' murder, and its conclusion that the family's bodies were completely incinerated, does not recognize the remains discovered in the forest as Nicholas's and his family's. No incense burns, no choir sings an akathist, and the only figures jostling to glimpse the tomb are foreign tourists.

✑   ✑   ✑

Is Russia indifferent, then, to the last tsar, whom the Church has canonized? Certainly, not only indifference but active forgetting, oblivion, was for seventy years the goal of Russia's Soviet authorities. With Bolshevik rule, Russia was thoroughly "de-Romanovized."[11] Statues and portraits (especially of the last three tsars, Alexander II, Alexander III, and Nicholas II) were removed, double-headed eagles burned and destroyed, and Petersburg's former palaces converted into art galleries, unions' headquarters, and meeting places for the Communist Party youth organization, the Pioneers, as if no Romanov had ever lived there (and, indeed, often enough as if the later members of the discredited dynasty had never

---

[9] For the story of the family's murder and the disposal, rediscovery and public reinterment of their remains, see Wendy Slater, *The Many Deaths of Tsar Nicholas II: Relics, remains and the Romanovs* (London: Routledge, 2007).
[10] Slater, *Many Deaths*, 29–30. As an observer of the cult of the Royal Passion-bearers, Slater is critical and unsympathetic: ibid., 106–27.
[11] See, especially, Orlando Figes and Boris Kolonitskii, *Interpreting the Russian Revolution: The Language and Symbols of 1917* (New Haven, CT: Yale University Press, 1999).

existed). Indeed, until the 1980s the very mention of Nicholas II was all but forbidden. When Soviet authorities did refer to Russia's last monarch, it was as that "tyrant" and "enemy of the people," Nicholas "the Bloody." Anastasia Edel, a Russian-American who lived through the last decade of the Soviet Union, recalls:

> Slowly but surely, the memory of the Romanovs was effaced from the nation's psyche. By the time I was growing up in the Soviet Union and studying history at school in the early 1980s, textbooks scarcely mentioned their name at all, preferring faceless terms like "czarism," "tyranny," and "autocracy."[12]

In short, everything appeared to confirm Trotsky's boast in his 1932 *History of the Revolution* that "the country had so radically vomited up the monarchy that it could never again crawl back down people's throats."[13]

Today, however, Trotsky appears to have spoken too soon. In the Winter Palace—as the official seat of the emperor until 1917 the most symbolically potent of the Romanov residences, but converted in the 1920s into hanging space for a much-expanded Hermitage Museum—the rococo chapel (closed in Soviet days) where Nicholas and Alexandra were married is again open, its magnificent gilded iconostasis gleaming after restoration, while the short nave serves as a repository for a changing menu of Romanov "relics" such as the torn, blood-stained tunic Alexander II was wearing when he died in 1881, or the bowler hat Nicholas II was wearing when he almost lost his life to a Japanese samurai on a tour of Japan in 1891. In the same spirit, the St George's Hall next door, which had functioned as the palace throne room until being "cleansed" of its monarchical trappings under the Soviets, has been restored to its former glory: the old map of the USSR in precious gemstones is gone and the throne, dais, and crimson, double-headed eagle canopy have been retrieved from storage. Above all, perhaps, Nicholas and Alexandra's first family home, the so-called "Flat" in the northwestern corner of the Winter Palace into which they moved immediately after their wedding in 1895, is not only marked once again on Hermitage maps but filled with furnishings, earnest but ersatz representations of the originals (looted in 1917) that are less interesting than the decision to reverse the policy of erasure to which they bear witness.[14]

---

[12] Anastasia Edel, "The remains of the Romanovs," *New York Times*, 10 July 2017: https://www.nytimes.com/2017/07/10/opinion/red-century-russia-romanov.html (accessed January 5, 2025).

[13] Cited in Figes and Kolonitskii, *Interpreting*, 72.

[14] Perhaps the most curious evidence of the rehabilitation of the Romanovs is visible in the long passageway that runs parallel to the great Neva enfilade; mounted portraits show the likeness of every ruling from the founder of the dynasty, Mikhail, to the last tsar, Nicholas II. Far the most interesting of these is the full-length canvas showing a young Nicholas II in a scarlet Hussar's uniform hung with gold braid on one side, and Lenin, in cap and trench coat, on the other. Painted by the Russian artist Ilya Galkin

The story is similar at the Anichkov Palace, at the other end of Nevsky Prospekt, with the twist here being that it was the home of the only Romanov more hated than Nicholas: his father, Alexander III, who had Lenin's elder brother Aleksandr (an eighteen-year-old member of a student terrorist group caught plotting an assassination attempt on the tsar) hanged in 1887.[15] In the 1930s, the Anichkov became the Leningrad headquarters of the local branch of the Pioneers. Today, although the Pioneers have gone, the Anichkov still resounds with children's voices, and every week, some 17,000 children come for lessons in drawing and music, creative writing, computer skills, ballet, and rhythmic dance in the renamed "St Petersburg City Palace for Creative Activity by Young People." Now, however, the former palace's Romanov connections have become a source of pride. "Thousands of Petersburgers spend their leisure hours dancing at balls held in the Palace's reception and drawing rooms, just as in the days of the Imperial Court," reads a plaque on the ground floor. Numerous reminders of the Romanovs have returned. In one hall, when I visited, a group of teenagers assembled in front of a Romanov family listened while an instructor explained the dynasty's history. In another, the products of a recent drawing class were displayed: Pollina (ten years old) had drawn a likeness of Empress Elizabeth and shaded it with pastels; Angelina (eleven) had drawn a seated Catherine the Great in black and white cross-hatching. But most striking of all was the wood-paneled library, or "digital resources center," dedicated to the memory of the once reviled Alexander III. On a mantle, a family photograph shows this once reviled emperor, bearded and thickset, surrounded by his family, the dainty, hourglass-waisted Empress Marie and their five children, including their eldest, the faintly mustachioed future Nicholas II. Before Russia's last tsar and his family could be venerated as saints, they had to be rehabilitated as people.

෨෨   ෨෨   ෨෨

Indeed, to grasp the significance of the phenomenon visible today in the Romanovs' former palaces, it is important to recall how recently most

---

in 1896, Nicholas's portrait hung until 1917 in a Petersburg trade school. Taken down in 1917, it was nonetheless neither defaced nor destroyed but rather saved when, in 1924 Vladislav Ismailovich covered Nicholas's portrait with a layer of priming, turned the canvas over, and used the other side for a full-length portrait of the USSR's recently deceased first leader, Lenin. Thus preserved, Nicholas's image was discovered, by chance, in 2017, the centenary of the Revolution. Today, with the canvas displayed so that both sides are visible, Nicholas and Lenin, joined like Siamese twins, offer a certain metaphor of Russia itself, a country that remained, perhaps, monarchical and theocratic even as, for seventy years, it wore the outer garb of the atheist and the revolutionary. For images of the double-sided portrait, see: https://www.nytimes.com/2016/11/15/arts/design/portrait-of-czar-nicholas-ii-beneath-lenin-portrait-stieglitz-art-and-industry-academy.html (accessed January 5, 2025).

[15] On the failed plot and the effect of his brother's execution on Lenin, see Robert Service, *Lenin: A biography* (London: Pan Books, 2000), 56–60.

Russians saw their first photographs of a ruler and his family whose faces were for decades far more familiar to publics in the West than they were in Communist Russia. "I first saw a photograph of Nicholas II and Alexandra in 1992," recalled one woman in a book I found for sale in one of Petersburg's churches: "In it, they were still young, and I simply could not take my eyes off those wonderful, gentle faces . . . I fell in love [with them] with all my soul: they stood for an ideal that until that time I had not had."[16] Said another: "When I saw my first photograph of the family I knew only lies about them. But they had my heart literally from the first moment." A third woman recalled how, as a girl in the 1940s, she had been told to throw an old book about the Romanovs on the fire. She complied, saving only a picture of the Tsarevich Aleksei "because he was so beautiful." Fifty years later, however, she declared: "It is enough to look at their photographs, and a wave of love and happiness fills the heart." Another story recounted what happened when, in the 1990s, one woman hung a portrait of the Romanovs over her desk at work. "One day," said a man who was the woman's colleague at the time, "when nobody else was in the room, I went and looked at the picture and, unexpectedly, it all became perfectly clear to me: truly, these really are holy martyrs!" The experience recalls Bulgakov's. In the impoverished and often chaotic 1990s, it seemed, many Russians were having their own "vision on the Yalta Embankment." "It's hard to say how I made my way to the idea of monarchy," said another witness, "but it was a path from atheism to faith and from faith to monarchy."[17]

Others have made the journey, so similar in structure to Bulgakov's, with him. Indeed, perhaps the most powerful testimony to the restoration of the Romanovs' memory can be found in Petersburg's Kazan Cathedral. On Nevsky Prospekt, roughly equidistant between the Winter and Anichkov Palaces, the Kazan Cathedral, designed by the serf architect Andrei Varennikov in 1811, has always been Petersburg's most sacred shrine, the house of one of Russia's most venerated palladia, the "Kazan" icon of the Virgin Mary (so called because it was said to have been found in the smoldering ruins of the Tartar capital of Kazan after the Russians conquered the city in 1558). Brought to Moscow with the Russian armies that expelled the Polish forces occupying the Kremlin in

---

[16] See Prot. Aleksandr Shargunov. *Tsar* (Zlatoust: Arvato, 2013), 235–369, where Shargunov, an archpriest in the Russian Orthodox Church, reprints depositions sent to the Moscow Patriarchate following the Canonization Committee's recognition of Nicholas and his family's claim to sainthood, and the call for the public to furnish Church authorities with evidence of posthumous miracles.

[17] Another man recalled seeing a portrait of Nicholas II for sale at a flea market. His thoughts returned to it constantly. "A strong desire flamed in my heart to have the picture I had seen in my own home. The association was not only with an understanding of the sainthood of the Tsar-Martyr himself (which at that time I did not fully understand) but of him as a visible symbol of that Old Russia I loved so much," he testified.

1612, the icon of the Virgin cradling the Christ-child was subsequently hailed as Protectress of Russia. After the foundation of St Petersburg, a copy of the sacred image was painted for Russia's new capital and the Kazan Cathedral (loosely modeled on St Peter's Basilica in Rome) erected as its home.

As the shrine of the capital's most sacred image, the Kazan Cathedral was, in tsarist days, the venue of choice for the celebration of divine services touching on the nation's destiny. In 1812, the Russian generals Mikhail Kutuzov and Bernard de Tolly departed for war against the French invader, Napoleon, directly after a liturgy in the building. (Kutuzov's body still lies in the building, the keys of the French and German cities he captured, and a disintegrating French battle standard, hanging above it.) It was here, in Nicholas and Alexandra's presence, at a liturgy held in thanksgiving for the dynasty's Tercentenary in 1913, that Rasputin caused a ruckus by presuming to sit, uninvited, on the chairs reserved for the outraged President of the Duma, Mikhail Rodzianko. When, a year later, Germany declared war, it was to the same cathedral that Nicholas and Alexandra immediately reported to implore the icon's help against the armies of the Kaiser.

Just inside the door, a blaze of candles indicated the location of the icon of Our Lady of Kazan, to the left of the icon screen in the Cathedral's darkened interior. In front of it, a queue fifty to sixty people long extended into the hushed, candle-lit interior, the faithful waiting patiently to press their forehead to the revered icon, kiss it, and pour out their hearts to the Mother of God. Others, having made their venerations, had left a burning candle in the stands in front of the image, the source of the blaze of candlelight I had seen on my way in. I walked about the interior, its space divided by parallel porphyry columns, where similar but smaller "blazes" indicated the whereabouts in the building of other popular saints. In the far corner, to the right of the iconostasis, a priest chanted vespers in the company of seven or eight laymen. And then on the cathedral's south wall, my eyes lit on some familiar faces. A century after Russia's last imperial family came to this temple to seek, in prayer, God's blessing on their empire at war, a large icon of Nicholas, Alexandra and their children as Royal Passion-Bearers looked serenely out at the cathedral's darkened nave, inviting the faithful to address their prayers to them; the candles burning on the altar in front of their icon indicate that two or three recently had done so. On a column opposite, an icon of St Serafim of Sarov — a sainted, nineteenth-century hermit with particular significance, as we shall see, for Nicholas and Alexandra — preserved the close historical bond between the last Romanovs and their chosen spiritual patron. But even more interesting is the stone throne carved into the column's other side: facing the iconostasis, this is where the tsar would stand during the liturgy (for even the tsar stood in church).

Even without other trappings, this throne would be a powerful reminder of the theocratic principle. But mounted above it was an icon of Nicholas II different from others I had seen. Unlike the image of the family hanging on the wall in the nave, this image above the throne showed Nicholas and Alexei alone, the heir nestled on his father's lap. Dressed in the coronation regalia of medieval Russia, Nicholas wore the so-called Cap of Monomakh, a pyramidal, sable-trimmed headpiece studded with sapphires, rubies, and emeralds and crowned with a golden cross hung with pearls that by tradition was reputedly a gift from Emperor Constantine "Monomakos" IX of Byzantium to his grandson, the medieval Russian prince, Vladimir Monomakh. Symbolizing the transfer of the theocratic ideal of the Constantinian regime from Byzantium to Russia, the medieval cap on Nicholas's head made this icon an undisputed representation of the very ideal of *teokratia* that the Church authorities, professedly at least, had sought to hold at a distance from the Royal Passion-bearers' cult. That which had brought the two together was the instinct of the Russian people.

CHAPTER THREE

Nicholas and Alexandra

NICHOLAS AND ALEXANDRA: THEIR STORY IS so familiar it hardly needs retelling.[1] He was born in 1868, the eldest child and first-born son of the Tsarevich Grand Duke Aleksandr Aleksandrovich, and his consort, Grand Duchess Marie Fyodorovna.[2] She was born Princess Alix in 1872, the fourth child (and third daughter) of Grand Duke Louis IV of Hesse and by Rhine and his consort, Princess Alice, the daughter of Queen Victoria.[3] Both grew up in the shadow of two of the nineteenth century's most powerful monarchs. When Alix was six, diphtheria swept her native Hesse, and her mother, who had trained in the "new" science of nursing, insisted on taking care of her own when the disease reached the Palace. Tragically, she died after having contracted the disease from her six-year-old daughter, May. Thereafter, Alix was raised by her English governess, Miss Jackson, under the strict supervision of her grandmother, Queen Victoria, with whom she spent long stretches of time at Osborne House and the castles of Windsor and Balmoral. She was intellectually curious, artistically accomplished, strong-minded, and preferred to speak English. Persuaded by the example of her grandmother (who reigned over the largest empire in world history), she took for granted that it was right for women to take a lively interest in politics. But she was also shy, introverted and, as a devout Lutheran raised in an atmosphere of judgment and death, possessed of something of a sullen, "otherworldly" disposition that was often interpreted as haughtiness, pride, and aloof indifference.

Meanwhile, Nicholas was twelve when student revolutionaries threw a bomb under his grandfather Alexander II's carriage in St Petersburg in 1881. The first bomb wounded one of Alexander's officer-guardsmen

---

[1] The classic account is, of course, Robert Massie, *Nicholas and Alexandra* (New York: Atheneum, 1967) and repeatedly republished. On Nicholas II himself, see, especially, Dominic Lieven, *Nicholas II: Emperor of All the Russias* (London: Pimlico, 1993) and on Alexandra (born Princess Alix of Hesse), Greg King, *The Last Empress: The life and times of Alexandra Feodorovna Tsarina of Russia* (New York: Carol Publishing, 1994). An anthology of excerpted primary sources can be found in Andrei Maylunas and Sergei Mironenko, eds., *A Lifelong Passion: Nicholas and Alexandra, their own story*, trans. Darya Galy (London: Phoenix Giant, 1996).

[2] Technically, the heir's specific title was *tsesarevich* ("son of Caesar") as all the tsar's male offspring were *tsarevichi* ("sons of the tsar"). But that title is foreign to English-language readers and I shall use "tsarevich" throughout as the title of the heir to the throne. For the biographies of Nicholas's parents, see Lieven, *Nicholas II*, 23–30.

[3] For Alix's parents, see King, *Last Empress*, 3–11.

but left the emperor unharmed. Alexander's mistake was alighting from his carriage to check on the wounded man. A second bomb was then thrown, which blew off one of the emperor's legs and pulverized the other. He was rushed to the Winter Palace, where he bled to death surrounded by his two families. By his wife, the pious Empress Alexandra Fyodorovna, Alexander II had had four sons and two daughters. In 1866, however, the emperor had created scandal by initiating a relationship with a nineteen-year-old schoolgirl, Princess Catherine Dolgorukova. She bore him four children and when Empress Alexandra died in 1880, the emperor waited only three months before marrying Dolgorukova, whom he titled Princess Yurievskaya. Though it was a morganatic marriage and her children were excluded from the succession, Alexander II's second family was shunned by his legitimate children. From the beginning, the extra-marital relationship had fostered a breach between the emperor and his heir the Tsarevich Aleksandr, Nicholas's father, who condemned the affair as contrary to the Christian morality incumbent upon an Orthodox tsar. Indeed, the abnormalities of Alexander II's private life encouraged the future Alexander III to break with his father's Enlightenment-inspired reforms and liberal, Europeanizing legacy in favor of the restoration of what he considered traditional Orthodox morality and the authentic, authoritarian social structure of pre-Petrine Muscovy.

The adolescent Nicholas was present when his grandfather Alexander II died, and the memory of his grandfather lying in a pool of blood stayed with him for the rest of his life. His father succeeded as Emperor Alexander III, and Nicholas himself suddenly became Sovereign Tsarevich. But otherwise, little in Nicholas's life changed. By comparison with other royal families in Europe, Alexander III's household was distinguished by the warm relationship between parents and children. Whereas the "liberal" Alexander II had styled himself in the way traditional among the Romanovs since Peter the Great as an "enlightened" European prince, Alexander III, embodied the nineteenth-century romantic reaction against the Enlightenment in its Russian, Slavophile form. (One gets the impression that the Romanovs' Orthodoxy had been a fairly nominal commitment for several generations.) Indeed, a year before ascending the throne, the future Alexander III had received Dostoevsky at the Anichkov Palace, and with his beard, bearlike build, and famed strength, his public image was that of the *tsar-muzhik* (the "peasant tsar") in a way that appeared to correspond to Dostoevsky's anarcho-monarchist ideal, even as the regime Alexander III headed was criticized as a police state.

Pious but intellectually incurious, he and his wife, Marie Fyodorovna, left their children's education to tutors of varying quality. But both emperor and empress enjoyed family life, and their children's memoirs are full of stories of fishing and hunting trips, relaxed family vacations in Denmark, and warm celebrations during the great Orthodox holidays of Easter and Christmas. Apart from his parents (from whom he took his love of Orthodoxy, Russian-ness and physical activity), the most formative influence upon Nicholas in these years was his English tutor, Charles Heath. As Aleksandr Izvolsky, Nicholas's contemporary and later Russian foreign minister, recalled, "though Alexander III permitted the presence of no tutor or governess between him and his wife and children, an exception was made for Mr Heath, who entered into great familiarity with the Imperial Family and became Nicholas II's true educator."[4] Possessing an appreciation for art, Heath was an accomplished watercolorist. He also implanted in Nicholas his distinctively Victorian love of fresh air, games, and physical activity.[5] Indeed, thanks to Mr Heath, Nicholas entered adolescence not only fluent in English but at ease in the manners of an English gentleman. With her own Victorian sensibilities, Alix appears to have found it an attractive combination.

The two young people first met in 1884, when Alix's elder sister Elizabeth ("Ella") married Nicholas's uncle, Grand Duke Sergei Aleksandrovich.[6] At the time of their first meeting at Ella's wedding, Nicholas was sixteen and Alix was just twelve. But already an attraction appears to have developed between them. A second meeting in 1891 confirmed their feelings. Ella noticed. Her husband, Sergei, was the youngest of Nicholas's father's four brothers, and, being close to Nicholas in age, Ella had formed a bond with Nicholas that was closer to that of sister than aunt. As her younger sister's confidante, Ella did her best to foster a match. But she knew that standing in the way on her sister's side was religion. Both princesses had been raised as devout Lutherans in an age that took the differences between Protestantism and other, non-reformed branches of Christianity seriously. When she married Sergei in 1884, Ella had not been required to convert to Orthodoxy. But as Nicholas was destined to be tsar, the luxury of keeping her Lutheran faith was not open to Alix; a future *tsaritsa* had to convert. The heartache this caused Alix is well known. She felt her very salvation was at stake; and yet, in an era when purely dynastic marriages were still being contracted, she had her father's permission to marry for love alone, and, as she believed, she loved Nicholas. Moreover, as Hesse was a small and impoverished grand duchy in a now united German Empire dominated

[4] Alexandre Izwolsky, "Souvenirs de mon ministère, IV: Nicholas II," *Revue des deux mondes* 55:1 (January 1920): 50.
[5] See Lieven, *Nicholas II*, 34–35.
[6] For Ella's story, see Christopher Warwick, *Ella: Princess, Saint and Martyr* (Chichester: Wiley, 2006).

by the overweening power of Prussia, the attractions (both material and psychological) involved in becoming empress of Russia must have been many and great. But it's a testament to the moral seriousness that defined Alix's life that she would trade her faith for none of them. Only after observing the effect upon her sister of her sister's conversion did Alix consent to marry Nicholas, which she did in 1894.

Once engaged, Nicholas and Alexandra spent several weeks at Alix's home in the English-style surroundings of Darmstadt's New Palace before traveling together to Windsor Castle as guests of Queen Victoria. The Queen initially opposed the match with Nicholas, as she disliked both Russia and Orthodoxy, and, in view of the revolutionary movements in the Romanov Empire, considered the Russian throne dangerous. But she was charmed by Nicholas, who returned her affection by referring to the reigning British monarch and Empress of India as "Granny" for the rest of his life. As soon as the summer of merriment was over, Alexander III dispatched an Orthodox priest from Russia to instruct the future *tsaritsa* in her new faith. By Alix's own report, she found it both intellectually fascinating and spiritually compelling. She also began learning Russian (although, for the next twenty-four years, Nicholas and Alexandra's domestic language as a couple would remain Alix's native English). Nicholas and Alix had planned to marry in the spring of 1895. But in October 1894 Alix was received into the Orthodox Church, made a Russian grand duchess, and given the name Alexandra Fyodorovna. A week later her would-be future father-in-law was dead and Nicholas, her twenty-six-year-old fiancé, was reigning emperor. With court protocol dictating twelve months' deep mourning, the couple wed on November 26 in the imperial chapel of the Winter Palace. Alexandra, the new Empress of Russia, was twenty-two years old.

Nicholas's journey to adulthood and marriage had not reflected the same intense, intellectually agonized piety as Alix's. From a young age, participating in the liturgies of Church and observing the feasts and fasts of the liturgical year, Nicholas was captivated by the sensuous beauty of the chants, incense, candles, and icons, and only later was he instructed in the intellectual tenets of Orthodoxy. Indeed, having absorbed the elements of Orthodox family life at home with his parents, Nicholas seems to have approached Orthodoxy as a ritual world to be enjoyed, rather than as an intellectual proposition to be assented to or a moral code to be rigidly observed.[7] Leaving home to serve as an officer in the prestigious Preobrazhensky Guards in 1887, therefore, Nicholas, who enjoyed the discipline and camaraderie of regimental life,

---

[7] His diary entries in these years are full of notes such as "Got up just in the nick of time for Mass" or "Got up half an hour before Mass." See Nicholas II, January 14 and February 4, 1890 in Diary (1) = *Dnevnik" Imperatora Nikolaia II* (Berlin: Slovo, 1923), 13, 17.

also made his own the flaws and foibles characteristic of the sons of the aristocracy across Old Regime Europe. He was a party boy, reveling in the daily succession of balls, concerts and ballets that made up the annual Winter Season. On January 15, 1890, he noted that this was "the first time in the New Year I spent the evening at home." Three days later, he wrote that his legs hurt because he had danced so much the previous night at the Vorontsov Ball. Lessons suffered. But the summers were full of revelry, too, especially once he had joined the regiment. On one occasion in July, he had to be carried home by his fellow officers from a party at which the regiment had gone through 125 bottles of champagne.[8] His infatuation with Mathilde Kschessinskaya, a student at the Imperial Ballet School, occurred at this time. The relationship became serious in 1892.[9] Though by this stage Nicholas believed he loved Alix and had resolved to marry her, for the next two years he and Kschessinskaya effectively cohabited a mansion previously owned by the composer Rimsky-Korsakov on Petersburg's leafy Petrograd Side. Indeed, Nicholas was still cohabiting with Kschessinskaya when, in April 1894, he departed for Coburg to ask Alix's hand in marriage. Once Alix had given him her hand, he confessed to her the nature of his relationship with Kschessinskaya and, making a gift to Kschessinskaya of the Petrograd mansion, broke the relationship off. No truth pertained to the portrayal by the 2017 Russian film *Mathilde* of Nicholas and Alexandra's marriage as a Charles-and-Diana-style scandal.

As man and wife, Nicholas and Alexandra's union was physically intense, fruitful, and exclusive. "Nicholas II was much more than a loving and devoted husband. He was literally the lover of his life partner," said Aleksandr Mossolov, a palace official who observed the couple at close quarters for more than a decade.[10] But it was also deeply spiritual. Even as Alexandra recalled the physical pleasures of her wedding night, by the morning after, her thoughts had turned to eternity. As she wrote in Nicholas's diary: "Never did I believe there could be such utter happiness in the world — such a feeling of unity between two mortal beings. No more separations. At last united, bound for life, and when this life is ended, we meet again in the other world and remain together for Eternity."[11]

A year later, in December 1895, having moved into in a specially renovated suite of rooms in the northwest corner of the Winter Palace, Nicholas noted that he and Alexandra had spent their first evening in

---

[8] See Nicholas II, July 30 and 31, 1890 in Diary (1), 31, 32.
[9] See HSH Princess Romanovsky-Krassinsky, *Dancing in Petersburg: The memoirs of Kschessinska*, trans. Arnold Haskell (London: Victor Gollanz, 1960), 38–39.
[10] A. A. Mossolov, *At the Court of the Last Tsar*, ed. A. A. Pilence, trans. E. W. Dickes (London: Methuen, 1935), 30.
[11] Maylunas and Mironenko, *Lifelong Passion*, 109.

their first family home hanging icons. Although Nicholas, as husband, father, and emperor, would always enjoy the officers' mess hall, the first night he and Alexandra spent in their first proper home as a couple foreshadowed the increasingly central place Orthodoxy would play in his and Alix's lives. Indeed, in addition to the new burden of bearing an office itself charged with sacred meaning, Alexandra's spiritual intensity, and the agony she had gone through in converting to Orthodoxy for his sake, seem to have quickened Nicholas's own religious inclinations. Others, however, saw the influence as flowing in the other direction. As the years passed, Alexandra's friend Sophie Buxhoeveden wrote that the young empress "became more and more attached to the Russian Church, throwing herself into the practice of its religion with all the fervor of her nature. In this she was encouraged by the Emperor."[12]

From the earliest years of Nicholas' reign, therefore, his diary entries reveal the emergence of a young man of striking Christian piety, one who always acknowledged God as his "first beginning and last end," the source of his happiness and the primordial principle over his life. On December 31, 1894, for example, he records some thoughts that ran through his mind during the Liturgy held to mark the closure of the year that had seen him become both tsar and married man. "It was difficult to stand in church with the thought of terrible transformation that had taken place during the year. But, trusting in God, I look without fear to the approaching year because the very worst thing that could happen to me, which I have feared my whole life, has taken place. And alongside such irreversible bitterness the Lord has blessed me with a happiness I could not have dreamt of. He has given me Alix."

Before marriage and accession to the throne, Nicholas mentions attendance at the Sunday Divine Liturgy irregularly in his diaries. Presumably, he attended, but the fact didn't always merit a mention. In what may have been a sign of Nicholas's increasingly religious mind, from 1895 the Divine Liturgy was noted every Sunday like a steadfast, weekly anchor, while Orthodoxy's liturgical calendar provided it with a sense of sacred form and meaning. As he wrote in his diary on the Monday before the beginning of Lent, 1895, he was looking forward to the season of prayer and fasting, because "my mood is such that I very much want to pray. To pray—whether in church or one's own private prayers—is the greatest consolation on this earth."[13] When Holy Week arrived, he attended the Liturgy daily. Later, in a letter to his mother, he described his feelings during Easter celebrations in Moscow in 1900. "What a joy it is to us, dear Mama, to prepare for Holy Communion

[12] Sophie Buxhoeveden, *The Tragic Empress: The authorized biography of Alexandra Romanov* (n. p.: Taylor Street Books, 2016), 60.
[13] Nicholas II, February 13, 1895 in *Dnevniki Imperatora Nikolaia II* (Moscow: Orbtia, 1991) = Diary (2), 64.

here in the Kremlin, with all its various churches, chapels and palaces… I never knew I would be able to reach such heights of religious ecstasy as this Lent has brought me to."[14] To write, as one historian has done that, Nicholas's "religious faith was personal, not the mediated religion of the Orthodox Church, ministered through prayer and sacrament, but a direct, unmediated bond with God" is an exaggeration that pries apart things that belong together: a Christian "faith" that was only liturgical prayer and sacrament, and never person, would hardly be either Christian or faith at all.[15]

In Nicholas's fundamental orientation towards God, the major events of family life all elicit outpourings, and Nicholas also reveals himself a man who thanks God for the good he sees around him. On Alix's birthday in their first year of marriage, he wrote that, "for all the Lord has already given us, for all that with which He has already blessed us in our short life together, it is necessary to thank Him for his great kindness and mercy." When the couple's first child, Olga, was born in November of the same year, Nicholas's first instinct was again to thank God. "I almost cannot believe that this baby is ours," he writes, elated. "God, what happiness!" Sensitivity of soul and the capacity for empathy mark him, too. Present at Olga's birth, he almost experienced his wife's birth pangs with her.

Thanksgiving, delight in the beauty of the natural world, sensitivity to others' sufferings — these are all fundamentally Christian dispositions, and they recur repeatedly in Nicholas's diary. His young wife was a shy empress. Recalling her discomfort at the great Winter Palace ball of January 1896, Nicholas wrote that he himself "suffered for poor Alix." The beauty of the created world also caught Nicholas's attention. "Everything in the park was so green and beautiful," he notes in the spring of 1895 at Tsarskoye Selo, while at Peterhof, on the Gulf of Finland, he noted the mirror-like quality of the tranquil water. On other occasions, he wrote about sitting with Alix in the Winter Palace watching the ice break up and float down the river and moonlit nights at Tsarskoye Selo. He and Alix picked anemones together in the park. As one Orthodox writer has put it, "Unless we start out with a feeling of awe and astonishment — with what is often called a sense of the numinous — we shall make little progress on the Way [of faith]."[16] By the early years of his marriage, at the latest, Nicholas seems to have been truly on that Way.

---

[14] Edward J. Bing, ed., *The Letters of Tsar Nicholas and Empress Marie: being the confidential correspondence between Nicholas II, last of the tsars, and his mother, Dowager Empress Maria Feodorovna* (London: Nicholson and Watson, 1937), 143–44.
[15] The quotation is from Richard Wortman, "Nicholas II and the Revolution of 1905," in Wortman, *Russian Monarchy: Representation and rule* (Brighton, MA: Academic Studies Press, 2013), 201.
[16] Ware, *Orthodox Way*, 13.

Nicholas's correspondence with his mother, the Empress Dowager Marie Fyodorovna, is also an important source of evidence for Nicholas's religious convictions. Marie's struggle to take pleasure in her eldest son's marriage and growing young family was aggravated by the deep grief she suffered for the loss of her husband, and by her misgivings (never allayed) about Alexandra's suitability for her son.[17] Like Nicholas and Alexandra's union, Marie's marriage with Alexander III had been loving, devoted, and exclusive, and on a visit to her father, the king of Denmark after her husband's death, she reported in a letter to Nicholas the sorrow that came over her when she stood during the Liturgy "next to Papa's vacant place." Nicholas replied with a reflection on his own marriage, writing to his mother that he understood how she felt. "I cannot be grateful enough to Providence, which has granted me such a treasure for life and thus comforted me . . . in the days of our dreadful sorrow."[18]

Both Marie's and Nicholas's grief was compounded by the poor health of Nicholas's younger brother and heir presumptive, the Grand Duke George Aleksandrovich. George, who had contracted tuberculosis in 1890, lived in an exile imposed by his health away from his family at Abastumani, a spa resort in Georgia's Lesser Caucasus Mountains. Three years younger than Nicholas, the two brothers had always enjoyed each other's company. In 1895, Nicholas wrote a note to his mother ahead of her departure with George on a visit to the family relations in Denmark. "I pray that you will be granted the consolation of seeing dear George well and happy as before. . .'Let not your heart be troubled; ye believe in God; believe also in Me' (Jn 14)." Despite the prayers Nicholas surely said for his brother, George died unexpectedly and alone in 1899, at the age of twenty-eight.

But the actions Nicholas took in the light of his Christian faith were not limited to the privacy of family sorrows. His faith also intruded on high politics. One example, perhaps, of this is an eyebrow-raising circular that Nicholas dispatched in 1898 to the governments of the other European powers calling for the world's first disarmament conference. "The maintenance of general peace, and a possible reduction of the excessive armaments which weigh upon all nations, present themselves in the existing condition of the whole world, as the ideal towards which the endeavors of all Governments should be directed," Nicholas advised his fellow European monarchs. In London, Vienna, and Berlin, where suspicions of Russian motives ran strong, statesmen wondered whether

---

[17] See letter from Marie Fyodorovna to Nicholas II on March 12, 1909 in Bing, *Letters of Tsar Nicholas*, 239: "It is too sad and painful to see her always ailing and incapable of taking part in anything. You have enough worries in life as it is, without having the ordeal added of seeing the person you love most in the world suffer. It hurts me so much for your sake, dear Nicky, and I pray God from the depth of my soul that she will soon recover and that you may be more at peace."

[18] Bing, *Letters of Tsar Nicholas*, 102.

Nicholas was mad or being tricky. But perhaps the most plausible explanation was that Nicholas was simply being a Christian. As a Christian and a ruler, Nicholas had apparently come to believe (in a way that should have encouraged Solovyov) that the preservation of the peace was simply part of his moral duty before God. As one historian has put it, "Fueled by the image of Russia's messianic role in the world promoted by the nineteenth-century Slavophiles and enlightened by the distinctively Orthodox emphasis on the humility of Christ, Nicholas also fervently believed in the divinely appointed nature of Russia's international status as a world leader."[19]

And yet, if Nicholas did take the moral obligations that flowed from his personal commitment as a Christian increasingly seriously after he had become tsar in 1894, it did not necessarily follow that he would come to perceive his *office* itself as a sacred one: that of an Orthodox-Christian ruler at the apex of a "Constantinian" regime that was ideally conceived as a *teokratia*. For the theocratic principle exceeds the merely private cultivation of Christian virtue (as important as that undoubtedly is). Since Peter the Great's secularizing reforms, other ancestors of his might have aspired to *that*. But such a (fundamentally Protestant and Kantian) view of religion does not suffice to build, and cannot amount to, a *teokratia*, in which, as Bulgakov put it, the "Tsar, too, bore his authority like the Cross of Christ" (and where, as Bulgakov continued, "obedience to him could also be the Cross of Christ and [carried out] in His name"). *Such* a theocratic conception of his office Nicholas seems to have adopted from very early on in his reign. It never left him, and he was always aware of the burden or binding obligation it placed on him and on his conscience. As Nicholas would put it to his foreign minister, Aleksandr Izvolsky, many years later, at the height of disturbances that potentially threatened the throne, "If you see me so little troubled, it is because I have the firm, the absolute belief that the fate of Russia, my own fate and that of my family is in the hands of God, Who has placed me where I am. Whatever happens, I will bend before His will, with the consciousness of never having had any other thought than to serve the country He has confided me."[20]

This book proceeds from the premise that Nicholas's conception of his office as being a theocratic one was so deeply and intuitively held that no account of his reign, and the tragedy with which that reign concluded, can ignore it. But whence had awareness of the theocratic principle at the heart of Russia's Constantinian regime come to Nicholas? The usual explanation — the lessons that Nicholas received as an adolescent

---

[19] John Mack, "Nicholas II and the 'Rescript for Peace' of 1898: Apostle of peace or shrewd politician?" *Russian History* 31 (2004): 83–103.
[20] Alexandre Izvolsky, "Souvenirs de mon ministère, II: Après la dissolution de la Douma," *Revue des Deux Mondes* 52:1 (July 1919): 105.

in religion and constitutional law from Konstantin Pobedonostsev, lay Procurator of the Holy Synod and leading arch-conservative of his age — seems insufficient. For all Pobedonostsev's horror at modernity, there was always something characteristically *modern* about his version of the Russian autocracy. A convinced pessimist as regards human nature, Pobedonostsev looked on the tsar's office as if it were a historical incarnation of Hobbes' Leviathan, a God-sanctioned repressive force for restraining humankind's ineradicable tendency towards sin, and little more.[21] But such a view has more in common with the Augustinian premises of Western political philosophy than it does with the broadly Platonizing vision of the Eastern Church Fathers. For them, as for Bulgakov later, the authority of the *basileus* had not merely a negative but also a positive value as a visible image of the rule of God over a cosmos characterized not by its inherent sinfulness and tendency towards disorder but by its fundamental and inalienable *goodness*, which was itself an image or icon of the goodness of God, Whose love for mankind (in the Eastern Christian mind) was maximally revealed when He mounted the Cross and died without dying. Unlike Bulgakov, then, for whom the *teokratia* was ultimately valuable as a *theophany* — that is, for what it revealed about the character of God — for Pobedonostsev power was essentially an end in itself. Given the human — and especially the *Russian* — propensity for anarchy and disorder, a baptized Leviathan was simply a practical necessity.

Not so for Nicholas. From Nicholas's diaries and letters, it seems that Nicholas assimilated the meaning of his office as tsar *intuitively* through living a life as an Orthodox Christian. In contrast to Pobedonostsev's lessons (or anyone else's), to which he nowhere refers, Nicholas's references to the liturgy of the Orthodox Church, whose rites and calendar provided the framework for his life, are constant and repeated. That is to say, it was simply by taking Orthodoxy to heart, week in week out at the liturgy, and daily in his prayers before the icons, that Nicholas absorbed the principles of the political theology of which his office as tsar was the expression. In the "bond of 'Orthodoxy' and 'Autocracy,'" then, Nicholas, we might say, found not the "great and overwhelming temptation" but, thanks to the Church's liturgical reconciliation of the two, a harmony that neither should nor even *could* be unyoked. As the Eucharistic Prayer of the Liturgy of St Basil, which Nicholas will have heard prayed repeatedly throughout his life, has it:

> Lord, think upon the mighty and Christ-loving Emperor whose reign upon earth Thou hast justified: gird him with the armament

---

[21] The classic study is Robert F. Byrnes, *Pobedonostsev: His life and thought* (Bloomington, IN: Indiana University Press, 1968), although my comments here are based more on my own conclusions than Byrnes's.

of truth and good will, shield him in the day of battle ... hold fast
his realm ...[22]

Provocatively, then, but not unjustifiably, what the religious philosopher Dmitri Filosofov said in 1907 of Nicholas's father, Alexander III,
could also be said of Nicholas II: "the principles of Orthodoxy [...]
were not for him hollow words, archaic vestiges [...] but the expression of the sacred duty of the Russian emperor who is Tsar first and
emperor second."[23]

But if we should single out *one* liturgical event likely to have left
an impression on Nicholas's imagination, it was his coronation. Held
in "theocratic" Moscow rather than "profane" Petersburg in May 1896
(two years before the *Rescript* described above), the coronation was a
pageant of *teokratia*, at the heart of which was both a wedding and a
sacrifice. Nicholas approached it with solemn trepidation. "May God
let this trying event pass smoothly and without misfortune and may
the Lord grant us to return here with gladness," he wrote in his diary,
ahead of his departure for Moscow.[24] But he need not have been so
anxious. The weather, when Nicholas and Alexandra arrived on May
9, was magnificent; crowds cheered the imperial couple's route to the
Kremlin enthusiastically. "There is nothing to say about our reception,"
wrote Nicholas: "it was joyful and festive, as only it can be in Moscow!"[25] Four days later, on the afternoon before the sacred coronation
liturgy itself, Moscow — a city of a million, the second largest in the
empire — resounded with the clanging of church bells, while priests in
every church in the Empire performed vigil services, and Nicholas and
Alexandra repaired to the Kremlin's seventeenth-century church of Our
Savior Behind the Golden Gates to receive the Eucharist. The following
morning, a twenty-one-gun salute rang out from the Kremlin as the liturgy's officiating clergy — the Metropolitans of St Petersburg, Moscow, and
Kiev, Nicholas and Alexandra's personal priest-confessor and attendant
priests and deacons — gathered to pray for the emperor.[26] From start to
finish, the coronation aspired to be a not merely human but *theandric*
(divine-human) event, one that aspired not to convert the sacred into the
political (by cynically "sacralizing the State") but to allow the political
to be seen as it truly was by elevating it to that divine realm (the "holy

---

[22] Cited in Schmemann, *Historical Road*, 219.
[23] Dmitry Merezhkovsky, Zinaida Gippius, and Dmitry Filosofov, *Le Tsar et la révolution* (Paris: Société du Mercure, 1907), 64.
[24] Nicholas II, Diary (2), 142.
[25] Nicholas II, May 5, 1896 = Diary (2), 142.
[26] The rite is recorded in the official publication *Chin" deiistviia kakim" obrazom"
sovershit'sia imeiet' sviashcheneiishee koronovanie ego imperatorskago velichestva gosudaria
imperatora Nikolaia Aleksandrovicha* (St Petersburg: Holy Synod, 1896). I am grateful
to have been able to consult this document, which originated in Nicholas II's private
library at Tsarskoye Selo, at the Library of Congress.

city") of which it was already the reflection, to the end that, in the tsar, through the ministry of the Church, the marred *imago Dei* in man, the naturally political animal, might better conform to its divine Archetype, Christ, the Logos, King (Russian: *Tsar*) of the Universe.

By tradition, the coronation was held in the Kremlin's Dormition Cathedral, a square, five-domed building at the heart of the Kremlin's Cathedral Square, dedicated to the Assumption of the Virgin Mary and constructed in 1475–79 by the Italian master Aristotele Fioravanti. Modeled on the twelfth-century Dormition Cathedral of the ancient Rus town of Vladimir, north of Moscow, the Kremlin's Dormition Cathedral was the repository of Russia's most revered Marian image, the Vladimir Mother of God. Painted in Byzantium, the Vladimir Mother of God, which had come to Russia with the daughter of the Byzantine Emperor Constantine IX Monomakhos (and mother, in turn of perhaps the most celebrated medieval Russian ruler, Grand Prince Vladimir Monomakh), symbolized, like the Cap of Monomakh that had come from the same source, the transferal of the theocratic ideal of the Constantinian regime from Byzantium to Russia, and was universally venerated as Russia's invincible Protectress.[27] (In 1916, Nicholas, perhaps recalling his coronation, would make his most personal contribution to Russia's war effort by ordering the holy image's conveyance along the whole front to implore the Virgin's blessing on Russia's incipient Brusilov offensive.) For now, it was the icon's value as a certain symbol of *teokratia* that may have impressed him. Further lending coronation the impression of unfolding, almost literally, beneath the very eyes of God, every inch of the cathedral's walls and ceiling were covered with images of Christ, Mary, the angels, and saints.

On its most basic level, the coronation was a wedding (*venchaniye*): of the tsar to his people at the hands of the Church, and of his people to God through the anointing of the tsar, the people's father and proxy. Afterwards, Russians would acclaim Nicholas as, among other things, their "God-wed tsar." And Bulgakov, declaring twenty years later in the wake of his vision on the Yalta Embankment that he would ever after love the tsar with "that love unto the grave that a bride and bridegroom share before the altar," will be revealed once again to have pronounced not a merely personal or idiosyncratic vision of the meaning of the office of the consecrated Russian ruler but the very mind of the Russian Church, spoken in the liturgy.

At this wedding, the first to arrive was the Imperial Crown itself, a miter-shaped piece encrusted with nearly five thousand diamonds

---

[27] After the Revolution, the Vladimir Mother of God was "cleansed" of its smoke and soot and put on public display in Moscow's Tretyakov Museum. Since 1993, it has been displayed in the Church of St Nicholas of Tolmakhi, a church building incorporated into the nearby Tretyakov, where it can once again be venerated.

created for the coronation of Catherine the Great in 1765 and other regalia, the very symbol of the kingship or sovereignty, one which was at once both *from* God and *of* the Russian people (for every extrinsicist representation of the phenomenon of ruling power must be avoided), to which Nicholas was about to be wed.[28] Only after this crown had taken its place, like a bridegroom, on a cushion in front of the towering iconostasis that separated the nave from the altar did Nicholas, the "bride," accompanied by Alexandra, arrive at the cathedral door. Meeting them were the four leading "hierarchs" or prelates of the Russian Church, the Metropolitans ("Archbishops") of St Petersburg, Moscow, and Kiev. Minutes later, the ceremony proper began when, like collective "fathers of the bride," the metropolitans conducted Nicholas and Alexandra down the aisle inside the church until, having reached the towering wall of icons that separated the nave from the altar, the whole party together made an act of adoration of God and Nicholas and Alexandra were seated on their thrones. Immediately afterwards, the Metropolitan of St Petersburg rose and asked the young tsar: "What do you believe?" In the Church's eyes, the only qualification for the consecrated office Nicholas to which had acceded was adherence to the Church's own faith.[29] This Nicholas proved by reciting alone in front

---

[28] By "extrinsicist," I mean any notion that the phenomenon of political order does not cohere naturally, by divine design, in the order of creation but appears in the world from a place beyond it arbitrarily and *ad extra*. Rather, the phenomenon of sovereignty is the image of a "procession" or "energy" from God's very nature graciously "written" by God into the very fabric of the cosmos when He created it as a visible, material manifestation, not of His being in Himself (His "essence"), but of His being for the world ("His energies"), His glory: on this distinction, see Ware, *Orthodox Way*, 21–23. This makes, the whole of creation — including, we argue here, the phenomenon of kingship, political order — a "great Burning Bush," a *theophany*: ibid., 118. As St Maximus the Confessor expresses it, "We do not know God in His essence. We know Him rather from the grandeur of His creation and His providential care for all creatures. For by this means, as if using a mirror, we attain insight into His infinite goodness, wisdom and power" (quoted in Ware, *Orthodox Way*, 25). If we are right to include the phenomenon of political order among God's acts of providential care for mankind, and the right to rule comes from God as a manifestation of His character, it nonetheless coheres in the order of the world through its peoples, of which the Russians are but one. Because of mankind's God-given freedom, every people (like every individual human being) has the capacity to *mar* the brightness of the image of God's ruling power entrusted to him. The purpose of Christian kingship is to *restore* and *enhance* that brightness through the deifying, remedial help of the Church and her sacraments. The coronation rite does that ritually. Inasmuch as they offer back up to God, through the tsar and the Church, the sovereignty that naturally coheres among them, this act of purification is the work of the Russian people too.

[29] *Chin" deiistviia*, 7 (NB: as no page numbers are printed in the order of service, the numbers given here are those I have given the text myself, with the count starting from the beginning of the description of the rite). On this point, see the work of perhaps the most insightful legal theorist of tsarism in Nicholas's reign, Lev Tikhomirov, *Monarkhicheskaia Gosudarstvennost'* (Moscow: Universal, 1905), Part II, 92: The monarchical regime "demands no special or outstanding administrative skills of the bearer of supreme authority... for there are always plenty of capable men to be found in the country to administer it under the supervision of the supreme authority, whose task consists precisely in setting the course his ministers should follow."

of the congregation assembled the Creed of Nicaea-Constantinople. "Yes, may the All-Holy Spirit be with you!," the Metropolitan intoned in reply when Nicholas had finished.

Then began a long litany of prayers chanted by the clergy. "For the blessing of his kingly [*tsarsky*] wedding by the King of Kings [*Tsarya tsarstvuyushchikh*] and Lord of Lords, let us pray to the Lord . . . For the reception by him from heaven, through anointing with all-holy Myron, of right judgment, strength, and wisdom for government . . . that the Lord would give him according to his heart and fulfil his every counsel . . . "[30] If we saw in all this nothing but empty ritual, we might expect Nicholas's mind to have wandered. He was, after all, only twenty-eight. But if the sensitive, already religiously inclined young man joined his spirit to this litany as he was expected to do, he would have found himself receiving the most important, and the most potent, lesson in his life on the theocratic ideal. As the analogical terms of these prayers themselves suggested, Nicholas, the earthly tsar, was implicitly the image of the heavenly tsar of tsars. Like him, Nicholas, not dominating or lording it over the people committed to him, was to *judge* them according to his conscience, consecrated (as it would be in a moment) through holy oil to God.[31] When, as we shall see, later in his reign, Nicholas would express his dependence on God in his conscience for his judgments as ruler, he was not expressing some strange and idiosyncratic "mysticism" but merely bearing witness to what he learnt from the mouths of Russia's bishops at his coronation.

The lesson in theocratic kingship continued with Scriptures then read (Is. 49:13–19, Rom. 13:1–7, Matt. 22:15–22). The first of these readings (Is. 49:13–19) was a promise of Zion's restoration given during the Jewish people's exile in Babylon from the Old Testament Book of Isaiah, a reading whose inclusion cast Russia as a second Israel waiting for the Lord to restore to its king (as if, since the death of the previous Tsar, Russia had been suffering its own "Exile"). The second reading (Rom. 13:1–7), meanwhile, from the New Testament Epistle of St Paul to the Romans, was a *locus classicus* of Christian political theology. "Brothers, let every soul be subject to the governing authorities; for there is no authority except from God, and those authorities that exist by God's institution. . . . " Truly, political authority, the right to rule, the *basileia*, came "down" upon the tsar from heaven.[32] But the choice of the third reading (Matt. 22:15–22), the Gospel story of the Pharisees' bid to tempt

---

[30] *Chin" deiistviia*, 11
[31] On political authority as an act of judgment, see especially Oliver O'Donovan, *Ways of Judgment* (Grand Rapids, MI Eerdmans, 2008).
[32] Indeed, this passage from Romans might have inspired the great Byzantine emperor Justinian's recasting of the sources of imperial authority in his famous novella on this subject: see further below.

Jesus into rebellion against the Roman authorities through the controversial question of the payment of taxes, may seem surprising, since
it concludes with Jesus's skewering of the Pharisees with his famous
injunction to " . . . render unto Caesar the things that are Caesar's and
unto God the things that are God's."

Among those who believe that the separation of "Church" and "State"
is a doctrine uniquely endorsed by Christian revelation, Jesus's injunction has the authority of a proof text, one which would destroy the
foundations of any theory of *teokratia*, apparently incontrovertibly.[33]
But such a separation has never belonged to the mind of the Eastern
Church.[34] Here, "Church" and "State," the ecclesiastical order and the
political (or what we might better call the orders of the *Church* and of
the *world*) do not flow from separate and discontinuous sources but are
both regarded as *from* and *for* God.[35] As St Paul writes to the Colos-
sians, the Christ who is the "head of the body, the Church," is the
same Christ in whom "all things were created, in heaven and on earth,
visible and invisible, whether thrones or dominions or principalities
or authorities — all things were created through him and *for* him . . . in
him *all things* hold together" (Col. 1:16–18; my italics).[36] Indeed, as the
modern Orthodox theologian Vigen Guroian points out, the Eastern
Church celebrates the complementarity of Church and world to each
other in the service of Christ when, in its annual commemoration of
the first Christian emperor, (St) Constantine, God's "apostle among
rulers," it acclaims him as one who "received not his call from men"
but Christ himself, directly.[37]

---

[33] See, as one eye-catching example among many, Alistair Kee, *Constantine versus Christ:
the triumph of ideology* (London: SCM Press, 1982); cf. Peter Leithart, *Defending Constantine: The twilight of an empire and the dawn of Christendom* (Downers Grove, IL:
IVP Academic, 2010), which expressly takes issue over the question of "Constantinianism"
with the pacificist-idealistic theory of politics (associated with John Yoder and Stanley
Hauerwas) dominant in academic American Protestantism. For another correction of
the dominant "separationist" school of thought from within the Reformed tradition,
see Oliver O'Donovan, *The Desire of the Nations: Rediscovering the roots of political
theology* (Cambridge: Cambridge University Press, 1996).

[34] Guroian, "Constantine and Christendom," 34. Nor for that matter has it belonged
to the tradition of the Western Church, as summed up definitively in Pope Leo XIII's
great encyclical, *Immortale Dei* (1885).

[35] Guroian, "Constantine and Christendom," 35.

[36] That "all things" includes political authority is also suggested when Jesus reminds
the Roman governor Pilate at the conclusion of his trial that, "You would have no
power over me unless it had been given you from above" (Jn 19:11).

[37] Guroian, "Constantine and Christendom," 23. See also the remarks to the same effect,
which Guroian quotes in support of his argument, by Alexander Schmemann, *Church,
World, Mission: Reflections on Orthodoxy in the West* (Crestwood, NY: St Vladimir's
Seminary Press, 1979), 35: "'Like Paul, thou hast received the calling not from men . . . '
This in the eyes of the Eastern tradition is the decisive factor in Constantine's conversion. He is called directly by Christ, not even through the Church, and he is chosen
not as an 'individual' but precisely as emperor . . . In him . . . the empire itself is called to
accept Christ and to become His *politeuma*." Cf. Schmemann, *Historical Road*, 116–18.

This, then, is the tradition that the Byzantine emperor, (St) Justinian, translated into law in his famous Novella Six, according to which the "greatest gifts that God, in his celestial benevolence, has bestowed on mankind are priesthood [*sacerdotium*] and sovereignty [*imperium*], the one serving on matters divine, and the other ruling over human affairs, and caring for them. Each proceeds from one and the same authority [i.e. God], and regulates human life."[38] Instead of the opposition, or rivalry, between the political and the sacred implied in the modern "separation of Church and State," then, the Eastern Church has historically looked for a *symphonia* ("satisfactory harmony") between the ecclesiastical and political orders, each conceived as sacred in its own way, within an integrated ecclesiastical-political whole, the Christian *teokratia*, that unites the *sacerdotium* and the *imperium*, we might say, unchangeably and unconfusedly, yet indivisibly and inseparably (to borrow four adverbs from classical Christology).[39] As Justinian has it, "The priesthood and the imperium do not differ very greatly. Nor are sacred things so very different from those of public and common interest."[40]

If, then, Jesus's injunction distinguishes but does not separate God and Caesar, the Gospel story's inclusion in the coronation liturgy reveals the latter as the ritual enactment of the *symphonia* that Jesus's injunction always paradoxically held out: the ritual conforming of Caesar (the natural image on earth of God's ruling power over the universe) to the divine Archetype, that the fallen human political order might "image" or manifest the true divine form, or "face" (Christ's), of sovereignty.

Thus, with the reading from the Gospel completed, the Metropolitans of St Petersburg and Kiev (bearers of the *sacerdotium*) approached Nicholas, the tsar (bearer of the *imperium*, whose title derived directly from the Latin *Caesar*), and fastened about his shoulders a dark purple mantle (known as the *porphyra* in Greek and *baryanitsa* in Russian).

---

[38] As Justinian's most recent annotators have commented, "more explicitly than any Emperor before him, Justinian asserts that the authority of both emperor and priest is derived from a common divine source": David J. D. Miller and Peter Sarris, eds., *The Novels of Justinian: A complete annotated English translation* (Cambridge: Cambridge University Press, 2018), 97, n. 1 Schmemann would offer the Justinianic formulation as a *malformation* of the Constantinian ideal: *Historical Road*, 144–46, 151–53. On the Russian situation, we may note James Billington, *Icon and the Axe*, 61: "It had . . . always been incorrect to speak even in Byzantium of 'Church' and 'State' rather than two types of sanctified authority (*sacerdotium* and *imperium*) within the universal Christian commonwealth. In Muscovy the two were even more closely intertwined without any clear commitment to the theoretical definitions and practical limitations that had evolved in the long history of Byzantium."

[39] See Russian Orthodox Church-Moscow Patriarchate, *Basis of the Social Concept of the Russian Orthodox Church*, 3.4: https://old.mospat.ru/en/documents/social-concepts/. For commentary, including on Patriarch Kirill's use of symphonia, see Betsy Perabo, "Russia's Unfinished Symphony of Church and State," Political Theology Network, July 2, 2018: https://politicaltheology.com/russias-unfinished-symphony-of-church-and-state/. Both accessed October 3, 2024.

[40] Novella Six. Cited in McGuckin, "Legacy of the 13th apostle," 283.

In a Christian setting, the symbolism of the mantle was dual, recalling at once as it did the porphyry cloak of the Roman emperors (of whom the Russian tsars, as heirs to Constantine, were successors) and the red centurion's cloak in which Caesar's soldiers had clothed Christ *as if he were Caesar* before "crowning" him with a mock crown, of thorns, in the same way.[41] That it was not Roman soldiers, however, but the metropolitans, successors of Christ's apostles, that did the mantling in Moscow in 1896 only heightened the dramatic analogy. In any case, Nicholas thus mantled was now a Caesar who (having symbolically conformed himself and his authority to the image and pattern of Christ the true King's true, *self-giving* kingship) had "rendered to God" what was his. This being the case, he was ready to receive his sovereignty back from God in a new, and Christo-form, way.[42]

Nicholas then bowed his head while the Metropolitan of St Petersburg made the Sign of Cross over the tsar. Then the metropolitan, having placed two hands in the shape of the Cross over the still bowing Nicholas, prayed a solemn prayer invoking the "Ur-text" (1 Sam. 16:13) of all theories of Christian kingship: the anointing of the shepherd boy David by the Prophet Samuel following David's election by God as King of Israel. "O Lord our God, Tsar of tsars and Lord of lords, Who through the Prophet Samuel chose Your bond-slave David and anointed him tsar over Your people, Israel: hear now the prayer of our unworthiness and look from Your holy dwelling place upon Your faithful slave.... Nicholas Aleksandrovich, whom You have been pleased to set up as emperor (*imperator*) over Your people and purchased with the Precious Blood of Your Only-Begotten Son . . . deign to anoint him with the oil of rejoicing, clothe him in strength from on high, place upon his head a crown of pure stone, give him many days, and having placed in his right hand the scepter of salvation, seat him upon the throne of truth, defend him with the shield of Your Holy Spirit, . . . place the fear of You in his heart . . . show him to be a true defender of the dogmas of the Catholic [*sic*] Church, to judge Your people in truth and Your poor in righteousness, to save the sons of the destitute, and to be an heir of Your

---

[41] Easy to miss, the Crucifixion narratives, especially John's, are coronation rituals in their own way: "And the soldiers plaited a crown of thorns, and put it on his head, and clothed him in a purple robe; they came up to him, saying 'Hail, King of the Jews!'" (Jn 19:2–3). Indeed, one wonders how far the Hellenistic notion of the king as incarnate Logos (see Baynes, "Eusebius and the Christian empire," 170) was in the Gospel writer's mind when he composed the Gospel of John's famous prologue. Was not Christ, the true Logos, also the true king?

[42] As a contemporary theologian has it, the mission given by God to the church is "to penetrate the world, every ontological inch of it, in order to give it the form of Christ.... The Church bears on the very form of existence in the world, communicating its own form to the world in an analogous way." And what happened in the coronation liturgy other than that? See David Schindler, "What is liberalism?" *New Polity: A journal of post-liberal thought* 1:1 (May, 2020): https://newpolity.com/blog/what-is-liberalism.

heavenly tsardom (Russian: *tsarstviya*)."[43] Again, the analogical relationship between his authority and that of God had been commended to
him by Russia's leading bishop. Nicholas kept his head bowed beneath
the Metropolitan's cruciform hands while a second clergyman prayed
over him. Only then was Nicholas invited by the Metropolitan to place
the imperial crown upon his own head, for in Russian practice the tsar
crowned himself, a sign that the *imperium* came directly to the tsar
from God without the delegatory mediation of the Church, just as
Constantine himself had been called directly. Hailed now as the "God-
wed, God-given, and God-adorned . . . Sovereign Emperor," Nicholas took
up the orb and scepter, seated himself upon his throne, and crowned
Alexandra empress.[44]

At that moment, the bells of Moscow's churches rang out, and the
Kremlin's garrison fired a salute of 101 guns. Then, when the noise
had died down, Nicholas rose from the throne, removed the orb and
scepter, and prayed alone the following prayer in a loud voice before the
assembly. "O Lord, Father God, Tsar of tsars. . . . You have chosen Me as
Tsar and Judge for Your people. I acknowledge Your inscrutable regard
for Me and worship Your Majesty. . . . Do You, my Lord and Master,
establish Me in the task You have set me upon. Teach and direct me
in this great service. May the Wisdom belonging to Your great Throne
be with Me. Send hither Your saints from heaven. . . . Let My heart be
in Your hands to establish everything for the sake of the welfare of the
people committed to Me and for the sake of Your glory so that on the
Day of Judgment I may give account without shame to You."[45] This was
Nicholas's solemn coronation oath. And when he had finished, while
Nicholas continued standing, all those assembled got down onto their
knees, and the metropolitan, "on behalf of all the people," replied by
saying that God had "filled" His people's "hearts with joy and gladness
by setting" His "slave," Nicholas II, to "rule" over them. While some
modern historians, and even theologians, write as if Eastern Orthodoxy
attributed no significance to tsarist authority that might have prevented
Russia's evolution towards Western-style liberal democracy, Nicholas can
hardly have been in any doubt that the Church, with all her authority, had now forcefully declared and ritually demonstrated the divine
source of an office that was his to bear and be faithful to, but hardly
to alter, change, or give away. Not his own, the tsar, Nicholas had just
heard, was God's *slave*, who had committed himself to give an account
to God at the end of days for the burden of the sovereignty conferred
by God uniquely on him. Should we blame Nicholas, twenty-one years

---

[43] *Chin" deiistviia*, 22.
[44] Ibid., 26.
[45] Ibid., 33.

later, for taking his oath and the Church's instruction seriously? What, given his commitments as an Orthodox Christian, could he have done differently? Or was it Nicholas's fault (in the dawning "age of secularization") for imagining that the words of the Coronation Liturgy could or even *should* be obeyed literally?

Perhaps, had the Coronation Liturgy had ended here, or had Orthodoxy been another kind of religion, a way could have been found out of this dilemma, a sleight of hand such as the one that had taken place centuries before in Anglican England. This prospect, which allowed a Christian monarch anointed by the Church in a similarly "theocratic" coronation liturgy drawing on many of the same biblical types and precedents to keep his (or, as it was in 1896, *her*) throne even as the people's representatives in parliament had long since started answering for the country, stalked the minds of Russian liberals, and the quintessentially English (and *Anglican*) notion of a merely symbolical monarch "who (nominally) reigns but does not rule" would be invoked directly during the final crisis of Russian theocracy at Pskov in 1917. But, as we shall see, it was a false hope. Such a sleight of hand was not available in Russia for the very reason that Orthodoxy was not that kind of (nominalist) religion. And, for those who cared to look, notice of that had already been given in 1896 at the coronation itself, and specifically in its character as a *liturgy*.

Indeed, for all its solemnity, Nicholas's crowning represented neither the coronation's climax nor its most solemn act. On the contrary, these, the sacramental anointing and the reception of Christ's Body and Blood itself in the Eucharist, were still to come. Thus, at the chanting of the priests that indicated the beginning of this Divine Liturgy, Nicholas removed his crown and remained bareheaded until that Liturgy had reached its climax in the consecration of the bread and wine as the Body and Blood of Christ in the Eucharist: after all, in the Real Presence, which the metropolitans as priests had now "confected," of the "Tsar of Tsars," marks of Nicholas's own merely *analogical* kingship were not needed.

With the very Body and Blood of God (truly, not merely "symbolically," as if that meant only "in name") now lying on the altar on the other side of the wall of icons that was the iconostasis, Nicholas's anointing was approaching.[46] When, therefore, the Royal Doors in the middle of

---

[46] On the Orthodox doctrine of the Real Presence, see Ware, *Orthodox Church*, 283: "the Orthodox Church believes that after the consecration, the bread and wine become in very truth the Body and Blood of Christ: they are not mere symbols but the reality." Cf. Meyendorff, *Byzantine Theology*, 203–4, who discusses the historical rejection in Eastern theology of merely "symbolic" representations of the Eucharist. Note the difference between Orthodoxy's "realist" ontology of the Eucharist and the purely nominalist one of the Church of England's Twenty-Eighth Article: "The Body of Christ is given, taken, and eaten in the Supper only after an heavenly and spiritual manner"

the iconostasis were opened, it was not for the priests to exit through the opening and distribute the sacrament to the laity but to fetch Nicholas and invite him to return with them to the altar. Moments before Nicholas did so, the party stopped on the *solea*, the step immediately in front of the open Royal Doors, on the laity's side of the iconostasis. Then, approaching from the altar, the Metropolitan, taking a special brush, daubed Nicholas's "brow . . . eyes, nostrils, lips, ears . . . and both sides of the hands" while saying the words, "Receive the Holy Spirit."[47] This was the mystery or sacrament of anointing, when, through the "holy Myron" or oil (*chrism*), the Holy Spirit was imparted to Nicholas to "seal" him forever in his office and to fortify him to carry out its duties through a new outpouring on him of God's own Spirit.

At that moment, Nicholas's office as tsar received a sacramental significance not extended to it in the previous act of crowning, and for a second time that day, the Kremlin garrison fired a salute of 101 guns.[48] By God's grace, the political and the sacred had been joined; and as if to seal it, Nicholas stepped through the Royal Doors into the sanctuary reserved for the clergy to consume God's Body and Blood there in the priests' company and as if, for a moment, he, too was a priest. Ordinarily, the Orthodox laity may not handle the consecrated elements; the Eucharist is served to them by a priest on a spoon, the Body and Blood mixed together. But alone on his coronation day, this was dispensed with for the tsar.[49] "Then His Majesty is permitted to receive . . . the Holy Mysteries, that is Communion in the Body and Blood of the Lord, in the Royal Way (*po tsarskomu chinu*)," that is, with his own hands, the Body first and the Blood second.[50] Indeed, that Nicholas as an honorary priest enjoyed the privilege of handling the Eucharist is denoted by the

(Book of Common Prayer, 1662). The suggestion here is that a people whose imagination has been formed by a Church that merely confects the Lord's Body and Blood "in name" and "symbolically" will have no trouble understanding royal authority (an image and manifestation of Christ's authority, after all) in the same, fundamentally nominalist, way. Hence the typically English (and Anglican) oxymoron whereby the monarch (literally, "sole ruler") "reigns" but does not "rule." The same cannot obtain in any Orthodox country.

[47] *Chin" deiistviia*, 42. Precisely when the anointing was introduced into the coronation liturgy is not known. The manuscript tradition would suggest that it was an established element of the Byzantine coronation rite by the eighth century: Peter Sarris, *Empires of Faith: The fall of Rome to the rise of Islam* (Oxford: Oxford University Press, 2011), 227. In any case, Schmemann believes that by the ninth century, the anointing had become "the fundamental, operative part in the coronation": *Historical Road*, 217.

[48] Upon the conclusion of this salute, Nicholas then moved slightly to the right of the Royal Doors so that he stood "in front of the local icon of the Savior." This allowed Alexandra to approach the Metropolitan, who then anointed her empress with the same words, "Receive the Holy Spirit." But this was a sacrament she shared only by association with her husband, and she was anointed on her brow only. See *Chin" deiistviia*, 44.

[49] Even Alexandra as empress was not allowed to penetrate the Royal Doors. Rather, she received Holy Communion "in the ordinary manner," by spoon, from the hand of the clergy, as a member of the laity.

[50] *Chin" deiistviia*, 43.

fact that the liturgy made provision for a priest to "wipe His Majesty's mouth and hands."[51] In line with the theory of Russia as a *teokratia*, Nicholas, aided by the Church, had now given all the "things of Caesar" to God and received in return all the world, i.e. God made man, Christ. Having been made a "Caesar" in the "form of Christ," the mockery of the Roman soldiers is set right, and God's rule over all things is vindicated.

With this, the coronation was complete and the ceremony moved towards its conclusion. Clothed again in their regalia, Nicholas and Alexandra were blessed by their confessor and presented by the Metropolitan with a cross to kiss. Then, when Nicholas had placed his crown back on his head, the assembly responded with an acclamation, the first and last time the laity had been involved in the liturgy at all: the tsar had come from the people, to be sure, but as a form of government Russia's *teokratia* was *from* God, *through* the tsar, and *for* the people. After this acclamation, the clergy conducted Nicholas and Alexandra for brief prayers in the Kremlin's other Cathedrals, of the Archangel (where they paid their respects to Nicholas's Romanov ancestors), and of the Annunciation (where further prayers of a private nature for themselves and their family were said). Finally, returning outside, and mounting the steps of the so-called Faceted Palace, Russia's newly God-wed tsar, the "Lord's Anointed," turned to face the crowd in and outside the Kremlin's walls, and made the customary bow to his people. The crowd responded wildly.

༄ ༄ ༄

Nicholas's perception of himself as a theocratic ruler responsible to God in his conscience remained throughout his life. In keeping with the coronation's image of the tsar as God's bond-servant, this perception of the theocratic nature of his office fostered in Nicholas not the capricious, high-handed attitude to power suggested by the early

---

[51] This was not because the Eastern Church made the tsar (or the Byzantine emperor before him) a priest in the ordinary sense or appointed him to a kind of "Caesaropapist" headship over the Church: never in his wildest dreams would Nicholas or any of his predecessors as far back as Constantine have presumed to offer the "bloodless Sacrifice" at the heart of the Divine Liturgy. That, on this his coronation day, the Church should invite the tsar to partake of some of the privileges of priesthood was a sign of that truth whereby, while the tsar's office, Justinian's *imperium*, was a "gift" that belonged to the "natural" order of creation, neither that order, nor the "graced" (and "supernatural") order of the Church established with the Incarnation, was intended by God to remain hermetically apart, the one interacting with the other as if the relationship between them were purely extrinsic and *ad extra*. Rather, the "natural" order of the creation was always originally supernatural; far from adding something "new" and arbitrary to it, the Incarnation restored it to its original vocation to become and to be truly supernatural *ad intra*: that is, graced, indeed, "deified," precisely as nature and endowed with all the properties (or energies) of God (Ware, *Orthodox Way*, 52–53). To put it another way, the boundary between the nave and the sanctuary existed to be crossed and now the tsar, who stood at the head of the natural order, had shown all the people the way.

modern West's idea of the "divine *right* of kings" (to do, presumably, as they pleased) but a constant, heavy awareness of the obligation that lay upon him to make an act of right judgment for the alignment of the earthly tsardom, Russia, with the Kingdom (Russian: *tsardom*) of God. We see it in a letter to his mother written in the context of troubles in Finland in 1902. "In the sight of my Maker I have to carry the burden of a terrible responsibility and at all times therefore be ready to render an account to Him of my actions."[52] He could not do what his conscience told him was wrong, even if in theory he as autocrat had the power to do almost anything. Indeed, if the absolutist regime that Peter the Great had founded had its fulcrum in the ruler's *will*, by contrast, the fulcrum of Russia's regime, as Nicholas imagined it, was not his right as ruler to do whatever he would, but his *obligation* to do whatever his conscience imposed. And this conscience was understood, moreover, not in the modern sense as the directive of a commanding, unreflective moral dictate (after all, Nicholas said his reason also told him that he was doing right) nor the irruption of an irrational and inarticulate subconscious (a misunderstanding that affected even Nicholas's own entourage) but in the classical Christian sense as the settled disposition of his mind at the end of its own internal dialogue with God.[53] In return for obedience to God in this inner dialogue of conscience, Nicholas looked for (and believed he received) a form of psychic consolation that confirmed for him that he was doing well. As he put it in another letter to his mother, a week after issuing the October Manifesto of 1905, "God Almighty will be our help. I feel Him supporting me and putting strength in me, which gives me courage and does not allow me to lose heart…"[54]

Beyond the walls of the Vatican, perhaps, commitment to such a model of Christian rulership was unusual. As we shall see, far from diminishing with the years, however, the centrality of religion to Nicholas and Alexandra's lives would only intensify. This is remarkable because, seen from the perspective of the history of secularization, the period between 1870 and 1914, when Nicholas and Alexandra reached adulthood, married, and formed a family, has been described as that of the "secularization of Christianity," one which "acted as a mediator for the transition from the Christian-secular world to that of natural irreligion, characterized by the loss of the sense of the sacred."[55] According

---

[52] Bing, *Letters of Tsar Nicholas*, 167.
[53] Cf. Mossolov, *At the Court*, 11.
[54] Nicholas II to Marie Fyodorovna, October 27, 1905, in Bing, *Letters of Tsar Nicholas*, 189.
[55] Augusto Del Noce, "The Dialogue between the Church and modern culture," in Del Noce, *Age of Secularization*, trans. Carlo Lancellotti (Montreal: McGill-Queen's University Press, 2017), 94.

to Del Noce, the vehicle for this secularization of Christianity was a
rediscovered Kantianism that insisted on the sufficiency of human reason for attaining the moral teachings of Christianity, which were held
to be universal precisely because they were rational, not because they
had been revealed by God or taught by the Church. The attraction
of such a neo-Kantian high culture was the separability it allowed for
between morality (which was considered rational and universally appli-
cable in its inherited Christian form), on the one hand, and dogma and
metaphysics (which Kant considered unverifiable by reason, and which
were deemed by his late nineteenth-century followers to be irrational),
on the other. From this point of view, the supernatural elements of
Christianity (from the Virgin Birth and Resurrection to priesthood
and sacraments) could be safely dispensed with by thinking people,
for the essence of Christianity was its moral teachings, which reason
affirmed anyway. The Church might remain a useful tool of social control for those elements of society that, lacking access to higher culture,
were deprived of the full enjoyment of their rationality. But for educated people to subscribe to the miracles and sacramental world view
of historical Christianity was a potentially disturbing sign of weakness
of mind, a penchant for "superstition." This created a sense of illusion
about Europe (including Russia) as a Christian civilization. For while,
says Del Noce, in these decades before the Great War, "Christianity
made its last stand on the trench lines of morality" and "practical judgments kept conforming to Christian morality," in fact, "cultivated people were convinced that claims about the truth of dogmas should be
dismissed, and were, at best, agnostic about supra-sensible realities."[56]

Insofar as the historical role of the Great War was to destroy this
illusion, the climax of the nineteenth century's "secularized Christianity" in the "realized atheism" of the Russian Revolution was entirely
fitting: modernist neo-Kantian morality and Marxism-Leninism were
stages in a single process of secularization that, in the wake of the Russian Revolution, would be viewed as the "judgment" of history, even
in those societies where Marxists did not succeed in establishing a dictatorship.[57] It is interesting, however, that despite their access, by way
of their social stations, to the neo-Kantian high culture of the period
1870 to 1914, Nicholas and Alexandra rejected it. This is not because, in
their sheltered worlds, they never met the alternative. On the contrary,
the neo-Kantian secularization of Christianity formed the backdrop to
their world. But unlike the bulk of their more "modern" friends and
family (and even important elements of the Russian clergy) — who, in

---

[56] Del Noce, "The common morality of the nineteenth century and the morality of
today," in *Age of Secularization*, 153, 159.
[57] Del Noce, "Secularization and modernity," in *Crisis of Modernity*, 83.

the setting of a society defined by the creeping secularization of Christianity, succeeded in combining an increasingly nominal commitment to Christian morality with a decidedly agnostic attitude towards the super-rational elements of historical Christian dogma and the supernatural elements of the Church's liturgical and sacramental life — Nicholas II and his family continued to subscribe to both. And it was a persistent feature of their lives that for this subscription they were deemed, according to the same neo-Kantian logic, to be dangerously superstitious and mentally defective.

Insufficiently sophisticated to see through the claims of dogmatic religion, Nicholas and Alexandra were, in the post-1917 emigration, cast by their more modern friends and family — who blamed Nicholas and Alexandra's superstition and lack of sophistication for the catastrophe of the Revolution — as "insipid," "reactionary," and "fatalistic." As Mossolov, who engaged almost daily with Nicholas from 1900 to 1916, recalled in bewilderment, Nicholas II believed that as tsar "his mission emanated from God. For his actions, he was responsible only to his own conscience and to God.... Responsible only to his conscience, his intuition, his instinct.... Responsible to elements that are not reason and at times are contrary to reason. Responsible to imponderables; to the mysticism that steadily increased its hold over him."[58] But what is mysticism in an age of secularization, if not another possible name for non-secularized Christianity?

By transforming religion into an affair of private conscience, the secularization of Christianity accomplished in European culture under the influence of Kant in the century before the Great War directly contributed to the effective separation of church and state even in Russia, where they remained formally united. For if religion was a private affair, then the public realm, the affairs of state, were, by definition, secular, and beyond the purview of religion in anything more than a purely Kantian, ethical sense. Ceasing to have at its heart the goal of realizing a concrete moral-religious ideal (Orthodox-Christian *teokratia*), political authority had, as part of this process, become a matter of skilled, technical administration — of foreign affairs and diplomacy, war, commerce and industry (i.e. the economy). And, naturally, this change carried with it implications for the standards against which the bearers of state office were to be judged. Competence and incompetence — the criteria by which the administrators of a secular state are measured — are not necessarily the yardsticks of *teokratia*, which are rather the mystical virtues of moral judgment, attention to God and conscience. This required, as one insightful theorist of monarchy put

---

[58] Mossolov, *At the Court*, 10–11.

it, "moral excellence" and "certainty in the permanence of his authority."[59] And if the first of these was best learnt in the home, the second was ensured by the dynastic principle, which, by making the burden of bearing the supreme authority hereditary eliminated all grounds for internecine struggle. Above all, said Tikhomirov, as a form of *teokratia*, the Constantinian regime demanded something else. "Essential to the monarch as supreme authority is the ability to establish a spiritual unity with his subjects so that he might give expression to the people's [moral-religious] ideal as well as the awareness of his duty incumbent upon him to give expression to this ideal in his government."[60] Servants of the rational and secular imperial state Peter the Great had created, imbued with the Kantian spirit of their age—men such as Mossolov—had forgotten that Russia (as its ritualized "constitution" nonetheless continued to proclaim), was first—and for Nicholas II, certainly—foremost a *teokratia*.

---

[59] Tikhomirov, *Monarkhicheskaia Gosudarstvennost'*, II, 92.
[60] Ibid.

CHAPTER FOUR

Pro et Contra, Bloody Sunday

ODAY, IF THERE IS A PLACE IN RUSSIA THAT recalls the intuitive sources of Nicholas's perception of Russia as a *teokratia*, it is the suburban palace of Gatchina, where, as an adolescent, Nicholas came of age during the reign of his father, Alexander III. Planted on a line of low hills forty-five miles south of St Petersburg, the Gatchina Palace is also in many ways a metaphor for Russia itself (and not only because its bulk, gathered in three rectangular blocks connected by two semi-circular galleries, seems to oppress the low hill on which it is built, in much the same way that Russia's cartographic mass seems to bear down on the globe's northern reaches). Designed in 1766 by the Italian architect Antonio Rinaldi, Gatchina was intended as a gift for the young guardsman and Catherine the Great's lover, Grigorii Orlov, who helped put her on the throne. After Orlov's death, the palace became the chief residence of Catherine's estranged son and heir, the ill-fated Paul I. Under him, the structure grew into its present squat appearance. Where Rinaldi had created straight, simple gables, Paul had the walls of all three wings pushed outwards, thickening their rectangularity. To the central wing he added another story, topped by a balustrade and a line of chimneys that from a distance appear as a kind of crenulation. Whereas the three, gently curving wings of the original palace had enclosed a meadow, where a flock of ewes and lambs grazed in idealized tranquility, Paul turned the sheep out and flattened the glade into a gravel-strewn parade ground, which echoed to the regular step of his own personal regiment of soldiers, whom he drilled in Prussian-style maneuvers daily. Insipid French pastoralism and the brutish Prussian parade ground: so Gatchina embodied two aspects of Russia's Europeanization.

Today, that space is littered with grey, Soviet-era apartment blocks, while the parade ground has been bisected by a busy road and half-transformed into a gritty car park. When I visited on a day made by the ambient damp to feel colder than it really was, a duckboard had been laid across the parade ground to cope with the spring melt, allowing visitors in Indian file to avoid the small lake of muddy, half-frozen puddles between the road and the palace. From up close, Gatchina — like Russia — appears a wounded giant, one still wearing a reminder of its traumas. Invisible from a distance but immediately apparent as soon as the visitor gets within a hundred yards of the palace are pockmarks — bullet holes and shrapnel divots — in its stone façade, left over from Gatchina's three years as headquarters of the occupying Nazis' regional Gestapo.

Along with the Anichkov, Gatchina was Nicholas II's childhood home. When in 1881 a student terrorist's bomb left his father, Alexander II, dead, the new emperor, Alexander III, Nicholas II's father, removed his family to this remote suburban palace for safe-keeping. Nobody had lived permanently at Gatchina since Paul had left. But watercolors produced in the late 1880s show how far the returned imperial family succeeded in making the enormous building, with its tasseled lamps, chaises longues and bear-skin rugs, a cozy family home. Nicholas was thirteen when the family moved in, and with his four younger siblings, he had an enchanted childhood at Gatchina, his sister Olga recalling in her memoirs a childhood of fishing trips and long walks through the estate's wild English park with their restless, physical father.[1] "Europe can wait. The Russian Tsar is fishing," Alexander III is said once to have told his foreign minister, when the latter had interrupted his angling on one of the Palace ponds.

After Alexander's death, Gatchina remained, like the Anichkov, the residence of the Dowager Empress Marie. Every Christmas, her son and grandchildren would arrive by train from Tsarskoye Selo to light a huge Christmas tree in the parlor. Then, ironically, during the October Revolution, Gatchina played host to the last stand of Russian liberalism, when Alexander Kerensky, the last prime minister of the Provisional Government, fled here in search of troops to send against the Bolsheviks. But the brief counter-revolution failed before it even began. Unlike Russian liberalism, the palace survived the Bolshevik takeover. For Lenin, the European culture the Romanovs had imported was to be preserved in its secular aspect, for the foundation it laid for (also secular and European) Marxism. As a result, rather than being ransacked and destroyed, Gatchina was, like St Petersburg's other suburban palaces, largely intact when the Germans crossed the Soviet border on June 22, 1941. Eight weeks later, as the Panzers were drawing a noose around the outskirts of Leningrad, Soviet authorities gave the order to pack the most valuable contents into crates and send them to Siberia. Anything of artistic value left in the buildings when the Germans arrived was plundered and sent in the other direction, to Königsberg in East Prussia, and Berlin. Whatever survived that was burned as firewood during the long Russian winter. Behind the lines, in the besieged city, 3.3 million Leningraders were trapped, and, by January 1942, dying at a rate of five thousand a day. The German soldiers holed up in Gatchina, enforcing urban genocide, had food to eat. But everything unessential (tables, chairs, wall paneling) was sacrificed in the effort to keep warm. Knowing that at some point

---

[1] Lieven, *Nicholas II*, 24–25.

retreat was inevitable, a German soldier scrawled in defiance on one of the stripped walls: "When Ivan comes, it will be empty." When Soviet troops returned in January 1944, it was.

Even today, Gatchina still presents a shocking quantity of bare brick wall. Through room after empty room, I crossed bare wooden floorboards. In some sections, the internal walls and staircases have collapsed, with the result that, at the end of any given hallway, I stared only into the darkness. As there are no window sills to keep the wind out, the draft sings and whistles hauntingly. None of Gatchina's original furnishings survive. But in a suite of rooms on the third floor, furniture has been brought in from stores conserved elsewhere. This made for an interesting, if forlorn, sight, tending only to emphasize the destruction that has taken place. A writing desk sat in a room with a few other objects suggesting that this was a study. In another, a child's cot, chair, and doll indicated that this was the nursery. Sometimes plaster and paper have been applied to walls to cover the bricks. But the room's "lived-in" feeling disappeared in the bonfires that followed the last shipment of plundered *objets d'art* back to Germany.

I found Gatchina's chapel by chance. Going down a flight of makeshift wooden stairs, I ended up at the end of a long and dark tunnel in what appeared to be a basement. A shaft of wan natural light at the other end of the room indicated the presence of another staircase leading back up to the surface. Climbing it to the top, I found myself in the company of four other people — a priest, and a couple with a newborn baby — concluding a ceremony that appeared to be the mother's post-partum purification. To call the chapel restored would be an exaggeration. But it was in a state fit for services. The ceiling and windows there were sealed, which meant that the draft at least had stopped whistling, and behind the makeshift iconostasis an altar had presumably been reconsecrated. Other icons — none hand-painted, many mere photostat reproductions — had been set up along the walls. In the nave, one of these icons showed the Royal Passion-Bearers, and on the bottom of the icon frame I noticed that someone had placed a typewritten "Prayer for Ukraine," asking God, the heavenly "king" (lit. tsar), to restore the broken unity of the Russian and Ukrainian peoples.

Nicholas was thirteen when he arrived at Gatchina in 1881. For the next decade it had remained his primary home. It was here that he was schooled, by private tutors of generally far higher ability than popular legend would have it, and it was here that he was inducted into the Orthodox religion.[2] Many of Nicholas's most formative religious experiences — the weekly Divine Liturgies, the daily prayers and special festal services for feasts and holidays — must have taken place in Gatchina's

---

[2] Ibid., 34–36.

chapel. It was here that he must first have intuited what it meant not only to be Orthodox but to be an Orthodox ruler. In this, Nicholas's first model was naturally his father, the reigning Emperor Alexander III. Though they were not especially close so long as Alexander was alive, Nicholas was devoted to his father's memory. Year after year until his own death in 1918, Nicholas's diary noted his father's birthday and death dates. Every year on the anniversary of Alexander's death, Nicholas attended a commemorative liturgy to commend his soul to God. It has been said that the essence of dynastic monarchy is the eternal self-sacrifice of the son for the father: that upon his father's death, his heir must "die" to himself and offer himself as a living image of his father.[3] "The king is dead; long live the king." Nicholas embodied this logic. And among those things that Alexander's example impressed most deeply upon Nicholas was the implicit, organic connection between the Russian tsar and the Orthodox Church.

Orthodoxy shaped the spirit of his father Alexander III's court and family life in a way that they had done with no Russian ruler since the time of Peter the Great.[4] In accordance with the traditional theocratic principle, Alexander III considered his office as tsar to be, properly speaking, a sacred one, given to him by God. Deeply influenced by the Slavophile movement that emerged in Russia during his own youth in the 1840s and 1850s, and which reacted against the secularizing trends in nineteenth-century European philosophy by reasserting the teachings and principles of Orthodoxy rather than aspirational European-ness as the proper source of Russian life and behavior, Alexander broke with the secular spirit of the European Enlightenment which had inspired most of his Romanov ancestors since Peter the Great, and sought instead a political style rooted in the sacred logic of Russia's own Eastern Orthodox culture. Thus, whereas as Peter the Great, desiring to import into Russia European modes of life and government, had abolished the traditional title tsar (which for centuries had located the imperial office within the Church) and substituted for it the new, more European title emperor (which established the ruler above and over the Church), Alexander by reference preferred to style himself as tsar rather than emperor, and his entire appearance, bearing and public image projected the traditional, religious and Church-inspired sources of the Russian ruler's role and power. As Dmitri Filosofov, an art critic and radical religious thinker from the turn of the century, put it in the 1907 tract *Le Tsar et la révolution* that we have already met: "Alexander III placed the Empire of Peter back under the Muscovite domination.... The principles of

[3] Ernst H. Kantorowicz, *The King's Two Bodies: A study in medieval political theology* (Princeton, NJ: Princeton University Press, 2016), 385–95.
[4] Wortman, *Scenarios of Power*, 282–302.

Orthodoxy, the coronation oath, were not for him hollow words, archaic vestiges . . . but the expression of the sacred duty of the Russian emperor who is Tsar first and emperor second." His son understood his office in precisely the same terms. As the same writer continued, "As an individual, Nicholas II is entirely innocent; as an emperor he is a curse. Being very religious and perfectly Orthodox, he understands all too well how far every concession to the spirit of the times is a betrayal of the principles of [Orthodox Tsarism]."[5]

෴   ෴   ෴

Can you canonize a tsar without canonizing the theocratic principle? Certainly, the Russian Orthodox Church, in declaring Nicholas II to be a saint, has seemed to try to do so. Officially, the Moscow Patriarchate has always stressed that in canonizing Russia's last monarch it was not seeking to endorse the old monarchy or promote its restoration, as if 1917 had never happened.[6] This position made sense politically. First, no significant popular movement existed then (or exists now) for a restoration of the monarchy. Secondly, the Church, like other organizations in contemporary Russia, must live with the fact that many Russians continue to fondly remember many of the elements of the Soviet system that the Revolution ultimately brought with it. Some of those people are also believers (indeed, some of them are also bishops), and not unnaturally, the Church does not want to alienate them.

One popular way, then, of thinking about the Romanovs' canonization is as the price the Patriarchate had to pay for reunion with the so-called "Russian Orthodox Church Outside Russia" (ROCOR). An émigré body with approximately 25,000 members, mainly in the United States, ROCOR, which glorified the imperial family as martyrs at a ceremony in New York in 1982, rejected the Moscow Patriarchate for its accommodation with the Soviet government for most of the twentieth century. When Communism collapsed, however, the reason for the schism between the Patriarchate and ROCOR collapsed with it, and pressure mounted on both parties for reunion. In subsequent negotiations, the ROCOR made the recognition of the Romanovs' sainthood a condition for reunion. This was not something the Patriarchate was willing to do automatically. Instead, the Moscow Patriarchate established a Canonization Commission,

---

[5] Merezhkovsky et al., *Tsar et la révolution*, 34.
[6] As the office of the Patriarchate said in 1996, when the Church commenced the official investigation to the family's claim to sainthood: "The canonization of the Royal Family within the assembly of Russian New Martyrs [should] not serve as an argument in the political struggle . . . [or] contribute to the nation's discord." See *Report of the Holy Synod Commission on the Canonization of Saints with Respect to the Martyrdom of the Royal Family* (Russian Orthodox Church, Moscow Patriarchate, 1996). Helpfully, the text can be found in English translation at: https://www.holy-trinity.org/feasts/nicholas.html. Accessed October 3, 2024.

to investigate the evidence for the Romanovs' claim to sainthood. Headed by the respected Metropolitan Yuvenaly of Kolomna, the Commission delivered its verdict four years later, in 1996. The result was universally interpreted as a compromise between a pro-tsarist ROCOR and more skeptical, even reluctant, and anti-tsarist, Patriarchate.

Appraising the evidence it had received, the Commission recommended Nicholas, Alexandra and their children indeed be glorified as saints, only not as martyrs but as Passion-bearers, and in their capacity as private believers only, not as the country's former tsar and ruling family. That Nicholas had been Russia's last tsar was, as far as the Canonization Committee was concerned, strictly accidental. No mention was made in its report of the theocratic principle. On the contrary, the Canonization Commission pointedly found more arguments against rather than for canonization in Nicholas's actions as ruler. Thus, while the Commission acknowledged that, "as a politician and statesman the Sovereign acted on the basis of his religio-ethical principles," it was precisely because Nicholas was "anointed for the Royal office [and] vested with the plenitude of power" that the "inescapable portion of personal responsibility for historical errors, such as the events of 9 January 1905 [i.e. the Bloody Sunday massacre] . . . rests on the Emperor himself."[7] Far from demonstrating any adherence to an Orthodox ideal of *teokratia* for which Nicholas deserved praise, the last reign, in the Commission's eyes, was a catastrophe. "The failure which overtook the Sovereign along the way, was not only and not so much his own personal tragedy, but . . . a prologue for the monumental historical drama of Russia."[8]

Things were scarcely better on the domestic front. Having already concluded that Nicholas had lapsed in his duties as an anointed monarch, the Commission now added to that indictment a charge that he had also lapsed in his duties as husband and head of the family: Nicholas, it found, had repeatedly tried to get rid of Rasputin, but at every attempt he had given in eventually to the stronger will of the empress. "Really, how was it possible," the Commission asked in disbelief, "that such a figure as Rasputin could have such an influence over the Royal Family and upon Russia's political and governing life of his time?"[9] Finally, the problem of the abdication reared its head. The Commission said that if Nicholas's divesting himself of the tsardom was not, strictly speaking, a sin against the canons of the Church, then it was certainly an irregular action in terms of the laws of the Russian Empire. In short, insofar as what it called the "governing and ecclesiastical activity" of Russia's last monarch was concerned, the Commission found no cause for Nicholas's glorification as a saint. Indeed, having also enumerated Nicholas's faults as a husband and father in the Rasputin affair, the Commission

---

[7] Ibid.   [8] Ibid.   [9] Ibid.

implicitly raised the question whether any claim to sainthood on the Romanovs' behalf be sustained at all.

The Commission solved this problem by invoking the Christian notions of repentance and atonement. "The Orthodox Church," the Commission observed in its report, "has examples of even those Christians who led a sinful life following Baptism but who were added to the ranks of saints. Their canonization took place precisely because they atoned for their sins not only by repentance but by special feats, through martyrdom or asceticism."[10] Such atonement for past sins, the Commission found, could be observed in the family's way of life between Nicholas's abdication of the throne in March 1917 and their murders at Ekaterinburg in July 1918. "The majority of witnesses of the last days of the Romanovs speak of... [them] ... as people who suffered and, in spite of all the insults and abuse, led a devout life."[11] Particularly weighty was the testimony (which the Commission found "very moving") of Father Afanasy Belyaev, the priest who served (as we shall see) as the Romanovs' confessor during their captivity in Tsarskoye Selo and the courage they displayed throughout their grim imprisonment in Ekaterinburg.

In the end, then, the Commission recommended that Russia's last monarch and his family should be canonized in view *not* of Nicholas's public acts as tsar but of their private virtues, and *not* as martyrs (since the Commission, having shut its eyes to the question of *teokratia*, found that they had died for no cause of Christian principle) but as members of a lower class of saints known as *strastoterptsy* (Passion-Bearers), who, while not "in the strict sense ... martyrs for Christ," nonetheless "demonstrated a superior example of Christian morality, endurance and personal bravery through their suffering."[12] This rejection of the title "martyr" was probably the Church's single most eloquent attempt to dissociate Nicholas's canonization from the theocratic principle.

All the same, with the Canonization Commission having found in favor of advancing the Romanovs' cause, the faithful were asked to submit evidence of miracles. Hundreds of these flooded in from across the country, and at a council of the Russian Church held in 2000 in Moscow's reconstructed Christ the Savior Cathedral, the Romanovs were canonized as Russia's sainted Royal Passion-bearers. Suddenly, in a country where the mere talk of Russia's last tsar and his family had been forbidden for seven decades, and where, when they were discussed, they were demonized as tyrants and class enemies, the same people were now held up as examples of Christian virtue to be venerated and prayed to — a dramatic reversal of judgment on the last representatives of tsarism that, in hindsight, can be seen as far more symbolically significant than the bishops may have desired or imagined. For as the hundreds of

---

[10] Ibid.   [11] Ibid.   [12] Ibid.

miracles bore witness, the canonization of Russia's last tsar, far from having been imposed on the Russian people from the top, had been effectively imposed on Russia's hierarchs by the Russian people.

෨෨ ෨෨ ෨෨

Eight kilometers long and clad with dark grey granite, the Obvodnyi Canal is St Petersburg's longest man-made waterway. Lined, a century ago, with factories, cattle yards, a power station, and two major regional train termini (the Baltic and Warsaw Stations), the canal formed in Nicholas II's reign the boundary between imperial St Petersburg and the capital's expanding working-class suburbs. Originally intended for navigation, by 1900 the Obvodnyi Canal had silted up, and served as little more than a sewer — a testament to that decade, the 1890s, when, almost overnight, Russia became an industrial power and St Petersburg was transformed from dynastic capital into industrial metropolis.[13] Even today, with the cattle yards and most of the factories gone, the grey embankment could never be called beautiful. But as an official government communication puts it, "without Obvodnyi Canal the perception of St. Petersburg would be incomplete. St Petersburg had always presented a dichotomy of two likenesses — the solemn, official, and beautiful, and the industrial, noisy, smoggy, and unkempt. Both likenesses, however, comprised the unique whole — the capital of the Russian Empire."[14] This is true. In 1917, it was workers from the slums south and west of the Obvodnyi who joined with their confreres from the factory districts on the northern side of the city to overthrow the monarchy.

All the same, few foreign tourists today walk the Obvodnyi's far from pretty embankment. But if they did, they would discover, in a yard beside a church opposite the now disused Warsaw Station, a full-length statue of Nicholas and Alexandra. Cast in bronze, the monument is not high art. Turned towards the viewer, Russia's last monarch and his consort stand stiffly, their hands almost touching, like a bearded Captain von Trapp and Maria, in a pose devoid of either human emotion or regal dignity. Nicholas's eyes capture nothing of the luminescence of his official portraits, the enchanting gaze that contemporaries frequently commented upon transformed into a kind of dull, lifeless stare, while Alexandra has lost the proud bearing and classical features that struck all those who met her, having been reduced to a mousy, nondescript figure, shorter and slighter than the husband whose equal she physically was. In short, the sculpture looks nothing like Russia's last emperor and empress. Indeed,

---

[13] Peter Gatrell, *The Tsarist Economy, 1850–1917* (New York: St Martin's Press, 1986), 43–45, 143.
[14] An electronic version of the pamphlet could once be found here: https://kgiop.gov.spb.ru/en/popularization/heritage-routes/obvodny-canal/. Unfortunately, the link seems to be broken.

as if the sculptor, too, realized that the viewer might need some help deciphering the couple's identity, the imperial crown, orb, and scepter have been laid, awkwardly, on an urn at their feet, and on the side of the granite plinth the ensemble stands on is a colorful mosaic of the whole family in medieval robes and the words, in gold lettering, "Holy Royal Passion-Bearers." Certainly, then, this is Nicholas and Alexandra. But as man and wife, characters from a sentimental film, an emperor and his empress, saints? The monument seems undecided.

For all its limitations, however, the mere fact of such a monument's existence is remarkable. Barely a mile and a half away down the Obvodnyi Canal from the sculpture of Nicholas and Alexandra, the Narva Gates, an oxidized triumphal portal of cast iron erected in honor of Russian victory over Napoleon in 1814, mark the site where, on January 9/22, 1905 ("Bloody Sunday"), the most notorious massacre in the history of the Russian Empire (other than that of the Romanovs themselves) occurred when troops opened fire on a column of unarmed factory workers and their dependents, marching on the Winter Palace to present a loyal "petition" to Nicholas II under the leadership of an Orthodox priest, Father Georgy Gapon.[15] Precisely how many people died that day, at the Narva Gates and at other places in the city, has been debated ever since but several hundred seems to be a reasonable figure.[16] Then as now, the event is widely regarded as having definitively discredited the myth of the tsar's paternal benevolence, on which the tsarist regime was founded.[17] And just over a hundred years later, our statue of Nicholas and Alexandra stood in a small car park beside a church (one of the more than seventy Russian-style churches raised in Petersburg with Nicholas's sponsorship,) a short walk away.[18]

Since the door was open, I entered the church. A tented, five-domed structure erected in 1908 and embellished with seventeenth-century-style *zakomarys* (stacked Russian gables), the building was closed in the 1930s, and its splendid mosaic interiors subsequently ruined. Even today, the congregation worships in largely improvised conditions. I had already left the semi-restored building and returned to the sculpture in the car park when a priest came out of the church and began to cross the muddy

---

[15] On Bloody Sunday, I have principally followed Abraham Ascher, *The Revolution of 1905*, vol. 1: *Russia in Disarray* (Stanford, CA: Stanford University Press, 1988), 74–101; and Andrew M. Verner, *The Crisis of the Russian Autocracy: Nicholas II and the 1905 Revolution* (Princeton, NJ: Princeton University Press, 1990), 141–83.

[16] Pipes, *Russian Revolution*, 25.

[17] See, for example, Leonid Heretz, *Russia on the eve of modernity: Popular religion and traditional culture under the last tsars* (Cambridge: Cambridge University Press, 2008), especially 157–90, which questions precisely this "myth" of the "myth of tsarism's" being discredited.

[18] On this church-building program as part of Nicholas's "apostle-like statecraft," see John Strickland, *The Making of Holy Russia: The Orthodox Church and Russian nationalism before the Revolution* (Jordanville, NY: Holy Trinity Publications, 2013), 110–12.

yard in front of the statue. I greeted him, an intelligent, humane-looking man in his thirties with light brown hair and short beard, and asked about the monument. He invited me for a cup of tea in a building that housed the parish offices behind the church. For the next twenty minutes, we sipped strong black tea, nibbled on sweet biscuits, and carried on such a conversation as we could in my broken Russian.

"As a young man, I had a low opinion of Nicholas II," he told me. "After all, I grew up hearing all the typical things that were said about him in Soviet times — that he was a tyrant, an enemy of the people, and so forth. Even after the Church canonized him a Passion-Bearer, I kept my distance from the cult until they had properly explained to me why the tsar had been sainted."

I nodded, surprised at his frankness. Articulate and well-educated, my interlocutor reflected the high quality of much of the contemporary Russian priesthood. His view on the Romanovs cleaved strictly to the terms set out by the Canonization Commission. The Church had not canonized tsarism; veneration of the Romanovs was not an endorsement of the theocratic principle.

"What's important to remember is that Nicholas II is venerated only on the grounds of the *last* years of his life, for how he conducted himself as a private Christian *after* his abdication, *not* for his actions as Tsar and emperor," said the priest, reinforcing the impression I had taken from the Canonization Committee's report. "As a Christian in captivity, he showed faith in God, forgiveness towards his captors. He was given the grace to imitate Christ in submission to God's will — and it is from this that he was able to pray, like Christ: 'Forgive them, Father, for they know not what they do.'"

The priest paused, shuffled restlessly in his chair, and looked out the window.

"His reign as tsar was full of mistakes," the priest continued. "Take Bloody Sunday, for example. All the people wanted to do was establish a connection with their tsar, remove the barrier between the tsar and the people. Instead, he left for Tsarskoye Selo. Why? Shouldn't he have welcomed them? Hundreds were shot — and they were all monarchists!"

His next comments pushed against the politer boundaries in which the committee had tried to contain the question of Nicholas's sainthood.

"Nicholas's problem was that again and again he put family ahead of his duties to the State. This came to a head in the abdication. Let's be clear. The abdication was a sin. Nicholas alone *was* the state, political authority. The officers would have remained loyal to the oaths they had sworn to him. But in abdicating, he betrayed those oaths and in doing so the state fell apart. He thought he was handing power to his brother. But the latter was an alcoholic and disqualified in any case for the throne through his marriage. The point is Nicholas *couldn't* abdicate. It was illegal. The crown and the state were his responsibility. That fact always has to be remembered against those who venerate his memory uncritically."

He emphasized the repentant sinner theory of Nicholas's sainthood.

"I think Nicholas was a Christian, a believer, but only in the last year or so of his life did he become a saint. Before that time there were parts of his life that are hard to call Orthodox. Some people hold him and his family up as models of Orthodox family life. But this fact should give them pause. Have you heard, for example, of the film called *Mathilde*?"

I had heard of the film, released during the centenary of the revolution in 2017, which depicted Nicholas and Alexandra's marriage as a Charles-and-Diana-style *ménage à trois* with Nicholas's old sweetheart, the primadonna Mathilde Kschessinskaya, in the role of Camilla. The priest's "some people" was a reference to Natalya Poklonskaya, the young and beautiful Ukrainian state prosecutor who resigned her position in Kiev during the 2014 Ukraine Crisis to pledge her loyalty to the government of Crimea, where she had grown up. Very public in her commitment to Orthodoxy, Poklonskaya achieved notoriety for the ardor of her devotion to the sainthood of Nicholas II, provoking national debate when, in 2016, she marched with an icon of his during Second World War memorial celebrations and denounced the film *Mathilde*. Despite Poklonskaya's leadership of the public campaign calling on the government to ban the film, the Kremlin refused and Orthodox vigilantes (not necessarily linked to Poklonskaya) threatened arson against theaters showing it. The same year, she claimed a bust of Nicholas II erected outside the buildings of the Justice Ministry in Crimea had begun to produce a miraculous secretion of myrrh. Presumably, it was such excesses as these that the priest I was talking to in St Petersburg wanted to distance himself from.

"We know that Nicholas had relations with Kschessinskaya. Why did his parents, who were supposed to be Orthodox, permit it? And another thing," he huffed, warming to his theme, "Nicholas smoked! Now, Orthodox people aren't supposed to smoke. It's a sin. And yet in every second photograph of Nicholas II, the 'Orthodox tsar,' can be seen smoking. Some of these pictures have been doctored so that you can't see the cigarette, but nobody's fooled!"

I was gaining the distinct impression that my priest didn't really set much store by Nicholas's claim to sainthood at all, that he saw it perhaps as a sop to traditionalists, a political concession. I suggested that the erection of a monument to Nicholas and Alexandra outside the church building might have been the subject of controversy within the parish.

"No," replied the priest, shifting despairingly in his seat. "There was no controversy, unfortunately. Most people don't know very much about Nicholas II. The congregation was apathetic. People were neither for nor against it when we put up the memorial. They were simply indifferent."

He offered me another biscuit.

"I don't think we should exaggerate the Russian state's receptiveness to Orthodoxy, either. The Church talks a lot about *symphonia*. This is a term taken from Byzantium to describe an ideal harmony between church and state, the ecclesiastical and secular authorities. But I studied Byzantium at the seminary. It wasn't the perfect, believing society it's sometimes held up to be. Outwardly, the Roman Empire became Christian. But did Byzantine *chinovniki* [civil servant, bureaucrats] really believe? Some of them, certainly. But not all. Again, it's like today. The Church likes to pretend that the state's servants are believers but mostly they're not."

He cited, as an example, the headmaster of the local primary school, who allowed him to come only four times a year to educate the students in religion. Far from being an adherent of a Bulgakov-style ideal of *teokratia*, my priest's experience of contemporary Russia had made him a partisan of the diametrically opposed principle of separation of Church and State.

"When Lenin came to power in 1917, one of his first acts was the separation of Church and State," said the priest approvingly. "Some modern Orthodox blame him for that. But actually, I think this was correct. It's the way it should be."

෴   ෴   ෴

Was the tsarist regime, then, an authentic expression of the Orthodox view of politics? Was there such a thing as the "theocratic principle"? Should Church and State be connected or separated? It was a debate as old as the Revolution, and in 1918, in a dialogue called "At the Feast of the Gods," Bulgakov tackled it directly. With the monarchy's collapse, something essential to Russia — the theocratic ideal — had been lost, and Bulgakov could not fathom his contemporaries' total lack of feeling for it. Even the Orthodox Church, it seemed to Bulgakov, had thrown in its hat with liberalism and democracy. And yet Russia could only really be Russia, that is, an *Orthodox* Russia, if the theocratic source and ends of political authority could somehow be retrieved, and the rightful analogical relationship between the earthly and cosmic orders be restored. But most Russians, even professing Orthodox ones, were oblivious to this.

To open his contemporaries' eyes, therefore, Bulgakov composed in the summer of 1918 his dialogue. A thirty-page exploration of the religious (i.e., spiritual and theological) meaning of the Russian Revolution, the dialogue recapitulates in eloquent terms Bulgakov's objections to the "received wisdom" of his age regarding tsarism's fall as an undiluted boon for Russia and for the Russian Church. Thus when one of the six participants in the dialogue, a figure known as the "Worldly Divine," asserts that the Russian Church has now embraced the truths of political liberalism and democracy, Bulgakov puts it into the mouth of another figure, known as the "Refugee," to object in terms that seem very closely to reflect Bulgakov's own thinking on the essential place of the theocratic principle in the Orthodox conception of politics. The following exchange between the pair follows.[19]

> *Worldly Divine*: You repeat the widespread prejudice that Orthodoxy and autocracy are linked together...[and yet] there is absolutely no link between Orthodoxy and autocracy, except the historical one, and this has been clearly confirmed now that Orthodoxy has finally received its freedom [i.e. with the fall of the monarchy in 1917].

> *Refugee*: But all the same a link did exist, not just an external one, but an internal mystical one, and this corresponds to the age-old conception of Orthodoxy, from St Constantine to the present. The Church concentrated special love on its anointed one, the beloved bridegroom of the Church from the line of David. Look closely at the liturgy which is now maimed by mechanical amputations and apart from the courtly rhetoric and servility, you will sense this mystical love. The Church recognized that in the 'external episcopate,' the 'vicar of God on earth,' it had the architect of the City of God, the keeper of the garden of the Church. Orthodoxy did not see its historic mission of creating the kingdom of God on earth in any other way. When Byzantium fell, the mantle of Monomakh was transferred to the midnight lands and our ancestors with full justification recognized Moscow as the Third Rome.

Lex orandi, lex credendi, Bulgakov is saying, pointing to the Church liturgies (from the coronation to the weekly commemoration of the tsar at Sunday Mass) that hallowed tsarism as a form of *teokratia*. In loving the Tsar, in anointing him as a Second David, in praying for him in the liturgy, as she had done since the conversion of Constantine, the Church had *not* betrayed herself or made a merely passing and transitory peace with the authorities that be, whether in Byzantium or medieval Muscovy. On the contrary, the Church's tradition was a true realization of its concept of politics. Her liturgies conveyed a love for "God's anointed," the tsar, that was real, and that anointing itself was no mere symbolic act in the nominal sense that modernity understands symbolism. On the contrary, says the Refugee. As far as the theocratic principle embodied in the tsar was concerned, one can "scarcely dispute that autocracy was given not only practical religious significance but also dogmatic significance in the history of Orthodoxy. Without this assumption, the history of Byzantium becomes unintelligible, particularly the ecumenical councils at which certain Church rights were recognized as the tsars', and so too does the entire history of the Russian autocracy. The Church glorifies

---

[19] Sergei Bulgakov, "At the feast of the gods," in William F. Woehrlin, ed. and trans., *Out of the Depths [Iz glubiny]: A Collection of Articles on the Russian Revolution* (Irvine, CA: Charles Schlacks Jr., 1986), 110.

St Constantine as the 'first tsar in Christendom to receive his scepter from God,' and conceives of him as an organ of theocracy."[20]

The Worldly Divine is not impressed with the Refugee's argument from Tradition, and it elicits from him an outburst. "Does it matter what cluttered up our divine services during the Imperial period?" the Worldly Divine asks, exasperated, revealing himself to be the representative of a typically modernist impatience with history, and of an urge to "cleanse" and innovate. The excision of references to the tsar in the liturgy had only improved the latter's standing in his eyes. "How the divine service shines now that there is no more of this! Like an icon that has been cleaned and liberated from age-old soot and dirt."

But Bulgakov knew that this urge to cleanse and liberate the Church from her accumulated "soot and dirt" was itself a manifestation of the secular mind. The soot and dirt accumulated on the surface of the icon were after all a material residue of the faithful's prayers and devotions before it.[21] And the same was true of the love for the tsar conveyed in the old tsarist-era liturgies with their roots in Byzantium a thousand years before. Like the loving veneration of the icon, the liturgy expressed and bore witness to an authentic *sensus fidelium*. If it had not, it would not have lasted so long. (Indeed, we might say that in the rite for the tsar's anointing and crowning, the Church *was* writing an icon, a liturgical one.) In any case, the Refugee replies in a way that captures the highhandedness that Bulgakov wished to criticize in modernity's engagement with Tradition.

> *Refugee*: We cannot dismiss everything that displeases us as an abuse, however. These anathemas enumerate the main dogmatic heresies which troubled and shook the Church — Arianism, Macedonianism, and so on. But among these under number eleven stand the following: 'Anathema to those who would think that Orthodox rulers ascend the throne other than through God's blessing, or that in anointment there do not pass to them the gifts of the Holy Spirit...; [and anathema too] *to those who would dare to rebel against or betray them.*'[22]

"Undoubtedly, this anathema is of political origin," sniffs the Worldly Divine in reply, "because with wise decisiveness it already has been excised by the new Church authority."

---

[20] Ibid.
[21] Probably, Bulgakov is parodying here the opinions of the liberal philosopher Prince Eugene Trubetskoi whose celebrated wartime publications, in 1916, acclaimed the discovery of the properly artistic qualities of the Russian icon, and the icons' liberation from "age-old layers of gold, smoke and tasteless, unskilled overpainting," as heralding the forthcoming liberation of the Russian Church, and Russian society itself, from the absurdity of tsarism: cited in Ouspensky, *Theology of the Icon*, 2:464. While Bulgakov and Trubetskoi had been friends and collaborators before the Revolution, even then they had begun to disagree on the benefits of liberalism: Williams, *Sergii Bulgakov*, 57–58.
[22] Bulgakov, "At the feast of the gods," III. My italics.

The anathema can be proved to have been empty all along, Wordly Divine is saying, because even in the most recent Week of Orthodoxy the Church, for the first time in a thousand years, did not pronounce it, *without ill effect or consequence*. The Church abolished this anathema, effecting its reconciliation with the principle of popular government or democracy, and no punishment arrived from God to check it. The demise of the monarchy and the Church's abandonment of the ideal of theocracy has been *approved by history*.

But this dismissal is merely the pretext for the Refugee to make perhaps his most devastating observation. The Worldly Divine has not understood the full cataclysm of the revolution. The latter itself, suggests the Refugee, is the consequence of (and God's punishment upon) the Church's loss of faith in a truly sacred politics. The secularization of Russia is wrongly understood as the effect of the revolution; it is its ultimate *cause* — and a cause that, disgracefully, the Refugee is saying, took hold first and foremost in the educated ("worldly") clergy. Thus, "even now there are those who propose that Russia brought this anathema upon itself, and who see in this the prime cause of all our misfortunes, for an anathema is not uttered in passing; it is not an empty word that falls powerless to the ground."[23]

As regards the Church's love for the Tsar, her bridegroom, therefore, Bulgakov's was an argument *for* the "soot and dirt," *for* the Tradition, and, therefore, *for* the tsar. But he also knew that, by 1918, he was barking at the wind. Popular sovereignty, democracy, authority *not* "by the grace of God but by popular dispensation," had won acceptance not only within educated, politically active Russian society at large, but also within the Church. Indeed, it's an acceptance that, a hundred years later, it would seem to have retained.

By comparison with Bulgakov's expansive ideal of *teokratia*, the official teaching of the modern Russian Orthodox Church is significantly more modest. While it is true that the relevant statement, the so-called Basis of the Social Concept of the Russian Orthodox Church (first published in 1997 and updated since), upholds monarchical "theocracy" (*teokratia*) as the ideal Christian political regime, it also actively discourages believers from seeking such a regime's practical restoration.[24] And yet perhaps the most striking difference between the content of Bulgakov's vision on the Yalta Embankment and the official teaching of the Russian Church today is the abandonment, by the latter, of the Christian Hellenism of the Fathers. As we have seen, these often spoke to or about Constantine and his successors as if a natural relationship of analogy existed between them as emperor (*basileus*) and the kingship (*basileia*) of God over the

---

[23] Ibid.
[24] Russian Orthodox Church-Moscow Patriarchate, *Basis of the Social Concept*, 3.7.

cosmos, whose source of unity and ordering principle was the Logos, just as that of the *oikumene* or empire was the *basileus* or emperor, the Logos's image. Not so, however, the modern Russian Orthodox Church, which sees kingship (*basileia*, sovereignty, the ruling authority) as a concession to sin.[25] But the alternative view — not only of Eusebius of Caesarea but of Cyril of Jerusalem, the Cappadocian Fathers, and John Chrysostom, not to mention such ante-Nicene apologists as Athenagoras and Melito of Sardis — is conspicuous for its absence, the victim, it would seem, of the discrediting effect of the Russian Revolution (and a testament again to the latter's fundamental religious meaning).

‽   ‽   ‽

Bloody Sunday, January 9th/22nd 1905: the event has been named already. To the Canonization Committee, it was perhaps the event that, more than any other, symbolized why no grounds for advancing Nicholas's cause for sainthood could be found in his "ecclesiastical and governing activity." That is, Bloody Sunday emblematized why Nicholas could not be canonized as tsar. But did Bloody Sunday disqualify Nicholas's "ecclesiastical and governing activity," as the Canonization Committee supposed? Moreover, is it really the case, as the Canonization Committee implied, that the courage and Christian virtue — the faith, humility and dependence on God — for which Nicholas was eventually canonized were only evident in his life as a private individual after events had forced him to surrender power? In the Canonization Committee's report, there seems just a hint of the modern prejudice in favor of the separation of Church and State, as only apart from politics, and in rivalry, as it were, with it, can the Christian attain virtue. Beyond the event itself, then, these are some of the questions that Bloody Sunday as a symbol of Nicholas's reign raises. And here, in the old workers' district by the Obvodnyi, the location of the homes, a hundred years ago, of many of the workers that died in the massacre, was a good place to raise them.

A mile or so along the Obvodnyi from the statue of Nicholas and Alexandra, Petersburg's Narva Gates, marooned in the middle of a busy traffic circle, stands one of the old Leningrad's few surviving Soviet murals. Painted on the side of a building facing the oxidized green gates, it shows a worker with a banner that reads "Proletariat of the world, unite!" against a backdrop of smoke-belching factories, while the man's fellow-workers defend a barricade against unseen government troops, and the symbols of tsarism — a double-headed eagle, an Orthodox cross — tumble around them. It is a memorial not only to the events of Bloody Sunday, which unfolded in the square, now a traffic circle, at its feet, but also

---

[25] Ibid., 3.1.

to the mythic importance attributed to it ever since, among liberals and Marxists alike, as the moment when the myths, not only of tsarism but also of Christianity were revealed in the hearts of the heretofore beguiled Russian people as being precisely that: as myths without foundation in reality. To educated men themselves, heirs to Kant and Feuerbach, such "truths" had long since been revealed. If they rejoiced, as we shall see, despite themselves, over Bloody Sunday, however, it was because with that event those truths had been revealed in a way accessible to the masses. To them, too, and not only to an Orthodox Christian such as Bulgakov, the meaning of the Russian Revolution, writ large, was *religious* — a negative theophany that confirmed atheistic conclusions of nineteenth-century European philosophy.[26] And what about Nicholas himself? Did Bloody Sunday occur because Nicholas was negligent towards the religious and theological meaning of his authority as tsar (as a certain reading of the Canonization Commission's report might lead us to believe)? Or is it truer to say that Bloody Sunday occurred *despite* his being so highly, if intuitively, conscious of it? Surely, part of the mystery of Nicholas's sainthood is that the very attitude of trust in and dependence on God, which Nicholas manifested during the time of his imprisonment (and for which the Russian Orthodox Church canonized him), was the *same attitude* of trust and dependence that defined Nicholas's inner life as tsar *always*.

～ ～ ～

Bloody Sunday, like the year-long revolutionary disturbances it would set in train, had its roots in the war with Japan. A contest between two rising industrial powers for access to the Chinese market, the war was inaugurated by the surprise Japanese attack on the Russian Far Eastern naval base, Port Arthur, on January 26/February 8, 1904. From the beginning, Nicholas's theocratic instincts were evident: Nicholas's conduct of the war, like his later response to Bloody Sunday, were framed and guided by them. Thus, when a battalion of East Siberian Rifles departed Tsarskoye Selo for the Far East, Nicholas personally blessed them with an icon of St Serafim of Sarov, at that time Russia's most recently canonized saint.[27] Then, when, a fortnight after the Japanese attack, Mass was held for the beginning of Great Lent, the forty-day Orthodox season of fasting in preparation for Easter, Nicholas recorded in his diary "what comfort" he received from "the Holy Mysteries of Christ . . . in today's

---

[26] Or, as Del Noce would have it, it was confirmation for such men, too, that "at the beginning of contemporary history there is an ideal causality" — that of the expansion of atheism: Augusto Del Noce, "Tradition and Innovation," in *Age of Secularization*, 64.
[27] Nicholas II, February 4, 1904, in Diary (2), 194. Strangely, a consideration of Nicholas's interior state does not feature in the only monograph dedicated to religion in the Russo-Japanese War: Betsy C. Perabo, *Russian Orthodoxy and the Russo-Japanese War* (London: Bloomsbury, 2017).

trying times."[28] Traveling to Penza in the Central Agricultural Region that summer for army maneuvers, he both appreciated the "beautiful places" in the Russian countryside he had seen through the windows of the train, and returned "pleased with all I had seen and with humble thanks to the Lord God for all his kindnesses."[29] To Russian troops in the Far East, he and Alexandra dispatched New Testaments, prayer books and icons. This attendance of Nicholas's on God did not please everyone, however. "The Japanese have guns and we are fighting with icons of St Serafim," War Minister Kuropatkin is said to have grumbled.

And yet for all Nicholas's faith, God seemed to turn His face against Russia. On March 31/ April 13, the battleship *Petropavlovsk* hit a mine at the entrance to Port Arthur, killing the admiral aboard, as well as most of the officers and crew. Nicholas "could not get this misfortune out of my head all day." But his faith was unshaken: "Let God's will be done in all things, but we must pray for God's mercy towards us sinners."[30] Then, barely a fortnight after his return from Penza, the Minister of the Interior, Vyacheslav von Plehve, was assassinated when the carriage in which he was traveling was blown up by the revolutionary terrorist group, the SRs (Socialist Revolutionaries). Again, Nicholas submitted to God. "How strictly the Lord is visiting us with his anger. But may His holy Will be done!" he wrote in his diary.[31]

The steadfastness of this conviction of Nicholas's is all the more remarkable for the misfortunes that continued to assail Russia. As 600,000 Russian soldiers were rushed to Manchuria to defend de facto Russian control of the Chinese territory against the vast, German-trained land army the Japanese were shipping to the Asian mainland, rumors filtered back to Russia proper that they were being deployed without adequate boots and uniforms, let alone weapons. Tales of incompetent and indecisive commanders indifferently squandering the lives of thousands quickly transformed the Japanese War from a patriotic cause into a humiliation for the government. Discontent spread. As factories were repurposed for the war effort, and government debt to finance war expenditures rapidly rose, consumer goods vanished from the shelves, and a rise occurred in inflation and unemployment. Life for Russia's new industrial proletariat grew more difficult than it already was, creating a ready, resentful audience for tales of government incompetence and malfeasance.

Then there were Nicholas's personal worries. Not the least of these was the birth, six months into the Japanese War, of the long-awaited but tragically diseased tsarevich, Alexei. "There are no words to thank God for

---

[28] Nicholas II, February 14, 1904, in Diary (2), 195.
[29] Nicholas II, July 3, 1904, in Diary (2), 218.
[30] Nicholas II, March 31, 1904, in Diary (2), 202.
[31] Nicholas II, July 15, 1904, in Diary (2), 220.

sending down to us such a comfort in this year of difficult experiences!" wrote Nicholas in his diary when the child was born on July 30/August 12.[32] According to Nicholas, the newborn was an "amazingly peaceful child. Almost never cries." By this time, Nicholas and Alexandra both were convinced that the child's birth was the result of the special intervention made on their behalf by their patron, St Serafim, in heaven. Yet if this was so, it soon became clear that, puzzlingly, the long-awaited Heir was ill. The first signs of hemophilia appeared only days after the birth. By September 1904, just three months before Bloody Sunday, they were a source of serious worry. Perhaps the dynasty's fate was insecure after all. Why would God, and Serafim, requite their faith and their prayers this way? A soul less faithful than Nicholas's might have questioned God's beneficence. But Nicholas, it appears, did not. Neither did he in October, when, having offered his prayers for the safe arrival of the Baltic Fleet in the Pacific ("Bless its path, Lord, and let it reach its appointed destination and there fulfil its heavy duty for the good and welfare of Russia!"), the war with Japan risked becoming a war with Britain after Russian sailors had panicked and opened fire on British fishing boats on the Dogger Bank.[33] "How everything has got complicated, how difficult everything has become!" he confided in his diary a little over a week after the incident: "But the Lord of mercies, after the testing He sends, [ensures that] then there will come times of calm!"[34]

In contradistinction, then, to the increasingly secular outlook of Nicholas's contemporaries, God, his existence, and sovereignty over human affairs remained the primary fact, the foundation, of Nicholas's worldview, from which all the rest proceeded. "May God bless the coming year and give Russia a victorious outcome to the war, secure peace and a tranquil life," he wrote in the opening lines of his diary for 1905.[35] Nine days later, Bloody Sunday littered the streets by the Narva Gates, and other locations within Petersburg were littered with the bodies of workers. As always, Nicholas's first instinct was to turn to God. "A dreadful day! Serious disorders broke out in Petersburg following the workers' wish to reach the Winter Palace. The army had to fire at various places within the city, many dead and wounded. O Lord, how painful and oppressive," he wrote in his diary. It was a Sunday, and, characteristically, he learnt of the massacre upon returning home from Mass.[36]

Significantly, Nicholas's piety contrasted sharply with that of the man usually presented as Bloody Sunday's "hero," the Orthodox priest and social agitator Fr Georgi Gapon who organized the march. A graduate

---

[32] Nicholas II, July 30, 1904, in Diary (2), 222.
[33] Nicholas II, October 2, 1904, in Diary (2), 232.
[34] Nicholas II, October 20, 1904, in Diary (2), 235.
[35] Nicholas II, January 1, 1905, in Diary (2), 245.
[36] Nicholas II, January 9, 1905, in Diary (2), 246.

of the prestigious St Petersburg Theological Academy, Gapon was an ordained Orthodox priest, and, as head of the Petersburg Mill and Factory Workers Assembly, a paid employee of the Ministry of the Interior (which had committed to him the twin task both of representing the needs of Petersburg's workers to the government, and of the Church's, and government's, solicitude for the workers, in a way that allowed for the peaceful rather than revolutionary development of the political consciousness of the capital's industrial workforce).[37] But he was also a conflicted, Janus-like figure, whose intention in organizing the march that led to Bloody Sunday was not to lead the peaceful march ("of monarchists") with which he is usually credited but to provoke a moral outrage that would justify revolution. So much, in any case, Gapon tells us himself in his *Story of My Life*, a memoir culminating in a description of the events of Bloody Sunday written by Gapon in exile in Switzerland.

First published in English in London in 1906, Gapon's *Story of My Life* offers itself as in many ways the photographic negative of Bulgakov's *Autobiographical Notes*, the tale, not of how Gapon was converted to the theocratic principle, but of how he was disabused of it. Thus, if *before* Bloody Sunday, Gapon tells us, he, as a priest, had "idealized the Emperor Nicholas II" both as an Orthodox tsar and a "good, kind and honest man," then the "massacres of January" were a "revelation that brought about a complete change in the mind," not only in himself, he claimed, but also in "the nation."[38] And yet despite how much Gapon was lionized at the time (and has continued to be since), a close reading of *Story of My Life* suggests that the significance of Bloody Sunday was not that it disabused Gapon of the myth of tsarism *as a consequence* of Nicholas's failure to live up to the tsarist ideal; it is rather that, as far as Gapon as the event's organizer was concerned, the calculated discreditation of tsarism was the day's *purpose* from the start.

The immediate justification for the march was the dismissal of four workmen belonging to Gapon's Assembly of Mill and Factory Workers at the massive Putilov arms factory south of the Obvodnyi Canal, in December 1904. With the men's fate transformed into a general political cause by the Socialist Revolutionaries (SRs), Gapon agreed to allow his organization to lead the call for the men's reinstatement. Across Petersburg, therefore, thousands of workers went on strike, and on January 6/19, 1905, Gapon declared that the following Sunday (January 9/22) a march on the Winter Palace would take place by the members of his Assembly. There, Gapon announced that he would demand the right to present to Nicholas II a "petition" for a vast range of political reforms that had nothing to do with the four workmen but precisely recapitulated

---

[37] For Gapon's biography, see Ascher, *Revolution of 1905*, vol. 1, 77–80.
[38] Georgii Gapon, *Story of My Life* (New York: E. P. Dutton and Co., 1906), 248.

the unrelated constitutional demands of the Union of Liberation, a recently formed alliance of radical and conservative liberals that sought a written constitution, the recognition of civil and political rights, and a national legislative assembly.[39] Significantly, for our purposes, Gapon's petition also included the Union's demand for the separation of Church and State, which Gapon knew Nicholas II could only reject along with all the others. Indeed, the sweeping nature of the political and constitutional demands contained in Gapon's petition, and the inevitability of their rejection, are the first indications that, rather than a peaceful march, Gapon envisaged from the start a conscious bid to provoke revolution: either Gapon would succeed in intimidating the authorities into capitulating to his stage-managed theatrics, or he would use the crowd to provoke an outrage that would demolish the government's moral claim to the right to rule. As Gapon tells us in *Story of My Life*, he also knew that such an outrage was best achieved by feigning an appeal to the regime's own ideology. For this reason, he says, it was agreed that the march would have, as Gapon had it, a "a distinctive religious character": the demonstrating workers would carry Orthodox icons and portraits of the tsar.[40] To the extent, then, that Bloody Sunday succeeded in discrediting tsarism, this discreditation was not merely the *result* of Bloody Sunday; for Gapon, it was its *purpose*. As Gapon put it in a note sent to Nicholas II himself the day before the march, if the monarch did not personally receive Gapon at the Palace, then the Russian people "will have no Tsar."[41]

Of course, the government, informed that the Assembly of Mill and Factory Workers that it had itself founded was being redirected towards revolutionary purposes did not merely sit on its hands and sadistically wait for an opportunity to shoot at working-class protesters. On January 7/20, the authorities instructed the workers not to take part in Gapon's march. The following day, they ordered the priest's arrest. But thanks to the SRs (the radical agrarian political-terrorist movement with which Gapon was also working), who hid him, Gapon evaded arrest and continued his agitation. When the scheduled Sunday arrived, therefore, Gapon was still at liberty to lead the demonstration, while the government, for its part, had decided that by this stage the march could not be prevented from going ahead. Rather, a cordon of troops would be placed around the monumental heart of the capital, where the palace buildings were located; the crowd, it was expected, would halt when it saw the army cordon. Unfortunately, this did not happen. But, again, Gapon cannot have expected anything less. On the contrary, to strengthen his

---

[39] On the Union's origins, see Ascher, *Revolution of 1905*, 1:34; Pipes, *Russian Revolution*, 18–19 ff.

[40] Gapon, *Story*, 176.

[41] Ibid., 162.

hand in this lethal game, Gapon encouraged the workers to bring their families with them. What such workers and their families didn't know, however, was that Gapon had also invited armed Socialist Revolutionary *provocateurs* to take part in the march. While the workers at the front of the crowd would carry icons and portraits of the tsar, the SRs would conceal their identity until the appropriate moment arrived to unfurl their revolutionary banners and brandish their weapons.

Certainly, not everything went as Gapon planned. As the workers were gathering at six advertised points in Petersburg's industrial outskirts on the morning of January 9, 1905, Gapon's plan to lend the march a religious character almost failed, when an Orthodox parish priest refused to surrender his church's icons. Not to be thwarted, Gapon and his associates had to seize them by force. Having obtained these sacred articles, however, Gapon cynically put them in the hands of the workers at the front of the demonstration. Setting off from the Putilov Works, the crowd encountered the army cordon at the Narva Gates. "Would they dare to touch us?" Gapon recalled asking himself in *Story of My Life* as the crowd approached Cossack lines, and the police standing by removed their caps at the sight of the icons.[42] For a moment, it must have seemed to Gapon that the troops might even *fail* to fall for the provocation and refrain from firing on the marchers. But Gapon needn't have worried. By now, the workers bearing the icons and Nicholas's portrait at the front of the crowd were only two hundred yards from the Cossacks at the Narva Gates. Persuaded by Gapon that the soldiers would never shoot on a crowd bearing the holy icons and images of the tsar, and one that, moreover, included women and children, the workers did not halt when they saw the soldiers but pushed on towards them. Having expected the crowd to retreat, the troops at the Narva Gates opened fire, just as they did at other points in the city where the crowd met the cordon. Journalists claimed that thousands were killed. But the truer figure seems to have been two hundred dead and another eight hundred injured.[43] Far from a peaceful march, it was from start to finish a vain, reckless, and reprehensible act of provocation in the extreme. Gapon fled, eventually to Switzerland.

≈   ≈   ≈

Despite the cynicism that motivated its organizers, Bloody Sunday united Russian society against the autocracy. By the middle of January, some 400,000 workers were on strike across the empire, threatening not only the production of armaments, and economic collapse in the war with Japan that Russia was then fighting tooth and nail in the Far East, but

---

[42] Ibid., 181.
[43] Pipes, *Russian Revolution*, 25.

also the breakdown of law and order, as the railway network was paralyzed, public transport in Petersburg, Moscow and other large cities ground to a halt, and the lights themselves frequently went out when work stoppages struck electricity power stations. In a bid to bring the strikes to an end, the government issued a series of manifestos foreshadowing the possibility of various reforms. One, in February, invited the Russian people to catalogue their grievances and send them to the tsar. Thousands responded. Another, in August, promised the establishment of an elected consultative Duma. But these failed to stem the urban unrest. Over the summer, the students went on strike, and, in the lower Volga, Right-Bank Ukraine, and Baltic provinces, a *jacquerie* erupted as, acting on longstanding grievances, the peasants began seizing lands left in the possession of the nobility by the 1861 Emancipation proclamation. Tax revenues plummeted, and only a massive French loan allowed the government to retain the army's loyalty and prosecute the ongoing war with Japan. When the United States, fearful of Japan's growing power in the Pacific, proposed a peace conference to bring the war to an end, Japan and Russia agreed, and a peace treaty was signed on September 5/18. But the treaty did nothing to bring Russia's domestic troubles to an end. On the contrary, in October, a general strike was called that saw workers, students and liberal professionals walk off work and withdraw their support for the government en masse.

In the end, it was the famous Manifesto of October 19, promising a Duma with legislative powers elected on the basis of universal male suffrage, along with sweeping and unheard-of civil liberties (freedoms of conscience, press, assembly, inviolability of the person from arbitrary arrest), that managed to force a split between the workers' and the liberal-bourgeois movements, and restore a measure of peace.[44] Cautiously, the Union of Liberation shifted its allegiance from the forces of revolution to the forces of order, and Russia's professional classes returned to work. Joined now by the Marxist Social Democratic Labor Party, the SRs tried to keep the revolution going on the streets. For the Union, however, led by the former University of Moscow historian Pavel Miliukov, the path towards the toppling of the autocracy lay through the representative institutions that Nicholas himself in the October Manifesto had created. Thus the Union of Liberation was re-founded as a political party. Formally called the Constitutional Democratic Party, it would be known as the "Kadets" (from the Russian spelling of "constitutional democrats"), and its leader would remain the same Pavel Miliukov. As for Gapon, having been feted in Switzerland by Plekhanov (the founder of Russian Marxism) and Lenin, and in France by the leading Socialists Jean Jaures

---

[44] The text can be found in Verner, *Crisis*, 242–43; and Ascher, *Revolution of 1905*, 1:228–29.

and Georges Clemenceau (the Third Republic's future Socialist president), Gapon took up residence in England. In 1906, he returned in secret to Russia, only to be murdered by the SRs that had co-opted him.

ᴓ   ᴓ   ᴓ

"Whose spirit dominates this or that historical figure? Whose 'seal' is stamped on this or that historical movement? Those are the usual questions which one must ask while reflecting on the complex phenomena of an ever more complicated life," wrote Bulgakov a year after Bloody Sunday in his essay, "Karl Marx as a religious type."[45] Written in the wake of the 1905 Revolution, the essay set out the reasons for Bulgakov's definitive rejection, at this time, of Marxism. If religion was, as Bulgakov had come to believe, the defining question of human life, then Marx (whose fundamental source of inspiration, Bulgakov believed, after careful study of Marx's works, was the German philosopher of atheism, Ludwig Feuerbach) was an atheist and a nihilist before he was a critic of capitalism — and Marx's whole philosophy was incompatible therefore with Bulgakov's increasingly important commitment to Orthodox Christianity.[46] Indeed, claimed Bulgakov, the primary and underlying source of man's unfreedom was not, to Marx, the bourgeoisie's control of the means of production but the very notion of God. That was why not the socialization of the means of production but the "annihilation of religion, as the illusive happiness of the people" represented Marx (and Marxism's) true goal (as Bulgakov quoted Marx himself as admitting).[47]

On the face of it, this would seem to have little to do with Nicholas II, Gapon, and the meaning of, and responsibility for, Bloody Sunday. Although Marxists played a greater role in events later in 1905 (Trotsky, for example, a convinced Marxist, was elected head of the St Petersburg workers' council, or soviet, in October), neither the SRs nor the Union of Liberation, nor even Gapon himself, was significantly inspired by Marx. And yet Bulgakov's essay is relevant all the same. Two passages, particularly, one at the beginning and another halfway through Bulgakov's essay, offer us a perspective from which to measure the two men, Gapon and Nicholas II, and the rival spiritual and ideational poles between which

---

[45] Sergei Bulgakov, *Karl Marx as a religious type: His relation to the religion of anthropotheism of L. Feuerbach*, ed. Donald W. Treadgold, trans. Virgil R. Lang (Belmont, MA: Nordland Pub. Co., 1979), 42.

[46] "As is well known," wrote Bulgakov, "the religious question occupies the central place in Feuerbach's philosophy. Its main theme is the rejection of the religion of theanthropism [i.e. historical mystical-dogmatic Christianity] in the name of the religion of anthropotheism [i.e. man as God]; it is a theomachistical, militant atheism. Especially this theme generated in Marx's soul the most profound resonance. Out of all the abundance and variation of philosophical schools . . . Marx's ear singled out the religious theme, namely the theomachistical one." See Bulgakov, *Karl Marx*, 79.

[47] Bulgakov, *Karl Marx*, 82.

Russia's fate oscillated throughout the revolutionary year of 1905 (and, as Bulgakov claims, beyond).

"I have often had to express my conviction," Bulgakov writes at the beginning of his essay, "that the determining power in the spiritual life of man is his religion—not only in the narrow sense of the word, but in a wider sense as well, i.e., the highest and ultimate values which one admits as being *beyond* him and *higher* than himself and also his practical relation to these values. To determine the real religious center in a person, to discover his genuine spiritual core, is to find out the most intimate and important things about him, and then everything external and derivative will be comprehensible."[48] And when we read and compare the diary of Nicholas II, on the one hand, and Gapon's memoirs, on the other, isn't this precisely what we obtain, the key to each man's outlook not only on God but also on politics and the best explanation of his motivation? Indeed, in Bulgakov's terms, Gapon reveals himself to have been not a Christian at all but a Marxist. As Bulgakov has it in the second passage of interest to us, if it is true that "in Marx's militant atheism, one can see the central nerve of his entire lifework,"[49] then in Marx's theory of revolution it is precisely the proletariat that is "entrusted with the mission of the historical realization of atheism, i.e. of man's practical liberation from religion."[50] Certainly, believed Bulgakov, this cynical instrumentalization of the not-unjustified grievances of the working poor "reveals the real Marx, the true 'secret' of Marxism, its genuine nature!"[51] And this would seem to be precisely what the Petersburg Assembly of Factory and Millworkers amounted to in 1905 for the SRs, the Union of Liberation, and for Gapon in their calculated effort to discredit the claims of a self-consciously theocratic autocracy: namely, *a weapon for the emancipation of mankind from religion*. Already, then, in 1905, the real meaning and ideational causation of the Russian Revolution can be seen to have been religious, a contest between "real mystical principles [which], being polar and irreconcilable, struggle with each other to govern the spirit and move history."[52] When, surveying the carnage at the Narva Gates after the soldiers had finished firing, Gapon tells us he screamed in outrage, "There is no longer a tsar for us!" he had already shown by his actions that for him there was no longer any God, either: he had got the massacre his every calculation had always countenanced and which he, more than anyone else, bore responsibility for.[53]

---

[48] Ibid., 41.
[49] Ibid., 61.
[50] Ibid., 85.
[51] Ibid., 85.
[52] Ibid., *Karl Marx*, 41.
[53] Gapon, *Story*, 185.

CHAPTER FIVE

The Duma Monarchy at Peterhof & Tsarskoye Selo

I T WAS LATE SUMMER, AND ON A GREY AND cloudy day I caught the bus to possibly the most famous of the Romanov suburban palaces, Peterhof, the dynasty's sumptuous summer estate on the Gulf of Finland. First laid out as an imperial property during the reign of Peter the Great, Peterhof acquired its superb great palace during the reign of Peter's daughter, Elizabeth (1740–61). The first of Rastrelli's many imperial commissions for Elizabeth, who transformed Petersburg from an administrative garrison into one of Europe's grandest imperial capitals, Peterhof was the progenitor of the Russian baroque or rococo immortalized as the dynasty's signature style in Rastrelli's crowning commission, the Winter Palace. In Nicholas and Alexandra's day, however, Peterhof was no longer lived in but used as the grandest of backdrops for imperial receptions: the last great one of these was the reception held in July 1914 as part of the State Visit to Russia of the President of France, Raymond Poincaré, which proved with hindsight to be the prelude to the Great War, Russian Revolution, and the demise of the dynasty. Today, Peterhof is one of St Petersburg's major attractions, and a permanent crowd gathers to watch the dance of its gilded fountains on the lawn in front of Rastrelli's palace. But the park at Peterhof is vast, and over the generations, in its various reaches, each reigning Romanov ruler had built his own smaller, more private, and more comfortable getaway. A three-story cottage built in 1897, Nicholas and Alexandra's contribution to this tradition was their so-called Lower Dacha. Twenty minutes' walk from the main palace, on a sandy bay lined by gently drooping birches, I find its ruins. Torn down in the 1930s, all that remains of the cottage is its foundations surrounded by grass. At the center of the ruins, an Orthodox cross stands in commemoration.

Before the Revolution, Peterhof's Lower Dacha had been one of Nicholas and Alexandra's favorite residences, a refuge. Typically, Nicholas, Alexandra and their children would spend two to three months a year here, during the "White Nights" of May and June, when the days were long and the weather was at its best on the gulf. In good times, Nicholas would swim daily from the beach or take his kayak out on the water. From the same beach, too, the stacks and chimneys of St Petersburg were clearly visible across the water of the shallow-bottomed gulf, as was the island fortress of Kronstadt, the station of Russia's Baltic Fleet, which guarded the capital. From Peterhof they would embark every July for their annual three-week cruise among the Finnish skerries aboard the imperial yacht, *Standart*.

Today, few visitors to Peterhof make the journey on foot out here to the ruins of Nicholas and Alexandra's Lower Dacha. In the quiet, empty parkland around me the tourist crowds at the main palace seem remote. Yet that may be about to change. After decades of covering Nicholas II's connections with Peter in oblivion, park administrators are preparing to turn the summer residence of Russia's last tsar into an attraction: the almost completely demolished building is to be reconstructed and opened to the public. Certainly, the site is not without historical interest: a notice on the wire fence notifies those who bother to read it that it was in this building, in August 1904, that Nicholas II's "long hoped-for Heir" Alexei was born, with all the unforeseen consequences that followed. Then, also here, by the waters, at Peterhof, on an evening in October 1905, Nicholas signed, amid great internal anguish, the famous October Manifesto that brought the revolutionary year of 1905 to a close.[1] Weighing on his mind, it seems, was the compatibility of the new order promised in the Manifesto with the promises to God that he had made in his coronation. As Nicholas wrote to a trusted advisor regarding the Manifesto and what it would mean for Russia's political order, "I recognize the whole solemnity and significance of the moment Russia is living through and implore the merciful Lord to bless with His Providence all of us and the great deed completed by my own hand."

❧   ❧   ❧

By way of the October Manifesto, Bloody Sunday, and the Revolution of 1905 that had followed it, clarified what was at stake in the confrontation between the autocracy and the forces of change. Was Russia a *teokratia*, a theocratic monarchy, a polity wherein authority was "by the grace of God, not by popular dispensation," or was it not? And if it was still the former, how could it be reconfigured to accommodate the demands of Russia's politically aware professional and working classes for a share in the country's government? What was the *minimum* to which the theocratic tsar's authority could be reduced for the sake of expanding the people's freedoms to the *maximum*, while preserving Russia as the *teokratia* it always had been (and Nicholas had sworn to keep it)? The answer, after much deliberation, was a hybrid regime known as the Duma Monarchy that was neither an autocracy as

---

[1] Alexandre Spiridovitch, *Dernières Années de la Cour de Tsarkoïe-Selo*, 1 (Paris: Payot, 1928), 64.

generations of Russians had known it (where all executive and legislative power remained in the hands of the tsar alone) nor a parliamentary regime with a constitutional monarch like the United Kingdom or the Scandinavian monarchies (where parliamentary majorities ruled in the monarch's name).[2] Rather, while remaining, as Nicholas insisted, an autocrat, who received the ruling power from God (and owed an account to God alone for his use of it), the Russian tsar established an elected body known as the State Duma and delegated his God-given legislative authority to it. As the October Manifesto stipulated, it was now an "inviolate rule" that "no law shall acquire force without the approval of the State Duma." In this, the Duma Monarchy did indeed resemble the British constitution. In contrast to the latter, however, executive authority, that is, the power to appoint ministers and direct government policy, was retained by Nicholas, as tsar. Unlike in Britain, Russian ministers, appointed by the monarch personally, not on the advice of a prime minister, were responsible to him, and not to the Duma, which had no part in their nomination or selection: as far as the composition of the cabinet was concerned, the balance of seats *there* was irrelevant. That Russia remained thus, in essence, a *teokratia* was underlined in the revised version of Russia's Fundamental Laws that the government issued before the country's first elections. To "the Emperor of All the Russias," its fourth article declared, "belongs the Supreme Autocratic authority. God Himself commands that he be obeyed, not only from fear of God's wrath, but also for the sake of one's conscience."[3]

〜 〜 〜

The new era of the Duma Monarchy opened in April 1906, when Nicholas, decked in the ermine-lined imperial mantle, and with the imperial crown on a stool beside him, commissioned its 478 deputies at a ceremony in the throne room of the Winter Palace. Not insignificantly, given the themes we have been evoking, his speech was preceded by a rite of blessing conducted by Orthodox priests, and his speech was peppered with hinted references to an undiminished theocratic principle. "Concern for the welfare of our native land, which Divine Providence has entrusted to Me, has prompted me to call upon the people's elected representatives to assist in the legislative process."[4] To be sure, Nicholas was aware that a new era in Russia's history had opened. But he did not

---

[2] On the ambiguities embedded in Russia's post-1905 political order, see esp. Geoffrey Hosking, *The Russian Constitutional Experiment: Government and Duma, 1907–1914* (Cambridge: Cambridge University Press, 1973), 1–13, whose analysis of Nicholas's state of mind is particularly insightful. Nicholas "wanted . . . to have both autocracy and the October Manifesto": ibid., 10.

[3] Cited in Pipes, *Russian Revolution*, 158.

[4] Cited in S. S. Oldenburg, *The Last Tsar: Nicholas II, his reign and his Russia*, vol. 2: *Years of Change, 1900–1907* (Gulf Breeze, FL: Academic International Press, 1975–78), 200.

for that reason imagine that Russia was anything but a *teokratia*, where God, tsar and people collaborated. "I pray that the Lord will bless the work which awaits Me together with ... the State Duma. May this day signify the renewal of Russia's morality — may it mark the rebirth of Russia's best forces.... God help Me and you."[5]

With the ceremony concluded, the Duma deputies proceeded across town to the building that had been provided for them by the government as the Duma's permanent home. A former imperial residence, the Tauride Palace had been built at the end of the eighteenth century as a gift from Catherine the Great to her lover, the great Russian statesman, Grigory Potemkin. In 1906, it had been completely refitted. Beneath a central dome, a great hall had been fitted with a rising series of semi-circular benches equipped with microphones. The benches faced a central rostrum. Here, the President of the Duma (elected by the deputies themselves) sat to umpire the chamber's sessions. Behind him hung a large portrait of the emperor, and to one side, facing the deputies, was a bench for government ministers to occupy when they attended Duma debates. The chamber exhibited the dignity with which the government intended to treat the country's new institution.

Unfortunately, the majority of the Duma's newly elected members never intended to treat the government with the same respect. Led by Pavel Miliukov, the voice of liberal-radical Russia, the Kadets never reconciled themselves to the Fundamental Laws as they stood.[6] A special grievance was that Russia had not become the British-style parliamentary regime they thought they had been promised in the October Manifesto. While the latter had decreed that the "people's representatives shall have an effective opportunity to participate in supervising the legality of the actions" of the tsar's ministers, the Fundamental Laws had not extended to the Duma the right of forming a government from among its own members, as was the case in Britain. On the contrary, ministers were to continue to be chosen by the tsar, as we have seen. Responsible to him, ministers could be called ("interpolated" was the technical term) to explain their policies and actions before the Duma, but the Duma could not vote to remove them if those policies and actions were not to its liking. Another source of grievance was that a majority in the Duma was not enough in itself for a legal project to become law; also needed was the approval of the so-called State Council, an upper chamber, half of whose members were appointed by the tsar, and the other half elected by various corporations (e.g. the clergy, nobility, universities, *zemstvos*, and trade and industrial associations).[7] And even if the State

---

[5] Cited in Oldenburg, *Last Tsar*, 2:200.
[6] Pipes, *Russian Revolution*, 149–52.
[7] Oldenburg, *Last Tsar*, vol. 3: *The Duma Monarchy, 1904–1907*, 5.

Council did approve a law initiated in the Duma, still the tsar was not *obliged* to give it his assent: like the American president or the German kaiser, the Russian tsar retained a veto. The Kadets' acquiescence in the Fundamental Laws was, therefore, tactical. From day one of the Duma's history, they agitated to *overthrow* them. Offered government portfolios in Nicholas's name, Kadet leaders turned them down. Instead, the Duma's very first motion (with a mere five deputies out of a total of 478 dissenting) after its convocation by the tsar in April 1906, was a vote to acquire the right to appoint and dismiss ministers for itself. From the beginning, the Duma, in the eyes of Russia's liberals, was, to paraphrase Clausewitz, the revolution by other means.

ᔕᔕᔕ   ᔕᔕᔕ   ᔕᔕᔕ

In July 1906, the squabble which the Kadets had picked with the government on the very first day of the new Duma's convocation ended in that body's dissolution: appointing a new energetic prime minister, Pyotor Stolypin, Nicholas II dissolved it and moved to call fresh elections. In response, the Kadets decamped to the Finnish town of Vyborg, where, in the so-called Vyborg Manifesto, they effectively called on Russians to reignite the previous year's revolution. By and large, the Kadets' natural constituency, the professional classes of Russia's cities, ignored this appeal. But the political drama incited a new round of violence in the Russian countryside. Responding to the Kadets' call to seize government-, Church-, and noble-owned lands, peasants, especially in the borderlands of western and north-western Russia, lynched landowners and burned noble estates that were hundreds of years old. Meanwhile, incited by the same Socialist Revolutionaries who had helped orchestrate the march that ended in Bloody Sunday, strikes once again broke out among industrial workers in St Petersburg. On July 19, the unrest spread to the capital's naval garrison: within sight of the bayside windows of Nicholas's Lower Dacha, the sailors at the island-naval base of Kronstadt mutinied.[8]

But the biggest threat to the survival of order came from Russia's thousands of professional terrorists. Unreconciled by the October Manifesto, the Social Revolutionaries transformed themselves into a properly terrorist organization, declaring effective war on the government and ordering vast shipments of munitions (from pistols to explosives) from supporters in Western Europe. Thus supplied with arms through Russia's Baltic ports, the Socialist Revolutionaries pursued a campaign of terror that amounted to nothing short of an armed insurrection against the government.[9] Russia's towns and cities were transformed into a

---

[8] Oldenburg, *Last Tsar*, 2:215. See further Ascher, *Revolution of 1905*, 2:227–38.
[9] In June 1906 alone, the police discovered a weapons cache composed of 223 bombs, 3,300 rifles and 400,000 cartridges of ammunition: Ascher, *Revolution of 1905*, 2:241.

virtual warzone. Before their suppression in 1907 by vigorous government counter-measures, terrorist attacks maimed or claimed the lives of 4,500 government officials and about the same number of civilians.[10]

Amazingly, however, despite these killings, the SR-Kadet alliance revived. Far from condemning the violence, Miliukov and the party leadership endorsed terrorism against government officials as a legitimate instrument of politics. Taking their cue from the Kadet leadership, Russian educated society—its liberal *obshchestvo* of lawyers, teachers, doctors, engineers, agronomists, veterinarians, and statisticians—raised money for such terrorist groups and turned a blind eye to their armed robberies and bank heists (such as the young Bolshevik Josef Dzhugashvili—the future Stalin—was performing in precisely these years on Lenin's behalf in the Russian Caucasus). The result was not class warfare so much as war on the principle of order itself (which, of course, lent this episode, too, of the Russian Revolution writ large an unavoidable theological significance: for what is order but an imprint of God on the world?).[11] In August 1906, a bomb tore through Stolypin's own dacha in the St Petersburg suburbs, causing twenty-eight deaths and gravely wounding his fifteen-year-old daughter. A plot to assassinate Nicholas himself was uncovered.

Against this incendiary backdrop, Russia's urbane foreign minister, Aleksandr Izvolsky, called that summer on Nicholas at the Lower Dacha. Echoing across the waters from Kronstadt, the sound of cannons could be heard clearly. And yet, recalled Izvolsky, Nicholas, although "he could hardly have been unaware that what was at stake only a few leagues from where we were sitting was his very crown," was calm.[12] Breaking protocol, which forbade the unsolicited enquiry of the emperor's state of mind, Izvolsky commented aloud, anxious to know the source of Nicholas's composure. Izvolksy's account of what happened next reads like the description of a failed vision on the Yalta Embankment—a moment when Izvolsky, afforded a vision of the theocratic principle, failed to see what was before him, for lack of religious sensibility to recognize its meaning. "Fixing on me that gaze whose extraordinary gentleness has often been commented upon," Izvolsky recalled, Nicholas replied with the confession of *teokratia* we have quoted earlier. "'If you see me so

---

[10] Pipes, *Russian Revolution*, 155. For the fullest treatment, see Anna Geifman, *Thou Shalt Kill: Revolutionary terrorism in Russia, 1894–1917* (Princeton, NJ: Princeton University Press, 1993).

[11] On this episode in Russian history, see also Gary Saul Morson, "Suicide of the Liberals," *First Things*, October 2020: https://www.firstthings.com/article/2020/10/suicide-of-the-liberals (accessed January 6, 2025). As Morson puts it wryly, in reference also to our own times, the university-educated, even if they did not do any of the killing themselves, nonetheless supported the terrorists because "doing so signaled advanced opinion and good manners." Supporting the killing of government officials was "virtue-signaling."

[12] Izwolsky, "Souvenirs de mon ministère, II," 105.

little troubled,'" Nicholas said, "'it is because I have the firm, the absolute belief that the fate of Russia, my own fate and that of my family is in the hands of God, Who has placed me where I am. Whatever happens, I will bend before His will, with the consciousness of never having had any other thought than to serve the country He has confided me.'"[13] Izvolsky, having served the tsar for decades, suddenly realized that his sovereign's conception of politics was not his own.

Certainly, then, in 1905, Russia had gained a Duma. But, to Nicholas II at least, the theocratic principle in Russian culture had *survived* the Revolution of 1905. For all the strikes, mutinies and the revived terrorist agitation of the summer of 1906, the latter *had not* succeeded in imposing on him a judgment *for* secularization. Nicholas, in his own mind, remained the living symbol of Russia's unchanged theocratic reality, rather than the symbolical emblem of a theocratic principle that had governed Russia's past. The sacred and the political remained intertwined, mingled, united. As a political community, Russia, through the tsar, continued to have one foot in this world and another in the unseen world of the spirit. Indeed, he might as well have quoted the words of his fifth-century Byzantine predecessor, Theodosius II:

> The stability of our State depends on the religion through which we honor God. The two are closely linked, as each depends on the other and thrives as each other flourishes. Since God has handed us the reins of government, and made us the link of piety and righteousness for all our subjects, we shall preserve the association between the two and watch over the interests of both God and men.[14]

That man was in rebellion was no reason for a Christian emperor such as Nicholas to desert his post. And Izvolsky, whose own religion bears all the marks of Kant's secularized Christianity, could not understand it. Considered from a secular point of view, Nicholas's behavior was *irrational*. Lacking, apparently, the formation in historical, mystical-dogmatic Orthodoxy to recognize in Nicholas's dependence on God a theological *principle*, Izvolsky instead ascribed Nicholas's behavior to personal idiosyncrasy, a "kind of mystical exaltation that... only increased under the influence of the tragic events of his reign."[15] In other words, the meaning of his exchange with Nicholas was mute to him: Izvolsky, a minister of the tsarist state, had, like most of the men who served Nicholas, in fact made his judgment in favor of secularization. For now, in 1906, such secular-minded bureaucrats continued to serve a theocratically-minded tsar whose conception of his own office

---

[13] Ibid.
[14] Theodosius II, convoking the bishops assembled at the Council of Ephesus (Third Ecumenical Council), AD 431. Cited in McGuckin, "Legacy of the 13th apostle," 281–82.
[15] Izwolsky, "Souvenirs de mon ministère, II," 106.

they did not understand but dismissed, as we have seen, as "mysticism": monarchical as opposed to parliamentary control of the executive was to such men simply more *efficient*. But eventually, many years later, the two parties would make common cause on this foundation, and, when they did, the Russian *teokratia*'s days would be numbered.

Later that afternoon at Peterhof, I made my way across the grassy slope that tended away from the Lower Dacha and the Gulf of Finland to the so-called Upper Dacha on the hill behind. The Upper Dacha—the holiday cottage of Nicholas's mother, the Dowager Empress Marie—had, it seems, never been demolished, and today its interior has been restored to its appearance when Marie used it. Homely rather than lavish, the building is of marginal interest to our story. And yet here in the garden, nestled among the rose bushes under a canopy of birches stands a life-sized bronze statue of Alexei, leaning in his trademark sailor suit against the stump of a tree. It remains the only freestanding statue of Russia's ill-fated late tsarevich that I know of in Russia. What are we to make of it? In his speech at the opening of the Duma, Nicholas had told the assembled deputies of his prayer to "pass on to My son the inheritance of a strong, orderly and enlightened State." To be sure, the disturbances of 1906 came to an end, as Nicholas had trusted, giving way, when they had, to half a decade of peace and prosperity, the "golden days" of the Duma Monarchy. And, while Nicholas's faith in God never wavered, we know this prayer of his for his son would not be answered.

෨෨ ෨෨ ෨෨

Tsarskoye Selo, the "Imperial Village." The words themselves are as inseparable from Nicholas and Alexandra's story as the enamels and Russian river pearls of a Fabergé egg. Spread on the other side of a line of low hills, eighteen miles south of Petersburg, Tsarskoye Selo was (and is) even grander and more captivating than Peterhof. It had been an imperial residence since 1710. In that year, Peter the Great's consort, the former Lithuanian peasant girl Marfa Mavronskaya, later to be known as Empress Catherine I of Russia, presented her restless, sea-loving husband with a small, two-story country house. Peter was delighted. Though he continued to prefer his seaside residence at Peterhof, Catherine liked to retreat to her "dacha" in the hills, and, on her death, she passed it to her daughter, the future Empress Elizabeth. By that time, a small village had sprouted around her mother's hermitage in the woods, and it was this immoderate and extravagant woman (from 1740, empress) who made that village truly imperial. Elizabeth took her mother's modest structure and, with the help of Rastrelli, transformed it into one of Europe's great palaces: a blue and gold rococo masterpiece, with a façade of muscle-bound atlantes almost two furlongs long, that Elizabeth named the "Catherine" Palace, after her mother. More than a palace, it was a statement. When her father had come to the throne of Moscow in 1682, Russia's tsars lived in almost permanent, windowless murk in the Moscow Kremlin, in a "palace" that most European princes would have found small even in the middle ages. By the time Rastrelli had brought to completion his work at Tsarskoye Selo in 1756, Elizabeth announced to all Europe her nation's arrival by receiving its ambassadors in a building whose size and gilded splendor were rivalled only by Versailles.

Even today, the Catherine Palace still impresses for its size and splendor. Against the turquoise blue of the walls, an apparently endless row of white stucco columns and pilasters a thousand feet long and three stories high creates a sense of infinity, while the five brilliant gilded onion domes that rise delicately over the palace's northern end suggest a fairytale world in the clouds, from which it has apparently descended. Inside an enfilade of parqueted, first-floor rooms embellished with a veritable forest of gilded linden wood carving, floor-to-ceiling windows alternated with mirrors beneath a vast *trompe l'œil* in a thousand square-foot ballroom. Of French inspiration, it constitutes a glorious testament to the early Romanov dynasty's improvident commitment to Russia's breakneck Europeanization.

That it survives to be visited at all, however, is a wonder. When the Germans invaded the Soviet Union in 1941, the Palace's splendor marked it out for destruction. The Slavs being "sub-human" in Nazi lore, the evidently European Catherine Palace was an aberration to be wiped from the earth. Working in teams, the Germans piled wagonloads of treasures on to trains bound for Germany, including the famed (if garishly ugly) "Amber Study" crafted by German masters between 1700 and 1710 in Berlin, presented to Peter the Great by the King Friedrich Wilhelm I of Prussia in exchange for 248 burly Russian guardsmen, and ultimately installed in the Palace on the orders of Elizabeth. (As this original was probably destroyed in Allied bombing of Königsberg in 1944, what visitors see today is a post-Soviet copy, part-paid for by a German gas company, Ruhrgas.) Then, as the Russian winter set in, and the supply of timber from the palace park was exhausted, the German soldiers burned the remaining furniture as firewood. When that had been consumed, long enfilades of gilded rococo carving—plump-faced cherubs, tendril-like candle stands—went up in smoke, leaving room after room of exposed brick. Having been shelled constantly from Soviet lines for two and a half years, the building, when the Germans finally abandoned their positions at the palace in January 1944, was (like Gatchina) little more than a roofless shell. The Germans mined it anyway, hoping to leave their Russian adversaries nothing more than a pile of rubble. Fortunately, the Soviet soldiers who liberated the palace assumed that it was mined and cut the wires before they detonated.[16] The end of the War brought with it decades of restoration.

But the Catherine Palace was not then, and is not now, Tsarskoye Selo's only palace and, in fact, Nicholas and Alexandra never inhabited it. Too draughty to heat, the "Big" (*bolshoi*) Palace, as they called it, served in Nicholas and Alexandra's day primarily as a jaw-dropping backdrop for court balls and receptions, while during the First World War its cavernous, gilded spaces were converted into hospital rooms for the wounded. It says everything about Russia's last empress that when all the hours are added up, Alexandra spent more time in Rastrelli's rococo wedding cake in a soiled nurse's uniform, cleaning vermin-infested wounds and assisting at amputations, than she did as a bejeweled hostess.

Lying at right angles to the Catherine Palace, beyond an expansive, canal-crossed park, the smaller, more subdued Alexander Palace is a masterpiece in neo-classical harmony and balance: two identical wings are joined by a colonnade of pure white Corinthian columns, set on the northern side across from a small artificial lake and, on the southern, the straight lines of a canal. Executed between 1792 and 1796 by Giacomo Quarenghi on the orders of Catherine the Great, it was a grandmother's gift to her favorite grandson, the future Emperor Alexander I, after whom the palace took its name. In 1866, Alexander I's nephew, Alexander II, gave it to his son, the future Alexander III and his consort, as a wedding present. The couple set up their summer home in the palace's left wing, and their first child, the future Nicholas II, was born here. As for Nicholas and Alexandra, they moved their family permanently to the Alexander Palace in the winter of 1904/5. The reason for this was Alexei, whose illness had to be kept secret even from the court. From that time, whether blanketed under a four-foot carpet of fresh snow, surrounded with new life in the wet and unsettled northern spring, or bedecked, in the autumn, in a breathtaking persimmon and butterscotch gown of fallen leaves, this leafy refuge of peace and tranquility would become Russia's *de facto* capital.

It may just be that it was November, that universal season of mortality, but as I crossed the damp, closely mown lawn, aroused in me was the feeling one gets when visiting a crematorium or war cemetery: somber, solemn, even sepulchral. During the Second World War, the Germans dug up the grounds for a Gestapo graveyard; but those bodies have long since been repatriated, and I like to think of the palace's solemnity as the spontaneous homage of the place itself to the tragic end met by the last family to have lived here, Nicholas and Alexandra's. Certainly, where the Catherine Palace is extravagant, gay, and frivolous,

---

[16] Christopher Morgan and Irina Orlova, *Saving the Tsars' Palaces* (New York: Polperro Heritage, 2005), 74–75.

the Alexander is angular, calm, and scientific. Because it sits sideways to the access street, its striking profile is only visible once well inside the perimeter fence. Giacomo Quarenghi, not seeking to imitate Rastrelli, did not construct a building to "overwhelm" the visitor's senses with color or statuary; there is nothing cinematic about the Alexander Palace's cool lines and mathematical symmetry. Indeed, the two wings, replicating the dimensions of Sicily's Greek temples, are nothing more than perfectly regular rectangles embellished with pilasters, engaged columns, and crowned with a triangular pediment. But the double colonnade of clean white Corinthian columns that connects them brings them to life with an air of subtle Attic grace. Whereas the Catherine Palace perfectly fulfils the requirements of modern tourism by asking nothing of the visitor other than to be cheaply dazzled, the Alexander Palace imposes a kind of hieratic discipline: the structure the visitor is about to enter was quite clearly never a tawdry "pleasure palace"; it was rather a temple — of piety, work and family. Even its color — pale peach and white — seems to soothe and purify.

The Alexander Palace has never been part of the standard tourist itinerary and, when I arrived (through the palace's almost absurdly small front door), it was as good as empty. Inside, there was a museum, but little sense of what it wanted to show visitors (or even whether it wanted them at all). Only half a dozen rooms were open, and no plan was available. Plastic sheeting laid across the floor indicated the designated route through the building, while temporary screens blocked the view down "forbidden" corridors. This was not at all what was originally intended when the last Romanovs departed. Just before dawn on August 1, 1917, only hours after the train that was to take them away into exile in Siberia had pulled away from the station, a team of curators belonging to the "Tsarskoye Selo Art Historical Commission" went to work to transform the palace as speedily as possible into a museum. Convinced of the historical significance of the building before him, Anatoly Lunacharsky, Bolshevik commissar for culture and education, imposed strict instructions on his team. Nothing was to be removed from its original location, the contents of every room were to be inventoried, and photographs taken of the appearance of every interior just as they were when the Romanovs vacated the palace. Within a year, a museum about Russia's last tsar had opened, and the first visitors arrived a month before the tsar and his family were shot in Ekaterinburg. Then, in the 1930s, all ideas of a museum were dispensed with. Instead, the Palace's left wing (where Nicholas's parents had had their apartments) was converted into a workers' sanatorium, while the right wing that Nicholas and Alexandra had themselves occupied was transformed into an orphanage. Tsarskoye Selo itself was re-named Detskoye

Selo, the "Children's Village." Less than ten years later, the Germans and their allies occupied the building. Graffiti found inside after the return of Soviet troops shows that it had housed a Spanish unit, sent by Franco (despite his denials) in aid of Hitler.[17] Fortunately, however, the fabric of Quarenghi's Palace emerged from the war in better condition than Rastrelli's. The plaster was missing from the walls, but the roof, walls and colonnade all survived. What the visitor sees today, therefore, is a modest, post-Soviet attempt at making the most of what it could of Lunacharsky's painstaking inventories and careful photography.[18]

ᖇᖇ   ᖇᖇ   ᖇᖇ

From the Oval Room, I followed the floor-sheeting through a labyrinth of temporary freestanding screens, to the right of the palace's two temple-shaped wings. From the time of Nicholas's accession as emperor, it was this wing that served as Nicholas and Alexandra's private apartments, and in 1902–3 they had it thoroughly renovated and redecorated in the period's reigning art nouveau (in Russian, *stil modern*) style.[19] What remains, therefore, is a precious window not only on Nicholas and Alexandra's inner world, but on the Russia over which the couple reigned. As the famous art critic Alexandre Benois, whom Lunarcharsky called on to inventory the Palace, put it, "Each and every detail [...] — the very juxtaposition of their objects — carries the stamp of the times, reflecting the melancholy spirit of the epoch, and speaking more eloquently of the causes for the downfall of the monarchy in Russia than historian can, no matter how brilliant or knowledgeable."[20] We might query the allegation of melancholy. But the rest of Benois's observation is correct. Unexpectedly, perhaps, the *stil modern* apartments of the Alexander Palace reveal how far Russia's last imperial couple were in often disconcertingly close touch with the spiritual and cultural currents of the so-called "Silver Age" of Russian culture, when, in the "golden days" of the Duma Monarchy, a country that nonetheless remained profoundly traditional and Eastern Orthodox in its habits and ways of thinking sought creative reconciliation with the new spirit of modernism that swept in from Western Europe.[21]

---

[17] Morgan and Orlova, *Saving*, 85.
[18] In fact, only weeks after my visit, the building and museum were definitively closed to visitors. The Palace, now fully renovated, has been open again to the public since 2022.
[19] This meant the destruction of what had been, in Quarenghi's original scheme, the Palace's concert hall. After the Romanovs had left the Palace, and still more after the Second World War, tearing out Nicholas and Alexandra's alterations and restoring Quarenghi's concert hall was discussed, but never carried out.
[20] Cited in T. S. Andreeva et al., *Tsarskoe Selo, 1917: Nakanunie...* (St. Petersburg: Russkaia Kollektsiia, 2017), 35.
[21] On the Silver Age, see Carl Proffer and Ellendea Proffer, eds., *The Silver Age of Russian Culture: An anthology* (Ann Arbor, MI: Ardis, 1971); and John E. Bowlt, *Moscow and St Petersburg, 1900–1920: Art, life and culture* (New York: Vendome, 2008).

It is easy to forget that Russia was perhaps the most culturally excit-
ing place in the world at the turn of the twentieth century, a land of
polarities, confrontation, intermingling that gave the world the *World
of Art* and *ballets russes*, composers such as Rachmaninoff, Prokofiev
and Stravinsky, and, in the visual arts, Malevich, Chagall, and Kandinsky. On the one hand, breakneck industrialization and urbanization
encouraged the growth of the new ideologies of Populism, Marxism, and
liberalism, in which, for all the differences between them, their sources
and proponents (Chernyshevksy and Chernov; Marx and Plekhanov;
Chicherin and Miliukov) were united in the debt they owed to the
atheistic conclusions of nineteenth-century European philosophy. On
the other hand, running counterpoint to these conclusions, Silver-Age
Russia witnessed a pronounced rebirth of interest in religion, metaphysics, mysticism. As Georges Florovsky, the greatest chronicler of the
twists and turns of Russian religious and spiritual life before the 1917
Revolution put it, in the first decade and a half of the twentieth century "many suddenly discovered in man a metaphysical being...The
religious theme became a theme of life, and not merely a category of
thought. People began to seek for more than just a religious worldview — a genuine thirst flared up for faith."[22] In philosophy, the original standard bearer of the new idealism was the prematurely deceased
Vladimir Solovyov. But his legacy lived on, and, indeed, gathered even
greater strength in the generation of disciples who succeeded him.[23]
These included the radical "God-seekers" such as Merezhkovsky (see
further below) and the literary Symbolists, such Akhmatova and Blok,
with whom they entertained close links, but also a growing band of
"neo-Idealist" thinkers and philosophers such as Peter Struve, Semyon
Frank, Nikolai Berdyaev, and ("our own") Sergei Bulgakov, who at this
time had not yet completed his return to Church Orthodoxy.

Capturing the spirit of what came to be called Russia's "Silver Age,"
Merezhkovsky described his generation as "witnessing a mighty and all-
important struggle between two views of life, between two diametrically
opposed worldviews. The final demands of religious feeling experience
a confrontation with the final conclusions of the experimental sciences."
[24] He meant the clash between the metaphysical claims of dogmatic
religion and those, hard and positivistic, of the natural sciences, whose
ascendancy at the end of the nineteenth century had only served to

---

[22] Florovsky, *Ways of Russian Theology*, in *Collected Works*, 6:233.
[23] Sergei S. Horujy (Khoruzhii), "Vladimir Solov'ev's legacy after a hundred years,"
Russian Studies in Philosophy 46 (2007): 9: "the whole period of the flourishing of
Russian religious philosophy, or the religious-philosophical renaissance was merely the
realization of the powerful developmental impulse that Solovyov's philosophy imparted
to Russian thought."
[24] Translated by Samuel Cioran in Proffer and Proffer, eds., *Silver Age*, 3–5.

demonstrate the extent of the dark void beyond positivistic human knowledge. According to Merezhkovsky, this clash was an invitation to a theosophical kind of mysticism, liberated from the constraining rigidities of the old religious dogmatism. Its language was to be that of the symbol, the sign that referred to the unknown reality beyond itself. With Merezhkovsky, it is clear how readily the religious revival of the Russian Silver Age always risked relapsing into a kind of revivified Gnosticism. Ultimately, Merezhkovsky and his fellow "God-seekers" (who included his wife, the renowned Symbolist poet Zinaida Gippius, and their mutual friend, Dmitri Filosofov), as they called themselves, would abandon historical Orthodoxy for what they called an a-dogmatic Christianity of the Holy Spirit, a "Third Covenant," that, in abandoning the "false" asceticism of the historical Church, purported to reconcile spirituality and sensuality, that is, religion and sex.

But before the breach between Merezhkovsky and historical Christianity was finalized, the Orthodox Church, sensing the missionary opportunities open to *it* in Russia's spiritual revival, attempted a dialogue with this generation of God-seekers and neo-idealist philosophers. The result was the founding, in 1901, of the so-called St Petersburg Philosophical-Religious Association, where, with the blessing of the Procurator of the Holy Synod Konstantin Pobedonostsev, the new generation of intellectuals (including Bulgakov) shaped by Solovyov and gathered round Merezhkovsky met for philosophical and theological discussions with some of the leading representatives of the empire's established Orthodox Church, including the head of the St Petersburg Theological Academy, Fr Sergei Stragorodsky. Discussing everything from the nature of revelation, freedom of conscience and the status of science to philosophy, asceticism, marriage, and the body, the Association's meetings were among the most quintessential artefacts of Russia's Silver Age. But if the Church hoped to see the God-seekers return to historical Orthodoxy and its rites and dogmas, the God-seekers hoped to see the Church *embrace* and not reject a conception of human liberty as the highest value, a conception that could not but throw those same dogmas and rites into irretrievable question. Ultimately unsatisfying for both sides, therefore, the meetings of the Religious-Philosophical Society were terminated by the authorities in 1903.

"The union of the Church and the world proved impossible, but was at least attempted," Merezhkovsky lamented. "Revolution without religion or religion without revolution; freedom without God or God without freedom," these were Russia's choices, Merezhkovsky thought.[25] But the Association's meetings had not been in vain. To be sure, in the ensuing decade or so before the Great War, Merezhkovsky, Gippius, and Filosofov

---

[25] Merezhkovsky et al., *Tsar et la révolution*, 241.

would leave Orthodoxy for good, in search of new testaments and new revelations that led them into ever-sharper confrontation with the Church and tsarist authorities. But others, including Bulgakov, would complete the passage that they had started and return to Church Orthodoxy. For Bulgakov, as we have seen, this had included, by 1909, the retrieval of the truth that had escaped Merezhkovsky: that in the Church and her ideal of *teokratia*, the union of the Church and the world had already been (albeit highly provisionally) completed as far as such a union was possible. In an age of secularization, in which the theocratic principle appeared to be passing out of history, the question before his generation was not whether a union of the sacred and the political could be achieved, but whether it could be *preserved*, the reverse of the problem as Merezhkovsky had conceived it. During the Silver Age, we might say, Russia's judgment in favor of secularization hung in suspense.

ᔆᔆ ᔆᔆ ᔆᔆ

The Maple Drawing Room was a spacious mezzanine whose upper half-story was carved out of smooth, warm maple, and installed as if a single unit at the near end of the room. Vegetal motifs sprouted at the joins of the architraves and ceilings, while the sinuous, curved beam that framed the view of it from the lower floor conjured the feel of a natural forest bower touched by the rays of the morning sun — a nook for Alexandra to read, embroider, draw, and do other work. Representations of this complex woman have always quickly lapsed into caricature. Like the *stil modern* which she chose for her family's apartments at the Alexander Palace, Alexandra's worldview was an eclectic combination of contradictions that looked aesthetically both backwards and into the future, and, as such, was as much a quintessential artefact of Russia's Silver Age as Merezhkovsky's and even Bulgakov's writings. As the leading historian of the period's arts has written, the *stil modern*, with "its organic motifs, botanical flourishes, and graphic references to the animal and vegetable world . . . captured and symbolized the very ethos of the flowering of [Russia's] Silver Age. . . . Like a persistent liana, [it] invaded the objects of the material environment from public buildings to private homes, from ashtrays to antimacassars, from set designs to bond certificates."[26] Indeed, the liana reached its tendrils all the way to the Alexander Palace. Far more than we would like to admit, the story of the Russian Revolution as the result of the self-isolation of a blind and suicidally out-of-touch ruling couple will not do. Far more than we would like to admit, Nicholas and Alexandra were early twentieth-century people, too, albeit at a time when that century had not yet made its historical judgment for secularization.

---

[26] Bowlt, *Moscow and St Petersburg*, 129.

The standard bearer of this aesthetic, and of the suspended judgment on the atheistic conclusions of nineteenth-century philosophy freighted with it, was the magazine known as the *World of Art*.[27] First published in 1898, *World of Art* was founded by the twenty-six year-old Sergei Diaghilev, an administrative employee at that time at the Imperial Ballet. His best-known claim to fame consists in the *ballets russes* that he founded, and toured Western Europe with, in 1906. An aesthete and a fixer, who dyed silver a shock of hair in his forelock, Diaghilev was a socialite and musician *manqué*, not a philosopher; he did not necessarily attribute a higher intellectual or religious purpose to his magazine, and, famously, *World of Art* had no manifesto. Its only rationale was beauty, anti-realism, eclecticism, art for art's sake, the organic unity of man's aesthetic experience. As Alexander Benois, who collaborated with Diaghilev in producing *World of Art*, put it, the spirit of the magazine was "not this, that, or the other in isolation, but everything together."[28] Alexandra could hardly have described her own aesthetic instincts better.

And yet, while the premises of *World of Art* always remained largely unexamined, they would, had they been systematically pursued, have been found to have been of a piece with the new Idealism of Russia's Silver Age. In his contribution to the magazine's very first issue, Diaghilev had taken aim precisely at Chernyshevsky, not for the atheism he adopted from Feuerbach *per se* (which did not trouble Diaghilev personally), but for the materialism and the positivist-realist approach to art which flowed from it. Diaghilev called Chernyshevsky a "barbarous image who approached art with unwashed hands, with the purpose of destroying it."[29] Instead, in issue after beautifully presented issue, *World of Art* presented Russian readers with forms, styles, and *objets d'art* that the realists had turned their backs on or despised: primitive Russian folk art; rococo miniatures; watercolors, wood cuts, and book illustrations; the latest *art nouveau*. And although *World of Art* (subsidized in the end by Tsarskoye Selo) existed for barely six years before its closure in 1904, the aesthetic that it midwifed defined the taste, set the tone, and captured the mood of much of the cultural and artistic life of late imperial Russia up to the Great War. Against the desiccating materialism of the old realist worldview, the *World of Art* aesthetic of Russia's Silver Age insisted on a mandatory subscription to the possibility of metaphysics, a world of ideas, spirit, and symbols, "beyond the physical." To be a *miriskustnik* (a *World of Art*-ist), therefore, was not necessarily to be religious, let alone Orthodox. But it did mean to reject the premises and consequences of materialism, and leave the door to the Church, myth, and religion (as well as theosophy, the occult, and mysticism) open. It fit Alexandra to a tee.

---

[27] See Stuart Grover, "The World of Art Movement in Russia," *Russian Review* 32 (1973): 28–42.
[28] Bowlt, *Moscow and St Petersburg*, 170.   [29] Grover, "World of Art," 33.

Seen from this perspective, perhaps what Nicholas and Alexandra's *stil modern* suite in the Alexander Palace indicates is that precisely Diaghilev's Silver-Age aesthetic, and the thought world behind it, was one with which Alexandra was perfectly at home. Stubborn, insecure, proud, Alexandra was (until her anxiety for Alexei overwhelmed her, at least) also curious and highly intelligent. She loved Wagner's operas.[30] She played Bach, Beethoven, and Tchaikovsky, and used to sing Rachmaninoff.[31] She read widely but did not share what she read with others. What she believed she knew about the Russian peasantry she learnt from her reading of the works of the "free-thinker" Tolstoy, excommunicated by the Holy Synod of the Orthodox Church in 1901.[32] Despite the protests of her confessor, she read Darwin's *Origin of Species*, and had a standing order for the latest works in science, mathematics, and astronomy.[33] Raised a strict Protestant, moreover, with a steadfast belief in miracles and the power of prayer, Alexandra nonetheless dabbled, apparently Madame Blavatsky-style, for a few years after her conversion to Orthodoxy, in theosophy, the kabbalah, and (possibly) the occult. As her closest friend and confidant, Anna Vyrubova, noted, the Russias' last empress had read "many books on all religions, particularly those of India and Persia," books in which she had presumably discovered the ancient mystical symbol of the swastika that Alexandra continued to doodle alongside the sign of the Cross in the margins of her diaries and spiritual notebooks right up to her death in 1918.[34] In this age of theosophy, therefore, where Europeans were discovering the previously little-known religions of the East for the first time, Alexandra's path followed the logic of Russia's turn-of-the-century spiritual revival. An eclectic and undefined movement, the Russian Silver Age could elevate its participants to true religion, mislead them towards the occult, or leave them to languish in an empty, decadent aestheticism.

In Nicholas and Alexandra's spiritual biographies, the typically Silver-Age temptation to occult Gnosticism is represented by the mysterious figure of Monsieur Philippe, a French occult healer to whom the couple turned for help in conceiving a son in 1901–2.[35] Having become a

---

[30] King, *Last Empress*, 121.

[31] Anna Vyrubova, *Memories of the Russian Court* (London: Macmillan, 1923), 9 [although the modern reprint I have used may not correspond to the original page numbers]; Spiridovitch, *Dernières Années*, 1:103. [32] Buxhoeveden, *Tragic Empress*, 60.

[33] King, *Last Empress*, 120.

[34] Vyrubova, *Memories*, 73. See also Lili Dehn, *The Real Tsaritsa* (Boston: Little, Brown and Co., 1922), 63: Alexandra's "fancy for the sign of the swastika was not for the swastika as a charm only as a symbol," recalled her friend and former lady-in-waiting, Lili Dehn: "She told me the ancients believed in the swastika as the source of motion, the emblem of divinity." Dehn recalled that Alexandra was wearing a ring with a swastika the day she first met her: ibid., 39.

[35] On Philippe, see Douglas Smith, *Rasputin* (London: Macmillan, 2016), 33–45, which shows the way in which Philippe was a certain forerunner in Nicholas and Alexandra's spiritual lives to Rasputin.

minor celebrity in his native France, Philippe was introduced to Nicholas and Alexandra in March 1901. Just a month before, Alexandra had been delivered of her fourth daughter, Anastasia; but she was desperate for a boy, and the idea from the beginning was that Philippe could help her produce an heir. Philippe won the couple's confidence quickly. "I met with one remarkable Frenchman, Mr Philippe!" Nicholas wrote in his diary on March 21, noting that they "talked for a long time."[36] Philippe returned to Russia in July, and Nicholas and Alexandra spent the evening with him that same day. They saw him the following evening, too. "What wonderful hours!" Nicholas recorded.[37] Philippe stayed in Russia for just under two weeks and Nicholas and Alexandra saw him every day. On one occasion, they stayed up listening to Philippe until 2:30 in the morning. They were known to pray with him too.[38]

What were they talking about? The widespread view at the time (and since) is that Philippe was a hypnotist, occultist and medium. According to the historian Douglas Smith, Philippe relied not only on prayer, but also on "astral fluids and psychic forces" in his healings. In his native France, Philippe had obtained an entrée into Parisian high society through the offices of Gérard Encausse ("Papus"), a scholar of the Kabbalah and practitioner of the occult, who re-founded two of France's leading masonic brotherhoods, the Martinists and Rosicrucians, and served as bishop in the Gnostic Church of France.[39] Papus claimed Philippe as one of his spiritual masters, and the immediate vehicle for Philippe's introduction to Nicholas and Alexandra was a graduate of Papus's school, the Montenegrin princess Anastasia who had married one of Nicholas's cousins, the Russian Grand Duke Nikolai Nikolaevich. Anastasia, or "Stana," as she was known, and her sister Militsa were widely credited with hosting seances, presided over by Philippe, at their St Petersburg palaces: at one, it was said, Philippe raised the spirit of Alexander III in Nicholas and Alexandra's presence. To French ambassador Maurice Paléologue, the story seemed to reveal the otherwise opaque source of Nicholas's irrational opposition to any diminution of his powers.

Did Philippe, then, induct Nicholas and Alexandra into the occult or the secret knowledge ("gnosis") of Papus's Gnostic Church of France? It

---

[36] Quoted in Smith, *Rasputin*, 36.   [37] Ibid.   [38] Smith, *Rasputin*, 37.
[39] Though it would be easy to write off Papus's esotericism as mere nineteenth-century pseudo-science (which, to be fair, it also was), there were also long ideational genealogies in play here: as higher order (i.e. mystical) Masonic fraternities, the Martinists and Rosicrucians became popular in Russia in the 1750s and 1760s as a reaction against the atheism of the French Enlightenment, and, particularly, the rationalism and skepticism of figures such as Voltaire (patronized as he was by Catherine the Great): Billington, *Icon and Axe*, 248–55. Meanwhile, in a similar spirit in late nineteenth-century Paris, the so-called "Gnostic Church of France" appears to have sought to spread the "secret teachings" of Jesus by reviving the dualist Cathar religion that the Catholic Church had suppressed in the middle ages: see Serge Caillet, *Monsieur Philippe, l'ami de Dieu* (Paris: Dervy, 2013), which summarizes French-language research on Philippe and his milieu.

goes without saying that that if he did, this would seriously undermine any perception of the tsar as a genuinely Orthodox monarch, possessed of an authentically Orthodox vision of Russia as a *teokratia*. But Paléologue is a notoriously unreliable source, known for his sensationalism and animosity towards Nicholas. A different picture of Philippe emerges from the writings of Aleksandr Spiridovich, a cavalry officer who was installed as the head of Nicholas's secret service. According to Spiridovich, Papus was a "black magician" with whom Nicholas and Alexandra never associated. Philippe, by contrast, was a Christian faith healer, a "gentle, good, and very pious man capable of healing a great number of people by prayer."[40] He rejected the story of Philippe's summoning of the spirit of Alexander III as a fabrication designed to disparage the reputation of Nicholas II, and linked Philippe instead with Russia's own wonder-working faith-healer, Fr John of Kronstadt, who, Spiridovich said, embraced Philippe as a brother when the two met at an Orthodox liturgy over which John was presiding. But if Paléologue's account is obviously hostile to Nicholas, then Spirodovich's seems too naïve, too obviously an effort of special pleading. It is worth noting, also, that both accounts were written after the Revolution, and more than two decades after the events in question.

Certainly, Phillippe *claimed* to be a Christian, and much of the time he spoke *like* a Christian. Connected to the conservative and royalist circles powerful at that time within the Catholic Church of France, Philippe joined the campaign for the canonization of Joan of Arc, a cause ultimately approved by Pope Benedict XV in 1920. One historian describes Philippe as a (fairly banal) French "religious nationalist."[41] That Nicholas and Alexandra might have sympathized with this milieu is not surprising. The Slavophilism in which Nicholas had been raised was also a form of religious nationalism; Alexandra kept a portrait of Marie-Antoinette over her writing desk. If Philippe had so quickly won Nicholas and Alexandra's confidence, it seems likely that he did so because — reassuringly from their point of view — he spoke a religious language that demonstrated that he shared their rejection of the epoch's drift towards secularization. Indeed, when Nicholas's cousin, the thoughtful if internally conflicted Grand Duke Constantine Konstantinovich, met Philippe in August 1902, he reported afterwards that the chief subject of Philippe's conversation was "the decline of religion in France and in the West in general."[42] Striking, too, in the descriptions Nicholas and Alexandra left behind of their meetings with Philippe are the ostensibly mainstream, rather than occult, Christian behaviors that

---

[40] Spiridovitch, *Dernières Années*, 1:99, 101–2.
[41] Wortman, *Scenarios of Power*, 356.
[42] Mylunas and Mironenko, *Lifelong Passion*, 207.

seemed to have framed the relationship as a form of naïve Christian pietism. Once, when Philippe had lunch with Alexandra and Nicholas, they took him afterwards to the nursery. "We showed him our daughters and prayed together with him in the bedroom!" wrote Nicholas excitedly.[43] The following day he spent three hours talking to Philippe alone. "The ways of the Lord are inscrutable!" he enthused afterwards.[44] Nicholas and Alexandra certainly also retained throughout the period of Philippe's influence the overtly Christian habits of thoughts and speech we saw them use in the years after their marriage.

Perhaps, then, Nicholas and Alexandra saw in Philippe only an unlearned faith healer with special knowledge of divine mysteries, and an ally in the defense of non-confessional Christendom against the threat, in their eyes, from the age's move towards secularization. And yet Nicholas and Alexandra seemed to appreciate Philippe precisely because he could offer them *something more* than what was available in the dogmas of the established Orthodox Church, a special knowledge of divine mysteries not revealed to all Christians. "I could listen and listen to him forever," Nicholas wrote after sitting up until the early hours with Philippe in March 1902.[45] When Philippe returned to France, Nicholas described himself and Alexandra as feeling "orphaned." "How rich our lives have become since we met him," wrote Alexandra in an epistle to Nicholas at this time; "it seems everything has become much easier to bear."[46] They referred to him as "Our Friend." This was not necessarily sinister in itself. But if the content of Nicholas and Alexandra's meetings and conversations with Philippe had been of a purely conventional kind, no need would have arisen for the secrecy in which those meetings were enveloped. Alexandra strove to conceal the content of her and Nicholas's conversations with Philippe even from her elder sister, the equally devout Orthodox convert Ella.

Either Alexandra was sworn to secrecy, or she knew that there was something in Philippe's teachings of which her sister would not approve. When Ella pressed her on Philippe, Alexandra wrote, in a letter to Nicholas in July 1902, that "I remained very quiet and gave dull answers, especially after she said she wanted to get to the bottom of it.... I stuck to the story of the remedy."[47] Did this mean that Nicholas and Alexandra's need for a boy was but a pretext for their relationship with Philippe, which was actually based on a thirst for the extra-dogmatic spiritual teachings he offered? The other thing Alexandra confessed to doing in order to deflect her sister's questions was to claim that the Grand Duke Nikolai Nikolaevich had long since given up his once well-known interest in "spiritism." "So the conversation never took that turn,

---

[43] Smith, *Rasputin*, 36.   [44] Ibid., 37.   [45] Ibid., 39.   [46] Ibid., 37.
[47] Maylunas and Mironenko, *Lifelong Passion*, 204.

which might have been more difficult to explain to her," she explained
to her husband. This confession of "spiritism" is the closest we get to a
description by Nicholas or Alexandra themselves of what drew them to
Philippe. Nicholas was equally evasive when pressed by his mother and
sisters. As historian Richard Wortman has observed, Philippe arrived at
Nicholas and Alexandra's court at the height of Alexandra's intellectual
interest in religion, mysticism, and spirituality, which her conversion, six
or seven years before, to Orthodoxy had not quenched but apparently
sharpened. "Her notebook from 1901 to 1905," Wortman notes, "includes
citations from German mystical and pietist writers Meister Eckhart and
Jacob Boehme, French religious philosophy, and even the Bhagavad-Gita.
In the last section, there are lengthy quotations from the *Lives of the
Fathers* of the Orthodox church and Serafim of Sarov."[48]

Thirst for this spiritism, which Alexandra's notebook suggests she did
not consider incompatible with a primary commitment to Orthodoxy
after her 1894 conversion, seems ultimately to have outweighed their
desire for an heir in their relationship with Philippe. But this did not
mean that the original desire had gone away, and, as if to back up his
claim to possess the special knowledge Nicholas and Alexandra were
seeking, Philippe apparently produced the desired pregnancy. After a two-
month visit to Russia by Philippe at the end of 1901, Alexandra became
convinced she was pregnant and that, thanks to Philippe's extraordinary
powers, the child in her womb was a boy. By the spring of 1902, her belly
was visibly swelling. But when Philippe returned to Russia in August
expecting to find Alexandra in the advanced stages of her pregnancy, the
child believed to be in her womb had not grown. Alarmed, their relatives
insisted that Alexandra submit to gynecological examination: there was
no child in her womb; she had suffered a false pregnancy. The public was
told she had had a miscarriage. Pressure from the family and the wider
government mounted for Philippe to be dismissed. Nicholas's mother, the
Dowager Empress Marie, commissioned the Palace Commandant, Pyotr
Gesse, to investigate. Gesse in turn enlisted Pyotr Rachkovsky, head of
the Okhrana, the Russian secret police, who reported that Philippe was
a Jew and a freemason linked to the Lodge Grande Alliance Israélite.
Nicholas and Alexandra were being taken in by a Jewish plot to bring
down the Russian monarchy, he alleged, but Nicholas dismissed the claim
and terminated Rachkovsky's investigation. "People talk such rubbish
about him that it's sickening just to listen to them, and I don't know
how they can believe the nonsense that they themselves are spouting,"
he wrote in his diary.[49] Perhaps Nicholas really did think of Philippe
as the orthodox Christian and faith healer that Spiridovich described?

---

[48] Wortman, *Scenarios of Power*, 356, n. 22.
[49] Quoted in Smith, *Rasputin*, 42.

Whatever the answer to that question, the disquiet which Philippe's mysterious presence generated was like a dress rehearsal for the Rasputin scandal a decade later. Finally, Prince Meshchersky, an old friend of Alexander III's who regarded himself as a key defender of the autocracy, obtained an audience with the imperial couple. He warned Nicholas and Alexandra that rumors were spreading that Philippe had diverted Alexandra from Orthodoxy, and that Nicholas, too, was inclined to abandon Orthodoxy in favor of Philippe's occult teachings. The people, Meshchersky said, believed Philippe to be a sorcerer.[50] This was a warning that Nicholas appears to have taken seriously, and in a way that suggests that, whatever the nature of the "wonders of God" he and Alexandra chatted about with Philippe, Nicholas had not ceased to think of himself as first and foremost an *Orthodox* tsar. He dismissed Philippe at the end of 1902, giving him an expensive French motor car as a reward for his services. Meanwhile, in the parting gifts that Philippe bestowed in return, the ostensibly Christian character of his ministrations asserted themselves: some dried flowers that he alleged Christ himself had touched, an icon, and a bell which Philippe said would ring whenever danger approached. Alexandra had the flowers framed and hung on the wall of her boudoir, a relic alongside her portrait of Marie-Antoinette. When, years later, Rasputin cemented his place in Nicholas and Alexandra's family circle: Alexandra would transfer to Rasputin the epithet she had once used for Philippe: "Our Friend."[51]

ⓔ   ⓔ   ⓔ

What we are to make of the presence of Philippe at Nicholas and Alexandra's court? Was their "faith" in Philippe a sign of how far out of touch with reality the couple was or a sign of how close, in a historical sense, they were to it? For what was the spirit of Russia's Silver Age, if not the rejection of the tyranny of the same positivistic scientism that Nicholas and, above all, Alexandra had also rejected in refusing the nineteenth century's otherwise prevailing judgment in favor of secularization? What was Merezhkovsky's and Gippius's, Blok's and Akhmatova's literary Symbolism but a more refined and sophisticated expression of the system of esoteric signs and symbols (such as Alexandra's beloved swastika) into which Philippe as a gnostic and higher order mason sought to induct Nicholas and Alexandra? Symbolism, Gnosticism, hermeticism, theosophy, the occult: interest in all these was the obverse of the nineteenth century's faith in science, progress, and purely materialist accounts of man and history, such as Marxism. Interest in them was not necessarily a sign of ignorance or backwardness. The unquestionably intelligent Vladimir Solovyov began a career that would see him recognized as Russia's

---

[50] Smith, *Rasputin*, 40–44.   [51] Ibid., 103.

greatest Idealist philosopher with a vision of a semi-Gnostic being called
"Sophia" while researching ancient Near Eastern mystery cults in the
British Library Reading Room. She would appear to Solovyov once again
later in his career, and the symbol-laden poetry Solovyov wrote in honor
of her was the direct impetus for the Symbolism that defined the literary
culture of the Silver Age and, even more significantly for our story, of the
distinct theosophical turn taken at the beginning of the twentieth century among some self-identified Orthodox thinkers, including Bulgakov.
But whereas Solovyov's and Bulgakov's paths ran from theosophy *back*
to Church Orthodoxy, Merezhkovsky, Gippius, and Filosofov followed a
path from theosophy to the rejection of the historical Orthodox Church.
This culminated, in exile, in an attempt to build an alternative, "free
Christianity" of the Holy Spirit, favorable to revolution, Socialism and
even, in the end, naïve endorsement of Nazism. To be sure, Monsieur
Philippe belonged to an altogether more popular level of Silver Age esotericism. But the "theosophical" temptation — a gnostic Christianity of
symbols and secret knowledge untethered from the rites and doctrines of
the historical Church — that he represented was essentially the same. In
this sense, Philippe embodied the danger to which not only Nicholas and
Alexandra, but all those who did not share the Kantian outlook of the
age, exposed themselves: namely, that *any* mysticism, even one untethered
from the dogmas and rites of the historical Orthodox Church, was an
ally and legitimate pursuit for those who held fast to the supranatural
and suprarational claims of historical, mystical-dogmatic Christianity.
Or, to put it another way, if we agree that Nicholas and Alexandra were
"mystical" Christians, who rejected the nineteenth-century reduction of
Christianity to an essentially rational system of ethics, then it is as if,
in Philippe (considered in relation to his ambiguous connections with
Papus) Nicholas and Alexandra faced the temptation of a vulgarized and
instrumentalized Idealism — a suprarational world of mind, spirit, and
will to power — unmoored not only from the disciplines of historical
mystical-dogmatic Christianity but also from the metaphysic that gave
authentic Christian mysticism its connection with rationality — the metaphysic to which the mysticism of historical Christianity had been tied by
its dogma — and which led in at least one compelling analysis to fascism.[52]
Nothing less than this was the significance of Nicholas and Alexandra's
overcoming of this temptation for a deeper entry into Church Orthodoxy.
For Alexandra, then, as for Bulgakov, rather than as for Merezhkovsky
or Diaghilev, Silver-Age theosophy was a station on the way to Church
Orthodoxy, not a final destination in itself. Anna Vyrubova, Alexandra's
later confidante, remembers being warned by Alexandra when the two

---

[52]   As Del Noce argues was the case with Mussolini: Augusto Del Noce, "Notes towards
a historical definition of fascism," in id., *Age of Secularization*, 106–7.

first became friends in 1905 that, despite Alexandra's interest in human *spirituality*, "if I wished for her friendship [I was] never to have anything to do with so-called spiritism."[53]

Indeed, Alexandra's spiritual journey seemed written into the décor of the next room (the Rosewood Drawing Room) I visited in the Alexander Palace. While the overall style was *art nouveau*, two Marian images, hung to either side of the mantelpiece. dominated the space. The one on the left was a traditional Orthodox icon of the Virgin and Child in the so-called "Hodegetria" style, the Mother of God tenderly fondling the toes of the divine Child seated on her lap with one hand and pointing to Him as the Way (hence this style's other name, "Our Lady of the Way") with the other. To the other side of the mantelpiece, meanwhile, Russia's last empress had hung as a pendant a painting of the Annunciation by the Austrian artist S. R. Granich, apparently an obscure member of the Vienna Secession movement that would have been entirely at home in the pages of Diaghilev's *World of Art*.

Because the veneration of Mary had had no part in Alexandra's Lutheran upbringing, these Marian images in her private rooms were visible legacies of her agonized conversion to Orthodoxy. But, perhaps, from the philosophical-historical perspective of the story we have been telling, they are also something else. To venerate Mary has, from earliest times, been to declare one's subscription to the dogmas of mystical-historical Christianity in its fulness. As the great Russian theologian Vladimir Lossky would later put it, "If the teaching about the Mother of God belongs to the Tradition, it is only through our experience of life in the Church that we can adhere to the unlimited devotion which the Church offers the Mother of God; and the degree of our adherence to this devotion will be the measure of the extent to which we belong to the Body of Christ."[54] For only if Christ is truly God made man, and not merely a good and wise human teacher (or some sort of cosmic spirit that merely *seemed* human, as the ancient Gnostics held) did it make sense to venerate Mary, the human Mother of God as, by the 1910s, Alexandra certainly did, deeply and devoutly. Indeed, the further we will follow Nicholas and Alexandra's spiritual biography, the greater part Mary will play in it. Alexandra communed with the spirit of Russia's Silver Age, but ultimately, in her choice for historical Orthodoxy, she transcended it. The Marian images of the Rosewood Drawing Room are a reminder of what set her apart from a figure such as Diaghilev. At the end of the day, art, for Russia's last empress, was never for art's sake alone: it had a *meaning*. Her earlier flirtation with the age's theosophy notwithstanding, Alexandra truly belonged, in the end, to Christ's Body, the Church.

---

[53] Vyrubova, *Memories*, 73.   [54] Lossky, *In the Image*, 210.

From the Rosewood Drawing Room, I followed the passageway into what was once the most infamous room in the Alexander Palace, if not the entire Russian Empire: Alexandra's notoriously "tasteless" Mauve Boudoir. Certainly, at first glance, the empress's inner sanctum seemed to bear witness to the crimes against taste her critics accused her of. Striped mauve and lilac wallpaper covered the walls. Chintz armchairs with lace-finished cushions filled the room, along with a profusion of sinuous Art Nouveau writing tables and picture stands, with legs in the shape of the fronds of lilies—all painted white and laden with photo albums, journals, letter-writing equipment, and frilly lamps. There was even an upright piano, also white. In the corner, a modern, in-built, wrap-around corner lounge, upholstered in the same lilac and mauve pattern that covered the walls, clung to the wall. A mantlepiece the length of the wall ran down the other side of the room, covered in masses of family photographs three deep and four or even five rows high. Palms stood in pots on the floor and all around the room could be found Art Nouveau vases overflowing with masses of fresh flowers (grown in the Crimea and dispatched daily by train to the palace). And then there were the icons: hundreds of sacred pictures bearing witness to man's encounter with the Divine in Christ, the Virgin and saints, and direct windows on to another, transcendent, yes, but crucially, also, *incarnate* and *sacramental*, reality.

In all, a scene more remote from the restrained classical elegance of Quarenghi that such visitors apparently expected to find would have been difficult to imagine, and the effect on visitors was disconcerting. Attempting to be both "this" and "that" (in perfect accord with Benois's precepts), the Mauve Boudoir was a space that was both modern and traditional, domestic and sacred, an Edwardian sitting room and an Orthodox chapel, an imperial residence and a family home. All that counted was that each item in itself be beautiful (and, one feels, even if the object, a vase, or a portrait frame, was itself "profane," in such beauty as it possessed lay, for Alexandra, its share of the sacred). The effect of the whole—of the icons, the frilly chintzes, and the lily-shaped stands—was beside the point. For Alexandra, what mattered in the first instance was beauty for beauty's sake, and in whatever form. This was entirely of the spirit of the Art Nouveau. But it was also, in the end, only a starting point for Alexandra. If Alexandra is Silver Age Russia's unacknowledged empress-*miriskustnik*, she not only understood the movement's source of inspiration, but also brought it to its otherwise unrealized fulfilment in the faith of the Church. "Beauty will save the world," Dostoevsky famously declared, in the mouth of the idiot-Prince Myshkin, in his 1868 novel, *The Idiot*, channeling both the spirit of Orthodoxy and that of the Hellenism (its roots in Plato's Form of the

Beautiful) that it had purified. Saving the world was not something Diaghilev had aspired to do. But everything we know about Alexandra suggests she had assimilated Dostoevsky's dictum wholeheartedly.

            ᔕᔕᔕ   ᔕᔕᔕ   ᔕᔕᔕ

Beyond the Mauve Boudoir, a hundred years ago, lay the imperial couple's bedroom, their private oratory or chapel, Alexandra's bathroom, a room for a maid, and a staircase providing access to the children's rooms on the floor above. When I visited, none of these was open to visitors. Returning instead to the central corridor, and following it to the end, I turned left, and entered the emperor's Audience Room. A dark room, with heavy oak paneling and a bronze chandelier (its lamps hung with tufted, almost 1970s-style tassels), and a small table capable of seating six on green, leathered-upholstered chairs, the style is somber and traditional. It was here that Nicholas received the ministers who traveled daily to Tsarskoye Selo from St Petersburg for routine audiences — the interminable *doklady* of Nicholas's diaries.[55] Going through a doorway at the end of the room, I entered Nicholas's "working" study, where he could consult papers alone before and after his meetings with ministers. Looking up from those papers, Nicholas had a view over the palace's internal courtyard: ironically, perhaps, for all Russia's last monarch's identification with the ideal of Byzantine-Muscovite *teokratia*, it was Quarenghi's orderly, eighteenth-century colonnade that framed that corner of Russia that Nicholas looked out on daily as he worked.

On the other side of the door, at the end of this working study, was Nicholas's bathroom. Equipped with a small swimming pool, where Nicholas swam short laps every morning after his prayers, this bathroom was effectively a home gym. Indeed, after his laps, Nicholas, in another surprising instance of affinity with the times, lifted weights and performed other gymnastics, reflecting a burgeoning contemporary interest in the "cult of body-building, gymnastics and martial arts" represented in some of the Silver Age's canvases.[56] The day I visited, the room's custodian was stocky woman in her early sixties; she had artificially curled brown hair and wore the plain clothes in primary colors characteristic of Russia's modest, post-Soviet working class, who, liberated from the state's apparatus of surveillance, but also deprived of its system of guaranteed work and welfare, live a precarious existence in the Soviet-era

---

[55] This Audience Room was not by any means a "cabinet room"; Nicholas always preferred to receive ministers individually at Tsarskoye Selo. As a group, the ministers met instead at the Mariinsky Palace, an imposing neo-classical pile opposite St Isaac's Cathedral in St Petersburg.

[56] The quotation is from Bowlt. *Moscow and St Petersburg*, 292. For example, a famous 1910 painting by the modernist, *miriskustnik* Ilya Mashkov shows himself and his fellow painter Petr Konchalovsky bared-legged and bare-chested with a pair of kettle bells and medicine balls at their feet: ibid., 281.

tower blocks that ring Russian cities. Unsure whether her sympathies were with the Revolution or the imperial regime it overthrew, I tested the waters (so to speak).

"Nicholas II — a very sad story," I said, motioning towards the swimming pool.

"Yes, very sad," she replied, with a sigh of apparently genuine regret. "They were such a wonderful family. Loved each other so much."

I nodded and mumbled an agreeing *da* ("yes"). It was the first statement of sympathy for the Romanovs I had heard a Russian express.

Beckoning to me from under the lintel of the next doorway was Nicholas's answer to Alexandra's Mauve Boudoir: the Emperor's State or "Parade" Study, his *kabinet* and inner sanctum. A spacious mezzanine like the Empress's Maple Drawing Room, Nicholas's *kabinet* is, of all the tsar's rooms in the *stil modern* wing of the Alexander Palace, both the most finely decorated and the most historically significant. Connecting it to the Maple Drawing Room on the other side of the corridor, an imposing Art Nouveau staircase in glossily polished oak elegantly descends from the upper floor, its balustrades finished in sinuous swan necks, while the mezzanine landing is connected to the oak-inset ceiling via massive "lumps" (stout half-columns on exaggeratedly high bases) of rutilated golden quartz, polished to suggest the shape of primitive columns, embellished with polished oak corbels "dripping" down their sides like long, slender tear drops of melted wax. Meanwhile, to the immediate left of the doorway into the room a billiard table stands positioned, while, tucked into the corner underneath the Art Nouveau staircase, an in-built, L-shaped lounge upholstered in stylized acanthus leaves wraps itself limberly around a fireplace, as if heralding that culture of informal entertaining that would reach its apotheosis in the villas of Frank Lloyd Wright on the other side of the Atlantic.

This, the most private of Nicholas's spaces, was both a workplace, where Nicholas spent most his working day, and where he held his most important and confidential meetings with individual ministers, and a refuge, a place to read papers, play billiards, and, crucially, as we shall see, *pray*. Indeed, perhaps the most important feature of the room in Nicholas's day was the icons with which Nicholas had hung it. An image of Christ the Pantokrator ("Ruler of the Universe") on the wall behind Nicholas's desk was particularly important, as the story of the following events, which took place in this room, will reveal.

Among the reforms the October Manifesto introduced into Russia's system of government was the increased importance of the Chairman of the Council of Ministers. A relatively minor office before 1905, the Chairman became in the era of the Duma Monarchy a post closer to that of a chancellor or prime minister, responsible for the day-to-day running of the Russian government, and equipped with powers to co-ordinate business across the government's various ministries. Appointed to this position at the height of the disturbances of 1906 was one of the great personalities of late imperial Russia and Russia's longest-serving Chairman of the Council of Ministers, Peter Stolypin. Until his assassination in Kiev in 1911, Stolypin was the most forceful and effective of all Nicholas's ministers, the restorer of order in 1906, and the stabilizer thereafter of the new Duma Monarchy. From his policy of rearmament flowed an extraordinary economic boom that already by 1909 made defeat in the war with Japan and the Revolution of 1905 seem distant memories.[57] And yet at the outset of 1906, Stolypin had been a mere regional governor (indeed, the youngest ever to have been appointed to such a post in Imperial Russia), albeit a remarkably successful one.[58] In April, Nicholas II, impressed with Stolypin's success in maintaining order in the otherwise rebellion-prone province of Saratov, appointed him Minister of the Interior. Impressed again, this time with the vigorous measures Stolypin employed to suppress the campaign of assassinations against government officials that were then rocking Russian towns and cities, Nicholas offered Stolypin the Chairmanship of the Ministerial Council in July. And he did so in the Alexander Palace Parade Study or *kabinet* we have just described at Tsarskoye Selo.

At that meeting in 1906, however, Stolypin, not a power-hungry man despite the resolve for which he was famous, initially sought to persuade the tsar to offer the Chairmanship to someone else. Nicholas was surprised but not deterred, and Vladimir Kokovtsov (Finance Minister from 1904 to 1914, and Chairman of the Council of Ministers himself from 1911 to 1914), who had the story from Stolypin himself, described what happened next, when, in apparently entirely unselfconscious keeping with the theocratic principle impressed on him at his coronation and a lifetime's attendance at the Divine Liturgy, Nicholas invested Stolypin with the unwanted burden. "Stolypin told us that he . . . attempted to point out his lack of experience and his unfamiliarity with the cross-currents of St Petersburg society, but the Tsar [did] not let him finish. 'No, Petr Arkadevich, here is the icon before which I often pray. Let us make the sign of the Cross over ourselves and let us ask the Lord to help us both in this difficult, perhaps historic moment.'"[59] Then, Kokovtsov continued, "the Tsar made the sign of the Cross over Stolypin,

---

[57] See Peter Gatrell, *Government, Industry and Rearmament in Russia, 1900–14: The last argument of tsarism* (Cambridge: Cambridge University Press, 2010), which provides impressive statistics to show that rearmament replaced railway construction as the main driver of economic growth in Russia after 1905.

[58] On Stolypin's character and career, see Hosking, *Russian Constitutional Experiment*, 21–23.

[59] Vladimir Kokovtsov, *Out of My Past: The memoirs of Count Kokovtsov*, ed. Harold Henry Fisher, trans. Laura Matveev (Stanford, CA: Stanford University Press, 1935), 153.

embraced him and kissed and asked him on what day it would be best to dissolve the Duma."[60]

It is worth pausing over this account. When it took place, Bulgakov had not yet had his vision on the Yalta Embankment. And yet the story of Nicholas, the Christian monarch, commissioning a prime minister by making the sign of the cross over him in the presence of an icon of Christ, shows how closely Nicholas's conception of Russia's form of government cohered with that vision of *teokratia* later revealed to Bulgakov. That political authority was properly "by the grace of God and not by popular dispensation" was, in Nicholas's mind, a truth from which neither himself nor his ministers could easily, if at all, be released. Not only that. As tsar, and Russia's autocrat, Nicholas's *modus operandi*, we learn, included frequent petitions for guidance from the Tsar of tsars, the universe's "Pantocrat," the Savior, Christ. And the image that forms in our minds as we imagine Nicholas at prayer before the Pantokrator icon is an icon, too, of *teokratia*: that is, of the consecrated ruler as "link" between the things of State and those of religion, and of the search for analogical conformity, through that ruler's prayers, between the human order and the cosmic, of the *mimesis*, as far as possible, of the earthly and sacred cities.

This was the first of Stolypin's several insights into Nicholas's theocratic conception of his office. Just how important the religious meaning of his office was to Nicholas continued to surprise all his ministers. Indeed, perhaps the most striking, and yet simultaneously the most tragic, demonstration of Nicholas's conception of his office as a sacred trust, and of Russia as a *teokratia*, involved Russia's Jews. Kept apart from the Russian Empire's non-Jewish subjects for centuries by a quasi-apartheid system that restricted their presence to the so-called "Pale of Settlement" (modern Ukraine, Belarus, central Poland, and Lithuania), Jews, under provisions most recently reiterated in the "May Laws" introduced by Nicholas's father, Alexander III, in 1882, were simultaneously barred from certain professions, while a maximum quota was imposed on Jewish enrolment in Russia's schools and universities.[61] In the changed circumstances of 1906, however, Stolypin obtained the Council of Ministers' support for the gradual according to the Jews of the same civil and political rights as other Russians, and a bill abolishing the most egregious provisions of the May Laws was sent to Nicholas for approval in October.

While Stolypin expected Nicholas to approve the bill quickly, the document appeared to vanish into the depths of the Alexander Palace.

---

[60] Ibid.
[61] On Alexander III's anti-Jewish legislation, see Hosking, *People and Empire*, 392–93. On the Muscovite roots of Slavophile anti-Semitism, see Billington, *Icon and Axe*, 72–75.

At his weekly meetings with the tsar, Nicholas never referred to it. Finally, in the second week of December, Nicholas returned the proposed legislation to Stolypin with a covering letter that revealed a previously hidden source of tension — the state, secularized or other, of Russia's political order — between Nicholas and his ministers.[62] Kokovtsov, to whom Stolypin had shown Nicholas's letter, copied it verbatim and reproduced it in his memoirs. "I am returning to you without my confirmation the recommendation of the Council on the Jewish problem," Nicholas wrote to Stolypin. "Despite most convincing arguments in favor of adopting a positive decision in this matter, an inner voice keeps on insisting more and more that I should not accept responsibility for it. So far, my conscience has not deceived me. Therefore, I intend in this case also to follow its dictates. I know that you, too, believe that 'a Tsar's heart is in God's hand.' Let it be so. For all laws established by me I bear a great responsibility before God, and I am ready to answer for this decision at any time."

Stolypin and the Council of Ministers were shocked. "None of the documents in my possession shows so clearly the Tsar's mystical attitude toward the nature of his imperial power," Kokovtsov commented using a word, "mystical," we have met before. The problem was not that Nicholas could not recognize the Council's arguments in favor of relieving the position of the Empire's Jewish subjects; he acknowledged that they existed, and was even persuaded, in a certain way, of their justness. Indeed, he had apparently even agonized over the competing claims of justice at stake in the issue. But in this instance he nonetheless found that the elimination of discriminatory legislation proposed by the Council conflicted with his religious conscience. If such measures were a step towards equality (such that Jews and Orthodox could marry, for example, without legal impediment or fear of social taboo), how far and for how long would Russia remain Orthodox? After all, discriminatory legislation against the Jews was as old as the Constantinian regime itself. Who was Nicholas to authorize its dismantling? Was it not, in its own way, a possible blow against the *teokratia*, the origins of the State in the moral community of Russia's Orthodox people, a dereliction from his coronation oath for which he would have to answer?[63] As Rowan Williams put it in reference to Bulgakov's alleged anti-Semitism, "what Judaism is always about is Christianity" — "a visible form of disobedience to God, a parody of what should be."[64]

---

[62] Kokovtsov, *Out of My Past*, 167.
[63] Laura Engelstein, *Slavophile Empire: Imperial Russia's illiberal path* (Ithaca, NY: Cornell University Press, 2009). 192
[64] Williams, *Sergii Bulgakov*, 299, 298. In this Williams likens Bulgakov's "anti-Semitism" (which term he uses advisedly so as not to equate it with Hitler's) to that of other European thinkers, from Karl Barth to Simone Weil — herself a Jew.

Whatever the precise questions Nicholas turned over in his prayers about the matter, his answer was a clear, and to his ministers apparently totally unexpected, reminder that Russia was a *teokratia*. The terms in which he addressed his note to them ("the Tsar's heart . . . ") went back, via St Gregory of Nazianzen's classic exegesis of the imperial office, to the Bible.[65] As the latter put it in an address to the Christian emperor Theodosius I in a passage considered ever after in Eastern Christian tradition as the *locus classicus* of Byzantine political theory:

> Emperors, respect your purple. For my oration lays down laws that also bind our legislators. Know how much has been committed to your conscience and what a mysterious thing your kingly power is. The whole world lies in your hands, however small the crown or weak the body. What is above you belongs to God; what is below you belongs to you. If I may express it this way: be as gods to your subjects (Ps. 81:1, 6). [For] the king's heart is in the hands of God (Prov. 21:1). It is there your strength should lie, not in your gold or your armies.[66]

The judge of his people, the tsar himself was under constant judgment.[67]

ᔉ   ᔉ   ᔉ

In the event, the establishment of a "merely" legislative Duma satisfied few. While the Kadets agitated for the Duma's control of the executive, parties further to the left demanded the confiscation of noble-held lands and their distribution to the peasantry. Nicholas and Stolypin, willing to do neither, dissolved the Duma and called new elections. To their chagrin, the Second Duma, which met in January 1907, and of which Bulgakov was an elected member, was even more radical and less willing to cooperate with the government than the first.[68] Faced

---

[65] On the Old Testament sources of Christian notions of kingship, see Dvornik, *Early Christian*, 1:288–310, which lays special emphasis on the Psalms of David.

[66] Gregory of Nazianzen, *Oration* 36.11. Cited in McGuckin, "Legacy of the 13th apostle," 264–65.

[67] As McGuckin comments, "The whole gist of this is to remind the monarch that his mimesis of God, and his validation from God, are conditional. He stands under judgement . . . The image of God holding the heart of the king is double-edged, signifying support as well as the ability to terminate that life in a moment." "Legacy of the 13th apostle," 265.

[68] The Second Duma was the scene of some of the Duma Monarchy's most memorable political exchanges. When, in March, Stolypin appeared before the chamber, in which the Kadets had lost their preponderance to a bloc of Socialist parties that turned out to be even more confrontational in their approach to relations with the government, to present the government's legislative program, he was met with stony silence from the Socialist bloc and denunciations from the Social Democratic Labor Party (the largest Socialist party in the Duma, of which Lenin's Bolsheviks were a faction). The session ended with Stolypin's famous remark: "All your attacks are calculated to cause a paralysis of will and thought in the government, and they boil down to two words: 'Hands up!' To these words, gentlemen, the government, confident in its right, calmly answers with two other words, 'Not afraid!'" Oldenburg, *Last Tsar*, 2:231. Stolypin's other famous retort, "You, gentlemen, want a great upheaval. We want a great Russia!" was also made in a session of the Second Duma, in May: McMeekin, *Russian Revolution*, 47.

with this, Stolypin concluded that the only way to break the deadlock was by changing the electoral law in favor of the propertied classes in the Russian core of the Empire.[69] Calling on the tsar's autocratic — indeed, *theocratic* — power to issue a new manifesto, Stolypin executed his plan in June 1907.[70] While the Kadets and others accused Stolypin of conducting a "coup," the country at large remained quiescent, and, in November, a Third Duma met in the Tauride Palace. Sitting until 1912, it was the only Duma in Imperial Russia to see out its full term. Had Russia discovered a remarkable, and perhaps even *ideal*, balance between the competing demands of cosmic order and human liberty?

Certainly, in the short term at least, the change to the electoral law worked. There was no new outbreak of unrest, and the Third Duma (1907–12), elected in October 1907, emerged with a solid liberal-conservative majority. The Kadets, with Miliukov at their head, retained some of their former, antagonistic attitude towards the Fundamental Laws. But their representation was much reduced and they could no longer hold the government to ransom. Instead, the biggest party in the Duma was now the so-called Party of October 17 ("the Octobrists") which dedicated itself to preserving the system of moderated monarchical government that had come into being with the October Manifesto.[71] Their leader was the swaggering Moscow-born lawyer and adventurer, Aleksandr Guchkov. Dominated as it was by the liberal-conservative Octobrists, the Third Duma achieved for the most part a serviceable relationship with the government. It voted on some 2,500 other pieces of legislation, including Stolypin's famous agrarian reform of 1907, which, by emancipating the peasantry from the commune, brought

---

[69] Whereas, under the old electoral law, the peasantry had elected 42 percent of the Duma's deputies, after the law of 1907, peasant representation was reduced to 22 percent. Meanwhile, the representation of the landowning classes (a vastly smaller percentage of the total population) rose from 32 percent to just over 50. And while the representation afforded the cities remained the same at 27 percent, this was divided into two curias or voting bodies, the first of which, representing those who met a certain property quota, elected most of the cities' deputies. The volatile urban working classes were left visibly under-represented. Also reduced were the number of deputies elected from among the national minorities on the Empire's peripheries, especially the Poles and the peoples of the Caucasus: the "State Duma must also be Russian in spirit," the Manifesto declared, not in a spirit of chauvinism, but as if taking steps to remedy the moral void Bulgakov had complained of by tapping into the resources of shared Russian culture. See Oldenburg, *Last Tsar*, 2:237; also, Hosking, *Russian Constitutional Experiment*, 42–45.
[70] As the June Manifesto had it, "only that Power that granted the first electoral law, the historic Power of the Russian Tsar, possesses the right to repeal and replace it... Our Tsarist Power over Our people has been received by the Lord God Himself, and We will answer for the fate of the Russian People before His Throne." Cited in Oldenburg, *Last Tsar*, 2:237–38. On Stolypin's commitment to preserving the tsar's autocratic rights, see Hosking, *Russian Constitutional Experiment*, 54.
[71] On the Octobrist program and its conflicted affirmations, see Hosking, *Russian Constitutional Experiment*, 50–54. On the one hand, the Octobrists pledged themselves as defenders of the monarchical principle; on the other, they sought the entrenchment and expansion of the practice of constitutionalism, the equalization of civic rights, and the rule of law.

about a dramatic upsurge of prosperity in the countryside.[72] In 1908, the Third Duma drafted a twenty-year plan for the introduction of universal primary school education.[73] It also approved Nicholas's project of extending the Trans-Siberian Railway east from Lake Baikal (from where it then dropped down into China) along the left, northern bank of the Amur River to connect Vladivostok by rail, finally, to the rest of the Empire: a huge public works program, the project, once commenced, would employ some 54,000 skilled workmen.[74] On 157 occasions, ministers appeared before it, to answer questions on government policy or explain legislation.[75] Between 1907 and 1915, the Duma Monarchy's synthesis of order and liberty seemed remarkably robust.

And yet it was not all plain sailing for the government. The Octobrist majority, while more conciliatory than the Kadets, had not given up the first two Dumas' ambition of wresting for itself executive control of the government: the Duma would gain control of the executive not in one fell swoop, but gradually, extending its rights and competences until the responsibility of the government to the Duma, rather than to the tsar, was a *fait accompli*, the result of a process of *evolution* rather than revolution (as it had been in their muse, England).[76] An obvious place to start was with the armed forces. While the Fundamental Laws of 1906 reserved control over them to the tsar, the same Laws had given the Duma the right to vote on monetary appropriations for the armed forces in the imperial budget, and Guchkov, the Octobrist leader, was alive to the opportunity this created to expand the scope of the Duma's powers.

Early in the life of the Third Duma, therefore, Guchkov chose a debate on army appropriations to criticize the presence in its general staff of persons "irresponsible by their very position at the head of . . . important branches of military life."[77] It was a reference to the tsar's uncles and cousins, the grand dukes, who held high office on the grounds of dynastic rank and relationship to Nicholas. Thus, Guchkov's speech antagonized Nicholas, Stolypin, and every other defender of the monarchy's historical rights: everyone was aware that the issue raised went to the heart of the constitution.[78] Although the army appropriations were passed in this instance without problem, Guchkov raised the issue again when the government presented its program for Russia's naval rearmament.[79] Having been destroyed by Japan in 1905, the Russian navy was in urgent need of new ships, and Nicholas had determined that these should be four new, dreadnought-type battleships. Guchkov saw in the

[72] Pipes, *Russian Revolution*, 183.
[73] Oldenburg, *Last Tsar*, vol. 3: *The Duma Monarchy, 1907–1914*, 42.
[74] Oldenburg, *Last Tsar*, vol. 3: 20; McMeekin, *Russian Revolution*, 48.
[75] Pipes, *Russian Revolution*, 183.
[76] As argued by Patrick Rollins in the introduction to Oldenburg's *Last Tsar*, vol. 1:xiv–xxxi.   [77] Oldenburg, *Last Tsar*, 3:20.
[78] Hosking, *Russian Constitutional Experiment*, 78–79.   [79] Ibid., 80–81.

government's urgency an opportunity to strike a blow for the principle
that Guchkov had outlined in reference to the grand dukes: the Duma
refused to authorize the appropriations until the government had conceded it a formal right to a say in the appointment of the staff officers
that commanded the navy. Alarmed, Stolypin saw the game Guchkov was
up to. However reasonable or innocuous it might appear, the Duma's
proposal would "establish invidious precedents to pave the way for an
unconscious transition to [parliamentarism]," he said.[80] Although not
involved in the day-to-day business of government, Nicholas observed
the situation closely, too. He was no less alive than Stolypin to the fact
that politics in Russia was often far more about principle than it was
about policy. And the principle that Guchkov had raised went to the
heart of the balance between the rights of God and the freedoms of
man in the Duma Monarchy.[81]

Legislation for the dreadnoughts went back and forth between the
government and the Duma for over twelve months. Guchkov would
not give way. In a much-publicized speech in the Duma chamber in
February 1909, he returned to his theme of parliamentary responsibility
by complaining that "in those areas of military affairs that are beyond
our power, the situation is not so promising." He even appeared to
question Nicholas's competence. The "agonizing question remains,"
Guchkov said, "does the Supreme Leader of our army know the state
of our defense establishment?"[82] Reviewed today from the perspective
of the years 1915 and 1916, Guchkov's speech reads like a dress rehearsal
for his part in the 1917 Revolution. Indeed, when the war minister, who
had appeared to answer questions in the chamber, seemed about to
concede Guchkov's point, Nicholas dismissed him, and replaced him
with a man he thought a surer hand: the chief of the Russian General
Staff, General V. A. Sukhomlinov. For Sukhomlinov's reasserting direct
imperial command over the armed forces, Guchkov, beginning in 1912,
unleashed against him a campaign of slander that would culminate, in
the Great War, in one of the scandals that did most to damage Nicholas's
prestige.[83] In any event, when Guchkov made his speech in 1909, Stolypin
was ill with pneumonia. Responsibility for the legislation passed to the
Finance Minister, Kokovtsov. Desirous of putting an end to the matter,
Kokovtsov, speaking on behalf of the Council of Ministers, advised the
State Council, Russia's upper house, to approve the legislation with
the Duma's amendments about its role in naval appointments. It did
so, by a slim majority; Guchkov was on the verge of victory. And then

---

[80] Oldenburg, *Last Tsar*, 3:21.
[81] Hosking, *Russian Constitutional Experiment*, 83.
[82] Oldenburg, *Last Tsar*, 3:58.
[83] See William C. Fuller, *The Foe Within: Fantasies of treason and the end of Imperial Russia* (Ithaca, NY: Cornell University Press, 2006), on which more below.

Nicholas used his veto: that ultimate authority in Russia remained with the tsar had again been asserted.[84]

In April, Nicholas II charged Stolypin, by imperial rescript, to spell out once and for all the crown's prerogatives regarding the armed forces, and the matters on which the Duma's right of supervision could be exercised.[85] Like the June Manifesto of 1907, it was another calm and self-confident exercise of authority that demonstrated to all that Russia remained in essence a *teokratia*. Accepted by Russian society at large, Nicholas's reassertion of his theocratic rights nonetheless secured for himself Guchkov's permanent enmity. Smarting from the blow to his pride, Guchkov resigned the Octobrist leadership, only to be re-elected by his party after the defection from it of conservatives dismayed at the increasingly revolutionary nature of his politics. When, in August, Stolypin, responding to Nicholas's rescript, presented regulations outlining the limits of the Duma's role in military affairs, Guchkov and the Octobrists raised no objections. For now, Nicholas had won; but the battlelines had been drawn.

The high point of Guchkov's career in the Duma came in March 1910, when he was elected the chamber's chairman or president. This had the disadvantage of requiring him to resign his party leadership. But it gave him a new right to direct audiences with Nicholas, through which he probably hoped, rating his power of influence highly, to sway the tsar toward the gradual surrender of his prerogatives. Alive, as always, to the question of principle at the heart of the existence of the Duma Monarchy, Nicholas distrusted him intensely. Their first meeting, in Nicholas's Alexander Palace *kabinet*, was tense. We can assume that Nicholas did not lead Guchkov over to the icon of the Pantokrator on the wall or make the sign of the cross over him in blessing. Significantly, the palace press release pointedly omitted the conventional adjective "cordial" from its description of the reception. For this "humiliation" Guchkov never forgave Nicholas, nor dropped from his list of goals his aim of completing the Revolution of 1905 by wresting executive control of the government from the tsar (and thereby, for our purposes, achieving the secularization of Russian politics against the theocratic principle). As Guchkov told the Duma in his inaugural address as president, "I am a convinced proponent of constitutional monarchy, and my convictions were not formed only yesterday.... We frequently complain about the external forces that impede our efforts ... we must not close our eyes to them: we will have to take them into consideration and, perhaps, we will have to reckon with them."[86] By "them," there's little doubt he meant Nicholas.

---

[84] Hosking, *Russian Constitutional Experiment*, 95–96.
[85] Oldenburg, *Last Tsar*, vol. 3:61.
[86] Ibid., 3:81.

CHAPTER SIX

The Fyodorov Sovereign Cathedral
NICHOLAS'S AND ALEXANDRA'S RELIGION

OULD A REFORMED RUSSIAN EMPIRE, SUCH as the compromise Duma Monarchy inaugurated by the October Manifesto, have survived? Who is to blame that it did not? A century after the Revolution, these questions, in much of the literature, would appear unsettled.[1] But nonetheless, one opinion emerges as a consensus: namely, if any hope existed for Russia to avoid revolution, it consisted in the steady transfer of rights and responsibilities from the tsar to the Duma, and the reduction thereby of the monarchy to a symbol in the modern, nominalist sense of that word—for, of course, the monarchy always was a *symbol* in the ancient sense, a "link" connecting the sacred and the political, and an image of God's ruling authority in the cosmos. Just this nominalist sleight of hand, whereby the monarch "reigns but does not rule," had saved the monarchy in England in favor of Parliament, which assumed its powers. Why did the "British solution" prove impossible to repeat in Russia? And why, above all, once a Duma had been created, did Nicholas refuse to allow it to develop into a parliament? Was it a lack of imagination, or an excess of it? Was the tsar bereft of the *ability* to conceive of a purely symbolic role for himself? Or was he hopelessly captive to the fantastical one—of a believing, Orthodox tsar ruling a believing, Orthodox people—he had fashioned in his imagination for himself? These seem to be the only answers to the question modern historiography, blind to the theological meaning of politics and, therefore, of the Revolution, permits itself.

---

[1] For a good, if inevitably somewhat dated, summary of the two sides of the argument, without venturing a verdict either way, see Arthur Mendel, "On interpreting the fate of Imperial Russia," in Theofanis George Stavrou, ed., *Russia under the Last Tsar* (Minneapolis: University of Minnesota Press, 1969), 13–41. More recently, a strongly optimistic assessment has been offered by Wayne Dowler, *Russia in 1913* (DeKalb, IL: Northern Illinois University Press, 2010). 279: "If Russia was still far from becoming a liberal capitalist democracy in 1913, it was even farther from socialist revolution. Severe stresses and tensions remained but the clear trend before the war was towards cooperation and integration." The assessment, by contrast, of Reginal E. Zelnik, "Revolutionary Russia, 1890–1914," in Freeze, *Russia*, 234–68 is strongly negative. Ultimately, I am inclined to concur with Hosking's conclusion that the underlying problem was that the clash of *principles* embedded in the differing interpretations of the meaning of the Duma Monarchy was simply insuperable: Hosking, *Russian Constitutional Experiment*, 243–46. Although these are not Hosking's terms, either Russia was a *teokratia* or it wasn't—as Bulgakov said he already saw in 1909.

For this reason, most historians, adopting the second option above, have been unsparing in the blame they have heaped on Nicholas. As one recently put it, the "prospect [of evolutionary modernization] was blocked essentially by the actions of one man, Nicholas, who would not countenance any diminution of his authority as autocrat.... The last quarter of a century of the Romanov dynasty...was ultimately a story of a modernizing regime overtaken by domestic and international forces that it had in part itself inspired.... But it was also a story of a tsar whose refusal to adapt to the new social and political realities of the regime he headed doomed that regime to extinction."[2] To another, the essence of Russia's tragedy is that "just as Russia was entering the twentieth century," its rulers were "trying to return it to the seventeenth. Here, then, were the roots of the Revolution: in the growing conflict between a society rapidly becoming more educated, more urban and more complex, and a fossilized autocracy that would not concede its political demands."[3]

But is it incompetence and anachronism, really, Nicholas's failure to bend with the winds of history? Or was the Russian Revolution, as Bulgakov saw it, a conflict of "real mystical principles...polar and irreconcilable," of the ideal of *teokratia*, the interpenetration of the sacred and the political orders, on the one hand, and of secularization, which required their separation, in the name of freedom and democracy, on the other? If so, then this conflict would have existed by the beginning of the twentieth century, whoever was seated on the Russian throne. That it came to a head the way it did, however, was due to the character of Nicholas II, who both intuited — more clearly and correctly than most of his contemporaries — the nature of the conflict that Russia was caught in, and also rejected as incompatible with *his* religion, Orthodoxy, the various, allegedly neutral and spiritually benign reforms that might have resolved it by emptying the tsar's office of anything but nominal, "symbolic" meaning, and transforming Russia into a British-style constitutional monarchy. Faithful to what Bulgakov called the "Christian concept of life and history," Nicholas II had no principled objection to the expansion either of his people's prosperity or their liberty, within acceptable limits. On the contrary, he approved measures that expanded both further than any Russian ruler before or after him (even including Gorbachev, whose liberty came at the price of economic collapse). Of course, every political regime and system comprises a certain balance between order and liberty. Distinctive of the Duma Monarchy was its aspiration to admit as large a margin of liberty as was compatible with the preservation of the theocratic principle. What the Duma Monarchy

[2] S. A. Smith, *Russia in Revolution: An empire in crisis, 1890–1928* (Oxford: Oxford University Press, 2018), 376–77.
[3] Orlando Figes, *A People's Tragedy: The Russian Revolution, 1891–1924* (London: Pimlico, 1997), 14–15.

did not permit, because its ruler could not countenance it, was that
Russia should cease to be Orthodox — and in order to remain so, it had
to remain a *teokratia*, where God's sovereignty over the universe was
acknowledged as the source of all political order. For this reason, the only
person in the Empire *not* free to leave the Orthodox religion after 1905
was "God's slave," the tsar, Nicholas II. This fact was central to his being.

❧　❧　❧

From the Palace, I followed a path through the Aleksandrovsky Park
that surrounds it, the golden rococo onion domes of Rastrelli's blue,
white and yellow Catherine Palace visible above the top of the trees in
the distance. It was Sunday, and the park, in brilliant autumn apparel,
was full of families. Beyond the paths, the maples, beech, and linden
trees had spread a dense carpet of leaves across the ground, and where
the wind had blown them together on an arm of the canals, the leaves
formed a mosaic of yellows and oranges reminiscent of the restored
Catherine Palace Amber Room.

The fabled Amber Room, the mirrored halls, the Atlantes and onion
domes: such are the stereotyped images of Tsarskoye Selo and, with it,
of the Russia of the Romanovs. But the grins, wild hair, and ruddy
cheeks of the local children also capture the spirit that once prevailed
here. Indeed, any reader of Nicholas's diary will be struck by the amount
of time he spent with his children, and especially his daughters, as if in
anticipation of the more relaxed nature of twentieth-century fatherhood.
To his children, Nicholas was not so much "His Majesty the Emperor,"
or even a distant, nineteenth-century "father," but something much
closer to a modern "dad." He played with them, read them stories, sat
with them when they were ill and took them with him to church. When
the youngest daughter, Anastasia, caught diphtheria in 1907, Alexandra,
imitating her mother in Darmstadt a generation before, cared in isolation for the family's Lower Dacha at Peterhof, while the rest of the
children went with their father to the Alexander Palace at Tsarskoye
Selo. With Alexandra gone for two weeks, Nicholas played "single dad."
Conversely, when Tatiana came down with typhus in March 1913, it was
Nicholas who sat with her every day until she was well again. As the
palace official Mossolov put it, "The paternal love shown by Nicholas
II was worthy of all praise. He adored his children and showed special pride in them."[4] Certainly, Nicholas never begrudged the sense of
wonder at the world that brings a childhood alive. His children filled
his thoughts and prayers. On his and Alexandra's twentieth wedding
anniversary in November 1914, he wrote in his diary: "Truly God has
blessed us with a rare family happiness; if only I might show myself

---

[4] Mossolov, *At the Court*, 29.

worthy of His mercy in that portion of my life that remains to me."[5]

By the time he wrote the words above, Russia was immersed in the war that would destroy tsarism. And yet Nicholas had, until then, had good reason to be confident about the future he was bequeathing his progeny. Indeed, if there was a golden era in the twenty-two years of Nicholas's reign, it was the half decade or so between 1907 and 1914 that coincided with that balancing act between *teokratia* and democratic liberty that was the Duma Monarchy.[6]

Demographically, Russia in 1913, with a population of 175m, was far and away the most populous country in Europe. But not only was its population three times as large as Germany's (the next most populous European country), it was also twice the size of the population of the United States — and growing, especially in the cities.[7] Since 1897, Russia's urban population had almost doubled. This was because, industrially, too, Russia, from 1908, went through one of the most dramatic periods of expansion witnessed by a major power in recent history: worldwide in these years, only Sweden and Germany grew more quickly.[8] By 1913, Russia was the fourth- or fifth-largest economy in the world, with a national output greater than that of France, about equal to Britain's, and double Austria-Hungary's.[9] While Russia remained the world's largest debtor, Russia's balance of trade was in surplus every year from 1901, and, from 1910, the State budget showed an annual surplus, too, allowing the government to begin paying its foreign debt off, such that by 1914 more than half of it was held by Russians.[10] Meanwhile, driven in large part by the government's need to rearm, old industries were revived and new ones, using new technologies, were born.[11] By 1913, Russia was the world's second-largest producer of oil and a maker of aeroplanes: indeed, the world's first wind tunnel and the world's first multi-engine aircraft (the sixty-foot-long "Russian Warrior") were constructed in Russia.[12] A French economist predicted that, if such growth was maintained, Russia would be the most powerful country in Europe by 1950.[13] In the countryside, too, the crisis of Russian agriculture had been solved. Not only was Russia the world's largest exporter of grain, but the peasants owned 90 percent of the land, grew 86 percent of all grain grown in the Russian

---

[5] Nicholas II, November 14, 1914, in Diary (2), 497.
[6] For a comprehensive account of the different facets of this "golden age," an account which my portrait of Russia in 1908–1913 largely follows, see Dowler, *Russia in 1913*.
[7] Dowler, *Russia in 1913*, 20–21.
[8] Ibid., 18–19, 27–28. In 1910, McMeekin gives an annual growth rate of 10 percent: *Russian Revolution*, 48.   [9] Dowler, *Russia in 1913*, 27.   [10] Ibid., 26–27.
[11] On the special importance of rearmament in driving Russia's post-1905 economic revival, see Peter Gatrell, *Government, industry and rearmament: The last argument of tsarism* (Cambridge: Cambridge University Press, 1994).
[12] The figure is from Pipes, *Russian Revolution*, 191. For the emergence of aeronautics, see Dowler, *Russia in 1913*, 219.
[13] Pipes, *Russian Revolution*, 191.

Empire and marketed 75 percent of all grain sold: at last, Russia had conquered the threat of famine.[14] For the first time in Russia's history, its population, though larger than ever, was, in both the towns and villages, receiving an adequate intake of calories. Not until the 1960s would Russians eat as well as they had done in the decade before the Revolution.[15]

Russia was rising in other ways, too. The final leg of the Trans-Siberian would soon connect Petersburg to Vladivostok, opening the maritime province of the Russian Far East to colonization, and the Pacific, potentially, to Russian goods.[16] Meanwhile, St Petersburg and Moscow, Warsaw, Kiev, and Odessa were transformed by the arrival of modern architecture, and the construction, for the first time, of public places of worship for the empire's newly emancipated non-Orthodox religions. The same cities gained modern transport networks of trolley buses, while, in Moscow, plans for an underground metropolitan railway (ultimately constructed by the Soviets) were drawn up. An empire-wide scheme for workers' insurance was introduced in 1912, and access to elementary education greatly increased. In the country's 124,000 elementary schools, 46 percent of children in the cities and 28 percent in the countryside received six years of elementary schooling (in Russian, religion, church-singing, and arithmetic), and the government had made universal literacy by 1922 an official goal.[17] Despite the preponderance of defense and rearmament in the State budget, as a percentage, spending on education increased three times faster.[18] The universities were expanded, and the popular press, freed from censorship, exploded. Conjured into existence through the relaxation of censorship after 1905 and the advances made in primary education was a new reading public. "By 1913," as one historian has noted, "Russia was the second-largest producer of books in the world, ranking close to Germany in the number of titles. Newspapers sought actively to shape public opinion and ministers were forced to justify their policies through them."[19]

In this setting, the Russian cultural and religious renaissance, heralded by World of Art and the Religious-Philosophical Societies respectively, became something approaching a mass phenomenon. Amid the explosion of popular literature, religious titles flourished. In elite circles, meanwhile, the eclectic aestheticism of Diaghilev's movement was already giving way, by the middle of this period, to the avant-garde. Figures such as Malevich, Larianov and Kandinsky put Russia at the forefront of the world's artistic

---

[14] Dowler, *Russia in 1913*, 28; Gatrell, *Tsarist Economy*, 139–40.

[15] Indeed, the decline in basic living standards brought about by the Revolution was catastrophic. In 1933, the average worker consumed less than half the amount of bread and flour than in 1913, less than two thirds the amount of sugar, and only one fifth as much meat and fish. See Sheila Fitzpatrick, *Everyday Stalinism. Ordinary life in extraordinary times: Russia in the 1930s* (Oxford: Oxford University Press, 2000), 41.

[16] McMeekin, *Russian Revolution*, 48.

[17] Dowler, *Russia in 1913*, 23.   [18] Ibid., 27.   [19] Smith, *Russia in Revolution*, 68.

development.[20] Meanwhile, borne along by a marked economic upswing, a new middle-class consumer culture was born. Indeed, Sofia Likhutina's cluttered and "perspectiveless" apartment, furnished with mass-produced pieces by Meltzer, in the Silver Age writer Andrei Belyi's well-known 1913 novel *Petersburg*, could almost be a critic's description of the Mauve Boudoir, albeit that Likhutina's, significantly, lacked Alexandra's wall of icons.[21] There was also an echo between the pleasure gardens, music halls, and popular theaters that became a feature of Russian urban life in these years and the pastimes that Nicholas II enjoyed with his children in the park of the Alexander Palace. On the other hand, the new consumer culture also tended to promote a process of secularization that alienated Nicholas and Alexandra from the empire's urban inhabitants. This was far less pronounced in the countryside and villages, where the bulk of the population continued to live, and where life, despite the noticeable improvement in people's levels of literacy, diet, and access to consumer goods, continued to revolve around the annual cycle of Church feasts and fasts, observed under the watchful eyes of every family's protective icons. But in Russia's cities, the secularization of Russia's worldview was proceeding apace.[22]

The changes affecting Russia left a sensitive observer like Bulgakov conflicted. He had no problem with the values of hard work, choice, and aspiration that the new mass-circulation newspapers tended to promote among the lower classes. But generally Bulgakov was much more pessimistic about the Russia of the Duma Monarchy than the glowing portrait of the preceding pages would seem to warrant. Russia, Bulgakov believed, suffered from a sickness, and that sickness emanated not from the tsar, the government, or whatever remained of the autocracy; it proceeded from people like Bulgakov himself, Russia's intellectuals. So at least Bulgakov argued in the famous essay collection, *Vekhi*, in 1909.

Appearing almost halfway through the life of the Third Duma, *Vekhi: a collection of articles on the Russian intelligentsia* aspired to take the pulse of the Russia that had come into being with the Duma Monarchy.[23]

---

[20] Grover, "World of Art," 32.

[21] The irony, as one commentator on Belyi's text has noted, is that the inspiration for the character of Sophia Likhutina was none other than the wife of the leading Silver Age poet Aleksandr Blok who was famous for alleging "horror" at the sight of the Meltzer factory on Petersburg's industrial Vyborg Side, a factory that produced so many of Petersburg's modernist furnishings. Doubly ironic was the fact that the same real-life woman of allegedly questionable middle-class tastes had also been the object of the sophisticate Belyi's own affections. See Olga Matich, *Petersburg/Petersburg: Novel and city, 1900–1921* (Madison, WI: University of Wisconsin Press, 2010), 296.

[22] See Gregory L. Freeze, "Religion and political crisis in late imperial Russia," *Journal of Modern History* 68 (1996): 308–50; Freeze, "A pious folk? Religious observance in Vladimir diocese, 1900–1914," *Jahrbücher für Geschichte Osteuropas* 52 (2004): 323–40.

[23] Its full name was *Vekhi: Sbornik statei o russkoi intelligentsia*. For an English translation, see Marshall S. Shatz and Judith E. Zimmerman, ed. and trans., *Vekhi. Landmarks: A collection of articles about the Russian intelligentsia* (Armonk, NY: M. E. Sharp, 1994).

Why, asked the contributors, for all the progress Russia had made, was social and political life in Russia so *poisonous*? Wherefore the gridlock of the first two Dumas, and the hatred that had manifested itself in the murder of 9,000 Russian subjects in two years of Social Revolutionary terror? Why, when Russia now had a long-awaited Duma, were the newly-authorized political parties determined to carry on the revolution?[24] The answer, Bulgakov argued in his contribution, "Asceticism and heroism," was the intelligentsia's false spiritual values, specifically the nihilism and revolutionary heroism that flowed from the religion it had made of atheism.[25] Atheism, Bulgakov argued, was the Russian intelligentsia's "most fundamental characteristic." Atheism created the "spiritual atmosphere of our universities and professional schools, where the younger generation of the intelligentsia is molded."[26] Atheism was the "common faith into which all who enter the bosom of the humanistic intelligentsia church are baptized."[27] It was "common knowledge" across Europe that there was "no intelligentsia more atheistic than the Russian." This mattered because, as he put it, "No culture has yet been built on such a foundation." The intelligentsia's atheism (its complete assimilation in our terms of the atheistic conclusions of nineteenth-century philosophy), not the autocracy, Bulgakov believed, was the source of Russia's woes.

Moreover, from the intelligentsia's atheism flowed the way of life characteristic of the Russian *intelligent*: the cult of the hero. And what was the hero, Bulgakov asked in "Heroism and Asceticism," but the god that man made *for* and, indeed, *of himself* in the absence of the

---

[24] *Vekhi*'s contributors were some of Silver Age Russia's leading philosophers and public intellectuals: Mikhail Gershenzon (1869–1925), a Jewish literary critic and historian; Nikolai Berdyaev (1874–1948), a philosopher of religion, who, until 1908, had been closely associated with Merezhkovsky, Gippius and their circle of radical "God-seekers" looking forward to the appearance of a "new" Christianity or "Third Testament of the Holy Spirit"; A. S. Izgoev (1872–1935), a liberal journalist and writer for the Kadet party newspaper, *Rech'* ("Speech"); Bogdan Kistiakovsky (1868–1920), sociologist, scholar of constitutional law, and moderate Ukrainian nationalist; Petr Struve (1870–1944), once a leading member of Russia's first generation of Marxists, but now a convert to liberalism who had served as Kadet member of the Second Duma, and, after its dissolution, taught economics at St Petersburg University; Semyon Frank (1877–1950), a philosopher and essayist who had grown up in a middle-class Jewish family in Moscow, embraced first Marx and then Nietzsche, and then worked with Struve on various Kadet publications before converting to Christianity in 1912; and Sergei Bulgakov, still reeling in the wake of his disillusionment with representative party politics as a Christian Socialist deputy from Kiev in the Second Duma. Uniting them was a common early embrace of Marxism, followed by a later repudiation of it (invariably under the influence of Solovyov) in favor of a return to the spiritual and metaphysical values found in classical philosophy and traditional religion, especially Orthodoxy. See Schatz and Zimmerman, *Vekhi*, xiii–xx.
[25] Sergei Bulgakov, "Heroism and asceticism: reflections on the religious nature of the Russian intelligentsia," in Schatz and Zimmerman, *Vekhi*, 17. Williams reproduces the essay, with an introductory discussion, in: *Sergii Bulgakov*, 51–68. He also notes Christopher Read, *Religion, Revolution and the Russian Intelligentsia, 1900–1912: The Vekhi debate and its intellectual background* (London: Macmillan, 1979), which I have found less helpful.
[26] Bulgakov, "Heroism and asceticism," 22–23.   [27] Ibid., 22.

God of transcendental religion? Solovyov, who had helped Bulgakov find his way back to Orthodoxy, had preached a religion of *Godman-hood* (inspired by the incarnation of God in Christ and the Orthodox-patristic doctrine of man's deification). But the Russian intelligentsia, Bulgakov believed, had substituted for this true dignity of man in Church Orthodoxy the false self-aggrandizement of *man-Godhood*, the delusion of human self-worship. It manifested itself in an intelligentsia which, as a class, saw itself as playing the role of Providence in Russia's history and, on an individual level, in the figure of the revolutionary hero, who, believing himself entitled to peddle any untruth or commit any act of treason needed to bring about his country's liberation from tsarism, cast himself as his country's unique savior or deliverer.[28] Perhaps, looking back to the Revolution of 1905, Bulgakov had Gapon in mind. But looking ahead to 1917, Bulgakov had already foreseen the silhouette of such figures as Guchkov, Miliukov, Lvov, and Kerensky. The Russian Revolution of 1917 would overflow with heroes.

Over against this atheism, and the cult of the hero that it inspired, Bulgakov, in "Heroism and asceticism," proposed the figure of the Christian monk or ascetic as an alternative for emulation. If only Russia could find its way back to such an ideal, her diseased polity might yet be healed. For the Christian monk or ascetic — the Orthodox *starets* — was the revolutionary hero's antithesis. "The basic difference between them is not so much external as internal and religious. The hero puts himself in the role of Providence, and by this spiritual usurpation he assigns himself a responsibility greater than he can bear and tasks that are beyond the reach of men. The Christian ascetic [by contrast] believes in God the Provider, without Whose will not a hair falls from the head. In his eyes both history and a single human life are a realization of God's plan, and even though he does not comprehend it in its individual details he humbles himself before it in an act of faith."[29] Instead of posturing before the world or giving himself over to the delusion of being his country or the world's savior, the ascetic "concentrates his attention on his true task, his real obligations, and their strict, absolute fulfilment"; the focus of his moral life becomes the "recognition of personal duty and its fulfilment" and "self-control." Rather than heroic self-aggrandizement, the mark of his presence in the world is humility.

Whether Bulgakov had a particular example of Christian asceticism in mind, he did not say. Perhaps it was Fr Zosima, the famous literary image of an Orthodox *starets* in Dostoevsky's *Brothers Karamazov*; perhaps it was the nineteenth-century hermits, Serafim of Sarov and Ambrosi of Optina, on whom Dostoevsky had based his character. But of this "ascetic" principle in Russian culture, Bulgakov made Russia's

---

[28] Ibid., 26.   [29] Ibid., 34.

patron, the thirteenth-century monastic founder St Sergei Radonezh, the symbol. Did it help prepare him for the discovery of the theocratic principle on the Yalta Embankment a year later? Certainly, *Vekhi* reveals Bulgakov as a man sick to the stomach with atheism, athirst for the alternative spiritual sources of a healthier politics. But striking, too, from our perspective, is how well the ascetic ideal Bulgakov explores in "Heroism and asceticism" functions as a description of what we have glimpsed of the inner life of Nicholas II.

Thus, in "Heroism and asceticism," Bulgakov praises the ascetic who, like Nicholas, trusted in God implicitly even though he had not been present three years earlier at Peterhof to hear the tsar declare to Izvolsky his "firm . . . absolute belief that the fate of Russia, my own fate and that of my family is in the hands of God, Who has placed me where I am. Whatever happens, I will bend before His will, with the consciousness of never having had any other thought than to serve the country He has confided me." Similarly, Bulgakov praises the ascetic who, like Nicholas, humbled himself before God, even though he never enjoyed the daily access to the tsar that would see an aide-de-camp testify of Nicholas's moral outlook (in a striking coincidence of allusions with Bulgakov's essay) that nothing "could shake his belief in the Lord or his conviction that 'not a single hair falls from one's head unless it is the will of the Most High God' (Lk 21:18)."[30] And yet on the Yalta Embankment Bulgakov seems to have been able to read these virtues in Nicholas's very bearing.

If all this makes sense, it is because, of course, the ascetic and the theocratic principles were — or ought to have been — intertwined in Russian culture, inasmuch as both flowed from Orthodoxy. As Rowan Williams, spotting the connection between Bulgakov's *Vekhi* contribution in 1908 and his vision on the Yalta Embankment a year later, has it, "what Bulgakov finds morally and spiritually compelling about the image of royal authority (and the reality of the monarchy in Russia in 1907 and the years following) could almost be characterized as its anti-heroic quality: Nicholas II is not the doer of great deeds, the self-conscious savior of the nation, but someone bearing what is laid upon him, like the monk bearing the duty or the penance imposed by a superior."[31] The truth of this remark resonates with what we have seen of Nicholas's interior. So much so, perhaps, that, if Bulgakov is right and true asceticism "consists in faithfully fulfilling one's duty, in bearing one's own cross in self-renunciation (not just outward but still more inward) and in leaving all the rest to Providence," then, in a secularizing revolution driven by

---

[30] Semyon S. Fabritsky, *Of Bygone Days: The memoirs of an aide-de-camp to the Emperor Nicholas II*, trans. William Lee (Bowmanville, Ontario: Gilbert's Books, 2016), 55.

[31] Williams, *Sergii Bulgakov*, 61.

atheism, and abounding, therefore, in deluded "heroes," Nicholas II was the hidden ascetic that Bulgakov was looking for—and perhaps, as the Russian Church has now proclaimed, even then a *saint*.[32]

 measure   measure   measure

But where did the "new Russia" leave the theocratic ideal? For all they shared with the new Russia, Russia's last monarch and his consort sat at a tangent to it, in that they did not share its secularization. On the contrary. During these same years, Nicholas and Alexandra, having overcome, in the way we shall see, the Gnostic temptation emblematized in Philippe, became ever more deeply Orthodox, and the symbol of this journey into Orthodoxy was the Fyodorovsky Gosudariev Sobor (or the Imperial Cathedral under the protection of Our Lady of Fyodorov), a church the couple built for themselves in the Alexander Palace park.

Set on the lip of an artificial oxbow lake, the cathedral is the "jewel" of the palace park. A triple-apsed building washed in white with blue corbelling, a green tented roof and a single, bulbous onion dome that glinted gold in the soft autumn sunshine of my visit, the cathedral was modeled on two masterpieces of medieval Russian ecclesiastical architecture: the 1489 Cathedral of the Annunciation in the Moscow Kremlin, and the 1198 Church of the Intercession on the Nerl outside the provincial town of Vladimir, north of Moscow.

Constructed between 1909 and 1912, as the regimental church for His Majesty's Consolidated Infantry and His Majesty's Own Convoy (the Cossacks), regiments stationed at Tsarskoye Selo for the protection of the imperial family, the Fyodorov Imperial Cathedral was, in reality, the family's private church. Entering through a specially constructed side entrance, in the form of a tented staircase embellished with gilded griffins (the Romanovs' dynastic symbol) and double-headed eagles (the Russian imperial arms), the family used to join the men for the Divine Liturgy here on Sundays, the infantry standing to the left, the Cossacks to the right, and the imperial family in a designated area of their own on the same side as the Cossacks.[33] But like so many of the other Russian Style churches erected during the last reign, the Cathedral was slowly erased from the landscape after the Revolution. In the 1930s, the building was turned into a cinema and storage depot for Soviet newsreels. During the Second World War, the roof collapsed, and its decorative scheme was destroyed. When communism itself collapsed in the 1990s, all that remained were bare walls overgrown with weeds.

Present both at the laying of the Cathedral's foundation stone in 1909 and at its consecration in 1912, Nicholas and Alexandra loved the

---

[32] Bulgakov, "Heroism and asceticism," 38–39.
[33] Spiridovitch, *Dernières Années*, 2:253–63. The foundation stone had been laid in 1909: 1:352–53.

original building dearly. "How good it is to pray in the Fyodorov with Cossacks and soldiers!" Nicholas confided in his diary.[34] Indeed, they had been so heavily involved in the cathedral's design and decoration that to say it was the rendering in bricks and mortar of Nicholas and Alexandra's inner worlds would not be incorrect. Every element of the building reflected that synthesis of dogma, mysticism, and folk religion that their souls had attained in the first decade of the twentieth century, and maintained up to and beyond the outbreak of the Great War. Especially dear to them was the crypt church beneath the main building dedicated to St Serafim of Sarov, the family's special patron. Here, the family prepared for communion and made their confessions. Alexandra, particularly, spent hours in prayer here in the flickering candlelight. But Nicholas frequently repaired to it for prayer, too. Indeed, in the summer of 1915, when Russian military fortunes were at their lowest, it was while at prayer here that Nicholas resolved to assume supreme command of the Russian Army.[35]

かな　かな　かな

It was a Sunday morning, and I had come for the Divine Liturgy at the restored Cathedral. The morning sky was clear, a luminescent white that couldn't yet be called blue, and above the gates at the end of the drive, a pair of gilded, double-headed eagles glinted softly. It might as well have been 1916. It was still early. Rather than going immediately inside, I walked anti-clockwise around the building. Where, only twenty-odd years ago, looting, neglect and war damage had left behind a shattered, roofless shell, today the cathedral's original decorative scheme has been restored, and, on the chaste whitewashed background of the northern wall, the first thing that greeted me was a mosaic in bold white, green, and blue tesserae, showing an old man with a white beard and stooped profile in a forest. It was St Serafim of Sarov.

If there was an event, still more a *person*, who both sealed and went on to symbolize Nicholas and Alexandra's overcoming of the occult temptation represented in Philippe, it was St Serafim, and the canonization festivities held in his honor in Sarov in 1903. Nicholas and Alexandra never "met" Serafim, who died long before either of them was born, but the place he occupied in their spiritual itineraries can't be underestimated: the most treasured relic the Fyorodov Cathedral housed was a piece of the simple, hand-carved wooden coffin in which the hermit had been laid upon his death in 1833. After the cathedral's consecration in 1912, Alexandra poured out her prayers before it almost daily.

---

[34] Cited in the official visitor's guide: *Feodorovskii Gosudariev Sobor v Tsarskom Sele* (St Petersburg: St Petersburg Eparchy, Russian Orthodox Church-Moscow Patriarchate), 10.
[35] As noted by Mark Steinberg, *Fall of the Romanovs: Politics and personal dreams in a time of revolution* (New Haven, CT: Yale University Press, 1995), 16.

Born in 1759 in the town of Kursk, the son of a wealthy provincial merchant and his wife, Serafim was one of the great spiritual figures of Russia's nineteenth century—and after his canonization (at Nicholas and Alexandra's insistence) in 1903, one of the great saints of Eastern Orthodox Christianity. A renowned hermit and seer, Serafim played a major role in reviving both the practice of hesychasm (the pursuit of union with God through the acquisition of the Holy Spirit by unceasing prayer) and the ideal of the *starets* or spiritual elder associated with it.[36] Seeking God, and obeying an instruction he had received from the Virgin Mary, Serafim lived for sixteen years alone in the forest in a state of constant prayer. He had visions and performed miracles. Eventually, returning to a monastery, Serafim took a vow of silence. For six years he said not a word to anyone, even visiting bishops. Only in 1813 was his silence broken, by a vision of Mary, who instructed Serafim to become a *starets* or elder: that is, a spiritual guide or director. By the 1820s, as many as two thousand people would come every day to seek blessings and spiritual counsels. He died in 1833.

According to the great twentieth-century Russian Church historian Georges Florovsky, Serafim was a "prophetic figure" who embodied a "certain inner and mysterious movement in the destiny of the Russian Church . . . Ascetic struggle and joy, the burden of battle in prayer and heavenly ethereality, the prefiguration of an unworldly light, marvelously combined to fashion this figure . . . his being, his whole life are manifestations of the Spirit."[37] Before Serafim, elite culture and the Orthodox Church were disconnected in Russia; after him, they drew closer together. With Serafim, true Christian mysticism revived at precisely that time when, in the works of Pushkin and Lermontov, Gogol and Glinka, Russian culture entered its "Golden Age." Indeed, the Russian nineteenth century would have been as unthinkable without Serafim, and the Russian spiritual revival he symbolized and helped set in motion, as it would have been without any of the better-known figures already named. In Fyodor Dostoevsky's *Brothers Karamazov*, that revival found its most famous literary embodiment in the figure of the hesychast *starets* Father Zosima.[38] Not least through Dostoevsky, Russia's nineteenth-century Orthodox revival made possible the conversion of those members of Russia's Silver Age intelligentsia, such as Bulgakov, who returned from Marxism via Solovyov to the Church.[39] At the deepest roots of that spiritual development that enabled Bulgakov to rediscover the theocratic ideal on the Yalta Embankment was Serafim (the real monk-ascetic of Bulgakov's essay in *Vekhi*).

---

[36] Florovsky, *Ways of Russian Theology*, in *Collected Works*, 6:156–61.
[37] Ibid., 164.   [38] Billington, *Icon and the Axe*, 203.
[39] Bulgakov made this debt to Dostoevsky clear in *Vekhi*: "Heroism and asceticism," 19.

Nicholas and Alexandra did not go untouched by this spiritual *ressourcement* of Russian culture, emblematized in Serafim. On the contrary. At a time when most Orthodox laity received Holy Communion perhaps no more than once a year, Serafim was a proponent of the benefits of frequent reception. "For the gift of Holy Communion is so great that even though a person be sinful, [yet] he may with humility and awareness of his sinfulness . . . approach the Lord who has redeemed us all," Serafim said.[40] The cause became Alexandra's too. Indeed, when we see the significance in Nicholas and Alexandra's lives of Holy Communion, and the increasingly vocalized store and comfort they put by it, we should think of Serafim. Above all, Nicholas and Alexandra believed they owed their son to Serafim; in this way, as we shall see, Serafim prepared the way for Rasputin, too.

In a mysterious way, Serafim "owed" his very canonization to the exercise of the theocratic rights of the emperor (in the sense that, apart from the tsar, the bishops might forever have resisted performing it). A popular movement for Serafim's canonization, unsupported by Russia's bishops, had existed almost since the day after the saint's death in 1833.[41] By the turn of the century, this was a well-organized operation, headed by the arch-conservative, religious-nationalist publicist, Sergei Nilus, who also happened to be the chief popularizer in Russia of that lamentable forgery of the Russian secret police, the so-called *Protocols of the Elders of Zion* (with its program for a Jewish-controlled world government).[42] In 1902, Nilus's movement for Serafim's canonization secured an official investigation into, and subsequent authentication of, Serafim's miracles by the Holy Synod. Though this should have sufficed to obtain Serafim's canonization, still the Holy Synod resisted, fearful as it was of the uncontrollable expressions of popular piety it might encourage. In the end, Nicholas had to order Russia's bishops to canonize Serafim — and he did so, in a twist that seems to defy explanation by any who have treated the subject, on the advice of Philippe, who (involved as he allegedly was in the campaign for the Catholic Church's canonization of Joan of Arc) apparently saw in Serafim, a Russian counterpart, a symbol of the national spirit, around which opponents of modernity could rally.[43] Indeed, when Nicholas dismissed Philippe, Philippe had counseled

---

[40] Helen Kontzevich, *Saint Seraphim, Wonderworker of Sarov and His Spiritual Inheritance* (Saint Xenia Skete, 2004), 29.

[41] See Richard Price, "The canonization of Serafim of Sarov: piety, prophecy and politics in late imperial Russia," in Andrew Louth, ed., *Studies in Church History 47: Saints and Sanctity* (Cambridge: Cambridge University Press, 2011), 346–64.

[42] On the forgery of the *Protocols* by the Okhrana's foreign division, and Nilus's role in the dissemination of them in Russia, see Norman Cohn, *Warrant for Genocide: The myth of the Jewish World-Conspiracy and the Protocols of the Elders of Zion* (New York: Harper and Row, 1967), 77–107.

[43] So Wortman, *Scenarios*, 356, which describes Philippe as an "active figure in conservative nationalist circles in France, and a champion of the canonization of Joan of

Alexandra, who still desperately wanted a son, to go to Sarov and bathe in the miraculous spring by Serafim's hermitage. A son would be born to her if she did this, he promised.[44] In any case, the Synod, having acquiesced in Nicholas's demand that Serafim be canonized, scheduled the ceremonies for July 1903 at Sarov.

Known as the "Sarov celebrations," Serafim's canonization was one of the great national festivals of late imperial Russia, as well as a watershed, as we shall argue, in the life of Nicholas II. Accompanied by government ministers and a large delegation of Romanov family members (including Alexandra's elder sister, the Grand Duchess Ella), Nicholas and Alexandra arrived in Sarov on July 17. Three hundred thousand pilgrims, mostly peasants, had preceded them. "It was a wonderful spectacle," recalled the court official Mossolov, who had traveled with Nicholas and Alexandra and the rest of the imperial party. "The crowds, in their Sunday best, greeted the Tsar as he passed with enthusiasm," while Nicholas, he said, returned the crowd's cheers with "short sentences full of good nature."[45] To Nicholas, the enthusiasm of the crowds at Sarov would confirm his perception that Russia was, fundamentally, a moral, and, indeed, a spiritual community united by Orthodoxy, while the role he was given to play in Sarov's various religious ceremonies would renew his existing understanding of his office as tsar as an inherently sacred and theocratic one. Above all, Sarov would redirect his internal spiritual compass away from the esoteric, para-ecclesial mysticism of Philippe, and back towards the historical, mystical-dogmatic Church Orthodoxy in which he had been raised and called to his office.

Almost from the start, it seems, Nicholas felt the hand of God. "At six o'clock we arrived at the Sarov monastery," Nicholas wrote. "There was something very special about going into the Cathedral of the Assumption and then into the Church of St Zosima and St Savatty, where we were able to pray to the relics of the holy father Serafim."[46] The following day, July 18, began, as Nicholas noted in his diary, with "the last solemn requiem for the *starets* Serafim," as Nicholas put it in his diary.[47] This requiem represented the last time the Church would petition God on Serafim's behalf as a common believer fallen asleep in the faith; after his

---

Arc," who "brought the example of French religious nationalism to the attention of the imperial family." According to Cohn, however, the religious-nationalist Nilus, who naively believed the Protocols were authentic, was inveigled by the head of the Okhrana's foreign division, Pyotr Rachkovsky, into Nicholas and Alexandra's acquaintance precisely in order to *displace* Philippe, whom Rachkovsky had identified as an undesirable French freemason: *Warrant*, 84–87. Of the two accounts, Cohn's sounds the more plausible. But then how to explain the encouragement Philippe gave to Serafim's canonization? Douglas Smith, the most recent scholar to have investigated Philippe's career in Russia, mentions Nilus in a vein that supports Cohn's account, but sheds no additional light on the mystery: *Rasputin*, 67.

[44] Freeze, "Religion and politics."   [45] Mossolov, *At the Court*, 133.
[46] Maylunas and Mironenko, *Lifelong Passion*, 218.   [47] Ibid., 219.

canonization, scheduled for later that evening, Serafim would be addressed instead as a saint capable of interceding before God in heaven on behalf of the Church here below. In the interval between these two ceremonies, Nicholas walked the two and a half miles through the forest to Serafim's cell. Then, returning to Sarov for the canonization liturgy, Nicholas assumed a role at the very center of the celebrations, as the bearer, along with three other members of the imperial family, of Serafim's sacred bodily relics. When the liturgy entered its fourth hour, the imperial party left the church building for refreshments, before attempting to return for the final part of the service. But the crowd was so thick with pilgrims that no path could be made through it, not even for the tsar. And having become a pilgrim like all the others, Nicholas did not insist on one being made. Through the Orthodox Church, the invisible wall that had always separated the monarch from Russia's common people had been overcome.

In the records Nicholas made before going to bed during these days, we can almost glimpse how, by degrees, the Sarov events reoriented his gaze towards the God not of Philippe (who is not mentioned in Nicholas's diary) but Serafim. "During the procession, when the relics were brought out of the church ... we carried the coffin on a litter. It was an incredible spectacle, to see how the crowd and especially the invalids, cripples, and unfortunates reacted to the holy procession. It was a very solemn moment when the glorification began and the kissing of the casket," he recalled before going to bed on the evening of the first day after he had borne Serafim's body.[48] The effect on him was strengthened the following day, when celebrations continued with another liturgy, which culminated this time in the exposure of Serafim's relics (his bones) to the crowd. More and more, it would seem, the disposition of Nicholas's heart was indistinguishable from that of any other pilgrim. "The holy procession was as moving as yesterday's," he wrote in his diary: "One felt an enormous lift, both from the event itself and the extraordinary mood of the crowd."[49] He was at one with the Orthodox faith and with Russia's faithful people. "God is miraculous in his saints! ... Great is his mercy towards dear Russia ... let us put our hope in the Lord for ever and ever," he wrote in his diary.[50] Everything Nicholas encountered strengthened in him his belief in the vitality of both Orthodoxy and the theocratic principle.

On the other hand, Philippe's instructions were not forgotten. Like thousands of other pilgrims on that final evening, Nicholas and Alexandra, along with other members of the imperial party (including Ella and Nicholas's sister Olga) went "in twos and threes" and "in the darkness [so] no one recognized us" and bathed in the spring where Mary had

---

[48] Ibid.   [49] Ibid.   [50] Ibid.

struck her staff for Serafim—which if she did, as we have seen, Philippe had promised that Alexandra would conceive a son.[51] Of course, they were not the only ones looking for a miracle, far from it. As Nicholas wrote solemnly in his diary later that evening, "We have heard of many people being cured today and yesterday." Would they be among them? Miraculously, in the event, they were: four months later Alexandra was pregnant with Alexei.

What is remarkable is how the couple appear to have interpreted this event. While this apparent miracle—"proof" of Philippe's credentials as a seer—might have confirmed Nicholas and Alexandra in the path of Gnostic temptation they seem to have been on, in fact (through the miraculous intercession of St Serafim himself, perhaps) it did not. Nicholas and Alexandra would always attribute the boy's conception not to Philippe but to Serafim. Indeed, it would seem that in 1903 their decision for Church Orthodoxy had been made: after the Sarov celebrations and the birth of Alexei, the temptation of the untethered, esoteric "spiritism" of the years 1901–2, associated with Philippe, was overcome. Others have observed how Alexandra's interest in Indian and Persian religions, evident in her spiritual diaries at the turn of the century, gave way thereafter to citations from the ancient Greek and Syrian Church Fathers—that is to say, to a wholly Orthodox spirituality founded ultimately on the *Philokalia*. St Isaac of Nineveh was a favorite. "The Empress was now more Russian than most Russians, more Orthodox than most Orthodox," said her friend and lady-in-waiting, Lili Dehn: "She was intensely religious. Her love of God and her belief in his mercy came before her love of her husband and her children, and she found her greatest happiness in religion at a time when she was surrounded by the panoply of Imperial splendor."[52] Dehn had experienced this intensity at first hand. In 1908, a year before the laying of the foundation stone of the Fyodorov Sovereign Cathedral, Dehn gave birth to her first child. Learning of its birth, Alexandra presented it with a pair of icons and expressed her wish to be the child's godmother. (One would wish to know whether one of them was an image of Serafim.) But although Dehn herself had been born and bred Orthodox, she had married a noble Russian officer of Swedish background, and to inherit certain family monies the child had to be baptized Lutheran. How much this fact pained the child's godmother, Dehn discovered on the child's seventh birthday. "The Empress told me that her dearest wish was that 'Titi' (as she called him) should be received into the Greek Church. 'It is more than a wish, Lili,' she said earnestly," Dehn recalled Alexandra telling her, "'it is a command. I insist upon my godson being Orthodox.'"[53]

There was a political dimension to this, too. The whole event at

---

[51] Ibid.   [52] Dehn, *Real Tsaritsa*, 54.   [53] Ibid.

Sarov had rehearsed the idea of Russia as a believing *teokratia*, united in a Church defended by her anointed tsar. Indeed, for Nicholas, the Sarov celebrations were, after his coronation, his own vision on the Yalta Embankment, when the meaning of the theocratic principle for Russian culture was again vouchsafed to him. It was significant in the same way for Alexandra, too, who, always looking at Russia "through the prism of Sarov," in the words of a lady-in-waiting, came to believe deeply "in the religious significance of autocracy... in the bonds of responsibility and affection that tied an Orthodox Tsar both to God and the Russian people."[54] When, bedridden years later, she protested, in a heated argument with Nicholas's cousin Sandro at the beginning of the revolutionary year 1917, "All this talk is ridiculous!... Nicky is an autocrat. How could he share his divine rights with a parliament?," it was *also* Sarov that Alexandra was thinking of.[55] Even Mossolov, a court official of significantly more secular outlook, who struggled, as we have seen, to comprehend the imperial couple's "mysticism," would later affirm, after what he had seen at Serafim's canonization, that he would "never cease to declare that the Sarov incidents are manifest evidence that the Bolsheviks are wrong when they claim that the people never manifested any other sentiments towards the dynasty than those of envy and hatred."[56]

❧ ❧ ❧

It has been said that "idea of the holy city as an ordering reality is essential in order to affirm the reality of the sacred."[57] If this is true, then it is a principle that the aesthetics of Russia's contemporary Orthodox revival constantly underlines in connection with the last Romanovs. So, from the steps where I had seen the mosaic of Serafim, I continued around the western wall of the Cathedral while the rising sun turned the eastern sky a shade of pale blue. Above a triple-arched Romanesque-style doorway carved with the quasi-Celtic motifs of medieval Suzdalia is a grand representation of the fallen Romanov dynasty's palladium, the so-called "Fyodorov" Mother of God, an icon of Mary under whose protection the dynasty's founder, Mikhail, accepted the Russian throne in 1613, and in whose honor Nicholas and Alexandra's cathedral was consecrated, three hundred years later, in 1913. Restored now, a mosaic of the Virgin and Child venerated by archangels, priests, kings (tsars), and queens (tsaritsas) stretches fifteen feet to the corbel, the figures' haloes shimmering faintly in the dull light on this side of the building. Serving as a backdrop to this scene are the golden domes of a holy city ("an ordering reality... that affirms the reality of the sacred") that could be Jerusalem, Constantinople, or Moscow, but which is, ultimately, as the Psalmist has it, the "city

---

[54] Lieven, *Nicholas II*, 164, quoting Kireev.
[55] King, *Last Empress*, 278.   [56] Mossolov, *At the Court*, 135–36.
[57] Del Noce, "The Death of the Sacred," in *Crisis of Modernity*, 118–19.

of the great King" whose "towers," "ramparts" and "citadels" proclaim from generation to generation that "this is God, our God for ever and ever" (Ps. 48:1–2, 12–14).

By now, parishioners were beginning to arrive, and as I stood watching, half a dozen people approached the mosaic on the western wall, bowed reverently, and crossed themselves before entering the church. As for myself, as I continued around the building and picked my way through the wet leaves and molehills that studded a lawn on its southern side, a splendid scene came into view: the profile of the cathedral with its narrow, "arrow-slit" windows and tented, tunnel-like side entrance, roofed in green and adorned with a mosaic of St George, Moscow's (and Russia's) patron saint. On the southeastern corner, a tented doorway, its roof painted blue to distinguish it from the others, indicated the imperial family's private side entrance to the church, its carved griffins and gilded, double-headed eagles restored as if expecting Nicholas and Alexandra's arrival any minute from the Alexander Palace, while, on the rear apse wall, a mosaic of Christ the Pantokrator seated on a golden throne, watched over all. In the other direction, a small grove of oak trees, their leaves seasonal shades of amber, stood in the middle of the lawn. Mounted on a plinth in the middle was the first monument erected in honor of Nicholas II after the fall of Communism, and one of the largest bronze busts of the Russian monarch that I had yet seen — four feet high, from the middle of Nicholas's chest to the top of his head. "The Holy Passion-bearer Tsar Nicholas," read the plaque.

At that point, the bells of the cathedral began to ring in their urgent, Russian manner — not the cascading peal of English church bells, or the low metronome of the Catholic angelus, but an a-melodic tingle, somewhat like the sound of a large xylophone. I left Nicholas's monument and the amber oaks, and wandered back towards the restored cathedral. Just inside the door at the top of the small flight of steps, watched over by Serafim, an icon of Nicholas and Alexandra as saints greets the visitor. Dressed in medieval Russian costume, the pair look up to heaven, while between them, in the middle of the icon, is a representation of the building I had just entered, the Fyodorov Sovereign Cathedral. In an iconographical convention going back to the Middle Ages, the couple present "their" church to God. Meanwhile, among the parish notices on the other side of the narthex, a sign advertised the existence of the "Tsarevich Alexei Sunday School," notifying parents of the time they are to deliver their children. Nicholas and Alexandra might have last visited the building days before the outbreak of the Revolution. But as saints they have very much returned as living presences to it.

I pushed through a second, heavy wooden door. The interior I discovered on the other side was without question one of the loveliest I had seen anywhere in Russia. A high, light-filled space, marked out by four great pillars decorated in a stylized floral pattern in white, royal blue, and red that is a distant, now wholly Russified, echo of the British Arts and Craft Movement that found expression in Nicholas and Alexandra's Winter Palace flat. Each pillar culminated in a capital painted with a yellow double-headed eagle on a blue background. Together, each pair of pillars supported an arch, also painted blue with a white scallop motif, and, in the center, naïve, early Christian-style, Greek crosses. Rising above the whole was the dome. But where I was expecting to find Christ the Pantokrator, I found instead, to my surprise, an image I had never seen before — or elsewhere since: a Christ Child seated on the lap of a bearded figure that, in contravention of a longstanding tradition in the Russian Church, can only be God the Father, His arms raised, against a blue sky dotted with stars.[58] On the eastern side, screening the altar from sight, a five-tiered iconostasis reaches all the way to heaven, its holy figures standing out against a background of rich gold leaf that at once intensified and radiated the golden light of the candles burning in front of its lowest tier.

Holy Communion — the reception of Christ's Body and Blood in the Eucharist — wasn't the only sacrament people had come for. Or, rather, a condition (along with fasting for up to four days) for receiving Communion was prior participation in the sacrament of confession.[59] Thus, behind the pillars on the far side of the church, a priest with a grey goatee in black cassock stood beside a small lectern holding the Gospel, hearing confessions. The Orthodox do not use confessionals as Roman Catholics do. Instead, the whole sacrament is performed as it were in public: the faithful approach, kiss the Bible in the priest's hands, and then whisper their sins in his ear, as, invariably, he leans down to hear them, the ringing of the church bells or the chanting of the liturgy providing such privacy as circumstances afford. As each penitent finishes, the priest covers his or her bowed head with a stole and, making the sign of the cross in the name of the Father, Son and Holy Spirit, absolves him of his sins.[60] A penance can be, but is not usually, imposed. When at ten o'clock the liturgy began in the Fyodorov Sovereign Cathedral, a queue of perhaps fifteen people stood waiting to receive this sacrament.

In all, perhaps forty people were in the building. But it is neither Russian nor Orthodox to be "at church" when the service starts. A grace period of almost an hour extends up to the conclusion of the

---

[58] On images of God the Father, banned at the 1666 Council of Moscow, see Ouspensky, *Theology of the Icon*, 2:371–409, which notes that despite the Council's ban, images of the "Paternity" continued to be painted and venerated in Russia.
[59] On the sacrament of confession in the Orthodox Church, see John Meyendorff, *Byzantine Theology*, 195–96; also, Ware, *Orthodox Church*, 288–90.
[60] In the Russian tradition, as opposed to the Greek, the Latin/Western-style *ego absolvo* formula is used: Ware, *Orthodox Church*, 289.

Great Litany, at least, and over the course of this time I watched as worshipers continued to arrive: middle-aged women in kerchiefs, the aged and invalid on walking sticks, but also pious-looking young families (with three, four, five or six children) and well-dressed singles of both sexes in their twenties and thirties. There being no pews (and no service or hymn books), people took up position on a part of the floor that suited them and their circumstances, the youngest children playing invented games among themselves at the back. Many adults joined the queue for confession, which the priest continued to hear right up until the distribution of the Eucharist. Before long, the queue was thirty or forty people long. Others, having bought two or three slender, beeswax candles from the shop to the side of the nave, went in search of the icons of favorite saints to venerate with a bow, a sign of the cross, and the lighting of one of the candles.

Known as the "Divine Liturgy of St John Chrysostom," the Orthodox "Mass," or Eucharistic service, is not said, but sung, in the somewhat modernized (and Russified) version of Old Church Slavonic that the Russian Church inherited from the "apostles to the Slavs," Saints Cyril and Methodius, who translated the Byzantine liturgy into a Bulgarian dialect in the early ninth century. [61] It is a truism that Orthodoxy cannot be seized apart from this liturgy, the public Sacrifice of thanksgiving — Eucharist — offered by the Church for, and on behalf of, the whole world. [62] Rather than being studied in books as an abstract theological proposition, God for the Orthodox is to be worshipped, met, known, and His divine Life personally assimilated in this Divine Liturgy, an ordered and orderly form of worship that crosses the boundary between heaven and earth, the created and the uncreated, inasmuch as the bread and wine offered by the people gathered as the "type" of Christ's humanity verily become, through the descent upon them of God the Holy Spirit, the true, deified human Body and Blood of God Himself. [63] Everything else that derives from this central Mystery — the contents of theological

---

[61] Dmitri Obolensky, *The Byzantine Commonwealth: Eastern Europe, 500–1453* (London: Weidenfeld and Nicholson, 1971), 131. For the text of the liturgy, I have used the Slavonic-English version published by Fr Sergei Sveshnikov of the Russian Orthodox Church Outside Russia and blessed by the Archbishop of San Francisco and Western America: https://frsergei.wordpress.com/wp-content/uploads/2013/04/master-dob1dobedob6dob5 d181d182dob2dob5dobddobddobod18f-dobbdob8d182d183d18odob3dob8d18f-slav-eng.pdf. For the structure and texts of the liturgy, I have also used the very helpful guide by Fr Jon Magoulias, *The Divine Liturgy of St John Chrysostom* (n. p.: Petersen Books, 2021).
[62] On the "for the world" nature of the Liturgy, see Alexander Schmemann, *For the Life of the World: Sacraments and Orthodoxy* (Crestwood, NY: St Vladimir's Seminary Press, 1973), 11–22, although the interpretation of the Liturgy given here as a ritual for the *reception of a king* is in many ways quite different from Schmemann's "pilgrimage of the People of God" approach: ibid., 23–46 and especially 26.
[63] Meyendorff, *Byzantine Theology*, 205–6; on the believer's need to assimilate (in the sense of "becoming consubstantial with") the deified humanity of Christ through the Eucharist, see Lossky, *Mystical Theology*, 181–82.

manuals and philosophical treatises — is mere knowledge "about" God, and of doubtful value. For the uncreated God, even after He has been "eaten" in the Body and Blood of Christ, ever remains, for the Orthodox, not only unknown but *unknowable* — a Being-beyond-being Who is absolutely outside the capacity of created human reason to comprehend, and Who can never be reduced to its categories or images (each of which, in fact, including *that of the king*, which, as we shall see, the Liturgy of St John Chrysostom constantly holds before the eyes of the faithful, must be renounced before the experience of true, interior, and super-rational knowledge of God is possible).[64]

Obeying its own time, the Liturgy was leisurely, unrushed, even slow. Among the first to arrive, I heard the choir chant the six psalms that constitute the service of Matins that is offered as an act of preparation. Close to an hour after I had entered the building, then, the Divine Liturgy proper began, with the singing of the so-called Great Doxology and Great Litany, a sequence of intercessions imploring God's mercy on myriad aspects of human life — from forgiveness of sins and the well-being of the Church, the political community and its leaders (including, of course, once upon a time, God's anointed, the tsar), to the weather, those traveling, the suffering and those in prison. During this time, the congregation's primary task, it seemed to me, was to attend to these litanies, bowing and making the sign of the cross every time the ornate, high-pitched voices of the mostly female choir intoned, "Gospodi, pomilui!" ("Lord, have mercy!") Impossible to squeeze into a morning like a duty to be ticked off on the day's list of things to do, the Liturgy, rather, absorbs the individual to-do lists of those in attendance into itself, creating a new temporal reality that, as the icons, the candles, and the incense manifest, is neither quite of this world nor of the next — but really of both at the same time. Although the gathered laity cannot hear him pray it, the prayer prayed by the priest at the culmination of this Litany perfectly captures not only the "atmosphere" or "spirit" but the very substance of the experience so produced: "Standing in the Temple of Your glory, we feel as though we are in heaven...!"

At the conclusion of the Great Litany, the so-called Prayer of the Little Entrance heralded the arrival of the clergy bearing the Holy Scriptures. Thus, proceeded by acolytes carrying glowing candles and swinging smoking censers, the priest, clad in brilliant gold and black chasubles, appeared through the smaller doors on the left side of the iconostasis facing the altar. Held up for all to see in his hands were the Scriptures. Proceeding to the center of the church in front of the Royal Doors in the middle of the iconostasis, he held the Scriptures higher and said a blessing in the direction of the altar. When he had finished, the people responded

---

[64] Ware, *Orthodox Way*, 14; and, perhaps supremely, Lossky, *Mystical Theology*, 23–45.

with one of the great hymns of the Eastern Church, the Trisagion or "Thrice Holy" ("Holy God, Holy Mighty, Holy Immortal, have mercy on us!") Then, from the ambon or lectern in front of the Royal Doors, the priest intoned the day's readings — the thirteenth chapter of St Paul's First Epistle to the Corinthians ("Love is patient and kind . . . "); and a passage from the sixth chapter of the Gospel of St Luke (the so-called "Sermon on the Plain"), which culminated in Jesus's famous exhortation, "Love your enemies . . . " (Lk 6:27). With these readings the first part of the Liturgy — the so-called Liturgy of the Catechumens — was completed, and while the choir, accompanied by some of the people gathered, continued to sing, the priest and acolytes made their way back behind the icon screen to the altar, where they would prepare and then offer the Gifts that would become the Body and Blood.

In its origins, the Liturgy of St John Chrysostom probably goes back to Syria. But before its export to Russia and translation into Slavonic, it was for centuries the liturgy of the Great Church (Hagia Sophia) of Constantinople, the imperial city, and, as such, greatly developed and expanded there.[65] Of course, with Hagia Sophia being, as it was, the "parish church" of the emperor, it should not surprise us that the Divine Liturgy in its current form should appear deeply impressed with the terms and images of kingship. Not only do parts of the Liturgy even owe their existence to the emperor's hand, such the great "Hymn of the Only-begotten" (which identifies the human Christ that "trampled down death by death" on the Cross as truly "Immortal God" and "One of the Holy Trinity"), composed by (St) Justinian in the sixth century.[66] The Constantinopolitan origins of the Liturgy of St Chrysostom would seem also to be manifest in its apparently fundamental intuition that the very ruling power of the emperor — and the court ceremonial developed at Constantinople to magnify it — was somehow willed by God as a certain image and representation of His own, far more glorious kingship, such that the whole Liturgy can be conceived, in a way, as a service of advent to mark the arrival of a King far greater than the emperor — the ceremonial of whose court was only ever a poor copy of the worship of God offered by the angels in the court of Heaven — Who is first named, supplicated and glorified by His servants before arriving in the very Flesh to impart to them the surpassing gift of Himself in the Eucharist.

---

[65] For the outlines of this development, see Hans-Joachim Schulz, *The Byzantine Liturgy: Symbolic structure and faith expression*, trans. Matthew J. O'Connell (New York: Pueblo, 1986), especially, 29–33, which (without speculating as I do about the direct influence of imperial court ceremonial on the current shape of the Divine Liturgy) gives special importance to the reign of Justinian (527–65), which coincided with the publication of the writings of Pseudo-Dionysius the Areopagite, the maturation of the Byzantine theocratic ideal, and the construction of Hagia Sophia as, in part, an expression of both the preceding. Also useful is Hugh Wybrew, *The Orthodox Liturgy: The development of the Eucharistic Liturgy in the Byzantine rite* (Crestwood, NY: St Vladimir's Seminary Press, 1990).

[66] Schulz, *Byzantine Liturgy*, 30.

To this intuition, the Liturgy's language and imagery would bear witness. Thus, the Great Litany, keeping one eye, as it were, on the emperor and earthly empire, and the other on the Great King of Kings Whose coming the people gathered are preparing, reminds the people that, not the emperor's but truly God's are the "Dominion, the Kingdom and the Power," while Little Entrance, which we have just described, begins with the priest supplicating the same God as "Master" and "Lord, Our God" Who, having appointed "in the heaven the ranks and hosts of Angels and Archangels," comes not only arrayed in a majesty that would outshine that of any earthly king, but in command of powers and forces that should make him tremble. And as the arrival of this Almighty One (Who is at once Three) approaches, the Liturgy grows, as it were, more urgent in its supplications. Thus, the priest, preparing to consecrate the bread and wine as the Body and Blood of this Great King, acknowledges that "none is worthy among them that are bound with carnal lusts and pleasures, to approach or to draw nigh, or to minister unto Thee, O King of glory, for to serve Thee is a great and fearful thing even unto the heavenly hosts themselves . . . for Thou alone, O Lord our God, dost rule over those in heaven and those on earth, art borne upon the throne of the Cherubim, art Lord of the Seraphim and King of Israel . . . " And the people, responding in song with the Hymn of the Cherubim, answer: "That we may receive the King of all, Who cometh invisibly upborne in triumph by the ranks of angels. Alleluia, alleluia, alleluia" — the same, of course, under Whose Face, painted on the dome above them, they have gathered.[67]

In any case, the Liturgy at the Fyodorov Sovereign Cathedral continued, and the priest, having been heard rather than seen by the congregation since returning to the other side of the iconostasis after the readings, now returned to lead the congregation in the recitation of the Nicene-Constantinopolitan Creed — the same as was read by Nicholas at his coronation to demonstrate his fulfilment of the only condition for his anointing, namely, that he be a right-believing Orthodox Christian. Standing at the foot of the iconostasis, the priest and acolytes, rather than looking towards the altar, faced the people for this recitation and together, in a curious, rhythmic meter, the whole assembly sang this profession of faith together, as one. The impression was one of the restoration, not only of a building but also, after almost a century of neglect and destruction, of an Orthodox believing community.

With the preparatory part of the Mass completed, the time for the Eucharist proper had arrived, and the priest returned behind the

---

[67] The Cherubic Hymn also bears witness to the hand of the emperor in shaping the Liturgy, added as it was to the rite by a decree of Justinian's nephew, Emperor Justin II (565–78): Schulz, *Byzantine Liturgy*, 35. It was a favorite of Alexandra's for family recitation: see below.

iconostasis to consecrate the elements and offer them in sacrifice. The Orthodox do not identify either *how* or *at what moment* the bread and the wine are transformed into the Body and Blood of Christ. What takes place, rather, they maintain, is, quite literally, a *mystery*, performed less by the priest than by the Holy Spirit, when He descends in response to the priest's prayer of *epiklesis*.[68] There is no elevation of the Host to the ringing of bells in the view of the laity, as in the Roman Mass; the iconostasis prevents anyone from seeing the priest and the altar. But the increasing solemnity and urgent tempo of the priest's prayers ("Bless, Master, the Holy Bread.... And make [it] the precious Body of Thy Christ") indicate clearly enough what is happening, and the people gathered responded by replacing the simple bows from the waist that sufficed until then with whole-body prostrations. Those mobile enough to do so dropped to their knees and touched their foreheads to the floor in total abasement. Imitating them, I, too, dropped to the floor and pressed my head to the ground.

As the King of All — in the form of bread that had become His Body, and wine that had become His Blood — had now entered His Holy City (in this richly decorated but still, by comparison with the court of Heaven, modest temple), another long sequence of supplicatory prayers began rehearsing the kingship of God in terms and images similar to those we have seen. (Indeed, before the Revolution, it was during these prayers, too, that, the earthly king, the tsar, was remembered.) Thus, after the people had prayed together the "Our Father" — with its request that God's Kingdom "come ... on earth as in heaven" — the priest humbly acknowledges that that for which he and the people had just prayed had in fact already, in an anticipatory, but nonetheless real, way, already happened: the Kingdom had come, because in Body and Blood the King is now among them. As the priest prays:

> We give thanks to Thee, O King invisible, Who by Thine immeasur-
> able might hast created all things.... Do Thou Thyself, O Master,
> look down from heaven upon them that have bowed their heads
> unto Thee, for they have not bowed down unto flesh and blood but
> unto Thee, the awesome God.... Attend, O Lord Jesus Christ our
> God, out of Thy holy dwelling place and from the glorious throne of
> Thy kingdom, and come and sanctify us, O Thou that sittest with
> the Father on high and visibly abidest here with us...

And, then, before he communed himself, the priest prays again: "Behold, I approach unto the Immortal King and our God." It may be that kingship is one of those images of the divine nature that must be "smashed" whenever the Orthodox Christian, following the apophatic way of his Church, wishes to ascend through the divine darkness to an

---

[68] Schmemann, *For the Life*, 43–44.

experience of God beyond human knowledge.[69] But that he must on the way contemplate God in the face of the king is something the Divine Liturgy of St John Chrysostom scarcely gives him the occasion to forget: truly, "King" is a Divine Name of special importance; the political order is, inherently, an act of sacred representation; and kingship — still more, *Christian* kingship, properly conformed to Christ — is a special theophany at the heart of the whole icon of creation.[70]

I was still on the floor when, looking up in snatched glances, I saw the priest now "burst" through the (for the first time) *open* Royal Doors at the center of the icon screen. Accompanied by the acolytes, he was holding aloft a golden chalice. Inside was the wine that was now the Blood of God, mixed with particles of the bread that was now the Body of God, which had been broken into it, and the congregation was invited to receive Holy Communion. Just as there were no pews, however, so there was no communion rail. Neither did the congregation form an orderly queue. Indeed, by comparison with the strict regimen of sitting, kneeling, and standing imposed on the laity by the Western Church, the Eastern Divine Liturgy seems a more "honest" depiction of mankind's frailty and the forbearance of the Divinity. Assisted by the deacons who held a crimson red cloth beneath the chalice to catch any particles of the Body and Blood that might have dropped from the believers' mouths, the priest stood in the center of the church with a crowd (now perhaps 250-strong) pressing in around him. He administered to them one by one, from the end of a long, thin golden spoon dipped anew each time into the chalice. In the Orthodox Church, the Eucharist is distributed to infants too and, touchingly, some parents lifted small babies up to receive it. Indeed, the convention seemed to be that children communicate first, their parents pushing them forward to the front of the crowd.

With the Eucharist distributed, the priest and acolytes retreated behind the icon stand. A few moments later, the priest reappeared among the congregation for the reading of the intercessions. Taking up a position on the floor in the middle of the congregation, they stood facing the altar, reading names from the slips of paper the people had filled out earlier and returned to the lady behind the shop counter. Finally, two and a half hours after the service had begun, a priest delivered the homily that marked the

---

[69] So, Ware, *Orthodox Way*, 25. "Through the apophatic way we smash in pieces all the idols or mental images that we form of him, for we know that all are unworthy of his surpassing greatness."

[70] On kingship as a Divine Name, see Pseudo-Dionysius the Areopagite, *Divine Names*, 12.2–3 in *Pseudo-Dionysius: The complete works*, trans. Colm Luibheid and Paul Rorem (New York: Paulist Press, 1987), 126–27; and on political order as *therefore* as an act of sacred representation, Matthew J. Dal Santo, "The analogy of kingship: a mystagogy of the coronation of Charles III," *New Polity: A journal of post-liberal thought* (2023): 35–42. Meanwhile, on creation as an icon or "theophany," see Ware, *Orthodox Way*, 118: "the whole universe is a cosmic Burning Bush, filled with the divine Fire but not consumed."

Liturgy's conclusion. There was no microphone and no pulpit. Instead, clutching a cross in front of this chest, he stood on the steps before the icon stand and spoke directly, without notes, to the congregation which was pressing in around him. Prompted by the day's readings, the priest's message was as old as Christianity itself: "Love thy enemies." But perhaps because for seventy years in Russia the Communist Party had hindered its hearing, those around me seemed to receive it with rapt attention.

ھ   ھ   ھ

As the church emptied, I followed a flight of stairs under the choir stalls at the back of the building down to the church's crypt, a location favored above all others by Alexandra as a venue for prayer. Today, the crypt has been as carefully restored as the cathedral above. Painted on the walls were patterns repeating the stylized flowers and foliage found in the upper church; the roof was painted royal blue with gold stars, like a vision of the early evening sky. Further along, a gallery that opened to my right displayed two large medallions of Nicholas and Alexandra mounted on the wall. Directly opposite, double wooden doors opened on to what was once Nicholas and Alexandra's private chapel, an inner sanctum where, before the Revolution, the most ancient icons in the family's possession had hung, and the relics of Serafim of Sarov had been preserved and venerated. Now, as then, an icon stand screens a second altar from view. To the right of it, an icon of Nicholas II shows Russia's last monarch dressed in the smart, white uniform of the Russian Imperial Navy, holding the imperial crown. Over his shoulders hang the red robes of martyrdom. "Holy Passion-Bearer, the Right-Believing Tsar Nicholas II," reads the caption in Church Slavonic. Taking a seat on a bench by the entrance, I watched as a handful of devotees arrived, crossing themselves and kissing Nicholas's image in turn. Having already been to Mass upstairs, they were there to extend the day's religious devotions by attending the weekly *moleben* or prayer service in honor of the imperial family.

I left the chapel, and retraced my steps along the corridor to the bottom of the steps leading back up into the upper church. Through the steamed-up windows of an underground canteen, kerchiefed women supped on soup and bread, making animated conversation with each other. Having fasted since Saturday night, they were hungry. The conviviality of the simple meal was reflected in their smiling faces.

Returning to the upper church, I left it for the fresh air, and walked back across the field towards the Alexander Palace. Inscribed on a tall wooden cross leaning against an oak tree on the other side of the oxbow lake were six simple words:

> *Za tsarya*
> *Za Rus*
> *Za vyeryu.*

"For the Tsar, For Rus, For the faith."

At a memorable juncture in "At the feast of the gods," the figure of the General laments the calamitous act of self-destruction that flowed, for Russia, from Nicholas's March 2, 1917 abdication. "Everything, everything, was already predetermined in those days, when the inner link of Russia, its historical tie, its determining form of life, was broken. Isn't that what philosophers call entelechy? Well, Russia lost its entelechy. Russia is a tsardom, or in general it is nothing."[71] No less than Trotsky, Bulgakov, in the General, appears to have spoken too soon.

ॐ　　ॐ　　ॐ

For some, perhaps, such a lengthy description of the Orthodox liturgy may seem unnecessary, out of place in a book on Nicholas, Alexandra, and the vicissitudes of the ideal of *teokratia* in Russia's twentieth century. And yet if we are to see Nicholas and Alexandra correctly, if we are to gain a true measure of their character and motivations, we must not see them *apart* from the Orthodox-Christian religion that from the beginning, and still more deliberately and consequentially after their experiences at the canonization of Serafim of Sarov, formed the constant backdrop of their lives. In fact, for them, the Orthodox Church and its liturgy was not the backdrop at all. It was the foreground, the foundation, the place from which the rest of their actions took their point of departure. To get them right, we must imagine them, week in, week out, in the setting I have just described, attending to the readings, crossing themselves and whispering "*Gospodi, pomilui!*" under their breaths with the Cossacks and regular officers who filled the rest of the building; kneeling as clouds of incense rose to the ceiling during the solemn consecration of the Eucharist; preparing themselves, through fasting, acts of forgiveness, and the confession of their sins to a priest, to receive, three or four times a year, the Body and Blood itself. As one court official commented, "The Tsar never stayed away from a religious service, however good a pretext he could have put forward in order to escape it."[72] The charge that while the "rite and images were Orthodox . . . Nicholas's faith was more broadly Christian and pietistic" simply cannot be sustained.[73]

Indeed, if there is something missing from existing biographies of Nicholas II, it is the depth and significance of his religion — the inner asceticism apprehended by Bulgakov at a distance at Yalta. One aide-de-camp described Nicholas's life as an "almost monastic existence." Week after week, year after year, attendance at the Sunday Divine Liturgy

---

[71] Bulgakov, "At the feast of the gods," 77–78.
[72] Mossolov, *At the Court*, 234.
[73] Steinberg, *Fall of the Romanovs*, 12.

(and, just as often, at Saturday evening Vespers) was an anchor holding
the rest of the week's duties in place. "The emperor was a true man
of faith, a convinced fatalist," the same aide-de-camp continued, using
"fatalism" in the same way as Mossolov and Izvolsky used "mysticism,"
as a cypher for historical, mystical-dogmatic Orthodoxy in an era of
Kantian religion: "Nothing could shake his belief in the Lord or his
conviction that 'not a single hair falls from one's head unless it is the
will of the Most High God' (Lk 21:18)."[74] The horizon of faith was
simply a constant in Nicholas's life. "During the direst moments of his
life, when for instance, his beloved son, the Tsarevich fell gravely ill, or
discord arose among the people he [Nicholas II] never lost his faith in
God and his Providence. It gave him the strength to hold up beneath
grief and horror . . . even during the most brilliant periods of his reign he
turned to the Lord with fervent prayers and fasted three times a year."[75]

The Church's sacraments (especially confession and Holy Communion) were so important to Nicholas that every time he received them,
he recorded the event in his diary. Thus, on Wednesday March 29, 1906,
Nicholas made a point of noting that he had gone "in the evening . . . to
confession after the general prayer service," while the following Sunday,
Pentecost, "I and all the children took the Holy Mysteries."[76] (Presumably,
"all the children" included the at that time infant Alexei, held up to the
priest to receive a tiny particle of the Body and the Blood from the end
of a long, thin, golden spoon.) Anything but mere formalities, Nicholas
looked on the Church's sacraments as genuine sources of spiritual and
psychic comfort. For example, after having received the Eucharist on Whit
Sunday 1906, Nicholas notes that "for a few hours, spiritual peace was
found," while a year later, receiving the Mysteries on Maundy Thursday
1907, he reported having "derived great comfort from the Eucharist."[77]

We will have opportunity to multiply examples of Nicholas's Eucharistic piety as they become relevant to events in later chapters. What is
important is that by the time the diary entries above had been written, the occult temptation represented by Philippe — of any mysticism,
even one untethered from the historical Church — had been overcome.
Nicholas II's judgment against secularization was not in favor of an
occult-flavored, theosophical mysticism of his own fancy but historical,
mystical-dogmatic Christianity in its early twentieth-century, Eastern
Orthodox form. His perception of Russia as a *teokratia* was not an
idiosyncratic fantasy but an essential element of this Church orthodoxy.

The same was true — fatefully — of Rasputin, the Siberian peasant

---

[74] Fabritsky, *Of Bygone Days*, 55.   [75] Ibid., 122.
[76] Nicholas II, March 29 and April 1, 1906, in Diary (2), 308.
[77] Nicholas II, April 19, 1907, in Diary (2), 362. Interestingly, Nicholas's own manner
seemed on occasion to recall that of a skilled confessor. "It was possible to tell the Tsar
anything, just as in confession and those to whom [he] had occasion to speak did not
hesitate to open themselves to him." See Spiridovitch, *Dernières Années*, 1:327.

hailed as a Serafim-like *starets* or holy man and introduced to Nicholas and Alexandra two years after the Sarov celebrations by their own confessor, Archimandrite Feofan, deputy head of the St Petersburg Theological Academy and one of the leading theologians of his day.[78] In the early days, nobody did more to promote Rasputin than Feofan, whose pet project was the identification of living holy men, *startsy*, for the spiritual strengthening of Russia. "God's men still exist on earth.... they are the mainstays of Holy Russia," Feofan is said to have told the seminarians under him at the Academy. When Rasputin, who had been wandering across Russia for a decade, arrived in Petersburg in 1905, Feofan was convinced that the Siberian peasant was one of these living saints. Indeed, so impressed was Feofan with Rasputin that he began introducing him to his spiritual children. The first of these was Militsa, the Montenegrin princess married to Nicholas's cousin, Grand Duke Pyotr Nikolaevich. With Feofan's approval, Militsa and Pyotr then introduced Rasputin to the emperor and empress. And so it was that, on November 1 1905, the fateful entry appeared in Nicholas's diary: "Tuesday . . . cold and windy. . . . Was occupied all morning. . . . At 4 o'clock we went to Sergeevka. Had tea with Militsa and Stana. We made the acquaintance of a man of God — Grigory, from Tobolsk province," reads the entry in Nicholas's diary that fateful day.[79]

The truth was that, after his experience at the Sarov celebrations, Nicholas was no less convinced than Feofan of the presence of wonder-working holy men in Russia, and throughout the turbulent years of 1904 and 1905 Nicholas welcomed many allegedly Orthodox holy men and women to the palace. These included now-forgotten figures such as the wanderers (*stranniki*, like Rasputin) Vasya and Matryona the Barefooted, and the so-called holy fool, Mitya "the Nasal Voice" Kozelsky, from the prestigious Optina Monastery (where Dostoevsky, Tolstoy and a dozen lesser stars of Russian culture had gone for spiritual illumination).[80] But they also included others now canonized by the Russian Church as saints. Indeed, on the day the October Manifesto had been signed, one of these, the future St John of Kronstadt, had come to pray with Nicholas at Peterhof.[81] "Lord, help us! Save and have mercy on Russia!" Nicholas wrote in his diary that day. Two weeks and a day later, he was introduced to Rasputin. Were all these, John's visit, the prayer and the introduction, in Nicholas's mind, connected?

As Douglas Smith has shown, in an exhaustive and compelling recent biography of Rasputin, Rasputin won his entrée into the palace not

[78] See Smith, *Rasputin*, 53–54.
[79] Nicholas II, November 1, 1905, in Diary (2), 287. Cited here as it appears in Smith, *Rasputin*, 65.   [80] Smith, *Rasputin*, 45.
[81] On St John of Kronstadt, a sainted priest and vehement monarchist, see Nadieszda Kizenko, *A Prodigal Saint: Father John of Kronstadt and the Russian people* (University Park, PA: State University of Pennsylvania Press, 2000), 235, 248.

as Alexei's healer but as a prophet, a man of God, raised up from an Orthodox people to steady the heart of an Orthodox tsar. We see this in the remarkably bold letter that Rasputin addressed to Nicholas just four days after their first meeting. In it, Rasputin said not a word about Alexei, but everything about the confidence that Nicholas as Tsar should place in God to guide him.

> Great Emperor, Tsar, and Autocrat of all Russia! Greetings to you! May God give you sage advice.... All Russia worries, she has descended into a terrible argument, she trembles in joy and rings her bells calling for God, and God sends us mercy and scares our enemies with awe-inspiring threats.... such is the power of God and His miracles! Don't disdain our simple words. You, as our Master, and we, as your subjects, must do our best, we tremble and pray to God to keep you safe from all evil, to protect you from all wounds, now and in the future, so that your life will forever flow like a life-giving spring.[82]

The theocratic principle, not Alexei's illness, laid the foundation for Rasputin's entry into Nicholas and Alexandra's world.

෴ ෴ ෴

All the same, if common allegiance to a picture of "Holy Russia" as an Orthodox land ruled by an Orthodox tsar guided by his priests (such as Feofan) and holy prophets from among the people — the *startsy* — secured Rasputin's entry into the palace, it was what he could do for Alexei that kept him there. And of this dimension of the drama, Bulgakov was entirely in the dark. Like everybody else in Russia, Bulgakov was utterly ignorant of the nature of the illness that afflicted Alexei until after the Revolution. With them, Bulgakov debated the source of his mysterious influence over the imperial family, with everyone else. "About the real character of his [Rasputin's] influence, people lied and argued a lot. Mostly, they hurled all kinds of dirt, which I didn't believe, but I almost never knew the real reasons for his strength," Bulgakov recalled later.[83] Of course, learning after the Revolution of Alexei's hemophilia, Bulgakov, "as a father," sympathized instinctively: what "an unceasing, secret martyrdom the illness of their only son was for the imperial family that that illness paralyzed and tormented simply never entered into my head," he could write. And yet while the revelation of Alexei's illness would never allow Bulgakov to justify Rasputin's spiritual and mystical aberrations (for, as Bulgakov wrote, Rasputin, as a Khlyst, "must not be defended or justified"), it did help him to understand it.[84] As regards

---

[82] Smith, *Rasputin*, 69. Unknown to earlier biographers, this remarkable letter lay in the archives until discovered by Smith.
[83] Bulgakov, *Avtobiograficheskie*, 84.
[84] Ibid., 84. The Khlysts were a heretical sect probably numbering around 100,000

Rasputin, Bulgakov, in his irrepressible, intuitive-theological commitment to the theocratic principle, and his sincere love for the equally sincere but equally "suicidal" Tsar Nicholas II himself, was constantly and forever conflicted between the worthiness of the *ideal* Rasputin represented and the sordid and tragic malignancy of the reality, the clash between which he could ultimately only explain as the work of demonic forces falsifying the true for the sake of perpetuating the lies of the Evil One.

As it was, Nicholas and Alexandra first invited Rasputin to come to the Palace as a personal guest in November 1907. After sitting briefly with Rasputin together, they took him to meet the children. Thanks to Nicholas's younger sister, the Grand Duchess Olga Aleksandrovna, who was also there, we have a record of what transpired that evening in the nursery. "When I saw him," Olga recalled, "I felt that gentleness and warmth radiated from him. All the children seemed to like him. They were completely at their ease with him. I still remember their laughter as little Alexei, deciding he was a rabbit, jumped up and down the room. And then, quite suddenly, Rasputin caught the child's hand and led him to his bedroom, and we three followed." Entering Alexei's bedroom behind Rasputin, Olga recalled that there was "a hush as though we found ourselves in church ... no lamps were lit; the only light came from the candles burning in front of some beautiful icons. The child stood very still by the side of that giant, whose head was bowed. I knew he was praying. . . . I also knew that my little nephew had joined him in prayer. I really cannot describe it — but I was then conscious of the man's utter sincerity."[85]

Olga, unhappily married to a cousin and already cohabiting with her future husband, the commoner Peter Kulikovsky, was not as intensely church-oriented as either Alexandra or Nicholas. Nonetheless, she was struck by many of the same features that had recommended Rasputin as a man of God to Feofan and others: as concerns his role in the demise of the Russian *teokratia*, Rasputin was, on the one hand, not so much a separate affair in himself as another embodiment of the religious and

---

adherents that existed on the edges of the Orthodox Church. Outwardly Orthodox, the Khlysts held, in addition to their attendance at the Church's public worship, private meetings, often in the cellars and basements of private homes. These meetings consisted in an energetic swirling dance, the women dancing in one direction in the inner circle and the men dancing in another in an outer circle, the aim of which was to induce a state of hallucination and ecstasy, under the influence of which members of the group would take it upon themselves to prophesy personal messages vouched to them by the Holy Spirit. Andrei Bely's 1910 difficult symbolist novel, *The Silver Dove*, purports to sketch the inner life of a cell of Khlysts. Allegedly, meetings ended in an orgy of group sex and even, in the wildest representations of the sect's excesses, cannibalism. One of the key teachings at the heart of "Khlystism" — that as there was no repentance without sin, sin itself was the path to salvation — was attributed to Rasputin by his accusers. See Smith, *Rasputin*, 82–88.

[85] Cited in Smith, *Rasputin*, 110.

spiritual currents that we have seen already. On the other, however, there was a deeply bodily, even visceral, element to Rasputin's place in the imperial family's confidences that with time allowed his part to become overshadowing: Rasputin's first invitation into the imperial home preceded by a matter of weeks his first healing of Alexei.

Olga was there that evening, too. "The poor child lay in such pain," Olga recalled, "dark patches under his eyes and his little body all distorted, and the leg terribly swollen." As night fell, the doctors told Nicholas and Alexandra that there was nothing they could do. Aware of Rasputin's reputation as a healer, Alexandra sent the peasant a message requesting that he come to the Palace. Olga had gone home before Rasputin arrived but the scene before her eyes when she returned the following morning bore no resemblance to that which she had left behind the night before. "The little boy was not just alive but well," she recalled: "He was sitting up in bed, the fever gone, the eyes clear and bright, not a sign of any swelling in his leg. The horror of the evening before became an incredibly distant nightmare. Later, I learned from Alicky [i.e. Alexandra] that Rasputin had not even touched the child but merely stood at the foot of the bed and prayed."[86]

Rasputin did not, then, win his way into Nicholas and Alexandra's confidence as a healer. But his healings made the place he had won as part of the spiritual economy of *teokratia* unshakeable. The timing was providential: barely a month before, in Pokrovskoye, the Church investigation launched by the local bishop had forced Rasputin to sign an affidavit denying that he was a Khlyst, and, as such, found salvation in sex.[87]

As it was, in 1908 the Siberian peasant became something like part of the Imperial family. When he wrote to Nicholas and Alexandra, he addressed them as "Mama and Papa" in his correspondence. He felt entitled to arrive unannounced at the Alexander Palace. And yet Alexandra knew she did not know as much about Rasputin as she ought. In February 1908, she initiated her own investigation, asking Feofan, her

---

[86] Cited in Smith, *Rasputin*, 111.

[87] Was Rasputin a Khlyst? Sent to Pokrovskoye by Bishop Antony to find out was an Orthodox priest by the name of Fr Glukhovtsev. After five days spent interviewing witnesses in Pokrovskoye, Glukhovtsev had conflicting evidence. When Fr Glukhovtsev filed his report to Bishop Antony in Tobolsk in January 1908, therefore, he recognized the inconclusiveness of his findings. Yes, Glukhovtsev thought, Rasputin and his followers formed a moral-religious group "distinct from Orthodoxy." But they were not necessarily Khlysty. To substantiate that allegation, more would have to be known about what exactly was said at the religious meetings held in the Rasputin, what the substance of the hymns sung and what the nature of the interpretation Rasputin put on the (otherwise apparently Orthodox) religious literature found there. Clearly, a second, more penetrating investigation into Rasputin would be required; in May, Bishop Antony gave his permission to its formation. And yet this second investigation, which would have probed Rasputin's links to the Khlyst movement, mysteriously never took place. According to Smith, the only explanation is that authorities in Petersburg, getting wind of it, intervened to quash it. See Smith, *Rasputin*, 123–25.

confessor, to go with Rasputin to his home in Pokrovskoye and report to her what he saw. Although a diocesan investigation into Rasputin was underway at the time, Feofan vouched for the authenticity of the "man of God" Rasputin when he returned. Questioned, therefore, by a member of her husband's entourage later that summer, Alexandra could answer with good conscience that Rasputin was "a very pious, far-sighted, real Russian peasant" who "knows church worship by heart."[88]

Another person who became Rasputin's confirmed adept in 1908 was Alexandra's friend, Anna Vyrubova. [89] Pious, and already devoted to the soon-to-be-deceased Fr John of Kronstadt (who, she claimed, had saved her from death by typhus by appearing to her in a dream when she was sixteen), Vyrubova was twelve years younger than Alexandra. She was well born — her mother a countess and her father, Alexander Taneev, hereditary head of His Majesty's Imperial Chancellery — but far from the first rank of the Russian aristocracy (in whose eyes, she and Alexandra should never have been friends).

To Vyrubova, just as much to Alexandra (and just as he originally was to Feofan and Vaniamin, too), Rasputin was a *starets*, a man of God, a living saint walking the land of Russia. And she never changed that opinion, despite what others said about him. "Just as all righteous men are recognized only after their deaths, so too will the holy deeds of the *starets* come to light after his death, and the people will understand who they have lost and who they failed to cherish during our dear father's life," she predicted.[90] And like Alexei, Vyrubova could claim herself to have been the beneficiary of one of Rasputin's miracles.[91] She would end her life an Orthodox nun in Finland.

Vyrubova never held any formal position at court, but lived in a grace-and-favor apartment in the grounds of the Alexander Palace. There, in March, and again in May 1908, Nicholas and Alexandra spent the evening with Rasputin. Among his gifts to them was an icon he had had painted. It showed Christ blessing Nicholas, Alexandra, and Alexei. They were to keep the icon, said Rasputin in a letter written to them at this time, so that "your faith will never run out . . . this [icon] will be a reminder to you that He is always with you, saving, protecting, and preserving." He concluded the epistle with the Jesus Prayer. Everything seemed very pious, wholesome, and, indeed, with the references

---

[88] Smith, *Rasputin*, 103.   [89] Ibid., 131.   [90] Ibid., 102.
[91] Crushed when a train derailed between St Petersburg and Tsarskoye Selo in 1915, and almost unconscious after lying for hours under the wreckage in the snow, Vyrubova, like Alexei in 1907, presented the doctors with a hopeless case. Those who treated her doubted that she would live. A priest delivered last rites. But after the arrival on the scene of Rasputin, who, visibly distressed to see her so close to death, prayed for her and assured her she would live, she recovered, albeit dependent for the rest of her life on crutches. The attending doctor in the hospital, who had given up on Vyrubova, vouched for the miracle: Smith, *Rasputin*, 293.

to Nicholas's "God-protected" ruling power, *theocratic.*

And yet nothing is easier than exaggerating Rasputin's influence. That year, Nicholas and Alexandra saw Rasputin on only three more occasions, in August, in November, and at Christmas. All the same, General Vladimir Gerasimov, the head of the Petersburg division of the Okhrana, the secret police, was concerned at what a peasant about whom the authorities knew so little was doing so close to Their Majesties. Okhrana agents began trailing Rasputin in Petersburg. Concluding that Rasputin was not a holy man, but a debauched and deceitful peasant, Gerasimov took his anxieties to Stolypin, Chairman of the Council of Ministers. Agreeing about the *potential* for scandal, Stolypin raised the matter with Nicholas. Although Nicholas was at first indignant, eventually he saw the point, and Stolypin issued an order prohibiting Rasputin's presence in the capital. But Rasputin ignored it, and with the help of at least one friendly grand duke. One half of the tragedy is that Rasputin, flouting the law, had begun to alienate Nicholas from his government.

The other half is that, on the face of it, all this was unnecessary; for in the following year, 1909, Rasputin's actual meetings with Nicholas and Alexandra remained relatively few and irregular. In February, Rasputin went with Feofan to the Palace to hear Nicholas name Feofan to the highest theological post in the Russian Empire, as rector, now, of the St Petersburg Theological Academy. Later in that same month in 1909, Feofan was made a bishop. But after this event, Nicholas did not see Rasputin again until June when Rasputin, together with Feofan — now a bishop and rector of the theological academy — arrived at Tsarskoye Selo with an undisputed real holy man in tow. This was the aged *starets* Makary, of the St Nicholas Monastery at Verkhoturye in the Urals, at whose feet Rasputin, the Orthodox *strannik* of 1897–1904, had probably learnt what he knew of Scripture and spiritual wisdom. By bringing Makary to the Palace now, Rasputin seems to have hoped to shore up his reputation with Nicholas and Alexandra, despite the rumors of sexual improprieties that Rasputin probably feared his imperial patrons might at this time have been hearing.[92] Nicholas enjoyed the meeting with Makary. But if it helped save Rasputin his reputation, it did not help him secure more frequent access to the couple. After the reception of Makary, almost six months passed before Nicholas and Alexandra saw Rasputin again (in January 1910). In the meantime, a crisis had taken

---

[92] Alexandra seems to have entertained doubts about Rasputin for longer than she is usually credited with having done. To assuage them, she dispatched in May 1909 a group of seven women to Pokrovskoye. After spending three days at home with Rasputin and his wife in Siberia, the party returned with a report for Alexandra at Tsarskoye Selo. Most of the group confirmed Rasputin's piety. But one at least wrote to Alexandra that Rasputin was not worthy of her confidence, albeit without accusing Rasputin of any named wrongdoing. After the revolution, another member of the group would accuse Rasputin of raping her on this trip. See Smith, *Rasputin,* 141–45.

place in Rasputin's relationship with Feofan.

It began on the very evening when Rasputin and Feofan left the palace with Makary: Feofan had heard the rumors after all. Having returned Makary to his hermitage, Feofan therefore made a pilgrimage to the cell of St Serafim of Sarov. There, Feofan said, Serafim had revealed to him that Rasputin was "on the false path."[93] Returning to Petersburg, Feofan summoned Rasputin twice to the Theological Academy for questioning. After issuing two warnings, Feofan cursed Rasputin and asked for an audience with Nicholas. It was granted; but rather than Nicholas, Alexandra, who utterly refused to accept Feofan's report, received Feofan instead.[94] Feofan never forgave himself for his part in introducing Rasputin to the tsar and empress. Far from strengthening the *teokratia*, the intelligent and well-meaning Feofan had become a vehicle for its moral demolition in the eyes of the public. With devastating consequences for the monarchy, the Rasputin scandal was about to break.

ro   ro   ro

It was in 1910 that Rasputin first became a truly regular presence at the Palace. Suddenly, at the beginning of 1910, his previously occasional visits to the palace became frequent: Rasputin called seven times at the Palace in January and four in February. And it's hard not to connect this increased tempo with Rasputin's knowledge that, having lost the confidence of Feofan, he could expect the Church authorities to begin to make a concerted effort to try to dislodge him from the imperial family's confidence. Indeed, they already *had* begun to try to do this. If they failed, it was because Rasputin showed himself to be a matchless reader of Alexandra's emotional needs and Nicholas's theocratic outlook. And yet the more familiar Rasputin's face became at the Alexander Palace, the more alarmed the Palace staff grew. The first to speak out, in March 1910, was the head of the imperial nursery, Sofia Ivanovna Tyutcheva. By now, Olga was fourteen, Tatiana thirteen and Maria and Anastasia eleven and ten, respectively. The honor of the older girls, especially, had to be guarded jealously. Given the rumors circulating about the advantage Rasputin was taking of his female acolytes, what was Alexandra, the girls' mother, thinking? Alexandra brushed off the implication. To Alexandra, of course, Alexei's life now depended on Rasputin, and she would allow

---

[93] Ibid., 146.

[94] For this episode, see Smith, *Rasputin*, 146–47. Not yet prepared to give up, Feofan presented his anxieties to the Metropolitan-archbishop of St Petersburg, Antony (Vadkovsky). Metropolitan Antony took Feofan's anxieties seriously, and, together, the bishop and archbishop made a representation to the Procurator of the Holy Synod, Sergei Lukyanov. Having collected incriminating evidence against Rasputin, the Metropolitan and Procurator then presented their accusations and supporting dossier to Stolypin, who used them when, almost exactly twelve months since his first representation to the Tsar on Rasputin, Stolypin raised the issue again with Nicholas. Again, Nicholas refused to listen.

nothing to change her opinion of him, for fear of jeopardizing the life of her son. But neither was it a question only of miracles. She could point to Rasputin's elevating effect on the boy's morale, too. "My dear little one!" Rasputin wrote to the four-year-old Alexei in 1909: "Look at our dear God, see his wounds. Once He suffered patiently, and then he became strong and all-powerful. And so you too, my dear one . . . will be cheery and we'll live together."[95]

ᔕ   ᔕ   ᔕ

Rasputin was discovered by the press and wider public in the spring of 1910 (a year, exactly, after "Vekhi").[96] Interestingly, the journalist who broke the story was Mikhail Novoselov, a member of the wider circle of the Solovyov-inspired Silver Age, and a friend of Bulgakov's (with whom Novoselov had shared his views on Rasputin). Novoselov had left the ancestral faith in adolescence, only to return to the Church later in life.[97] Moreover, the story appeared in a monarchist-conservative *Moscow Gazette*, edited by the other main intellectual figure who, in addition to Vladimir Solovyov and Bulgakov himself, had dedicated himself to the problem of *teokratia*: Lev Tikhomirov.[98] Called "The Spiritual Touring-Actor Grigory Rasputin," Novoselov's piece appeared in March. In it, Novoselov purported to "unmask" Rasputin before the Russian public. Citing the (probably invented) evidence allegedly provided to him by three independent but unnamed sources (a journalist, a student, and a real *starets*), Novoselov created the image of Rasputin that the Russian press clung to until the Siberian peasant's death: Rasputin was a fraud interested only in bettering his financial position and climbing the social ladder. He used hypnotism and other charms to obtain sexual favors from his women followers. Despite presenting the outward appearance of an Orthodox holy man, he was a Khlyst. Moreover, Rasputin was a terrible husband and father: he had abandoned his own family, and his children were godless and corrupted by vice.

Novoselov's purpose was not revolutionary; he did not allege that Rasputin held any influence over the tsar, or name the imperial family. With Tikhomirov, he thought he was performing a service to the monarchy, opening Nicholas and Alexandra's eyes to the dangers of association with such a figure. This is doubtless why Novoselov felt entitled to invent sources and make allegations that better informed acquaintances of Rasputin's knew to be untrue: Rasputin, for example, had not abandoned

[95]   Smith, *Rasputin*, 160.   [96]   Ibid., 168–70.
[97]   Bulgakov says he first heard of Rasputin when Novoselov raised the subject with him in 1907: *Avtobiograficheskie*, 84.
[98]   We have already met Tikhomirov, the revolutionary-cum-tsarist apologist whose four-volume 1905 work *Monarchical Statehood* provided the closest thing anyone ever came to providing for a modern rationalization of and program for sustaining Russia's Constantinian regime.

his family; on the contrary, he had just bought a large new home for them in Pokrovskoye, and brought his daughter Maria to the city for her education. His children were neither godless nor corrupted by vice. And in this lay the downfall of Novoselov and Tikhomirov's strategy: Novoselov's sensational portrait of Rasputin contained so many things that Nicholas *knew* to be untrue that, not for the last time, he dismissed the warning worth heeding that the sensational portrait did contain.

Worse, Novoselov and Tikhomirov had opened a floodgate. Every group and political party in Russia looking to pare back the power of the monarchy naturally gravitated to the Rasputin story. The Siberian peasant was a godsend for the monarchy's opponents in the Duma. That summer, Miliukov's Kadets ran no fewer than ten articles on Rasputin in *Rech'* ("Speech"), the party's newspaper.[99] These articles included fabricated interviews with members of a harem of twelve young women whom Rasputin allegedly kept prisoner at his house in Pokrovskoye. They were so popular that they were reprinted in local newspapers up and down the country. By the end of 1910, Rasputin was a household name in Russia, for all the wrong reasons. Indeed, it seems that the press campaign did, for a time, dent Nicholas and Alexandra's confidence in him. In May 1910, Rasputin left Petersburg for Pokrovskoye, and didn't appear at the Palace again until February 1911. Moreover, Rasputin won Nicholas and Alexandra's confidence back in a way that can only testify to the degree of his instinctive intelligence: by using the press itself to present another side of himself, one that, he perhaps knew, both Nicholas and Alexandra would find hard to condemn or reject. Thus, there appeared in December 1910 a short tract in the Russian press written by Rasputin himself. He called it "My Life in Fear with Jesus." "I have trust in You, God, and I am not ashamed of it. I will praise You, my enemies don't leave me in peace.... I will say in my soul: Jesus, be my Creator and Protector, and the enemies will follow me and will have raids to catch me and will shoot arrows into my soul and will penetrate me with their sly gazes and will want to take the truth away; but they cannot, they won't be able to take it ... Jesus! Save those close to you!"[100] In the religious inner world of Nicholas and Alexandra, externalized for us in these years by the motifs of their cathedral at Tsarskoye Selo, the message was welcomed as authentic instantly. Alexandra never let go of the portrait Rasputin painted of himself in that piece as a martyr reliving the insults hurled at Christ himself; when others, even those closest to her, would later bring their accusations against Rasputin to her, she would quote this image drawn by Rasputin of himself in 1910 back at them.

But the press would not let Rasputin go. On the contrary, when

---

[99] Smith, *Rasputin*, 172.　　　　[100] Ibid., 182.

Rasputin began an acquaintance with the firebrand monk, extreme Orthodox religious-nationalist and vehement anti-Semite, Iliodor, public interest snowballed. One of the most unsavory figures of late imperial Russia, Iliodor was probably the most visible representative of the so-called Black Hundred movement that opposed all the reforms inaugurated in the wake of the Revolution of 1905 — the Duma, and civil, political, and religious liberties.[101] Believing himself the savior of Russia, Iliodor called for a violent purge of foreigners, Jews, and European influences. At the end of 1910, he had been imprisoned in a monastery for his public attacks on Stolypin, on the leaders of the Church, and on government ministers. In early 1911, however, Iliodor broke out of prison and traveled halfway across the country, where, occupying another monastery with his followers, he declared open rebellion against the government. Stolypin wanted to use force to expel Iliodor and return him to incarceration. But Nicholas II refused, and, instead, issued Iliodor with a pardon that reversed the previous year's order for his imprisonment. Iliodor regained his liberty and ended his rebellion, and when Rasputin returned to Russia from Palestine in June, he went straight to Iliodor to congratulate him in front of the cameras. (The two, having met while Iliodor was a student at the Theological Academy in 1905 and 1906, maintained an on-again, off-again friendship.)

The press immediately identified Rasputin as the author of Nicholas's decision. This was incorrect. At the beginning of 1911, Rasputin was not even in Russia, but in the Holy Land, on pilgrimage, from which he did not return until the start of the summer. Significantly, too, Rasputin, though endorsing the Union in a pamphlet in 1911, was never, at heart, an anti-Semite, and later turned decisively against the politics of Iliodor and the Black Hundreds.[102] The real problem was Nicholas's chronic inability to distinguish the true defenders of the theocratic principle from those who reduced it to xenophobia, dictatorship, and anti-Semitism.[103]

---

[101] When, in the setting of his vision of Nicholas II on the Yalta Embankment, Bulgakov said that, in his conversion to *teokratia*, there never was any element of "police-Black-Hundredism," it was figures such as Iliodor that he had in mind. See Bulgakov, *Avtobiograficheskie*, 82.

[102] Smith, *Rasputin*, 225, 535–41.

[103] He was not alone in this. At the height of the Revolution of 1905, the saintly Fr John of Kronstadt, too, called for the forcible destruction of the revolutionaries who attacked the "true monarchical order established by God," and until his death he would associate himself on and off with the Union of the Russian People, the organization, often identified as proto-fascist, that was founded at the end of the year to defend the autocracy and the exclusive established status of the Orthodox Church. It published anti-Jewish literature, and its unofficial armed wing, the Black Hundreds, taking advantage, when it could, of the connivance of the police, unlawfully organized pogroms. In 1905, Nicholas II accepted the Union's insignia, and, like Fr John, forever took a naïve but not terribly active interest in the group's lawful activities. See Kizenko, *Father John*, 247–48; Pipes, *Russian Revolution*, 48, 154. And although this does not excuse them, the Union's anti-Jewish policies were not as bad as those of the splinter group, the

Nonetheless, the newspapers generated the impression that Rasputin, the imagined power behind the throne, was now running the country. When Stolypin was shot dead at the Kiev opera in August 1911, some newspapers sensationally insinuated that Rasputin was now in a position to have prime ministers assassinated.[104] Knowing this to be fiction, Nicholas asked the Chairman of the Council of Ministers, the highly competent former Minister of Finance Count Vladimir Kokovtsov, to stop the publication of these false stories. But the principle of freedom of press enshrined in the October Manifesto made this impossible; all Kokovtsov could do was to call the editors to his office and ask them to stop damaging the monarchy. But Rasputin stories sold, and the sensational reportage continued. At Livadia in November 1911, Feofan, still Nicholas and Alexandra's confessor, tried a final time to open Alexandra's eyes to the dangers she and her husband were courting, remonstrating with her in the palace for an hour and a half. But Alexandra refused to listen.

Rasputin, or the figment of him, was beginning to take over Russian public life. In 1912, another bishop tried to dislodge Rasputin from Nicholas and Alexandra's confidence. This attempt also failed, largely because, once again, the accusations which Rasputin's accusers levelled against him included what Nicholas knew to be sensational untruths, which inclined him to dismiss as untrue even allegations with a solid foundation.[105] In response to Nicholas's refusal to listen, the Okhrana

---

Union of St Michael, which called for the complete disenfranchisement of all Jews: Oldenburg, *Last Tsar*, 3:196, n. 22.

[104] On the assassination, see Pipes, *Russian Revolution*, 187–91. Nicholas's behavior toward Stolypin before, and, especially, after the shooting have often been criticized, fairly it would seem, as they are by Pipes. But Oldenburg notes that his actions were perhaps those we would expect of him. Before returning to Kiev to pray "for a long time" by the side of Stolypin's body, Nicholas II went to the shrine of a saint who had been canonized in the year of his coronation, Feodosia of Uglich, at nearby Chernigov: Oldenburg, *Last Tsar*, 3:103.

[105] The bishop was Germogen of Saratov. A churchman favorable to the Union of the Russian People, Germogen had once considered Rasputin a true *starets*. In 1911, however, Germogen concluded that Rasputin was a fraud, and a threat to the tsar. Resolving to remove Rasputin from influence, Germogen (together with Iliodor, who now turned against his former friend) confronted Rasputin in December. The meeting, it was said, ended in violence. A month later, in January 1912, the Holy Synod removed Germogen from his diocese. Incensed, Germogen blamed Rasputin, whom he publicly denounced now as a Khlyst, and took his accusations to the press. The papers covered it with glee. Rasputin, the peasant-pilgrim from Pokrovskoye, so it seemed, was now picking and choosing bishops. In fact, the two events, Germogen's confrontation with Rasputin and his removal from episcopal office, had nothing to do with each other. The cause of the Holy Synod's actions was Germogen's resistance to various church reforms that the Holy Synod had agreed upon, but Germogen considered heretical. As tsar, Nicholas backed the Synod, and Germogen was exiled to a monastery in Minsk province, where, though a bishop, he carried out the duties of a parish priest until 1915. On the other hand, it does appear that in 1911 Rasputin succeeded in securing, by way of his influence with Nicholas II, his first appointment of a friendly candidate as a bishop: Varnava, the archimandrite of a Moscow monastery, who was named bishop of Kargopol in Russia's north over the

itself began composing sensational stories of Rasputin's exploits, which it then distributed to the newspapers. Some included entire invented monologues, as if they were the Siberian peasant's own words and confessions. But by far the most politically significant aspect of this storm was the part played by Aleksandr Guchkov. Consistent with his goal of wresting executive control of the government from the monarchy, Guchkov was the first to identify for the opposition the opportunities that existed in instrumentalizing the Rasputin scandal to achieve constitutional ends.

He launched his attack in the first days of 1912 with the publication in the letters section of his newspaper, *Golos Moskvy* ("Voice of Moscow"), of a summary of the allegations made in a recently suppressed booklet-length manuscript entitled *Grigory Rasputin and Mystical Libertinage* by Novoselov, the publicist, and Bulgakov's friend, whom we have already met.[106] In arguable breach of the law, however, the Okhrana seized the *Golos Moskvy* print run. Guchkov was both incensed and triumphant. With the Rasputin scandal having now become a free speech issue, he was free to raise the matter publicly in the Duma.[107] Thus, Rasputin (though never named) became the subject of Duma debate for the first time. "Russia is going through dark, difficult days," Guchkov declared to the chamber: "Some sort of evil spirit from the middle ages has risen before us.... Duty demands that we raise the voice of our conscience so that it will allow public indignation, which is steadily growing, to be heard."[108] Until January 1912, Rasputin had been a story for the gossip pages; from that day onwards, however, Rasputin became a constitutional issue.

Then, in a turn of events devastating for public perceptions of the imperial family, Guchkov began circulating copies of letters allegedly written by Alexandra and her daughters, and given to him by Iliodor, who allegedly had them from Rasputin, to whom the letters were allegedly originally written. In them, Alexandra could be read apparently calling Rasputin her "beloved and unforgettable teacher, savior and mentor," allegedly longing to "kiss" Rasputin's hands and lay her head on his "blessed shoulders." She wished "for only one thing—to fall asleep, fall asleep forever" in his "embrace." Were the letters authentic? In the fact of their existence, yes, but they were probably doctored for effect when copied and circulated. Certainly after the Revolution, Duma president Mikhail Rodzianko claimed that the copies of the letters circulating

head of the Holy Synod's objections. See Smith, *Rasputin*, 236–42.

[106] On the allegations, see Smith, *Rasputin*, 253, who says Novoselov's pamphlet was "quite fairly characterized," even at the time, as a "bunch of lies and extreme exaggerations." Bulgakov says that Novoselov spoke to him about the publication: *Avtobiograficheskie*, 85.

[107] In 1915, it was the *Voice of Moscow* that led the campaign against the "traitors" Miasoyedov and Minister of War Sukhomlinov.

[108] Cited in Smith, *Rasputin*, 256.

in Petersburg in 1912 differed in certain respects from the originals he still had in his possession. But if that was the case, Rodzianko did not come to Alexandra's defense in 1912. Instead, the letters "released into society the poisonous notion that the empress was having sex with a debauched Russian peasant in the palace, for this is how they were read in salons and drawing rooms across the country...." As one courtier commented, "all respect for the tsar" had been "lost."[109]

The theocratic principle was also, implicitly, imperiled; a cuckold tsar, who could not even keep his wife's lusts in check, could hardly claim to be the Lord's anointed. Thus, the Rasputin scandal began poisoning Nicholas's relationship not only with the Duma, which had always been strained, but also with his ministers. The Chairman of the Council of Ministers, since Stolypin's assassination, had been Vladimir Kokovtsov. When he urged Nicholas to send Rasputin away, because of the damage it was doing to public perceptions of the monarchy, Nicholas refused. Nicholas knew that no liaison between his wife and Rasputin existed, and to send Rasputin away in such circumstances would damage the theocratic principle in another way, by setting a precedent for the Duma to seek to pressure the tsar by concocting scandals. On the other hand, Nicholas did give the Duma Chairman Mikhail Rodzianko, an Octobrist, permission to conduct his own secret investigation into Rasputin, including unimpeded access to all Church files on the alleged holy man. A month later, Rodzianko returned with a report for Nicholas that he believed demonstrated that Rasputin was a fraud and a Khlyst—and an immediate danger to the imperial family. Rodzianko expected gratitude, but got none, apparently because Nicholas believed that Rodzianko, betraying Nicholas's trust, had shared his secret report with the Octobrist party leader, Guchkov.

Certainly, the very day after Rodzianko had delivered his allegedly secret report to the palace, Guchkov rose in the Duma to denounce Rasputin in the most direct terms yet. "One wants to talk, one wants to shout that the Church is in danger and the State is in danger too," Guchkov inveighed, in a speech taken down and reprinted in the newspaper:[110] "You all know what terrible drama Russia is going through ... and in the center of this drama is a mysterious tragicomic figure who seems to have come back from the other world, or is some vestige of the Dark Ages.... Perhaps he is a fanatical sectarian spreading his dark deeds, perhaps he is a roguish swindler busy making profit. What paths has this person taken to reach this key position, having seized such influence that even top state and church authorities bow down before him? ... Facing such a scenario, it is our duty to shout words of warning: the Church

---

[109] Ibid., 247.   [110] *The New Times* (Novoe Vremya).

is in danger and the State is in danger!"[111] The chamber erupted with approval. The speech made Guchkov a household name as a warrior for truth and decency. In Bulgakov's terms, Guchkov had staked his claim to being a "hero." Knowing such claims to be without the least foundation, however, Nicholas viewed the same events through the lens of the controversy over the navy in 1908 and 1909. Having concluded that Rodzianko and Guchkov were working together, and that the reasons behind their attack on Rasputin were political, he refused on principle to move a finger against Rasputin. The stage was set for 1915–17.

As it was, Nicholas and Alexandra tried to escape the storm (the "false rumors, ill will, and bizarre and scabrous intrigues" that "reigned in St Petersburg at the beginning of that year") through an earlier than usual departure for Livadia, in Crimea.[112] Extraordinarily, although he traveled by public train and never stayed at the palace, Rasputin followed them. The conditions for the drama of 1915 and 1916 were being laid. Scurrilous cartoons began to circulate. The myth of Rasputin, the power behind the throne, had been created, and yet the only even reasonably secure evidence of his influence was the appointment of a single provincial bishop. In this sense, the significance of that year's scandals was not the extent of Rasputin's influence, for that influence was marginal and insignificant, but the way the suggestion of that influence was "weaponized" for the sake of bringing about constitutional change. Quite simply, Rasputin was "the perfect tool . . . to bring down the [tsarist] regime."[113]

෨   ෨   ෨

And yet that Nicholas was, throughout all this, in his own self-conception, simply Russia's Orthodox tsar, comes through in the closest thing history has left us to an authorized biography of Nicholas II: an illustrated, 132-page booklet entitled *The Reign of the Sovereign Emperor Nicholas Aleksandrovich*. Written by Professor Andrei Elkhaninov, with direct access to Nicholas himself, the book's chief interest lies in the fact that it tells us precisely what Nicholas wanted us to know about himself. Of course, we should not expect to find in this text an unvarnished account of the tsar's weaknesses and shortcomings. Conventions had to be observed; no faults could be permitted to be identified in the emperor. But the things for which Nicholas is *praised* in the text we may accept as things he genuinely *wished* to be praised for—a genuine if necessarily idealized representation of the vision Nicholas entertained of himself and the nature of his office. And in this regard, Elkhaninov's biography, appearing as it did in 1913, the same year the Fyodorov Sovereign Cathedral was consecrated, adds a written witness to the one

---

[111] Smith, *Rasputin*, 272.
[112] Spiridovitch, *Dernières Années*, 2:210.   [113] Smith, *Rasputin*, 257.

already provided by the Cathedral of the centrality of Orthodoxy in Nicholas's life. "The Emperor and the whole Imperial Family revere Sundays and feast days as holy, and always attend Vespers [the proceeding day's vigil] and the Divine Liturgy," Elkhaninov tells us: "During the service, the Tsar and his family are a model of attention and piety. The Sovereign especially appreciates simple, clear services and loves the ancient chants and rites. At every meeting, the Monarch kisses the hands of the clergy, as they also kiss his. Prayers are said daily, in the morning and before bed, by the Sovereign alone, and by the Imperial children . . . together with their august mother."[114]

Elkhaninov never uses the term *teokratia*. But, clearly, its substance was his ideal. "Tsarist authority has been received from the Lord God over our people. Before His Throne We will give an account for the fate of our Power," writes Elkhaninov, citing the opening lines of Nicholas's Manifesto of June 1907.[115] Indeed, for our purposes, his biography can be taken as amounting to a portrait, painted by the tsarist authorities themselves, of what Nicholas II might have understood by the term. Certainly, Elkhaninov agreed that the tsar's only essential qualification was confession of the Orthodox Christian faith.[116] "Deeply believing," Nicholas, says Elkhaninov, "begins not a single day nor project without turning in prayer to God. In the Lord God, he seeks admonition and support in his affairs; as God's Anointed he exercises his authority as from God. This deep faith in the source of Tsarist authority, this sober, holy, and sincere conviction in the protection of the Most High find their reflection in all the important State affairs of the current reign."[117]

But the most touching example, perhaps, of the Orthodox inspiration of Nicholas's inner life, and the humility and common cause it fostered in his relations with his subjects, is the story Elkhaninov tells of a group of Orthodox peasants from the Polish province of Kholm.[118] Alarmed by rumors that the tsar was planning to abandon Orthodoxy, they traveled during Easter 1905 to Petersburg, to find out for themselves whether "Orthodoxy still existed on the earth." Received first by the Minister of the Interior, the peasants greeted him with the customary Orthodox Easter salutation "Christ is risen!" But when the (doubtless Kantian-minded) minister replied, not with the customary "He is risen indeed!," but a restrained *Zdravstvuitye* ("Good day"), their fears appeared to be founded. The leader of the party, an abbess from a convent in their local district, insisted on seeing the tsar. Ushered into a reception room, the peasants greeted Nicholas II with the same Easter greeting that they had addressed to the minister. "He is risen indeed!"

---

[114] Andrei Georgievich Elkhaninov, *Tsarstvovanie Gosudaria Imperatora Nikolaia Aleksandrovicha* (C.PB [Sankt-Peterburg"]: Sel'skago Viestnika, 1913), 68.
[115] Ibid.   [116] Ibid., 5.   [117] Ibid., 66.   [118] Ibid., 69–70.

Nicholas replied instinctively before, Elkhaninov writes, "kissing each according to Orthodox custom." The peasants fell to their knees. "The faith lives! The Tsar is Orthodox! The Orthodox people is alive!" they allegedly cried through tears of joy.[119]

In this "aliveness" to the Divine Liturgy, in their response to the Church's sacramental and liturgical rites as something utterly real and transformative, Nicholas II and Bulgakov were one, and they were so often in isolation from their contemporaries, even Orthodox ones, who tended to downplay it as an empty, malleable ceremony. Indeed, if we have lingered so long here on the liturgy, it is because when looking for a source of Nicholas's own conception of Russia as a *teokratia*, it is to the liturgy that we should turn. "The Church concentrated special love on its anointed, as the beloved bridegroom of the Church from the line of David," Bulgakov urged in the voice of the Refugee in "At the feast of the gods." "Look closely at the liturgy, which is now maimed by mechanical amputations, and apart from courtly rhetoric and servility, you will sense this mystical love." The argument here is that Nicholas did "look closely at the liturgy" and, doing so, felt its "mystical love" for the bearer of his office deeply. His mistake, if mistake it was, was to take it too seriously. In an age of secularization, he staked his, and his family's, life on it.

Indeed, whether the choice was Elkhaninov's or Nicholas's, it is surely significant that the opening page of his biography begins not with Nicholas's birth in 1868, but with a summary of the Coronation Liturgy of 1896. "Yes, establish, instruct and direct him in the great service, as Tsar and Judge of the All-Russian Tsardom; yes, *let his heart be in the hands of God, let him direct everything to the benefit of the people committed to him and to the glory of God so that in the Day of Judgment he may not be ashamed to render Him account*," the text reads, italicized in the original, as if to underline for the text's readers in 1913 that nineteen years after his coronation Nicholas II was living "with prayer on his lips, with deep faith in his heart," and, more than ever, in the reality into which the liturgy had conducted him.[120] Barely four years later, in the train station at Pskov, and as bread riots in Petrograd occasioned the Duma's demand that he relinquish executive control of the government into their hands, Nicholas would still be thinking of his Coronation Liturgy and the account he and he alone would be obliged to render to God for Russia as a result of it.

෨ ෨ ෨

Rather than proving the perversion or idiosyncrasy of Nicholas's

---

[119] Ibid., 70–71.
[120] Ibid., 5–8. The text, which begins on page five, is broken up by two illustrations.

religion, then, Bulgakov believed the Rasputin episode could only be understood by reference to the same, authentically Christian, theocratic principle. *Pace* the later findings of the Canonization Committee, the alleged holy man occupied, not a false place in Nicholas's heart and understanding of his office as tsar, but an authentic one — falsely. As an authority, Bulgakov cited his master, Vladimir Solovyov, who, in his 1888 tract on the theocratic ideal, *La Russie et l'Église universelle*, had sketched a tripartite vision of what true *teokratia* in Russia should look like. According to Solovyov, the theocratic principle was composed of three essential components: the charisms or personal offices of *priest*, *king*, and *prophet*. While Solovyov argued that the first office (that of priest) belonged, properly speaking, to the pope in Rome, as successor to St Peter, and the second to the Russian tsar, as heir to (St) Constantine and Byzantine emperors, the third office would be filled by a representative from the ordinary, believing Christian people. Such a prophet would speak with the authority, not of Holy Orders or sacred anointing, but of the *sensus fidelium* — the common sense of all the faithful — inspired by the Holy Spirit.[121]

Of course, Nicholas never read Solovyov's text. But Bulgakov believed that the theocratically-minded Nicholas was instinctively recreating Solovyov's system. In this sense, therefore, Bulgakov believed Rasputin was not so much a separate affair in himself, as, in many ways, the embodiment of all the religious and spiritual currents that we have seen already, the emblem, however unworthy, of the legitimate religious meaning of the Russian Revolution. Years later, Bulgakov put it this way in a fictional exchange between himself as the Refugee and a Public Figure of liberal-Kantian sympathies in "At the feast of the gods":[122]

> *Public Figure*: It is really nightmarish to recall this evening now. Rasputin — there is the real inspirer of the revolution, not the Kadets.
>
> *The Refugee*: You are right, perhaps more than you realize, insofar as Rasputin was the point of application and the medium for the operation of mystical forces. And nevertheless this fatal influence expressed all the historical character and even the significance of the last reign. The tsar called for a prophet of theocratic inspirations — after all, even according to Solovyov's scheme, he was supposed to do this. Was it his fault alone that in answer to his call, which came from out of the depths, he received only a false prophet? And here, was not the whole people equally guilty, and their entire historical Church with

---

[121] See Vladimir Solov'ev, *La Russie et l'Église universelle* (Paris: A. Savine, 1889), especially chapter 9; also, Kantor, "Vladimir Solov'ev." It is not suggested here that Solovyov's theory expresses, in the terms Solovyov represented it, the mind of the Eastern Church on *teokratia*.

[122] For what follows, see Bulgakov, "At the feast of the gods," 80. We shall return to this passage later.

the hierarchy at its head? Or perhaps no one is personally guilty here, and if one may even speak of guilt then it is only about tragic guilt, more accurately about fate, about a certain sacrificial doom which befell the most worthy, and hardly the incompetent.

Indeed, Bulgakov would maintain to the end that the Rasputin scandal redounded, in a roundabout way, to Nicholas's credit. "For myself," Bulgakov repeated at the end of his life in *Autobiographical Fragments*, "I was ready to love the emperor even more for Rasputin, and even now I attribute to him as an asset, that with him such a figure as Rasputin was possible, not, of course, as [Rasputin] actually was, but as the embodiment of the principle of a saint and prophet from the people before the tsar. The tsar has called for a prophet, I said to myself I do not know how many times, and is he to blame if, instead of a prophet, he met a Khlyst? The tragic guilt in this matter is that of the weakness of the Church, the intelligentsia, the administration, all Russia. But that this tsar, in our dry and unbelieving age, should have managed to raise himself up to this ideal [i.e. of the appearance before the tsar of a prophet sent by God from the people], even as far as lending obedience to this 'Friend' (as in her tragic blindness the empress called him), this was majestic, momentous, prophetic."[123] To be sure, Rasputin the man was an aberration who exposed himself dangerously to demonic forces that very probably ended up using him to bring down the *teokratia*. But the fact that he was possible at all as a figure in an age of such "secularized," Kantian religion did not falsify but proved the depth of Nicholas's internalization of the theocratic principle. Rasputin, we might say, was the corrupted symbol and symptom of Nicholas's healthy refusal of his contemporaries' judgment in favor of secularization.

---

[123] See again Bulgakov, *Avtobiograficheskie*, 84–85.

CHAPTER SEVEN

Crimea

§O FAR, WE HAVE ARGUED, TO BE UNDERSTOOD properly, the history of Russia's twentieth century—and, indeed, of the twentieth century *in general*—must be understood *theologically*. The Russian Revolution in its widest sense, flowing from the rejection of the theocratic principle by Russia's intelligentsia and governing elite, represented a *crisis of the sacred in the world*. Manifest above all in the demise of the world's last Constantinian regime—the Russian *teokratia*—that had sought, via the political order, to keep the two, the sacred and the world, together, the revolution of 1917 "transhistorically" realized the atheist conclusions of nineteenth-century philosophy, inasmuch as it proceeded from and in turn represented a collective *judgment for secularization*—in the first instance of the political order, but through the latter *of the world*. Shaken by the force of this event, all the twentieth century proceeded under the value of this sign. Today, reinforced by the completeness of the West's ideological victory over the Soviet Union in the Cold War, the cultural and political development of the West continues to affirm and extend this judgment in favor of secularization according to an ever more accelerating tempo. But in Russia the reverse has occurred. Making a saint of the last bearer of the theocratic principle, Russian culture has symbolically *reversed* its judgment in favor of secularization. But what evidence was there of this symbolic reversal of judgment, outside the limited environment of Petersburg and its suburbs, where the memory of the last Romanovs was strongest? To answer that question, I determined to follow the footsteps of the Romanovs themselves to find out—to retrace, as it were, the historical geography of the *collapse* of the theocratic principle in Russian culture a hundred years ago in order to trace, today, the extent of the same principle's *revival*. The first challenge this presented me was that of the historical-geographical consequences of the Revolution itself. The borders of modern Russia no longer coincide with those of Nicholas and Alexandra's. If this is significant, it is because before 1917, that part of Russia dearer to Nicholas and Alexandra than any other was the disputed modern peninsula of Crimea.[1] Not for nothing, perhaps, did Bulgakov have his vision of Nicholas II in Crimea's leading seaside resort, Yalta.

ஐ   ஐ   ஐ

---

[1] Vyrubova, *Memories*, 17–18.

In the cool but humid air, a wiry, brown-haired man in jeans and navy polo held a piece of paper with my name scrawled in uncertain Latin letters on a piece of paper in his right hand; he was the driver of the taxi sent to collect me by my hotel.

"Is this your first trip to Crimea?" he asked, apologizing for the rain that had begun falling again as we drove through the streets of Simferopol, the regional capital. "It's usually warmer this time of year. What are you doing here?"

I paused before revealing the purpose of my visit. There was no reason to think that popular sentiment in Crimea today should be automatically pro-Romanov. To be sure, before the Revolution, Nicholas and Alexandra's white, Italianate palace at Livadia was among the imperial family's best-loved residences. Well-liked in nearby Yalta, the family were at ease, and often appeared with a minimum of barriers and chaperones in public. This accounted for the human scale of the Romanovs' proximity, which made Bulgakov's 1909 encounter with Nicholas II possible. But local good will towards the dynasty was neither universal nor inexhaustible. In 1905, and again in 1917, the Black Sea Fleet stationed at nearby Sevastopol proved a hotbed of revolutionary agitation. In addition to Nicholas and Alexandra, many Romanov grand dukes had palaces in Crimea. When the monarchy fell in February 1917, even formerly trusted servants in these grand ducal palaces cheered the proclamation of a republic, and pinned red ribbons to their liveries.[2]

Decades later, after the clash of Soviet and Nazi armies in the Second World War had left the peninsula a battle-scarred ruin, Crimea was rebuilt as the jewel in the Soviet crown, a sliver of the USSR with a Mediterranean-style climate colonized year-round by workers on State-funded holiday from Moscow and Minsk, Kiev and Leningrad in a vast network of concrete Soviet sanatoria. Gorbachev himself was on holiday here, in a State-owned villa not all that far from Nicholas and Alexandra's Livadia Palace, when a KGB-led plot to oust him in August 1991 instead precipitated the final collapse of the Soviet Union.[3] But unable to think of a different reason, I explained to the taxi driver my desire to see the Romanov residences, particularly Livadia. Again, I needn't have bothered worrying.

"Livadia? That's funny!" he exclaimed. "I have a friend who works in the museum there. She's a curator. When you visit the palace, ask for Nadia. Tell her that Grigory sent you."

༄   ༄   ༄

---

[2] Prince Felix Yusupov, *Lost Splendour* (London: Jonathan Cape, 1953), 255.
[3] The story, with its Crimean angle, is well told by Serhii Plokhy, *The Last Empire: The final days of the Soviet Union* (New York: One World, 2015).

Geographically, the Crimean Peninsula is shaped like a flattened dia-
mond. The upper two thirds continue the flat, dry grasslands that
extend from the Carpathians all the way to Manchuria. Simferopol lies
at the steppe land's most southerly point. Beyond it, the grass gives
way to the foothills of the mountains that make almost make Crimea's
southern coastline — a sub-tropical micro-region of emerald-green and
turquoise — an island unto itself. The Peninsula has been inhabited for
millennia. Its first recorded native inhabitants were a people called the
Tauri, whom Greek writers considered to be savages who made human
sacrifices to their gods. From them the peninsula gained its classical
name of Tauris. Between 600 and 400 BC, however, Greek colonists
from Anatolia founded a string of settlements in the Peninsula's south,
settlements that thrived on the cultivation of grain, vine and fruit, fishing, and the raising of livestock for leather.[4] While the grasslands in the
Peninsula's north became the home of the feared Scythians, a hundred
years either side the birth of Christ the Greek settlements of the southern coast were folded, like the rest of the Greek world, into the Roman
Empire. Cicero called them the "hem of Greece sewn on to the fields
of the barbarians."[5]

For all of Russia's debt to Byzantium, Crimea's southern coast is the
only part of the Russian Empire that was ever ruled by the emperor in
Constantinople. The leading Greco-Roman city on the Peninsula was
Chersonesos, and when, in the fourth century AD, the pagan empire
of Rome became the Christian empire of Constantinople (the "New
Rome" on the Bosporus), Chersonesos followed suit and became Christian too. Within its walls, life continued, as it had done for centuries,
to follow rhythms set in the Mediterranean. Though a constant flow
of "barbarians" streamed across the steppes to Crimea's north, under
Byzantine rule, Chersonesos exported fish, hides and honey to Constantinople. But as the empire's listening post on the volatile politics
of the steppe, the city had another function too, that of informing
the emperor of advancing armies of horsemen before their mounted
archers appeared before the walls of the capital. In the fourth century, that threat came from the Goths; in the fifth, it was the Huns;
in the sixth, the Avars — and so on and so forth, down the through
centuries: Bulgars, Magyars, Pecheneg Turks, Cumans. Some of these
nomadic tribes, such as the Goths, settled on the Peninsula and survived there until modern times. Others plundered what they could and
left. But over against this ever-present threat from the steppe, in the
south Chersonesos held on, and in 988 it performed perhaps its greatest

[4] Glen Mack and Joseph Coleman Carter, eds., *Crimean Chersonesos: City, chora, museum and environs* (Austin, TX: Institute of Classical Archaeology of The University of Texas, 2003), 17–28.   [5] Obolensky, *Byzantine Commonwealth*, 25.

contribution to world history, by providing the setting for the baptism of Grand Prince Vladimir of Kiev to Byzantium's Orthodox variant of the Christian faith.[6] It was this event that Russian President Vladimir Putin was referring to when, seeking to justify Crimea's annexation in a speech at the end of 2014, he called it Russia's "Temple Mount." Two years later, he and Patriarch Kirill unveiled a colossal statue of Grand Prince Vladimir outside the Kremlin.

In the thirteenth century, Crimea was lost to Byzantium and the Rus alike. Four and a half centuries of Muslim-Tatar rule commenced in 1313, when Genghis Khan's son Juchi and grandson Batu made Crimea part of an empire of grass and horses, the fabled Khanate of the Golden Horde, stretching from central Siberia to the borders of Lithuania and Poland.[7] In 1440, the Golden Horde broke up, and Crimea became a khanate of its own, its rulers subject to the Ottoman Sultan at Istanbul.[8] The Russians arrived — or returned — in 1783 when the armies of Catherine the Great, led by Catherine's lover, Prince Grigory Potemkin, conquered the peninsula. It remained Russian until Khrushchev had it transferred to the Ukrainian Soviet Socialist Republic in 1954.

But it was the Peninsula's more recent history that imposed on me as, with the sun in my eyes, I walked to the nearby intersection of Catherine Street and Kirov Avenue. Named after the Leningrad party secretary whose 1935 murder provided Stalin with the pretext for his Purges, this is Simferopol's main thoroughfare. Strung across the street above the passing Ladas and second-hand Audis were swathes of banners and bunting celebrating the second anniversary of Russia's second, more recent annexation ("re-unification") of the Peninsula in March 2014.

> *Russia, peace, unity!*
> *When we're united, we're invincible!*
> *With Russia — forever!*
> *Unity of spirit is Russia's strength!*
> *It pleases us to live in Russia. To work and raise children. To love*
>   *one's native land and believe in the oneness of thoughts.*

A hundred or so meters further up the road, I reached Simferopol's central "Lenin Square." On this expanse of concrete, under the gaze of a giant bronze Lenin, in the weeks before the referendum in March 2014, several thousand local residents gathered to cheer on the sailors of Russia's Black Sea Fleet. Rival pro-Ukrainian demonstrations later

---

[6] Ibid., 43–51.
[7] Charles Halperin, *Russia and the Golden Horde: The Mongol impact on medieval Russian history* (Bloomington, IN: Indiana University Press, 1985), 25.
[8] The best introduction to Crimea's Tatar history remains Alan W. Fisher, *The Russian Annexation of the Crimea, 1772–1783* (Cambridge: Cambridge University Press, 1970), 1–16.

made use of the same square.[9] Every year since the annexation, it has served as the venue for Simferopol's anniversary celebrations. And — a sign of not only of the times but, it would seem, of the Kremlin's determination to reach a younger, online crowd — I spotted a large board that still displayed the event's official hashtag: *#KrymRossiyaNavsegda* (CrimeaRussiaForever). If such sentiment has its way, the moving tableau of empires will have ended.

At the other end of Catherine Street, flanked by chestnuts coming into leaf, the octagonal shape of Crimea's late Soviet regional assembly came into view. In February 2014, this beige, steel and concrete building became the ground zero of the Peninsula's annexation drama, when pro-Russian biker groups took it over in a bid to force its members to vote for a referendum.[10] In the garden to its right, a stone plinth mounted by a Soviet T-40 tank, and surrounded by a half colonnade of Doric columns, forms a memorial to Simferopol's liberation by Soviet forces in 1944. Fresh flowers lay at the foot of the plinth. Beyond the memorial, five glinting helmet cupolas drew my attention. They belonged to a large neo-classical church, chastely painted in white at the far end of the garden. With its Doric-colonnaded portico and fine entablature, the 1816 Cathedral of St Alexander Nevsky was originally commissioned by Emperor Alexander I and was, before the Revolution, the seat of Crimea's local Orthodox bishop. In 1930, Simferopol's Communist Party blew it up as part of Stalin's war on the Church. What the visitor sees today is an in-progress reconstruction whose sponsor is none other than the current occupant of the Kremlin himself. Prominently placed in front of the building, a large sign sports the Russian flag and double-headed eagle. "The restoration of the Cathedral of Grand Prince St Alexander Nevsky the Pious is being carried out under the sponsorship of the President of the Russian Federation, V. V. PUTIN," it reads. After seventy years of Communist dictatorship, was it a distant echo of Bulgakov's *teokratia*?

◈　◈　◈

Simferopol's main train station is a grand, late imperial building in neo-Ottoman style, fronted by a graceful, arched colonnade hung with plants and an imposing clock tower decorated with Ottoman-style motifs. Because of Ukraine's transport embargo when I visited, its platforms lay quiet. The few shabby bays of the bus terminus in its car park, however, were busy with the arrival and departure of packed minivans. To reach

---

[9] Tom Porter, "Thousands gather for rival pro-Ukrainian and pro-Russian rallies in Crimea," *International Business Times*, March 9, 2014: http://www.ibtimes.co.uk/thousands-gather-rival-pro-ukrainian-pro-russian-rallies-1439538 (accessed January 9, 2025).
[10] For a narrative of the annexation and its context, see Richard Sakwa, *Frontline Ukraine: Crisis in the borderlands* (London: I. B. Tauris, 2015), 100–13.

the enclave of Romanov palaces at Livadia, I had to take a bus from the terminal in front of me south across the coastal ranges, a journey of about 80km. This was not how the Romanovs usually arrived. Typically continuing aboard the imperial train through Simferopol, the emperor and his family would disembark at the port city of Sevastopol. There, waiting for them at the imperial wharf directly opposite, at the far end of the southern arm of Sevastopol's many-fingered harbor, would be the magnificent, low-slung imperial yacht, *Standart*. Having boarded the yacht, Nicholas, Alexandra, and their children would sail a few hundred meters to the grand, neo-classical ensemble of the city's famous Count's Steps, Sevastopol's ceremonial gateway. Disembarking from the imperial yacht, the family would be met by Crimea's governor, imperial officials and, as was almost always the case, an enthusiastic crowd. Usually, official engagements would detain them a couple of days. When they had concluded, the imperial family would re-board *Standart* and sail four hours to the fashionable coastal resort of Yalta, from where a short drive brought them to their cliff-side palace at Livadia.

Even from the window of a dilapidated 1970s minivan, however, the overland route by minivan from Simferopol to Livadia was a pretty drive. Twenty minutes out from Simferopol, the terrain began to rise into wooded hills, studded here and there with the golden onion domes and blue and white painted walls of newly constructed Orthodox churches and monasteries. At regular intervals, billboards appealed for Crimeans' electoral loyalties, providing a window onto local political life in the aftermath of the annexation. To read them was to imagine Crimea as a stronghold of Communist Party sympathy. "Thank you, Soviet Soldier, for the Victory," proclaimed a board paid for by the Russian Communist Party in reference to forthcoming Victory Day celebrations. "Defend the interests of the working man," another called out. But these were the sentiments of the Kremlin's loyal opposition, not the government. "Build the new, Russian Crimea," demanded a United Russia billboard. "Russia — that's us," read another. All the same, it would be wrong to suggest that politics was the only thing on locals' minds. The majority of the billboards were dedicated to more banal purposes, and the view across the wooded hills was disfigured by advertisements for a world of private commerce utterly foreign to the old Soviet Union: supermarkets, wedding expos, pool and spa showrooms.

Climbing into the mountains, we passed through farming country: houses made of rough-hewn stone or brick with corrugated iron roofs; diminutive, snow-white goats with heavy udders; a heavily pregnant dog; and fruit trees in white and pink blossom. At length, however, the farmland and broadleaf woods gave way to Scots Pine, then scrub and grassland as mountains rose out of valleys below. As the minivan climbed the road through the coastal range, thick cloud closed in, only to then part, as if biblically, when we crossed the ridge at the top and began a swift descent towards the Black Sea. I had entered an entirely new ecological zone. Shielded by the mountains at its back from the icy blasts of the winter winds sweeping off the steppe, the thin coastal plain basked in the warm southern sun. Cypresses appeared along the roadside, soon joined by showers of bright pink and purple bougainvillea. Spread across a diminutive, sunny plain halfway down the mountain was my first vineyard. Together, these things revealed the Black Sea stretched out beneath me for what in human terms it has been for centuries: an extension of the Mediterranean and the civilizations it has cradled.

ↁ ↁ ↁ

A coastal enclave spread heedlessly along the Black Sea shoreline at the foot of a steep escarpment. Yalta is a town of bottle-green cypresses and electric pink bougainvillea, lilac wisteria, spreading cabbage-tree palms — and cars. Lots and lots of cars. Set on a series of foothills, what used to be the tsarist empire's premier holiday resort is a labyrinth of twisting lanes and steeply rising terraces, intersected by half a dozen fast-gushing streams that race down the mountain towards the sea. Every few hundred meters, the bridges built to cross them funnel traffic to choke points jammed with idling vehicles. I commented on the traffic to the driver who had bundled me into his taxi when I left the minivan. It was the start of the tourist season, he explained, and things were getting busy. I asked whether the annexation had affected tourist numbers, but he shook his head at the suggestion.

"Most tourists come from Russia, anyway," he explained. "We still get some from Ukraine too but, you know, normal people, not the crazy ones." He was referring to the "fascists" who are commonly held to rule from Kiev in the wake of the Euromaidan. We passed homely two- and three-story villas lining the street, shielded from the road by often luxuriant vegetation (very little of which is sufficiently well-tended to claim the status of garden). A hundred years ago, the grandest of these were the dachas of St Petersburg's and Moscow's rich and famous, who, following the lead set by the imperial family, made the "Crimean Riviera," with Yalta at its center, the focus of their spring and summer pleasures. In time, guesthouses for the middling classes mushroomed alongside them, jumbled stories of rough-hewn stone. Being in a valley, Yalta is dark and damp, and local architecture has traditionally favored a kind of Ottoman-style wood paneling with large windows to catch as much light as possible.

During the 1917 Revolution, Yalta was cleared of its dispossessed aristocrats, but this did not bring its history to an end. On the contrary, the town became home to the Soviet Union's most sought-after health spas and holiday resorts when the old tsarist-era building stock was transformed into sanatoria for party members. Soon, however, the demand for Yalta's relaxations exceeded its supply of accommodation. The solution in the 1930s, and again in the 1960s, was the construction of a vast network of hospital-type structures, which crawled up the side of the mountain overlooking the town. In the 1970s a handful of ugly eight- and nine-story concrete boxes sprung up, disfiguring it forever. My hotel, however, was an old tsarist-era pile at the end of Yalta's famous embankment. Built during the reign of Alexander III (after whom it was originally named), this 1.5km-long seaside promenade put Yalta firmly on the holiday-seekers' map. Decades ago, it was renamed in honor of Lenin, and Lenin's (not Alexander's) Embankment it remains today. A typical bronze statue of the Bolshevik leader still presides over the angular, Soviet-era square at its main eastern end. Ironically, it was here, in 1909, that Bulgakov saw Nicholas II for the first time and, seeing him, was a convert forever to the ideal of *teokratia*.

෨෨ ෨෨ ෨෨

A natural beauty spot located on a high bluff to the south overlooking Yalta, Livadia had been an imperial property since Emperor Alexander II (Nicholas's grandfather) bought it as a gift to his wife, Empress Marie Alexandrovna, in 1860. She fell in love with it, and commissioned architect Hippolyte Monighetti to build a two-story villa overlooking the sea. Later, a smaller building was constructed alongside, so that there were in fact two imperial residences at Livadia; and it was in this smaller building, alongside the main house, that Alexander III died, with the still unwed Nicholas and Alexandra in attendance, in 1894. Unwilling, perhaps, to be confronted with the painful memories associated with the property, and preoccupied with their wedding, coronation, and the birth of the first two of their children, Nicholas and Alexandra would take four years to return to the Crimea. They first did so in 1898. For the couple, and, later, for their family, Livadia was above all a holiday destination, an escape from the grind of the court, government, and bureaucracy in St Petersburg. If, at Tsarskoye Selo, the emphasis was on duty, at Livadia it was on rest and relaxation. All the same, danger lurked. When Nicholas and Alexandra next returned two years later in 1900, Nicholas contracted typhoid. For days, it seemed Livadia would witness the death of a second emperor. On another occasion, Nicholas fell off his mount when it slipped on wet clay during a ride in the mountains, injuring his side.[11] After two visits in the spring and autumn of 1902, however, another long break (occasioned by the effort to conceive

---

[11] Mossolov, *At the Court*, 237.

Alexei, his birth and the discovery of his illness, the outbreak of the war
with Japan, the Revolution of 1905 and the turbulent, opening years
of the so-called "Duma Monarchy") intervened before the family again
returned to Crimea in 1909.

By this time, the old palace was beginning to show its age. Dark,
damp and too cramped for Nicholas and Alexandra and their five children, the house lacked running water on the upper floor, and hot water
had to be carried up in pails for the emperor's bath.[12] Presented with a
choice between extensive repairs or total reconstruction, Nicholas and
Alexandra chose the latter, and commissioned the head of the Imperial
Academy, Nikolai Krasnov, to build an entirely new palace, modeled on
the summer residence of the Italian king, Victor Emmanuel III, in the
Ligurian Riviera.[13] When it was finished in 1911, Nicholas and Alexandra loved it from the start. Setting his eyes on it for the first time
that spring, Nicholas wrote to his mother in Petersburg that he could
not "find the words to express our happiness and satisfaction in the
possession of such a house, built exactly as we wished it."[14] Voeikov,
the Palace Commandant, remembered it as "full of light," and "one
of the most beautiful places" he had ever seen. As Robert Massie put
it, "to every other palace in Russia Nicholas and Alexandra preferred
Livadia."[15]

Today, it's easy to appreciate why. As one approaches along the
path from the discreet access road, the palace emerges from behind
the spreading branches of mature redwoods and sycamores. Together
with the slender, banded trunks of the palm trees that stud the emerald
lawn in front of the building, the effect of this is to lend the Romanovs' Crimean home an air of California, as if, even in this redoubt of
Europe's Old Regime, the outlines of the dawning "American Century"
were already being foreshadowed. The architectural language of the palace itself is, however, eclectic. With its Ionic colonnade and Renaissance
balustrading, the building appears to have been chiseled out of a single
block of fine, white, sun-bleached marble (it is actually local limestone),
like a miraculously preserved villa of ancient Greece or Rome. What
is indisputable is that the natural setting is spectacular. To the left of
the palace as the visitor views it, the ground slopes away gently at first
before—beyond marble fountains, rose beds and fir trees—disappearing
absolutely into the waves of the Black Sea.

---

[12] Spiridovitch, *Dernières Années*, 1:375.
[13] It is said that it was built with such haste precisely because the increasing scrutiny of
the Romanovs' finances that had arisen with the advent of the Duma in 1905 was deemed
likely to make the construction of further imperial palaces more difficult in the future.
[14] N. N. Kalinin and M. A. Zemlianichenko, *Romanovy i Krym. 'U vsekh nas ostalas'
toska po Krymu ...'* (Simferopol': Biznes-Inform, 2021), 149.
[15] Massie, *Nicholas and Alexandra*, 162.

൞   ൞   ൞

The afternoon sun was dipping, the shadows growing long across as the grass. Individual visits are not permitted at the palace, and I was just in time for the last guided tour of the day. A guard invited us to wait for our guide beyond a barrier of flimsy aluminum gates in the exiguous space between the portico and the bottom of the steep terrace facing it. As a private residence, Livadia was entered not by grand staircase, but directly from the courtyard through a pair of warm, cedar-colored wooden doors flanked by fluted white pilasters and guarded by two Egyptian-inspired white marble lions. Still in place, and set in delicate, scalloped roundels decorated with tendrils of acanthus, the stylized "N" and "A" of Nicholas and Alexandra's personal monograms recall the palace's first and last owners. Opposite this doorway, my eyes fell on a bronze bust of a bearded figure in military uniform, grandly set on a white marble plinth beneath the branches of a magnolia tree. It was Nicholas II, or, more precisely, as the accompanying plaque would have it, using both the tsar's secular and sainted titles, "The Sovereign Emperor Nicholas II, Holy Passion-bearer." It was dated 19 May 2015 — the second anniversary of Nicholas's birthday *after* the annexation; and the monument's primary sponsor was the Moscow-based Imperial Orthodox Palestine Society, an Orthodox missionary society founded by the imperial family before the Revolution and revived since the fall of communism.[16]

Our guide arrived, and the tour began. Livadia is about more than the last Romanovs. During the Nazi occupation of Crimea, from 1941 until 1944, Livadia served as headquarters of the German Army's 22nd Infantry Division. In February 1945, it was the venue of the famous Yalta conference between Stalin, Churchill and Roosevelt, at which the future of post-War Europe was largely decided. In homage to this world-historical event, in the first room we entered, the flags of the United States, Great Britain, and the Soviet Union sprouted from a single stand in the middle of a large round conference table spread with a felt bottle green cloth. In the next, three leather-bound folders lay on a long cherry-wood table, one each for each of the British, US, and Soviet leaders. Photographs showed the three men sitting at that very table — Roosevelt in the middle with Stalin and Churchill on either side — while their delegations raised vodka glasses in a toast.[17] From there we proceeded

---

[16] On the Society, see Strickland, *Making of Holy Russia*, 81–85.
[17] On the Yalta agreements, see Serhii Plokhy, *Yalta: The price of peace* (New York: Viking, 2010). Putin held the agreements up as a model for diplomacy in his address at the seventieth anniversary of the United Nations: Russian President Vladimir Putin, "70th session of the United Nations General Assembly," September 28, 2015: http://en.kremlin.ru/events/president/news/50385 (accessed January 10, 2025).

into Nicholas's formal study, decorated with neo-classical furniture and hung with light yellow wallpaper. The tsar used it for receiving ministers and ambassadors on official business from St Petersburg, and in 1945 Roosevelt, who occupied the palace with the American delegation for a week that February, used it as his dining room.

Leaving this room behind, we walked out into a gloomy, green-carpeted hallway, and up a flight of broad, shallow stairs carved in dark, heavy oak. The upper floor was the location of the family's private rooms. As in Gatchina and Tsarskoye Selo, none of Livadia's original furnishings survived. Instead, photographs show the family's private rooms decorated with an avalanche of roses, family photographs, and the English-style fabrics that Alexandra loved. A lifeless waxwork of Nicholas II in white naval uniform greets visitors in a room that was once his informal study or *kabinet*. Cabinets filled informatively, if unimaginatively, with black-and-white photographs lined the four walls. More interesting was the small dining room we headed to next: an intimate, light-filled space with a superb view of the sea, where, around a table laden with trappings of home, the Romanovs would once have taken breakfast *en famille*.

Descending the stairs to the ground floor, we passed through a warren of blind passages before entering a sunny cloister. Around a large central fountain, paths bordered by beds of white pebbles formed a geometric pattern, while neatly trimmed hedges enclosed carefully laid rose beds punctuated with waxy green cycads and ficus trees. In each corner, a tall cabbage palm rose towards the sky, which was turning a darker and darker shade of blue as the sun set. From this inner sanctuary, a narrow passageway led to the palace chapel, a wonderful neo-Byzantine structure of finely carved white marble, and the only part of the original palace to survive the 1911 reconstruction. It was here that, the day after the death of Nicholas's father, Alexander III, the twenty-four-year-old Princess Alix of Hesse was received into the Orthodox Church and took her new name, Alexandra Fyodorovna. A liturgy was underway when we peered inside, a handful of mainly older people standing at random points between the door and icon screen. Above their heads, a cloud of incense hung in the air. When the tour ended, I turned back to the chapel and went inside.

Religion played no less a part in Nicholas and Alexandra's lives on holiday in Crimea than it did elsewhere. Before setting foot in their new palace in 1911, they insisted on its being blessed by a priest. The rest of the family's first day in the new building was spent hanging icons.[18] Just as departure from Tsarskoye Selo was always preceded by a service to ask blessing on the journey, so arrival in Livadia was

---

[18] Vyrubova, *Memories*, 21.

always marked by a service of thanksgiving for safe arrival in the palace chapel. Returning in 1912, in time for the last week of Lent, the family attended services twice a day during Holy Week, while on Holy Thursday, "a very solemn day in the Orthodox ... calendar, their Majesties took communion, ... turning from the altar to the congregation and bowing on all sides. After this, they approached the holy images and kissed them." [19] Two days later, on Easter Saturday night, "there was a procession with candles through the courts of the palace and on Easter Sunday for two hours the soldiers, according to the old custom, gathered to exchange Easter kisses with the Emperor and to receive each an Easter egg. Children from the schools came to salute in like manner the Empress. For their Majesties it was a long and fatiguing ceremony, but they carried it through with all graciousness ... " On their visit in September 1913, a succession of Church feasts in the lead-up to Sunday saw them at the Divine Liturgy (itself never shorter than three hours in duration) three days in a row. [20] As always, their usual weekly practice was Saturday Vespers (the "all-night" service) and Sunday Mass. [21]

Today, the chapel is the most beautiful and apparently best-loved part of the restored palace. On a bright blue mosaic background, gold stars covered the concave ceiling. Halfway down the length of the nave, two slender, white marble columns were capped with stylized acanthus capitals. At the center of the triple arch, these columns support the Chi-Ro, a Christian symbol first used by Constantine. Two circular, brass candelabra threw a flickering light over the stone icon screen at the church's far eastern end, the reflection of its candles dancing in the gold leaf of the icons with which it is inset. I imagined Nicholas and Alexandra kneeling in private prayer before it. Today, their presence is signified by an icon of themselves, the Royal Passion-Bearers, halfway down the nave on the left-hand wall facing the altar. Three or four small beeswax candles were burning on a stand in front of it, the memory of a recent supplicant's prayers. Though the palace is a museum, the chapel is a place of pilgrimage.

To the immediate right of this icon, a low door with a white marble lintel led to a small icon shop. Among the images on sale was a range of icons of the Romanovs in all sizes and to suit all budgets—from small, laminated cards to traditional painted olive-wood boards and the even more expensive enameled diptychs, housed in soft, faux velvet boxes with golden clasps. Gesturing towards the books I saw were also for sale, I asked the woman behind the counter to show me what they had on

---

[19] Ibid., 23.
[20] Nicholas II, September 13, 14, and 15, 1913, in Diary (2), 423.
[21] In the spring of 1914, Nicholas noted in his diary that he didn't go to the Saturday evening all-night vigil ("Vespers") precisely because it was a departure from his usual practice. Naturally, he attended the Divine Liturgy the following morning, Sunday. Nicholas II, May 3 and 4, 1914, in Diary (2), 461.

the Royal Passion-Bearers. She called out to a man with a grey, pointed beard packing boxes in the small room behind. "Are you Orthodox?" he asked, eyeing me with a mixture of curiosity and suspicion. The confession that I was not prompted the woman to try to persuade me to buy a Bible. I assured her that I already had one, and beat a retreat.

Outside, I followed the paving along the side of the chapel towards the sea. At the furthermost edge of the terrace in front of the palace, a Soviet-era sign marked the start of the "Sunny Path." A popular walk among the sanatoria crowd of the 1960s and 1970s, this path had been known to Nicholas and Alexandra as the "Horizontal Way," a 6.7km trail along the hilltop overlooking the sea that provided the route for their daily stroll. Before too long it would be dark, but I followed the path anyway through the waxy-leafed camellias and rhododendrons. After a few hundred meters, the clear, well-defined path of grey paving stones became a trail of stone and dirt beneath a canopy of bright-green spring foliage — lindens and oak interspersed with the dark green needles of Scots pine.

But for its use by Russia's last tsar a century ago, it could have been any coastal beauty spot the world over. An athletic young woman in a pink singlet top and running tights loped past, while in the other direction a middle-aged couple in raincoats with a Labrador walked hand in hand. As the hillside steepened, the trail negotiated a rocky cliff-face high above the coastal village of Oreanda, where the narrow coastal plain has broadened down below. Oreanda was the location of the original imperial estate on Crimea.[22] In 1881, however, the palace was destroyed by fire, and the imperial family decamped permanently to Livadia. A few hundred meters further along, I discovered a half-peristyle of white Doric columns that served as lookout. This romantic folly is all that remains of the Romanovs' original Oreanda Palace. Some of the best-known photographs of the last of the Romanovs show Nicholas and Alexandra enjoying this same view, uncluttered, then, by the scores of boxlike apartment complexes that now sprout up and down the coast from Yalta. The sun having now dropped below the level of the cloud bank that hovered over the sea, I retraced my steps to Livadia.

∽ ∽ ∽

The clouds that were closing in the previous night had completely vanished by the following morning. The sky was royal blue, the sea a fine cobalt. By 9.30 it was already warm enough for short sleeves, and I

---

[22] Kalinin and Zemlianichenko, *Romanovy*, 11: 46. Acquired by Emperor Alexander I (the vanquisher of Napoleon) on his 1825 visit to the peninsula, on Alexander's mysterious death a few weeks later the estate passed to his younger brother, the new Emperor Nicholas I, who gave it to his wife when, in 1837, he in turn visited. Completed in 1852, the Greek-style palace she had built marked Yalta's transformation into an empire-wide holiday resort.

asked reception to call another taxi for the palace. I wanted to go back and try to make contact with the "Nadia" commended by my original driver from the airport, Grigori.

When, half an hour later, a taxi emerged from the snarl of traffic, there could be no doubt about its owner's loyalties. The Russian tricolor and double-headed eagle were plastered on the dashboard, and an orange and black ribbon of St George's tied around the rear-vision mirror. The driver was a wiry, wizened figure with darting, lively eyes. He was also talkative. Born to Russian parents in Grozny, he fled to the peace of neighboring Georgia when the first Chechen war broke out in 1993. After a few years in Tbilisi, he moved to Moscow and, after fourteen years there, to Crimea. Like everyone I met in Yalta, he loved his city and delighted in its climate.

I asked him how people felt about the annexation.

"I tell you," he said, gesticulating with one hand while hanging on to the wheel with the other, "it was like returning to a mother. We never felt part of Ukraine here. Whenever people used to ask me where I was from, I'd never say 'Ukraine,' always 'Crimea.'"

At Livadia, a woman in the ticket booth phoned through my request to see Nadia, relaying the introduction Grigori had given me. Miraculously, after a pause, the said Nadia agreed to meet me. A tall, slim woman in her thirties, she had long, straight, light brown hair and jade green eyes set in a small, round face. As Grigori promised, she was a member of the museum's board of curators, but, confusingly, she had no idea who Grigori was, and looked embarrassed to be speaking to a foreigner introducing himself as an acquaintance of an unknown taxi driver from Simferopol.

I made a gesture in the direction of the palace, and asked about the newly erected bust of Nicholas II. She confirmed that it had been a gift the year before, from the local historical society. I asked whether it reflected a lot of local interest in the Romanovs.

"Well," she replied: "We have a lot of visitors. Mostly Russians, very few foreigners — for obvious reasons," she added furtively, with reference to the sanctions. "Before [the annexation] people used to come to Yalta on cruises and visit the palace. Now there are no cruises, but Russians come anyway."

I asked whether she had a sense of the sort of questions people were interested in when they visited. She tilted her head thoughtfully to one side before answering.

"Hmmm. Well, firstly, we give them a lot of information on the tour. The questions they ask are mainly to do with details about the imperial family's everyday lives. What sort of food did they like to eat? What pastimes did they engage in? Were they a loving family? Did they really care for each other, or were they cold and formal? These are the sorts of questions we can answer," she concluded, proudly.

The description corresponded with my own experience the previous day, but what remained unclear was whether those visitors came positively or negatively disposed towards the Romanovs. When I put this to Nadia, her answer suggested to me that she had begun to enjoy the questioning. In spite of my dubious connections to the unknown "Grigori," it seemed she had decided I was a serious person.

"You know, during Soviet times, there was a very negative attitude towards the Romanovs, and Nicholas II in particular. They were called 'enemies of the people' and so forth," she began to explain. "But now people have access to much more information. Attitudes are changing. Older people still tend to come with negative views, but younger people are much more positive. It's still a surprise for many to learn that before the revolution, the economy was growing, industry was getting stronger, for example."

I asked about the palace itself, and whether, now that the family had been canonized as saints, it had become more than a museum — a religious site, a place of pilgrimage.

"Yes, you could say that," she answered reflectively, as though I was the first to present the idea to her in those terms. "We do get a lot of pilgrim groups. They come on tours organized by the Orthodox Church. As the family are now saints, it's a big deal for them to see the church where the Tsar-Martyr, as the Church now calls Nicholas II, actually prayed. As the Romanovs' private church, it's an important thing for them to see."

Her words confirmed the impression I had gained the day before, in the chapel's icon shop.

The interview having run its course, I wandered through the redwoods, drinking in the fresh air blowing up off the sea that rolled gently towards the shore below. At length, I found a taxi outside the palace gate. Smoking a cigarette in the shade opposite his old Lada, the driver was a chubby, stubble-cheeked, middle-aged man wearing a grubby, ill-fitting t-shirt.

"Oh, you're a foreigner?" he asked, as if surprised, on hearing my accent.

I then asked him whether he was a local.

"No," he replied, "I'm from Zaphorizhia, in Ukraine. Have you heard of it?"

I had: it was the home of Ukraine's fiercely Orthodox, and fiercely independent, Cossacks, their *sech'*, or warrior's council, a symbol, in Bulgakov's *Vekhi* essay, of *volia* (self-will) — of wanton rebellion against established order — that always competed in Russian culture, he believed, with the rival principle of *askesis*.[23]

---

[23] Bulgakov, "Heroism and asceticism," 46. Cf. Hosking, *Russia and the Russians*, 17–18, which represents Russian history and culture as the push and pull between

It struck me that he was the first self-identified Ukrainian I had so far met in Crimea. Everyone else referred to themselves "Russians" or "Crimeans." I asked him his view of the Russian annexation.

"I'm Ukrainian. It's as simple as that. But the thing is, I came to Crimea *after* the annexation had already taken place. There's no work in Ukraine. The country's a mess. Why stay in Zaporizhia and be unemployed? From here I send money home to my mother and my family."

Since the annexation, stories about the flight of Ukrainians from Crimea to Kiev and elsewhere in Ukraine have occasionally appeared in the Western press. But my driver's story ran counter to them. I asked him whether he thought Crimea would one day return to Ukraine.

"No, I don't think so," he confided. "They've lost it for good—and Donetsk."

At that moment, we passed a white, Grecian-style rotunda, standing in the middle of a grassy traffic island, where the local road met the main coastal highway. An Orthodox cross crowned its small dome. I asked the driver to stop. Darting between passing cars to reach it, I found a golden, double-headed eagle hanging above the rotunda's open entrance. Inside, thousands of tiny, glittering tesserae formed a mosaic of the Virgin spreading her veil around the Romanovs, who were gathered in front of the Livadia. Offering surprisingly naturalistic renderings of Russia's last imperial family (tired and balding, Nicholas is shown as the weary middle-aged man he was in 1917, not as the fresh-faced emperor he had been twenty years before), it is the work of an experienced mosaicist, and the materials costly.

Outside the rotunda, I found a plaque with the date of the monument's unveiling: 2013, the 150th anniversary of the consecration of the Livadia palace chapel and the 400th anniversary of the dynasty's 1613 election to the Russian throne. It was also the first evidence I had found that the local cult of the Romanovs had predated the annexation. As a symbol of a certain kind of Russianness, the Royal Passion-Bearers, then, were not a post-annexation import.

༄   ༄   ༄

According to Mossolov, the great tragedy of Nicholas II's reign was the wall (*sredosteniye*) that separated the imperial family from the ordinary people—the Russian *narod*—despite the community of sympathies that united them in Orthodoxy. Lifted temporarily though this wall was at Sarov, no matter how much each side sought to overcome it, still it remained, breeding incomprehension, distrust, and, ultimately, hatred.

---

pravda ("truth," "right," "justice," "God's law") and *volia* ("freedom," "anarchy," "self-will"). On the nineteenth-century origins of Cossackdom as an element of specifically Ukrainian rather than Russian identity, see Serhii Plokhy, *The Cossack Myth: History and nationhood in the age of empires* (Cambridge: Cambridge University Press, 2012).

Indeed, if there was one reason why Nicholas and Alexandra loved Crimea so much, it was because it was here, almost alone in their vast empire, that they felt that the wall separating them from the people momentarily slipped away. In this sense, life at Livadia was like a permanent Sarov, where Nicholas and Alexandra could enjoy the popular, demotic, human side of *teokratia* as they imagined it was meant to be: a communion of genuine affection between the Orthodox *narod* and the tsar God had set over it as the keeper and guardian of its moral-religious ideal.[24] In Petersburg or Tsarskoye Selo, this desire to "go to the people" could only be a source of scandal; at Yalta, it was part of the course of daily life, as when Alexandra bundled her daughters into a car and had themselves driven to Yalta for an afternoon's shopping. So lacking were mother and daughters in airs that they were not always recognized.[25]

But the supreme manifestation of this "going to the people" was the charity bazaars that Alexandra held on the pier at Yalta every year from 1911 to 1914. The bazaars involved months of preparation. Alexandra, her daughters, and invited members of her entourage, such as Vyrubova and Dehn, spent untold hours knitting the scarves, hats, and socks, executing the careful embroidery and needlework, painting the watercolors, and drawing the postcards that she and her daughters would sell off in a specially erected tented pavilion, in aid of the local charities that the empress sponsored. When the long-awaited day arrived, usually in spring, when the weather was at its finest, Alexandra was in the thick of the action, presiding over her own table — receiving money and giving change — "with energy and enthusiasm," like any Victorian matron at the annual church fete, despite her own often fragile condition. (By 1909, constant, unrelieved anxiety for Alexei's health, coupled with long-term sciatica, had drastically undermined Alexandra's mental and bodily strength.) If such church fetes were a scene that Alexandra had witnessed during her childhood in England, for a Russian empress to engage in something so common and middle class represented an almost unimaginable upending of conventions. And yet, it seems, Yalta loved it.

"The crowds around her booth were enormous," Vyrubova recalled, "the people pressing forward almost frenziedly to touch her hand, her sleeve, her dress, enchanted to receive their purchases from the hand of the Empress."[26] Vladimir Voeikov, the palace commandant responsible for the imperial family's security, concurred: "You had to see to

[24] Spiridovitch, a sensitive observer of the imperial couple for almost a decade, believed that, after the Sarov celebrations in 1903, Alexandra had always harbored a religiously-motivated desire to "divest herself of her personality . . . lose herself in the crowd [and] 'go to the people.'" Spiridovitch *Dernières Années*, 1:351.

[25] Spiridovitch, *Dernières Années*, 1:396–97.

[26] Vyrubova, *Memories*, 22.

believe with what enthusiasm the people of Yalta met the appearance at the bazaar of Their Highnesses, in order that they might receive from their hands some trinket. The Imperial Family conducted itself with everyone . . . very simply." [27] The monies raised went to the poor, especially the tuberculosis patients under treatment in Yalta's many hospitals and sanatoria.

Many of these were Alexandra's own foundations, and she took a serious interest in them. "One of the first duties laid on me when I first visited the Crimea was to spend hours at a time visiting, inspecting and reporting on the condition of buildings, nursing and care of patients," reported Anna Vyrubova, Alexandra's confidante: "I was particularly charged with discovering patients who were too poor to pay for the best food and nursing." [28] Another opportunity for breaching the wall was a fundraiser for these tuberculosis hospitals called "White Flower Day," when society ladies went from door to door selling white flowers for the inmates of the empress's sanatoria. Incredibly for a Russian empress, Alexandra and her daughters participated in the event like anyone else, "spending the whole day driving and walking, mingling with the crowd and vending their flowers . . . enthusiastically. . . . The crowds surged around them eager and proud to buy a flower from their full baskets. But the buyers were no whit happier than the sellers." [29]

Bulgakov describes his vision of Nicholas II on the Yalta Embankment as a moment that included only himself, the reigning emperor, and the theocratic ideal. But it seems entirely possible that the unnamed setting of the encounter that opened Bulgakov's eyes was a crowded White Flower Day, or one of Alexandra's charity bazaars. For Nicholas, too, attended Alexandra's bazaars, and, while she and his daughters were in their element in the pavilion, Nicholas sought his own communion with the people in a humble stroll along the embankment. His manner, too, was easy and accessible. "The Emperor looked at the passersby, greeted them, and shared a kind smile with the most enthusiastic," Spiridovich recalled. [30] Does this help us better imagine the scene that so transfixed Bulgakov?

Certainly, Bulgakov was not the only Russian who came to see their sovereign in another light in Crimea. Voeikov describes a trip by motor car that he and two other attendants took with Nicholas to the Askania

---

[27] V. N. Voeikov, *S Tsarem i bez Tsaria: vospominaniia posliedniago Dvortsovago Komendanta Gosudaria Imperatora Nikolaia II* (Helsinki: publisher not identified, 1936), 63. Spiridovitch described the scene in similar terms: "Making an effort to overcome the effects of her illness, the sick Empress forced herself to be friendly and even charming. The Grand Duchesses handed over their objects gaily, writing their names in the postcards. . . . The public was delighted. Many of the peasants couldn't hold back their tears." Spiridovitch, *Dernières Années*, 2:144.

[28] Vyrubova, *Memories*, 22.   [29] Ibid., 23–24.

[30] Spiridovitch, *Dernières Années*, 2:144.

Nova wildlife park in the spring of 1914.[31] There, on the Ukrainian steppe on the other side of the Isthmus of Perekop, zebras, American bison and various kinds of antelope wandered freely on the grassy plains. The owner was a naturalized German by the name of Falz-Fein, who lived with his brother, sister, and daughter in a simple, one-story building. The Falz-Feins were not used to socializing with emperors. Nonetheless, Nicholas and his party stayed the night, and "a very delicious lunch was given, during which the Emperor, with his knack for bewitching everyone, created a really wonderful atmosphere." The following day, the tsar paid a visit to the local peasant village. Instinctively, the villagers knelt on the ground and crossed themselves. "Get up, my friends," Nicholas said, greeting them "with gentleness and simplicity," recalled Spiridovich, who was among the small party that accompanied Nicholas on the visit. As in Yalta, it was the "simplicity of the emperor [that] surprised the peasants the most."[32]

The naturalness with which Nicholas undertook such acts of condescension surprised the Falz-Feins, too. Thus, in another upending of convention, a few days after Nicholas's departure from Askania Nova, the Falz-Feins received an invitation asking them to lunch with the imperial family at Livadia. They accepted, and, to their even greater surprise, Nicholas, appreciative of their "services to the country," conferred on the immigrant family the status of hereditary nobility.[33] The experience gave them an entirely new view on the character of Nicholas II from the one to which they had become accustomed. Voeikov recalled the reaction of the newly ennobled head of the family: "Falz-Fein came up to me with tears in his eyes. He said that he had never expected to establish such gracious relations and was struck by the Tsar's charm." "The Emperor indeed should show himself more to his subjects," Falz-Fein told the Palace Commandant, "so that each could judge him on their personal impression rather than on the lying rumors spread about." For rumors, as we have seen, of the grubbiest kind, *were* now spreading.

෴   ෴   ෴

The following morning, the sky was once again royal blue, the pine-studded mountains rising crisp and clear behind the town, their peaks unobscured by the slightest wisp of condensation. I went for a final walk along the Embankment. Halfway along, I found open a chapel I had passed on previous occasions and found shut. A small, helmeted, neo-Byzantine tower in grey stone looking out over the sea, it looked

---

[31] For the trip, see Voeikov, *S Tsarem*, 63–66.
[32] Spiridovitch, *Dernières Années*, 2:439.
[33] The motivation for this was Nicholas's appreciation for Falz-Fein's conservation efforts. Falz-Fein ran a breeding program for two species of duck that had otherwise disappeared from southern Russia: Spiridovitch, *Dernières Années*, 2:440.

older than it really was. Erected—as a plaque informs the passer-by—"by the donations of the grateful citizens" of Yalta, it was opened by the Patriarch of Moscow in 2009.

I ascended three shallow steps to the open side door, entered and found a man kneeling on the floor in prayer. On the wall in front of him was a fresco of the Virgin robed in blue with a crimson mantle and seated on a jewel-studded throne flanked by two green-robed archangels, her hands raised in a sign of prayer and blessing. The hand of God descended over the Virgin's head. To either side of her was a pair of pomegranate trees, their red fruit an early Christian symbol of suffering, and I noticed that, in a concertina-ing of history, the Mother of God had been given Nicholas and Alexandra for companions. With his distinctive beard, Russia's last tsar wore the white robe of a martyr and a red cloak. A caption in Greek above his head identified him as *ho hagios Nikolaos* (St Nicholas). Opposite him Alexandra (*he hagia Alexandra*) wore a red and gold kaftan and long white veil beneath a jewel-studded crown. At the apex of the arch between them was Aleksei. Looking like a figure out of a late Roman glass, the heir wore a diadem, his hands raised in the ancient Christian *orans* position. Between him and each of his parents were images of his sisters—Tatiana and Anastasia to the left, Olga and Maria to the right. Barely a century ago, the Yalta Soviet was pressing for the execution of the Romanovs detained in the palaces in the hills surrounding the town. Today, by contrast, the modern-day citizens of Yalta have raised a shrine in their honor.

The kneeling man rose to his feet. I recognized him, with his pointy goatee, from my visit to the icon shop at the Livadia Palace chapel two days before. He recognized me, too. We exchanged pleasantries. Remembering the guarded reception I had received at our first meeting, I expressed my sympathy for the tragic fate of the Romanovs and observed that Livadia seemed to have become a place of pilgrimage for those who wanted to honor their memory.

"Yes," he replied, "this is true. Many pilgrims come to Livadia for that purpose. People love and honor the Romanov family. They were a very good family, a Christian family. People who knew them described the children as angels. For that reason, many people come here and to Livadia to pray to them for happiness in their own family lives, for help in their difficulties."

His open face suggested an unexpected willingness to talk. I asked him if this meant that people had now changed their minds about Nicholas, and considered him to have been a good tsar.

"It's hard to say. Opinion is divided. He was a good man, certainly. But perhaps if he had listened to Stolypin, there wouldn't have been a revolution. In Russia," he added, repeating wisdom recycled through the ages for all visitors, "a ruler must be harsh (*zhetskoy*). Nicholas II gave the country too much freedom. The anarchists and revolutionaries took advantage of this. So perhaps the tsar made a mistake."

I suggested that perhaps Nicholas's father, Alexander III, could be considered a good tsar. "Perhaps," he replied. Then suddenly his eyes brightened. "A good tsar would be someone like Putin! He is a hard man, I think. But he maintains order and this country needs a hard ruler."

Certainly, Putin, who has commented only very seldom on Nicholas II, seems to have conceived an admiration for Nicholas's father. He unveiled a bronze statue of Alexander III at Livadia in 2017, and recast a man dubbed, for half Putin's adult life, an "enemy of the people" as a far-sighted patriot.[34]

I asked instead whether he thought the dynasty could ever be restored. His answer was equivocal, reflecting the divisions that still plague the remnants of the dynasty almost a hundred years after the Revolution.

"I don't know. Perhaps. People talk about Grand Duchess Marie [grand-daughter of Nicholas's uncle, Kirill] being made empress. But the problem is she isn't really a grand duchess. Despite what some people say, she isn't the heir."[35]

Perhaps my interlocutor had even seen her. Within two years of Russia's annexation of the Peninsula, both the leading claimants to the headship of the dynasty had visited Crimea. The first to do so was a Danish citizen, Prince Nikolai Romanov, who returned to Crimea the year following the annexation. "It's great for you. It's great for me. Because Crimea is Russian." he told the cameras, beaming as he stepped off the plane that had brought him to the disputed Peninsula.[36] In 2016, the other leading contender, the Grand Duchess Marie, referred to above, did the same. Answering questions on the 400th anniversary of the Romanovs' election to the Throne, Patriarch Kirill affirmed that "none of the descendants of the Romanovs are pretenders to the Russian Throne. But in [Grand Duchess] Marie and her son George the Romanov succession has been preserved — not to the Throne of the Russian Empire, but rather to its history."[37] She had come to Crimea

---

[34] See Russian President Vladimir Putin, "Unveiling of monument to Alexander III," 18 November 2017: http://en.kremlin.ru/events/president/news/56125 (accessed January 10, 2025). Note, significantly, the date, one week after the centenary (unmarked by Putin) of the "Great October Revolution."

[35] Grand Duchess Maria Kirilova, grand-daughter of Grand Duke Vladimir Aleksandrovich (brother of Alexander III and Nicholas II's eldest paternal uncle) is one of several self-proclaimed heads of the Romanov house.

[36] Simon Kruse, "Prins Romanoff og det symbolske besøg," *Berlingske*, September 12, 2015: https://www.b.dk/globalt/prins-romanoff-og-det-symbolske-besoeg. Accessed October 6, 2014. Neither the Danish government nor the Danish royal family supported the visit.

[37] Patriarch Kirill of Moscow and All Rus', "Pastoral Message," May 9, 2013: http://www.patriarchia.ru/db/text/2926965.html (accessed January 10, 2025). Two problems (at least) allegedly stand in the way of Marie's claim: first, her grandfather's marriage

to underline her claim to that history but, clearly, not all Yalta's monarchists were willing to be wooed.

"There are prophecies," the man tending the chapel continued. "They
say that a tsar *will* return to Russia. I for one hope so. I'm a monarchist.
Monarchy — not capitalism, not socialism, not democracy — is the best
form of government."

He advanced the arguments used by defenders of monarchy everywhere: tradition, historical continuity, a connection with the past. Indeed,
so important to him was this continuity that his sense of history even
had room for the Romanovs' executioners.

> Keeping our history is important. That's why I don't think we should
> remove Lenin from the square at the end of the Embankment. We
> should let him stay with information panels telling people what he
> did, how many people he killed. You know he killed more than a
> million people? Terrible! People should learn about that when they
> see his statue.

I asked whether he felt the same way about Stalin. His eyes fell to
the ground and for a moment, he looked unsure.

"Khrushchev removed all Stalin's monuments. But was Stalin good
or bad? I don't think it's black or white. He did a lot of bad things.
Thousands of people died when he purged the Party."

I mentioned the millions also left dead by Stalin's collectivization
of the farms.

"Yes, I know that. But on the other hand, he was responsible for the
Great Victory [of 1945]. So, whether he was good or bad, I can't say."

Conflicting currents of patriotism were at war in his heart. "In any
case," he said, as if finding his balance, "I believe the tsar is given to us
by God. We must honor whomever he sets over us."

≈   ≈   ≈

On a sunny day, the drive along Crimea's southern coast ranks among
the world's most glorious. Against a backdrop of green, pine-clad crags,
the sun's rays reflect off the calm, blue waters of the Black Sea, with a
fresh breeze carrying the scents of mountain and sea, in a way that is
reminiscent of the Amalfi. My driver's name was Sasha. He was a tall
man in his mid-fifties, who once served as a military engineer with Soviet
forces in Afghanistan. How he ended up working for the hotel I never
found out, but our fifty-mile journey from Yalta to Sevastopol revealed
him to be a gentle, well-educated man. This part of the coast remains
studded with reminders of the Romanovs, and when I explained to

---

in 1912 to a divorcee, which never received Nicholas's blessing before the revolution,
automatically disqualified his descendants; second, as a woman she is not qualified to
inherit the throne under Paul I's revision of the laws of succession in 1796.

Sasha the nature of my interests, he swung sharply to the left, and we began a long and windy descent down the side of the mountain towards the narrow hem of land by the sea. We pulled up in a gravel car park in the shade cast by a thicket of elder trees.

In front of us was a small, white-washed stone church surrounded by a colonnaded gallery. Halfway up each of the columns, a variety of subtropical creeper had wrapped its tiny, green-leafed tendrils around the smooth stone. The church was built in 1885 by one of the sons of Nicholas I. A modern bust of St John of Kronstadt stood by the door. During his attendance on the dying Alexander III at Livadia, the acclaimed wonderworker liked to say the Divine Liturgy here. Closed in 1924, and stripped of its valuables, the building lay abandoned for seventy years and, inside, the evidence of its suffering was easy enough to spot. Beneath the row of high windows that run the length of the nave, stretches of bare wall broke up a mosaic enfilade of saints, the result of unrepaired looting and neglect. But as in hundreds of similar places across Russia, regeneration was underway here, too, and, to either side of the single-tiered white marble screen that served in Byzantine style as the iconostasis, an *ad hoc* collection of icons had been piously assembled. Alexandra used to come here to sing the Liturgy with her daughters, and, today, a large image of the Royal Passion-Bearers is among the church's collection of icons.

We got back into Sasha's shiny black four-wheel drive, and climbed back up through the pines to the main highway, before continuing along the coast towards Sevastopol. Not more than fifteen minutes later we passed a stretch of roadside restaurants and kiosks, positioned to take advantage of the view of the so-called Swallow's Nest, a Gothic fantasy of towers, portcullises, and crenulations built on a slender promontory above the waves for an eccentric German baron in 1912. Half an hour further along, we veered off to the right and followed a steep road to the top of the mountainside. This was the old, imperial-era road from Sevastopol to Yalta. As the Aleppo pines gave way to a scrub of holm oaks, a church came into view that was even more spectacularly positioned than the Swallow's Nest.

Perched 400m above the plain, on the flattened summit of rocky crag with sheer cliffs making up three of four sides, the five-cupolaed Church of the Resurrection was erected between 1888 and 1892, as one of hundreds built at private expense across the empire to give thanks for the deliverance of the lives of the imperial family in a train crash outside the small village of Borki in the Ukraine on October 17, 1888.[38] They had boarded the train in Sevastopol. In 1898, Nicholas and Alexandra's first return to the Crimea since becoming emperor and empress

---

[38] On the unfortunate journey, see Wortley, *Scenarios of Power*, 309.

coincided with the tenth anniversary of the train's derailment, and the young emperor and empress marked the occasion by attending a service of prayers here at Foros.

We got out of the car and walked to the edge of the viewing platform. A puff of fresh wind filled with the scent and moisture of the sea buffeted the side of the cliff, and our faces, as we peer over the stone railing. On the coast below, the individual rooftops of the town of Foros were visible. Sasha pointed to one.

"That was Gorbachev's," he said, indicating a shiny silver tessera on the edge of the turquoise sea, which was separated from the rest of the town by a sizeable wood. Built in 1988 at great expense in a technically challenging location, the villa at Foros (officially known as State Resort No. 11, or the Sunrise Building) was where Mikhail Gorbachev came to enjoy the Crimean sun. Connected by escalator to a beach at the foot of the cliffs directly below, the Foros villa was "utmost luxury by Soviet standards," and Gorbachev and his wife Raisa, understandably, loved it. Gorbachev and his family were here on the last day of their holiday when, on August 18, 1991, a clique of KGB hardliners set a coup in motion in Moscow.[39] For two days, the eyes of the world were fixed on the same sunbaked silver tessera by the sparkling sea that Sasha had pointed to. I took a picture and turned my attention to the church behind me.

Built in the neo-Russian style favored by Alexander III, the clifftop Russian Style church was a splendid sight. Five onion cupolas, crowned with shimmering Orthodox crosses, glinted in the midday sun. Inside, rays of sunlight streamed through the southwestern windows, dancing in the clouds of incense that filled the small chamber. Closed, like the church at Oreanda, in 1924, it was converted into a roadside canteen until the German invasion of 1942, and subsequent Soviet re-conquest of the peninsula left it a virtual ruin. It was restored to the Church in 1990.

We resumed our journey. Persuaded, by then, of my interest in the Peninsula's history, Sasha proposed that we continue along the old road, over the mountains to Sevastopol, rather than returning to the coastal highway. Leaving the church behind, the road rose until it had reached the watershed. Like an ice-age diorama, the earth's folds swept upwards from the plains below in a great, bowl-shaped shield crowned with forested crags. The narrow strip south of the ridge was emerald, yielding to the blue of the sea; north of it, the land, cloaked in dry, tan-colored grass, stretched away to the horizon. In modern times, Crimea has often been seen as the key to control of the whole northern shore of the Black Sea, and a roll call of empires has fought for dominion over it: the Tatars

---

[39] Plokhy, *Last Empire*, 79–80. The site was so steep and unstable that every year new soil had to be brought in to replace that which had run off into the sea during the winter rains.

and Ottomans against the invading Russians in the eighteenth century; the Russians against the invading British and French in the nineteenth; White Russians against Red, and the invading Germans (twice) against the Soviets in the twentieth.[40] The tawny plain that now stretched out in front of me was where many of those armies had done battle.

Descending the road leading north across the plain to Sevastopol, we passed a camp of bikers, perhaps fifty or so caravans, decked out with Russian flags. A large hand-painted sign read, *Krym nash!* — "Crimea is ours!" These were the Night Wolves, who stormed the Crimean assembly in February 2014 to force a vote on the referendum. Sasha, who appeared not even to notice them, passed the encampment without suggesting that we stop. We passed a low hillside planted with 5,000 beige stone crosses in orderly rows — the Nazi cemetery of Goncharnoye.[41] In 1942, this was the scene of a grinding three-week battle between the 30th Armeekorps of Hitler's Wehrmacht, assisted by Romanian auxiliaries, and two divisions of Stalin's Red Army.

Half an hour later we were crossing the floor of the bowl-shaped valley, traveling northwest into the burning afternoon sun. In his 2014 speech marking Crimea's annexation, Putin said that for Russians "Crimea is Balaklava and Kerch, Malakhov Kurgan and Sapun Ridge. Each one of these places is dear to our hearts, symbolizing Russian military glory and outstanding valour." It happened that on the fifty kilometers of road between Foros and Sevastopol we passed three of them. The first was Balaklava. Crossing an old railway line, and on either side of the highway, bright lime-green vine leaves appeared — the Balaklava vineyards. To the west, a cleft visible in the steppe was Balaklava bay, a long and deep fjord, which served as the main British base during the 1854–55 Anglo-French siege of Sevastopol, the primary theatre of the 1853–56 Crimean War, which, despite its name, was waged over half the globe. Its origins lay, obscurely, in a squabble over whether the Russian-backed Orthodox, or the French-backed Catholics, should guard the keys of the Holy Sepulcher; the war was, in essence, a combined British and French attempt to forestall the Russian dismemberment of the Ottoman Empire.[42]

Sasha pulled up on a narrow strip of red earth between the highway and the train line, and pointed to the vineyard, which was visible through the windscreen. "This is where the Russians defeated the charge of the British cavalry in 1854," he told me, referring to the Charge of the Light

[40] Robert Forczyk, *Where the Iron Crosses Grow: The Crimea, 1941–44* (Oxford: Osprey, 2014), 6.

[41] Ibid., 220–21. For decades after the Second World War, the remains of Nazi soldiers were stored in warehouses outside Sevastopol. Most were returned to Germany. But in 1998, Ukrainian authorities granted permission for the construction of a war cemetery for the remains of 5,000 German soldiers. Mack and Coleman Carter, *Crimean Chersonesos*, 202.

[42] Orlando Figes, *Crimea: The last crusade* (Harmondsworth: Penguin, 2011), xx–xxi.

Brigade immortalized in Tennyson's famous ode. Twelve hundred men were killed or wounded that day.

"The British erected a monument to their dead soldiers. It's still there. Would you like to see it?" I nodded, eager to walk the battleground.

"There's a path just on the other side of the railway line," Sasha told me, with his bluff, trusting smile, apparently pleased that he had been able to cater so well to my specialist historical interests. "A few hundred meters, no more."

The path was really a clearing beneath a row of grey, weathered telegraph poles stringing their way across the vineyard from one side of the valley to the other. I followed them up the hill into the early afternoon sun. A tough, sedge-like grass grew around the base of the poles, and the earth beneath the vine stocks was a deep, rich red. The air was warm — but for the slight, chill breeze on my back, it would have been hot. Away from the little-traveled road and disused train line, all was quiet. I was alone with the memory of the dead. After about ten minutes, a white, somewhat squat obelisk came into a view, a modest but dignified example of mid-Victorian graveyard architecture. A four-sided pyramid on a cubed plinth set upon a base of three steps, it was enclosed by a respectful cast iron rail, half a foot high. I stepped over it. The simple Victorian inscription read: "In Memory of those who fell in the Battle of Balaklava, 25th October 1854."

Russian success at Balaklava was no prelude to ultimate victory, however, and the war dragged on for another year before Sevastopol eventually fell, after a withering 349-day siege that left the city little more than a pile of burnt-out rubble. A few months later, Russia sued for peace. By that stage, 120,000 British, French, and Sardinian troops, and a quarter of a million Russian ones, were dead. Nobody kept a tally of civilian losses inside the besieged city.[43]

With the afternoon sun on my back, I retraced my steps beneath the telegraph wires and across the vineyard to the car. Again, the car moved off. At this point, the road began to climb back up out of the valley, crossing the line of low hills that separate it from Sevastopol. As we crested the low summit, Sasha again pulled over into a car park. On the other side of the road, an open-air collection of tanks, plans and cannons served as the attraction. This was the Sapun Escarpment, an open-air memorial to Soviet victory in the massive clash between Soviet and Nazi forces that played itself out on the valley we had just crossed in 1944. To Russians, the Crimea campaigns, hardly known in the West, and the staggering forces both sides threw into controlling the Peninsula, are an integral part of the Second World War. During the Nazi siege of Sevastopol, from October 1941 to July 1942, the Soviet army lost 200,000 men (or just over

---

[43] Figes, *Crimea*, xix.

eight hundred per day), while the Germans, who dropped twenty thousand tons of bombs on the city, lost, with their Romanian allies, 32,000 men of their own.[44] By 1942, Hitler identified Crimea as a higher strategic goal than Moscow. Not only would the Peninsula enable Hitler to forge a direct route across the Caucasus to the Caspian oilfields; it also represented a kind of German spiritual homeland. Before departing to play their role in the fall of the Western Roman Empire, the fourth-century Goths had for centuries lorded it over the Crimean grasslands. For this reason, Hitler planned to rename the Peninsula "Gothia," connect it to Berlin by Autobahn, and use Nicholas and Alexandria's white Italianate palace at Livadia as his summer retreat.[45]

The memorial at the Sapun Escarpment where I was standing was a monument to the Soviet men who perished when, just under two years later, the Red Army wrestled control of this ridge, the gateway to Sevastopol, back from the Nazis on May 7, 1944.[46] Three years of fighting for control of Crimea cost the Soviet Union no fewer than five armies and 700,000 casualties.[47] A people more sentimental than the Russians might have remembered the battle with individual crosses for the 17,500 men who fell in or around Sapun in 1944. But, not being a sentimental people, the Russians have not. Not the sum of a thousand personal tragedies that it has become in the West, war remains in Russia the supreme demonstration of collective might, of the sacrifice of self, even in death, for the Motherland.[48]

Back in the car we headed off on the final stretch of the journey. Off to the side of a large roundabout on the outskirts of Sevastopol, a man in his twenties stood beside his car, which was decked out with the red, blue, and white banner of Russia, the old hammer and sickle of the Soviet Union, and slogans in celebration of the approaching May 9 Victory Day celebrations. Beyond the roundabout, the narrow two-lane highway on which we drove to cross the valley merged with the grander new road that we had left behind at Foros. We passed underneath a monumental Soviet-era aluminum arch in honor of the 1983 bicentenary of Sevastopol's foundation, its massive hammer and sickle insignia still firmly in place, and then, abruptly, on either side of a wide verge covered in knee-high grass and fruit trees in blossom, humble stone cottages with corrugated iron roofs fringed the surprisingly modest road leading into the heart of the port-city proper.

---

[44] Mungo Melvin, *Sevastopol's Wars: Crimea from Potemkin to Putin* (Oxford: Osprey, 2017), 532–33; Forczyk, *Where Iron Crosses*, 243–47.
[45] Melvin, *Sevastopol's Wars*, 251–52.
[46] Ibid., 561.
[47] Forczyk, *Where Iron Crosses*, 336–37.
[48] Melvin, *Sevastopol's Wars*, 568. In the crucial year of 1942–43, the Crimea tied up a German army of 300,000 men that could have turned the Battle of Stalingrad in Hitler's favor.

At the foot of the southern arm of Sevastopol harbor, the road swung sharply to the left; continuing the roll call of "Russian military glory," the hill over our right shoulder was the famous Malakhov Kurgan, a defensive redoubt whose storming by French forces on September 8, 1855 heralded the beginning of the end of the first siege of Sevastopol, and the city's fall four days later.[49] Then, we rounded the bay and entered Sevastopol's main thoroughfare, Ulitsa Lenina. Fronting the street, an elegant ensemble of colonnaded facades and Corinthian capitals belonged to Sevastopol's grand nineteenth century. Nearby, the neo-classical colonnade of the Count's Landing Steps marked the ceremonial entry to the port-city from the sea, and, opposite, the 1970s polished steel and granite of the Eternal Flame to Soviet Victory watched over the memorials and garden beds of Nakhimova Square. In 2014, the largest pro-Russian demonstrations in the Peninsula took place in this square, and so did the biggest celebrations, held when the later referendum results were announced.

Indeed, around the corner at Artbukhta (short for Artillery Bay) the party didn't seem to have ended. Warm spring weather had brought people into the street, and the approach of Victory Day encouraged the patriotically minded to bring their Russian and Soviet flags with them. Young men in sheepskin bomber jackets and blue jeans had transformed a truck in the gritty carpark by the ferry wharf into a blaze of Russian patriotism. Along the Kornilov embankment, older folk and families with children strolled or listened to the busking musicians as they soaked up the rays of the afternoon sun, reflecting off the dark, oily waters of the bay. The elegant white colonnade of the waterside Hotel Sevastopol glimmered in the same solar broadside.

But I had a booking in a less glamorous guesthouse in a residential area a few blocks back from the harbor. Turning the car away from the water, Sasha and I drove a short distance back out of the city, where it changed dramatically. Despite the grandeur of Sevastopol's historical center, modern, everyday Sevastopol is poor. In the suburbs, rotting concrete apartment blocks stood alienated one from another in a sea of knee-high grass. Stripped back to the blue metal beneath the tarmac, the worn road itself was full of tire-sized holes. As Sasha turned a corner, an old man in a worn grey suit crossed the road, leading a goat.

෨෨   ෨෨   ෨෨

A city of almost 400,000, Sevastopol is Crimea's largest. Only fifty miles separate it from Yalta, but the two places couldn't be more different in spirit. If Yalta is a town of the last golden days of tsarism, then Sevastopol is the city of the Soviet regime that sent Russia's last tsar to his grave, a city whose inhabitants, it seemed at first glance, would have preferred it if the golden days of the USSR had never ended.

---

[49] Figes, *Crimea*, 391.

For all the homage locals render to the vanished Soviet Union (and the drama of more recent events), however, Sevastopol owes its existence to the Romanovs. Located on the southern shore of a deep and sheltered inlet, six miles long and two miles wide at its mouth, the city spreads across a series of bays and headlands on each shore, which gives the impression, when seen on the map, of two jaws of jagged teeth. Despite Russia's enormous size, when, on the threshold of the modern era, the navies and merchant fleets of Western Europe were discovering whole new continents, the country was essentially landlocked. In 1702, Peter the Great's victory over the Swedes opened the frigid Baltic Sea. But it was his most gifted successor Catherine the Great's stunning victory in the Russo-Turkish War of 1768–74 that brought Russia to the temperate shores of the Black Sea. Nine years later, a formal act of annexation made the Crimean Peninsula Russia's, and it was here, at Sevastopol, that Russia really exacted revenge on its geography: until the later nineteenth-century acquisition of Vladivostok, Sevastopol's superb natural harbor was easily the finest anchorage in the empire, and unlike the waters of the Baltic, those of the Black Sea do not freeze in winter. Destiny, too, seemed to commend Sevastopol to the Russians. Only 160 miles of open sea separated Crimea from the Turkish coastline on the Black Sea's southern shore, and as a base for Russia's as-yet-unbuilt Black Sea Fleet, the construction of Sevastopol acquired the character of a down payment on the tsar's restoration of the cross over the old Byzantine capital at Constantinople ("Tsargrad," the "tsar's city," as Russians used to call it, in reference to the Byzantine emperor whose sacred authority their tsar inherited). Looking out across the sea towards the fabled Hagia Sophia, Sevastopol's very existence was, in its own way, also a testament to the ideal of *teokratia*.

I made my way back to the harbor. As the sun set, Russian and Soviet flags fluttered in the breeze, blowing up off the glinting gunmetal of the sea, while at souvenir stalls bomber-jacketed hawkers sold all manner of annexation mementoes. *Krym Nash!* fridge magnets, coffee mugs, baseball caps, and T-shirts are displayed alongside the same with an image of Putin, either alone in sunglasses and bomber jacket, or in presidential suit and tie alongside the balding head of Nikita Khrushchev (the Communist Party General Secretary who, in 1954, "gave" Crimea to Ukraine by redrawing the Soviet Union's at that time largely meaningless internal borders), with the ironic caption, "One gave it away — the other took it back." Two years now since Russia's 2014 reannexation of the disputed Peninsula, and "justice" is still being served, courtesy of the Chinese manufacturers of trinkets and cheap clothing. Other souvenir sellers do a trade in images of a black-mustachioed Stalin, glorified as victor over the Nazis. Given Russia's depiction of the

Ukrainian authorities in Kiev as "fascists," the reference isn't merely historical. It is an accepted truth of Western reporting that Putin has presided over the "re-Sovietization" of Russian society. But perhaps only in Sevastopol does "Soviet" feel justified as an adjective, a situation that reflects the longstanding facts of local sociology.[50]

Located on a deep natural harbor, and strictly closed to foreigners until the early 1990s, Sevastopol was the Soviet Union's premier naval base. On the eve of the Soviet collapse, the Soviet surface fleet was based in the city, while a secret base at nearby Balaklava housed nuclear submarines. Thousands of Soviet sailors and their families called Sevastopol home. Even by Soviet standards, the city was unusually dependent on the fate of the armed forces. When the USSR collapsed in 1991, Sevastopol's fortunes collapsed with it. With the Soviet Black Sea Fleet split between the new nations of Russia and Ukraine, a wave of poverty broke across a formerly proud and prosperous port city, and Sevastopol's almost exclusively Russian-speaking residents found themselves citizens of a country many had never considered existed: Ukraine. With the Soviet Union gone, Khrushchev's 1954 redrawing of the border assumed a significance it had never previously enjoyed. And yet the reckoning with history was deferred, when Russia obtained, from Ukraine, a lease on Sevastopol's port facilities, and the right to anchor what remained of Russia's Black Sea Fleet in Sevastopol harbor. In this way, Sevastopol, a legally Ukrainian city on the Crimean Peninsula that was also legally Ukrainian, became home to what were now thousands of Russian citizens, almost all of them sailors and other military personnel, while Ukraine itself inched closer and closer towards alignment with NATO. Ukraine-NATO marine exercises were even held in the city, within view of Russian sailors and warships. As a far-sighted analyst warned at that time, the disputed city of Sevastopol "could [...] prove to be the stone that upsets the entire Eurasian applecart."[51]

Of course, that prophecy almost came to pass in 2014, when, following the overthrow of the government of Viktor Yanukovych in Kiev by pro-Western protesters, Russian military personnel stationed in Sevastopol fanned out from the city, forced the surrender of their Ukrainian counterparts and sealed off the Peninsula from contact with Ukraine. After a rushed and irregular referendum gave Crimeans' blessing for annexation by Russia, Putin signed a formal treaty of "re-unification" in a grand ceremony in the Kremlin on March 18. Nowhere in Crimea was this turn of events greeted with more enthusiasm than

---

[50] The best discussion of the history and sociology of Crimea is Gwendolyn Sasse, *The Crimea Question: Identity, transition, conflict* (Cambridge, MA: Harvard University Press, 2007).
[51] Anatol Lieven, *Russia and Ukraine: A fraternal rivalry* (Washington, DC: United States Institute of Peace Press, 1999), 159.

in Sevastopol. In fact, the Russian law admitting Crimea to the Russian Federation admitted Sevastopol separately from the rest of the Peninsula: like only two other Russian cities, Sevastopol is a federal subject in its own right. And immediately after signing the law on reunification, Vladimir Putin flew here directly, taking to the harbor aboard a Russian warship, to the cheers of the flag-waving crowd on the foreshore.

Today, the Kremlin displays its armed forces confidently in Sevastopol, as a city under Russian administration. On the harbor opposite the tourist stalls, a Russian warship cruises out to sea through the dark breakwaters, while, in the sky above, a pair of Russian jets rumble and scream overhead, appearing and then disappearing again behind the thin clouds that partly obscure an otherwise golden sunset. I watch them dive-bomb an imaginary foe, racing towards the ground before arching back on themselves in return ascent to their bastion in the clouds. Yet whatever their actual feelings about this state of affairs (and outwardly, to be fair, most seemed very pleased), the people of Sevastopol moderate the melodrama of geopolitics with the same kind of leisure activities familiar on seaside promenades the world over. Merging into the crowds, I watch as a clown performs for a crowd of families on the wharf beneath the white Corinthian columns of the Hotel Sevastopol. Further along, where a small hill on the headland has been reshaped into a concrete amphitheater, three scruffily bearded twenty-year-olds play Russian punk rock, while a fourth member of the band sings his tunes into the wind.

   ◊ ◊ ◊

The bright spring sun danced on the water, a shade of light turquoise by the shore and deep cobalt out at sea. An arid headland strewn with rubble half an hour out of town, the ruins of the ancient city of Chersonesos are outwardly an archaeological site like hundreds of others from Greco-Roman antiquity. Disembarking the local bus from Sevastopol, I entered the site through a hole in the typically stout late Roman walls, made of thousands of hard, thin bricks. Flowers sprung up among the ruins: small red poppies, their petals like fragile tissue paper, bobbed in the gentle breeze off the water alongside the swaying, heavily seeded heads of a carpet of grass. It could have been any marble-studded seaside plain from Spain to Italy, Greece, and Turkey.

Local tourist literature calls Chersonesos the "Slavic Pompeii." Founded in 422 BC, Chersonesos was among the northernmost of ancient Greek colonies.[52] Moving along paths through the site, I wandered through a ruined Greco-Roman streetscape boasting all the

---

[52] Mack and Coleman Carter, *Crimean Chersonesos*, 17–19.

amenities typical of ancient Mediterranean civilization: a theatre, soldiers' barracks, baths, mills and bakeries, cisterns, shops and inns, all
roofless, but with their walls evocatively preserved to shoulder height,
as at Pompeii. Whereas Pompeii was destroyed before Constantine's
conversion to Christianity, life carried on in Chersonesos for another
millennium, and, instead of ruined pagan temples, Chersonesos reveals
a multitude of Byzantine churches, recognizable with their triple apses
and finely stylized capitals. In the elegant stone half-circle of an ancient
theatre, built in around 300 BC to seat 2,000, and where, in Roman
times, bloody gladiatorial battles entertained the crowds, I found a
Christian chapel built directly on top of the stage floor.[53]

From the theater, my eyes followed the ruin-strewn headland that
stretched away to the east, providing a natural breakwater for the small,
protected harbor known as Quarantine Bay that was the heart of the
life of the ancient city. Enriched by the nutrients carried down the
Danube, the Dnieper and the Don, the surrounding waters of the Black
Sea were plentiful in fish, and for centuries Chersonesos's fishermen
hauled their catches ashore here. Here, too, merchants from the cities
of the Mediterranean assembled to exchange their goods for the honey,
wax, amber, furs, and slaves of the "barbarian" traders of the steppes
and northern forests. But such traders were just as often raiders, and
I traced with my eyes the line of the fifteen-meter-high curtain wall of
dressed limestone constructed by the Byzantine emperor Theodosius II
(the same whose instructions to fathers at the Council of Ephesus we
have already quoted). As wave after wave of barbarians swept against its
walls in late antiquity, the ancient city took on the look and feel of an
embattled military camp. Today, Chersonesos still possesses an edge-of-
the-world feeling, and it and a handful other Crimean settlements are
the only sites on the territory (legally, or otherwise) of modern Russia
with a direct connection to antiquity.

If there is a paradox to this, it is that it was Chersonesos's overrun-
ning by barbarians that sealed its claim as a cradle of Russian civilization.
For, by the tenth century AD, among the barbarian peoples who "traded
and raided" with Byzantium and its Crimea outposts were the "Rus,"
Scandinavian warriors who lorded it over the Slav peoples who lived
in the forest clearings along the banks of the Dnieper, and whose chief
trading post was a palisaded settlement called Kiev, on the high bluff of
a bend in the same river. [54] Failing in his desire to unite his people by
way of their existing pagan religion, in AD 987 the Rus high chieftain
Vladimir sent envoys throughout the known world to investigate other

---

[53] Ibid., 76–77.
[54] On the origins of the Rus, see Janet Martin, *Medieval Russia, 980–1584*, 2nd ed.
(Cambridge: Cambridge University Press, 2007), 7–8.

people's religious customs. Their report sealed Constantinople's place in the Russian mind as the special dwelling place of God among men and the symbol of *teokratia*. "We knew not whether we were in heaven or on earth.... For on earth there is no such splendor or beauty and we are at a loss how to describe it," they said, describing the Divine Liturgy they had witnessed in the Emperor Justinian's apparently miraculous, domed basilica, Hagia Sophia: "We only know that God dwells there among the people, and their service is fairer than the ceremonies of other nations."[55] Accounts vary as to what happened next. But according to the medieval Russian tradition, Vladimir then laid siege to the nearest, geographically, of Byzantium's possessions: Chersonesos. Seizing the outpost, Vladimir demanded the hand of Emperor Basil II's sister in marriage, as well as bishops and priests to baptize and instruct his people. Basil consented, and in 988, a Greek bishop baptized Vladimir into the Orthodox faith in Chersonesos's cathedral. Returning to Kiev, Vladimir ordered all his subjects, Slav and Scandinavian, to be baptized in the Dnieper.[56] United in allegiance to Vladimir and adscription to Orthodoxy, the Rus had become a people. In 2014, Putin dubbed the site Russia's "Temple Mount."[57]

❧ ❧ ❧

Chersonesos's history came to an end when a great fire (probably lit by invading Mongols) swept through the old Greco-Roman city in the thirteenth century. For the next few centuries, fishermen would continue to use its harbor, but civic life itself was extinct, and a protective layer of grass and sedges grew over the rubble.[58] So it remained until the Russians returned and, eventually, excavations began, unearthing the maze of streets, houses and churches that the visitor sees today. The most important items uncovered can been seen in the archaeological museum that stands among trees at the center of the site. A practical, oblong-shaped brick building, the museum was originally the residence of the abbot who headed the monastery established here in 1852 — a reminder that the idea of Crimea as the sacred cradle of Russian civilization is far from being a recent private invention of Putin's. On the contrary, when the Russians arrived (or returned) in 1783, Crimea had been Muslim for 450 years, and from the 1850s, the Russian government and Church cooperated to "re-Christianize" the peninsula.[59] Through an ambitious program of church construction,

[55] Obolensky, *Byzantine Commonwealth*, 253; Martin, *Medieval Russia*, 7.
[56] Obolensky, *Byzantine Commonwealth*, 253–58; Martin, *Medieval Russia*, 8–9.
[57] Russian President Vladimir Putin, "Presidential Address to the Federal Assembly," December 4, 2014: http://en.kremlin.ru/events/president/news/47173. Accessed October 6, 2024.
[58] On the French, see Figes, *Crimea*, 271–72.
[59] See Mara Kozelsky, *Christianizing Crimea: Shaping sacred space in the Russian Empire*

archaeological excavations, and monastic foundations, the authorities hoped that Crimea would become Russia's own holy land, a "New Athos," where, by recovering Russia's Byzantine roots and fostering a pure Orthodox religion, the religious sources of the Russian State would be strengthened. As part of this project, then, a monastery was built at Chersonesos, and a great, Russian Style cathedral on the traditional site of Vladimir's baptism was consecrated in the presence of Alexander III in 1892.[60] As tsar, Nicholas II visited in 1898, when, to the tolling of the great Cathedral bell, he and Alexandra were presented with an icon of Vladimir the Great and the Virgin Mary, respectively, before both inspected the archaeological finds in the museum. In 1902, the couple, returning to venerate the site of Vladimir's conversion, were presented, this time, with an icon of the Seven Holy Martyrs of Chersonesos. "By the prayers of these blessed last and those of Saint Vladimir, Equal to the Apostles, the Illuminator of All Rus who was baptized here, may the Lord preserve your going out and your coming home now and forever more," said the *higoumen* (abbot) of the monastery, who solemnly prayed over the imperial couple on the occasion.

Of course, the new "Crimean Athos" did not survive the Bolshevik conquest of the peninsula in 1920. Closed and stripped of their valuables in the 1930s, the Chersonesos monastery and cathedral were then as good as destroyed in the Second World War. Afterwards, Soviet victory saw the ruined monastery reconstructed as an archaeological museum, while a marble statue of Stalin was erected in front of the untended cathedral ruins. Not until Communism collapsed in 1991 could Chersonesos be revived as a holy site, when the cathedral — but not the monastery, which remained the archaeological museum it had become — was restored.[61]

The late Soviet period was a golden age of archaeology at Chersonesos, and the collection was extensive and well presented. As a result, it was early afternoon by the time I left the building. Heat and stillness had descended upon the ruins. In Chersonesos, only the northern end of the town had been excavated. South of the museum, scrubby parkland awaited the archaeologists' shovels and picks. Among the trees, however, a church was visible, its rectangular floor plan, steeple, and chaste yellow and white stucco recalling the church architecture of eighteenth-century Protestant northern Europe far more than it did Byzantium. Built in 1852, it was, however, the Chersonesos monastery's original church. I wandered inside. Eyes that, moments before, had

---

and beyond (DeKalb, IL: Northern Illinois University Press, 2010).
[60] Kozelsky, *Christianizing Crimea*, 149.
[61] Mack and Coleman Carter, *Crimean Chersonesos*, 57.

been frozen in an uncomfortable squint dilated with immediate relief in the sanctuary's interior shade. Recently restored, the smooth marble floor possessed the antiseptic spotlessness of a private home.

As I got my bearings in the narthex, an old woman appeared. *Zdravstvuite* (hello), she said, in a friendly voice. We engaged in pleasantries about the weather and the beauty of the site. Then, pointing to the wall behind her, she took my arm and drew my attention to a fresco on the church's wall. It showed the faces of Chersonesus's seven holy bishops, to whom the church is dedicated.

"Our saints are very powerful," she knowingly intoned. "They help a lot of people. Many come here to pray for their families or other worries and the saints hear them. You should buy their icon. It would be good for you."

She then showed me a wall of shiny, new, pewter-framed icons.

"Aren't they beautiful?" she said, turning to me, eyes glistening. "It's a collection custom-made by a single artist using modern methods. The artist donated them to the church."

The icons were certainly modern. Executed in colors so bright they looked almost fluorescent, they also came dangerously close to being three-dimensional. Each of the faces was a kind of miniature relief map, with raised surfaces for forehead and cheeks, and plastic beads marking the eyes, teeth, and cheeks. Among them was one of the Royal Passion-Bearers, Nicholas, Alexandra, and Alexei. It was the first evidence I had seen of the family's being venerated at Chersonesos.

"Chersonesos is a very interesting place," I remarked. "President Putin called it a Russian Jerusalem, didn't he? What do you think?"

She looked at me carefully, considering her answer.

"I don't know," she replied. "That might be his opinion. But for me, I don't want any problems with Ukraine. You know, Russia and Ukraine are friends — family. We are like one country," she said, locking the fingers of her hands together to illustrate the point. "The most important thing is peace between us."

Chersonesos might have borne the weight of Russia's rhetorical claims for its controversial actions regarding the disputed Peninsula, but this woman, at least, who tended for the site, didn't care to shoulder them.

She walked over the desk in the icon shop, and returned with a small tourist souvenir plate. It was painted with a picture of the church and an icon of the seven holy bishops — the same icon, incidentally, that the ill-fated Nicholas had received when he visited the monastery here in 1902.

"Go back to your country," she urged me gently. "Tell them about our church and our saints, and tell them we want peace. It has been so good to meet you. Your presence here has truly been a gift."

   ◈  ◈  ◈

Writing to his patron, Catherine the Great, to vaunt his conquest of
Crimea in 1783, Potemkin lauded Chersonesos as the "origin" of Russia's
Christianity, "and hence of our humanity."[62] Was he right? Since his
return to Orthodoxy from Marxism at the beginning of the twentieth
century, Bulgakov had thought so. That Orthodoxy was the source of
the spiritual values that humanized and elevated Russian culture was
the foundation of the criticism that he and other Silver Age intellectuals
had made of the Russian intelligentsia, and its ultimately *dehumanizing*
atheism, in "Vekhi." By 1921, however, Bulgakov was no longer sure,
and in an unpublished dialogue entitled "Under the Walls of Chersonesos" he dramatized his inner conflict. Set on a moonlit night in the
very archaeological site where I had been walking, "Under the Walls of
Chersonesos" is remarkable for presenting as close as Bulgakov came
to a repudiation of the ideal of *teokratia* — and, indeed, much more
besides of Bulgakov's spiritual itinerary.[63] Whereas in "Heroism and
asceticism" (Bulgakov's essay in *Vekhi*), Bulgakov had traced the roots
of Russia's ills to the intelligentsia's atheism, in "Under the Walls of
Chersonesos," Bulgakov identifies those ills differently and traces them to
Eastern Orthodoxy. Whereas, then, Bulgakov had once seen Orthodoxy
as a source of spiritual truths to *oppose* to the false, atheistic conclusions
of nineteenth-century European philosophy, he now began to look on
Orthodoxy itself as the *source* of the spiritual errors that had led Russia
to revolution. Rather than being something to celebrate, Vladimir's baptism at Chersonesos became, frankly, something to *regret*. As Bulgakov
put it, speaking once again through the figure of the Refugee we have
met before, "The key to the Russian tragedy is not to be found in
Petersburg, Moscow, or Kiev, but in Chersonesos.... [T]he historical
chain of events that culminates in our day departs from here; it's here
that it begins and here that it is mystically established."[64]

This extraordinary about-face reflected the spiritual crisis that enveloped Bulgakov as the revolutionary catastrophe he had long feared
unfolded. First, a coalition of liberals and moderate Socialists replaced
the *teokratia* of Nicholas II in March 1917 with the impeccably Kantian
"Provisional Government," and then, in October, a carefully executed
coup d'état raised Lenin, and his Bolshevik faction of Russia's Social
Democratic Labor Party, to power. The following year, Bulgakov, apparently completing his return to Orthodoxy, was priested in Moscow. And
yet Russia was traveling in the opposite direction. With the Bolsheviks
installed now in "Holy Moscow," Russia's judgment for secularization

---

[62] Ibid., 50.
[63] Translations are my own, from the French translation by Barnard Marchadier: Serge
Boulgakov, *Sous les remparts de Chersonèse* (Geneva: Ad Solem, 1999).
[64] Boulgakov, *Sous les remparts*, 22.

became a judgment for extreme, State-imposed atheism, and Bulgakov fled for Crimea. There, while a brutal civil war raged between the Bolshevik Red Army and the disunited forces of opposing White armies for the right to decide Russia's destiny, Bulgakov took up a teaching post at the University of Simferopol, and served as a priest in a parish in Yalta. In 1920, however, Bulgakov watched as the Reds, whipped into a fighting force by Trotsky, caught up with him, and the Bolshevism he had fled in Moscow brought its brutal, atheist regime — with its seizures of private property, summary executions, and suppression of religion — to Crimea.

The Bolshevik takeover of Crimea precipitated in Bulgakov a profound spiritual crisis. Dismissed from his post at the university, Bulgakov dedicated himself to his parish.

Before this time, Bulgakov had apparently had little contact with non-Orthodox Christian clergy. At Yalta, however, Bulgakov found himself inspired by the example of Yalta's Roman Catholic priest, a certain Pole by the name of Fr Matthew, and his small but devout and disciplined congregation. Whereas the Orthodox Church seemed either to collapse before the Bolshevik onslaught or seek false accommodation with it, Yalta's Catholics, it seemed to Bulgakov, quietly but patiently resisted Bolshevik attempts to split or to suppress them. By comparison with his own Orthodox flock, Catholics seemed to possess more deeply implanted Christian virtues, while the Catholic Church's tightly organized structure, centered on the pope in Rome, gave it the strength to resist State interference. Thus, Bulgakov, his observations reinforced by conversations with Fr Matthew and his own historical-theological research, subjected his existing understanding of what the Church fundamentally was, as well as the competing (from an Orthodox point of view) claims of the Bishop of Rome (i.e. the pope), to searching examination. His dialogue "Under the Walls of Chersonesos" was the result.

According to Bulgakov in "Under the Walls of Chersonesos," it was Russia's misfortune to be baptized into an Eastern Orthodoxy that Byzantium had already all but corrupted. Far from being something to celebrate, Vladimir's baptism at Chersonesos was something Russia should "flee."[65] The two chief sins of the Russian Church were nationalism and caesaropapism, and both flowed from the "cursed" Byzantine legacy imparted to Russia at Chersonesos — above all, Byzantium's rebellion against the legitimate authority of the Bishop of Rome. The latter was the true head of the Church on earth, and, without the pope, the Orthodox Church suffered an insoluble crisis of internal authority. From this crisis, Bulgakov now believed, flowed a gamut of spiritual consequences that Bulgakov held responsible for the revolution: a false

---

[65] Ibid., 45.

messianism and national-religious chauvinism that failed to recognize that the Russian Church was but *one part* of the greater Church universal, *not the whole*; a lack of discipline, as a result of centuries of imperial interference in the life of the Church, which undermined the proper authority of bishops; an excessive focus on and idealization of monasticism, at the expense of the basic moral formation of the laity; and, in short, general spiritual, moral, and dogmatic *paralysis*.

Indeed, the very things that generations of Russian Orthodox writers had praised as the *truths* of Russian Christianity had proved to be figments or, worse, delusions.[66] Even such apparent glories of Russian Christianity as its holy *startsy*, or elders, were contaminated by the Russian Church's defects. Whereas the Roman ideal was one of submission to the objective authority of the ordained clergy, the operative principle in Russia was a subjective and self-willed lay individual. After all, the Russian layman not only *chose* this or that holy man for her spiritual advisor; he (or she) also *effectively usurped the right to canonize* this person as saint. As the Refugee put it, the basis of the choice of a *starets*, he said, is "the will, an anarchic liberty . . . for me the *starets* is the incarnation of the Church, but I am the one who chooses it; as a result, *I* am the Church."[67] In this sense, the "thirst for *startsy* as anchors of salvation" that characterized the life of the Russian Church before the revolution had not come about by chance: Russians, Bulgakov said, "had the sense of the Church, but did not know how to realize it."[68] Self-will, excessive spiritual subjectivity, the lack of a proper sense of Church authority: Bulgakov might have been talking about Alexandra and Rasputin.

Also symptomatic of Russian Christianity's defects was the place of the tsar in the Church. Indeed, at times, in "Under the Walls of Chersonesos," the tsar almost appears to be those defects' universal *source*. If on the Yalta Embankment in 1909, therefore, Bulgakov believed that his eyes had been opened to the truth of "holy tsarist authority," now in "Under the Walls of Chersonesos," in 1921, he recast Russia's pre-revolutionary Church-State regime as aberrant "caesaropapism," the unlawful usurpation by the Russian tsar or Byzantine emperor of the pope's rightful place in the Church. Of course, this was the very claim that Bulgakov, speaking through the mouth of the Refugee, had only recently sought to

---

[66] Thus, in "Under the Walls of Chersonesos," Bulgakov argues that Aleksandr Khomiakov's famous ideal of *sobornost'* ("conciliarity") was mere Protestantism, one that left the Church without the true, internal sense of authority and discipline that it needed to survive times of persecution. Meanwhile, Dostoevsky's idealization of the Russian people as God's elect, a Second Israel, with a special purpose in history, was a relapse into a kind of Judaism, with the additional perverse historical effect of promoting Russia's notorious national exclusivism and anti-Semitism: Bulgakov, *Sous les remparts*, 76. He later changed his mind, of course, and the piece we are discussing was never published.
[67] Bulgakov, *Sous les remparts*, 77.   [68] Ibid.

rebut in his 1918 dialogue, "At the feast of the Gods." And yet now, in "Under the Walls of Chersonesos," the same Refugee reversed his earlier argument. What's more, he pointed specifically to references to the tsar in the *liturgy* (which Bulgakov had earlier adduced as evidence of the endorsement that Orthodoxy had rightly but implicitly lent the theocratic ideal) as evidence now, of the caesaropapist error. "If you take all that the tsar represented for the Church in the Orthodox liturgy, not only from the perspective of courtly etiquette and conventional courtesies but in perfectly serious and authentic rites and prayers, you will see that not only for the [Russian] Church there was nothing superior to the tsar, but supremacy in the Church belonged to him, at least insofar as the representation of the body of the Church was concerned."[59] Far from manifesting a truth, Caesaropapism gave a "fundamental and dogmatic character" to something, the imperial regime, that was mere *oikonomia*, "only historical and temporary."[70]

But this was not, perhaps, Bulgakov's most biting criticism in "Under the Walls of Chersonesos." True, the Refugee concedes drily, people will say now that the old caesaro-papism was harmful and unwanted, and that the revolution was in fact a good thing, a *deliverance*. But the truth that Eastern Orthodoxy as a whole was yet to face up to, Bulgakov believed, was that, so long as it lasted, the old caesaropapism was not unwelcome at all. It was not so much that the ruling authorities had imposed the caesaropapist error on an unwilling Church. Rather, in the Byzantine emperor or Russian tsar, the Eastern Church itself found a substitute for that true, internal sense of authority that the Church had lost when in 1054 it broke with the papacy. To put it another way, those who wanted to put tsarism behind them spoke and acted as if, for centuries, the State had kidnapped the Church. But the truth, thought Bulgakov, was that the Church's leaders themselves, the bishops, had identified in the State an escape route from the legitimate obedience they owed to the pope. On the verge, it seems, of becoming Catholic, Bulgakov, by 1921, was already commemorating the pope's name in secret when he celebrated the Divine Liturgy for his parish in Yalta.

Albeit never published, "Under the Walls of Chersonesos" was a stinging indictment of many of the beliefs that Bulgakov had made his own

[69] Ibid., 60.

[70] Ibid., 60–61. That all the Eastern Church's veneration of the tsar represents mere "oikonomia," pragmatic accommodation to historical circumstances without the least theological significance, is also McGuckin's argument. See "Legacy of the 13th apostle," 287: "The idea of the symphonia of the two kingdoms is a dominant idea of Byzantine Christian thought. This has sometimes been read as if it was a continuation of the Hellenistic political theory of the King as the mirror of God and the earthly kingdom's affairs as paralleled to those of heaven. It is not this.... The sacrality of the emperor, and the apostolic status of Constantine as model for subsequent emperors, were both put forward as 'economic' theological positions."

in his return to Orthodoxy, as well as of the Church to which Bulgakov
as a priest had devoted his life.

~~~   ~~~   ~~~

Nicholas's last visit to Sevastopol took place, against the backdrop of the
Great War, in 1916, for a fleet review. "The ships in great order produced
a mighty impression," Nicholas wrote in his diary, before noting that,
next day, he and Alexei personally inspected twenty-five vessels: "On
each, I went around to all the officers and crew and thanked them for
their service."[71] Maintaining the fleet's morale was essential. Vast sums
were being spent on building Russia's first *Imperatritsa Maria*-class
super dreadnoughts, and had Russian planning not been thrown into
disarray by the collapse of Nicholas's regime, in 1917 Sevastopol was to
have been the launching pad for the massed Russian naval forces that
would, it was hoped, seize Constantinople from the Ottomans, and
impose Russian control on the Straits. By restoring the cross to the
dome of Orthodoxy's greatest church, the sixth-century Hagia Sophia,
it would open a new "Byzantine" (as opposed to Petersburg) period in
Russian history that would have seen Nicholas hailed as the tsar who
recovered "Tsargrad."[72]

Though often omitted in Western accounts of the Great War, the
plan to seize Constantinople captured the Russian people's imagination.[73] Bulgakov's 1918 dialogue "At the Feast of the Gods" reflected this
excitement. "I believe that Russia truly is called to show the world a
new, religiously united community, and the hour of its birth may have
been anno 1914 . . . participation in the World War may prove to be the
great service to humanity which opened a new period in Russian and
universal history — namely the Byzantine period . . . We were already on
the eve of the march to Constantinople," declared the Writer, a moderate Slavophile, in the dialogue.[74]

But it is the figure of the General who captures the pathos of the
situation as Bulgakov (who dared not reveal his "tsarist" sentiments even
to his friends) experienced it. For as the source of Russia's Orthodox
religion, Constantinople ("Tsargrad") was also a symbol of *teokratia*, and
perhaps repossession of it alone could have saved Nicholas's Russia as
a "theocracy." Now that the monarchy was gone, however, there would
have been nothing to celebrate in a putative Russian capture of Constantinople, no meaning or higher, religious-historical purpose. "With

---

[71] Nicholas II, May 12–13, 1916, in Diary (2), 586–87.
[72] On the advanced state of Russian military planning, see Sean McMeekin, *The Russian Origins of the First World War* (Cambridge, MA: Harvard University Press, 2011),
223–25; McMeekin, *Russian Revolution*, 89. The five divisions assigned to the capture
of the Ottoman capital would be led into battle by the so-called "Tsargrad Battalion."
[73] McMeekin, *Russian Origins*, 225.
[74] Bulgakov, "At the feast of the gods," 68, 69.

the revolution, all my hopes collapsed at once," confessed the General: "Really, what the devil would I do with Tsargrad without a Tsar? Am I supposed to go there with Papa Miliukov and dear Kerensky? Better let the Turkish sultan sit there with the surviving old Turks, the protectors of ancient Islamic piety."[75] Like Bulgakov's vision on the Yalta Embankment, these sentiments are more robustly conservative than those we are usually inclined to attribute him. And yet the General's remarks are so close to the record of Bulgakov's own thoughts that there is no doubt that the General's sentiments, at this moment in the dialogue, are Bulgakov's, too. As Bulgakov has it in *Autobiographical Notes*, "I loved the Tsar, wanted Russia only with the Tsar, and without the Tsar, Russia was to me no longer Russia. My soul's first movement — half-conscious, it was so deep — when the Revolution was completed and the first exhortations were being shared was: Yes, war to a victorious end is like this. But what was the point? What was victory now without the Tsar *for*? What is the point of Tsargrad when there is no Tsar? To be sure, for the Tsar, Tsargrad was fitting. The Tsar was the high priest who alone could go that altar, only he and he alone. And the thought that into this Tsargrad might arrive the Provisional Government with Kerensky and Miliukov was to me such a disgusting, such a painful and distressing thought that I felt in my heart a cold and deathly emptiness."[76] In short, the thought of the Revolution's leaders walking Constantinople's sacred streets would only confirm the hollowness of the Revolution's freedoms, "purchased" as they were, he believed, at the price of *teokratia*, the abandonment of the theocratic ideal that had for so many centuries nourished the Russian soul.

Converted, then, to the theocratic ideal in Crimea, Bulgakov also came to doubt it profoundly in Crimea. And yet, in the end, Bulgakov never became a Catholic, and from his *Autobiographical Notes*, we know how strongly he later reaffirmed his belief in *teokratia*. But how were his doubts resolved? Even after having become convinced of the claims of the papacy in 1921, Bulgakov had not wanted to turn his back on Russian Christianity altogether, or to cease to be culturally, theologically, and spiritually *Russian*. Then, in exile first in Prague, and then in Paris, Bulgakov discovered that the specifically Russian character of the spirituality and theological culture that Bulgakov had imagined he could retain while submitting to the pope weren't acceptable to the representatives of the Catholic Church that he encountered. Reunion, he discovered, meant reunion on Rome's terms only, and, in the 1920s, that meant the acceptance of a rationalizing, neo-Scholastic style of theology that he could not make peace with. The very internal sense of discipline and authority that he once praised and admired he

---

[75] Ibid., 80.   [76] Bulgakov, *Avtobiograficheskie*, 73.

now found oppressive. Precisely in order to inculcate the inner sense of discipline that so distinguished the lives of Catholics, Bulgakov now believed, Rome put too much emphasis on the external forms of authority at the expense of the inner life of the spirit.[77] In the end, therefore, Bulgakov did not become Catholic, and "Under the Walls of Chersonesos" was never published.

Instead, Bulgakov gained in exile a new appreciation for Eastern Orthodoxy — and, indeed, a certain new vision of *teokratia*. When Bulgakov quit Crimea for exile in 1922, his first stop en route was Tsargrad itself, the old Byzantine capital, Constantinople. And while history had since ensured that Miliukov and Kerensky never bestrode the streets of Tsargrad in place of the tsar or the floors of Hagia Sophia, Bulgakov the refugee *did*. The experience anchored him forever in Orthodoxy's fundamentally Christian-Platonic view of the cosmos as a theophany, an orderly hierarchy of meaningful symbols radiating a knowledge of the divine nature, its *energies*. "Of all the wonderful churches I have seen, this is the most absolute, the universal church. . . . Human tongues cannot express the lightness, the clarity, the simplicity, the wonderful harmony which completely dispels all sense of heaviness. . . . A sea of light pours from above and dominates all this space, enclosed and yet free. The grace of the columns and the beauty of their marble lace, the royal dignity — not luxury, but regality — of the golden walls and the marvelous ornamentation: it captivates and melts the heart, subdues and convinces. . . . This is indeed Sophia, the real unity of the world in the Logos, the coinherence of all with all, the world of divine ideas. It is Plato baptized by the Hellenic genius of Byzantium."[78] Suddenly, the specific path and historical task of Orthodoxy made sense. "Here one understands anew the whole force and convincing self-evidence of the testimony of St Justin Martyr. . . . The church of St Sophia is Plato's realm of ideas in stone rising above the chaos of non-being and subduing it through persuasion: the whole pleroma as a single, whole, pan-unity. Here it is manifested and shown to the world. O Lord, how holy, how marvelous, how precious is this manifestation!"

Ultimately, the theocratic principle was part of this Christian-Platonic worldview. It was a *tsar* — the Byzantine emperor Justinian — who had had Hagia Sophia constructed, and for centuries Byzantine emperors, publicly acknowledging the receipt of their authority from God, had been anointed and crowned beneath its vast dome. This

---

[77] See Bernard Marchadier in Boulgakov, *Sous les remparts*, 16–17.
[78] Bulgakov, *Avtobiograficheskie*, 95. The English translation here is from Sergius Bulgakov, *A Bulgakov Anthology*, ed. Nicholas Zernov and James Pain (London: SPCK, 1976), 13–14. Though critical of anything smacking of "Hellenism," Meyendorff makes the same observation regarding what he describes as the "Neoplatonism" of Hagia Sophia: *Byzantine Theology*, 208.

liturgical act underlined their role in the cosmic scheme of Holy Wisdom. The tsar was both a symbol of the monarchy of God over the cosmos, and the consecrated human agent of God's transcendent order of justice on earth. Power properly exercised had to be theocratic, in the sense of being exercised for man on behalf of God, because justice itself was not man's invention but a cosmic gift to be received and discovered.

Indeed, even at his most despairing of Russian civilization in 1921, Bulgakov never identified anything other than *teokratia*, the theocratic principle, as of the essence of Russia's vocation as a Christian people, culture, and civilization. "The history of the Russian people, marked as it is by the idea of a power that operates in virtue of the holy unction and which considers itself theocratic, as well as the religious expectations present in the Russian consciousness, bear witness to this theocratic vocation and mission — and it's a point on which I do not have to burn what I have loved ... The revolution has buried the question [*teokratia*] without suppressing it and at the first occasion it will return to the historical scene given its status as [Russian culture's] *faculté maîtresse* [organizing idea]."[79]

And yet, Bulgakov believed, at stake here was something more than the revival of the theocratic principle in Russia. Russia's destiny was to reveal, in its attachment to *teokratia*, a truth about the true nature of political power relevant to the whole world. As he put it, "What awaits us here, of course, is a new creative historical and dogmatic effort, and, God willing, a new dogma of power, confirmed one day by the infallible authority of the successor of St Peter."[80] Bulgakov may have abandoned, as unnecessary, the second part of that affirmation. But there is no reason to believe that Bulgakov abandoned the first. Russia's *truth*, the truth vouchsafed to Eastern Orthodoxy for itself and for the world, was the true theocratic nature of all human power: an integral element of a cosmos willed by God as a manifestation of His ruling power and other energies, politics is always already an act of sacred representation.[81]

---

[79] Bulgakov, *Sous les remparts*, 285–86. French in the original Russian.

[80] Ibid., 287.

[81] Which is precisely why Meyendorff, who otherwise opposes natural and revealed theology, is right to identify, in the Palamite distinction of essence and energies, a permanent dogmatic bulwark against secularization: John Meyendorff, *A Study of Gregory Palamas*, trans. George Lawrence (Crestwood, NY: St Vladimir's Seminary Press, 1964), 27. On Bulgakov's errors regarding the essence/energies distinction, see however Lossky, *Mystical Theology*, 80.

CHAPTER EIGHT

Belarus

I HAD CROSSED THE BORDER WITHOUT A GUIDE-book. So far as I was aware, none existed. A popular publisher covered Belarus in its guide to Eastern Europe, but the whole country received only eight pages, and my first stop, the eastern industrial town of Mogilev, none. Russia was a known quantity, familiar. But Belarus was not, and I had boarded the sleeping car in Moscow's Belorussia Station with misgiving. Known in Soviet days as Belorussia ("White Russia"), and in earlier times as Ruthenia, Belarus is a flat, 80,000 square-mile lozenge of factories, forest, and farmland forming a land bridge between its giant neighbor to the east and the eastern reaches (Lithuania, Poland) of Central Europe to the west. An independent country only since the Soviet collapse of 1991, Belarus has been ruled for all but three of those years by its tall, mustachioed president, Aleksandr Lukashenko. A left-leaning authoritarian populist of the old school who was once the manager of a Soviet collective farm, Lukashenko has been credited with making Belarus "the closest approximation of Soviet polity and economy in the post-Soviet space."[1] Proverbially, Europe's "last dictatorship," a "black hole," "anomaly in the region," "bastard in Europe," "outpost of tyranny," "authoritarian cesspool," Belarus has become a byword for the heavy-handed, backward-looking authoritarianism Eastern Europe was supposed to have put behind it when it threw off Soviet tutelage a generation ago.[2]

Why was I going? The answer was that as the headquarters from June 1915 of the Russian Army's high command ("Stavka"), the town of Mogilev, in Belarus's east, was among the last nerve centers of tsarism. Until that time, Nicholas and Alexandra had visited Belarus (known, since the Polish uprising of 1831, merely as the "North-West Provinces") only rarely. From the point of view of the court, the land was a marginal place, notable primarily for the ancient forest of Belovezha in the far west, where for the sake of its rich game (including the rare European bison or wisent) Nicholas annually hunted in the autumn. In 1914, however, Belarus's marginality was transformed drastically by the outbreak of war with Germany.[3] With Poland (a land to which

---

[1] Andrew Savchenko, *Belarus: A perpetual borderland* (Leiden: Brill, 2009), 223.
[2] This list of unflattering epithets is from Grigory Ioffe, *Understanding Belarus and Why Western Foreign Policy Misses the Mark* (Lanham, MD: Rowman and Littlefield, 2008), xii.
[3] See Joshua A. Sanborn, *Imperial Apocalypse: The Great War and the destruction of the Russian Empire* (Oxford: Oxford University Press, 2014), 28–31.

Belarus had for centuries been deeply connected), Belarus lay at the center of the fighting. Originally, "Stavka," Russian staff headquarters, was established at Baranovici, a small town in the Belarusian far west, near the modern border with Poland. Owing to German victories in the spring of 1915, which saw all Poland and much of western Belarus lost to the Germans, Stavka was relocated hundreds of miles east to Mogilev.[4] To bolster morale, and demonstrate Russia's commitment to victory, Nicholas assumed personal command in July. For the first time in his reign, this brought Nicholas to Belarus for extended periods. Living modestly at first in the imperial train, Nicholas was finally prevailed upon to move into the local governor's mansion. On a hill overlooking a bend in the lazy Dnieper River below, the few rooms he occupied here became Nicholas's effective second home. Often he brought Alexei with him, and Nicholas's diary allows us to imagine father and son falling asleep after their nightly prayers, side-by-side in their simple camp beds. Alexandra and the girls regularly visited. In short, in Mogilev, the Russian *teokratia* went to war. Indeed, for eighteen months between August 1915 and the collapse of the dynasty in February 1917, it was Imperial Russia's unofficial second capital.

In the demise of Russian *teokratia*, then, the role played by Mogilev — and by extension Belarus — was large: it was here, as we shall see in a later chapter, that Nicholas, having assumed for himself (out of obedience to what he believed was the message addressed to him through the icon of Christ in his and Alexandra's Fyodorov Sovereign Cathedral) supreme command of the Russian Armed Forces, presided over the recovery of Russia's wartime fortunes in 1916, permitting himself, for several sweet months, to believe in Russian victory (and just possibly, with it, the return of a Christian emperor to "Tsargrad," Constantinople). It was in Mogilev that, symbolically, Nicholas's assimilation of the theocratic meaning of his office reached its fulfilment, and also in Mogilev that the first plots to unseat Nicholas were hatched. In February 1917, it was from Mogilev that Nicholas departed to rescue his family and restore government sway in Petrograd — and also from Mogilev that Nicholas, a week later, departed as an "ex-emperor," Citizen Romanov, for exile in Siberia, and, subsequently, gruesome death. It was in Mogilev, Belarus, then, that the theocratic principle in Russian culture attained its apotheosis, and also in Mogilev, Belarus, that it died.

Since Nicholas's time, however, Belarus has been occupied by Germany (twice), Poland (once), and was part of the USSR for seventy years. Between the two world wars, its western half was subject to Polish colonization, while its eastern half suffered the standard Soviet cocktail

---

[4] Sanborn, *Imperial Apocalypse*, 65–108. Sanborn sees in this retreat the beginning of the collapse of the Russian Empire itself.

of nationalization, collectivization, industrialization, and purge. In 1941, the Germans invaded. Across Belarus as a whole, nine tenths of all built structures were destroyed between that year and the Soviet liberation of 1944. Mogilev was no exception, and when the war was finally over, the historical center of "old" Mogilev (where Nicholas had made his wartime home) was so ruined that the modern city was reconstructed, in high Stalinist-Gothic style, half a mile east: like Belarus as a whole, post-war Mogilev is essentially a Soviet creation, without obvious connection to its pre-communist past. In such a place, could there be any memory of the time when Nicholas II called Mogilev home? And in a land that is no longer *Russia* politically, is there any recollection of the Russian ideal of *teokratia*?

∾   ∾   ∾

As the train trundled on through the night, however, I was thinking about the more recent history of the lands beyond the windowpanes. Thanks to the winds that were blowing one fateful day, no territory in the world had received more of the poisonous fallout from the meltdown of the nuclear reactor at Chernobyl than Belarus. Spurred on by that terrible capacity of the night to disarm the rational mind, I indulged an increasingly preposterous vision of the Soviet dystopia frozen in time into which I imagined the sleeper train carrying me. I needn't have bothered. When, just after dawn, my train pulled into Mogilev station, the scene I had imagined failed to materialize. The morning sky was a baby blue and gentle pink, and of the successors of the KGB there was not a trace anywhere on the platform. Disappointingly, no one bothered to look at the hard-won visa in my passport. Half an hour later, I was sipping a cup of Nescafé pod coffee in an almost surgically clean hotel, close to what was left of Mogilev's "historical center." Through the floor to ceiling glass that formed one side of my seventh-floor room, I watched the city, bisected by two enormous Stalinist-era boulevards (the typically Soviet-named 1st May Street and Peace Avenue) and ringed by the familiar curtain wall of gray, Khrushchev-era apartment blocks, stir to life. Was there anyone out there who would relate to the purpose of my search?

Lukashenko, it turned out, did not rule by oppression alone because he did not have to. The perpetuation in Belarus of a broadly Soviet way of life has always enjoyed widespread support and consent. There was good reason for this. Belarus was one of the Soviet Union's great success stories. Chernobyl notwithstanding, the late Soviet period had been a good time in Belarus, with employment and cradle-to-grave welfare. A "model republic," Belarus produced the USSR's best dairy and agricultural produce, its most fashionable knitwear, and its most sought-after tractors and television sets. Per head of population, no other

Soviet republic had as many high-tech factories or as many institutes of higher education. Whereas, therefore, in the West, the very word "Belarus" conjures unfortunate associations, among Russians, who know it better, the word retains the cachet it held in Soviet days, a marker of craftsmanship (for the older generation, Belarusian knitwear, *beloruskii trikotazh*, remains the fashion gold standard) and quality, particularly in agricultural goods. Served in the immaculate hotel buffet, breakfast at the hotel my first morning justified the Russian rather than the Western imagination: ham, eggs, bread, yoghurt, and deliciously warm *dranniki*, shallow-fried potato pancakes stuffed with onion and dill and served with sour cream that are the local specialty.

As for Mogilev, the town began life as a fort on the Dnieper River, an outpost of the Rus principality of Polotsk, and, by extension, the greater Rus commonwealth of Kiev, of which the Polotsk principality was part. By the 1350s, however, Kievan Rus had disintegrated, and, marking the moment at which the history of the future Belarus diverged from that of modern Russia, Mogilev, with the rest of the old Polotsk principality, fell under the sway of Lithuania and its still-unbaptized rulers or grand dukes. Converted to Catholicism and acceding through marriage to the throne of Catholic Poland in 1386, Lithuania's grand dukes drew the future Belarus into the orbit of Catholic Western Europe. For residents of towns like Mogilev, this had advantages. When, in 1569, an act of union created a unified Polish-Lithuanian Commonwealth, Mogilev, like many other former fortresses and trading posts of the old Rus west that had fallen under Lithuanian domination, became a handsome, Central-European town that enjoyed, under the so-called "Magdeburg Law," a form of local self-government that left municipal administration in the hands of local merchants. By the 1630s, therefore, Mogilev's profile was that of a prosperous, high-walled town on the banks of the Dnieper, sheltering an eclectic collection of new baroque steeples, old Rus onion domes, and the wooden, pyramidal roofs of the town's synagogues, filled out with the neat half-timbered merchants' houses.[5] Frayed and faded, much of this survived into Nicholas's day.

Union with Poland, then, was good for business. But it also brought about a fateful religious split in Belarus's population.[6] Fearful of the connections between his kingdom's Orthodox bishops and their metropolitan ("of *all Rus*") across the border in Orthodox Moscow, the Catholic kings of Poland sought to secure the religious unity of their realm through the 1596 Union of Brest, whereby the Orthodox bishops of Belarus transferred their allegiance to the pope. In many ways, this made

[5] Adding to the local religious diversity was an influx of Jewish refugees from Reconquista Spain throughout the sixteenth century.
[6] On the religious history of medieval Belarus or Belorussia, see Florovsky, *Ways of Russian Theology*, Part 1 in *Collected Works*, 5:33–37, 52–74.

sense: much of the Belarusian nobility and urban gentry, impressed by the superiority of Polish culture and education, had already converted to Catholicism. Beyond Mogilev's city walls, however, the peasants, monks and lower clergy refused (despite being allowed under the terms of the Union to keep their icons and traditional Slavonic liturgy) to follow their bishops, and remained defiantly Orthodox. When they then appealed for help to the tsar in Orthodox Moscow, Polish authorities inevitably identified attachment to Orthodoxy as a threat to the realm, outlawed non-conformity, and resorted to coercion to achieve the acceptance by the peasantry of what was known as the "Unia" or Greek-Catholic Church. Practiced by approximately eight percent of the Belarusian population, it survives today mainly in the west, near the border with Poland.

For that part of the population that resisted, however, coercion fed the cause of rebellion. In the 1650s, an Orthodox insurrection against Polish-Catholic domination, led by the Cossacks, attracted Moscow's support, and the forces of Muscovy invaded. During the decades of warfare that followed, the foundations of local prosperity were destroyed, and the lands of the future Belarus, including Mogilev, began a long decline. In 1709, a Polish-Swedish army passed through during Charles XII of Sweden's failed invasion of Russia. In 1762, the Russian Empress Catherine the Great annexed the region to Russia. Orthodoxy was restored, but local self-government was quashed in favor of rule by a Russian governor from Petersburg. In 1812, Napoleon, having assembled the largest army Europe had ever seen, transited on his way to Moscow, the retreating Russians scorching the earth in their wake. Four months later, the remnants of Napoleon's Grande Armée picked their way back across the same burnt-out territory, chased now by the Russians on their way to Paris. Discontented with Russian rule, in 1833 and again 1864, the local Polish gentry rebelled, only to be beaten down, twice, by the Russian army. In 1839, the region's peasantry, having been herded against its will into the Uniate or Greek Catholic Church under Polish rule, was herded back, by order of the tsar, into the Orthodox one. By this stage, who they were, Catholic Poles or Orthodox Russians, many seem not to have known. Perhaps for this reason, since the fall of communism, the revival of Orthodoxy in Belarus has not been as sweeping as that seen next door in Russia. But it has nonetheless happened, and, today, just over half the population identify as Orthodox, up from just over a third in 1991. As members of the Belarusian Orthodox Church, Moscow Patriarchate, they belong to a church organization with its head, the patriarch, in Moscow, represented in Belarus by an "exarch," the metropolitan-archbishop of Minsk.

෨ ෨ ෨

Given Belarus's conflicted history, did the theocratic principle ever have a chance to take root? Was Belarusian culture different on this point from Russia's — and was there any place in it for the Royal Passion-bearers? My search for them began, unpromisingly, it might have seemed, in Mogilev's Soviet Square, a windswept concrete platform overlooking a bend in Dnieper on what is now the western side of town, but which, in Nicholas's day, had been the town center, and, as such, the location of Stavka and of the governor's mansion, where Nicholas had his rooms. Flattened with the rest of old Mogilev in 1941–44, the area had emerged from the Second World War a ruin. Today, a towering, sword-bearing Amazon — a post-War Soviet representation of the Motherland defending itself against the German invaders — stands on a granite plinth erected on the site of the old governor's mansion, where Nicholas had once lived, and dominates the amorphous space. Yet while the governor's mansion had been demolished, the unremarkable, neo-classical building on the other side of the square where Stavka had met still stood, serving today as Mogilev's regional historical museum.

Unfortunately, I had arrived on a Monday, and the building was, in principle, closed. Noticing, however, that the main door was ajar, I slipped inside, where I found a young woman sitting behind the ticket desk.

"Would you like to visit the museum?" she asked cheerfully, raising my hopes. "Unfortunately," she continued, dashing them just as quickly, "our museum is shut on Mondays and Tuesdays. Can you come back later in the week?"

I explained that by Wednesday I would be gone, and I had come far to see the museum. Appealing to local pride, I said I understood the world-historical significance of the building it was housed in and yet, alas, I might never be back. Could an exception be made for a foreigner?

"Hmm, I'm not sure," she replied: "Let me call the guard."

As I heard her sympathetically repeat the details of my case down the phone, my confidence grew. My cause had won an advocate.

"The guard says you should speak to the director. Perhaps he will give you permission. Follow me."

We proceeded down a corridor of 1970s faux-wood paneling and heavy, dark green acrylic carpet. Far from deserted, the building was full of curators and administrators. Walking through a pair of frosted glass doors into the anteroom of the director's office, I repeated my story to his middle-aged secretary.

By the time I had finished, this new gatekeeper was on my side, too.

"I understand," she said, smiling kindly. "The problem is that the director is busy. But take a seat and wait until his meeting has finished. I'll make sure he understands the significance of the situation, and that it's impossible for you to wait until Wednesday."

She swung her chair back round to her desk before pivoting almost immediately back again.

"But why do you have so little time in Mogilev? You'll just have to come back!" she said, smiling broadly, as if she had solved the problem.

Over the next twenty minutes, people came and went through the office. The director's friendly secretary repeated my story to them all, while I made eyes that expressed my disappointment. Everyone agreed it was unfortunate. But what to do if the director never finished with his appointment? At last, my new champion took matters into her own hands. With a smile, she suggested that we forget about the director and go and see the chief of security instead. We entered a neighboring office where a middle-aged woman with greying, shoulder-length hair turned out to be chief of security. My new sponsor explained the situation.

"But perhaps it's not possible?" the secretary asked, concluding her plea.

"Why impossible? (*Kak nevozmozhno?*)" the chief of security replied after a minute's reflection: "Call Galina. She knows more about what he's interested in than anyone else. Give her the key and let her show him everything."

Galina soon arrived. An older woman apparently nearing retirement, she walked with a pronounced hobble, and gestured that we should go upstairs.

"This is our exhibition," she said, turning the lights on as we entered the first large room at the top of the landing. Even with the lights on, the effect of the dark laminate paneling, green carpet, and lack of windows made it a heavy scene.

"This is the Russian Western Front in 1915.[7] Mogilev is here. The Sovereign (Russian: *gosudar'*) arrived in Mogilev in August, in the wake of that year's spring retreat, when military headquarters were permanently moved here. A month before, Nicholas II had taken over supreme command of the army for himself. From that time," she continued, "Mogilev was effectively the military capital of the Russian Empire."

The story put a certain spring in her step. Galina was evidently proud of her town's place in world history. Still, Galina's age placed her as a product of the Soviet education system that knew only "Nicholas the Bloody," and I had no real idea how Nicholas would be remembered in Belarus. And yet, in the first of what would become many refutations of many stereotypes, she pointed to a photograph taken on the day of his arrival in Mogilev as commander-in-chief.

"You know, for the first few months he was in Mogilev, the Sovereign lived aboard his train. Of course, as tsar, as emperor, he had every right to use the governor's mansion. But he didn't want to put the governor or

---

[7] What the Russians call their Western Front is what the Allied powers referred to, more generally, as the Eastern Front.

the generals sharing the building with him out. The train seemed like the ideal solution. Every day, he would drive in to confer with the military staff working in this building." She pointed to the floor under our feet.

"Eventually, however, the local governor threatened to resign if the Sovereign didn't move into the governor's mansion. So, the tsar agreed and took over two rooms, a bedroom, and a neighboring office. In the bedroom were two beds, one for himself and the other for the tsarevich Alexei."

We walked over to a display cabinet showing a copy of the decree in which Nicholas II proclaimed himself commander-in-chief. The proclamation provoked the first great crisis in relations not only between Nicholas and the Duma politicians, who vehemently opposed the decision, but also between Nicholas and his ministers, all but one of whom sided with the Duma. To many historians, it was the act that put Russia on the path to revolution.[8] But a hundred years later, Galina offered praise, not criticism.

"Never before in history had a ruler taken command of an army in retreat," she said admiringly: "Nicholas's mother, the Council of Ministers, all of them tried to talk him out of it. But his wife supported him. Nicholas believed that, whether he took personal command or not, he was responsible for the army and the country, anyway. By showing that he was completely committed to victory, Nicholas II believed that he would raise army morale. And, in fact, he was right. When the troops learned that the Sovereign had taken personal command and had himself come to live at the front, they began to believe that the Germans could be defeated. In fact, it saved the country. After the tsar took command, the front was stabilized. The Germans made no further advances until after he was betrayed by his generals in 1917."

Such praise of Nicholas — and, by extension, tsarism itself — would have been a potentially criminal act in Soviet Belorussia. Evidently, modern Belarus was not quite as "Soviet" as is sometimes claimed. Above all, listening to Galina, I was struck by the utter insignificance of the border I had crossed earlier that morning. The defunct Russian Empire was not a foreign, "colonial" entity that her country had been liberated from by way of the 1991 Soviet collapse but, in her words, "the country." Nicholas was not the "Russian Emperor," a historical third party, but instead "the Sovereign." It was as if Belarus was the name of the modern state Galina lived in, but the community of historical destiny to which she instinctively imagined herself belonging was a "Russia," a community that was not necessarily continuous with the modern Russian Federation.

Galina pointed to a photograph of the bald, mustachioed General Mikhail Alekseev. A commoner and professional soldier, Alekseev

---

[8] See, for example, Pipes, *Russian Revolution*, 228.

had risen from peasant stock to Nicholas's chief-of-staff and *de facto* commander-in-chief of the Russian Imperial Army. It elicited more praise for Nicholas.

"Despite making himself supreme commander, Nicholas II was under no illusions that he was expert in military affairs. The meaning of his position as Supreme Commander was moral and symbolic. He left military planning to Alekseev. The fact is that as far as the Imperial Army itself went, Nicholas's assumption of Supreme Command led to its professionalization."

Although disputed by some historians, the point could be defended.[9] In 1917, however, Alekseev, who would play a decisive role in persuading Nicholas to abdicate, was informed of plots to overthrow Nicholas, and yet did nothing to warn his Sovereign. I asked Galina whether the tsar had made a mistake in abdicating. The question provoked a brief pause in our conversation. Inhaling deeply, she looked me in the eyes as if to emphasize the seriousness of what she was about to confide.

"When the Sovereign abdicated at Pskov, he was entirely alone. He asked all his generals by telegram whether they still supported him, and they all, with the one exception, replied that he should abdicate, even Alekseev, who owed his very appointment to Nicholas. The result was a great tragedy. Had the Sovereign reached Tsarskoye Selo as planned on February 28 with the detachment of loyal troops with which he intended to march on the capital, I'm convinced there would have been no revolution, and the country would not have endured all the suffering that came after it."

It was now clear. Galina had revealed to me — a foreigner about whom she knew nothing — not only her knowledge of history but also, unavoidably, her historical-political sympathies: she regretted the Revolution, wished the tsar and tsarism had not fallen, and, implicitly, regretted the subsequent process that had formally separated Belarus from Russia.

I followed my guide into a new room. Dominating the wall at the far end, a modern, painted mural showed scenes from the lives of Nicholas and his family, emphasizing not their remoteness from ordinary people, but their humanity. On the left, Alexandra and the four grand duchesses, dressed in nurses' uniforms, tended the wounded in wartime hospitals; to the right, Alexei sat surrounded by his sisters, in an image that combined a sense of childhood innocence with a message of dynastic continuity. But it was the central image that held my attention: Nicholas in military uniform standing flanked by his generals, while on the large desk behind

---

[9] See, for example, Dominic Lieven, who notes that, "the Emperor was a much more calming influence at headquarters than his nervous uncle." Lieven also notes the positive effect the move had on the coordination of civilian and military authority: *Nicholas II*, 213; Lieven, *Towards the Flame: Empire, war and the end of Tsarist Russia* (Harmondsworth: Penguin, 2015), 347. For a similar assessment, see Heretz, *Russia on the Eve*, 227–28.

him a small white bust of Lenin sat in a pool of blood. The Revolution inaugurated not a bright new future beyond tsarism, the image seemed to be saying, but suffering and bloodshed. With every passing minute, Belarus appeared less and less the unreformed outpost of Soviet life it is routinely portrayed as being.

We left the exhibition rooms and wandered out to the main connecting corridor.

"Do you see those wooden doors over there?" Galina abruptly asked, pointing to a pair of doors at the end of the first-floor landing. "When Nicholas came back from Pskov, he took leave of his generals in a room inside this building. It's on the other side of those doors. It's now an exhibition room, but not connected with the First World War, and I'm afraid I haven't got the key."

She looked around at the floor we are standing on, nodding in the direction of the wide, carpeted stairwell.

"All the same, he would have come up those steps; his very spirit (*dusha*) is in this place."

We had not spoken of God directly. But Galina's reverence for the spirit of Nicholas II struck me as implying some sort of religious commitment.

I followed Galina down the stairs and back to the main door. By now, the morning cloud cover had burned off, and the noonday sun was shining brightly as I crossed a square that, a hundred years before, had been the nerve center of the final, great act of exertion of one of history's most ambitious and successful empires.[10]

෨෨ ෨෨ ෨෨

Behind the museum, a park spread across the top of the hill overlooking the Dnieper. Benches lined a shady path beneath the trees, and at the far end was the outline of a small white church with a single brass onion dome dedicated to "the Royal Martyrs and . . . the New Martyrs and Confessors of the Twentieth Century." A stone's throw from the demolished governor's mansion where Russia's last tsar made his Mogilev home, there was now a church dedicated to his memory. I pushed on the door and went inside. Above a floor of shiny white tiles, the mechanically reproduced rather than authentically hand-painted icons that hung on the plain concrete walls suggested a budget that stretched only so far. But the sacred space was nonetheless clearly loved. Everything was spotless, and the flowers decorating the ambon were fresh. To the left of the iconostasis, a large icon showed Nicholas II wearing a medieval robe and Cap of Monomakh; an inscription identified the subject as "St Nicholas, the Tsar-Martyr." The same image was repeated on a processional banner on the step in front of the iconostasis, while on the wall on the other

---

[10] For a compelling account of the success of the Russian imperial project, see Dominic Lieven, *Empire: The Russian Empire and its rivals* (London: John Murray, 2000).

side of the nave another large icon showed Nicholas, Alexandra and their children as a family: the "Holy Royal Passion-Bearers." Nearby, an icon of St Serafim, their heavenly patron, as well as an image of "Our Lady in Majesty," the copy of an icon of the Virgin Mary, seated on a throne, and holding an orb that was said to have descended from heaven to a church in Moscow the day Nicholas abdicated. The icon is interpreted as meaning that, when the monarchy fell, the Mother of God — Queen (Russian: *tsaritsa*) of Heaven — assumed for herself the tsar's sacred authority over Russia (to preserve it, apparently, for a time when it might be restored). In this small corner of Belarus at least, it seemed, not only Orthodoxy but the theocratic principle were back.

I walked from corner to corner of the church, examining the images. As I did so, a woman wearing a pink kerchief emerged from a crypt I hadn't previously noticed, to the left of the iconostasis. A second woman followed her out, followed by a man sporting a shock of wavy grey hair. His black cassock identified him as a priest. I wanted to ask him about the church and about the meaning to the Orthodox faithful who attended it of Nicholas II and his family's sainthood. But the three were engaged in conversation and I decided to try to find him again later.

No sooner had I stepped out of the church, however, than a voice behind me called out: "*Gospoda*! Wait!" (*gospoda* means "sir," and was the standard form of address before the revolution, after which it was suppressed in favor of *tovarishch*, "comrade." Like the Romanovs, its use has been partially rehabilitated since the collapse of communism.)

It was the priest. He held out my map, which must have somehow fallen out of my pocket.

We shook hands. His broad smile suggested a willingness to talk. I explained my purpose in Belarus. I did not use the terms *teokratia* or "theocratic." But the priest nodded his head intently as if he knew what I was getting at.

"Yes, this is correct. To those who come here, the Sovereign [*gosudar'*], Nicholas II, was God's anointed [*bozhii pomazannik*], a God-fearing man and Orthodox Christian," the priest replied. "He was murdered because he was God's tsar, and, therefore, his death was a true martyrdom."

But wasn't he a *Russian* tsar, I asked, and this Belarus?

A man, evidently, of flamboyant gestures, the priest pulled his wallet out of his pocket and showed me a fistful of Belarusian banknotes.

"This is Belarusian paper," he said, "but, culturally, we are *Russians*, pure and simple. And Russians must have a tsar. For Russians, monarchy is the only legitimate form of government — not socialism or democracy but *monarchy*. Of course, we don't mind if other countries have different systems. But for Russia and for Russians, it must be *monarchy*."

The priest began rehearsing the standard arguments in favor of monarchy, wherever it is found: continuity, impartiality, a horizon of decision-making longer than the next election cycle.

And yet neither Bulgakov nor Nicholas II would have located the essence of the Russian tsardom in this. As revealed to Bulgakov on the Yalta Embankment and intuited by Nicholas from earliest age, the defining element of tsarism was the theocratic principle: the tsar as the human image and bearer of an authority over the world — a *cosmic kingship* — that was properly God's. Without that, wasn't monarchy just another form of arbitrary dictatorship? I pointed to Vladimir Putin. In the West, I said, it was common to call Putin "a tsar." Was he one?

The priest saw where I was going. Yes, he said, Russia's president *was* a "strong leader," but he was adamant nonetheless that Putin was "*not* a tsar." A tsar, he continued, "is sent from God and anointed by the Church. That is what Nicholas II was, God's anointed [*bozhii pomazannik*], and why he refused to capitulate to the demands of the Duma. They wanted Nicholas to be tsar in name only while they took all the power for themselves. What they did not see was that the *tsar*," he said stressing the word, "could not give *them* what he himself had received from God. No one can be a true tsar without recognizing this."

Less elegantly put, perhaps, than by Bulgakov, the theory the priest was expounding was nonetheless that of *teokratia*, of an authority "by the grace of God, not popular dispensation."

And yet it was one thing to recognize the claims of *teokratia* and call oneself a tsarist, as Bulgakov had done, so long as the monarchy existed. But to do so today, wasn't *that* to hope for something that could not be?

"Not at all," he said, fixing his single good eye on me. "God is merciful. When the time is right, He will give the Russian people a new tsar. Only first of all we must prove ourselves *worthy*. God will not give us one until we have repented of ours sins and returned as a people to Orthodoxy."

There was a pause in the conversation.

"Have you seen our chapel?" he asked, his eyes brightening.

A smaller, timbered building, the chapel was the original place of Orthodox worship erected on this site, as soon as it had become possible to do so, after the collapse of communism in 1991. Now that the new church had been built, this chapel had been repurposed as what the priest called an "education center" designed to disseminate the truth about Russia's last tsar and his family.

The priest drew a key from his pocket and unlocked the doors. Inside, the walls were covered with black and white photographs of the Romanovs: engagement and wedding photographs from the early 1890s; the 1896 coronation; the birth of the grand duchesses, and, at last, the heir; the 1913 Romanov Tercentenary; Nicholas appearing on the balcony of the Winter Palace in July 1914 to announce the declaration of war on Germany; the tsar at Mogilev, reviewing troops and awarding medals. They were not originals, but copies, many of which I recognized from the plates of books I had read years before. But to local people of the older generation who had been raised during the ban on images of the last Romanovs under the Soviet Union, they were very likely new, and perhaps even revelatory.

"These photographs are a crucial part of our educational center," explained the priest, pointing at the walls. "Unfortunately, there are still many people in Mogilev and in Belarus who don't know the truth, who say that Nicholas II was either a weak ruler, who did everything his crazy foreign wife told him to do, or, alternatively, that he was 'Nicholas the Bloody,' a callous and heartless tyrant who hated the workers and peasants, the ordinary people. That's why we have assembled these pictures and information panels, to show those who come here that these people, the right-believing [*pravoveryuushchii*] Tsar Nicholas II, the right-believing Tsaritsa Alexandra and their children, were a true Orthodox family, and Nicholas II was a true Orthodox tsar, God's anointed [*bozhii pomazannik*]."

To demonstrate interest, I looked more closely at the pictures he and his friends had assembled.

"See, they were beautiful spirits!" the priest said, singling out a photograph of two, luxuriantly long-haired teenage girls in long dresses bouncing a pair of peasant children on their knees—a photograph I had not seen before.

"This is Nicholas II's two youngest daughters, Grand Duchess Maria and Grand Duchess Anastasia, playing with peasant children in a village not far from here. When they visited Mogilev, they loved to drive out to the surrounding villages and mix with the common people. Although their father was the tsar, they did not think of themselves as above anyone. We were all Orthodox then, all believers. That was all that mattered."

It was, indeed, a touching photograph. The girls seemed perfectly relaxed and happy. It was difficult to imagine that, no more than two years after the picture had been taken, the two beautiful girls could be murdered in cold blood in the distant Urals.

He paused for a minute as his eyes scanned the wall of photographs, before alighting on another one.

"This is a photograph of Alexei, the heir to the throne, the tsarevich. Yes, he was very ill. Hemophilia. We know that now. But what a good tsar he would have made! During the war, he spent many weeks here on and off with his father despite his illness. When he went, wearing his little uniform, on visits to the front with his father, the troops always gave him a huge hurrah. People who knew or met him said that he was a very good little boy, kind and full of concern for the ordinary people."

He sighed, and the direction of his eyes fell to the floor.

"We have a mission, to tell the truth about the Tsar-Martyr Nicholas II and his holy family. You see this exhibition? We have taken it all over Belarus, all over Russia. We set ourselves up in the parish halls of churches. And wherever we go, people come and leave amazed. They have simply never been told the truth. Right now, we are preparing to take a selection of material to Nizhny Novgorod."

Nizhny Novgorod was a large and old Russian city, known in Soviet times as Gorky, on the banks of the Volga River, hundreds of miles away, northeast of Moscow. The man taking the exhibition there was called Vasily, and the priest believed I should meet him.

"Vasily can tell you everything. I'll call him. With luck, he can see you before he leaves for Nizhny."

Barely a few hours before, I had left the hotel unsure whether I'd find a single person in Mogilev who remembered Nicholas II. Now, it seemed, I had stumbled upon a network of devoted admirers.

The priest called Vasily. I listened to the disjointed conversation that ensued, as my new-found priest-friend tried to explain the nature of my interest in Nicholas II to an evidently skeptical and impatient Vasily.

"He is writing a book on the Sovereign [*gosudar'*] and has lots of very interesting questions. I think you would like to talk to him," the priest tried to persuade his friend.

Audibly harried and impatient, Vasily nonetheless consented. The priest gave me his phone number.

"Call him before five o'clock. He doesn't have much time because he must leave tonight with the exhibition. But he would be glad to talk to you about the tsar and why we venerate him."

A trail that I had feared had not existed had suddenly become very hot indeed. We shook hands warmly. Then I made my way to the icon shop, which I found staffed by an old woman who practically fell over herself when she discovered that I was a foreigner. To her, that meant a potential convert, and she did her best to force various edifying tracts upon me.

"St Innokentii of Alaska. Do you know him? He is very good. What about Nikolai of Serbia? He was a prophet, he had visions. You should read them. They talk about the return of a tsar and the anti-Christ who will oppose him."

I handed over tens of thousands of Belarusian rubles (the exchange was five thousand to a dollar) and forced a small library into my daypack.

"Do you get many pilgrims coming to pray, here, in Mogilev, to the Royal Martyrs?" I asked, using the Romanovs' local name.

She assured me they did. "From Belarus, from Russia. Sometimes from Serbia. They love our tsar in Serbia. But very few foreigners. No one from the West. Oh, but they were such a wonderful family. Have you been down to the St Nicholas women's monastery yet? You must. It's the oldest in Mogilev. The Sovereign often prayed there while he was in Mogilev. Do you know the story about the coin?"

She looked at me expectantly. I shook my head.

"They closed the monastery in 1934. It was looted and almost destroyed. Then, when the Soviet Union fell in 1991, a local movement immediately arose to re-open the monastery. Not long afterwards, a local man came forward. As a boy, he said, he had been on his way to Divine Liturgy at the monastery church, one Sunday before the Revolution, when the tsar and tsaritsa arrived for the same liturgy. He stood by the entrance and bowed as they passed, and when the Sovereign passed in front of him, he gave the boy a gold coin. He had kept it, never parting with it despite all the troubles we have been through since. Years later, hearing that the monastery was to reopen, he came forward with the coin and gave it to the sisters. Isn't it a wonderful story?"

It was clear that, in the old woman's eyes, the story amounted to a miracle.

"The coin is on display in the St Nicholas Monastery church. Go and see it for yourself," she said in a tone that was more instruction than suggestion. "Then write to us when you get home, won't you, and tell us what you learnt from our books? It would make me so happy."

I followed the path away from the church. As I did so, a dark-haired man I had paid little attention to when I first went into the church — he had been sweeping the floor — ran up behind me and asked whether it was true that I was from abroad. I replied that it was.

"I was born here," he said, almost breathless, as if there were something urgent he had to tell me. "But my family are Cossacks, from the Don. They tried to force my grandfather into a kolkhoz, but he didn't want to go. Instead, he came here, to Mogilev. I don't really know whether I'm Russian or Belarusian or Cossack. It doesn't matter, anyway."

Then he got to the heart of what he wanted to say.

"The most important thing is that we have peace. We don't want problems with anyone. We do not want a war. Will you tell that to people when you return to your country?"

෨   ෨   ෨

To reach the monastery meant retracing my steps back through the park to the square with sword-brandishing Amazon. There, I picked up a path that led to an unsealed trail across the Dnieper floodplain, a picturesque scene of meadows, tidy wooden houses, and carefully tended kitchen gardens. The early afternoon sun was shining in full force now, and here and there the black dials of sunflowers rose to meet it. Dogs behind fences barked as I passed. The place and the moment seemed timeless, some sort of unchanging, eternal Russia, the village Russia, perhaps, of Dostoevsky's *Brothers Karamazov*. It was hot, and I began sweating profusely. Fifteen minutes later, the sight of the gates of the monastery completed the scene.

Nestled as it was behind a high, white-washed wall, the first thing I saw of the St Nicholas Monastery was the five golden onion domes of its chapel gleaming brilliantly in the sun. Founded in 1663, with a charter granted by the king of Poland, the monastery was not originally Orthodox at all, but Uniate Greek-Catholic. It was awarded to the Orthodox after Catherine the Great's annexation of the eastern half of the future Belarus, just over a century later, and remained home to a community of monks until the latter were expelled at the height of Stalin's war on religion in the 1930s. Re-founded in 1994, it was re-established as an Orthodox nunnery.

When I arrived, all was still and hot. A small platoon of khaki-clad army cadets exited the complex. Momentarily dazzled from the glare of the white-washed walls as I passed through the gate, I was surprised by a lurching figure who suddenly accosted me from the right, grunting something I couldn't make out. I jumped away in fright. Almost instantly, an old, black-robed woman with a frail, bird-like face, framed by the high black fez-like head gear of an Orthodox nun, came to my rescue. Handing the man a thick slice of black bread, she told him to sit still and leave the visitors alone. Meekly, he did as she commanded. Was I, after all, in one of Dostoevsky's novels?

I surveyed my surroundings. To the left of the church, the monastery's two single-story residential buildings formed the other two sides of a cobbled yard, at the center of which were garden beds. Everything was neat, orderly, and tidy. Behind an ornamental row of bright red tulips, a healthy crop of vegetables grew in the beds: tomatoes, green beans, cucumbers. Considering that the place was a ruin when restored to them, the nuns had worked wonders. As a rule, Orthodox monasticism is strictly contemplative, liturgical. The nuns did not teach school, or double as nurses. They prayed, sang the Church offices together, and tended with their own hands the territory they inhabited. The cheerful appearance of the monastery-church reflected the careful, God-fearing work of *their* hands.

I followed a path lined with the same red tulips to the church building. In front of the doors at the narthex was a covered porch, protecting a drum that had been filled with holy water from a spring in the monastery grounds. A sign encouraged pilgrims to take from it liberally. On the wall behind, a fresco of Nicholas, Alexandra, and their children stood watch over all who came and went.

Inside, the church walls enclosed a surprising large, high space. At the other end of the church, a tall, gilded iconostasis, of seventeenth-century origin glinted in the light that entered from the bright day outside through the high windows. Between me and it, a handful of black-robed nuns in their fez-like headgear scampered here and there over the Persian-style carpets spread on the floor, tidying up from the morning's service. On the walls and the supporting columns that marked off the light-filled interior into smaller units, every available space was covered with images: Christ in many and varied poses, the Mother of God, the Archangels, saints. Three or four of these showed Nicholas II alone or Nicholas, Alexandra, and their children. One large icon of the family that looked out over the congregation from the lowest row of the iconostasis, kept exalted company with the Mother of God and Christ himself, while, on the southern wall, a prominent fresco of the Romanovs, with their feet at a standing person's eye height stared down from above. Embroidered in gold on scarlet cloth, a processional standard allowed the family to be held aloft, while another displayed the image of Nicholas II standing alone.

An image different from others I had seen caught my eye. Mounted on a stand in front of the northern wall, it looked more like an official portrait, of the kind that might once have hung in a government office before the revolution: Nicholas, in navy blue military uniform and heavy gold epaulettes, stood with his weight on one leg and his hands poised on the hilt of his sword in the drawing room of one of the imperial palaces. The inscription identified the subject as "The Holy and Blessed Tsar-Martyr, Nicholas." What was it, then, an icon?

A sign on a stand beside explained that nobody knew who painted the image, or why and when it was painted. It had been discovered in the basement of an old Soviet workers' canteen in Mogilev on the very day when Nicholas and his family had been declared saints five hundred miles away in Moscow, in 2000. Hailed as a confirmatory sign, the image was blessed by Mogilev's bishop, and transferred to its current location in the monastery church for veneration. Affixed to the bottom left corner of the image was the small golden coin the old woman at the icon shop had described. Beneath it a plaque told the story I already heard, adding only the name of the boy, Simeon Khalimov, and the year of his encounter with the tsar, 1916.

As I stood reading the story, a young man came and stood beside me, bowing from the waist in veneration before the mysterious portrait-icon and its miraculous coin-relic. When he was finished, he lit two beeswax candles burning on the stand before the image and walked away.

Seeing a nun standing behind a stall selling books and icons at the rear of the church, I walked over and attempted to initiate a conversation, but she was uninterested in talking and called a younger woman in plain clothes and kerchief over to talk to me instead.

A laywoman by the name of Maria, she came often to the St Nicholas Monastery to venerate the icons. When I asked her the questions I had put to the priest earlier in the day, she repeated what I had heard before, that as an Orthodox people, Russians must have a tsar; and that despite what many people continued to think, Nicholas was a good tsar, with a beautiful family. In their love of God, they were role models, she said. Then she began the story of the gold coin.

"When Simeon came forward with the coin, we knew that it was a sign from God," she said, smiling broadly.

Guessing that she might be a mother, I asked her what local children learn about Nicholas in school. A frown drove away the smile that had previously lit up her face.

"I have three children in school in Mogilev," she said. "They learn a little bit. But it's not very good. The textbooks still say many things that are wrong — that the tsar was weak and indecisive and so on. They blame him for taking Russia into the war, the revolution that followed, with all its hardships. But the truth is he didn't want the war. He tried to avoid it."

To make up for the defects in the education the children received at school about Russia's last tsar, believers such as herself, she said, taught their children to learn "the truth" in Sunday school.

"There are many prayers and hymns written in honor of the Royal Passion-Bearers, and we encourage everyone to say them."

Every Wednesday a group gathered in the church to say their *akathist*, a dedicatory hymn, she said.

Our conversation came to an end. I thanked her, then bought a candle and returned to the portrait-icon to light it. As I turned away, however, the woman came running after me.

"I want you to have this," she said, pressing a little blue book into my hand. On its cover was a picture of Grand Duchess Elizabeth Fyodorovna, Alexandra's elder sister, now also venerated as a saint.

"It's a collection of her sayings and thoughts," she explained. "Take it and read."

❧　❧　❧

A few hours later, I called Vasily as instructed by the priest. An impatient, distracted voice answered the phone.

"Yes, yes, I remember. Where are you? I have very little time. I must go to Nizhny Novgorod later tonight. Can we meet now? I can be at the square in ten minutes. I'll be in an old Volga," he said, before abruptly hanging up the phone.

The Volga was easy to spot. Old and beige, it was less a car and more a kind of iron skeleton on wheels. Approaching, I spotted him — a gaunt man about my age, with hard, skeletal features to match his car — behind the wheel. His dark hair had been shaved roughly and close to the skull. His eyes were thin and raven black. They sparkled with the intensity of a higher, divine cause. I recognized the glint, with its latent suggestion of fanaticism, from my years in an Evangelical youth group. A blonde-headed boy, clearly his son, sat quietly on the cracked acrylic of the rear seat, an icon of St Nicholas the Wonderworker hanging by a white string in a frame around his neck. He looked restless but evidently knew better than to try to hurry his father. Vasily also wore an icon. Unlike his son's, Vasily's had been fastened to his chest with what appeared to be a kind of white webbing tape resembling a bandage. Fittingly, in view of the subject of our planned conversation, the figure it depicted was St Serafim of Sarov, the Romanovs' special patron.

"Get in," he said through the open window.

I did as I was told, half afraid that when I opened the passenger door, it would fall off. Vasily picked up on the involuntary raising of my eyebrows.

"See. I said it was an old Volga. It's good for you to see a proper Russian car!"

His humor broke the ice, but only for an instant. Within moments, his humorless, piercing gaze was again fixed on me.

"So, you're writing a book about Nicholas II. What do you want to know?" he asked, firing off the question as he turned the ignition.

I explained that I was interested in how people remembered his reign a hundred years after the Revolution. I said that it seemed to me that what they thought about Nicholas as a man and ruler would reveal much about the way they approached many other things — their world view and sense of national identity.

"Look [*smotritye*]. You're a historian, right? I don't think that the veneration of the tsar is something that you can approach as if it were just facts in a book. It's something spiritual. You have to feel it with your soul. In fact, I think you have to be Orthodox to be able to really understand it. Are you Orthodox?"

"No," I answered apologetically.

I had a feeling Vasily saw me as being as little a Christian as the church's medieval missionaries had thought the local heathen.

"Who knows," I said hopefully, "perhaps one day I will."

But the effort to meet Vasily halfway rhetorically failed. Attempting a different tack, I explained that one of the reasons why I thought what I was doing was important was because in the West, they say that Russia was reviving the Soviet Union and that there is a new cult of Stalin. I said that I didn't think that this was correct. I thought we could learn a lot more by looking at a cult that really *did* exist — like that of the last tsar. The only problem was that no one really knew very much about it, or understood what I said when I tried to explain it to them, which suggested to me that I didn't know enough myself.

I sensed I had won his attention.

"For example," I continued, more confidently, "I think the cult of the imperial martyrs is the opposite of the cult of Stalin. I prefer to compare Nicholas II to Saints Boris and Gleb, as sufferers of non-resistance."

Vasily looked thoughtfully out of the windscreen. I imagined that he believed I had entered further into the spirit of the Royal Passion-Bearers than he thought possible for a non-Orthodox.

"Yes, the cult of the imperial martyrs is like that of Boris and Gleb. They are all *strastoterptsi* ["passion-bearers"]. But Stalin, on the other hand, is a more difficult question. I don't think you can say that he was either black or white. He did many terrible things. But he also won the war."

The profound duality of Stalin's reputation among Orthodox Christians is something that has struck me before. Perhaps no person in world history martyred as many Christians as Stalin, the man on whose orders 35,000 priests were shot during the Second Five Year Plan of 1933–38. And yet Russia's modern Orthodox are often among the first to credit Stalin for his patriotic and successful defense of the country against the Germans. Soon, Vasily was rattling off a list of redeeming virtues I had heard before.

"Stalin also re-opened the churches. Lenin, Khrushchev, they closed the churches down. But Stalin re-opened some of them. He died Orthodox, too, you know," Vasily said, taking the story to a conclusion I hadn't heard before.

All the same, the first part of Vasily's story was true enough. Very early on, Stalin appears to have realized the war against Germany could only be won if waged as a war, not for the defense of what Stalin had already begun calling "Marxism-Leninism-Stalinism," but for the salvation of Orthodox *Russia*, Holy Rus. As Stalin put it to American diplomat Avery Harriman in 1941, "We are under no illusion that they are fighting for us [the Communists]. They are fighting for Mother Russia."[11] The very day German troops crossed the border, Soviet authorities authorized and published a statement by the patriarch likening the defense of the USSR to the great defensive wars of Russia's past, and declaring that the "Church of Christ will bless all Orthodox who defend the holy borders of our Motherland."[12] A few days later, the League of the Militant Godless was wound up (the last issue of its newspaper, *The*

---

[11] Steven Merritt Miner, *Stalin's Holy War: Religion, nationalism, and alliance politics, 1941–1945* (Chapel Hill, NC: University of North Carolina Press, 2003). 67.
[12] Ibid., 69.

Godless, ironically dedicated to condemning Nazi persecutions of Christians), taxes were reduced on the few still-functioning churches, and some of the "anti-religion" museums the Party had opened since 1917 were closed.[13] Then, in 1943, the dictator had the patriarch unexpectedly brought to him at the Kremlin. Given that the patriarch himself had only barely survived the previous decade's executions, he naturally enough expected to be interrogated and then shot; instead, Stalin invited him to re-open the churches, on condition that the Church prayed for Soviet victory and encouraged the people to do the same. They did so, and Stalin, keeping his end of the bargain after the war, allowed around 22,000 Orthodox churches to remain open, albeit strictly for Sunday services only.[14] Khrushchev, anxious to return to Marx and Lenin's original atheism, closed most of them again in the 1960s.

"But, *ladno* ["in any case"]," Vasily said, as he swung the car down the street, "we're talking about the tsar and his family, not Stalin. You know that we have two different names to refer to the family by? The Russian Orthodox Church Outside of Russia calls them "martyrs." The Moscow Patriarchate, on the other hand, calls them "Passion-Bearers." This was a concession made for political reasons. There are still people opposed to the idea of venerating them at all. Personally, I consider them martyrs."

There was a pause as Vasily was seemingly turning over something important. Then he woke from his momentary reverie.

"How much time have you got?" he asked.

I replied that I had all afternoon.

"Come on then. Let's go to my place. We can keep talking there while I get things ready to take with me to Nizhny Novgorod."

Taking out a small 1990s Nokia mobile phone he made a call to his wife. They would have company for dinner.

෴   ෴   ෴

Vasily lived on the other side of the Dnieper, in one of Mogilev's residential satellites. The afternoon sun shone almost white, as the Volga crossed the iron bridge leading over the floodplain, and then the Dnieper itself. A century ago, Nicholas took Alexei boating on this river, stopping here and there to swim at its sandy beaches. Today, a patch of *khrushchevki* — the box-like concrete and steel apartment blocks named after Soviet leader Nikita Khrushchev, who introduced them to the Soviet Union's post-war housing crisis in the 1960s — had long since mushroomed on the opposite bank of the river.

Coming to the end of the bridge, and turning down a street on the left, we drove past row after row of them. Every block looked the same,

---

[13] Ibid.   [14] Pospielovsky, *Russian Church*, vol. 2, 349.

five to six stories high, and constructed of visibly rotting concrete and rusted iron. Grass grew thick in the strips between them. At length, we pulled up in front of one of them and got out.

Entry to Vasily's block, I discovered, was less by any main door than through what appeared to be a gaping hole in the grey concrete. In the stair well, the concrete floor had been painted green. The family of four — Vasily, his wife, and two small boys — resided on the third floor in an apartment consisting of four small rooms and a modest hallway crammed with shoes and jackets.

After removing my shoes and receiving a pair of slippers in their stead, I was invited to go inside. The whole floorspace probably measured five hundred square feet in total, maybe less. The furniture was made of a light, chestnut-colored timber that I supposed was birch. The small windows were hung with frilly lace curtains. An odor of unwashed bodies and cooking hung in the air. The largest room was Vasily and his wife's bedroom, which, with a brown and orange acrylic bedspread laid over the bed, doubled as the apartment's only living room. It was here that I was invited to sit.

Around me, scores of black and white photographs of Nicholas II and his family jostled each other for a place on the walls, bed, windowsills, and floor. To the left of the door, in an elaborate gilded frame, hung a large portrait of a still-young and beautiful Alexandra. A callow happiness, later lost amid the cares of life, shone from her eyes. From the other side of the room, half a dozen smaller portraits of Nicholas in military uniform answered the image of his wife's. Leaning against the wall on the head of the bed, an icon showed the image of a bald, round-faced man in a white suit.

"Botkin," I said aloud, recognizing the face of the Romanovs' faithful physician, who, though offered his freedom, insisted on accompanying them into exile, and was finally murdered at their side in the same hail of Bolshevik bullets in 1918. This was the first icon of the doctor I had seen. The campaign to canonize him too had clearly succeeded.

"Yes, it's Botkin," said Vasily, now actually smiling and appearing to relax. In naming the figure correctly, I guessed I had won his respect.

He told me to sit on the bed and began plying me with books and A4-sized photographs of the Romanovs. Many of the photographs had accompanying texts, and I realized that spread around me on the bed, the floor, and walls was the exhibition that he would take, that night, six hundred miles east, to the banks of the Volga. Of all his exhibits, Vasily was particularly anxious to show me some photographs of the bullet-holed and blood-stained basement where the family of seven was shot. Taking one in his hand, he pointed to what he described as a symbol drawn on the torn wallpaper above a couple of holes left by revolver fire.

"Do you see these marks?" he asked. "They're a symbol. The White investigators found them when they entered the house. They also found this graffiti. Can you read it? It's a quotation from the Bible. It says: 'And then Balthasar was betrayed and killed by his own servants.' Do you know the story? Balthasar was king of Babylon and the Jews arranged to have him killed by his servants. They didn't kill him themselves but were responsible for it. It's symbolic because this is the same thing that happened to the tsar."

My heart sank. Ritual murder was the accusation at the heart of one of the most ignoble affairs of Nicholas's reign: the notorious Beiliss trial of 1913.[15] Two years earlier, when an Orthodox Christian boy was found dead in Kiev, the authorities, apparently lacking the ability to identify any other culprit, arrested Mendel Beilis, a Jew, and accused him of murdering the boy as part of a dark, anti-Christian ritual. The trial created a sensation that attracted the attention of both the Russian and world media. Lacking any proof, and faced with expert witnesses who denied the whole notion, Russian police, apparently assuming that they enjoyed the tsar's unspoken support, brazenly fabricated the evidence. Even the conservative newspapers that usually defended the police were appalled. To its credit, however, after the innocent man had spent two years in prison awaiting trial, the jury acquitted Beilis, and the trial judge in Kiev upheld the jury's not-guilty verdict.[16] Moreover, it seems that the police misread Nicholas's attitude to the Jews. According to Spiridovich, when Nicholas learnt of Beilis's acquittal, his first reaction was to declare his satisfaction that the liberty of an innocent man had been restored.[17]

Implied in Vasily's pictures was accusation of "ritual murder" that would make the Jews responsible for Nicholas and his family's murder. Vasily must have registered the look of alarm and disappointment on my face because, changing tack, he continued in a more apologetic tone.

"I don't mean to say that the Jews are to blame for killing the tsar. I have met Orthodox Jews [*Yevrei*]. They are honorable people. What I mean are the Yids [*Zhidy*]. The Bible uses this term a lot, especially in the Gospel of John. The Yids are not real Jews [*Yevrei*] but plotters, hypocrites. Anyway, I don't want to put those pictures in our exhibition. They're too controversial; they require wisdom to understand properly. They will lead some people astray. I don't want anything in the exhibition to distract from the Orthodox nature of the tsar's life and his family's love for God and each other."

---

[15] Dowler, *Russia in 1913*, 185–87; Pipes, *Russian Revolution*, 70–71.
[16] Indeed, Pipes notes that the trial became a surprising demonstration of the independence of the Duma Monarchy's courts: *Russian Revolution*, 71, asterisked note at the bottom of the page.
[17] Spiridovitch, *Dernières Années*, 2:447.

Vasily's desire to avoid rousing the slumbering demons of Russian anti-Semitism struck me as betraying a sensitivity I had not necessarily expected to find. But how honestly did he mean it? I later noticed that, despite his earlier avowal, the pictures of the cabalist symbols and graffiti *were* packed along with the rest for the journey to Nizhny Novgorod.

This was a shame, because Nicholas II, although sometimes caricatured as a "virulent anti-Semite," could transcend the prejudices typical of his age and background. And if there is a *place* that represents a shift in Nicholas's attitude towards his Jewish subjects, it is Mogilev, where Alexandra wrote to him in 1916 on behalf of a Russian Jew who, having emigrated to the United States, had returned to Russia when the war broke, enlisted to fight the Germans, and lost an arm in the Carpathian campaign. Hospitalized in Petrograd, and decorated by tsarist authorities for his bravery, the man had been discharged. But despite the service he had rendered his country, he remained subject to the legal restrictions against Jews (including a ban on settling in Moscow or Petrograd) that had driven him to America in the first place. Alexandra's innate sense of injustice was aroused.

"One sees the bitterness, and I fully grasp it—surely such a man ought to be treated the same way as any other soldier who received such a wound," the empress wrote to her husband: "He was not obliged to fly over here at once.... [O]ne would like him to be treated justly and not different to the others with similar losses of limb."[18] Nicholas felt the force of his wife's arguments, and, although the justice touched only one man, in a reply dated the same day, Nicholas told Alexandra that he had personally instructed the Minister of the Interior to release the man from all and any restrictions.[19]

❧ ❧ ❧

At length, Vasily's wife appeared. A young woman with long straight brown hair hanging plainly down the middle of her back, she wore a white kerchief over the top of her head and tied under the chin, a dark

[18] Maylunas and Mironenko, *Lifelong Passion*, 462.

[19] Other stories corroborate the absence of anti-Semitic feelings in Alexandra at this time. See, for example, Princess Paley, *Memories of Russia, 1916–1919* (London: Herbert Jenkins, 1924), 14. As for Nicholas, another contemporary bears witness that the tsar's attitudes were changing. Before the Revolution, Russian law excluded Jews from holding the rank of officer. In 1916, however, the case of two young men was forwarded to Nicholas. Though the men were baptized, their father was Jewish, and the relevant military authorities were arguing that this disqualified the men from entry to the Empire's officer training school. But Nicholas was having none of it. Ignoring the boys' accusers, the tsar ruled in the young men's favor: Georgii Shavel'skii, *Vospominaniia: poslednego protopresvitera russkoj armii i flota*, vol. 2 (New York: Chekhov Publishing, 1954), 57–58.

green, ankle-length dress, and a crimson-colored waistcoat. She offered no greeting, and Vasily never introduced us. Dinner, she informed Vasily, would be ready in half an hour. He should start packing if he intended to leave as planned, she warned matter-of-factly, and I imagined I heard irritation in her voice at being left at home with the children while Vasily peddled his exhibition. Shortly after, a friend of Vasily's named Igor arrived to help. The two men were a study in opposites. Where Vasily was the image of the zealot, thin, dark, and restless, Igor was the down-to-earth peasant, fair, barrel-chested, and placid. A practical man, he brought a sense of imperturbability and calm into the agitated room. He had a small daughter with him who slipped away to play with Vasily's son. This time, I was introduced.

"He even recognized Botkin," said Vasily, referring to me: "He might help us with the catalogue too."

Vasily's wife, whose name, I learned, was Sveta, announced that dinner was ready, and Vasily led us to a tiny, narrow kitchen. A steaming saucepan of *pelmeni* sat in the middle of a table that took up most of the floor space. Beamed into the room from a small television perched on top of the fridge, an Orthodox tele-evangelist harangued us along with his studio audience. Vasily turned the volume down and proclaimed the Easter blessing, *Khristos Voskrese!* Sveta and Igor answered with the same. Then all three begin singing a lengthy hymn for the meal we were about to receive, ending in a hearty "Amen" from Vasily.

"That was the Easter grace," he informed me, with his characteristic machine-gun delivery.

Over dinner, Vasily ran through the various things he needed to have with him for Nizhny. Of a piece with his innate, zealous restlessness, he ate little and declared that he had finished eating long before the rest of us.

"You know," he said abruptly, "we don't get any help from the state for our exhibition. Here in Belarus the government is not communist, per se. But it's still Soviet in the way it thinks. It doesn't like us making too much of the time before the revolution. They consider it divisive."

I volunteered that it seemed to be different in Russia, where the government did quite a lot to promote Orthodoxy. Vasily jumped to his feet, as if in a physical rush to disabuse me of the misperception that the modern Russian Federation is in any fundamental way more hospitable to Orthodoxy than the modern Belarusian state.

"In Russia," he intoned, "Putin is surrounded by a liberal elite. They don't get it. They're not really Orthodox believers. They go to church, perhaps, but they don't really believe. Putin is Orthodox; that is for sure. He is a strong leader too. But the people who surround him are liberals."

I had heard similar views from people less outwardly zealous than Vasily in Moscow too. But in the lips of this resident of provincial Belarus, its implications were interesting. If modern Belarus remained too fundamentally "Soviet," the opposing problem with the Russian Federation was, somewhat unexpectedly, that it was too liberal, too Western. He slunk off to resume his packing, leaving the rest of us to continue the conversation.

"Don't worry about Vasily," said Igor: "He doesn't always wait for an answer when he asks a question."

I asked Igor how he came to be involved with Vasily's project and he replied that he had known very little about the tsar — only what he had learnt at school in the Soviet Union about "Nicholas the Bloody" — until he saw Vasily's exhibition in Mogilev.

"I am just a simple person, not a historian or a theologian. I have my own business as a mechanic. But thanks to the exhibition I learnt that Nicholas II was an Orthodox tsar. He loved God and he loved his family. In Soviet times, the Communists accused him of all sorts of things. But I know now that he was a man of peace. I love my family and when you have a big family the way he did, you want peace for your country and for your children."

Then, with a palpable sense of urgency, and in a way that reminded me of my encounter with the man of Cossack origin at the church, Igor switched his attention to the present day.

"You have to understand that here in Belarus, and in Russia, we don't wish anybody any harm. We don't want a conflict with anyone. But Russia has to be strong in order to be able to defend itself. You must tell people that when you get home."

Noting once again the utter immateriality of the border separating Belarus from Russia, I promised that I would.

After dessert, a second friend arrived to help with the boxes.

"Take this," instructed Vasily: "It's a present."

It was a fridge magnet with citations from Nicholas II and Alexandra, clearly intended for a souvenir stall.

A few minutes later, in the middle of throwing shirts into a sports bag, Vasily interrupted his packing to present me with an armful of fat, dog-eared scrapbooks. They were home-made visitor books, recording the impressions of visitors to Vasily's exhibition in Mogilev, Moscow and elsewhere.

"Have a look at these," he said.

I leafed through pages and pages of thanks "to God and the organizers . . . for this wonderful exhibition," "beautiful photographs," "informative texts," etc , along with heartfelt wishes that "God save all those involved" and "forgive us our sins."

Vasily had become a missionary for the Romanovs' cause, and these visitor books provided an opportunity to see inside the minds of his converts.

"I'm grateful for your love, which with such joyfulness of heart you share with us." "We thank everyone for this wonderful, clear exhibition. We very much enjoyed it. The pictures and photographs were very beautiful. May the holy imperial martyrs pray to God for our sins!" "Vasily—may God save you! The Tsar is holy. He will always help us!" "What beautiful people, both in spirit and in appearance!!!" "Thank you for your blessed work. May God turn the hearts of as great a number of people as possible to this family." "Holy father, Tsar Nicholas II, pray to God for our sins!"

Others thought in terms of politics. I doubted that Vasily knew of Bulgakov, or would have known of the term *teokratia*. But he had intuited its import and struck a deep cultural nerve in communicating it to his fellow Russians.

"We thank God for this exhibition. It is of great significance, for the restoration of the monarchy in Russia will be impossible without the removal of the shroud of slanders that has covered God's anointed tsar and his family," one visitor had written. Another concluded her note with the remark that she had been "shaken to the roots of my soul."

෴   ෴   ෴

By 8:30 p.m. we were ready. Two cars were needed to transport the boxes filled with photographs and texts on the Romanovs. By common agreement I went with Igor. His car, an old Renault, was a moving mechanic's work shed. The dashboard's standard plastic covering had been removed, exposing all the car's internal machinery from the steering wheel deep into the engine. A pile of metal rods intended for some unknown purpose lay lengthways down the middle of the vehicle. The rear seat was spread with hardware and fitted with a child's safety seat into which one of Igor's daughters had been strapped. We drove back into town together to put Vasily on the overnight bus to Moscow and from there, Nizhny.

At the last minute, Vasily invited me to join him on his trip to Nizhny. For a moment, I was torn. But thinking of the journey I still had planned before, I declined. Vasily was not the kind of man to disguise his disappointment, but watching him squeeze his wiry frame in the coach's stiff, cramped seats, I was glad, as the coach pulled away, to be staying put.

Igor drove me back to my hotel.

"Have you got a few minutes?" he asked quietly, as if something was on his mind as we pulled up. I nodded that I did.

"What you're doing is very good," he said, turning round in his seat to check that his daughter was still sitting patiently in the safety seat behind, then shifting so that he his eyes could meet mine. "It is good that you are trying to understand Belarus, that you are trying to understand Russia. You see those people out there," he added, pointing through the car windows to the passers-by in the street, "they don't want any problems. They don't want a war. But the Russian mind is different from the Western mind. Russians think differently."

He was speaking softly, sincerely, from the heart, and the subject seemed to pain him.

"You see that we live simply," he said, gesturing at the car. "My wife and I live in a small hut, just a few rooms in the forest. We grow our own vegetables. I don't like the city. There are too many distractions, too many temptations. When we look at Western Europe, we don't understand it. You know the Roman Empire, ancient Rome? It's like that. When people get too comfortable, too rich, when they have too much, they forget God. In Russian, by contrast, we have a saying: 'Keep your body cold, your stomach empty, and your heart warm.' You understand what it means? It means that when you have too many things, too many nice clothes, too much nice food, you forget how to love — how to love other people and how to love God. I think Europe has forgotten how to love. It has forgotten God."

In his simple and direct way, he was asking me to explain the spiritual logic of the foreign world that I was from. Gay marriage, then receiving a lot of coverage in the Russian-language news, exercised him especially. Also perplexing to him was why women felt the need to work outside the home when their calling was to be wives and mothers, or why it was that Europeans were so unconcerned, apparently, by Muslim migration. Did they want Europe to become *Islamic*?

Over the half an hour that followed, I did my best to set out the philosophical sources of the sexual revolution of the 1960s, and how the continued unfolding of that event underlay many of the points of difference between Russia and the West that he identified. Easily forgotten in the West is how sheltered the former USSR and Eastern Bloc were from the changes that swept the West during the seventy years they were behind the Iron Curtain. Catching only glimpses of them through chinks in the wall, Russians only really discovered the full, radical amplitude of them in the 1990s, and by then they had missed all the steps in the development of the Western logic.

But it didn't appear to help.

"But why do people in the West say that white is black and black, white?" he asked, dismayed. "The Orthodox Church has black and white, good and bad. But in the West, people now say there's no such thing as good and bad. It just depends on how you look at it. That's not true. It's a lie."

In Russia, we might say truth remained what it had been to Plato and his Christian continuators: an objective, transcendent ideal, written into the cosmos itself, to which human society had to conform, not something merely immanent to man's mere *experience* of the world, to be redefined, as it were, at will, according to a fundamentally Kantian notion of the world as phenomenon only.

As remarkably patient as his daughter had been amid the encroaching mountain of hardware on the back seat, at length she grew restless. Igor took note and agreed it was time for him to get her home. I was not sorry. I had first hopped in alongside Vasily in his clapped-out Volga a full five hours before. With a final *dobrii nochii* ("Good night"), I got out of the car and walked into the hotel.

෴   ෴   ෴

The following day, I boarded the regional train for Minsk. The modest coupé, dating, it seemed, from the 1970s, consisted of two vinyl-covered benches with overhead luggage racks facing each other, beside a small window hung with a forlorn little red and white checked curtain. The compartment was dark, and I spent the entire, almost three-hour journey alone. But through the window, the trip was a pretty one, and as we rolled over the flat Belarusian land, almost every scene disabused my expectations of Chernobyl-style environmental disaster. Tall straight poles of birch and pine forests. Roadside memorials to the war dead: a Soviet soldier seated in the forest, rifle laid over his knees. Farmland. Herds of Frisian cattle. Fields of rapeseed coming into bloom. White-blossomed fruit trees. Towns of small cottages with corrugated iron roofs and long backyards diligently cultivated as family garden plots. Bogs, meadows, ponds, streams. More farmland. On a country road a lone truck traveled towards a village of a hundred or so houses surrounded by fertile dark green fields. A man fly-fishing. A horse grazing in the shade. Cottages with chickens. A horse with a foal. A pair of white goats. A storm gathering, turning the bright blue sky gunmetal grey. Four men in bright lifejackets paddling kayaks on a lake. A field of bright, lipstick-red tulips. The outskirts of Minsk, the capital. Grey apartments. Factories and rail yards.

෴   ෴   ෴

Minsk dominates modern Belarus like no other city. Located roughly at the country's geographical center, it's the hub of its networks of roads and railways. But it is not Belarus's "ancient capital." When Nicholas's empire broke up, nationalists wanted Vilna (modern Vilnius) — the leading city of the old Lithuanian grand duchy — for the new nation's

chief city. But Poland occupied Vilna in 1920, and Polish it remained
until, by a clause of the infamous Molotov-Ribbentrop Pact of 1939, it
was renamed Vilnius, and made capital of the Soviet Socialist Republic of Lithuania. As a national capital, therefore, Minsk was a run-
ner's up prize, a city of 100,000 that until 1917 had been the site of a
Russian governor's mansion, and whose most widely spoken language
was Yiddish. After the Revolution, Soviet rule brought administrators,
factories, and higher education institutions. By 1939, the population
had more than doubled. Of its 239,000 inhabitants, a third was Jewish.
Five years later, Minsk, like the rest of Belarus, stood in ruins. Minsk's
crater-ridden streets were lined with little more than mounds of burnt-
out rubble. Post-war Soviet reconstruction was thorough, efficient, and
determined. As early as 1946, the first factories were reopened; Minsk
quickly became the "symbol of Soviet Belarus's success."[20] By 1959, its
population was already half a million, and it was on its way to becoming the capital of the model republic described earlier.

Today, Minsk is a city of two million people, and to arrive, as I
had half done, expecting a vision of rotten concrete apartment blocks
and grey, smog-ridden skies, was obviously a mistake. Neatly organized into wide, tree-lined boulevards, Minsk could even be elegant.
At European-style outdoor cafes, a smattering of well-dressed customers
enjoyed Italian-style coffee and biscotto in the sun. To the city's north,
a broad sweep of parkland spread around an attractive bend in the
River Svislach that a weir had turned into an artificial lake, with an
encircling cycle path and riverside beer gardens. Not far away, my hotel
seemed to me a model example of contemporary Belarusian "euro-chic,"
decked out in the imitation Scandinavian-style minimalism that I had
often seen in Russia. As president, Lukashenko has built his popularity
on the alleged "economic miracle" over which he has presided. This is
sometimes dismissed as propaganda. But for the moment, Minsk's part
in the Belarusian miracle seemed real enough.

I left my bag in the room, and walked back down to the edge of
the lake I had seen from the taxi window. An ice hockey match was
about to start at the stadium here, and the place pulsed with fans and
spectators. Those without tickets found substitutionary diversion at
a string of open-air trestle tables with beer and shashlik. And yet the
city's Soviet bedrock is never far beneath the surface. Among those
in the ice hockey crowd, an aged serviceman passed me, leaning on a
Zimmer frame, his chest draped in medals. On the roof of a prominent
building in the distance, giant white letters spelled out in Russian the
city's official, Soviet-era designation: "Minsk: Hero City." In Minsk's
fundamentally Soviet-built environment, traces of the Romanov rule

---

[20] Ioffe, *Understanding*, 109.

could only be highly prized fossils trapped in a landscape of more recent shale.

So far as I can tell, Nicholas II first visited Minsk in October 1914, the third month of the Great War. Though he must have passed through its railway station earlier, on this occasion he stopped, and was driven round the city in a car to visit its war hospitals. We know from a record in his diary that he was particularly impressed with the hospital that had been erected inside the Russian governor's mansion.[21] He was back later that December, noting, in the thoughtful tone frequently encountered in his diary, the "echelon of recovered wounded soldiers returning to the war" that he saw through the windows of the imperial train.[22] Nicholas was in the city again in the summer of 1915.[23]

But otherwise, with so little to build a local legacy on, in Minsk the Romanov trail went cold. Explorations turned up nothing more than a single icon in Minsk's Orthodox Cathedral of the Holy Spirit. A Western-style basilica-shaped building with two very un-Orthodox baroque bell towers rising from the western end above white-washed walls and a pitched green roof, the cathedral was built at the high water mark of Polish influence in Eastern Europe in the 1630s, to house a Catholic monastery. It had been confiscated and awarded to the Orthodox after the Russian annexation, and is, today, the seat of the Exarch, or metropolitan-archbishop, of the Belarusian Orthodox Church, Moscow Patriarchate. There, hanging from a column on the northern side of the aisle, was an icon of Nicholas II as "Tsar-Martyr." Alone without his family, he was dressed in medieval robes with the fur-trimmed Cap of Monomakh on his head. As I stood watching, a woman in the ubiquitous kerchief, no longer young but not yet middle aged, came forward and crossed herself before it. But the cathedral's mainly female worshipers directed most of their devotions toward the large image of the Virgin with Child, encased in a thick armor of tarnished silver to the left of the iconostasis. After a short while, I went back outside, and made my way — as had by then become my habit — towards the icon shop, where a cheerful young woman bid me welcome with a warm smile. I asked her whether she had for sale an icon of Nicholas like the one on display in the cathedral.

"Unfortunately not," she said: "But I have this one here."

Extracting a painted wooden icon from behind a pile of clutter, she showed me an image of the tsar in coronation robes, holding a scroll on which were written the words from St John's Gospel, "No greater love hath man than this, that he lay down his life for his friends."

---

[21] Nicholas II, October 22, 1914, in Diary (2), 493.
[22] Nicholas II, December 13, 1914, in Diary (2), 504.
[23] Nicholas II, June 10, 1915, in Diary (2), 533.

I asked whether the tsar was a popular saint among locals.

"In Minsk?" she asked. "No, not really. People prefer more local saints. But in general, in Russia, yes, he's popular. Where are you from? Serbia? Czech Republic? Poland?"

Perhaps my lousy accent led her, too, to guess that I was a Serbian pilgrim: this Orthodox nation is the only other to rival Russia in its devotion to Nicholas's memory.[24] But it was her ambiguous reference to "Russia" that intrigued me. Does this "Russia" include Belarus, or is it a *tertium quid*, something entirely separate? Belarusian political scientist Yury Drakokhurst has resolved the dilemma by pointing not to any purported Russian colonization of Belarus, but to Belarusians' own mental colonization of Russia. "At least some of Russia's space has always been within Belarusians' mental map. Russia is not *to the east* of Belarus; rather, Russia *is the east* of Belarus."[25] To Belarusians, it seems, Russia is a land populated by a people that are no longer "us" but who are not yet "them" either.

Thanking the young woman, I left the cathedral and walked back down the so-called Boulevard of Victors towards the glass-and-steel domed Museum of the Great Fatherland War, on the edge of the lake on the other side of the ice hockey stadium. Along the boulevard, and the one it cut across just before the museum, posters for the approaching May 9 Victory Day celebrations competed for the attention of pedestrians and motorists: *Ya pomnyu, i ya gorzhus'* ("I remember, and I take pride"). At intersections, light posts were decked out in the national colors, and, on the ground, a carpet of "ferns," with fronds formed out of dense clusters of the red and green national flag, had sprouted along the footpaths. It has been said that in Soviet Belorussia, the memorialization of Soviet victory in the Soviet Second World War was practically the "raison d'être of the republic."[26] It would seem to remain so today.[27] Indeed, if, in Belarus, Victory Day is a secular Easter, Minsk's Museum of the Great Fatherland War is the religion's chief cathedral. From its

---

[24] In 2014, a life-sized statue of Nicholas II was raised in Belgrade, where he is celebrated as the "tsar-liberator" for risking war with Germany (and ultimately his throne) in defence of Serbian independence in July 1914. "The role that Tsar Nichols II played in saving Serbia and Europe as a whole is too great to describe in just a couple of words. He sacrificed his crown, his reign and his life to save Serbia and to save Europe," said the guest of honor, Patriarch Kirill of Moscow, on that occasion. See Natalya Mihailova, "Russian, Serbian patriarchs sanctify monument to Nicholas II in Belgrade," *Pravmir*, November 17, 2014: http://www.pravmir.com/russian-serbian-patriarchs-sanctify-monument-nicholas-ii-belgrade/. Accessed October 9, 2024.

[25] Drakokhurst is cited in Ioffe, *Understanding*, 204–5. On the inadequacy of "us" and "them" categories: ibid., 90.

[26] Simon Lewis, "The 'Partisan Republic': Colonial myths and memory wars in Belarus," in Julie Fedor, Markku Kangaspuro, Jussi Lassila, Tatiana Zhurhenko, eds., *War and Memory in Russia, Ukraine and Belarus* (London: Palgrave MacMillan, 2017), 377.

[27] See, above all, David Marples, "History, memory and the Second World War in Belarus," *Australian Journal of Politics and History* 58 (2012): 443.

flagpole, the hammer-and-sickle banner of the old Soviet Union still flew over the city. A black granite sculpture of Glory—a woman with a surprisingly round, kindly face—guarded the entrance. Viewed from the ground, however, the trumpet she held aloft looked eerily like a machine gun. The building pullulated with school groups being cate-chized into the nation's foundation story, the climax of which was the great steel-and-glass dome opening to the cloud-skidded sky above—a distant Soviet act of homage, perhaps, to the enduring claims even in this once-model Soviet republic of the "sacred city."

෴ ෴ ෴

The following day, I continued my journey by regional train across Belarus to Brest, a fortress town by the Polish border in the far south-west. When I alighted, the air was even warmer than it had been the day before. Something about the place spoke of having crossed an unseen climatic or geographical watershed. Though still six hundred miles from the Black Sea, Brest in early spring seemed to pulse with the relaxed warmth of the south running through its veins, in a way that made Mogilev, three hundred miles away, seem both distant and more Russian. I had come to Brest because, apart from Mogilev, the only other part of the territory of modern Belarus that Nicholas and Alexandra had vis-ited frequently was the ancient forest, now national park, of Belovezha, seventy-five miles to Brest's north.

Crossing town in a taxi I picked up at the station, I arrived at my hotel, a communist-era establishment prosaically called Otel' Molo-dyozh ("Hotel Youth"). A pretty girl with a moon-shaped face and long, straight chestnut hair greeted me from behind the reception desk.

"*Zdravstvuite.* Where have you arrived from today?"

That I had arrived from Minsk surprised her.

"Minsk? I thought you were on the Moscow train."

I explained that I had boarded it in Minsk. On the other hand, I added, I am often in Moscow and, as a city, I liked it. Did she, too, like Russia's fast-paced capital?

"Me? Oh, I've never been to Moscow," she confessed, an innocent, half-embarrassed smile creeping over her face.

Inside the hotel, the mood was 1975. Cleaning ladies in bright blue cotton uniforms scurried along brown-carpeted corridors decorated with plastic palm trees, while my narrow, university-style bedroom with its clunky timber veneer furniture turned out to be scarcely big enough to house both me and my backpack. It was easy to imagine Brezhnev ruling "One Big Country" from the Kremlin.

Outside, Brest was a sleepy place, broad footpaths and gracious, tree-lined avenues lending it the feel of a big country town. Originally located on an island in the waters of the broad River Bug that today forms the border with Poland, Brest was the most westerly town of the old grand duchy of Lithuania, and, by virtue of its location on a juncture of Eastern Europe's riverine trade routes, one of its most prosperous. Like the rest of the future Belarus, Brest became Russian under Catherine the Great. In the nineteenth century, Russian authorities demolished the old medieval island-town to construct a sprawling military fortress in its place, while the town itself was relocated to its present position, a mile or so away east. In Soviet days, Brest might have been on the edge of Soviet territory, but the Polish state visible on the either side of the river was a Soviet satellite, and an extension of the Eastern bloc. Today, by contrast, Brest exudes a distinctly edge-of-civilization feel. On the far bank of the Bug begins not only Poland but, in the form of NATO and the EU, the Euro-Atlantic community known as "the West." A city whose inhabitants uniformly speak Russian, even if they've never set foot in Moscow, Brest stands on Europe's primary geopolitical fault line.

ᐒ ᐒ ᐒ

The following day dawned warm and sunny, and I found a local bus going in the direction of Belovezha. When the core of the nuclear power plant at Chernobyl in neighboring Ukraine imploded in 1986, the winds swept a vast cloud of lethal radioactive gases over the rich Belarusian countryside. Indeed, in purely statistical terms it was Belarus, not Ukraine, that bore the brunt of the disaster: seventy percent of the radio isotopes released by the explosion landed on Belarusian territory, contaminating one third of the republic's land mass, and exposing a fifth of its population (circa 2.2m people) to elevated levels of radiation.[28] Today, however, the countryside around Brest is some of the loveliest in Belarus. Leaving the city beneath a deep blue sky, the bus headed through lush green fields broken with copses of ash and elder. Belarusian dairy goods were the pride of the Soviet Union, and are still in strong demand in Russia today, and either side of the bus spread out dairy country. After about an hour, we stopped in a small village overshadowed by a medieval watchtower. On the bench in front of me sat a woman in her late sixties or early seventies. I leant forward and asked her how much longer it would be until we reached the national park.

"Twenty minutes, I think," she replied. "I'm not going that far but you should be there by ten o'clock."

She seemed glad to talk. A retired schoolteacher, she was on her way to a nearby church to celebrate the feast of St George. A lace shawl to cover her hair when she got there lay on her lap.

---

[28] David Marples, *Belarus: A denationalized nation* (London: Routledge, 1999), 28.

"Are you Czech?" she eventually asked. "Slovak?" The usual guesses. She was clearly enjoying the conversation. Then, pointing to two young men on the seat in front of her, "Are you traveling alone or are you with others?" I shook my head and said I was traveling solo.

"There are a lot of faces on the bus today I don't recognize. It's nice to talk with a younger person. The older generation here is very friendly. But the young people don't say anything."

She nodded in the direction of a few young people seated nearby.

"Why not?" I asked.

"They have their computers. They're always . . . "

She made the gesture of someone absorbed in reading from the screen of their telephone.

By then the morning cloud had burnt off, and a blue sky hung over the verdant countryside.

"You're lucky," she said. "It's a sunny day. In winter, it can be very tough."

She spoke about the history of her town and her life in it. She hadn't been born there, but in a neighboring village, and had only moved when she married. This was the first and last mention she made of a husband. I assumed he was dead. She made no reference to children.

"I hate sitting at home. I would love to travel. I have been to Poland and Germany. But that's all."

I assumed that these were Soviet-era trips, and that the Germany she referred to was the now-vanished GDR. I asked her where she would go first if she could go anywhere. The answer shot straight off her lips: "Jerusalem."

I could not know whether her faith was something newly discovered or long-held, but her answer echoed the longing of generations of Russian peasant-pilgrims. But, again, there was the same ideal: the sacred city.

The bus ground to a halt, and she gathered her things to hop off.

"She's going to the church too, I can see," the woman said, nodding in the direction of another older woman with a similar lace shawl. As the bus pulled away, I watched the two of them already locked in conversation. She looked up and waved as we passed, cracking a broad, open-faced smile.

We reached Belovezha five minutes later, entering through a great wooden archway, as if it were a kind of Belarusian Serengeti. During the Second World War, Nicholas and Alexandra's palace was destroyed, but the forest's dense thickets provided cover for thousands of Soviet partisans. Afterwards, Soviet authorities returned the forest to its previous status as a hunting reserve, and built a new lodge at a secluded spot known as Viskuli. Khrushchev, Brezhnev, and other Soviet leaders used it for hunting. Indeed, it was at a secret meeting at Viskuli in Belovezha in December 1991 that the new leaders of Russia, Ukraine and Belarus, Boris Yeltsin, Leonid Kuchma and Stanislav Shushkevich, pulling the rug out from underneath Soviet president Mikhail Gorbachev, signed the so-called "Belovezha Accords" that dissolved the Soviet Union.[29] A quarter of a century later, when people across the old USSR hear the name Belovezha, it's this meeting, and the destruction of a country many remain proud of, that they think of.

Near the entrance, a museum told the park's story, with every Russian emperor from Catherine the Great to Nicholas II receiving a large portrait. Perhaps even more than Russia, Belarus is the heir to the Soviet Union. But nobody at Belovezha has thought to cast Nicholas and Alexandra in the terms of the Bolshevik newspaper *Pravda*'s 1918 death-notice editorial, the "symbol of a brutal regime of blood and violence against the people . . . in which the brothel and the divine worship were both elevated to the throne."[30] On the contrary. A model of their demolished chateau was accompanied by half a dozen photographs of Nicholas, Alexandra, and their children on holiday in the national park. The impression was one of a time of peace, domesticity, and innocence, before the all-destroying storm of the twentieth century.

A well-maintained network of paths crisscrossed the park, and I spent the afternoon cycling them on a rented bike. Stretches of cold, swampy water meadows were broken up by oak and beech forests, as well as great expanses of grass, shimmering in the sun. On the back roads, all was quiet and deserted. Nicholas and Alexandra never spent as much time at Belovezha as they did at Livadia, in Crimea. Yet as a cool breeze began to whip up late in the day, a sign with a black and white photograph of two figures in an open sedan captured my attention. It was a picture of a young Nicholas and Alexandra, beaming with the joy of their tragic romance, on their way to Belovezha in 1897. Even in this remotest corner of the old USSR, it seemed, the monarchy was crawling back down people's throats.

෨ ෨ ෨

After the outbreak of the Great War terminated visits to Belovezha, Nicholas returned to Brest in September 1914 to pin the St George's Cross, Russia's highest military honor, on the breast of the local commander, General Ivanov.[31] Three years later, Ivanov would head the division dispatched to put down the armed insurrection in Petrograd that would lead to the collapse of the monarchy. From Brest, Nicholas

---

[29] Plokhy, *Last Empire*, 301.   [30] Slater, *Many Deaths*, 52.
[31] Nicholas II, September 24, 1914, in Diary (2), 487–88.

traveled to the fortress at nearby Osovets, where he gained his first, sobering impression of the destructiveness of modern warfare. "A peculiar feeling came over me when I saw the destruction produced by German bombardment of the different buildings and the masses of craters in the earth," he wrote in his diary.[32] But Brest played perhaps its most significant role in Nicholas's life as the venue for the signing of the treaty struck in March 1918 between Russia's fledgling Bolshevik government and Kaiser Wilhelm II's Germany. This Treaty of Brest-Litovsk handed 2.5 million square kilometers of Russian territory to Germany and its ally Austria-Hungary, including four tenths of the Russian Empire's pre-war population, nine tenths of its coal mines, half its industry and about a third of its railways. At a stroke, it undid three centuries of Russian expansion by Nicholas's ancestors.[33] When news of the treaty reached Russia's last monarch in exile at Tobolsk, Pierre Gilliard, the Swiss tutor who went with them into captivity, recorded in his diary that Nicholas considered that the Treaty of Brest amounted to Russia's "suicide."[34] "Up until the Brest treaty, the sovereign believed in the future prosperity of Russia. After the treaty, he . . . lost this faith," Gillard confided.

Back in Brest the day after my trip to Belovezha, I found the building in which the treaty was signed, a modest white cottage that is now Brest's local historical museum. Then I turned towards the western edge of town, where, as the streets run away to meet the River Bug, Belarus — and, with it, the whole "Russian World" — gives way to Poland. My goal was the heavy, five-sided red brick fortress on the Bug. Constructed between 1833 and 1842 as part of a great line of fortresses designed to repel an attack on the empire's Polish territories, the fortress is in fact a tsarist-era structure consisting of a series of interlinked forts constructed across a series of islands cut by arms of the Bug and Mukhavets rivers and various man-made canals between them. With walls two meters thick, even in its ruined state, the old fortress projected grim defiance. The fortress, however, never saw active duty under Nicholas II. When the Germans pushed eastward in the spring of 1915, it was abandoned without a fight.

Instead, Brest Fortress is celebrated today for the mythic resistance it offered in the face of the 1941 Nazi invasion of the Soviet Union. After the surprise attack by Hitler's forces on 22 June, the fortress's 9,000 Red Army defenders held out for thirty-two days against the 17,000

---

[32] Nicholas II, September 25, 1914, in Diary (2), 488.
[33] Alexander Watson, *Ring of Steel: Germany and Austria-Hungary at War, 1914–1918* (London: Allen Lane, 2014), 494.
[34] Pierre Gilliard, *Thirteen Years at the Russian Court* (n. p.: Leonaur, 2016), 133. While authentic, the quotation that follows does not appear in the abridged version of Gilliard's memoirs that I used, and I can no longer find the source for it.

men of the German Army's 45th Infantry Division.[35] Whereas Soviet defenses collapsed across the rest of the front, these "heroes of Brest" endured artillery bombardment, air attack, thirst, injury, and hunger, preferring death over surrender. When, in the 1950s, the rubble was cleared, the terrible conditions in which the last defenders were killed were brought to life by Sergei Smirnov in a popular book that itself became the inspiration for a wildly popular film extolling the patriotic values embodied in the "legend of Brest" on which generations of Soviet children were raised. In 1967, the fortress was awarded the title of "hero-city," and the fortress officially renamed the Brest Fortress Memorial Complex.[36] In 1971, a colossal Soviet realist monument was unveiled. Entitled "Courage," it shows a Red Army soldier with bulbous knitted brow and angular, gritted jaw pushing his way doggedly through a wall of concrete.

Today, however, the fury of the 1941 siege has been replaced by the sounds of families picnicking on the pleasant lawns in front of the fortress entrance. Through an archway made of huge slabs of 1970s concrete in the shape of a five-pointed Soviet star, I penetrated the fortress wall, listening to the speakers blaring patriotic music as I passed through the darkness into the museum complex proper. On the other side, local tourists and families with small children wandered along the cobbled paths in a mixture of reflection and relaxation, and a young couple donned rented Red Army uniforms at the hands of the enterprising owners of costumes stalls set up alongside the T-34s. Among the site's most famous exhibits were two defiant, heart-rending pieces of graffiti ("We'll die, but won't leave the fortress"; "I'm dying but won't surrender. Farewell Motherland. 20.VII.41"), discovered in the rubble after the war.

I visited the fortress's museums and other memorials. Then, late in the afternoon, clouds veiled the sky, and an abrupt shower forced me to take refuge in the large church standing at the center of the grassy expanse in the middle of the fortress. Incinerated during the wartime siege, for decades it remained a burnt-out shell. Today, however, with the Orthodox Church having begun its colonization of this Soviet monument too, it is once again functioning, dedicated, as it was during tsarist times, to St Nicholas the Wonderworker. Restored to services in the 1990s, the building's internal walls remain scorched and blackened from the war. And to my surprise, on a battle-scarred

---

[35] Rostislav Aliev, *The Siege of Brest, 1941: A legend of Red Army resistance on the Eastern Front*, trans. Stuart Britton (Barnsley: Pen and Sword Military, 2013), 1–3. Recent research suggests that the Soviet-era legend of a thirty-two-day siege is a myth. See Christian Ganzer, "German and Soviet losses as an indicator of the length and intensity of the Battle for the Brest Fortress," *Journal of Slavic Military Studies* 27 (2014): 449–66.
[36] Marples, "History, memory and the Second World War," 443.

column towards the center of the nave, I found an icon of a youthful Nicholas II in his 1896 coronation robes. If we can imagine retreating Russian officers taking Nicholas's portrait as emperor away with them when they evacuated the fortress in 1915, now his image has returned to Brest, as an icon, it would seem, of *teokratia*. Beneath the image of Nicholas in the dazzling Imperial Crown, with its two great diamond-studded hemispheres, a Cyrillic inscription hailed the "God-Crowned" tsar, and implored his intercession from heaven for the "resurrection of the Orthodox and Autocratic Russian Tsardom."

The rain ended as quickly as it had begun, and in the sticky post-tempest heat I followed a path out of the citadel over a bridge across the main channel of the Bug. This was the South Island, or "Volhyn" Fortification. A gravel road continued through farmland grown high with spring-time weeds and flowers until, a few hundred yards from the border with Poland, it arrived at a small country house that was a recently dedicated Russian Orthodox convent. There, at the most westerly outpost of "Holy Rus," the nuns seemed to staff a kind of new, spiritual Brest Fortress on the very doorstep of the West. I wandered around, curious, through the carefully tended garden plots. In the middle of the lawn in front of the house, a perspex- and pinewood-walled gazebo had been transformed into a semi-open-air chapel. On the wall hung an icon of the Romanovs. A hundred years after news of the Treaty of Brest-Litovsk had appeared to break Nicholas's spirit, Russia's last monarch had returned to these borderlands, not only as a saint but as a symbol, it would seem, in Belarus, too, of a regenerate theocratic principle.

෨ ෨ ෨

The next morning the breeze blew warm again from the south. Calling a taxi, I was driven to the station to catch the train to Poland. Of course, Nicholas and Alexandra's world had not recognized the watery line of the Bug as a border: in their day, Russian rule was extended as far as Warsaw. Indeed, the family's visits to Belovezha typically concluded with the family traveling two hundred or so miles west, to a hunting lodge they had had built for themselves at Spała (pronounced *Spa-wa*), a village surrounded by dense forest in the Polish salient itself, seventy-five miles southwest of Warsaw. What remained of it, I wondered? Was there any trace there of some sort of memory of *teokratia*, or any sign of its resurgence, not necessarily among Poles, who, as a nation, were and remain Catholic, but among possible Orthodox visitors? How far were pilgrims prepared to go in their search for a point of contact with the Royal Passion-bearers? How well did they know Nicholas and Alexandra's *story*?

Three hours from Brest, we arrived in Warsaw, where I boarded a bus for Tomaszow Mazowiecki, a prosperous town of 60,000 in the green Polish countryside, seventy miles southwest of the capital. From there I took a taxi for the final five or so miles to Spała.

A glorious spring evening coincided with my arrival, the sky above the trees of the forests that still ring the village having turned a deep, evening cobalt. With its fresh air and network of gentle walking and cycling trails, Spała is today a popular weekend getaway for Varsovians. Chosen because of the reference in its name, Dvor Carski ("Tsar's House"), to the period in the town's history I was interested in, my hotel was an upmarket bed and breakfast that traded on Spała's Romanov connections. Photographs and facsimiles of Nicholas and Alexandra and other Romanov tsars lined the walls alongside framed copies of what appeared to be authentic Imperial Russian government bonds, with their attractive late nineteenth-century fonts and elaborately stylized double-headed eagles. Opposite the reception desk, I noticed a photograph of Patriarch Kirill of Moscow, beside an icon of Nicholas II.

The following morning, I went in search of Nicholas and Alexandra's hunting lodge, or whatever of it remained. Spała was the most modest of all the Romanov residences.[37] Alexandra's friend Anna Vyrubova described it as "one of the dampest and gloomiest palaces" she had ever seen.[38] Nobody called it homely. "In all, there was something non-Russian about it that shocked those who came from the interior of the country," said Spiridovich, who had also accompanied Nicholas and Alexandra there.[39]

Today Spała consists of little more than a single, straight main road with a Catholic church and a smattering of hotels and guesthouses, gifts and groceries shops, cafés, and bike rentals. Finding the location of Nicholas and Alexandra's Spała lodge was not difficult. Of the lodge itself, however, only the sandstone foundations have survived, overgrown with grass. The flat patch of land they frame is now a makeshift basketball court, a sign marked in Polish, English, and Russian indicating its former purpose beneath the floor of Nicholas and Alexandra's hunting lodge. And, yet, at some point in the not-too-distant past, some pilgrim must have passed: wedged between the timber frame and the perspex cover of the sign was a little paper icon of Russia's Royal Passion-Bearers.

∽   ∽   ∽

Despite its modesty, however, the Spała lodge played a larger role in Nicholas and Alexandra's story, the story of the internal collapse of the

---

[37] Robert Massie described it as a "small country inn . . . lost at the end of a sandy road . . . cramped and dark": *Nicholas and Alexandra*, 172.
[38] Vyrubova, *Memories*, 44.   [39] Spiridovitch, *Dernières Années*, 2:288.

Russian *teokratia*, than might be expected, and it is with an incident that occurred at Spała that this chapter must conclude. Although not physically present, the primary protagonist was Rasputin.

Seeking rest after that summer's tiring Borodino centenary celebrations, Nicholas, Alexandra, and their children returned to the now-demolished chateau at Belovezha for the first time in seven years in September 1912. During the fortnight there, Nicholas hunted in the ancient forest, walked with his daughters, or took them rowing on the little lake in front of the chateau. Alexei, who had not had a life-threatening attack of hemophilia since his apparently miraculous healing at the hands of Rasputin in 1907, joined in most of these activities with his sisters. But then disaster struck. Playfully imitating the sailors on the imperial yacht, he climbed, one bath time, up on to the edge of the bath in the Belovezha chateau and jumped from there into the water. As he did so, he slipped, hitting his groin, to the horror of all watching, on the tap.[40] An internal hemorrhage opened, and the boy passed out a few minutes later.

In the days that followed, the boy seemed to improve. Confined to his bed by the imperial physician Botkin (the same, now sainted layman whose icon I had seen on Vasily's wall in Mogilev), the boy regained consciousness, and the swelling in his groin subsided. It was decided he was well enough for the family to continue its holiday in Spała. Little did they know that the little dark lodge would form the site of one of the family's most terrible passions before their murder, just under six years later, at Ekaterinburg.

The Romanovs arrived by train from Belovezha on September 16. Outwardly, Alexei's condition continued to improve. Sitting up in bed, he resumed his studies. The swelling continued to subside. But Alexei longed to go outside. Unable to walk, he was placed in a carriage with his mother and Anna Vyrubova, who had joined the family at Spała, and taken on a short drive, when a sudden jolt on the uneven country road tore the internal wound back open. The bleeding began again, Alexei's groin swelling even faster than it had in Belovezha. In minutes, the collected blood was the size of a grapefruit. The boy was in agony. "That return drive stands out in my mind as an experience of horror," recalled Vyrubova: "Every movement of the carriage, every rough place in the road, cause the child the most exquisite torture, and by the time we reached home he was almost unconscious with pain."[41]

Upon reaching the lodge, Alexei was laid on one side in bed; one of his legs had bent up beneath him as the skin had stretched to cover the swelling and then stiffened in place. Meanwhile, surgeons, who

---

[40] Spiridovitch, *Dernières Années*, 2:284–85.
[41] Vyrubova, *Memories*, 45.

generally acknowledged how little they could do, were called to Spała from Petersburg. Alexei groaned and shrieked from the pain. "For fully eleven days these dreadful sounds filled the corridors outside his room, and those of us who were obliged to approach had often to stop our ears with our hands," Vyrubova recalled, noting that during the entire ordeal Alexandra "never undressed, never went to bed, rarely even lay down for an hour's rest. Hour after hour, she sat beside the bed." Such moments of crisis brought out all the strength in her character; she martyred herself for the boy she believed God through Serafim's prayers had given her. Nicholas, by contrast, struggled to bear his son's suffering. "Once, when the Emperor came into the room seeing his boy in this agony and hearing his faint screams of pain, the poor father's courage completely gave way and he rushed, weeping bitterly, to this study,"[42] said Vyrubova. Alexei himself believed that he was going to die. "When I am dead, build me a little monument of stones in the wood," he allegedly said to his mother.[43]

The surgeons' arrival from Petersburg changed little. Two days after they began administering the few procedures available to them, Alexei's temperature had only risen. The leading surgeon declared the situation hopeless. Only a miracle could save the boy, he apparently told his parents. Perhaps the tumor would go down spontaneously by itself, but such an eventuality occurred "only once in a hundred times."[44] God, who had given Nicholas and Alexandra an heir, was about to take him away. The local Orthodox priest was called to confess the boy, and a large green tent erected in the garden, as a makeshift chapel for the Divine Liturgy. "After the first celebration," recalled Vyrubova, "he walked in solemn procession from the altar to the sickroom bearing with him Holy Communion for the sick boy." Death appeared imminent. Fr Aleksandr administered Alexei the Church's last rites, and a death notice was prepared for publication in Petersburg. But Alexandra refused to give up.

So far, Alexandra had not sought to involve Rasputin in the drama. At that time, he was two thousand miles away, in his home village of Pokrovskoye, Siberia.[45] Only when every other avenue had been exhausted did she call on the intervention of the man she had decided was a *starets*. Surely, God would hear *him*. "The Empress declared that she could not believe that God had abandoned them and she asked me to telegraph Rasputin for his prayers," Pierre Gilliard, Alexei's Swiss tutor, recalled. A few hours later came Rasputin's calm, laconic reply. "God has seen your tears and heard your prayers. Do not grieve. The Little One will not die. Do not allow the doctors to bother him too

[42] Ibid., 45.   [43] Ibid., 45.   [44] Spiridovitch, *Dernières Années*, 2:289.
[45] Smith, *Rasputin*, 290.

much."[46] Two days later, according to the testimony of at least three eye-witnesses (Vyrubova, Gilliard, and Spiridovich), Alexei's condition began to improve. As Vyrubova put it, the boy "lay wasted and utterly spent, but alive."[47]

Was it a miracle? Some have suggested that it was just a coincidence, or, more plausibly, that the calming effect on Alexandra of Rasputin's short, reassuring telegraph was unconsciously noticed by Alexei. Seeing the change in his mother's demeanor, the boy, too, it is suggested, relaxed, and, with this, the internal bleeding, made worse by the boy's state of panic, also, at last, began to subside. Certainly, this was the only treatment for hemophilia known in medical handbooks before the discovery of plasma treatment.[48] But Alexandra was not privy to this theory. Precisely Nicholas and Alexandra's aloofness from their generation's judgment for the purely ethical, secularized Christianity of Kant precluded the possibility of such an interpretation. It was a *miracle*; Rasputin's prayers had saved her son's life a second time. As Spiridovich put it, "From that moment, the Empress's faith in Rasputin became unshakeable and no force existed in the world that could alienate the *starets* from the imperial family's sympathies."[49] Just eighteen months before the outbreak of a world war that would see the Duma launch another bid for executive control of the government through an attack on the figure of Rasputin, it was a fateful conclusion for Alexandra, and Nicholas with her, to have made.

And yet even after Spała, we still should not exaggerate the extent of Rasputin's influence. Between June 1912 and February 1913, Nicholas and Alexandra did not even see the Siberian peasant.[50] In all, Rasputin saw Nicholas and Alexandra only six times in 1913, and conversed with them even fewer. In May, he followed Nicholas, Alexandra, and their children to Kostroma for the Romanov Tercentenary, and was in Moscow for its climax. But in neither place was he received by them. Nicholas and Alexandra saw Rasputin at the Alexander Palace on June 1, and again on July 17. The reason for the latter meeting was again Alexei. The day before, the boy had hurt his hands playing tennis and Nicholas and Alexandra called Rasputin for help. "He stayed a little while with Alexei and Alexandra," Nicholas noted in his diary on that occasion, "and spoke a little with me and the girls, and then left. Shortly after his departure, the pain in Alexei's hand started to pass and he himself calmed down and began to sleep." The boy's condition

---

[46] Massie, *Nicholas and Alexandra*, 176.
[47] Vyrubova, *Memories*, 46.
[48] Massie, *Nicholas and Alexandra*, 177–78.
[49] Spiridovitch, *Dernières Années*, 2:290.
[50] Smith says that Nicholas and Alexandra received Rasputin in January 1913. But the first record in Nicholas's diary in 1913 of a visit from Rasputin is in February.

continued improving. The family saw Rasputin again once in August and in September (at Livadia, in the Crimea), respectively. Most meetings lasted for not much more than an hour, and were squeezed for Nicholas into a daily schedule filled with many other meetings with men he saw much more frequently.

It was significant, therefore, that stories about Rasputin's "influence" were, on the eve of the Great War, capable of being recycled at all. In Bulgakov's scheme, a prophet might pray for the tsar, encourage, warn, and advise him, but not dictate to him or take over his will. At no time before 1915, at the earliest, did Nicholas's relationship with Rasputin ever exceed the bounds of this scheme. And yet the problem was that men such as Guchkov and Rodzianko were convinced, as early as 1912, that it had, and they insinuated as much in the papers. Rasputin's influence was discovered in everything. Meeting no denial from the palace, which refused to discuss private matters, or any punitive action from the government, which felt its hands to be tied by the October Manifesto, every invented story was left standing in the public memory as a proven charge against a man who was, after all, one of the imperial family's occasional intimates. Even when, on rare occasions, some of the more fanciful stories published in the less reputable papers were challenged by writers in other journals, and the original story found to be baseless, the apologies and retractions later issued were buried in the paper's back pages, and never attracted the degree of public attention they should have.[51]

As a result, Rasputin was, by 1914, one of Russia's most famous people. On the eve of the Great War, the newspapers covered his comings and goings between Petersburg and Siberia as if he were the tsar himself. And then, suddenly, the Rasputin circus almost lost its star. At home in Pokrovskoye in Siberia in June, Rasputin was enjoying Sunday lunch with his family on June 29/July 12, 1914, when the postman called with a letter. Answering it quickly, Rasputin ran out of the house to have the postman take his reply. He was passing through the gates on to the street when a woman approached him and drove a knife through his stomach. Rasputin was badly wounded but not killed.

Two weeks before these events, meanwhile, the Serbian nationalist Gavrilo Princip had shot the heir to the Austrian throne in Sarajevo, and from his hospital bed in the Siberian town of Tyumen where he recovered from his wounds, Rasputin opposed with every muscle he could muster the drift towards war in the capitals of Europe. The telegrams he sent Nicholas prophesied disaster should Russia go to war with Germany. When Nicholas ignored the warning, Rasputin composed the following telegram:

[51] Smith, *Rasputin*, 326.

Dear friend, I'll say again a menacing cloud is over Russia, lots of sorrow and grief, it's dark and there's not a ray of hope. A sea of tears, immeasurable, and as to the blood? What can I say? There are no words, indescribable horror. I know they all want war from you, evidently not realizing that this means ruin. Hard is God's punishment when he takes away reason, it's the beginning of the end. You are the Tsar Father of the people, don't allow the madmen to triumph and destroy themselves and the people. Yes, they'll conquer Germany, but what of Russia? If one thinks then truly never for all time has one suffered like Russia, drowned in her own blood. Great will be the ruin, grief, without end. Grigory.[52]

It has been called the "most remarkable and prophetic letter ever written to a Russian monarch by one of his subjects."[53]

---

[52] The letter, which is now in Yale University Library, is translated in Smith, *Rasputin*, 362–63.   [53] Smith, *Rasputin*, 362.

PART TWO
COLLAPSE

More on the Kantian Background to the Russian Revolution

O FAR OUR TRAVELS ACROSS RUSSIA—ACROSS the Russia of time and place, but also the Russia of the mind, in the writings of Sergei Bulgakov—have allowed us to assemble the elements of the theocratic ideal, *teokratia*, and suggest what it might mean for that ideal to have been the "spontaneous feeling of the Russian people, on which the Russian Statehood had been built" (as Bulgakov put it). This, in turn, has enabled us to grasp two things. First, it has shown us the religious meaning of the Russian Revolution, as an event whose fundamental causes can be regarded as *ideational*: that is, the clash between the theocratic ideal of Eastern Orthodoxy and the atheistic conclusions of nineteenth-century European philosophy, each of which extended incompatible claims over politics because they extended incompatible claims over the *world*. Second, it has enabled us to regard the canonization of Nicholas II and his family as saints in Russia today as sociologically significant, as a sign or a symbol of the regeneration (or perdurance) of the theocratic ideal in Russian culture. Indeed, this book would have it that the story of the collapse and regeneration of the theocratic principle in Russian culture is the red thread that ties Russia's history in the twentieth and twenty-first centuries together, that lends everything else its meaning, and in the light of which everything else is explained. *Apart from this story, contemporary Russia, her internal political and social evolution and the meaning and sources of her external behavior, cannot be properly understood.*

Certainly, Bulgakov seems to have been convinced that the collapse of tsarism, not only as a regime but as a religious ideal, possessed a defining significance of this kind. As we have seen, Bulgakov, overcoming his earlier rejection of tsarism, became a tsar-lover on the Yalta Embankment, when the true meaning of tsarism as an expression of Russian culture's aspiration, through an authority "by the grace of God, not popular dispensation," to a politics that fulfilled its calling to be an act of sacred representation—a disclosure of God's ruling power in the world—impressed itself on him. To the extent that tsarism (however imperfectly) expressed and sought to realize an image of the City of God on earth, Bulgakov was, in the full meaning of the word, a "tsarist," the proponent of a view of politics that affirmed the reality of the sacred and its rightful sovereignty in all human affairs. At the same time, however,

Bulgakov also believed that it was his misfortune to become, as he put it, a partisan of the theocratic principle at just the time the ideal of *teokratia* "was departing from history"—and it says everything about how closely Bulgakov identified himself with the theocratic ideal that he considered himself "doomed to the torment of a slow death with it."[1] As Bulgakov put it, describing his interior response to the events he lived through as Russia careened towards revolution, "I could not and did not want to love anything as much as tsarist autocracy, as the tsar, as an authority that was mystical and sacred, and yet I was doomed to watch, as this *teokratia* failed in Russian history and even departed from it, how it was secularized, substituted, and left its place to the intelligentsia."[2] But why *was* tsarism, as an authentic form of sacred politics, doomed? Why was *teokratia* passing out of history?

To Bulgakov, the question of the possibility of a sacred politics was inseparable from another question: how was religion, belief in God, possible in modernity *at all*? For clearly if God could not be rationally believed in, there could be no rational foundation for a sacred politics, and (as Nicholas II's opponents in the Duma quite clearly intuited) quite apart from the merits or otherwise of the reigning emperor, tsarism stood denuded of every justification. The fate of the Russian regime and what we would call the phenomenon of secularization were tied together, not in a merely sociological way, but on a deeper level of ideational or philosophical causation. People did not have to stop going to church or thinking of themselves as "good Christians" for tsarism to collapse. But if they began to *represent to themselves* that what they did in church and what they believed as "good Christians" was somehow less real (because they believed it, perhaps, on the grounds of "faith alone," as if revelation did not form a unity with the witness, when properly understood, of the world of the senses) than what they saw with their own eyes around them, read in the paper, or argued about with their neighbors, then the collapse of tsarism *was* inevitable. And that in turn raised questions about how the advent of modernity changed the way people looked at and acted in the world: what it was that people thought the world *meant*. Thus, in asking himself what the rise of the Russian revolutionary movement signified about the possibility of religion, Bulgakov tells us in *Unfading Light*—a miscellany of theological and philosophical reflections written between 1911 and 1916 that represented Bulgakov's first book-length work of theology—that he was thinking primarily, in these years before the Revolution, of the legacy of the Prussian philosopher Immanuel Kant, father of all nineteenth-century (and, indeed, all *twentieth*-century) philosophy.[3]

---

[1] Bulgakov, *Avtobiograficheskie*, 82.   [2] Ibid., 74.
[3] Sergei Bulgakov, *Svet Neverchenii: Sozertsaniia i umozreniia*. English translation in Sergius Bulgakov, *Unfading Light: Contemplations and speculations*, trans. Thomas

Kant, it will be recalled, established what we might call modern, "critical" rationality. Distinguishing his own approach from the "dogmatic" worldview that had prevailed since Plato (according to which, truth, being located objectively in a cosmic order transcendent of the human mind, was first *that which man discerned* by an act of dialectical contemplation and then *that to which man conformed himself* through a self-imposed act of discipline, or *askesis*), Kant affirmed that nothing could be established as true that could not be isolated, observed, measured by the human eye and other human senses. To these sense perceptions, the human mind then applied various "transcendental" categories of analysis that the individual human mind itself generated. The result was that the existence of a thing (*anything*) was verified *not* through a universal human faculty of intuition (refined through dialectical contemplation) existing in analogous relationship with that wisdom of God in which the order of the cosmos had been believed (since Plato and the Church Fathers who followed him) to inhere, but by the critical, analytical judgment of independent human minds reaching agreement on the meaning of the world through "dialogue," or demonstrating unilaterally that they had understood what the world was by successfully manipulating the world to expose its secrets (typically, in ways that magnified human power over intrinsically "meaningless" matter).

All this is to say that Bulgakov seems to have recognized, with his friend and younger contemporary Vladimir Ern, who in 1915 wrote a famous essay, "From Kant to Krupp," that we know impressed Bulgakov, the many strengths, and still more the even greater defects, of Kant's so-called "critical" approach.[4] All this is to say that first in Kant's native Germany, and then in Europe generally, Kantian method had led to great advances in both the basic and applied sciences. But, like Ern, Bulgakov also believed that Kant's rationality could be destructive of the human civilization it purported to improve. This was why Ern (and apparently Bulgakov) concluded that Kant led inevitably to the awesome weapons of the renowned German arms manufacturer, Krupp. Worse, with the embrace of Kant's critical rationality, Europe, starting with Kaiser Wilhelm II's Germany, not only acquired new mastery over nature; it also

Allan Smith (Grand Rapids, MI: Eerdmans, 2012). In his book on Bulgakov's political theology, Rowan Williams offers an important discussion of *Unfading Light* and the circumstances of its production. But he nowhere discusses the polemic that Bulgakov addresses against Kant on the possibility of religion in the opening chapter. See Williams, *Sergii Bulgakov*, 113–31.

4 Vladimir Ern, "Ot Kanta k Kruppu," in Ern, *Mech i Krest: Stati o sovremennikh sobytiiakh* (Moscow: I. D. Sytina, 1915), 20–34. It can be found in modern reprint in A. A. Ermichev, *V. F. Ern: Pro et Contra: Lichnost' i tvorchestvo Vladimira Erna v otsenke russkikh myslitelei i issledovatelei* (St Petersburg: Izd-vo Russkoi khristianskoi gumanitarnoi akademii, 2006), 415–24. On the essay and its context, see Matthew J. Dal Santo, "From Kant to Krupp—and Kiev: Vladimir Ern on Kantianism as a Source of War, 1914 and Today," *Telos* 205 (Winter, 2023): 128–49.

traded the last vestiges of the traditional Christian-Platonic view of the world as the manifestation of given ("dogmatic") truths rooted in a transcendent cosmic order (and, hence, ultimately in the divine nature itself, whether the essence or the energies — or, as for Bulgakov, the mysterious "hypostasis" of Sophia) for a view of the world as a vast reservoir of potential meanings (or none) whose actuality was to be realized by the activity upon it of the human will. This presented itself to contemporary Europeans as "enlightened" and "humanistic." But very far from the wondrous theophany it had been for his ancestors, the world as represented to himself by modern man became, Bulgakov believed, a formless waste awaiting man's activity upon it in a way that only announced God's absence, the divine non-existence, the negative theophany of atheism. (For example, considering advances in physics, we might say that splitting the atom reassures man that the world is only a bundle of atoms.) Thus, in a spirit very much akin to that of Ern, Bulgakov can say, when preparing *Unfading Light* for publication in December 1916, that the Great War was the outworking of Kant's critical method, a "spiritual catastrophe, unexpected and devastating," that was nonetheless a symptom of that "humanist worldview, triumphally asserted in 'modernity.'" [5]

For himself, Bulgakov was concerned most of all about what Kant's method meant for the philosophy of religion. Clearly, all material bodies (from man himself to the stars, insects, stones, and plants) were susceptible to such a critical analysis. But God, lacking a material body subject to human sense perception, could never be rationally "analyzed" or manipulated according to the criteria Kant's critical rationality demanded. This in turn meant that God — whether the God of the philosophers or the God of the Bible and of the Church — lacked, according to Kant's criteria for truth, the objective, empirical quality that allowed even his existence to be accepted on any grounds other than philosophical necessity or pious, private opinion. Indeed, Kant himself affirmed that as a philosophical postulate God *did* belong to a handful of notions that were necessary to accept without "critical" proof being possible.

Of course, Kant died in 1804, before the full implications of his philosophical revolution had been worked out. But once they had, the consequences would be revolutionary. By locating truth in man's internal act of intellection itself, Kant had finally abolished the very possibility of rationally establishing the existence of God himself. Rationality henceforth would be secular, the only role allotted to the God of the Bible being that of the guardian of a bloodless Christian morality that Kant and his followers generally regarded as harmless and universal. As we have seen, men as they were of the Kantian nineteenth century, even

---

[5] Bulgakov, *Unfading Light*, xxxix.

Nicholas II's closest aides, his ministers, and officials in the Russian government, subscribed to this secularized, Kantian worldview (even while, presumably, they continued to go to church). At root, then, Bulgakov's purpose in *Unfading Light* was to show how wrong-headed this was. Over against the atheist conclusions of his age's judgment for secularization, Bulgakov would make the case for God.

On the non-existence — impossibility — of any proof of God's existence, Kant, believed Bulgakov, was simply wrong. Every human culture posited the existence of a world of spirit beyond the perception of the bodily senses, but not necessarily (especially in the world's organized religions) beyond the scrutiny of the mind. *Contra* Kant, religion was, empirically, the most widely attested feature of human civilization of all. In this sense, the implicitly atheist frame of reference of modern European, especially *German*, civilization after the Kant was the exception. To accept *its* rationality would be to accept a drastic amputation of what it meant to be human. As Bulgakov, not accepting this act of amputation, put it, "Kant's schemas are valid for characterizing not human being in general with all the inexhaustible fullness of its spirit, but only the 'scientific human,' i.e., only one side of this spirit and its activity."[6] To investigate what religion is, Bulgakov continued, it is necessary "only to have no prejudice, either metaphysical or speculative, dogmatic, or empirical . . . to look at life with open, simple eyes and allot to the universal-historical fact of religion that attention which naturally belongs to it, if only because of its prevalence."[7] And in doing this, the philosopher of religion had at his or her disposal centuries and centuries of empirical human testimony. "The life of the saints, ascetics, prophets, and founders of religions — literature, cult, custom, in a word, that which can be called the phenomenology of religion . . . side by side with the personal experience of each person" — these, Bulgakov believed, represented the empirical "proofs" of God's existence.

Far from being an irrational or superstitious *accretion*, then, religion resulted from the apparently *innate* and *universal* human intuition that One other than the world of the senses existed and could be sought — and that such a religious sensibility was essential to what it was to be human. As Bulgakov put it, it was man's universal experience in religious matters that every human being enjoyed from the moment of birth the "sensation of a higher, divine reality," which would be real for him or her if only he or she would acknowledge it. After all, as Bulgakov continued, while the "sense of God" is universally given, it is given "not in general, *in abstracto*, but precisely for a given human being: the human in himself and through himself discovers a new world before which he trembles from dread, joy, love, shame, repentance."[8] To

---

[6] Ibid., 2.   [7] Ibid., 5.   [8] Ibid., 17.

propose as a "humanism" a form of rationality that denied the reality and significance of that universal human intuition was to endorse a vision of modern man as a creature less than human, less than fully man, not merely *naturally* as a species but also individually, as a *person*.

For Bulgakov, then, *contra* Kant, the universal human intuition that God existed, and the human person's experience of God as Other when that intuition was acceded to, were the empirical proofs of God's existence that Kant was looking for but could not find because he defined the faculties of human sense-perception too narrowly. Were the eyes or the hands more reliable guides to reality than the soul or the heart? Imagine the truncation of what it meant to be human that would follow if that proposition were rigorously accepted; it was so all-destroying of human life — of love, family life, and friendship, among other things — that it never could be. Kant had ignored the witness of his own being. "God is — outside me but also for me — far higher than my subjectivity, and yet he communicates with it," said Bulgakov, using the terms of Kant's own critique: "This proposition is not only an analytical judgment deduced on the basis of an examination of the concept of religion, but at the same time a religious synthetic judgment *a priori*. YOU ARE — in religion this stands prior to any analysis but at the same time as the object of analysis." In such terms, Bulgakov's theory of religion should, perhaps, be thought of as a version of the so-called "ontological argument" also being explored at that time in Catholic circles connected to the legacy of the nineteenth-century priest and theologian Antonio Rosmini (1797–1855) in Italy, and another apparent witness to the influence on Bulgakov of Ern, who in 1914 had returned from several years' study of Rosmini in Milan.[9]

In any case, Bulgakov did not believe that the "proof" of God's existence (*pace* Aquinas and the Thomistic tradition that followed him) could be derived from deductions made extrinsically by the rational mind on the grounds of its empirical observations of the world of the material senses (a view which already conceded too much to Kant), such that belief in God could somehow be deductively "impelled." Rather, if, for Bulgakov, it was the intuition apparently universally intrinsic to being human that another such as God must exist, and could be sought after in the universal human phenomenon of prayer and religion, then because, according to this intuitive argument, belief

---

[9] For Ern's biography and Rosmini's place in his thought, see Ermichev, *V. F. Ern*, 7–56. On Rosmini ("undoubtedly the greatest Italian philosopher of the first half of the nineteenth century"), see Gerald A. McCool, *Nineteenth-century scholasticism: The search for a unitary method* (New York: Fordham University Press, 1977), 119–25. While Rosmini's propositions, which challenged the reigning neo-Thomist account of religion in the nineteenth-century Catholic Church, were proscribed by Pope Leo XIII, Rosmini was declared blessed by Pope Benedict XVI.

in God's existence was not reduced to a rational deduction from the objects of sense perception, God himself was revealed, Bulgakov believed, as the One who liberated man from any and all forms of either natural, rationalistic necessity, or the apparently also universal human temptation to occult "knowledge" and magic. As Bulgakov has it, "The religious path in this sense is necessarily the path of miracle and grace. God is the transcendent ... the sole and authentic not-I," and there "is not and cannot be any 'spiritual knowledge' that leans on *method* ... For God is Wonder and Freedom, while all knowledge is method and necessity."[10] The man who believed in God's ability as Other to intervene freely in the world, including by performing miracles, was not for that fact a childish or weak-minded "mystic," but a human soul that had responded rationally to man's innate intuition regarding God's existence, encountered this Other in prayer, and put his faith in Him. Only such a man's rationality was not the truncated atheistic rationality of Kant, but the authentically human rationality of man as a being made *for* God and life with Him.

Hence, the other elements of religion that Kant had dismissed — prayer and faith — were not symptoms of a mind captive to "dogmatic" superstition, but the features of a human life adjusted to true rationality. Just as, for Kant, the body's senses were the organs that allowed a person knowledge of the world, so, for Bulgakov, the corresponding organ in respect of God was what the Bible called "the heart," the spiritual center of a person's total being, and if the bodily senses could give rise to a proper human response to the material world, so the spiritual senses of the heart could lead man to a proper response to God. That response was faith. Faith was man's proper response to that encounter with God as Other that follows man's yielding to the innate human desire to search for Him. In Bulgakov's terms, the "I believe" of faith is the authentic subjective response to the objective "YOU ARE" disclosed when, in the heart's encounter with God through the spiritual senses, man's innate intuition that God exists is confirmed by God Himself. In this sense, said Bulgakov, the decisive moment in the religious life was "the encounter with God in the human spirit, the contact of the transcendent with the immanent, the act of faith. *God exists.* This is what resounds in the human heart, the poor, little, wretched human heart; *God exists,* sing heaven and earth ... *God exists,* respond the abysses of human consciousness and creativity. Glory to him!"[11]

Such faith, which was authentic, Christian faith, said Bulgakov, could never be the fruit of a merely rational deduction from extrinsic truths. Such a rationalistic "possession" of God, the transcendent, the Other, the Not-I, man has not been given to seek (and, in fact, does

---

[10] Bulgakov, *Unfading Light*, 23.　　　[11] Ibid., 24.

not want). Rather, faith is the surrender of oneself to God, an "act of freedom, madness, love, bravery... the tossing of the end of life's thread into heaven in the certainty that it will hang there without any reinforcement." Different from the occult, different from theosophy, both of which sought (no less than rational proofs of God's existence) to enclose the otherness of God in man-made methods of knowing and manipulating, faith, said Bulgakov, was the "highest and final sacrifice of a human being to God — himself, his reason, will, heart, his whole essence, the whole world, all evidence... a completely disinterested exploit, giving away everything and demanding nothing. It is the love of humankind for God exclusively and for the sake of God himself."[12]

Indeed, only in the light of Bulgakov's prodigious account of what religion is, of what is at stake in believing, we might say, can the significance of much of what we have seen already in this book be appreciated: the significance of Nicholas and Alexandra's refusal of their age's merely moralizing "Kantian" Christianity; of the occult temptation presented by Philippe; of the Sarov celebrations and their decision for Church Orthodoxy (including the door this left open to the "prophet," Rasputin); of the structuring centrality to their lives of the Church's calendar and sacraments; and, above all, perhaps, the place in their lives of prayer.

Prayer (which Kant had dismissed, as we have seen, as "idolatry"), Bulgakov was convinced, remained "insufficiently understood and valued" as the "foundation of religious experience."[13] This was unfortunate, Bulgakov believed, because if the "fundamental givenness of the religious in general is the transcendent," then prayer was "the fundamental form of religious achievement." Because prayer consisted in the "striving of all the spiritual forces of a human being, of the whole human person, for the Transcendent," every prayer "realizes the command: go beyond yourself." Because, in prayer, man made the "effort to come out himself, to rise above himself," prayer was an essential part of the realization of that sacrifice of self to God that is faith. How short-sighted Kant had been, therefore, to dismiss prayer as idolatry, a falling away from what it was to be human! "The thunderous fact of prayer — in Christianity and in all other religions — must finally be understood and valued in its philosophical meaning." Far from being an act of weakness, a talking to oneself or into the air, prayer, was "connected with the very foundation of the human person in its unbreakable wholeness." Indeed, if the one truth that Bulgakov opposed to Kant was that the capacity to encounter the sacred in religion was the mark of what it was to be human, the second was that, as he put it, italicizing the words in the text of "Unfading Light" itself, "*Where there is no prayer, there is no religion.*"[14]

---

[12] Ibid., 32–33.   [13] Ibid., 24.   [14] Ibid., 25.

What does this mean for us, and our study of the Revolution and Russia's subsequent history in the twentieth century as the demise and regeneration, in Russian culture, of the theocratic principle? Obviously, there is the point we have already made: if religion is irrational, and if rationality is secular *by definition*, then, whatever the personal merits or flaws of the reigning monarch, Russia's theocratic regime, underpinned as it was by religion, could never be anything but "dogmatic," irrational, illegitimate, a deluded clutching at straws, a *myth* in the most cynical and power-hungry meaning that modernity is inclined to attribute to that word. And wasn't that how the autocracy's opponents, in the Duma and in the press, represented it? And yet, to follow Bulgakov, there is an irony here. The liberal politicians, the intelligentsia, the revolutionaries: all of them prided themselves on being the representatives of a rationality that did not have to justify itself before history; they were the disciples merely of the *critical* truth. But were they? Bulgakov did not believe so. United above all in ending the ongoing executive control of the government by the tsar, which they considered "irrational," the opponents of tsarism were, ideationally, merely the uncritical disciples of Kant, and, as such, Bulgakov believed, the heirs not only to all Kant's undoubted greatness, but also to the German philosopher's blind spots and errors, including an altogether inadequate account of religion. Nicholas II, by contrast, according to Bulgakov's alternative account of religion, was altogether more rational than his opponents. Naturally enough, this *more human* rationality of Nicholas's could not be without political consequences.

Again and again, in our account so far, we have noted the prayers which Nicholas II has left behind in his diary, for himself, his family and for Russia. Bulgakov helps us recognize their significance. In a "Kantian" world in which religion, as Bulgakov recognized, was no longer possible, Nicholas II remained instead a man assured by experience "of the reality of another, divine, world," who assumed as a matter of course a "living, immediate bond with religious reality." As Bulgakov put it, "Only the man who really has encountered divinity on his life's journey, who has been overtaken by it and on whom it has been poured out with its prevailing force has embarked on an authentically religious path."[15]

If Nicholas's prayers tell us anything, it is that he was such a man. At the end of the day, Nicholas's own personal religious experience, and the conviction that flowed for him from that experience that religion (*pace* Kant) *was* possible, was why Russia had its revolution, and why she had *had* to have it. To have consented to the secularization of the Russian *teokratia* — a regime that assumed the reality of religion — would have been to deny the reality of his entire religious experience,

---

[15] Ibid., 7.

including God himself, from his childhood at Gatchina to his coronation, the Sarov celebrations and beyond. That is why, if this book is the
story of the "logic" of Russia's recent past as Russian culture's *judgment
for secularization* and its later reversal, then it also aspires to being a
spiritual biography of the man, Nicholas II, at the center of the drama.
For inasmuch as it was Nicholas II's fate to be Russia's last theocratic
ruler, it is in his life that the theological and philosophical-historical
themes which this book follows assume an approachable human form
and scale. For the story of this clash will move us little if we treat those
ideas as merely disembodied theological or philosophical postulates;
only if we allow the ideas we are dealing with to assume human bodies will the religious meaning of the Russian Revolution strike us fully.
And it is to that story that we shall now turn. Providence had placed
on the throne perhaps the only man of a certain background in Russia
who, while outwardly sharing his ministers' and officials' participation
in late nineteenth- and early twentieth-century European culture, did
not accept either Kant's impossibility of religion or his substitute, a
"secularized," "Kantian" Christianity (a religion of morality but not the
supernatural). On the contrary, the outbreak in 1914 of the Great War
would show, as never before, that Nicholas was one who had "encountered divinity on his life's journey... been overtaken by it and on whom
it [had] been poured out with its prevailing force."

CHAPTER NINE

The Russian *Teokratia* Goes to War

WHEN IT FINALLY CAME, AT THE END OF 1914's long "July Crisis," on July 19/August 1, Germany's declaration of war on Russia, and Russia's reciprocating declaration later the same day, produced almost ubiquitous outbursts of loyalty to Nicholas and Russia's tsarist regime.[1] Workers who, only a few weeks before, had been striking, called off their pickets, while the Duma, calling a truce in its undeclared war for executive control of Russia's government, proclaimed a "Sacred Union" by which its members swore to prosecute the war to the end as one with the tsar and his ministers. Indeed, the outbreak of the Great War provided the occasion for the last great pageant of *teokratia*, in the form of a three-day visit by Nicholas and Alexandra to Moscow. There, crowds several hundred thousand strong pressed into Red Square, straining to be part of the carefully choreographed sequence of ceremonies that included no fewer than four liturgies in different Kremlin cathedrals.[2] Completing the *mise-en-scène*, Nicholas and Alexandra, on their journey home to Petersburg, stopped to pray at the Trinity-Sergius Monastery, north of Moscow. There, the abbot blessed Nicholas with an image of the Virgin painted on the burial board of the great fourteenth-century hermit St Sergei of Radonezh.

And yet, despite the comfort Nicholas doubtless found in these prayers and liturgies, spiritually and psychologically the strain of the preceding July Crisis (the month-long round of diplomatic exchanges and preparations for war among the European Great Powers precipitated by the ultimatum addressed by Austria-Hungary to Serbia on July 11/24) eventually caught up with him. On 9/22 August, Russia's last monarch recorded in his diary a sensation of nervous exhaustion, mixed, perhaps, with a sense of evil premonition: "I felt giddy with nausea and lay down all evening. At about midnight the foul feeling passed."[3] Was it a premonition of the horrors to come? Nine days later, news reached Nicholas of Russia's first major debacle: the destruction of the Russian Second Army under General Samsonov at the Battle of Tannenberg on August 15/28, when 70,000 men were killed and 92,000

---

[1] Up to the last moment, Nicholas II had sought to avoid war with Germany. On Russian behavior during the July Crisis, see, especially, Dominic Lieven, *Towards the Flame*, 313–42.

[2] Voeikov, *S tsarem*, 104–5.

[3] Nicholas II, August 9, 1914, in Diary (2), 480.

more captured in a failed Russian invasion of East Prussia.[4] But it is typical of Nicholas that the "foul feeling" did not shake his faith in God's providence. Just three days after Tannenberg, the Russian Third Army's victory over Austro-Hungarian forces in the southwest delivered the major town of Lvov into Russian hands. The capital of the Austrian Crownland of Galicia, Lvov had been the seat of a Rus principality in the days when a Grand Prince had sat at Kiev. As always in such occasions, Nicholas gave thanks to God. "Thanks be to God. I'm incredibly happy for this victory and rejoice in the celebrations of our army."[5] For the rest of the month good news continued to arrive from Galicia. At Tsarskoye Selo, he received ministers and visited military hospitals. But he longed to be with Russia's soldiers, whom he considered the embodiment of courage, chivalry, and patriotism. "In body, you are alive here, but in spirit you are completely there with our heroes, fulfilling their heavy duty gallantly and uncomplainingly," he wrote referring to himself with a degree of candor we are not accustomed to meeting in his diary.[6]

Journeys to the different fronts on which Russian troops were fighting granted Nicholas his "longstanding wish to be closer." In September, he made his first trip to Russian Army headquarters ("Stavka") in the Belorussian town of Baranovici. From Baranovici, Nicholas traveled to the Belorussian town of Rovno where his sister, Grand Duchess Olga, a trained nurse, had served since the opening of hostilities, and thence to the fortresses of Brest-Litovsk, Ivangorod, and Osovets. At Osovets, the fighting was only eight miles distant, and as the fortress had only just repelled a German attack, Nicholas's visit so soon after gave rise to a popular patriotic belief that he had himself led the fortress's defense.[7] It was Nicholas's first direct observation of modern warfare, and it is a testament to his fundamental humanity that it was modern warfare's destructiveness, not its efficiency, that featured that evening in his diary: the "sight of buildings destroyed by artillery fire, the enormous quantity of crosses scattered in the fields and forests" weighed on him heavily. As Voeikov, the Palace Commandant responsible for Nicholas's security, who traveled daily with him, recalled, "on account of the sensitivity of his [i.e. Nicholas's] character and his innate love of peace," such visits to the front (which his cousin, by contrast, the Supreme Commander Grand Duke Nikolai Nikolaevich, avoided at all costs) "aroused in the Sovereign a deep sorrow for the death in the field of battle of the faithful officers and men of the Imperial army."[8]

---

[4] McMeekin, *Russian Revolution*, 63.
[5] Nicholas II, August 25, 1914, in Diary (2), 483.
[6] Nicholas II, October 22, 1914, in Diary (2), 493.
[7] Voeikov, *S Tsarem*, 112.
[8] Ibid., 113–14.

Indeed, Nicholas seemed to intuit that the Great War was, in a way past wars had not quite been, a moral void, its very existence an outrage against God. A symbol of this was the blown-out church that Nicholas and his entourage visited near the fortress of Ivangorod (modern Deblin, in Poland), where wind whistled through the gaping holes that German shells had punched in the walls. In these western provinces of the Russian Empire, the local population was not Orthodox but Polish and Catholic. But this fact didn't stop Nicholas expressing solidarity with the people whose church the building was. How could services continue in view of such damage, Nicholas asked the local Catholic priest who accompanied them? The priest's reply, "The wind will blow through, but we will pray," hit a nerve with Nicholas, who ordered that 3,000 rubles be given to the priest for the church's restoration.[9] And yet, despite the alarm he felt at the destructiveness of modern weaponry, the journey to the Polish fortresses seemed to have a consolidating effect psychologically. As he recorded on his return to Tsarskoye Selo, "Since my return from my trip, an inner peace has arisen."[10]

By the time Nicholas returned to Stavka, at Baranovici, in October, Russia was also at war with Ottoman Turkey. With the receipt of two British-built dreadnoughts in July, Turkey enjoyed naval superiority in the Black Sea, and, on October 16/29, Ottoman warships shelled Sevastopol. But on land Russia had the advantage, and in eastern Anatolia the Russian army was advancing. On November 14/27, at Stavka, Nicholas celebrated his and Alexandra's twentieth wedding anniversary with a Mass of thanksgiving. "Truly God has blessed us with a rare family happiness," the tsar wrote in his diary, "if only I might show myself worthy of his mercy in that portion of my life that remains to me."[11] Four days later, he was back in church for prayers, ahead of his departure on the 19th for the Caucasus: fulfilling his duty as tsar, he would meet the men of his army fighting the Turks.

Thus, traveling by train via Kursk, Kharkov, the Kuban, Derbent, Baku and Tbilisi (where, Nicholas noted in his diary, there was a "mass of people" in the streets to see him), Nicholas arrived on December 1/14 in what is now the town of Sarikamis in modern Turkey, but was then Russian territory. This was as close to the front as it was possible for Nicholas to go, and, to him, "the most significant day in my trip to the Caucasus."[12] He talked to the men, distributed medals, and visited hospitals and churches. Nicholas, it seems, brought a touch to these visits that boosted morale and made them memorable for all concerned. "Wherever the Tsar happened to be, there was felt unfeigned gladness

---

[9] Ibid., 114.
[10] Nicholas II, September 27, 1914, in Diary (2), 488.
[11] Nicholas II, November 14, 1914, in Diary (2), 497.
[12] Nicholas II, December 1, 1914, in Diary (2), 501.

and good disposition," said Voeikov, at least.[13] As evidence, he described
an exchange between Nicholas and an ordinary soldier in Sarikamis that
is extraordinary if true. Inspecting the Russian troops involved in the
capturing the town only a few weeks before from the Ottomans, Nicholas was pinning St George Crosses on the breasts of the men cited
for bravery, when one man, the medal already pinned by Nicholas to
his uniform, raised his voice, daring to address the Sovereign who was
about to move on to the man beside him. "Your Imperial Majesty," the
officer said, making a confession, "I was not present at the battle." One
feels that Nicholas's entourage held its breath. But not missing a beat,
Nicholas responded with a wisdom not usually attributed to Russia's
last Tsar. "You did well to tell me," he said, commending the man's
honesty, "But you soon will be."[14] He left the medal in place. Nicholas
always considered Russia's soldiers her real heroes.[15]

Returning via Vladikavkaz, Nicholas stopped in Voronezh to venerate the relics of the local saint, Mitrophan, an eighteenth-century bishop,
in the company of Alexandra and the couple's two eldest girls, Olga and
Tatiana. From there, the Imperial family proceeded together to Tambov,
and thence to Moscow, for prayers in the Kremlin's cathedrals, and the
inspection of the city's military hospitals. From Moscow, Alexandra
and the grand duchesses returned to Tsarskoye Selo, while Nicholas
proceeded directly, via Minsk, to Stavka. He had been on the move
for almost a month. By the time he had returned to Tsarskoye Selo
for Christmas, he was ill, bedridden with exhaustion from his constant
concern for the fortunes of the country and welfare of his soldiers. As
Voeikov, who accompanied Nicholas on these journeys, put it, Nicholas
"spared neither his strength nor his health out of his desire personally
to see everything and transmit by his visit to the troops that faith in
victory over the enemy that he was himself filled with."[16] In doing this,
Nicholas was enacting what he considered to be an essential duty laid
upon him as tsar by Russia's theocratic regime: to be an example of
faith in God. As the bishop of Ekaterinoslav (modern Dnipro-Petrovsk,
in Ukraine) put it, in a speech delivered in Nicholas's presence in 1914:
"This is your feat, Your Imperial Majesty, your labor: to display Russian
life, the spirit of the Orthodox man, in our bitter but holy days."[17]

Can anyone doubt that Nicholas did not acquit this duty faithfully?
To read Nicholas's diary is to encounter constantly signs of one who
had "encountered the divinity in his life's journey" and "been overtaken
by it." More and more prominent in Nicholas's piety was the place
of the Virgin Mary. On September 8, he noted in his diary the Mass
held for the feast of the Virgin's Nativity, while on his visit to Vilna/

---

[13] Voeikov, *S tsarem*, 117.   [14] Ibid., 116.
[15] See diary for September 5, 1914, in Diary (2), 484.
[16] Voeikov, *S tsarem*, 113–14.   [17] Ibid., 120.

Vilnius during his trip the Northwestern front in September, for example, he recorded making a special visit to the city's Orthodox cathedral
"to venerate the Ostrobramsky Mother of God," a local icon of "Our
Lady of the Gate of Dawn" specially revered by the city's Orthodox
and Catholics alike.[18] Another sign is given by stories like that related
by Voeikov, about an incident during a visit by Nicholas and Alexandra together to St Petersburg's Peter and Paul Fortress in October 1914.
Having traveled into the capital for a memorial service in honor of the
soul of Nicholas's father, Alexander III, Nicholas, Alexandra and their
children were returning along the Neva embankment, when, passing by
the so-called "log cabin of Peter the Great" (a wattle and daub building,
now protected inside a brick enclosure, where Nicholas's ancestor had
first established his residence in Russia's new northern capital), Nicholas
unexpectedly ordered their driver to stop. The log cabin, Nicholas knew,
housed a revered icon of Christ, and Nicholas and Alexandra wished
to venerate it. Voeikov described what happened next. "The Imperial
motor cars stopped . . . at the entrance to the chapel. The Emperor,
Empress and two Grand Duchesses walked through the crowd of those
praying at the shrine. I bought candles, which they placed in front
of the icon. Those praying only recognized the Imperial Family when
they got down on their knees in the middle of the chapel."[19] But perhaps the most moving records of Nicholas's fundamental orientation
towards God throughout the Great War are the short notes that pepper
his diary about his own prayers. With Europe now enveloped in war, on
New Year's Eve 1914, the year ended with Nicholas saying his prayers in
church. He recorded their content in his diary. "I prayed to God that
He would grant us victory in the coming year and a calm and peaceful
existence after it. Bless and strengthen, Lord, our incomparable, gallant,
and uncomplaining armed forces until their last feat!"[20]

⁓ ⁓ ⁓

Another person whose worldview the Great War failed to secularize
was Alexandra. Sparing nothing for the good of Russia, Alexandra at
her best embodied a Martha-like *teokratia* of practical charity. Ten
years earlier, during the Russo-Japanese War, Alexandra had thrown
herself into the work of Russia's women auxiliary committees, transforming the Winter palace into a collection center for bandages and
other medical supplies, and turning its vast halls into hospital wards for
wounded officers [21] She repeated the feat in 1914. All around Tsarskoye

---

[18] Pope Pius XI authorized its crowning as a Mother of Mercy in 1927.
[19] Voeikov, *S Tsarem*, 113.
[20] Nicholas II, December 31, 1914 in Diary (2), 506.
[21] Buxhoeveden, *Tragic Empress*, 105–6. Cf. Vyrubova, *Memories*, 8, who recalls watching
Alexandra sew bandages in similar workrooms at Tsarskoye Selo.

Selo, buildings were converted, at Alexandra's insistence, into hospitals, which Alexandra funded out of her own personal resources. The largest Tsarskoye Selo hospital was the Catherine Palace, Russia's answer to Versailles, whose vast parqueted floors and gilded interiors became the backdrop for row after row of hospital beds. This time round, the couple's two eldest daughters, Olga and Tatiana, were old enough to be involved in such work, and each established a charitable foundation to raise money for the relief of the wounded, war widows, and war orphans, while the Empress's special cause became that of the hospital or sanitary train. Alexandra also saw to it that, together with her friend Anna Vyrubova, she and her eldest daughters formally trained as nurses. Enrolling immediately after the outbreak of the War, the Empress was a qualified "Sister of Mercy" two months later.[22] It was an achievement of which Alexandra was rightly proud.

Nursing was one of those rare activities in her life as an empress in which Alexandra's personal skills and temperament were given an opportunity to shine. She loved the work and threw herself into it, spending her mornings preparing the wounded for surgery, assisting at operations, or changing dressings, and her afternoons sitting with the convalescing. Indeed, it is as if it was only with the Great War that Alexandra finally came into her own, and finally discovered *her* way of being Russian empress. Certainly, the new sense of purpose that nursing lent her seems to have helped her put away some of the character traits — the shyness and self-consciousness, often interpreted as arrogance and indifference — that had crippled her relations with Russian society.

Of course, she could not disguise the pain she felt now that the land of her birth and that of her adoption were at war, nor her fears for her brother, the Grand Duke of Hesse, and the shame she felt at reports of German atrocities.[23] But, as she says in a letter to Nicholas in November 1914, "Our work in the hospital is my consolation."[24] Nicholas noticed the change that had occurred in her as a result and encouraged her to persist at her duties: "Do not fear," he advised, "but be more sure of yourself when you are alone, and everything will go smoothly."[25] The operations she assisted at included amputations. Her first "big" one of these — an arm — took place a few days after her letter to Nicholas above in November 1914. While she passed the instruments to the surgeon, her eldest daughter, Grand Duchess Olga, threaded the

[22] Vyrubova, *Memories*, 52, 53.
[23] See Alexandra to Nicholas II, September 19, 1914 (A. 9) in Joseph T. Fuhrmann, ed., *The Complete Wartime Correspondence of Tsar Nicholas II and the Empress Alexandra, April 1914–March 1917* (Westport, CT: Greenwood Press, 1999), 15.
[24] Alexandra to Nicholas II, November 17, 1914 (A. 57), in Fuhrmann, *Complete Wartime*, 41.
[25] Nicholas II to Alexandra, November 18, 1914 (N. 59) in Fuhrmann, *Complete Wartime*, 42.

needles. Mother and daughter returned to the surgery room to assist at a second amputation that afternoon. In the meantime, Alexandra had spent the middle part of the day binding dressings for soldiers who were "scarcely men anymore" on account of the wounds to the groin they had sustained. "I did three such — and one had a little tube in it. One's heart bleeds for them [and] being a wife and a mother I feel for them quite particularly," she wrote to Nicholas.[26] In *Quiet Flows the Don*, the Soviet novelist Mikhail Shokholov imagines the horror that comes over the face of an unnamed Romanov visiting a military hospital in the Great War when the wounded Cossack and budding revolutionary who is the hero of the story informs her of the location (the groin) of his wound. But Shokholov knew nothing of the heroism of Russia's empress. Alexandra, who thought nothing of treating officers who had suffered a hernial rupture, wouldn't have been so easily shocked.[27] Indeed, she wouldn't have been shocked at all. "I have seen the Empress of Russia in the operating room of a hospital . . . taking from the hands of the busy surgeons amputated legs and arms, removing bloody and even vermin-infested dressings, enduring all the sights, and smells, and agonies of a military hospital in the midst of war," her friend, Anna Vyrubova, wrote years later.[28]

Conjured in such reports are scenes of a kind almost impossible to imagine any other European Sovereign at the center of, and, indeed, while Nicholas was supportive, Alexandra's mother-in-law, the Dowager Empress Marie Fyodorovna, objected. But Alexandra continued her work undeterred. Indeed, she was feeling stronger than she had done for years. "I feel it's the time to do such things. God has given me better health and I find that we must all, big and small, do everything we can for our touchingly brave wounded."[29] It was serious, sobering work. She and her two eldest daughters witnessed their first death on the operating table that same month of November.[30] The transformation was so complete that, for a moment, Alexandra became, quite unselfconsciously, "mother" of all Russia's brave, young men, unstintingly lavishing her strong internal instinct to motherhood on any wounded Russian officer who found himself in one of her hospitals. She met the sanitary trains as they arrived at Tsarskoye Selo from the front, and helped receive the wounded. On such occasions, she heard from the doctors and nursing orderlies who had embarked the wounded men

---

[26] Alexandra to Nicholas II, November 20, 1914 (A. 66), in Fuhrmann, *Complete Wartime*, 46.
[27] Alexandra to Nicholas II, January 29, 1914 (A. 164) in Fuhrmann, *Complete Wartime*, 79.
[28] Vyrubova, *Memories*, 53.
[29] Alexandra to Nicholas II, November 28, 1914 (A. 92), in Fuhrmann, *Complete Wartime*, 57.
[30] Alexandra to Nicholas II, November 25, 1914, in Fuhrmann, *Complete Wartime*, 53.

about conditions at the front, gaining a first-hand impression of the nature of modern warfare and soldiers' reactions to it. "Six versts [four miles] from the battle and the windows shook from the artillery. Aeroplanes were flying there over Varsovie [Warsaw]," she reported to Nicholas.[31] And the Siberian troops, having never seen an airplane before, concluded it was a spiritual being, and a sign that God was on the German side. As a result, she said, they refused to fight.

But it was the plight of the wounded that concerned her the most, and she was growing in her judgment as a nurse. "Dear me, what wretched wounds. I fear some are doomed men; but I am glad that we have them and do all in our power to help them." She had already assisted at two operations that day, and done the rounds among the wounded. She treated the men as if they were her own sons. Especially dear to her was an "officer of the Second Rifles whose legs are already getting quite dark and one fears an amputation may be necessary. I was with the boy yesterday during his dressing—awful to see—and he clung to me and kept quiet, poor child."[32] Making herself a second mother to the young man, she visited him daily in his ward in the Catherine Palace until his death four months later. "He will pass away gradually—I only hope not while we are away," she wrote to Nicholas.[33] Indeed, she became so close to him that his death was announced to her in a premonition while she lay in her bed, sleepless, in the nearby Alexander Palace the night before. The letter to Nicholas about it that resulted was an occasion for the Empress to reiterate her motivation as a nurse. "Thank God we have the possibility of at least making some comfortable in their suffering and can give them a feeling of homeliness in their loneliness. One longs to warm and help them, brave creatures, and replace their dear one who cannot come."[34] Two days later, she wept as she, Empress of Russia, attended the young officer's funeral.

By the second half of 1915, Alexandra had become too tired—and too distracted by politics—to assist daily at operations the way she had done in 1914. But she still visited the wards to sit with the dying. As she put it herself in a letter to Nicholas, "My consolation when I feel very down and wretched is to go to the very ill and try to bring them a ray of light and love."[35] A second motherly attachment developed. This time, the young officer had a septic leg that was beyond amputation, and death was inevitable. Daily Alexandra sat with the "boy" (as she called

---

[31] Alexandra to Nicholas II, November 19, 1914 (A. 62), in Fuhrmann, *Complete Wartime*, 43.
[32] Ibid.
[33] Alexandra to Nicholas II, November 27, 1914 (A. 89) in Fuhrmann, *Complete Wartime*, 56.
[34] Alexandra to Nicholas II, March 2, 1915 in Fuhrmann, *Complete Wartime*, 86–87.
[35] Alexandra to Nicholas II, October 1, 1915 (A. 504) in Fuhrmann, *Complete Wartime*, 257.

him) while he lay dying. At her prompting, Nicholas sent the young man a personal message, thanking him for the sacrifice he had made for his country. And when he died, Alexandra telephoned his mother herself from her phone in the Alexander Palace. Again, the absence of any horror at disease or death, the absence of any fear of touching or being touched by a commoner, is remarkable in a woman who was, after all, a Sovereign's consort.[36]

Indeed, if the sufferings or "passion" of such young men are taken as symbolical of those of their generation, then to read these stories is almost to picture Alexandra, veiled in the nun-like uniform of the Sisters of Mercy, cradling the broken bodies of Russia's war dead in her arms, as at the center, symbolically, of a wartime Russian *Pietà*: while the flower of Russia's youth "clings" (in Alexandra's own words) to her in their final breaths, Russia's last *tsaritsa*, grieving over the human face of Imperial Russia's stricken youth, "strokes" their heads in trust that God will receive Russia's sacrifice.[37] And if this analogy is not blasphemous it is because for Alexandra, nursing was a Christian vocation, and, by training as a nurse, she was allowing herself to become an instrument of God's own love. "I wanted to go to church every day [this week]," she wrote to Nicholas, "and only got there once, such a pity as it is such a help when the heart feels sad. We always place candles [before the icons] before we go to the hospital and [I] like to pray for God and the Holy Virgin to bless the work of our hands and to let them bring healing to the ill "[38] The Church's faith was simply the center of her life. On her and Nicholas's twentieth wedding anniversary in November 1914, she asked, in reference to the Russian tradition of devotion to Mary's veil, the "sweet Virgin [to] spread her mantle of love around" her husband.[39] When she heard the bell of the nearby Church of Our Lady of the Sign beginning to toll for the liturgy, she was inspired to go and light a candle in front of the icons for her husband.[40] Back at the hospitals, the wounded and dying called out for her if she was passing. Alexandra, apparently, never refused any of them. "With her arm under his head she would speak words of comfort and encouragement, praying with him while preparations for the operation were in progress, her

---

[36] Indeed, it wouldn't be repeated in a senior member of a major European royal family until the time of Diana, Princess of Wales, eight decades later. Only, of course, in 1915, there were no television cameras.

[37] Given the prominence of references to Mary in her letters, it cannot have been lost on Alexandra that, as *tsaritsa*, she shared her title with the Mother of Christ, "Queen," or, to Russians, *tsaritsa*, "of Heaven."

[38] Alexandra to Nicholas II, September 24, 1914 (A. 24) in Fuhrmann, *Complete Wartime*, 23.

[39] Alexandra to Nicholas II, November 17, 1914 (A. 57), in Fuhrmann, *Complete Wartime*, 39.

[40] Alexandra to Nicholas II, April 8, 1915 (A. 236) in Fuhrmann, *Complete Wartime*, 108.

own hands assisting in the merciful work of anaesthesia ... the dying smiled as she knelt beside their beds murmuring last words of prayer and consolation."[41]

And in a way that tends, again, to refute the idea that her religion was somehow less than fully Orthodox, at the center of her spiritual life were the Church's sacraments. "Thank God we shall have the blessing of Holy Communion together tomorrow—it will give strength and peace," she wrote to Nicholas in October 1914. As we have seen, at that time, it was customary for the Orthodox laity to receive the Body and Blood of Christ only once or twice a year. But in this respect, too, Alexandra was anticipating some of the trends of modern Orthodoxy. She rejected, as she wrote in the same letter to Nicholas, the idea that receiving the Holy Mysteries should be looked on as a "duty" to be performed only out of obligation, only occasionally. On the contrary. Alexandra looked on the Holy Mysteries in much the "pioneering" way Father John of Kronstadt had done, as a source of joy and comfort that the soul should avail itself of whenever it needed it. "Shyness and false pride keep many away," she said, Alexandra wrote to Nicholas. But as a nurse she would make it part of her mission to encourage "everyone" to take Holy Communion regularly. To Alexandra, this included not only the wounded in hospital, but also the soldiers fighting at the front. So fearful was she that Holy Communion wasn't being offered the troops frequently enough that she sent bread and wine to the army chaplains on the front line at her own expense. The issue still preoccupied her almost a year later.[42] At Easter 1915, she wrote to Nicholas that she would encourage all the officers in her hospitals that were well enough to "come to church with her on Sundays and receive Holy Communion."[43]

Neither was it the souls of merely *Russian* soldiers she was concerned for. When she heard that Catholic German and Austro-Hungarian prisoners-of-war, while being offered the opportunity of seeing a priest for confession, were nonetheless being denied Holy Communion, she wrote to Nicholas in protest, declaring the practice "quite wrong," and begging him to do something about it.[44] True to the British side of her upbringing, Alexandra was nothing if not a Victorian missionary, only for Eastern Orthodoxy. Traveling to Vilnius/Vilna to visit military hospitals, she distributed icons and Bibles. It was another activity in which she had her husband's full support. A letter from him to her in April has him asking her to arrange for the sending of no fewer than

---

[41] Vyrubova, *Memories*, 53–54.

[42] Alexandra to Nicholas II, August 26, 1915 (A. 399) in Fuhrmann, *Complete Wartime*, 183–84.

[43] Alexandra to Nicholas II, January 29, 1915 (A. 164) in Fuhrmann, *Complete Wartime*, 79.

[44] Alexandra to Nicholas II, May 10, 1915 (A. 309) in Fuhrmann, *Complete Wartime*, 130.

13,000 icons for the men of the eleven *plastuni* regiments of dismounted Cossack marksmen he had just reviewed.[45] We might think of it as a kind of "charity" *teokratia*.

In addition to her nursing duties and self-appointed "mission work," in the first twelve months of the war Alexandra had a small empire of her own to administer — an empire of hospitals, at Tsarskoye Selo, and sanatoria, in Crimea, that she had founded and which she was, at least notionally, ultimately responsible for administering. One Sunday alone she visited no fewer than forty medical establishments in Tsarkoye Selo and nearby towns after church. Sleepless that night on account of the various administrative questions still running through her mind, she got up and spent the remaining night hours packing devotional literature for distribution among the soldiers at the front. At last, she told her husband, she understood something of the demands upon him as emperor.[46]

Reflecting the newfound sense of confidence and purpose her nurse's costume gave her, Alexandra, having rarely appeared in public for years, traveled about Russia far more than she had ever done before the War. Traveling between Tsarskoye Selo and Stavka, she insisted on stopping overnight at towns such as Pskov, Luga, Vilnius/Vilna, and Vitebsk, to visit their military hospitals and schools for nursing sisters. On one such visit to a hospital, she sat down and spent the morning setting bandages. In such settings she was in her element. Visiting Vilna, she inspected the local hospitals, as well as "two completely overcrowded sanitary trains."[47] Totally focused on nursing, she reported to her husband the number of wounded and the often inadequate conditions she believed they were being held in. She knew that her nurse's uniform wouldn't "be welcome at Stavka": *there* she knew she had to be *empress*.[48] But she wanted to be of use, and her gift, she believed, was nursing. "Such a pity I cannot get off now in a sanitary train! I long to be nearer the front... they should feel our proximity and gain courage."[49]

Naturally observant of life around her, Alexandra offered herself at this time as her husband's eyes and ears, reporting to him what she believed to be the human realities of wartime that he might otherwise have missed. In December 1914, she urged Nicholas to allow American observers into Russian prisoner-of-war camps, and begged him to put pressure on his cousin Grand Duke Nikolai Nikolaevich to improve the arrangements for the wounded granted leave for recovery. These

[45] Nicholas II to Alexandra, April 18, 1915 (N. 275) in Fuhrmann, *Complete Wartime*, 122.
[46] Alexandra to Nicholas II, November 21, 1914 (A. 71 and 72) in Fuhrmann, *Complete Wartime*, 47–49.
[47] Alexandra to Nicholas II, November 22, 1914 (A. 321) in Fuhrmann, *Complete Wartime*, 49.
[48] Alexandra to Nicholas II, October 31, 1914 (A. 56) in Fuhrmann, *Complete Wartime*, 41.
[49] Alexandra to Nicholas II, November 24, 1914 (A. 79) in Fuhrmann, *Complete Wartime*, 52.

should be returned to the towns from which they came, she advised, so that they might be cared for by their families, not deposited "where by chance the sanitary train has brought them."[50] She protested against any inhumanity in the treatment of prisoners, and was determined to "make a good row," as she put it, about the decision to transfer convalescing German and Austro-Hungarian troops from Moscow to the provincial center of Kazan. Many were not fit to travel so far and risked death. When she heard reports in the hospital that Russian officers were being punished by the commanders for not returning quickly enough to the front, she was equally distressed and begged her husband to "help out here." Such men were risking life and limb for their country, and "one doesn't want bitterness setting in their poor hearts."[51] She took their cause up again the following year. Whereas the law provided for an officer to keep his pay for up to nine months of convalescence, Alexandra pointed out that some needed treatment for up to a year. "They lose their pay—and some are so poor they have no fortune of their own—it does seem unjust. Crippled, not always for life, but for a time, doing their duty bravely, wounded and then like beggars—their moral sufferings become so great. Others hasten back [to active duty] too early in order not to lose all and many completely lose their health for that."[52]

Then, back in Tsarskoye Selo's hospitals, the ever-vigilant Alexandra also noticed that officers discharged from the hospital and sent back to the front were returning a second time for treatment. One she had often sat with while convalescing earlier in the War had just died, after returning, wounded again, to her in the Catherine Palace, she reported to Nicholas in January 1915.[53] "Would to God that this hideous war could end quicker," wrote Alexandra.[54] "Well, we all knew that such a war would be the bloodiest and most awful one ever known and so it has turned out," she wrote, at a time when many of her contemporaries were still inclined to think of it as a "gallant" undertaking, soon to be concluded.[55] The first year of Russia's Great War was Alexandra's finest hour.

 basic ses basic

---

[50] Alexandra to Nicholas II, December 12, 1914 (A. 111) in Fuhrmann, *Complete Wartime*, 61.

[51] Alexandra to Nicholas II, March 2, 1915 (A. 184) in Fuhrmann, *Complete Wartime*, 85.

[52] Alexandra to Nicholas II, May 12, 1915 (A. 315) in Fuhrmann, *Complete Wartime*, 133.

[53] Alexandra to Nicholas II, January 29, 1915 (A. 164), in Fuhrmann, *Complete Wartime*, 79.

[54] Alexandra to Nicholas II, November 21, 1914 (A. 72), in Fuhrmann, *Complete Wartime*, 48.

[55] Alexandra to Nicholas II, November 26, 1914 (A. 55) in Fuhrmann, *Complete Wartime*, 55.

A hundred years on, Russia's Great War remains, in the popular imagination, a litany of disasters, one that, by finally and decisively exposing the incompetence of tsarism, led to the latter's justified collapse. But did the War really expose the incompetence of the "Old Regime"? Or was it merely cast as doing so by those wishing to establish a new one? The impression that, from the start, Russia's war performance was uniformly disastrous is incorrect. To be sure, there were defeats. At the Battle of Tannenberg (26–30 August) and again, fourteen days later, at the Battle of the Masurian Lakes (7–14 September), the Germans devastated the Russian Second Army and drove the Russian First Army back across the border. But in Russia in 1914, no one believed that these defeats in the forests of East Prussia foretold general Russian defeat. On the contrary, Russian morale remained high, buoyed by sweeping victories over Russia's other adversary, Austria-Hungary. As we have seen, just as Tannenberg was reaching its climax, the Battle of Galicia pitted the Russian and Austro-Hungarian armies against each other on the rolling farmland north of the Carpathians. In mid-September, the battle resulted in a great and decisive Russian victory, when the Russian army, fulfilling a centuries-old Russian ambition, occupied the Galician capital of Lemberg/Lvov, the westernmost of all the lost territories of the old Kievan commonwealth. Thereafter, the Russians laid siege to the last surviving Austro-Hungarian fortress on the northern side of the Carpathians at Przemysl, in modern Poland. Austro-Hungarian authorities rushed an army from Serbia to the Carpathians, to try to hold off the Russians. But Przemysl fell the following February, 1915, to general Russian rejoicing. Austria-Hungary had been dealt a body blow.

Indeed, to an external observer, it was not Russia but Austria-Hungary that began 1915 looking down the barrel at defeat. The Habsburg empire had lost an entire province. One third of the total forces with which the Habsburgs had begun the war in all theaters were dead, wounded or prisoners. Moreover, the victory in Galicia was seen in Russian eyes as reflecting the judgment of God, in a way the East Prussian battles were not. Certainly, Nicholas II was deeply attuned to what he called the "historical and religious significance of Galicia's return to Mother Russia," words he never used of the battles in East Prussia.[56] Nicholas, we might say, was reading the war symbolically, taking it on faith that God was a providential participant in it, and that its outcome would have a religious-historical meaning. From the outlook of such *faith*, tsarism remained a very much going proposition — and so did Russia.

And yet for all that his opponents had created the impression of an emotionally stunted monarch, indifferent to his people's sacrifices and

---

[56] Alexandra to Nicholas II, April 11, 1915 (A. 248) in Fuhrmann, *Complete Wartime*, III.

plight, Nicholas II never forgot the cost at which the great victory in Galicia had been bought: God acted in history, but he did so through ordinary human lives, the tragic cost of which did not go unnoticed by Nicholas. Indeed, while the battle for Galicia was still raging, Nicholas, who was visiting Stavka at Baranovici at the time, drove out to an army encampment on the village's outskirts, recently deserted on account of its occupants' transfer to the front. Nicholas's recorded impressions reveal to what extent the men of his army were never, for him, mere cannon fodder. "Yesterday, I motored out for twenty-four versts [sixteen miles] and walked in a pretty wood and through the camp of the Fourth Army Corps.... The little huts in which officers live bear their names, surrounded with little gardens with benches, gymnastic and different amusements for children. I thought with anguish of those who shall probably never return there." The same concern for the human cost of war, even in victory, returned when, in early April 1915, Nicholas embarked on a victory tour of conquered Galicia. Thus, traveling from Tsarskoye Selo for Lvov in early April, he noted in his diary that the journey through the battlefields of Galicia left him "full of the deepest impressions . . . lots of graves of our soldiers."[57] And, typically, arriving in Przemysl, Nicholas's first act was to attend a local hall that had been converted into an Orthodox church for a *Te Deum* or formal liturgy of thanksgiving.

In the early spring of 1915, therefore, Nicholas and Alexandra's general sense was that, thanks to God's Providence, Russia's war was just going well, and would, in time, result in a general Russian victory. Much of the Russian population appeared to believe the same. Thus when, from Galicia, Nicholas proceeded through Ukraine to Odessa on the Black Sea, he received an enthusiastic reception, with cheering crowds lining the streets. "On the way to the cathedral [for another *Te Deum*] there was a mass of troops, officials and people. The arrival was amazing," he recorded in his diary.[58] From Odessa he continued to the shipyards at Nikolaev, to inspect the *Imperatritsa-Mariya* dreadnoughts under construction there. It is "wonderfully interesting and comforting to see what our people are capable of when they set to work in earnest," he wrote to Alexandra, brimming with optimism after visiting the shipyards.[59] And when he continued from there to Sevastopol in Crimea to review the graduation of officers and Cossacks, the men's evident loyalty and goodwill made it what Nicholas called "a singular pleasure to look into their faces."[60] By the twenty-second of the month, he was back at Tsarskoye Selo, and full of thanksgiving and confidence. "What

---

[57] Nicholas II to Alexandra, April 9, 1915 (N. 242) in Fuhrmann, *Complete Wartime*, 110.
[58] Nicholas II, April 14, 1915 in Diary (2), 524.
[59] Nicholas II to Alexandra, April 18, 1915 (N. 271) in Fuhrmann, *Complete Wartime*, 120.
[60] Nicholas II, April 16, 1915, in Diary (2), 524.

a bright joy it is to see the family," Nicholas wrote in his diary. Alexandra attributed it all to God. "You have personally conquered thousands of hearts, I feel, by your sweet, gentle and humble being and shining pure eyes," Alexandra had written to him during the journey: "Each conquers through what God gives him — each in his own way."[61] For Nicholas, Alexandra believed, that gift was not a great or commanding personality, which she knew her husband did not have, but rather something much more precious. *faith.* Bulgakov would have recognized its significance: in the presence of the God he had encountered. Nicholas's confession was a continual "YOU ARE" and "I believe."

ཐ   ཐ   ཐ

As 1915 wore on, however, both Nicholas's and Alexandra's faith was tested. Would God bring the war to a victorious conclusion for Russia after all? Even as the great victories in Galicia were unfolding, there had been hints of brewing trouble. The first was that by the end of December 1914, Russian arms stores were gravely depleted. The Russians, like all the Great War's belligerents, had reckoned with a short war of, at most, several months' duration. They had prepared accordingly, but now that those weapons stocks were exhausted, Russia, unlike the more industrialized Britain, France, and Germany, lacked the industrial base to replenish them. Moreover, thanks to the German blockade of the Baltic, and the failure of the British attempt to take the Dardanelles in the Gallipoli campaign, Russia was now isolated from its Allied partners, Britain and France. Without the ability to import armaments from them, or from the United States, a potentially disastrous shortage of arms was looming.

Then, in February, the Germans mauled another Russian army in East Prussia. This was no more a body blow to the total Russian army than other engagements in East Prussia. Altogether more worrying, from the point of view of Russia's political stability, was the response adopted to it by Stavka. Rather than allowing the army's upper command to accept a portion of the blame, Nikolai Ianushkevich, chief of staff to the army's supreme commander, Grand Duke Nikolai Nikolaevich, found a scapegoat in a minor Russian intelligence service officer by the name of S. N. Miasoyedov, who was accused of passing secrets to the enemy. If this was dangerous to Nicholas and the future of tsarism, it was because Miasoyedov was a client of the current Russian War Minister, Sukhomlinov, whom Nicholas had appointed in 1912 to thwart Guchkov's bid at that time to wrest military appointments from the tsar. Indeed, in accusing Miasoyedov of treason, Ianushkevich was merely reviving an accusation that the Octobrist leader Guchkov had

---

[61] Alexandra to Nicholas, April 11, 1915 (A. 248) in Fuhrmann, *Complete Wartime*, 112.

first made three years before, in 1912, when, in a bid to discredit Suk-homlinov, and, through him, the monarchy, Guchkov falsely accused Miasoyedov of passing secrets to the Austrians.

Today, historians have concluded that both accusations, Guchkov's in 1912 and Ianushkevich's in 1915, were false, and that both Guchkov and Ianushkevich themselves knew it.[62] Miasoyedov was convenient merely for striking at Sukhomlinov, a man both Guchkov and Ianushkevich detested, albeit for different reasons: Guchkov, because Sukhomlinov, as a crown appointee, offended his belief that the Duma and not the tsar should possess executive control of the armed forces; Ianushkev-ich, because he resented Sukhomlinov's right, as Minister of War, to interfere in Stavka's prosecution of the war. In any case, the stratagem worked. When, at the end of a hastily convened court-martial, Miasoye-dov was found guilty and hanged the same day, suspicion fell inexorably on his patron, Sukhomlinov. It was the Duma's turn to fan the flames of outrage. It duly did so, with established critics of the government, such as Guchkov and the Duma President, Mikhail Rodzianko, joining the young Socialist Revolutionary deputy Aleksandr Kerensky to denounce Sukhomlinov as, in effect, a German spy, protected by unnamed forces at court. Given the empress's background as a German princess, this could only mean Alexandra herself.

Finally, there was Rasputin. As we have seen, the Siberian *starets*-pilgrim had seen relatively little of Nicholas and Alexandra when he was stabbed in the stomach two weeks before the assassination of Archduke Franz-Ferdinand in June 1914. Despite all Rasputin had done to dis-suade Nicholas from allowing events in the Balkans to entangle Russia in war, Nicholas had ignored these warnings, and followed his own course: in 1914, Rasputin, despite Guchkov's shrill claims of two years before, was *still* not a politically significant figure. But later, it seems, after the fighting had broken out, Nicholas could not help but recog-nize Rasputin's wisdom. Perhaps for this reason, then, when Rasputin, having recovered from his wounds, returned to the capital (a city the authorities had now renamed Petrograd, to erase the German overtones of its original name) in September 1914, Nicholas began receiving him regularly. The first such visit by Rasputin to Nicholas II during the Great War took place at the Alexander Palace on September 14/27, when Nicholas recorded in his diary that he sat "a long time" with the peas-ant. A fortnight later, Nicholas "saw and long talked" with Rasputin again. On October 7/20, Nicholas had another "good discussion with Gregory." Nicholas clearly derived comfort from these discussions. This was never clearer than ten days later, on October 17 (the day after the

---

[62] See William C. Fuller, *The Foe Within: Fantasies of treason and the end of imperial Russia* (Ithaca, NY: Cornell University Press, 2006).

Turkish shelling of Sevastopol), when Nicholas found himself in a "violent mood on account of the Germans and Turks." As he recorded in his diary, "Only in the evening under the influence of a calming conversation with Gregory did my soul retrieve its equilibrium."[63] Just over a fortnight later, Nicholas, seeing Rasputin again, had another "comforting talk." Under the spiritually intensifying effects of the Great War on Nicholas, Rasputin was recovering the role that had originally seen him enter Nicholas's confidence, as a prophet from among the ordinary Orthodox people, sent by God to help him bear the burden of the Russian *teokratia*.

This pattern of visits continued in 1915, with Nicholas noting a conversation with Rasputin in his diary every two to three weeks. These conversations apparently remained of a purely spiritual nature. They did not touch on politics; there is no evidence that Rasputin made suggestions for ministerial appointments or offered advice on policy, except where it concerned Nicholas's prestige as tsar. And even then, Nicholas received Rasputin's counsels as advice, not instructions. Thus, when Rasputin questioned the advisability of Nicholas's tour of Galicia (which Rasputin considered premature: the war, after all, Rasputin pointed out, had not yet been won), Nicholas ignored him, as he had done during the July Crisis, and proceeded with the tour anyway.

And yet despite the limited nature of Rasputin's influence at the beginning of 1915, some in Nicholas's entourage and the Okhrana — which had long since concluded that Rasputin was a gift in the hands of tsarism's enemies — were alarmed at Rasputin's increasingly frequent pattern of meetings with Nicholas. Their fears seem to have given rise to one of the most infamous, extraordinary, and damaging scandals involving Rasputin of all time: the incident at the Yar Restaurant in Moscow, where, on March 26, 1915, Rasputin, allegedly drunk and surrounded by gypsy prostitutes, was said to have exposed himself before the packed restaurant, before boasting of his sexual exploits over the empress.

෮෮   ෮෮   ෮෮

On April 18/May 1, the German army unleashed the first instance of "saturation shelling" of the war, on a weak point in the Russian line southeast of Cracow. Designed to relieve the pressure on Germany's embattled Austro-Hungarian ally, the German offensive quickly developed into a devastating and apparently unstoppable onslaught. On May 21/June 3, the Central Powers re-entered Przemysl. On June 9/22 Lvov fell to them, too. By that stage, the Germans had inflicted 250,000 casualties, and had swept the Russians out of all their new conquests in Galicia. Naturally, given their religious outlook, Nicholas and Alexandra prayed that God

---

[63] Nicholas II, October 17, 1914, in Diary (2), 492.

would intervene to help Russia's army. "All our prayers must be heard no matter how hard it is now... I know your faith and trust in God," Alexandra wrote consolingly to Nicholas on May 9.[64] And yet it was to no avail; the rout continued. Nicholas's "humble" conquest — so recently a sure sign of God's favor! — had proved stunningly brief.

The problem was Russia's guns, or lack of them. The one Russian army corps holding the original center of the front southeast of Cracow possessed only four heavy guns to oppose to the two hundred of the Germans. The Germans possessed shells in such quantities that the Russian trenches would emerge from hours of continuous shelling utterly demolished; the Russians themselves were so short of munitions that they had to limit their reply of their heavy guns to a maximum of ten shells per gun per day. Whereas the Germans were capable of firing 700,000 shells in a few hours, it took Russian factories six months to produce an equivalent amount.[65] This crushing shortage of arms was of the essence of the notorious "Munitions Crisis" of 1915, during which the Russians often struggled to provide their men even with rifles.[66]

As the summer advanced, the news only worsened. There was little the Russians could do to fight back. Warsaw was abandoned on July 23/ August 5, and the great fortress at Brest a fortnight later. Vilnius, capital of modern Lithuania, fell in September. With these cities, territories that had been Russian for hundreds of years were lost. The turn of events weighed on Nicholas and Alexandra's spirits. "One gets at times so tired from suffering and anxiety and yearns for peace — oh, when will it come, I wonder? How many more months of bloodshed and misery?... God is not unjust, and I place all my trust in Him unswervingly — but it is such pain to see all the misery," wrote Alexandra to her husband.[67] Of course, she did not give up her faith. "One prays and one prays and yet never enough," Alexandra sighed during a brief respite in the German advance in June, "God must surely hearken unto our supplications and then send some success at last."[68] The only problem was that by the time God, apparently, did answer her and Nicholas's supplications, in spring 1916, it would be too late. In the meantime, the Great Retreat had precipitated the political crisis that would lead to the fall of tsarism — and this *despite* the government's astonishing success in resolving the munitions crisis that was the immediate cause of the Great Retreat itself.

---

[64] Alexandra to Nicholas, May 8, 1915 (A. 303) in Fuhrmann, *Complete Wartime*, 129.

[65] Oldenburg, *Last Tsar*, vol. 4: *The World War, 1914–1918*, 28–29.

[66] See Norman Stone, *Eastern Front, 1914–1917* (Harmondsworth: Penguin, 1998), 144–64.

[67] Alexandra to Nicholas II, May 4, 1915 (A. 287) in Fuhrmann, *Complete Wartime*, 124–25.

[68] Alexandra to Nicholas II, June 12, 1915 (A. 329) in Fuhrmann, *Complete Wartime*, 140–42.

The first symptoms of this political crisis were the anti-German riots that swept Russia's cities in May.[69] Alexandra was appalled. She herself had come to Russia as a German princess. Where did her loyalties lie? Were Russian soldiers being slaughtered in their thousands at the front, and the Russian army in headlong retreat, because Russia's war effort was being sabotaged *at the very top*? As nobody knew about Alexandra's care for the Russian wounded, these doubts, which, in time, crystallized into certainties, were firmly lodged from the spring of 1915 in the Russian public's mind.

Making it worse, responsibility for stoking these fears lay with Russia's own army high command, Stavka. Just as Ianushkevich had used Miasoyedov to deflect responsibility for Russia's difficulties in February, so, now, in May, it was Ianushkevich's idea to deflect responsibility for the Great Retreat by whipping up fears of fifth-columnist Jews and Germans. Millions of such people were therefore summarily expelled from their homes, precipitating a refugee crisis that threatened to overwhelm the capacity of the Russian home front to cope. Across Russia that spring, such a mass of humanity — 3.3m people — were on the move that some have described it as a "whole empire walking."[70] Once again, Alexandra rose to the occasion, reporting the human suffering she witnessed in the course of her relief work to Nicholas. "Masses of Jews and trains arrive with them from Courland [modern Latvia]," she wrote to Nicholas during a visit to the military hospitals of Vitebsk, then a Jewish-majority town in western Belarus: "A painful sight, with all their packages and wee children." She urged Nicholas to make sure the government did something to help these people discreetly, so as to prevent anti-Jewish pogroms. By the end of the summer, she was thinking in more concrete terms. "One ought really to do something more for the refugees — more food stations and flying hospitals — masses of children are homeless on the high road and others die.... It's bitterly painful to see. The government is working out questions for the fugitives [i.e. refugees] after the war, but it's more necessary to think of them [now]," she advised.[71] She made visits to five refugee camps in Russia's renamed capital of Petrograd, and made a point of reporting to Nicholas the difficulty refugees had in finding work. Those from

---

[69] On May 29/June 11, a violent crowd in Petrograd looted five hundred shops, offices and factories owned, or perceived as being owned, by Germans. In Moscow, more than two hundred private apartments were ransacked and six hundred people killed, most of them Russians with foreign-sounding surnames: McMeekin, *Russian Revolution*, 67.
[70] Peter Gatrell, *A Whole Empire Walking: Refugees in Russia during World War I* (Bloomington, IN: Indiana University Press, 2005), 3. Gatrell notes that once a further half million had been added to their number before the end of 1916, there were, in 1917, more refugees in the Russian Empire than there were members of the industrial proletariat.
[71] Alexandra to Nicholas II, August 28, 1915 (A. 413) in Fuhrmann, *Complete Wartime*, 190–92.

the Baltic provinces, she reported to her husband, often couldn't speak Russian.[72] The relief organization founded in the name of their second daughter, Grand Duchess Tatiana, would end up distributing aid to many of them.[73]

The second symptom of the political crisis precipitated by the Great Retreat was the renewed attack on Sukhomlinov, a minister of the tsar whose position was already weak through his associations with Miasoyedov. Now, Sukhomlinov was blamed for Russia's shortage of weapons.[74] Leading the attack was Guchkov. In *Golos Moskvyi*, Guchkov painted Sukhomlinov as hopelessly incompetent, even criminally negligent, thereby succeeding in reviving that spirit of liberal public opposition to the dynasty that had gone into abeyance the previous July with the declaration of the war against Germany. Nicholas understood the dangers. Yielding to the newspaper campaign, therefore, the tsar dismissed Sukhomlinov on June 12/25. Concessions were needed, and Nicholas was prepared to make them, so long as the fundamental theocratic nature of the Russian regime was not altered. Nicholas even agreed to the formation of a legal commission to investigate formal police charges against Sukhomlinov for negligence leading to the Munitions Crisis and, if evidence arose, treason.

It was a huge win for Guchkov and the re-emergent liberal opposition. In Sukhomlinov's place as Minister of War, Nicholas appointed Guchkov's close ally, Sukhomlinov's former deputy, Aleksandr Polivanov. Repaying the favor to his ally, Polivanov then appointed Guchkov to head the newly-founded War-Industry Committee, a body set up to promote cooperation between the government and private industrialists in the production of armaments. No longer a member of the Duma, Guchkov thus gained a platform that enabled him to present himself as a leader of society. But Guchkov's ambitions went further even than that. With its base in Moscow, Guchkov's War Industry Committee

---

[72] Alexandra to Nicholas II, September 5, 1915 (A. 435) in Fuhrmann, *Complete Wartime*, 206–7.

[73] Gatrell, *Whole Empire*, 125–26. Gatrell, rather meanly, seems to question how interested a royal princess could have been in such work, and complains that her part in it "reinforce[d] prescribed gender roles among those who volunteered to assist refugees." He does not mention Alexandra's efforts or her interest in refugees' plight, either. On the Tatiana Committee, see also Helen Rappaport, *The Romanov Sisters: The lost lives of the daughters of Nicholas and Alexandra* (New York: St Martin's, 2014), 235, 255–56.

[74] This was grossly unfair. Far from incompetent, Sukhomlinov oversaw during his time as minister a thirty-three percent increase in military spending: the Russian army's supplies of machine guns quadrupled, the first military airplanes were commissioned, and the Army's fleet of trucks and cars was enlarged. Indeed, says the leading historian of Russian grand strategy under the Romanovs, "Sukhomlinov was determined to prepare the Army for either of these eventualities to the best of his ability.... Sukhomlinov's reforms resulted in the optimal exploitation of reserve manpower.... If this system did not lead Russia to win the war in its first six months, it arguably at least prevented Russian defeat in the same period." See Fuller, *Foe Within*, 73. But that is not how it was seen in 1915.

was consciously being readied by Guchkov as Russia's "shadow govern-ment."[75] Meeting frequently with the heads of other civil society orga-nizations, such as Prince Georgi Lvov, head of Zemgor (the All-Russian Union of Zemstvos and Municipal Councils) and a prominent leader in the liberal Kadet Party, the mayor of Moscow and the rich industrialists, A. I. Konovalov, at whose mansion the group met, Guchkov and his friends plotted ways of discrediting the government while enhancing the reputation of their own organizations. When, eventually, the tsar capitulated to the pressure, and surrendered executive control of the government to civil society, the leaders of the War Industry Committee, Zemgor and the other groups mentioned above, would be ready to fill the vacated posts of the tsar's ministers.

That this win had been bought at the cost of one innocent man's life (Miasoyedov's) and another's freedom (Sukhomlinov would later be arrested) seemed in no way to trouble Guchkov, Polivanov, or their associates. On the contrary, the lesson they took away from it was that, if pushed sufficiently hard with accusations that, if unaddressed, threatened the Russian war effort, Nicholas would capitulate to society's demands. Wartime, Guchkov and others concluded, was the perfect time for the Duma to resume its pursuit of wresting from the tsar the holy grail of executive control of the government, the transformation of the Russian *teokratia* into a purely constitutional monarchy run, in fact, by professional politicians.[76]

Indeed, in mid-1915 Russia's politicians found the truth of this con-firmed everywhere they turned. In June and again in July, Nicholas made further concessions, in a bid to unite government and society for the sake of the war effort. Ignoring the advice of both Alexandra and Rasputin (who, for reasons we will address below, was now assuming a more decisively political role as the imperial couple's advisor), he dis-missed three further ministers (of the interior on June 6, holy synod on July 5, and justice on July 6) known for the hostile views held of them in the Duma. Meanwhile, on June 14/27 Nicholas announced that the Duma, in recess since January, would reconvene to help the government prosecute the war. Censorship of the press was relaxed. Yet rather than promoting the reconciliation of government and society, Nicholas's actions in mid-1915 only furthered the country's political polarization. As we shall see, rather than stabilizing, Russian politics were entering

---

[75] McMeekin, *Russian Revolution*, 71.
[76] Cf. Lieven, *Towards the Flame*, 349: "Liberal politicians were well aware of the fact that failure in the Crimean and Japanese wars had led to a weakening of the autocratic regime and progress to what they saw as Russia's predestined liberal future. They hoped that Russia's setbacks in the First World War would have the same result." Of course, it's a short step from *hoping to exploit the opportunities created by setbacks* to *hoping for*, and *helping to bring about*, the setbacks themselves.

a period of unrelieved crisis that stemmed from disagreement between the tsar and society's representatives in the Duma about fundamental constitutional principles.

One symptom of this was a change in the ambitions and role of Rasputin. For it was at this time, when the pressures on the monarchy arising from the Great Retreat were at their severest, that Rasputin's enemies in Nicholas and Alexandra's entourage decided to act to discredit the peasant once and for all, by concocting the story of Rasputin's night at the Yar mentioned above. Rasputin, we now know as a fact, *was* at the Yar that night. But he was not drunk, was not surrounded by prostitutes, did not expose himself and did not boast of sexual intimacy with the empress. Rather, those elements of the story were invented by the Moscow Okhrana on the order of the deputy minister of the interior, Major-General Dzhunkovsky, between the end of May and the end of the beginning of June, two months *after* Rasputin was in Moscow.[77] Dzhunkovsky then presented Nicholas with the doctored police report of Rasputin's allegedly gross misbehavior a few weeks later, on June 21, exactly a week after Nicholas's gesture of conciliation to reconvene the Duma. Dzhunkovsky's plan, it seems, was to deny the revived liberal opposition the opportunity of using Rasputin as a weapon in their ongoing plan to discredit the government, by removing him from Nicholas's confidence once and for all, on the grounds, if need be, of fictitious allegations.

It had precisely the opposite effect to the one Dzhunkovsky intended. When Nicholas communicated the contents of Dzhunkovsky's doctored police report to Alexandra, it elicited from her an outburst usually taken as an example of reactionary politics and conspiratorial delusions. Thus, she wrote to her husband:

> "Ah, my Love, when at last will you thump them with your hand upon the table & scream at Dzh[unkovsky] & others when they act wrongly? — one does not fear you — & one must — they must be frightened of you.... If Dzh[unkovsky] is with you, call him, tell him to tear it up & not dare to speak of Gr[igory] as he does & that he acts as a traitor & not as a devoted subject.... Oh, my Boy, make one tremble before you — to love you is not enough, one must be afraid...!"[78]

And, indeed, paranoid and reactionary is precisely how such a letter would seem if we did not know, as we do now, that Dzhunkovsky was concocting evidence to frame Rasputin and, with outright lies told to Nicholas's face, trying to deceive his own tsar, in the middle of a world war. As it is, however, we must give Alexandra credit for seeing through Dzhunkovsky's stratagem, and for urging on her husband the importance of finding better and more trustworthy servants.

---

[77] See Smith, *Rasputin*, 376–77.   [78] Quoted in Smith, *Rasputin*, 378.

For this reason, although the Yar affair never happened, it was of decisive political significance.[79] In its aftermath, Rasputin obtained the complete immunity from accusation in Alexandra's eyes that he had lacked before. Henceforth, Alexandra would dismiss any and every report of Rasputin's misdoings as calculated inventions, and would have little trouble in persuading her husband to do the same. No less significantly, Dzhunkovsky's bid to abuse his powers as a government minister to dislodge Rasputin from his cozy position inside Nicholas and Alexandra's family circle for the first time aroused serious political ambitions in Rasputin himself. Before the early summer of 1915, Rasputin had not been involved in politics, because there was no reason for him to be; his position rested on his personal favor with Nicholas and Alexandra, not the council of ministers. Dzhunkovsky's report changed this calculation. Rasputin now knew a minister could use his position to move against him. To look out for himself, therefore, Rasputin now had to take an interest in ministerial appointments, while, in Alexandra, he acquired a means to press them upon Nicholas. In this sense, Rasputin's political influence was a myth that became a reality through the very effort summoned to defeat it. Like Sukhomlinov's "incompetence" and Miascyedov's "treachery," that Rasputin's "influence" was an illusion hadn't stopped the Duma from alleging that it was real. It suited their political goals too well. On the chess board of history, all the pieces necessary to bring about the downfall of Russia's theocratic regime had been assembled.

Someone who appears to have intuited this meaning of events was Alexandra. Doubtless influenced by the false incident at the Yar, her attention shifted in the middle of 1915 from relief work to constitutional politics, her letters to Nicholas swelling with a new emphasis on "autocracy," on Nicholas's need to "command" and to impose his will on those around him. "If only you could be severe, my Love, it is so much necessary," she wrote to him in June 1915, in response to Nicholas's comments, in a letter to her, about the disarray prevailing at Stavka as the Germans advanced: "They must hear your voice and see displeasure in your eyes. They are too much accustomed to your gentle, forgiving kindness."[80] She began spending less and less time in

---

[79] As for Dzhunkovsky's concocted Yar incident, this did not enter into histories of the revolution until a version of it was reproduced in the 1920s in the memoirs of Bruce Lockhart, a British secret agent active in Russia during the Great War. In that memoir, Lockhart claimed to have been an eye-witness to Rasputin's behavior at the restaurant. And yet, extraordinarily, as Smith, Rasputin's most recent biographer, has demonstrated, the British secret agent was also lying: on the evening when the incident at the Yar was supposed to have occurred, Lockhart's secret service diaries, stored in London, show that he was not in Moscow at all, but hundreds of miles away in Kiev. Smith, *Rasputin*, 380.
[80] Alexandra to Nicholas II, June 10, 1915 (A. 320) in Fuhrmann, *Complete Wartime*, 134–35.

the operating room, and the attention she once devoted to questions of an organizational character she now lavished increasingly instead on political and constitutional subjects.

The source of Alexandra's half-understood conception of Russia as a *teokratia* was Rasputin. "He speaks much and beautifully," she writes to Nicholas a few days later, "and on what the Russian Empire is. Though other Sovereigns are anointed and crowned, only the Russian one is the real Anointed since three hundred years."[81] In garbled form here is, apparently, the idea that, while other European monarchs may be crowned and (some of them at least) anointed in a grand Church-administered coronation rite (as Alexandra's grandmother Queen Victoria was in the Protestant Church of England), only the Russian tsar ruled a polity that was still, institutionally, a *teokratia*, rather than some sort of internally secularized, parliamentary, and constitutional regime. (The reference to the "three hundred years" surely reflects the Romanov Tercentenary of 1913, but also, on Alexandra's part, a misunderstanding: Russia did not *become* a *teokratia* with the election of the first Romanov in 1613; a "theocratic" polity was what the first Romanov was elected *to*.) In any case, if this theory of sacred kingship (of "holy tsarist authority") was what Alexandra had been hearing from Rasputin, then it is worth noting that Rasputin seems to have intuited that the demand for a "ministry of public confidence" soon to be made by a coalition of liberal and Socialist parties in the Duma known as the "Progressive Bloc" possessed a theological significance that has often escaped later commentators.[82] Like all the constitutional strife that had roiled Russia since at least 1881, the Progressive Bloc's demands were motivated by a prior judgment for secularization.

For all its crudeness, then, Alexandra's lecturing of Nicholas on the religious basis of autocracy was a thermometer of the countervailing pressures raised by the Progressive Bloc. Slower than her husband, but quicker than many around her, Alexandra realized that the Bloc's formation in the summer of 1915 had brought into focus what the contest between Tsar and Duma was all about: whether political authority in Russia proceeded from God via the tsar (whether *political order* was, to speak more theologically, in fact a divine *procession*, even a Divine Name, *imaged* in the tsar) or was, in a Kantian sense, a phenomenon merely immanent to the human consciousness, not tied (how could it be?) to any higher metaphysics. And in this sense, the renewed contest between the tsar and the Duma of the summer of 1915 was a contest about *secularization*. Did the claims of God still extend to politics? How, in the

---

[81] Alexandra to Nicholas II, June 14, 1915 (A. 336), in Fuhrmann, *Complete Wartime*, 143–45.
[82] On the Progressive Bloc, see further below.

wake of the conclusions of nineteenth-century European philosophy, which all sensible people must surely subscribe to, could they? In her own way, Alexandra had had her "vision on the Yalta Embankment," only without Bulgakov's corresponding intellectual refinement, moral sensitivity, and sense of tragedy: for Alexandra in 1915–16, the autocracy (theocratic tsarism) was something to be clutched at all costs, as an end in itself rather than an *image* of the divine nature — an *idol* rather than an *icon*. For Bulgakov, by contrast, who grasped the distinction, Russia's tragedy flowed from the conflicting claims of a "Tsar-love" (devotion to the cosmic order and authority of God imaged in the tsar) and a "freedom-love" (commitment to a notion of human liberty, especially of conscience, that understood the latter as itself an image of the supra-cosmic *freedom* of God) that were both posited by the same deposit of Christian faith; for Alexandra, by contrast, there was no tragedy because there was, at least at this stage, Tsar-love *only*: order and authority, but no freedom.

Here, in Alexandra's lopsided conception of *teokratia*, there lay great danger, one that Bulgakov sensed, and wrote of in *Unfading Light*. For over against what he called "Germanism" — the false deification of man through the false, Kantian-style immanentization of reality in the "critical" (i.e. rational) human consciousness — Bulgakov identified a native Russian temptation that was this "Germanism's" twin opposite. He called it "Khlystism," the equally false deification of man through fetishization of the dogmatic (i.e. the "uncritical" or the irrational) and the sacred. Precisely the heresy of which Rasputin had been accused, "Khlystism" represented to Bulgakov the "ever-lurking temptation of Orthodoxy," in which "anthropology is replaced by anthropolatry, prayer by rapture . . . sacrament by ecstasy, religion by mysticism."[83]

Before the Great Retreat, it would not have been right to describe Nicholas's and Alexandra's religion in these terms. But from the middle of 1915 until the murder of Rasputin at the end of 1916, we are close, especially regarding Alexandra. Focused as the Empress was on the *man* who held her son's life in her hands, Alexandra was tempted not by the German, but by the Russian "immanentization" of religion: the reduction of Orthodoxy to fetish, the sacred embodied in a Siberian peasant. Indeed, in its own way, Khlystism had no quarrel with Kant, for Khlystism, too, conceded the *rational* impossibility of religion. To reject "Germanism," then, in the name of Alexandra's lopsided view of the Russian *teokratia*, wasn't enough. To do so *and* reject "Khlystism" *at the same time* — this was the mark of true Orthodox faith, of true Christianity — and, hence, of a properly assimilated theocratic principle. As Bulgakov put it, "To unite the truth of the one (i.e., the *critical*

---

[83] Bulgakov, *Unfading Light*, xl.

and the *immanent*: author's note) and the truth of the other (i.e., the *dogmatic* and *transcendent*), to find not a 'synthesis' but a vital unity, in lived experience to know God in the world and the world in God, this is the ultimate task of religious consciousness posed by its history."[84] The tragedy of 1915–17 is that Nicholas and Alexandra, whose religion as individuals and as a couple was never really reducible to Rasputin, failed to achieve it. Of course, they do not bear the blame alone. Uniting the "truth of God" and the "truth of the world" requires the world's cooperation too. In 1915–17, that responsibility was the Duma's and the Bloc's.

ळ   ळ   ळ

Throughout the summer of 1915, an intensification in Nicholas's whole spiritual life is discernible. Thus, the day before the Duma was to resume sitting, and on the eve of the feast of the family's special patron, St Serafim of Sarov, Nicholas and his daughters attended Vespers at the Fyodorov Sovereign Cathedral, and the following cross procession. The following day, the anniversary of Germany's declaration of war on Russia, the Duma met, and the Progressive Bloc first made its appearance. For Nicholas, it was doubly significant for being St Serafim's feast day, and the whole family attended Mass and took part in another cross procession. "All prayed very fervently," Nicholas noted in his diary.[85] Three days later, a Sunday, Nicholas was at Divine Liturgy again, and on the 23rd Warsaw was evacuated. The city would never return to Russian sovereignty. A week later, Alexei, Nicholas's heir, turned eleven. As usual, the family attended a liturgy at church in celebration, and Nicholas, mindful, perhaps, of the sacred duties that would one day form an integral part of the boy's inheritance, recorded this prayer in his diary: "Bless him, Lord, with health and the growth of his spiritual qualities."[86] Over the next week, the family was back in church twice, first for the baptism of the infant daughter of one of Nicholas's more distant cousins, the last member of the Romanov dynasty born before the Revolution, and then again for the Divine Liturgy on the Feast of the Transfiguration. Two days later still, Nicholas saw his priest for confession ahead of Holy Communion at the Sunday Divine Liturgy the following day, August 9/22: "Went to Mass at nine a.m. in the cave church [i.e. the crypt beneath the Fyodorov Sovereign Cathedral] and partook of the Holy Mysteries. What great comfort in these heavy days!"[87]

    In fact, it was likely that, at the conclusion of the Divine Liturgy mentioned above, Nicholas made one of the most fateful and widely criticized decisions of his reign: to dismiss his cousin, Grand Duke

---

[84] Ibid., xli.
[85] Nicholas II, July 19, 1915, in Diary (2), 539.
[86] Nicholas II, July 30, 1915, in Diary (2), 541.
[87] Nicholas II, August 9, 1915, in Diary (2), 542.

Nikolai Nikolaevich, from the Supreme Command of Russian armed forces, appoint himself in his place, and thereby fulfil his sacred duty to Russia. How Nicholas reached that decision, however, he did not relate in his diary, but in a letter he wrote to Alexandra a year later, on the event's anniversary. Significantly, the letter supports Stolypin and Kokovtsov's earlier eye-witness accounts of the "theocratic" style of Nicholas's governing habits. Thus, in August 1916, Nicholas wrote to his wife the following note:

"My thoughts surrounded you particularly last evening and this morning when you went to Holy Communion in our cozy underground church [at the Fyodorov Sovereign Cathedral]. It must be a year ago that we took it together during those hard days before my coming here. I remember so well that I was standing opposite our Savior's big picture upstairs in the big church when an interior voice seemed to tell me to make up my mind and write about my decision to Nikolasha [Grand Duke Nikolai Nikolaevich]."[88]

Recalling, then, the way Nicholas invited Stolypin to find in prayer before Christ's icon in his office at the Alexander Palace the courage to assume the chairmanship of the Council of Ministers, Nicholas, he tells us himself this time, was led to make what would be perhaps the single most important decision of his reign out of obedience to a message that he believed was addressed to him while in prayer before Christ's icon. This likely took place after Divine Liturgy in the lower chapel of the Fyodorov Sovereign Cathedral on August 9/22, a Sunday on which he, having purified his soul through confession the evening before, had also received Holy Communion. Truly, Nicholas knew *from the inside*, to quote again the words of St Gregory of Nazianzen, "what a mysterious thing kingly power is."

And yet if Nicholas felt led to assume the supreme command that day, he did not in fact make that decision immediately. Rather, for the better of two weeks, it seems, he sought confirmation of the message addressed to him through the icon, through attendance at the liturgy, and through private supplicatory prayer. Certainly, we know that, six days after the experience before the icon, Nicholas was back at Divine Liturgy for the Feast of the Virgin's Dormition (August 15/28). The same evening, he returned for Saturday Vespers ahead of the following Sunday's Divine Liturgy. Evidently, his heart was building towards the momentous decision: as if to obtain God's final blessing of it on August 21/September 2, he made, with Alexandra, a special visit to Petrograd, to pray before the capital's two most revered images: the icon of Our Savior in the chapel of the same name at Peter the Great's log cabin

---

[88] Nicholas II to Alexandra (N. 311), August 8, 1916, in Fuhrmann, *Complete Wartime*, 553–54.

(where, as we have seen, Russia's last monarch and his wife had surprised supplicants in 1914); and the icon of Our Lady of Kazan in the Kazan Cathedral on Nevsky Prospekt. Then, fortified, apparently, in the certainty of his decision through these prayers, Nicholas made his decision. The decisive day was August 22/September 3. "Lord, bless my trip and my decision!" he wrote that day in his diary.[89] The following day he left for Stavka, at its new location in Mogilev, and on the 24th he made the decision public and official. "Signed a rescript ... and a *prikaz* regarding the assumption by me of Supreme Command.... Lord, help and teach me!"[90] Nicholas had shown he believed that the "tsar's heart is in God's hands" as implicitly as Gregory of Nazianzen; indeed, he staked everything on it. Just as a version of Kant's nakedly "secular" rationality was uniting the opposition, God had moved to the center, not only of Nicholas's being, but of Russia's government.

As Nicholas surely knew it would, his decision to assume the supreme command met protest and consternation from Nicholas's ministers, from the Duma, and even from his own mother. When they learnt of the project, the Council of Ministers took the unprecedented, and frankly once inconceivable, action of writing collectively to Nicholas, begging him to change his mind — and of indirectly threatening to resign if he did not.[91] Significantly for our purposes, when Nicholas then rejected their appeal in a Council meeting two days later, he did so, it was said, "clutching an icon and sweating profusely."[92] Was it a smaller, portable version of the one through which he believed Christ had spoken to him? Certainly, he always remained obedient to the instruction he believed Christ had addressed to him.

The plan also had undeniable merits.[93] The first of these was that, precisely because Nicholas labored under no illusions regarding his own talents as a day-to-day commander, effective supreme control of operations would lie not with himself but with General M. V. Alekseev, a professional soldier of humble social background whom Nicholas appointed his chief-of-staff. Day to day, Alekseev was, from August 1915, the Russian Army's real supreme commander. Rather, the purpose was to end the bickering between the War Ministry and Stavka that had undermined Russia's ability to respond to the Germans during the Great Retreat, by unifying the direction of Russia's civilian government and active military operations under the unitary authority of the

---

[89] Nicholas II, August 22, 1915, in Diary (2), 544.
[90] Nicholas II, August 24, 1915, in Diary (2), 544.
[91] Pipes, *Russian Revolution*, 225.				[92] Ibid.
[93] Lieven enumerates many of these: *Towards the Flame*, 347. For what follows, see also Oldenburg, *Last Tsar*, 4:39–42.

tsar. With the one supreme authority overseeing both the War Ministry and Stavka, the harmful shifting of blame and cultivation of false accusations of treason that had characterized relations between them during the spring of 1915 would now become impossible. The dispassionate coordination of policy could be achieved, and morale would be strengthened. Moreover, with effective command of the army now in the hands of a professional, Alekseev, rather than in those of a grand duke who owed his appointment to membership of the dynasty, the quality of Russian dispositions would improve. Indeed, as the leading historian of the Great War's eastern front has noted, "constant talk of shell shortage, and the blaming of everything on upon it, concealed a much more important factor [in Russia's setbacks in 1915]: the increasing crisis of authority in the Russian army."[94] Nicholas's decision to assume personal command solved that crisis. With the tsar behind him, Alekseev's authority was clear and could not be questioned.

Contra many representations of events, therefore, professional soldiers, in contrast to the politicians, *welcomed* Nicholas's decision. Thus, Admiral Kolchak, when later interrogated by the Bolsheviks in Irkutsk the night before his execution, explained that the change of supreme command in 1915 had meant the professionalization of Stavka: the very fact, said Kolchak, that the emperor could be counted on *not* to interfere in the decision-making of a professional soldier, his chief-of-staff, General Alekseev, was "the guarantee of success in the war."[95] Indeed, the only mystery about the ministers' reaction to Nicholas's decision is why it horrified them at all: barely a month before they had recommended something remarkably similar, a "Supreme War Council" headed by the tsar that would put an end to what Katkov called the "high-handedness and incompetence" that new War Minister Polivanov had identified as prevailing at Stavka, with crippling effect on Russia's war effort.[96]

The real reason, then, why the Council of Ministers (save its Chairman Goremykin) reacted so violently to news of Nicholas's decision to assume the supreme command was political: the act frustrated the bid for power by the Duma's newly formed "Progressive Bloc"—a tactical coalition of the Duma's major parties that that brought Guchkov's Octobrists and Miliukov's liberal Kadets together with selected representatives of *both* the more right-wing nationalists *and* left-wing socialist revolutionaries. United in the goal of wresting executive control of the government from the tsar, the bloc had come into existence just days before Nicholas's announced assumption of the supreme command, when the Duma reopened on July 19/August 1 (the first

---

[94] Stone, *Eastern Front*, 165.
[95] Cited in George Katkov, *Russia, 1917: The February Revolution* (New York: Harper & Row, 1967), 141.   [96] Katkov, *Russia, 1917*, 141 ff.

anniversary of Russia's entry into the war). Nicholas had intended the reconvened Duma to help rally the Russian public to Russia's government-led war effort. But radicalized as they had been by 1915's events, the deputies had no intention of leaving Nicholas's authority uncontested. On the contrary, the formation of the Progressive Bloc, under the leadership of Duma President, Mikhail Rodzianko, was the most significant political event of the summer of 1915. Its plan to use the difficulties created by the War to force the liberalization of Russia's constitution made prolonged and embittered conflict with the government prosecuting that war inevitable (not least because an essential element of the Bloc's strategy consisted in discrediting that government without scruple, whether the allegations it hurled at it could be proved as true, or whether, like the earlier attacks on Miasoyedov and Sukhomlinov, it knew they could not).[97]

On August 25/September 3, the Bloc published a long list of demands. Connecting the Bloc to the thrust of Duma politics before the War, these included the Duma's oversight of military appointments that Guchkov had sought in 1908, as well as rights for the Empire's religious and ethnic minorities (including Jewish emancipation), the release of political and religious prisoners, autonomy for Poland, and enhanced local self-government in Finland and Ukraine. But its fundamental and governing demand was for a government "of persons enjoying the confidence of the public," a mixed "bureaucratic-parliamentary regime," in which Nicholas's existing ministers would co-operate transparently with the Duma and in which, when new ministerial appointments had to be made, the opinion of the Bloc would be respected. All of which is to say that, in practice, a "government of confidence" was to be a government over the appointment of ministers to which the Bloc would have a veto. It was also a calculated step towards a British-style constitutional monarchy, a path that would be extremely difficult for Nicholas to reverse after the War. Indeed, a few days later, in newspapers (such as Guchkov's) controlled by the Bloc, the Bloc published the names of a "dream ministry" that included its leading members and supporters from the voluntary organizations. Tellingly, the men named in these lists would be the same to take over the government of Russia in March 1917. As Pipes comments, "in terms of both personnel and program, the first revolutionary government may be said to have been conceived as early as August 1915, when Tsarism was still in charge and revolution seemed a remote prospect."[98]

---

[97] McMeekin, *Russian Revolution*, 69, who notes that this turn of events — the bid by the opposition to use the war to discredit the government and demand constitutional reform — had been as good as predicted by the conservative statesman Peter Durnovo, in a memorandum he circulated in February 1914. On the latter, ibid., 55–56.
[98] Pipes, *Russian Revolution*, 226.

Of course, Nicholas was unlikely to agree to this unheard-of, publicly declared challenge to the tsarist authority by a sitting Duma. But even more shocking to him was the support the Bloc evidently enjoyed among his own ministers. Indeed, it seemed that a relationship of near-transparent co-operation between the Duma and the tsar's ministers already existed. Thus, at a meeting of the Council of Ministers, the day after the publication of the Bloc's demands, the aged chairman, Ivan Goremykin, was shocked to discover that rather than rallying to the tsar, a majority of ministers wanted Nicholas to reach an accommodation with the Bloc. "The Bloc has been created to seize power," the often derided but prescient Goremykin warned: "Its barely concealed aim is the limitation of the tsar's power."[99] It said everything to Nicholas that his leading ministers—including Polivanov, the war minister, Sazonov, the foreign minister, and Krivoshein, the highly competent minister of agriculture touted as a new Stolypin and future council chairman—did not deny this charge. Apparently, the idea, common to the Duma and ministers alike, was simply to force Nicholas to carry out the revolution by his own hand. Nicholas considered it a great betrayal: his own ministers had voiced their lack of confidence in Russia's governing system; the tsarist regime that employed them (in which authority was "by the grace of God, not popular dispensation") did not command their loyalty.

It is worth pausing over the brazenness of these developments. The *de facto* formation of a shadow government by the Bloc and his own ministers was a challenge to tsarist authority that no tsar who wished to preserve that authority could ignore. And Nicholas did not ignore it. Rather, he reasserted his prerogatives. Thus, on September 3/16 the Duma was prorogued. Then, the same month, Nicholas began dismissing the ministers who had favored capitulation to the Bloc. For the sake of Russia's war effort, Nicholas stayed his anger against Polivanov and Sazonov, who held on to their posts until dismissed in March 1916.

Thus, the imprudence of the course of action that the ministers, in combination with the Bloc, had embarked on in the summer of 1915 became immediately clear. A sovereign cannot have, as advisors, men or women who dispute the very nature of the regime the sovereign heads. By presenting Nicholas with an ultimatum, they had left him isolated, failing to recognize the immovability of the religious conviction on which his commitment to the existing tsarist regime was founded; but Nicholas, as sovereign, refused to blink. If the only men left who shared that vision were less competent than their predecessors, then so be it, Nicholas must have reasoned; these last must be the ones God had given. Ministers, however competent, will have to be chosen from among *them*. But how could Nicholas identify candidates for ministerial

---

[99] Cited in Katkov, *Russia, 1917*, 143–44.

appointment loyal to the theocratic principle? The full consequences of the council of ministers' collusion with the Progressive Bloc in the late summer were seen when, in answer that question, Nicholas filled the holes that had emerged in his cabinet by relying for advice on ministerial appointments, for the first time, on someone whom until now he had, despite the legend to the contrary, held at arm's length from the business of government: Rasputin. By the end of 1916, the nefarious influence of "Dark Forces" on Russia's government would be a chief item in the Bloc's charge sheet against the monarchy. What the Bloc had conveniently forgotten was that in attempting to force Nicholas to abandon a vision both of politics and of Russia that he could not in good conscience abandon without abandoning his religion, the Progressive Bloc and its allies in the Council of Ministers were themselves the one who had handed those "Dark Forces" that influence on a platter.

CHAPTER TEN

The Crisis of the *Teokratia*

I N 1915, A SATIRICAL ESSAY DID MORE THAN A
thousand speeches to demolish the authority of Nicholas II. Faced
with the apparently incomprehensible acts of a monarch whose
motivating considerations their own implicit judgment in favor of
secularization prevented them from understanding, the leaders of
the Progressive Bloc proceeded to ascribe Nicholas's decisions not to a
genuine conflict of principle but to "madness." Nothing put about by
Russia's liberal opposition popularized that idea better than the allegory of the "Mad Chauffeur" published by Vasily Maklakov—a lawyer,
freemason, and Kadet member of the Duma—in the Moscow newspaper, *Russkiye Vedemosti* in September 1915. Almost every student of the
Russian Revolution is familiar with it.

"Imagine that you are driving in an automobile on a steep and narrow road," Maklakov invited his readers. "One wrong turn of the steering wheel and you are irretrievably lost. Your dear ones, your beloved
mother, are with you in the car. Suddenly you realize that your chauffeur is unable to drive. Either he is incapable of controlling the car on
steep gradients, or he is overtired and no longer understands what he
is doing.... Fortunately, there are people in the automobile who can
drive, and they should take over the wheel as soon as possible. But it
is a difficult and dangerous task to change places with the driver while
moving. One second without control and the automobile will crash
into the abyss. There is no choice, however, and you make up your
mind; but the chauffeur refuses to give way... he is clinging to the
steering wheel.... Can one force him?... he mocks your anxiety and
your helplessness: 'You will not dare touch me!'"[1]

Printed in Moscow, a city teeming with the disgruntled members of
Russia's Voluntary Organizations close to the Bloc, and smarting from
the prorogation of the Duma, Maklakov's allegory was an extraordinary
piece of propaganda. On the one hand, like so much radical-progressive
rhetoric before and after it, it tied an existential outcome (in this case,
Russia's very survival: avoidance of the "abyss" that on all sides surrounded it) to what it claimed to be the making of a minimal, merely
technical or procedural change. Like an automobile, Russia was a piece of
machinery, one crucial but nonetheless small and interchangeable element
of which no longer functioned properly. Removing the tsar from behind

---

[1] Cited in Katkov, *Russia, 1917*, 178.

the wheel was, therefore, no big deal. No significant question of principle or "total functionality" was raised. Once this change had been made, all could continue as before, only healthily. As such, Maklakov's fable perfectly captured the self-confidence of the Bloc. Its members, of course, were confident they *did* know how to drive. Because of this confidence, no fewer than *three* secret plots for a palace coup ("to change the driver") would ultimately proceed from Maklakov's liberal, progressive milieu.

On the other hand, the terms of the allegory itself also adverted to (while, of course, still trivializing) a question of principle. Nicholas, after all, was "mad" only metaphorically. As anyone who met or saw him would have known, there was nothing wrong with his mind physiologically. Rather, Nicholas's "madness" was a reference to Nicholas's failure to adhere to the only kind or standard of rationality which men such as Maklakov and the rest of the Bloc respected: that is to say, Nicholas was "mad" because, in his "dogmatic" commitment to "authority by the grace of God, not popular dispensation," he did not subscribe, in the political domain, to the "critical" rationality of Kant. In short, Russia was careening to destruction because its ruler (who should have realized that he was merely an *administrator*) insisted instead on attributing his authority religious meaning because he confused what was in truth the naked human phenomenon of politics for some sort of substantial metaphysical reality founded on a fairy tale: God. Disguised beneath the rhetoric of minimalist, procedural change, the Bloc and its adherents wanted to change Russia fundamentally, *from within*.

Their project for a so-called "change of driver" was a revolution of theological-philosophical significance — if only, perhaps, they themselves could see it (which, of course, blinkered by the certainty of their own Kantian assumptions, they could not). For, as Bulgakov did not hesitate later to point out in the "rubble" of 1918, however, Maklakov was tragically and irretrievably wrong. As Bulgakov put it in the mouth of the conservative General who plays the advocate for the Old Regime in "At the Feast of the Gods," if men such as Maklakov "had understood anything about Russia, they would have known the stakes when they whispered about a 'change of driver' ... the vulgar expression of the day. ... They spoke of how a 'change of driver' would be painless for the army and the country. And I, an incorrigible romantic about autocracy, a utopian, felt myself to be the only sober one among madmen. They imagined that to change a ruler anointed by God is as easy as changing a coach driver, and that, having changed, they could go wherever they wanted. And off they went! ... Is it unpleasant now?"[2] Bulgakov's complaint was not only that although the men of the Bloc and Voluntary Organizations thought they could drive the car, it turned out that they

---

[2] Bulgakov, "At the feast of the gods," 79.

didn't know how to after all: within weeks of their coming to power in March 1917, power slipped from Maklakov and his associates' hands. (Maklakov himself, who had hoped to be Justice Minister in the Provisional Government, but was passed over in favor of Kerensky, ended his career as Russian ambassador in Paris; but once the Bolsheviks refused to recognize him as their man, he was in the less than ideal position of being an ambassador without a government to represent.) Far from recovering its proper course, the automobile careened more and more wildly under their direction towards the deepest and blackest corner of the abyss. Rather, Bulgakov's complaint was that the men of the Bloc had been induced to make this colossal mistake because they simply didn't understand what kind of regime Russia was or how, outside their own narrow, "Kantian" circle, Russians continued to conceive of politics in the "maximalist" terms inherited from centuries of exposure to the claims of Christian theocracy.

In the end, Bulgakov was saying, it was not "sensible" figures, such as the liberal (and "European") Guchkov, Miliukov, and Rodzianko, but a crank, an "unhinged" firebrand, such as the radical religious philosopher Dmitri Merezhkovsky, who had proved that he understood Russia, and the likely course of her future, better. As Merezhkovsky had hissed, nonetheless presciently, as far back as 1907:

> All the events of our revolution are known in Europe in the minutest detail, but their underlying meaning remains a mystery. Europe sees the body but not the soul of the Russian revolution . . . the Russian revolution is not only a political phenomenon; it is a religious one. This is what Europe understands only with difficulty. In your [European] eyes, we are merely going through the ordinary growing pains of social development, such as, in their time, all European countries have gone through, and we will end up the way you have; we will set our house in order and bridle ourselves with the muzzle of a parliament; we will rid ourselves of the extreme Socialists and anarchists and content ourselves, in place of the "City of God," with the old shop of constitutions, with the "even mean" of bourgeois democracy; that's the way it has been everywhere else and that is the way it will be with us.[3]

But, Merezhkovsky added, this was a mistake.

> We won't stop at a constitutional monarchy . . . even if it wanted to, the Russian monarchy could not give us a constitution. Only together with Orthodoxy can the Autocracy be toppled . . . And when both have fallen, a void will open in the people's political and religious conscience that the existing European forms of government will not be able to fill — not only constitutional monarchy

[3] Merezhkovsky, *Tsar et la révolution*, 73.

but also the bourgeois, democratic republic. By the same token, to overthrow these two, age-old monoliths, the Autocracy and Orthodoxy, an earthquake so violent will be required that all the old parliamentary stalls will collapse like a house of cards. The revolution will not stop at any of them...When you Europeans realize that, you will rush to extinguish the fire. Then, watch out![4]

When, a few decades later, Stalin's tanks stood on the Elbe, the history of the twentieth century would appear to have borne him out.

As for the man at the center of this drama, Merezhkovsky's collaborator, Dmitri Filosofov, completed his friend's thought: "Nicholas II cannot give a constitution because this would be for him the act of a traitor. He would heroically mount the scaffold and suffer for 'his faith,' but he would never consent to the only act that is terrifying for him as a faithful member of the Church.... Primary responsibility for the chaos currently prevailing in Russia lies with Orthodoxy, and, however strange this statement may seem, it is Orthodoxy that will cause the tsar to perish."[5] Not unreasonably, one of the overriding goals of Orthodox theologians who have written on politics in the twentieth century appears to have been to refute this charge. But were Merezhkovsky and Filosofov, for all their undoubted exaggeration, nonetheless in some sense correct? Was Nicholas the martyr, ultimately, of an authentic theocratic principle?

の の の

By 1918, to suggest, as Bulgakov did, that the "mad chauffeur," as tired as he was, was the only one who could hold the whole thing together after all was not as controversial as it had been in 1915. But even in 1915, and still more 1916, the false and ultimately self-serving nature of the idea of the mad chauffeur should have been apparent. The dramatic turn-around in Russia's fortunes that followed (even without being directly caused by) Nicholas's assumption of the supreme command should have served as a warning to those members of the Progressive Bloc and wider Duma-led opposition: a warning that to identify Russia's difficulties in the Great War as a direct function of its regime type was to misdiagnose the source of the country's problems, as well as to misidentify the nature of their remedy. As it turned out, the "Munitions Crisis" was not a permanent or insuperable feature of Russia under its existing regime; Russia did not have to cease to be a *teokratia* to take the fight back to the Germans.

On the contrary, the "mad chauffeur," Nicholas II, and his ministerial Chairman Goremykin had been right. Russia could only recover if the tsarist authority that held the country together was maintained as the

---

[4] Ibid.   [5] Merezhkovsky, *Tsar et la révolution*, 78.

directing aegis under which the undoubtedly great contribution the Duma and Voluntary Organizations could make was directed. Indeed, this *was* the formula in accordance with which Russia staged, from the end of 1915, an extraordinary turnaround in the war's fortunes. In September, the German advance came to an end, and even, in places, reversed. Parts of Austrian Galicia, albeit not Lvov, were reconquered. Russia had borne the burden of the war in 1915 and survived: while the more industrially advanced powers, Britain and France, had remained inactive in the face of 85 German infantry divisions and one cavalry division on the immobile Western Front, in the east Russia had fallen back before, but ultimately checked, an offensive driven by 137 German and Austro-Hungarian infantry divisions and 24 cavalry. Among the liberal opposition, *mea culpas* were rare but not unheard of. "We blundered badly over the change of command," Count D. A. Olsufiev, a Moscow landowner prominent in opposition circles, confessed in October: "All of us were wrong. The emperor was more far-sighted. The change was for the better.... [T]he military situation has improved. The influx of refugees has ended, Moscow will not fall, and that is infinitely more important than who will become minister and when the Duma will be reconvened."[6]

How was this achievement possible? Part of the answer is that at the same time that he assumed personal command in August 1915, Nicholas II also authorized the establishment of a series of Special Councils, designed to bring government, private industry, and society's representatives in the Duma and Voluntary Organizations together, to rectify the shortages that had made Russia so helpless before the Germans' guns.[7] By the end of August, four of these councils had been brought into existence, for defense, transport, food, and fuel, each chaired by the relevant government minister. The most important of them was the Special Council for Defense, whose brief was to coordinate government and private industry for the sake of increased munitions production.[8] Nicholas attended its first meeting in person. Thereafter, its usual chair was War Minister Polivanov. Working closely with him was his friend and ally Guchkov: in return for Guchkov's unscrupulous role in the judicial murder of Miasoyedov, and his dismissal of the former War Minister, Sukhomlinov, fate had appointed him head of a second, subsidiary body established by Nicholas at this time, the Central War Industry Committee, charged with marshalling Russia's small and medium-sized firms for the war effort.

---

[6] Cited in Oldenburg, *Last Tsar*, 4:56.   [7] Pipes, *Russian Revolution*, 230.
[8] It was empowered to seize and re-organize underperforming firms, hold management to account, and adjust wages. Consisting of around forty members, ten of them from the Duma as selected by Duma President Mikhail Rodzianko, it met twice a week.

The Special Councils were a great success. If, in 1914, the maximum capacity of Russian industry had been 150,000 shells, by the end of the following year, 1915, that had more than trebled to 950,000 shells, and, by the end of 1916, production had doubled again, to 1,850,000 shells. To be sure, just as large a part in overcoming Russia's weapons shortage was the government's success in placing orders with British and American firms for munitions. But even here the Special Council for Defense assisted. Foreign armaments were not much good if they could not be shipped from their port of entry to the battlefield. After the Germans had sealed the Baltic and the Turks the Black Seas, Russia relied on the sub-Arctic ports of Archangelsk and, from 1916, of Murmansk (originally, Romanov-on-Murmansk). But the former had only inadequate rail links with the rest of the country, and the latter, none at all. The Special Defense Council saw to their construction. The three other Councils (transport, food, and fuel) also did important work, as did a further body authorized by Nicholas in November 1915: the All-Russian Union of Zemstvo and Municipal Councils. This so-called "Zemgor" united Russia's previously separate zemstvo and municipal Voluntary Organizations into a single body, and, supplied with generous funding by the Imperial government, assumed chief responsibility for Russia's military hospitals and refugee relief centers. While Zemgor's work was undoubtedly important, under the leadership of the earnest, but overly self-regarding, Prince Lvov, a political liberal with close links to the leaders of the Progressive Bloc, it came increasingly to think of itself as an alternative government.

But be that as it may, the fact is that if, by the New Year of 1916, anyone was left looking discredited, it should have been the ministers and the Progressive Bloc. The German advance had petered out. The Russians had dug in, and, with the imposition of Alekseev's steady hand professionalizing Stavka, Russia gained the breathing space that she needed in order to regroup. The fact that she so obviously succeeded in doing so was Nicholas's greatest achievement as Supreme Commander.

ഇ   ഇ   ഇ

As we have seen, when Nicholas assumed the supreme command in August 1915, not he but his chief-of-staff, Mikhail Vasilievich Alekseev, became operational commander. A commoner only one generation removed from the peasantry, whose father had broken into the officers' corps after twenty-five years among the Army's rank and file, Alekseev epitomized the surprising openness of the Russian Army as a route of social advancement to non-nobles.[9] Even as Nicholas's Chief-of-Staff, Alekseev adopted few social graces: Alekseev spoke neither French

---

[9] Stone, *Eastern Front*, 21.

nor English and felt uncomfortable in exalted company, avoided the
officers' mess (populated as it was by the sons of counts and princes),
and employed as his subordinates men of a similarly humble social
background. His defect was that he delegated too little work for these
subordinates to do. Instead, Alekseev worked himself to the bone by
micro-managing every event along the front, in unrelenting eighteen-
hour days.[10] All the same, says Stone, "It is difficult not to regard his
Stavka . . . as a great improvement on its predecessor. . . . Alekseev was
an incorruptible man with only the good of Russia at heart . . . a charm-
less effigy of the virtues his predecessors ought to have displayed . . . if
the Tsar wanted an apolitical Stavka, he undoubtedly got one in Alekseev and his aides."[11] But if Alekseev's appointment professionalized
Stavka, it also clarified Nicholas's own role as tsar, too.

From August 1915, Nicholas effectively lived at Stavka in Mogilev,
occupying the two rooms in the now-demolished governor's mansion,
as we have seen. Every morning, Nicholas received a briefing from
Alekseev before signing orders and reading dispatches from his ministers in Petrograd. Lunch was taken, communally, in the officers' mess.
Afterwards, Nicholas and his entourage would drive out to walk in
the surrounding woods for fresh air or, occasionally, go cruising on
the Dnieper. He prayed daily in his own two small rooms, and, at least
twice a week, though often more, in church. In the evenings, he was
available for any of his generals to talk to in confidence. In other words,
like the king on a chess board, Nicholas, though invested with complete
power as tsar and supreme commander, did not play an active role in
day-to-day military planning and operations. But *doing so* was not his
purpose. Rather, amid the flux of war, Nicholas's purpose was to be
the symbol of God's sovereignty and the constancy of his Providence,
the anchor of the Russian State and war effort in a reality — God —
greater than itself. And this he did, unself-consciously, through the very
"Godward-ness" of his outlook and being from the very moment of his
arrival in Mogilev. Not least through his unfailing attendance at available liturgies, Nicholas as tsar was Russia's constant, sacred metronome.

Nicholas liked Mogilev. Formally received by Mogilev's archbishop
and clergy on August 27, he noted that its location on a bend in the
Dnieper was very attractive. In October 1915, Alexei arrived. Two days
later, it was Alexei's birthday, and, after a special liturgy of thanksgiving,
father and son walked along the bank of the river.[12] On Saturday evenings there were Vespers and on Sundays, the Divine Liturgy, while the
feasts of the Elevation of the Cross and Virgin's Intercession (September
13 and October 1, respectively), saw him again in church midweek, to

---

[10] Ibid., 223.   [11] Ibid., 192.
[12] Nicholas II, October 5, 1915, in Diary (2), 550.

mark feasts that, in their origins, were acts of thanksgiving for God's deliverance in times of war and foreign invasion. Returning for a few days to Tsarskoye Selo, Nicholas repaired for prayers to the place where his weighty decision to assume the supreme command had been made: "Went to Vespers," he wrote in his diary: "Wonderful to pray once again in the Fyodorov Sovereign Cathedral."[13] A sense of consolation in that decision was, it seems, strongly with him.

At Stavka in 1915 and 1916, Nicholas retained his confidence in Russia's future, and his admiration for the courage of the men serving in Russia's armies. From his new base at Mogilev, he resumed his visits of inspection. When he and Alexei visited the Southwestern Front that October, he was disappointed that "heavy fog" prevented his being able to see the Austro-Hungarian positions, only four miles away. But that scarcely detracted from the pleasure he derived from being back among the troops. As he noted in his diary, the "gloriously bright expressions on their faces . . . gladdened the heart." On the same trip, the front commander, Ivanov, awarded the twelve-year-old Heir the St George Medal, on account of his coming "in proximity to military positions," and, a week later, sent Nicholas himself the St George Cross, fourth class, for the same reason. Nicholas was so gratified that he described the day when the decoration arrived, with a note from Ivanov instructing the tsar to pin it to his own chest, as "unforgettable."[14] Later the same month, Nicholas and Alexei were in Revel (modern Tallinn) to review submarine crews ("ours and English") and left the fortified harbor town with "the best of impressions," before continuing on to Riga, which, at the height of the Great Retreat, had seemed destined to fall to the Germans, but which a dogged Russian defense had ended up saving. The crisis of the spring and summer having been surmounted, optimism about Russia's war effort was clearly returning.

From Riga, Nicholas returned to Mogilev via Pskov, where he stopped to receive a report from General Ruzsky, the Northwest Front's commander. Eighteen months later, in February 1917, Ruzsky, as we shall see, would act as the agent of the Duma in seeking to persuade Nicholas of the merits of constitutional monarchy, and the two men would part from each other embittered; but in late October 1915, Nicholas's authority was unquestioned at the Front's command headquarters in Pskov, and Ruzsky showed Nicholas every respect. After a week at Stavka, Nicholas and his son departed again for the south, this time to visit the port city of Odessa, where Alexei was greeted wildly by crowds crying out "The Heir! The Heir!" in the streets, and where in his diary Nicholas again recorded his great admiration for the common Russian

---

[13] Nicholas II, September 26, 1915, in Diary (2), 549.
[14] Nicholas II, October 17 and 25, 1915, in Diary (2), 548, 549.

soldier. "It is difficult," he confided, recognizing that the task to which the infantrymen serving in his army had been called demanded significantly more physical courage than the role he had himself been called by God to assume, "because one would wish to thank units, especially when there are so many of them, but the soul shrinks in awe."[15]

A month later, at a lunch on St George's Day for holders of the St George Cross at Stavka, however, Nicholas put aside this "awe," and gave expression to his admiration. "Excellent to see so many young heroes in one place," he noted in his diary. "In the two rooms [used for the luncheon] there were more than 170 men. I spoke to each one of them."[16] Of course, it would have been possible for Nicholas to admire the courage and bravery of Russia's soldiers without referring that admiration to any religious commitment. But the fact is that this simply wasn't the case for Nicholas, who constantly united Russia's war effort to faith in God's deliverance. Thus, on the move again a fortnight later, he was inspecting troops on the Central Front: "Left in the best impressions. In three reviews, I saw 84,000 men. . . . Help them, Lord!"[17] Returning to his family at Tsarskoye Selo on Christmas Eve, he made it in time for Vespers ("What a joy I managed to arrive home for the festivities," he noted) only to depart again for Stavka on New Year's Eve. Arriving late that night at Mogilev, the tsar went directly to church in order, in accordance with his longstanding custom, to see the New Year in with a liturgy before the icons. "I prayed ardently that the Lord would bless Russia with a decisive victory and strengthen us in faith and patience," he recorded.[18]

Early in the New Year 1916, it seemed God had heard him. Munitions production was expanding and, on February 3, news reached Nicholas of a great victory over the Turks: Russian troops had stormed and taken the fortress-town of Erzerum in Eastern Anatolia. This represented the high watermark of Russian penetration of the Near East, leaving only a demoralized and poorly led Ottoman army between Nicholas's buoyant troops and the realization of the longstanding Russian dream of retaking Constantinople: as one historian has put it, in early 1916 the Russian Empire was at its historical zenith.[19] Jubilant, Nicholas made his first (and, in the event, last) visit to the Duma's meeting place in the Tauride Palace, for a liturgy of thanksgiving for the fall of Erzerum. Despite the hostility between monarch and Duma engendered by the formation, the previous summer, of the Progressive Bloc, Russia's recent victory over the Turks gave everyone something to unite around, and

[15] Nicholas II, Dnevnik, 8 November 1915, in Diary (2), 557.
[16] Nicholas II, Dnevnik, 26 November 1915, in Diary (2), 560.
[17] Nicholas II, December 12, 1915, in Diary (2), 562.
[18] Nicholas II, December 31, 1915, in Diary (2), 565.
[19] McMeekin, *Russian Origins*, 221.

the speech that Nicholas made on this occasion was received with unusual warmth by the Duma deputies. For a moment, it appeared that the conflict between them might have been healed. Indeed, Nicholas described it as "an original and successful day."[20]

A week later, Russian success over the Ottomans occasioned the visit to Stavka of the British diplomat Mark Sykes, whose name would be later given to the Sykes-Picot Agreement dividing the former Ottoman Near East between Britain and France. The restoration of the Cross over Hagia Sophia — now an official Russian war aim recognized by Britain and France — began to look like *destiny*. Indeed, Russia had so completely recovered from the Munitions Crisis that Russian forces enjoyed superiority over the Germans in both men *and* arms all along the front.[21] With Russia's fortunes again rising, Nicholas expressed his inner condition in prayer. "Lord, help and bless our gallant army!," he wrote in his diary, drawing the sign of the Cross in the margin.[22] Surely, he must have felt God was blessing the act of faith and obedience by which he had assumed the supreme command. It was simply a *new* army and, it seemed, a *new* war.[23]

At the head, now, of an army whose fortunes were rising, Nicholas spent Easter (Pascha) 1916 at Stavka, the meaning — and perhaps also the *fate* — of his own ruling authority at that time in Russia seeming to be illumined symbolically at moments in the light of that of the "King (Russian: *tsar*) of Israel" and "Lord of the Seraphim" (to use the titles attributed to Christ, as we have seen, in the Liturgy of St John Chrysostom), whose arrest, trial and execution the Church that week not only commemorates but, as far as possible, symbolically re-enacts. It began with Nicholas's attendance before the icons at Divine Liturgy on Palm Sunday (the feast of Christ's triumphant entry into the Holy City as Son of David and rightful King of Israel), and Nicholas was again before the icons in church for both the morning and evening liturgies on Great and Holy Monday, as well as for a morning liturgy on Great and Holy Wednesday (when the Church marks the same rightful King's betrayal by his servants and closest friends). Nicholas appears to have attended these liturgies alone. He mentions Alekseev "and other members of Stavka" first at the morning liturgy on Great and Holy Thursday. Marking, as it does, Christ's institution of the Eucharist, this day's liturgy is a very sacred one, and Nicholas noted that his generals

---

[20] Nicholas II, February 9, 1916, in Diary (2), 572.
[21] Stone, *Eastern Front*, 211.
[22] Nicholas II, March 7, 1916, in Diary (2), 576.
[23] Stone, *Eastern Front*, 224: "A new Russia was indeed beginning to emerge in 1916." Also, Katkov, *Russia, 1917*, 142: Nicholas's assumption of the supreme command was the "turning point after which the fighting capacity of the army steadily increased until it broke down under the strain of the revolutionary events of February, 1917."

that day "partook of the Holy Mysteries."[24] Having already received Holy Communion at the beginning of Lent, Nicholas on this occasion did not, not because he viewed the Sacrament as a thing of minor importance, but precisely because he revered it so highly: he would have wished to make his confession before receiving the Sacrament, and, as he explained in a letter to Alexandra, he wished to observe the Church's general rule that, where possible, only one's own personal confessor should hear one's confession lest (through the temptation to conceal or give only a selection of one's sins) "instead of bringing peace and calm it might have the contrary effect."[25] That evening Nicholas returned apparently again alone when to church for the one-and-a-half-hour-long Liturgy of the Twelve Evangelists.

The following day, Good Friday, the commemoration of Christ's final abandonment by his friends and death on the Cross, is the most solemn in the Christian year. Again, Nicholas was twice before the icons in church, in the morning for the solemn spreading of the burial shroud over the altar to mark Christ's death on the Cross, and in the evening for the ritual carrying out and "burial" of this shroud, in the Church's ritual re-enactment of Christ's burial in the Tomb. To help bear the shroud that has lain this day on the altar is a solemn responsibility, one that implicitly identifies the believer with his Lord's suffering and death. There is great poignancy (and perhaps even something strangely prophetic) in the fact that, on this last Holy Week and Easter of Imperial Russia, Nicholas (though he had attended Good Friday liturgies all his life) should make the first reference in his diary to bearing this shroud himself, which he as earthly king (Russian: *tsar*) did with the help of his own friends and servants, Alekseev and the generals Nilov and Ivanov. Only a year later, these men having betrayed him, Nicholas would celebrate Easter 1917 as a prisoner.

Seen in hindsight, then, Easter 1916 seems to overflow with symbolic significance, as if, in its rituals and liturgies, something of the spiritual struggle Nicholas was engaged in was mystically signified, while the tragic shape of things to come was also foreshadowed. In the hopeful conditions of 1916, however, such a sequel must have seemed absurd. Sentiment at Stavka was buoyant: on Great and Holy Tuesday, news arrived that Trebizond, an ancient, Greek-majority town in far eastern Turkey, that many centuries before had briefly served as the capital of the Byzantine Empire, had fallen to Russia's army. The joy of Easter morning seemed to announce the steady arrival of a new "Byzantine" period in Russian history, when the cross over Hagia Sophia might

---

[24] Nicholas II, April 7, 1916, in Diary (2), 581. On Alekseev's piety, see Shavel'sky, *Vospominaniia*, vol. 1, 395–400, and, especially, 2:234, where he says: "I never before or after saw such sincere and ardent faith as I saw in this great statesman."

[25] Nicholas II to Alexandra (N. 932), April 4, 1916, in Fuhrmann, *Complete Wartime*, 436.

be restored (and Russia's theocratic regime thereby resoundingly vindicated). We can only speculate, however, as to whether Nicholas himself felt this way.

Certainly, on the following morning, Holy Saturday, Nicholas was back before the icons in church. Then he drove out "out of town" to a "telegraph station" from where he walked back "through the fields and woods, hills and valleys" to the bend in the Dnieper before Mogilev. At a quarter to midnight, Nicholas was again standing before the icons in church, awaiting the commencement of the solemn Easter liturgy — the celebration of Christ's Resurrection — that would end at ten minutes to two on Easter Sunday morning. With Christ having now "trampled death by death" and risen from the grave, the mood at the liturgy was hopeful and joyous, but the suggestive illumination of Nicholas's kingship in the light of Christ's was not for that reason terminated. On the contrary, in thanksgiving for Christ's resurrection, long-established custom called on the tsar to act as it were *in persona Christi*, and bless all his friends and even his least servants with a triple kiss, personally. Completing this duty took Nicholas three days. He began with Alekseev and the other generals. As he has it in his diary, immediately after the completion of the Eastern morning liturgy, "Everyone gathered in my rooms, I blessed them, and then we broke the fast." [26] Then, rising after a few hours' sleep at 9.30 on Easter morning, Nicholas spent an hour giving the customary triple "kiss of peace" (*khristosovanie*) to the rest of his staff, the Orthodox clergy, municipal administration, and Mogilev's leading citizens, before walking in the afternoon down to what he describes as the "lower monastery" on the banks of the Dnieper (the same monastery that today preserves as a relic the gold coin Nicholas handed out to a village boy on a visit to the same monastery in 1916). But it wasn't only the higher ranks that received a blessing from the tsar. On Easter Monday alone, he gave the triple kiss of blessing to the "Cossacks and lower ranks of all units present in Mogilev — in all 860 men." So many men of lower ranks were present in Mogilev, however, that the ritual blessing continued on Easter Tuesday. [27] In short, as long as the theocratic principle remained alive in Russian culture, Nicholas could find his role as supreme commander in becoming his staff's symbolic "moral anchor" and "sacred metronome," vicariously attending the liturgy even when his staff could not, and demonstrating, in the faithfulness of his own person, that it was truly in God (and "not in gold and armies" to paraphrase, again, Nazianzen) that not only Nicholas's but also Russia's strength lay. Nicholas's virtue was to intuit this duty and to embrace the resulting activity as essential to his office.

---

[26] Nicholas II, April 10, 1916, in Diary (2), 581.
[27] See Nicholas II, April 11–12, 1916, in Diary (2), 581.

From April to October 1916, Nicholas was, apart from short tours of inspection of Russia's various fronts, at Stavka in Mogilev. His role continued as before: to embody, as monarch, Russia's religious-moral ideal as an Orthodox *teokratia*, and, as far as possible, to see to the realization of that ideal in practice. By this stage, Nicholas seems to have come to know Mogilev sufficiently well for favorite locales to emerge for his afternoon walks. The "lower monastery" on the banks of the Dnieper was one such locale, and it may of course have been on one of these afternoon walks, in the spring and summer of 1916, that the local boy received the coin he would later present, decades later after the fall of Communism, to the re-established monastery.

Beyond Mogilev, too, in the army and country at large, morale remained high, and Nicholas had every reason to remain hopeful for Russian victory. At Bender (in modern Moldova's "breakaway" region of Transnistria) in May, Nicholas, reviewing troops, noted that "all presented excellently," and that he was "very satisfied." Similarly, in Odessa, a day later, he recorded that "The troops presented themselves excellently, the people did very well, and the horses were good." Reviewing the upgraded Black Sea Fleet at Sevastopol, he wrote that "the ships in great order produced a mighty impression," and he spent that evening "long outside in the air, talking with sailors who came to dinner." And he remained as keen as ever to convey to his men his personal respect, gratitude and admiration for them. Inspecting twenty-five warships in Sevastopol harbor, he noted that "On each one, I went around to all the officers and crew and thanked them for their service." A day later, he sought to convey the same admiration and thanks to the navy's newly-founded fleet air-wing. What Nicholas knew, but the rank and file he reviewed did not, was that in barely a few weeks, Russia's boldest, most innovative, and most successful operation in the Great War — the Brusilov Offensive — would begin, and the men he was reviewing would find themselves in the thick of the fighting. On May 23/June 6 it began. "Bless, Lord, our troops with the farthest success!" Nicholas wrote in his diary.[28]

Nicholas's hopes were not in Brusilov and his innovative methods alone, however. Rather, Nicholas (a man, as we have suggested, who had truly "encountered divinity on his life's journey... been overtaken by it and on whom it [had] been poured out with its prevailing force") had himself taken steps to help ensure victory — steps that again reveal his profoundly theocratic conception of his office, as well as how far his own "historical, mystical-dogmatic" Christianity differed from the increasingly merely secularized, "Kantian" moralism of his contemporaries. Thus, while Brusilov's plans were being laid, Nicholas instructed

---

[28] Nicholas II, May 23, 1916, in Diary (2), 588.

Fr Nikolai Shavelsky, head chaplain of the Russian armed forces, to have the Vladimir Mother of God — Russia's holiest icon and national protectress, credited, as she was, with having saved Moscow from attack by the Tatar ruler Tamerlane in the fifteenth century — brought at once to the front. Now, one might expect a *priest* to have been pleased to execute such an instruction. And yet Shavelsky — a modernist-minded priest who admired Wilhelmine Germany's industrial and scientific prowess, and entertained reservations about icons — considered Nicholas's instruction the symptom of possibly a dangerous "superstition" that could only have come from Alexandra.[29] Of course, Shavelsky had no choice but to carry out Nicholas's orders anyway, and the icon's transfer to Stavka was arranged to coincide with the opening days of Brusilov's offensive. "I hope she will arrive soon, just in time for the serious times approaching," Nicholas wrote in anticipation to Alexandra.[30]

To Nicholas, then, God was, as we have seen, a reality — a YOU ARE — Who could not be written out of the course and conduct of the Great War. On the contrary, Lord as He was of history, *God*, not man, Nicholas apparently believed, would ultimately determine its outcome. "Today they bring the Holy Image . . . to our church. I feel sure her blessings will help us much," Nicholas wrote in just this spirit to Alexandra on May 28/June 8.[31] Indeed, Nicholas seems to have been in this regard far closer to the spirit of the Russian people than were modernist-inclined priests such as Shavelsky: according to Alexandra, who had the information from her sister, the Grand Duchess Elizabeth Fyodorovna, who ran a convent-cum-hospital in Moscow, "great crowds" had turned out to mark the Vladimir Mother of God's ceremonial departure from the Kremlin.[32] At Stavka, too, the image was received with solemnity and reverence. "At about 10 a.m. I went with Alekseev to church," Nicholas wrote to Alexandra: "When Mass ended, the icon of Our Lady of Vladimir was transferred to the square in front of my quarters and the Staff Building. A prayer service was held and everybody made their venerations."[33] Hundreds, he said, queued to kiss it.[34] Moreover, events in the days that followed seemed to vindicate not the modernist Shavelsky's, but the "superstitious" Nicholas's, view of religion, the Mother of God apparently responding in power to the honor lavished on her image.

---

[29] Georgii Shavel'skii, *Vospominaniia*, 2:73. On his pre-War admiration for Wilhelm II and Germany, see 1:78–79.

[30] Nicholas II to Alexandra (N. 1045), May 26, 1916, in Fuhrmann, *Complete Wartime*, 474.

[31] Nicholas II to Alexandra (N. 1065), May 28, 1916, in Fuhrmann, *Complete Wartime*, 480–81.

[32] Alexandra to Nicholas II (A. 1063), May 28, 1916, in Fuhrmann, *Complete Wartime*, 481.

[33] Nicholas II to Alexandra (N. 1075), May 30, 1916, in Fuhrmann, *Complete Wartime*, 487.

[34] Nicholas II, May 28, 1916, in Diary (2), 589. The picture is confirmed in Shavel'skii, *Vospominaniia*, 2:80–81.

Brusilov's offensive was extravagantly successful.[35] To be sure, Brusilov was a new kind of commander, using new kinds of methods, a reflection of the change in tone and approach that had come over Russian military operations in Alekseev's more professional Stavka. With Brusilov deploying a crack force ("60,000 men of the highest physical standard"), and enjoying a superiority in shells (the Russians now had six shells to every German one) and aircraft, Nicholas kept a running daily tally of the number of Austro-Hungarian troops Russian forces taken prisoner. And yet he seems not quite to have believed what his eyes were reading in his generals' reports: 25,000 prisoners taken at the end of the first full day of fighting on May 24; 40,000 by the 25th; 51,000 a day later, etc. On the 25th, a *Te Deum*, a liturgy of thanksgiving, was held, Nicholas naturally attending. Then, as if providentially, the day after the arrival of the Vladimir Mother of God, the largest single-day increase of prisoners taken was recorded: from 71,000 on May 28 to 106,000 on the 29th. A similar "coincidence" occurred the day after the icon departed Stavka for a tour of the southwestern front, when in one day the total number of prisoners increased by one quarter (from 120,000 on June 1 to 150,000 on June 2). Then, on June 4, 1916, six days after the Vladimir icon's arrival at Stavka, the Russian Eighth Army broke through the Austro-Hungarian lines near Lutsk in Volhynia, while the Ninth Army did the same further south at Czernowitz. One third of the Habsburg Empire's forces were now sitting as prisoners in Russian camps.[36] As an independent belligerent, Austria-Hungary was finished; it survived only as a German auxiliary. Incredibly, Russia enjoyed a two-to-one advantage in the field over the Central Powers.[37]

At last, God was smiling on Russia's cause. Or so at least it not unreasonably seemed to people of faith like Nicholas and Alexandra. "To me, it is like a second war. We are beginning again ... In the hospital one says ... they scream hurrah with joy," Alexandra wrote from Tsarskoye Selo to her husband.[38] Nicholas agreed. "In the official announcement made [regarding the offensive's successes] the word 'victory' was used for the first time!" he reported in return.[39] Others caught the new mood, too. "Yesterday, the Vladimir *Bozhe Mater* image [i.e. the Vladimir Mother of God] returned from the front," Nicholas wrote to Alexandra at the end of the first week of June: "The old priest of Moscow [who accompanied the image] is quite in rapture with the

[35] For a military historian's account of the Brusilov Offensive, see Stone, *Eastern Front*, 247–61.
[36] Stone, *Eastern Front*, 254.
[37] Ibid., 261.
[38] Alexandra to Nicholas II (A. 1059), May 27, 1916, in Fuhrmann, *Complete Wartime*, 478.
[39] Nicholas II to Alexandra (N. 1062), May 27, 1916, in Fuhrmann, *Complete Wartime*, 478.

troops he saw and their spirit."[40] Nicholas and Alexandra's war was reaching its climax.

By the end of June, Russian forces had taken 266,000 Austro-Hungarian prisoners, and were advancing on the passes over the Carpathians. On the 20th, the British and French, hoping to emulate Russia's victories, opened a new offensive on the Somme. "Help them, Lord!" Nicholas wrote the same day in his diary. True, a recently launched Russian offensive against the Germans in the center, opposite the old Stavka headquarters at Baranovici, had failed to replicate Brusilov's successes further south. All the same, having assumed supreme command when Russia's fortunes were at their lowest ebb, Nicholas had overseen the rebirth of Russia's war effort, even while those of her allies languished: the Italians were on the back foot on the Isonzo, the great British offensive on the Somme ended in a bloodbath, and in the Battle of Jutland the apparently invincible Royal Navy obtained a disappointing stalemate (if not a defeat). Alone among the Entente, Russia enjoyed decisive battlefield victories against the Central Powers. "Oh, how happy I am!" Nicholas recorded in his diary at the beginning of July. He also felt needed. In the thick of things at Stavka, Nicholas felt uniquely placed as supreme commander to be able to listen and thereby right some of the wrongs that came to his attention. "I continually see officers, colonels, and generals who come from the front and invite them to lunch and dinner. Many of those who are put out of their places come here with complaints and their affairs are looked through. Mogilev is like an enormous hotel where people pass through and one always sees any amount of different sorts and types."[41]

For all these reasons, then, Nicholas approached Alexei's birthday at the end of July with an optimism not seen since 1914. The boy's health was so good that, on the day before, Nicholas had watched with pleasure as his son played a game of soccer with twenty local boys in the square in front of Stavka in provincial Mogilev. On other days, father and son walked down to a sandy beach on the riverbank that Alexei had dubbed "Evpatoria," in allusion to the seaside Crimea resort he had recently visited when inspecting his mother's veterans' sanatorium. "May he grow, Lord, and may You strengthen him spiritually and bodily, and may God's blessing be always upon him," he prayed for him.[42] And while he could evince exasperation at the low quality of his generals' leadership ("after two years of war they cannot learn the simplest lessons of warfare! I cannot tell you how angry I am with them"),[43]

---

[40] Nicholas II to Alexandra (N. 1108), June 7, 1916, in Fuhrmann, *Complete Wartime*, 496–97.
[41] Nicholas II to Alexandra (N. 1221), July 4, 1916, in Fuhrmann, *Complete Wartime*, 530–31.
[42] Nicholas II, July 30, 1916, in Diary (2), 594.
[43] Nicholas II to Alexandra (N. 1172), June 22, 1916, in Fuhrmann, *Complete Wartime*, 514.

he had every confidence in the man, Brusilov, whose bold ideas had translated Russia's newfound strength into victories. "He talks about everything cleverly and rightly. His ideas about the war are also very sound. Our walks and teas are the most convenient time for these conversations," Nicholas wrote to Alexandra.[44]

Wisely, Alexandra didn't expect Russia's recent successes to lead to a speedy end to the war. "God alone knows when the end will be," she warned in a letter to Nicholas, at the height of Russian successes in 1916.[45] Her spirits buoyed, however, by the good news from the front, Alexandra, too, recovered from some of the exhaustion that had crippled her, and, resuming her nursing duties in Tsarskoye Selo's hospitals, she took more young officers under her motherly wing. Assisting at operations in the morning and visiting the wards to sit with the convalescing in the afternoons was as demanding as it had been in late 1914. But she did it anyway. "Now another youngster who suffers awfully lies next door and wants me also to bring my work and sit, so that I shall be torn to pieces now [by his suffering]."[46] She was in her element, and she would occasionally write to have some of the officers she had nursed and grown fond of received by Nicholas when they returned, via Stavka, to the front.[47] "Ah, how I miss you both," she wrote to Nicholas and Alexei at Stavka at the end of June: "The hospital is my real saving and consolation. We have many heavy wounded, daily operations, and much we want to get through before leaving." The last was a reference to her and her daughters' forthcoming departure for Mogilev, where they arrived on July 10, residing for three nights in the Imperial train. Certainly, Alexandra was happier than she had been in years. Planning as she was to add a wing to one of her Tsarskoye Selo hospitals, she had, it seemed, found an outlet for her natural, administrative talents, as well as her nursing ones: "Thank God that He has given me the strength to be of use again — such consolation in one's work," she wrote to her husband.[48] On her journeys to and from Stavka she resumed her custom of stopping *en route* to inspect army hospitals, as she did, for example, in Smolensk.

Quite simply, God remained at the center of the Imperial family's public and private lives. None of Alexandra's enthusiasm for the sacraments had slackened. "I long for this moral strength," she wrote to Nicholas from Tsarskoye Selo on August 6: "One goes through so much

---

[44] Nicholas II to Alexandra (N. 1238), July 14, 1916, in Fuhrmann, *Complete Wartime*, 534.
[45] Alexandra to Nicholas II (A. 1262), July 20, 1916, in Fuhrmann, *Complete Wartime*, 540.
[46] Alexandra to Nicholas II (A. 1102), June 6, 1916, in Fuhrmann, *Complete Wartime*, 491.
[47] See Nicholas II to Alexandra (N. 1221), July 4, 1916, in Fuhrmann, *Complete Wartime*, 530–31.
[48] Alexandra to Nicholas II (A. 1266), July 21, 1916, in Fuhrmann, *Complete Wartime*, 541.

and has to give out such a lot. Confession, Sunday evening at ten."[49] Nicholas's thoughts were on God, too. The first weeks of August 1916 coincided with the anniversary of his decision to assume the supreme command. To mark the event, a liturgy was held at Mogilev on the 23rd, followed by a "good and simple" lunch in Mogilev's Hotel Bristol. Alexandra and the children had returned to Stavka for the anniversary and Nicholas's diary entry the following Sunday began simply but contentedly: "Excellent. Went all together to Mass . . . "[50] How in the late summer of 1916 God must have seemed to have blessed his decision!

ﾍﾉ   ﾍﾉ   ﾍﾉ

Throughout July and August, the rout of Austria-Hungary continued. By the end of August, Russia, occupying almost the whole of Bukovina, had moved its line forward to the passes through the Carpathians guarding the way to Hungary. Russian losses, too, had been monstrously high, as they also were on both the Somme and the Isonzo on the Western and Italian fronts in 1916. But unlike their allies, the British, the French, and the Italians, the Russians at least had something to show for them. *How* to beat Germany in the field had essentially been worked out — by the Russians.[51] Indeed, as Stone reminds his readers, when the British later broke through German lines on the Western Front in November 1918, it would be using the techniques Brusilov pioneered in 1916.

And then suddenly, unexpectedly, the wheels fell off. In the autumn of 1916, Nicholas abruptly abandoned the running tally he had been keeping of Austro-Hungarian prisoners captured. The Russians' very success in reaching the Carpathian passes, and the invasion and possible partition of Hungary it seemed to portend, brought about, first, Romania's entry into the war against the Central Powers, and then Romania's just as swift collapse. It was a disaster for Russia. Lengthening the already distended front Russia had to defend, the Romanian front forced Stavka to divert resources to "save" an ally incapable of defending itself.[52] On September 21, Nicholas ordered Brusilov to halt his offensive. God had withdrawn his blessing just as swiftly as He had given it. Not only had Romania's collapse overstretched the army; food was growing increasingly short in Russia's cities.

In truth, food supply had been a problem that had grown in inverse proportion to Russian successes against Austria-Hungary in the summer, and Nicholas was at a loss as to how he and his ministers should fix it. "Confound these affairs, from thinking about them so much my brain

---

[49] Alexandra to Nicholas II (A. 1300), August 6, 1916, in Fuhrmann, *Complete Wartime*, 551.
[50] Nicholas II, August 23, 1916, in Diary (2), 600–1.
[51] Stone, *Eastern Front*, 235–38.
[52] Ibid., 274.

does not grasp any more where is the true solution," he had written
as early as June.[53] By September, however, Alexandra was reporting
"great disorders in the streets on account of food," and recommending
a system of pre-ordering bread to reduce the amount of time people
spent in queues.[54] Extraordinarily, Nicholas II's Russia had no system
of wartime rationing. And from her work in the Tsarskoye Selo hospitals, Alexandra began to sense that the officers' morale was beginning to
crack. "They feel one sacrifices them for nothing," she wrote to her husband, noting with alarm the increasing signs of insubordination, theft
of army *materiel*, and the distribution of political propaganda.[55] At
Stavka, Alekseev, his chief of staff, delivered the same message, revealing
to Nicholas the "quantity of letters he gets from officers, their families,
soldiers, etc., and also anonymous ones — all begging him to draw my
attention to the difficulties of life in the towns and small places on
account of the high prices of food stuffs."[56]

The fact was that redressing the Munitions Crisis of 1915 had come
at a price, and now Russia was paying it.[57] The problem was inflation,
as a flood of new government spending saw Russian industrial production expand and factories attract new workers by offering higher
wages. Thousands flooded in from the countryside to take advantage,
only to have the value of the wages they had come for undermined by
rising prices, shrinking consumer good production, and the seizing up
of commercial exchange between the cities and the countryside, as the
peasantry discovered there was nothing to buy with the money merchants from the towns were offering. This "Scissors Crisis" (the widen-
ing divergence between the prices of consumer and agricultural goods)
would hold the Russian economy in its grip until Stalin solved it, with
extraordinary brutality and loss of life, by collectivizing the farms and re-
enserfing the peasantry. But short of such violence (unimaginable as it
was to Nicholas), what was the government to do? Certainly, Nicholas
grew only more frustrated, venting his exasperation to his wife when
the head of the Supplies Committee informed him that they "cannot do
anything to help the situation." With the Agriculture Ministry obstruct-
ing his instructions, he called the food supply crisis gripping Russia's

---

[53] Nicholas II to Alexandra (N. 1126), June 11, 1916, in Fuhrmann, *Complete Wartime*, 499–500.
[54] Alexandra to Nicholas II (A. 1405), September 14, 1916, in Fuhrmann, *Complete Wartime*, 582.
[55] Alexandra to Nicholas (A. 1413 and 1418), September 16 and 17, 1916, in Fuhrmann, *Complete Wartime*, 586–87.
[56] Nicholas II to Alexandra (N. 1440), September 22, 1916, in Fuhrmann, *Complete Wartime*, 600–1.
[57] Stone, *Eastern Front*, 282–301; Smith, *Russia in Revolution*, 93–97; and, most fully, Peter Gatrell, *Russia's First World War: A social and economic history* (Harlow: Pearson, 2005).

industrial centers the "most damned question I ever came across. I have never been a merchant and simply don't understand these questions about provisions and stores."[58] Nicholas intuitively understood the essence of his office as theocratic ruler as cohering in a lifelong duty of "judgment" for the realization of the country's moral-religious ideal, not the expert-technical management of an industrial economy. Industrialized warfare was demanding courses of action and a style of government not provided for in his conception of *teokratia*.[59] But surely God would help?

Characteristically, Russia's last monarch turned to the sacraments. At the end of September, Alexandra urged Nicholas to return to Tsarskoye Selo, for the sake of making his confession and receiving Holy Communion.[60] Arriving on Saturday evening, he went directly to confession and Saturday evening Vespers at the Fyodorov Sovereign Cathedral. "How wonderful it was to pray in it once again," he noted in reference to the beloved church building. And the following Sunday morning, he was back with Alexandra and the children. "Had great comfort from receiving the Sacred Mysteries together as a family," he wrote in his diary.[61] This was just as well, for the petering out of the Brusilov Offensive would expose how isolated Nicholas had become politically, a fact obscured amid 1916's successes.

❦ ❦ ❦

The underlying clash between Nicholas and the Bloc had not gone away. If anything, it had only grown worse. In January 1916, Nicholas, in twin gestures of conciliation towards the Duma, authorized the Duma's first convening since the August crisis of 1915 for February, and dismissed Goremykin as Chairman of the Council of Ministers. Buoyed by the stabilization of the front against Germany the previous autumn, the dramatic improvement in armaments production, and the promising outlook for Russian arms in the Caucasus, Nicholas considered the moment a good one for attempting to patch things up with the country's representatives on terms acceptable to the monarchy, a *modus vivendi* with the Duma that would unite the country's resources in the war for the Motherland *and* preserve the theocratic principle at the foundation of Russia's regime. To carry out this task, Nicholas turned to the sixty-eight-year-old former governor of Tver province, Boris

---

[58] Nicholas II to Alexandra (N. 1431), September 20, 1916, in Fuhrmann, *Complete Wartime*, 593–94.

[59] Indeed, to be fair to Nicholas personally, Stone notes that the government itself "barely understood what was happening and certainly lacked the statistical apparatus that might have produced a more suitable policy": *Eastern Front*, 288–89.

[60] Alexandra to Nicholas II (A. 1465), September 28, 1916, in Fuhrmann, *Complete Wartime*, 611–13.

[61] Nicholas II, October 21, 1916, in Diary (2), 608.

Stürmer, a member of the State Council and the mayor of Moscow, who was named Chairman of the Council of Ministers in Goremykin's place.

Typically, in histories of Russia's descent into revolution, Stürmer plays the part of fool, incompetent, and stooge of Rasputin. But Stürmer was an altogether more serious figure than the caricature that appears in most histories. Experienced, moderate, and principled, he represented a return to the vision of Stolypin, even if his manners were considerably gentler.[62] As Katkov puts it, "The appointment of Stürmer...was intended by the emperor as an attempt to appease the Duma" by replacing the previous, disliked chairman with a "soft-spoken, diplomatic personality."[63] Certainly, McMeekin concludes that "there seems to have been no better reason for the vilification campaign against him than his Germanic name."[64]

Unfortunately, however, rather than eliciting a spirit of compromise and cooperation, the conciliatory overtures that Stürmer addressed to Rodzianko appear to have raised expectations among Bloc members that the government was on the verge of capitulation to its terms, that is, to the creation of the "government of public confidence" that would have had the Duma appoint a ministry in the tsar's name. Thus, when Nicholas made his first visit ever to the assembly on February 22/March 4, 1916, he was met by men laboring under the expectation that executive control of the government would soon be in their hands.[65]

---

[62] For the briefest of résumés of Stürmer's career, see Pipes, *Russian Revolution*, 241. Pipes, however, likens Stürmer's politics to those of the reactionary Plehve rather than those of Stolypin. But the appointment of a second Plehve would hardly have raised the (albeit in the end exaggerated) expectation of compromise that Stürmer's appointment evidently did raise among the members of the Bloc. See below.

[63] Katkov, *Russia, 1917*, 187.

[64] McMeekin, *Russian Revolution*, 76 — although McMeekin does add, in parentheses, "and the fact that he maintained relations with Rasputin."

[65] Thanks to an account of the event left behind by Rodzianko, we can reconstruct it in detail. Entering the Catherine Hall, where the deputies were assembled, to cries of "Hurrah!," Nicholas's first act was to kiss the cross that had been erected in front of the rostrum for the liturgy of thanksgiving (the short *Te Deum* service) that was about to take place. Together, tsar and chamber sang, "Lord, Save thy People," and then, when the choir began a hymn in honor of the souls of all those who had fallen in battle, Nicholas, as Duma President Rodzianko movingly recalled, "fell to his knees, followed by all the Duma." When they got to their feet, Rodzianko noticed that Nicholas had tears in his eyes. Amazingly, Rodzianko thought this the right moment to press the Bloc's demand for a government responsible to the Duma — an act that went way beyond the terms of compromise that Nicholas envisaged. "You cannot imagine the greatness of such an act, its quieting influence on the country, and its effect on the successful outcome of the war," he said approaching Nicholas. But when Nicholas, deflecting Rodzianko's brazen bid to milk the emotion of the day for the sake of political concession, replied that he would merely "think about it," Rodzianko, his hopes for the historic day dashed, understood that this was a polite way for Nicholas to say that he intended to do nothing of the kind. Russia would remain the *teokratia* the whole chamber had just dedicated to God. In an instant, thanksgiving gave way to resentment, and Rodzianko began to rank himself among Nicholas's enemies. For the description of the incident, see Mikhail

Then, when it became clear that Nicholas was not prepared to cede his authority to the Duma, the Bloc turned in fury and without scruple on Stürmer, exploiting his German name to create the image of the toadying, Rasputin-dependent incompetent that has been passed down to us in most histories today.[66] Far from reconciling government and Duma, as Nicholas had hoped, then, Stürmer's appointment had been seized on by the opposition to torpedo any chance of cooperation on terms that might have been acceptable to Russia's monarch. In the name, paradoxically, of "saving" Russia's war effort, the Progressive Bloc and its allies in the Special Councils, Central War Industries Committee, and Zemgor declared war on the very government leading that effort.

Politically, this "war" between the monarchy and the opposition (which liked to think of itself as representing "the country") set the tone for the rest of 1916: so poisoned by bad faith and suspicion was the relationship between the two bodies (including layers of "fake news" believed, and often disseminated, by the Bloc) that the achievements of the Brusilov Offensive did nothing at all to relieve the tensions between them. In the opposition's eyes, the victories of Russian arms against Austria-Hungary in the summer of 1916 were achieved *despite* Nicholas's government, which, left to itself, was straining every sinew to betray Russia to the Germans. This belief had disastrous consequences, which ultimately dashed any hope of Russian victory. By the time the Brusilov offensive ground to a halt in the autumn of 1916, no fewer than three distinct conspiracies—plots for a palace coup to exile Alexandra to a monastery, force Nicholas to agree to a government responsible to the Duma, or remove him from the throne—were afoot among different groupings of the opposition: one centered on Guchkov, Nicholas's long-standing enemy; another centered on the so-called "Kadet grandee" Prince Lvov, who, since the organization's creation with Nicholas's permission the previous November, headed Zemgor; and another on President of the Duma Mikhail Rodzianko.[67]

Precisely when these plots were hatched is unknown. Historians a century later have not been able entirely to penetrate the thicket of secrecy the conspirators erected around their plans. But what is clear is that, following their defeated attempt in the August Crisis of 1915 to impose a government of public confidence, the leaders of the Progressive

---

Rodzianko, "Memoirs," in Frank Alfred Golder, ed., *Documents of Russian History*, trans. Emanuel Armstrong (New York: Century Co., 1927), 107.

[66] In fact, although the surname was German in origin, Stürmer's family itself had been in Russia for generations. Foreseeing the problems his name might create, Stürmer had applied to Nicholas for permission to go by his mother's name, Panin, an old Russian name of impeccable patriotic credentials: Nicholas agreed in principle but the law required obtaining consent from each head of the extensive branches of the existing Panin clan, a time-consuming bureaucratic process in the best of times.

[67] See esp. McMeekin, *Russian Revolution*, 71–72, 85–88.

Bloc and their allies in the Voluntary Organizations had met in private in Moscow and formed (possibly with the knowledge of War Minister Polivanov and other members of the Council of Ministers) in September 1915 a secret society that aimed at establishing a "government vested with public confidence to wrest power from the hands of those leading Russia to its destruction, slavery and shame."[68] With the society infiltrated by the tsarist police, the content of its program was known but apparently not taken seriously by the Interior Ministry until, in the first months of 1916, the Interior Ministry's attitude may have changed. By that stage, the secret society's planning appears to have advanced to a stage where an alternative, revolutionary government in the form of a "dictatorial directorate" had been envisaged. Certainly, a document identifying it and its future leaders ("Messrs. Guchkov, Lvov, and Kerensky") was obtained by German intelligence in January 1916, and we are probably safe in assuming it was known to the Russian government, too.[69]

What further embittered relations between the Bloc, on one hand, and Nicholas, on the other, was Nicholas's dismissal of the remaining two ministerial "renegades" of 1915: War Minister Polivanov, who was dismissed in March, and Foreign Minister Sazonov, who was dismissed in June. Certainly, these dismissals were punishment for the support both ministers had given the Bloc's demand for a government of public confidence in the August crisis of 1915. But was it also the advance in the conspirators' planning, and Guchkov's known proximity to Polivanov, that saw Polivanov retired? Certainly, when Nicholas appointed Polivanov War Minister in 1915, he had warned him against taking Guchkov into his political confidence. Nonetheless, Polivanov had nominated Guchkov as head of the Central War Industries Committee. Nicholas had consented to this. But in the wake of the failure of his attempt at reconciliation, through Stürmer, was the benefit of the doubt Nicholas had lent Polivanov and Guchkov's association beginning to run out? Sazonov, too, continued to entertain relations with the Bloc; his portfolio was given to Stürmer.

But none of this was enough to discourage Guchkov, who, still in charge of the Central War Industry Committee, even tried to induct Nicholas's own chief of staff, Alekseev, into his conspiracy. Thus, in a secret letter to Nicholas's chief of staff in 1916, Guchkov described Stürmer as "if not an actual traitor" then at the very least a man "ready to commit treason." But if any treason was afoot, it was indisputably Guchkov's: this overture to Alekseev was unquestionably designed to sound out Alekseev's willingness to lend the army to the plot Guchkov was hatching against Alekseev's Supreme Commander — Nicholas.

[68] Katkov, *Russia, 1917*, 158.
[69] Ibid., 165–66; McMeekin, *Russian Revolution*, 72.

Discovered, as usual, by the tsarist police, Guchkov's communications with Alekseev were reported to Nicholas, who called Alekseev in to explain himself.[70] Thus, Guchkov's bid to politicize the army failed (for now). But if it is remarkable that Guchkov himself, despite his attempts at sowing sedition, was left in charge of the War Industries Committee, the fact is probably to be found in Nicholas's low opinion of Guchkov's qualities as a leader (he was regarded as a firebrand) and the relatively marginal contribution of the organization he headed to the war effort, which Guchkov, however, was prone to exaggerate.[71]

By September 1916, therefore, the optimism reflected in Nicholas's diary during the summer had given way to the frustration created by the emergence of an apparently intractable food supply problem, and an undeclared "war" between the government and the Bloc. As regards the first problem, it was not that there was no food in the Empire; it was the failure to get it from the countryside, where it existed in abundance, to the cities.[72] Not unwisely, Rasputin, who knew the plenty the peasants enjoyed in Siberia, advised cancelling all train traffic between Russia and the front for a period of three days, to allow food deliveries to the cities to travel unhindered and put fears of shortage to rest. Nicholas ignored the advice. Persuaded, however, that a man with a background from outside the Imperial bureaucracy might be better placed to resolve the supply problems the Empire was facing, he did make an unprecedented gesture of reconciliation with the opposition by appointing the fifty-year-old Aleksandr Protopopov Minister of the Interior on 19 September.[73]

Significantly, Protopopov was an Octobrist (a party, as we have seen, of which Guchkov was leader, taking its name from the October

---

[70] For this whole episode, see McMeekin, *Russian Revolution*, 77. Katkov speculates that the general did not inform his supreme commander himself because the strain of command affected Alekseev's moral judgment: *Russia, 1917*, 181.

[71] The War Industry Committees, whose central committee Guchkov headed, filled at best two to three percent of government munitions orders: Pipes, *Russian Revolution*, 230.

[72] See Gatrell, *Tsarist Economy*, 138.

[73] In my account here, I follow Semion Lyandres, "Progressive Bloc politics on the eve of the Revolution: Revisiting P. N. Miliukov's 'Stupidity or Treason' Speech of November 1, 1916," *Russian History* 31 (2004): 447–64. An apparently intelligent and energetic man only fifty years old who had built a personal fortune on textiles, Protopopov had been recommended to Nicholas from many quarters. Everyone from Rasputin (whose nomination of Protopopov as early as November 1915 Nicholas had ignored) to former foreign minister Sergei Sazonov (a known liberal, dismissed in June, as we have seen, for being too close to the opposition) and Britain's King George V had praised Protopopov's abilities, the last because, from April to June 1916, Protopopov had led a Duma delegation to Russia's wartime allies Britain and France, and the king had written to his cousin to inform him of the impression Protopopov's intelligence and professionalism (his "state wisdom," as the king called it) had created in London. Sazonov had recommended him for the same reason, as a man in whom Russia's allies could have confidence by burying the rumors spread abroad by German misinformation that the Tsar was seeking a separate peace. As Lyandres shows, Russia's own opposition would, ironically, end up being completely taken in by these rumors.

Manifesto of 1905), Deputy President of the Duma and a leading member of the Progressive Bloc. His appointment seemingly expressed Nicholas's hope that government, Duma, and Voluntary Organizations could work together to provision Russia's cities. It was, in short, another conciliatory gesture.[74] As Nicholas put it in a letter to Alexandra after his first meeting with the Deputy President of the Duma in July 1916, Protopopov was an attractive candidate for the Interior Ministry because "I always dreamed to have a Minister of the Interior who could cooperate with the Duma."[75] If this was so, then a new era in the history of Russia's war effort appeared about to dawn. Presumably, Protopopov's would be the first of many appointments from the Duma, Voluntary Organizations, and the Progressive Bloc. With one of "their own" elevated to the head of Russia's most powerful ministry, the Bloc's long-standing demand for a government of public confidence seemed only a heartbeat away from realization—albeit, crucially, as a gift from the tsar, rather than as the product of his capitulation to the Bloc's ultimatums.

Certainly, when news of Nicholas's appointment of Protopopov first broke, it was received as a blow *for* the Bloc. None other than Guchkov, the opposition's chief conspirator, hailed it a "colossal victory of the public," while his associate (and fellow conspirator), the wealthy Moscow industrialist Aleksandr Konovalov, considered it a "capitulation" comparable in constitutional consequence for Russia to the Manifesto of October 17, 1905.[76] "The best that one might have expected," Konovalov gushed at a meeting of Kadets in early October 1916, "was the appointment of some liberal-minded bureaucrat. And all of a sudden it is the Octobrist Protopopov, a man essentially alien to the bureaucratic world.... After an Octobrist minister, a Kadet minister will no longer be such a fright.... It all depends on us. It is all in our hands."[77] Certainly, in its "war" with the monarchy for control of the executive, the Duma, it seemed, had as good as won. A leading historian has called Protopopov's appointment "the Crown's supreme effort at compromise."[78] Installed in office, Protopopov then outlined a program "that had much . . . in common with the Bloc's," including the full legal emancipation of the Empire's Jews, the distribution of lands confiscated from exiled German landowners to the peasantry, and a project for the judicial responsibility of the government to the Senate as a kind of supreme court that picked up directly on ideas then circulating at the heart of the Bloc's leadership.[79] Food supply, meanwhile, it was later

[74] Katkov, *Russia, 1917*, 189.
[75] Cited in Lyandres, "Progressive Bloc politics," 453.
[76] Lyandres, "Progressive Bloc politics," 454.
[77] Cited in Pipes, *Russian Revolution*, 247–48.
[78] Pipes, *Russian Revolution*, 247.
[79] Lyandres, "Progressive Bloc politics," 453.

announced, was to be transferred from the Agriculture Ministry, which clearly lacked the means to deal with it effectively, to the Interior Ministry, which controlled the police force.

Expecting the Duma to rally the country behind the new Octobrist Interior Minister, Nicholas authorized the reconvening of the Duma for November 1. But if a day is a lifetime in politics, then, in the fevered conditions of 1916, the month and a half between Protopopov's appointment and the opening of the Duma proved to be an eternity, for the opposition had since turned 180 degrees in its opinion of Protopopov. Speaker after speaker, enjoying the benefits of parliamentary privilege, rose to denounce what was now deliberately framed as "the Stürmer-Protopopov government," tarring the former Deputy Duma President and Progressive Bloc member with the brush that had been used to discredit Stürmer as an enemy agent on the grounds of his German name. The thirty-six-year-old Social Revolutionary Aleksandr Kerensky, an implacable opponent of the monarchy, and future head of Russia's Provisional Government, went first, denouncing Stürmer, Protopopov and the other ministers—who had left their seats in the Catherine Hall, having been informed in advance that accusations of treason were about to be made—as "hired killers" and "betrayers of the country's interest," "men suspected of treason... fratricides and cowards."[80]

Even more damaging was the speech that followed, by the Duma's elder statesman, the admired historian, liberal "moderate," and leader of the Constitutional Democratic or Kadet Party, Pavel Miliukov.[81] Miliukov's fundamental charge was that the tsarist government was incompetent, because the Bloc had been excluded from playing a proper role in it. Observing that "all the Allied Powers have summoned to the support of the Government the best men of all parties, all the confidence, and all those organizing elements present in their countries," Miliukov asked, "[w]hat has our own Government accomplished?"[82] And yet Miliukov ignored the fact that, at the end of 1916, which had seen the French Army bled white at Verdun, the British stalemated on the Somme and off the coast of Jutland, no Allied Power could point to victories against the Central Powers equal to Russia's against Turkey in Anatolia, or Brusilov's against Austria-Hungary in the Carpathians: while the British and French measured success in terms of hundreds of square feet captured from the Germans, Russia, under Brusilov, had seized from the Habsburgs an area larger than Belgium. To Miliukov

---

[80] Cited in McMeekin, *Russian Revolution*, 78. On the ministers' leaving the assembly, see Katkov, *Russia, 1917*, 191. Rodzianko, similarly informed, also left the Chamber. They foresaw the seditious character of the forthcoming speeches.

[81] An annotated version can be found in English in Pavel Miliukov, "Speech of 14 November 1916," in Golder, *Documents*, 154–66.

[82] Miliukov, "Speech," in Golder, *Documents*, 155.

and the Bloc, it was as if none of it counted, because executive control of the government still belonged to the tsar and not the Duma. As Sean McMeekin has observed, "the improvement of Russia's strategic position in 1916, by all political logic, should have cooled down tempers on the home front."[83] The fact that it did not reveals how far Russia's Duma politicians were primarily occupied in fighting another war: not against Germany but against the tsar and, still more, *against the theocratic principle.*

To discredit the tsar and this principle Miliukov accused the government not only of incompetence, but of complicity with the Germans. "From one end of the Russian land to the other," Miliukov claimed (quoting, as evidence, a speech of his own from 1915), "there are spreading rumors of treachery and treason . . . rumors [that] reach high and spare none." By that, everyone knew that Miliukov meant the German-born Empress and the allegedly pro-German Chairman of the Council of Ministers, Stürmer. To support this claim, Miliukov pointed to a document which he had become aware of on a recent visit to Western Europe. This, he claimed, was a blueprint for the sabotaging of the Russian war effort from within, which the pro-German party in the Russian government (i.e. Stürmer and the empress) were now in practice following. "Gentlemen," Miliukov appealed to the chamber, "if our own Government wanted deliberately to set itself a task, or if the Germans wanted to employ their own means for the same purpose . . . they could not do better than to act as the Russian Government has acted."[84] To "substantiate" these extraordinarily serious claims, Miliukov then produced newspaper clippings from the enemy press in Berlin, Cologne and Vienna, which speculated hopefully that Stürmer would prove to be a pro-German.

But Miliukov's primary evidence consisted of conversations he had had with unidentified "people" in Switzerland (a country he acknowledged as a "place where all kinds of propaganda meet"). Purportedly, these "people" had revealed to Miliukov the "lines of communication" whereby the German government had succeeded in installing Stürmer.[85] Miliukov then referred to the *Berner Tagwacht,* a Swiss newspaper that had published a series of articles during the summer of 1916 claiming that secret negotiations were taking place even now between the German and Russian governments for a secret peace that would betray Russia's war dead and its foreign allies.[86] What Miliukov did not reveal, however, probably because he did not know it, was the fact that the *Berner Tagwacht* was the organ of the Swiss Social Democratic

---

[83] McMeekin, *Russian Revolution,* 76.
[84] Miliukov, "Speech," in Golder, *Documents,* 155–56.
[85] Ibid., 161–62.　　　　[86] See Katkov, *Russia, 1917,* 191–93.

(i.e. Socialist) Party, which had long since been subverted by the German government. Indeed, its editor in 1916, was one Robert Grimm. Less than twelve months later Grimm would accompany Lenin on the famous "sealed train" put at his disposal by the German government to take him from exile in Switzerland (where Lenin had close relations both with the very Swiss Social Democrats who published the *Tagwacht* and, it is now clear, their German handlers) to revolutionary Petrograd, while the German Marxist Karl Radek, one of the *Tagwacht*'s frequent contributors, was the future head of Lenin's Comintern.[87] Far from uncovering a German plot to subvert the Russian war effort, the duped Miliukov had instead become the instrument of a German misinformation operation.

The other target of Miliukov's speech was Protopopov, the newly appointed Minister of the Interior, an Octobrist and former deputy president of the Duma. As we have seen, many members of the opposition had hailed Protopopov's appointment in September as a victory. But we now know that Miliukov had not. On the contrary, apparently sensing the danger that Protopopov's appointment represented to the unity of the Bloc and its hope of forcing Nicholas to submit to a properly constitutional, English-style regime, Miliukov, even in September, had not joined in the celebrations when Protopopov was named interior minister. Back then, as new evidence has shown, at a meeting between the former Deputy President of the Duma and his former Progressive Bloc colleagues at Rodzianko's apartment on October 19, Miliukov accused Protopopov of "plunging a knife into the Bloc's back."[88] "At this [difficult] moment you, a person endowed with the Duma's trust, became part of the Stürmer cabinet. At such a [crucial] moment it is impermissible to uphold the confusion [about a public cabinet] that may result from your appointment," Miliukov continued. Significantly, Miliukov made no mention of Rasputin, or of Protopopov's meeting with a German businessman named Warburg while traveling with Miliukov on a Duma delegation to Western Europe. On the contrary, it was precisely the *risk* that Protopopov's appointment might have *succeeded* in reconciling monarch and Duma, that Protopopov's might indeed have been the *first* of *many* appointments from that body, and that such a ministry of men enjoying "public confidence" through their membership of the Duma might have been brought into existence by the *tsar himself* without a fundamental change to Russia's constitution having first been enacted, that was the issue.

---

[87] On the extent of Lenin's co-option by and cooperation with the German government for the sake of fomenting revolution in Russia, see McMeekin, *Russian Revolution*, 127–36.
[88] For what follows, see Lyandres, "Progressive Bloc politics," 458–64.

With his November 1 speech, Miliukov made this hostility public. Thus, Protopopov, too, Miliukov claimed, was a traitor and agent of German influence. As evidence, Miliukov drew the chamber's attention to Protopopov's meeting with Warburg. Now, Miliukov, who had been aware at the time of Protopopov's (apparently chance) meeting with Warburg, had never before raised any suggestion that that meeting might have been compromising. On the contrary, Miliukov had continued for months to support Protopopov as deputy president of the Duma. Moreover, a Duma-led investigation into the Warburg meeting had cleared Protopopov of any wrongdoing. Only now, a month and a half *after* Protopopov had gone to work for the government, did Miliukov find Protopopov's actions suspicious. As regards the attack on Protopopov, then, Miliukov's November 1 speech was the product of Miliukov's failure to browbeat Protopopov into stepping aside. It aimed to discredit any idea that the *tsar*, and not the leaders of the Bloc, could appoint a popular ministry from among the members of the Duma before it took root.[89]

So, Miliukov posed his famous rhetorical question in regard to what Miliukov considered to be Russia's abysmal war effort. "What is it, stupidity or treason?" Though Miliukov later denied that this was his intention, his audience in the Duma in 1916 took the hint. "Treason!," the stenographic report records a voice crying in reply from the floor. Hammering his message of betrayal and foreign interference home by a citation, Miliukov read against Duma rules in the original German, from the *Neue Freie Presse*, a Viennese newspaper, in which the original author exulted in the Central Powers' luck in cultivating the pro-German faction "said to gather around the young empress." No matter her services to Russia, no matter how many bloody amputations she assisted at or how many dying Russian officers whose final moments she had eased, Alexandra had now been identified as the enemy. As Miliukov well knew, it was enough to justify a revolution. For in naming the empress in the context of treason, Miliukov had crossed the line no public figure had dared before to cross. And he was fully aware of what he was doing. "You ask, 'How can we start a fight [against the government] while the war is on?,'" Miliukov put it to the chamber in conclusion. "But, gentlemen, it is only in wartime that they [i.e. the government] are a menace. They

---

[89] Miliukov's speech opened the floodgates for all manner of *ad hominem* attacks on Protopopov. It was now alleged, for example, that Protopopov was mad, possibly on account of the venereal disease which he allegedly sought treatment for from one of Rasputin's shadowy associates, the Buriat "doctor" and dispenser of Tibetan medicine, Badmaev. And yet nothing had been found to be wrong with Protopopov's mental condition just months before, when he had won accolades in London and Paris for his leadership of the Duma delegation. As Lieven comments, "Nicholas can be forgiven for his remark that the disease must have come on rather rapidly in the days since he had chosen Protopopov to be his minister." See Lieven, *Towards the Flame*, 351.

are a menace to the war, and it is precisely for this reason, in time of war and in the name of war . . . that we are fighting them."[90] His fellow deputies loved it. *"Cries:* 'Bravo!' Stormy and prolonged applause, on the left, in the center, and the left section of the right," the session transcript recorded.[91] When the government demanded a transcript of Miliukov's speech, Rodzianko, in an act of defiance, simply refused to hand it over. But typed up, copied, and distributed on broadsheet, the speech reached millions of Russians at home and in the trenches at the front.[92] Miliukov's speech was the first, calculated act of the Revolution.[93] Indeed, the verdict of a recent historian is damning: "Like Guchkov and Kerensky, Miliukov attacked the government ostensibly to root out corruption and improve Russia's chances of winning the war, in reality to increase [his] own power and influence. They [i.e. all three men] should have been more careful what they wished for."[94]

෨෨ ෨෨ ෨෨

The monarchy's isolation as the revolution approached is impossible to ignore in the sources. But it was isolated, to a very large extent, because the opposition rejected every gesture of rapprochement that might have brought monarchy and country together. Nicholas made two final gestures of conciliation. First, he sent the ministers of War and the Navy to the Duma to appeal for cooperation, reassuring the Duma of the armed forces' adequate provisioning, and thanking the Russian people "and their representatives" for their support in meeting the army's needs.[95] But, as always, Duma leaders preferred to interpret the gesture as one of weakness, a covert signal that the two men wanted to flee the sinking ship of the Council of Ministers and make common cause with the Bloc.[96] Then, a fortnight later, Nicholas dismissed the demonized Stürmer, and installed Aleksandr Trepov in his place as Chairman. Until that time Minister of Transport, Trepov, whose bearing some compared to that of Stolypin, had been regarded, even by the Duma, as a competent and patriotic minister. As Chairman, Trepov intended to form a ministry acceptable to the Duma, carry through the emancipation of Jews, and improve the conditions of workers. Meeting privately with Rodzianko, he even obtained the Duma's support on condition that he obtained the dismissal of Protopopov and other ministers not to the Bloc's liking. Appearing in person before the chamber, Trepov made

---

[90] Lyandres, "Progressive Bloc politics," 165.   [91] Ibid., 166.
[92] Pipes, *Russian Revolution*, 255.
[93] As believed at the time by Voeikov, *S tsarem*, 166.
[94] McMeekin, *Russian Revolution*, 79.
[95] Pipes, *Russian Revolution*, 257.
[96] Rodzianko, "Memoirs," in Golder, *Documents*, 114: "The idea back of their speeches was this: 'If the other ministers disagree with the Duma, we two, representing the army and navy, wish to go hand in hand with the people.'"

a speech asking the Bloc to join the government in "forget[ting] our squabbles" and "postpon[ing] our feuds. In the name of the government, I declare directly and openly that it wishes to commit its energies to constructive, pragmatic work in cooperation with the legislature."[97] As a pledge of the government's determination to see the war through to victory, he confirmed what had, up until this time, only been rumors: that England and France had indeed promised Russia sovereignty over Constantinople and the Turkish Straits.

And yet, for his troubles, Trepov was hissed and booed at for forty minutes like a traitor.[98] Leading the heckling was future Provisional Government Minister of Justice, Kerensky. Then, Vladimir Purishkevich, a hot-headed right-wing deputy who loved to declare his loyalty to the monarchy but did more than most to undermine it, got to his feet to deliver an excoriating denunciation of Alexandra and the Siberian "holy man" who was her spiritual advisor. It must all have seemed absurd to Nicholas: in appointing Trepov, he had gone pointedly against the advice offered him by his wife and Rasputin.

Meanwhile, between Nicholas and Trepov, the sticking point became Protopopov. Still believing that the Duma could be induced to cooperate with the government on Rodzianko's terms, Trepov succeeded in persuading Nicholas to dismiss Protopopov, only for Alexandra, at Rasputin's bidding, later to pressure Nicholas into reversing his decision. In fact, Nicholas's appointment of Trepov ended up representing a last example of that independence from his wife in political matters that Nicholas had heretofore maintained. Traveling by train for the special purpose of imposing her judgment, Alexandra prevailed by boiling the question down to one of *teokratia*. At stake, she said, she said, "is the question of the monarchy and your prestige. . . . The Czar rules in Russia and not the Duma."[99] She was right. That *was* the significance of her husband's "quarrel" with the Duma. But she was utterly wrong in believing that the advice of the Siberian holy man was the right ground to fight it on. "To follow our Friend's counsels, I assure you, is right," she told him a day later. "A country where a man of God helps the Sovereign will never be lost and it's true — only one must listen, trust and ask advice — not think He does not know. God opens everything to Him . . . and when He blesses an undertaking, it succeeds."[100] It's a measure of how far, for Alexandra, Rasputin's word had become the only touchstone of *teokratia* that the capitalized pronouns ("He," "Him") in this letter refer not to God but the Siberian peasant.

[97] Pipes, *Russian Revolution*, 257.   [98] Ibid., 258.
[99] Alexandra to Nicholas II (A. 1591), November 12, 1916, in Fuhrmann, *Complete Wartime*, 652–54.
[100] Alexandra to Nicholas II (A. 1600), December 5, 1916, in Fuhrmann, *Complete Wartime*, 657–58.

ᕀ   ᕀ   ᕀ

Bulgakov, looking back in 1918 on the sequence of events that led to the revolution, concluded that it was a mistake to view them only as a failure of politics. A truly spiritual struggle was going on beneath them, between good and evil. In that spiritual struggle, Rasputin was the symptom, but not in a true sense the cause of the evil. As Bulgakov put it in "At the feast of the gods," Rasputin was "the point of application and medium for the operation of . . . mystical forces.... The tsar called for a prophet of theocratic inspirations . . . Was it his fault alone that in answer to his call, which came from out of the depths, he received only a false prophet?"[101] The terms in which Bulgakov framed the question show that he did not think it was. Rather, his picture of Nicholas calling "out of the depths" for a "prophet of theocratic inspirations" was a reference both to the words of King (in Russian, *Tsar*) David in Psalm 130, and to the title of the essay collection, *Iz glubiny* ["Out of the Depths"], in which Bulgakov's dialogue was first published; as such, Nicholas's words, and his true but misdirected piety, was intended in the dark days of 1918 as a metaphor for Russia itself. Not for the last time, Bulgakov was eliding the fate of Russia's last tsar with the fate of Russia itself. And, remarkably, although Bulgakov had in these years no access to Nicholas's thoughts, it *was* also a good description of his inner condition: as 1916 drew to an end, the impression reflected in Nicholas's diary is of a man exhausted, certainly, but perhaps also inwardly broken. The nausea that had sent him to bed way back in August 1914 seemed once again to seize him. "Felt feeble [*ramol'no*] and went to bed before dinner," he wrote on November 24/December 7: "In the evening the feeling left."[102] Physically and spiritually worn out, he slept the following morning until ten.

As a recent historian has noted, however, all this was in a way very odd. The Russian Revolution need not have happened — certainly not for the reasons with which much of it was justified at the time. As that historian notes, "1916 was Russia's best year yet in the war, and her prospects for 1917 appeared bright."[103] To be sure, the food supply problem in the cities, especially Petrograd, persisted. But (and in contrast not least to conditions in Germany) no one was starving. Arms production remained up, specialized supplies of equipment from Russia's Allies were flowing in along new railways, and the German war effort itself was so strained by the effects of the British naval blockade, that, from the Baltic to the Black Sea, Russia now enjoyed a sixty percent superiority over the enemy in both guns and men. A major

---

[101] Bulgakov, "At the feast of the gods," 80.
[102] Nicholas II, November 24, 1916, in Diary (2), 613.
[103] McMeekin, *Russian Revolution*, 76.

offensive for the spring of 1917, that included a Russian amphibious attack on Constantinople, and which, in coordination with British and French offensives in the West, might have brought about an end to the war, was even then in planning. As the historian cited above continues, "Russia's problems, as the third winter of the Great War approached, were real. But they were made to seem worse than they actually were by ambitious politicians who claimed to have easy solutions for them."[104]

Moreover, as 1917 would prove, the easy solutions those politicians claimed to possess did not exist: gaining power, all these men would fail spectacularly in the exercise of it. Indeed, none of them would do any better at all than Nicholas; most of them far worse. And yet it was precisely these politicians who, at the end of 1916, were beginning to win the public argument. Even in the wider Romanov dynasty, the opinion had formed that only the very politicians who were accusing the government not only of incompetence but of treason, could steer the country out of the jaws of the collapse which everyone agreed now threatened *if only* Nicholas did not give way on the constitutional question. In November, no fewer than two grand dukes, Nicholas's cousins, including former Supreme Commander Nikolai Nikolaevich, visited him at Stavka to persuade him to give in to the Duma's demands. At assemblies of the United Nobility in Moscow and Petrograd, Russia's counts and princes publicly declared their transfer of their political allegiances to the Progressive Bloc.[105] Nicholas and Alexandra's political isolation was almost complete. Indeed, to the reader of Nicholas's diary and letters, there is the strong sense that, at the beginning of December 1916, Nicholas had reached the end of his endurance. He would and could not, out of conscience, concede control of government to the Duma, for to do so would be to betray the entire theory of politics he had sworn to uphold at his coronation. On the other hand, after more than twenty years of personal responsibility for Russia's fortunes, he was tired and isolated. The only political advisors he had left were his wife and a Siberian peasant. In "normal" times, he would not have (and had not) made himself their prisoner. But who else was there who intuited the principles at stake?

That winter, then, Nicholas did his best to keep the combined wheels of Russia's war effort and its *teokratia* ticking over. On November 26, he, Alexandra, and Alexei joined 20,000 recipients of the St George's cross for three prayer services, after which bags of food and other items were distributed.[106] In early December, he spent two hours at a factory specializing in producing optical glass for the War and Navy Ministries and came away "very happy with the state of affairs."[107] On December

[104] Ibid., 77–78.   [105] Pipes, *Russian Revolution*, 256.
[106] Nicholas II, November 26, 1916, in Diary (2), 613.
[107] Nicholas II, December 4, 1916, in Diary (2), 614.

4, he returned to Stavka, not intending, it seems, to do anything other than remain the bearer and guardian of Russia's moral-religious ideal.

Increasingly, he placed his hopes in the Virgin Mary. Mary, the *Bogoroditsa*, "God-bearer," or "Mother of God" in Russian, had assumed a central role in Nicholas's inner life. References to her and her images become more and more frequent in his correspondence. During Alexandra's stay at Stavka in the happier days of the summer 1916, it had come to her attention that one of Mogilev's monasteries (the seventeenth-century Annunciation-Brotherhood Monastery) possessed a wonder-working icon of the Virgin.[108] She made frequent visits to pray in front of it. So, thereafter, did Nicholas.[109] Back at Tsarskoye Selo, Alexandra sought similar consolation in a visit to the ancient Russian town of Novgorod, where she attended Mass and venerated Novgorod's ancient icons. When she returned to Tsarskoye Selo, she sent an image of the Virgin ("so lovely... her face is so sweet") that she had acquired to Nicholas at Stavka, suggesting that he hang it above his bed. Writing to thank her in a letter of the 13th, Nicholas II again bore witness to the special place assumed in his prayers at this time by Mary. As Nicholas reported to Alexandra, he had now determined to dismiss the Chairman of the Council of Ministers, Trepov, and "I on purpose went to pray before this conversation at the Virgin's image and felt quiet after."[110]

But if this was the *form* of *teokratia*, its substance had been subverted from within. The place from which a *teokratia* ought to be ruled is the Orthodox monarch's consecrated conscience in unobstructed dialogue before God. Deciding that her husband's conscience wasn't up to the task, however, Alexandra had succeeded, by the end of 1916, in transferring the burden of rule to the conscience of a would-be prophet (of possible, unintended, demonic inspiration). So it was that in December 1916, Nicholas had dismissed the competent Trepov not truly out of a "dialogue of prayer" in his own heart with God, but at Alexandra and, still more, Rasputin's behest. This was because Trepov, seeking to put

---

[108] The monastery was founded under Polish rule, closed after the Bolshevik Revolution of 1917, and badly damaged during the Second World War. Rather than restoring it, Soviet authorities chose to tear the ruins down, and build an apartment block on the site. The monastery's wonder-working icon of Mary was, however, saved, and is today on display for veneration in the Cathedral of the Three Holy Hierarchs (Basil the Great, Gregory the Theologian, and John Chrysostom) in the center of Mogilev. This transferal of the icon is doubtless at the root of the tradition that Nicholas "frequently prayed" here. He did not. He frequently prayed before the icon which was then located in a monastery in another part of Mogilev that has now been destroyed. See Sergei Somov, *Pravoslavnye Monastyri Belarusi* (Minsk: Chetyri Chetverti, 2003), 107.

[109] Writing to Alexandra from Stavka on December 10, Nicholas noted the special trip he made to the monastery to pray before the image: Nicholas II to Alexandra (N. 1626), December 13, 1916, in Fuhrmann, *Complete Wartime*, 668.

[110] Nicholas II to Alexandra (N. 1638), December 13, 1916, in Fuhrmann, *Complete Wartime*, 673.

an end once and for all to the rumor mill surrounding Rasputin, and judging that the supposed holy man's chief motivation was pecuniary (that is, the bribes and kickbacks he received from ministers keen to indulge him), decided to offer the peasant a "bribe to end all bribes" — a quarter of a million rubles — on condition that he leave Petrograd and return, for good, to Siberia.[111] It says much about what motivated Rasputin that while he was at first tempted to accept Trepov's money, he decided in the end to inform Alexandra, who now viewed Trepov as a threat to the life of her son. Rasputin, meanwhile, in view of the scale of the bribe the Siberian peasant had turned down, had vindicated himself in her eyes as, indeed, a holy man, a model of righteousness. "We have been placed by God on a Throne and we must keep it firm and give it over to our Son untouched," Alexandra persisted in a letter to her husband on the issues at stake.[112] Worrying over Nicholas, she said, as over a "tender, soft-hearted child, which needs guiding," she urged him to be a "real Tsar" ("Be Peter the Great, John [i.e. Ivan] the Terrible, Emperor Paul — crush them under you"). She knew he would find such role models ridiculous ("now don't you laugh, naughty one!"), but her insistence that her husband should harken to Rasputin as the guide God had sent them was serious.[113] "I know he leads us right," she reassured him.[114]

And yet there were also signs that might have given Alexandra pause to question her confidence in Rasputin's guidance. What had taken Alexandra to Novgorod was the presence there in a convent of a recluse renowned for her capacities as a seer. According to one source, when introduced to the empress, the holy woman had blurted out "Behold, the martyred Empress Alexandra."[115] In her own account of the trip, Alexandra said that the *staritsa* greeted her as "you, the beautiful one," and urged her "not [to] fear the heavy cross."[116] The old holy woman also gave the Empress an apple, the eating of which was supposed to bring her a blessing. Alexandra sent it on to her husband at Stavka, along with the icon of the Virgin that Alexandra suggested Nicholas hang above his bed at Mogilev. But, ostensibly at least, no blessing ensued but a curse: the day after Alexandra's letter, and the apple from the holy woman, reached Stavka, the news broke that Rasputin was dead, having been poisoned, shot in the back of the head, and drowned in the freezing Neva by Nicholas's favorite nephew, Grand Duke Dmitri

---

[111] Smith, *Rasputin*, 568.
[112] Alexandra to Nicholas II (A. 1642), December 14, 1916, in Fuhrmann, *Complete Wartime*, 674–76.
[113] Alexandra to Nicholas II (A. 1637), December 13, 1916, in Fuhrmann, *Complete Wartime*, 671–73.   [114] Ibid.   [115] Vyrubova, *Memories*, 72.
[116] Alexandra to Nicholas II (A. 1633), December 12, 1916, in Fuhrmann, *Complete Wartime*, 669–71.

Pavlovich, and his niece's husband, Prince Felix Yusupov, on the very day when Nicholas had eaten the *staritsa*'s apple.[117]

ري   ري   ري

Fr Vasiliev, the imperial family's current confessor, buried Rasputin in a grave within the grounds of Tsarskoye Selo on December 21. To the rest of his extended family's outrage, Nicholas insisted on punishment for the holy man's killers.[118] Now more isolated than ever, the imperial couple prepared for Christmas in an atmosphere of gloom and mourning. All around Nicholas, people advised him to give up his prerogatives and surrender to the opposition. But in his own heart, Russia remained what it always had been, a *teokratia*. As usual, Nicholas saw the New Year in in church. "At 11.50 p.m. went to prayers. Ardently prayed that the Lord would have mercy on Russia!" he wrote in his diary.[119] Five days later, on the eve of the Feast of the Epiphany, Fr Vasiliev sprinkled the family's home in the Alexander Palace with holy water. It was an annual custom. But as one that was at root an exorcism, its meaning had never seemed more immediate than at the beginning of 1917. As Nicholas told Prince Golitsyn, his last Chairman of the Council of Ministers, at their audience, "all is in God's hands — His will be done."[120]

---

[117] On the murder, see Smith, *Rasputin*, 590–96.
[118] Nicholas exiled Felix Yusupov to his estates near Bryansk, and Dmitri Pavlovich to Persia to serve with the Russian Army.
[119] Nicholas II, December 31, 1916, in *Diary* (2), 617.
[120] Cited in McMeekin, *Russian Revolution*, 84.

CHAPTER ELEVEN

Pskov

TOMBSTONE OF
THE RUSSIAN *TEOKRATIA*

F OR MILE AFTER MILE, THE BUS MADE ITS WAY through the same flat, desolate landscape: beige fields, mud, stripped trees, concrete apartment blocks, filling stations, panel beaters and mechanics, machinery sales yards, the withered stalks of unidentified crops clinging to rocky soil. It was the morning service to Pskov, and I had almost missed it. Outside, the temperature hovered sullenly around zero; the air was cold but humid from the melting snow. Inside the bus, however, a scorching, dry air blew relentlessly from the brown plastic vents overhead, condensation dripped down the panes of cracked double glazing, and I sat uncomfortably on a rust-colored acrylic seat tilted at an irremediable forty-five-degree angle, the adjusting side lever having long since jammed or broken.

We left St Petersburg behind and, eventually, somewhere beyond Gatchina, the conifers returned. The ordinarily faintly sinister sight of their dark green needles was welcome relief from the relentless dystopian landscape closer to the city. We crossed half-frozen rivers and streams. Out in the forest, the earth was still covered in a layer of snow. Winter had not yet released its grip. An hour out from Pskov, the temperature dropped, and it began to snow. "Defend the Interests of the Working Man!" shouted a Communist Party campaign poster from a roadside hoarding as we entered the city. Elections for Russia's State Duma were scheduled in six months' time, and the country's remaining communists were trying to position themselves as a real left-wing alternative to the ruling United Russia Party. (That year, they ended up winning 17 percent of the vote, lower than expected.)

When we reached Pskov, the bus didn't stop, as I had expected, at the city's inter-city bus terminal, which was located next to the main train station I had gone to see. We appeared to be somewhere in the suburbs. Complaining to the driver as he unloaded my pack into a foot of snow, I pointed out that I thought the bus service stopped at the bus station.

"It stops at *our* bus station," he replied, gesturing towards the company logo on the small building behind his shoulder. "It's a pity I didn't know you wanted to go to the main bus station," he continued. "We drove straight past it. But don't worry. There's a public bus stop four hundred meters down on the other side of the road. Bus number six. I don't know whether it goes to the station but you can ask the driver."

With the snow falling again, I heaved my pack onto my shoulders and trudged through the mixture of mud and ice along the roadside. I didn't make it the full four hundred meters. Spotting a standing taxi, I decided that I could afford the luxury of private transport. Ten minutes and 150 rubles ($3) later, I was dropped in the main square of Pskov in front of the green and white stucco train station that was the sole reason for my journey. It was here, on March 2/15, 1917, while the imperial train sat impounded amid the snow at one of the station's platforms, that Nicholas signed his name to a document renouncing the throne. This was it: the struggle, and an age in the history of mankind was over. As Bulgakov put it in "At the feast of the gods," "the Constantinian epoch ended for Byzantium in 1453, and for the entire Orthodox Church on March 2, 1917." And it did so in Pskov. Pskov is the tombstone of Russia's *teokratia*, the place where the theocratic principle expired in Russian culture

Just as it was that afternoon in 1917, the sky when I visited was leaden, the snow silently falling. My feet were beginning to get cold, and if I was to explore the station and town for vestiges of the momentous event that took place there, I needed to find a place to store my pack. I entered the main station, and laid my rucksack on the conveyor belt for the mandatory security screening. Five police officers in navy uniforms and pointed hats loitered off to the side of the main concourse. I addressed one standing somewhat apart from the rest of the group. In his early twenties, the seriousness of his junior rank still studiously composed on his still boyish face, he listened shyly as I enquired about the existence of a left-luggage room. When I had first visited Russia a decade and a half before, these had invariably been located in dimly lit concrete basements, reached only after hauling your luggage down two flights of cold concrete stairs, and were invariably staffed by middle-aged women in pink tracksuits covered, as a rule, by brown aprons. But things had since changed here in Pskov.

"Come with me," said the policeman. In Pskov, the track-suited matrons and the dungeon-esque left-luggage rooms of other cities' train stations were now a thing of the past, phased out in favor of the kind of automatic steel lockers you might find in any Western European city. Kindly, the policeman made sure I understood how it worked so that I would have no problems retrieving my bag later. It occurred to me that a dozen years before, a policeman like him would have asked me for a bribe.

We struck up a conversation. His name was Pavel, and he had been born and raised in Pskov. Did he know, I asked, whether there was a memorial in the station to the tsar's abdication?

At first, he seemed not to have understood. But the event was so momentous, I felt there must be some record of its having taken place, so I rephrased my question, this time by telling a story. "*In 1917, at a platform in this station, the last Russian tsar signed a document renouncing the throne..."*

He signaled that I should follow him. Crossing the concourse, we left the shelter of the station and were once again in a world of white, where the sky was the same dirty white hue as the snow lying on the platform and tracks. A train stood idle at an outer platform. Pavel pointed to a bronze plaque under an ornate lamp halfway up the green and white stucco station wall.

> *On 2nd (15th) March 1917 at*
> *15 hours and 05 minutes in the saloon wagon*
> *of the imperial train in station at Pskov*
> *Emperor Nicholas II abdicated*
> *the throne*
> *of the Russian State*

The snow fell silently around us.

I asked Pavel what he thought. Was Nicholas a good tsar or not?

"I don't know," he modestly replied. "At school I found history boring. But I'm interested in it now."

School, for Pavel, could not have been more than five or six years ago, and, as a police officer in training he would have had to study national history after leaving, too.

"I really don't know very much about the last tsar," he continued. "But perhaps because of living here, I've always felt somehow close to his time. They say that he issued a decree to build schools for simple people, you know, peasants, who had no education. If he did that, then he was a good tsar. And after the Revolution there was so much suffering."

It was a simple yardstick, but defensible enough on its own terms. The expansion of literacy is often touted as one of the great achievements of early Soviet Russia. But like many others, it was built on foundations laid by the late imperial regime. Between 1895 and the outbreak of the First World War in 1914, spending on education rose from two million to 82 million rubles. As a proportion of the fast-expanding imperial budget, education more than doubled the share it received during Nicholas's reign.[1] As we have noted already, when the government set itself the goal of universal adult literacy by 1925, it was entirely realistic.

Pavel was clearly proud of his town.

"Pskov has a very long history," he said. "Its kremlin is very strong. No one has ever conquered it."

"Yes," I replied. "But didn't the Germans occupy the town in the Second World War?"

---

[1] The figure is from Peter Waldron, "State Finances," in Dominic Lieven, ed., *Cambridge History of Russia*, vol. 2: *Imperial Russia (1689–1917)* (Cambridge: Cambridge University Press, 2008), 473.

"That is true," he admitted: "from 1941 until 1944 they were here . . ." The crackling of his radio interrupted his thoughts.

"Will you visit the chapel?" he asked when the crackling stopped.

"What chapel?" I asked.

"For the tsar. It's on the other side of the station building, in the square."

That there was a shrine at all to Nicholas anywhere in Pskov came as news to me.

"Yes, of course," I replied. "Is it open?"

"It's open every day. It's just over there, back out through the main door."

                                                  ~ ~ ~

Retracing my route through the station, I found myself back in the square in front of the station. Most of the space was given over to a car park and a bus stop. But, on a raised platform in the middle of it, beneath the bare branches of a linden tree, there was a small but ornate building, painted in the same green and white livery as the station, which I had somehow missed before. A perfect square in the style of St Petersburg baroque that gave way to a masonry dome topped in turn by a bronze onion mounted with an Orthodox cross, this was, I discovered from reading the plaque affixed to the side of the building, Pskov's "Royal (lit. tsarist) Chapel." Erected on March 17, 2003 — the eighty-sixth anniversary of the abdication — it had been consecrated by Pskov's metropolitan in the presence of the local governor.

Pulling on the right of the pair of honey-colored doors that formed the entrance, I entered. Inside, the chapel glowed with the invisible energy of an active place of pilgrimage. In front of the cross-shaped window in the apse, lamps hanging from the ceiling shimmered before three large icons: of Christ's Resurrection (in the center), the Mother of God (in a place of honor to the right), and Russia's Royal Passion-bearers (to the left). Between the glass covering each icon and the wooden frame surrounding it, pilgrims had inserted a range of smaller images of their own printed on card or paper, "votives" or tokens of devotion and thanksgiving to God for the sainted family's intercessions. There were so many such votives that they cascaded onto a small table set in front of the icons, while on the small stand positioned in the center of the space, another icon of the Romanovs lay decorated with yet more votives. I crossed myself and lit two candles before the main image of the family.

Looking around the room, I noticed behind me, silently perched behind a counter, a plump old woman selling icons.

"Have you had many visitors today?" I asked.

"No, not so many today," she replied. "It's not the season for traveling. We get many more in summer."

"Are you from far away?," she asked, having picked up on my accent.

I replied that I was Australian, and, hoping to bridge the cultural gap between us, observed that our own queen was a distant relation of Nicholas II.

"Ah," she sighed, unsurprised. "Your queen has Russian roots!" she concluded, reflecting the widespread Russian belief that every decent person had to have some connection to Russia and its good people.

"You could say that," I replied, realizing the futility of attempting a better explanation. "It's a tragic story," I added, pointing towards the Romanovs' icon.

"Yes, it is. They shot them all: Nicholas Aleksandrovich; Alexandra Feodorovna; Alexis and the girls."

"Was Nicholas a good tsar?" I then asked, putting to her the same question I had put to Pavel.

"Of course!," she replied as if the question were beyond dispute, before drawing a connection to Russia's present. "And, today, we have a good president too. He goes to church, prays to the icons, looks after his wife and family, helps the poor."

I nodded. In fact, Putin had divorced his wife two years before. I told the lady that in the West many people say that Putin is a bad man.

"But how?," she replied: "We Russians are simple people. We help. Where people are in need, we help. Like in Syria. We help them. Russia has never claimed anything for itself."

I did not doubt that she believed this.

"What else will you see in Pskov?" she asked: "The cathedral?"

"Yes," I said: "and the Spassko-Trinity Monastery on the other side of the river."

"*Molodets!* ["Well done!"]," she said, approving of my itinerary: "Do you know the number of the bus? I'll write it down for you."

I thanked her and took a final look at the shrine.

"God be with you," the woman said behind me as I left.

As I descended the shallow steps, two women, elegantly-clad in long mink coats, passed me in the other direction. Crossing themselves, they entered.

"So long as there is a Russian God, there will be a Russian Tsar," Merezhkovsky had asserted in 1907.[2] It seemed he was right, only now that tsar was present in the form of a saint's cult. Tombstone in 1917 of the theocratic principle, Pskov was also a certain window on that principle's revival.

∽ ∽ ∽

About a century before Constantinople fells to the Turks in 1453, Grand Prince Basil I (1359–89) of Moscow, apparently already seeing

---

[2] Merezhkovsky, *Tsar et la révolution*, 155.

the writing on the wall for Byzantium, wrote to the patriarch to notify him that the Muscovites would henceforth cease to commemorate the Byzantine emperor in the liturgy. In reply, Ecumenical Patriarch Antony IV (1389–97) issued one of the most famous statements of Eastern Christian political theology. "It is not a good thing, my son, for you to say 'We have a Church but no Emperor,'" the patriarch wrote to the grand prince: "It is not possible for Christians to have a Church without an Emperor, for the imperial sovereignty and the Church form a single entity and they cannot be separated from each other."[3] To justify his teaching the patriarch then quoted the words of Scripture: "Fear God, honour the Emperor" (1 Peter 2:17). But is Eastern Orthodoxy wed to *teokratia*, the theocratic principle, to authority "by the grace of God, not popular dispensation," as the patriarch, and this book, would have it? The question, much disputed then and since, was raised by the very location where Nicholas's abdication took place.[4] That the Russian *teokratia* expired in 1917 at the train station in Pskov was, strictly speaking, a coincidence: if the leaders of the Revolution had played their cards differently, Nicholas's train might have been stopped at any one of northern Russia's provincial stations, and the abdication have taken place there. But it was not, and in the end, it was in the ancient city of Pskov that the drama played out.

One of the original principalities of Kievan Rus', Pskov was already 1,100 years old when Nicholas arrived in 1917. Like nearby Novgorod, to which it was linked, it had a history different in many ways from that of the rest of Russia. Ruled by merchants and burghers through an elected *veche* (assembly), Novgorod and Pskov were Russia's "northern republics"; rather than theocratic-autocratic Moscow, their electoral-oligarchic political arrangements resembled the self-governing towns of the German Hanseatic League with which Novgorod and Pskov had traded for centuries. In Pskov, there was no tsar, God's image and anointed, until, in 1399, the city, though nominally still an autonomous republic, accepted the presence of a viceroy from Moscow (to which city Pskov definitively surrendered its independence in 1510). Did Pskov, and nearby Novgorod with it, "prove," then, that Orthodoxy and democracy were compatible? Such at least was the claim made by the Worldly Divine in an exchange with the Refugee in Bulgakov's "At the feast of the gods."

---

[3] Cited in George Ostrogorsky, *History of the Byzantine State*, rev. ed. (New Brunswick, NJ: Rutgers University Press, 1969), 535; also, Obolensky, *Byzantine Commonwealth*, 342–45. A translation of the whole relevant passage from the Patriarch's letter can be found in Ernest Barker, *Social and Political Thought in Byzantium* (Oxford: Oxford University Press, 1961), 194–96.

[4] For the most recent denial of this connection, see the "Declaration on the Russian World Teaching" by Public Orthodoxy, the Eastern Orthodox Christian Studies Center at Fordham University, on March 13, 2022: https://publicorthodoxy.org/2022/03/13/a-declaration-on-the-russian-world-russkii-mir-teaching/. Accessed October 9, 2024.

Sparking the debate between the two figures is the Refugee's claim, summed up in his affirmation that "the Constantinian epoch ended ... for the entire Orthodox world on 2 March 1917," that the tsar had genuine theological significance in Eastern Orthodoxy and that, therefore, as the meaning of the Russian Revolution was inseparably religious, the product of a clash between the (supernatural) faith of the Church and the (atheist) conclusions of modern, especially, nineteenth-century, European philosophy.

To this, the Worldly Divine replies as follows.

Worldly Divine: You repeat the widespread lie that Orthodoxy and autocracy are linked together, just as it is alleged by the Black Hundreds or the open enemies of the Church, by politicking writers such as Merezhkovsky, who carried on a flirtation with the revolution until it showed its teeth. [But] there is absolutely no link between Orthodoxy and autocracy except the historical one, and this has been clearly confirmed now that Orthodoxy has finally received its freedom, and no one can reproach it for an alliance with autocracy.

Then, when the Refugee, not accepting this answer, suggests that the revolution could itself be considered as a kind of mysterious vindication of his claim (since with it Russia had "brought on itself" the Church's longstanding anathema of all those who "think[ing] that Orthodox rulers ascend the throne not through God's blessing or that in the anointment there do not pass unto them the gifts of the Holy Spirit ... would dare to rebel against or betray them"), the Worldly Divine, reiterating his case, points to other considerations.[5]

Worldly Divine: All the same, I see nothing mystical in the union of Orthodoxy and autocracy. Orthodoxy flowered not only in Moscow but in the Northern Russian republics [he continued] where a great surge of national creativity was realized: icon painting and church building. It [Orthodoxy] lived under Batu [the Mongol conqueror of Kievan Rus]. It lived under the Sultan [who subjugated Byzantium in 1453] just as now under the Bolsheviks. It's possible to link its [Orthodoxy's] fate to autocracy only by closing one's eyes to history.[6]

In other words, the Worldly Divine alleges, the Refugee, making an error made by many before him (including, as today's Worldly Divines would doubtless have it, by the author of this book), has reduced the historical experience of Eastern Orthodoxy to that of Moscow, and thereby erected the theocratic principle evident in the history of the Muscovite tsardom into a political-theological "dogma" binding on all Eastern Orthodoxy. The history of republican Novgorod and Pskov, however, shows that the claim that theocracy is the "natural" political ideal of Eastern Orthodoxy is untrue and arbitrary: the Eastern Church

---

[5] Bulgakov, "At the feast of the gods," 111.   [6] Ibid., 112.

has embraced many different political regimes during its history. No single "political ideal" of Eastern Orthodoxy or unified Eastern Orthodox "political theology" exists. No religious meaning attaches, then, to the downfall of the Russian monarchy and Eastern Orthodoxy is at least as compatible with modern, European-style liberal democracy as it was with Byzantine and Muscovite theocracy. Indeed, to the extent that the politics of medieval Pskov and Novgorod were also electoral and democratic, even to call such democracy "modern" and "European" is misleading. It is authentically *Russian*, too, if only "mystics" such as the Refugee would open their eyes to see it.

Now, while it is true that Bulgakov, later in his career, would appear to have endorsed a version of the Worldly Divine's reasoning, in "At the feast of the gods," he rejected it.[7] There, argues the Refugee, the theologian's task is to consider the experience of the Church as a whole, not selectively. One swallow does not make a summer.

> *Refugee*: You point to the provincial centers of Orthodoxy. They exist with the center but the main line does not go through them. From the time of Constantine, Orthodoxy has had a universal-historical task: to found an Orthodox theocracy, unified as the Church. That was the drift of the idea of the Second and Third Rome.[8]

To the Refugee, then, the Russian Revolution did not somehow reveal the falseness of the Byzantine and Muscovite ideal of theocracy, let alone that Orthodoxy's true political ideal was democracy or republicanism all along. It was rather that, with the Revolution, the world notified the Church that it was withdrawing *its* consent to the project embarked upon in its name by Constantine — and without the world's consent and cooperation, the Church could not build her vision of a rightly ordered Christian society *freely*. (Bulgakov, remember, in becoming a "tsarist" never renounced his commitment to Christian *freedom*.) Christians should not expect, therefore, that an era of harmonious co-operation with modern society was about to dawn just because the Church had dropped its alliance with Constantine's successors. To be sure, "in 1917, the Constantinian epoch of Church history ended," but "the next period, which . . . has [already] begun," the Refugee affirmed, "has its analogy in the epoch of persecutions and the catacomb existence of the Church."[9] In view of the Bolsheviks' coming attack on the Russian Church, the statement may be considered prophetic. For all the flaws and failures of historical *teokratia*, its demise heralded for the Church, Bulgakov believed, an era of marginalization and even suffering. No lasting concordat with the political face of atheism was possible.

---

[7] On the abandonment of the ideal of *teokratia* by the (apparently "liberal") later Bulgakov, see Regula M. Zwahlen, "Sergii Bulgakov's Reinvention of Theocracy for a Democratic Age," *Journal of Orthodox Christian Studies* 3:2 (2020): 175–94.
[8] Bulgakov, "At the feast of the gods," 112.   [9] Ibid.

For Bulgakov, this did not mean that the Russian theocracy, having collapsed in the Revolution, should be restored. But the "theo-logic" on which it had been built should not be despised or ignored: it had been an entirely legitimate development, and an authentic historical realization of Eastern Orthodoxy's understanding of the apostolic deposit of faith (much as the medieval papacy had been for Roman Catholicism). "Of course, the single, *sobornyi* Apostolic Church will abide up to the end of time," says the Refugee, concluding his exchange with the Worldly Divine in "At the feast of the gods": "But whether present-day Greco-Russian Orthodoxy is adequate for that is hardly beyond question. I myself propose that, in fact, we have already gone beyond the limits of historical Orthodoxy, and that a new epoch has begun in the history of the Church, an epoch at least as different from that which preceded it, as, for example, the Constantinian epoch differs from that which came before it."[10] To be sure, as Bulgakov acknowledged, this new era is upon the Church because "theocracy in the form of a holy empire did not succeed; more accurately, its significance proved to be only preliminary, transfiguring, but not conclusive." But in answer to the Worldly Divine's original contention, the theocratic ideal must not for that reason be considered to have been an *error*. For its principles were embedded in the Church's faith itself, and "one can [not] consider as failure any lawful development which plays itself out to the end."[11]

❧   ❧   ❧

Later that day, I hailed a cab for the Spaso-Preobrazhensky ("Transfiguration of the Savior") Monastery, on the other side of the Velikaya River which bisects the city. Nine hundred years old, the riverside monastery is notable for its central church, the twelfth-century Cathedral of the Transfiguration, an ancient, white-washed brick cube surmounted by a squat black onion dome that preserves some of the only frescoes from Kievan Rus to have survived the thirteenth-century Mongol conquest both intact and in situ in all Russia. Painted by the famous Byzantine monk, Theophanes the Greek, the frescoes are widely regarded as some of the most beautiful in the Orthodox world. Crossing the bridge across the river on foot, therefore, I arrived to find the monastery sitting white-on-white amid the snows, as the skies overhead grew darker and darker until they were almost the color of the brooding onion dome. Pushing on the cathedral door, however, I discovered that the cathedral was shut. I tried the doors several times, doing nothing to muffle the sound of my banging, in the hope of forcing the repetition of the good luck I had had in Mogilev. Perhaps a resident monk would hear and take pity on me. But nobody came to open the door for me, and Theophanes's frescoes

---

[10] Bulgakov, "At the feast of the gods," 113.   [11] Ibid.

went unadmired. Poking around the rest of the grounds, I climbed a creaky wooden staircase and, pushing on another door halfway along the external timber landing, found myself in a tiny, upper-story timbered chapel, where I disturbed a middle-aged woman at her prayers in a room warm and fragrant with the scent of pine and beeswax. Excusing myself, I went back out onto the wooden landing and descended the stairs.

Back in the bi-chromal world of white-on-white against black sky, I followed a snow-bound path back past the squat cathedral towards the river. Children in snow boots and winter jackets were starting to come home from school, kicking the dirty brown slush by the side of the road. I crossed the bridge over the Velikaya back to Pskov's eastern side. At that point, the black river was probably one hundred and fifty feet wide, and, in the relatively mild tail-end of winter, not frozen but flowing quickly. The view was splendid, a vision of a vanished medieval Rus. On the eastern bank ahead of me, the conical tower of the restored "Bashnya" or city bastion, the tallest of the towers of the old city walls, answered the onion domes of the Transfiguration Monastery. Downriver were the towers and onion domes of the Krom. Descending a flight of Soviet-era concrete stairs to the riverside, I made the latter my destination. Russian cities were once known for the degraded quality of their public amenities. In their free time, Soviet citizens were expected to rest rather than relax, let alone cultivate the Western cult of personal fitness. But laid out ahead of me was a pleasant riverside promenade that, without the onion domes in the distance and the three inches of snow blanketing it, wouldn't have been out of place in any provincial town in northern Europe. Every hundred yards, the promenade widened to accommodate pairs of modern, steel benches, while modern streetlamps that stood at regular intervals suggested that the renovated promenade was intended as a pleasant place for the citizens of Pskov to walk or jog, even after dark. Halfway along the waterfront, the modern boat houses of the Pskov City Rowing Club, with their view across the river to the domed church and monastery complex, consolidated the impression of Pskov I was forming, as a more prosperous, more relaxed, even more "Western" kind of Russia than I had seen before. The border with Estonia and NATO — only twenty-five years ago a mere administrative boundary — lay a mere twenty-five miles to the west.

At length, I reached the Krom, the walled core of the old city sitting sheltering beneath grey-hatted conical towers on a promontory where the smaller Pskov River, a tributary, enters the Velikaya. The site, a natural stronghold, is the oldest part of the town, the work, in its current form, of a thirteenth-century Lithuanian prince called Daumantas, who, having stormed the town with his followers in 1266, defected from the still pagan society of his native Lithuania, adopted Orthodoxy, was accepted as Russian, and became immortalized as one of Pskov's ablest rulers. Inside the walls, preserved beneath perspex, are the excavated foundations of the cluster of trading stalls, houses, and workshops that grew up within the Krom over the following two centuries. These were the heyday of Pskov's prosperity, when the *veche*, or municipal assembly, ruled the city, and German, Swedish, and Danish merchants sailed up the Velikaya from the Baltic to trade with Pskov's own, the products of Northern Europe being exchanged for the furs and forest products in which the city specialized. But apart from the grey stones visible through the perspex, almost nothing from this heyday survives, and the Krom, being deserted on account of the inclement March weather, felt lifeless and morose, the commercial spirit that animated this once self-confident republic having long since been chased out of its historical encampment.

At the heart of the Krom today is, instead, a monument, as it were, to *teokratia*: the 1682 Cathedral of the Holy Trinity in Muscovite style. A tall, almost flat-roofed building with a central, oversized onion dome positioned among four outer onion domes in rigid symmetry, the cathedral appears to hold the rest of the citadel in self-conscious subjection, its spirit, like that of "theocratic" Moscow itself, stressing not the horizontal bonds of Pskov's local democracy, but order, verticality. Entrance is by a raised staircase, enclosed, gallery-style, with a roof. Going up the steps, I entered a church apparently devoid of visitors. Instead, I found company in an image that was, by now, a familiar backdrop to the world I had been exploring: the Icon of the New Russian Martyrs. Canonized for veneration by the faithful at the same assembly of the Russian Church that glorified Nicholas II and his family as saints in Moscow in 2000, the icon shows six rows of bishops, priests, monks and nuns representing the several thousand Orthodox Christians martyred during the 1920s and 1930s Anti-Religion Campaign, when Russia's new communist authorities, flushed with the confidence of history's apparent judgment in favor of Marx's atheism, sought to make the Orthodox Church go the same way as the monarchy, arresting priests and closing monasteries and churches. Implicitly drawing the same connection between the collapse of the monarchy and this attack on the church (of which Bulgakov seems already to have had an intuition when he prophesied the approach of a new "catacomb existence" for the Church in the era inaugurated by the demise of *teokratia*), in the icon's foreground stands a lone family group, Russia's Royal Passion-Bearers, a handful of laity among a sea of clergy, monks and nuns.

༄ ༄ ༄

Was Nicholas himself aware of the theological significance of the events he was living through at the beginning of 1917? He had spent the first month and a half of the New Year at Tsarskoye Selo. On January 21 he received a telegram from Alekseev, his chief of staff, requesting his return to Stavka at Mogilev to discuss unnamed matters. The request appeared odd. Everything was quiet at the front. Morale was high, Russia's troops looking forward to victory.[12] Indeed, of the more than 16,000 letters sent by officers to their families in January 1917, a mere seventeen, it has been found, "criticized the conduct of the war in a serious way, and only four were critical of senior military leadership ... overall, a military censors' report concluded in January 1917 [that] 'morale and the material situation is superlative.'"[13] The same was true among the rank and file. As one gunner wrote to his wife, "We hear that on your side [i.e., among people in the rear] there is talk of peace, but among us we talk only of the upcoming offensive. When we win, beat the mighty Prussians ... and take Berlin ... then there will be peace."[14] In contrast to the optimism at the front, however, the situation in the capital remained tense following Rasputin's murder, with the Bloc making daily attacks on the government in the Duma. Nicholas himself was at a loss as to why Alekseev needed his presence at headquarters. Not without reason, Alexandra already doubted the loyalty of Russian high command.

She was right to be nervous. By this stage, two more plots, in addition to Guchkov's for a palace coup, had reached various stages of activation. One centered on the leader of the Voluntary Organizations, Prince Lvov, in Moscow; the other, on the President of the Duma, Mikhail Rodzianko, in Petrograd.[15] All three conspiracies aimed at isolating Nicholas and browbeating him into granting the government of public confidence that the Bloc demanded. Indeed, in a sense, there was really only one big plot, for uniting the ringleaders and keeping them informed of each other's planning was a Masonic order called the "Grand Orient of the Peoples of Russia," which had been founded in the aftermath of the August Crisis of 1915.[16] The problem for the conspirators was that army high command

---

[12] See esp. McMeekin, *Russian Revolution*, 89–90. "The mood among frontline troops was ... robust. On the northern front—closest to Petrograd ... there was little sign of defeatism. Among letters sent home by soldiers ... in the first two weeks of January 1917, military censors noted a 'substantial rise in cheerful spirits' over the previous year ... the soldiers were well fed and clothed. Only nineteen out of 151,963 letters from ordinary soldiers expressed dissatisfaction with food rations, and only twenty-two complained about the winter clothing.... The most common sentiment over the New Year's holidays was that Russia would finally settle accounts with the Germans in 1917. Far from buying the argument of Russian liberals that change was desperately needed at the top, officers on the northern front were generally pleased with how things were going."
[13] Ibid.   [14] Ibid., 90.
[15] Rodzianko's involvement in a conspiracy to unseat the Tsar has only recently become known to historians. Published for the first time in 2013 was the transcript of an interview Rodzianko gave to a sympathetic, liberal journalist in May 1917, when personal responsibility for toppling the tsar was still something to be trumpeted rather than kept quiet. In it, Rodzianko speaks quite openly about his involvement in a secret plan to remove Nicholas from power. See Mikhail Vladimirovich Rodzianko, "Interview," 16 May 1917, in Semion Lyandres, *Fall of Tsarism: Untold stories of the February 1917 Revolution* (Oxford: Oxford University Press, 2013), 104–13.
[16] Katkov, *Russia, 1917*, 167–68; McMeekin, *Russian Revolution*, 72.

remained uncommitted, though not for the want of the conspirators' trying to recruit them. At the end of 1916, Alekseev had temporarily retired to a sanatorium in Crimea, to convalesce from overwork-induced stress. Nicholas visited him there, and sat by his bedside.[17] But so, too, had Guchkov, who again sounded Alekseev out about his plot. According to Voeikov, Alekseev promised Guchkov that he would "neither help nor stand in the way" of a palace coup, while General Gurko, Nicholas II's acting chief-of-staff in Alekseev's absence from Stavka, had allegedly already promised Guchkov his support.[18] If this is true, then Nicholas's two most senior subordinates at Stavka, although knowing of the existence of an extensive and increasingly well-organized plot against their supreme commander, did nothing to alert their Supreme Commander. And yet Stavka was also unwilling simply to surrender Nicholas to Guchkov and the Bloc. So long as Nicholas was at Mogilev, the freedom to shape Russia's future lay with the army's generals. This, it seems, is why Alekseev had requested Nicholas's return to Stavka.

That something was amiss or being kept from the emperor continued to impress Nicholas and his entourage after they had arrived at Stavka on January 23. There was little for Nicholas to do and his aides-de-camp felt that the sovereign was being deliberately "cut out" of what planning for the spring offensive there was going on. In 1916, Nicholas had felt himself an integral part of life at Stavka, hosting lunches and dinners for his generals, receiving a daily briefing from his chief of staff, and forming a point of moral and symbolic focus and stability through his regular and representative attendance at the Divine Liturgy. Now, in his first appearance there in 1917, Nicholas could think only of going home. Three of the five children were ill — dangerously so — with the measles. Once the moral center of life at Stavka, Nicholas, ceasing to be the king on the chessboard, had become a mere pawn. At Stavka, the Russian *teokratia* was already leaking legitimacy. Nicholas intended it to be a short trip. "I shall not stay here for long," he assured Alexandra.[19]

The first suggestion of trouble in Petrograd appeared in a letter from Alexandra on February 24/March 9, which complained about radical speeches "by Kedrenskii" (Kerensky) in the Duma, and described the outbreak of what she called a "hooligan movement" in the factory districts. When, the following day, February 25/March 10, workers called a general strike, and the police and Cossacks came under attack from the crowds, Rodzianko telegrammed Nicholas, predictably asking for the formation

---

[17] Nicholas II, November 20, 1916, in Diary (2), 616. Alekseev's illness was so serious that Shavel'sky, who also notes Nicholas's attendance on the ill general, administered last rites: *Vospominaniia*, 2:234.

[18] Voeikov, *S tsarem*, 189.

[19] Cited in Tsuyoshi Hasegawa, *The February Revolution: Petrograd, 1917* (Seattle, WA: University of Washington Press, 1981), 431.

of a "government of public confidence" as the solution.[20] Rather than constitutional concessions, however, Nicholas was for using force, and authorized "all necessary measures" to restore order. The course of action, not lightly decided on, appears to have been the fruit of agonized prayer. "I went yesterday to the Virgin's image and prayed hard for you, my Love, for the dear children and for our country," he wrote to Alexandra a day later, referring to the Mogilev icon Alexandra had discovered in 1916.[21]

The mutiny of the Petrograd garrison (February 26/March 11) dramatically changed Nicholas's estimation of the seriousness of events. Still unwilling to contemplate constitutional change, Nicholas decided instead to deploy loyal troops from the front to Petrograd. Unlike the mutinous garrison itself (mostly recent peasant recruits billeted in overcrowded barracks in an unfamiliar city), these frontline troops, being well-fed, well-clothed and well-armed, were increasingly confident of victory in the war with Germany, and evinced the high level of morale we have seen. Chosen to lead this operation was General Ivanov (a popular commander whom Nicholas had personally decorated).[22] Consisting of three companies of the St George Battalion, four infantry regiments, four cavalry regiments, two machine-gun detachments and four artillery batteries, it was a serious fighting force—and precisely what the Bloc, hoping to profit constitutionally from the disturbances, feared. "One disciplined division from the front would have been enough to quell the uprising," recalled the Duma deputy, A. Bublikov.[23] Nicholas, having reached the same conclusion, had dispatched precisely that: Stavka was to remain on standby to dispatch other forces if necessary.

The jolt to his authority appears to have been precisely what was needed to rouse Nicholas out of the despondency that had descended upon him. Correctly seeing the disturbances in Petrograd for what they were—a garrison insurrection—Nicholas was not about to stand by and surrender the reins of government—Russia's *teokratia*—either to the rabble, or to opposition politicians such as Rodzianko, who might seek to use it as a weapon to extort from him the constitutional change that they had long ago elevated as their priority. On the contrary, as we shall see, Nicholas seems not to have held any less firmly than he did in 1906 to the "absolute belief" that "the fate of Russia, my own fate and that of my family is in the hands of God, Who has placed me

---

[20] Indicating how far Nicholas's authority had already eroded, Rodzianko also wrote separately to Russia's generals, urging them to petition the tsar to grant the desired ministry. Even more remarkably, two of them agreed: Brusilov, whom Rodzianko appears to have continued to consider the general most amenable to the palace coup Rodzianko was toying with, and General Ruzsky, the Commander of the Northern Front, who, in just a few days' time, would seek to browbeat Nicholas into transforming Russia into a constitutional monarchy in Pskov. See Hasegawa, *February Revolution*, 433.
[21] Nicholas II to Alexandra (N. 1679), February 26, 1917, in Fuhrmann, *Complete Wartime*, 695–96.   [22] Hasegawa, *February Revolution*, 461–62.
[23] Cited in Hasegawa, *February Revolution*, 293–94.

where I am." Constitutionally speaking, this was precisely the problem: a monarch less impressed with the duties and obligations of *teokratia* would have had much less trouble accepting the handing away to elected politicians of the power that Nicholas believed he had himself received mysteriously from God.

Having decided to dispatch Ivanov and his troops to Petrograd, Nicholas then decided to return to Tsarskoye Selo himself. The prospect of losing control of Nicholas produced alarm in Alekseev, who pleaded with Nicholas to remain at Stavka. But while alluding vaguely to the "dangers" Nicholas might expose himself to by making a train journey, Alekseev nonetheless did not inform him of Guchkov's plot. Nicholas dismissed the warning. Then, before Nicholas, still at Stavka, went to bed on February 27/March 12, the political situation reached a temporary summit. Requesting a telegraphic conversation with Nicholas, his younger brother, Grand Duke Mikhail Aleksandrovich — having consulted Rodzianko — made the cause of constitutional change his own. For the sake of saving the dynasty in the *appearance*, if not the reality, of its power (i.e. as a symbolical, constitutional monarchy), Mikhail, who neither attributed any religious significance to events, nor identified any theological principle (i.e. *teokratia*) as being at stake, urged his brother to dismiss the existing government, and appoint another acceptable to the Duma, with the leader of the Voluntary Organizations, Prince Lvov at its head. Nicholas rejected Mikhail's suggestions. This created an opportunity for the first direct sign of insubordination on Alekseev's part vis-à-vis his supreme commander. For while Nicholas had rejected his brother's constitutional recommendations, Alekseev signaled to Mikhail his *own* substantial agreement with them: increasingly, Alekseev, who was still ill, viewed himself as his own supreme commander. Charged with supplying troops for Ivanov's operation, he would act more and more on his own initiative to secure a political solution acceptable to Stavka. It was a conflicted, and conflicting, position.[24]

Nicholas's train drew out of the station in wintry Mogilev at five o'clock in the morning on Tuesday, February 28/March 13. So as to leave the direct route between Mogilev and Petrograd for Ivanov's forces, the imperial trains (there were always two in wartime) would take a roundabout journey, proceeding west, cross-country, to the Petrograd-Moscow line. Outwardly, there was no sign that Nicholas was traveling to his abdication. "As the train left the station, soldiers assembled on the platform for departure to the front shouted enthusiastic hurrahs. Spontaneously, they began singing a hymn," a leading historian has written, describing the scene.[25] According to the recollections of the commander of the imperial train, Colonel von Thal, "There was

---

[24] Hasegawa, *February Revolution*, 436.   [25] Ibid., 437.

absolutely no sign of disturbance or confusion either along the railway or in the cities [Orsha, Smolensk, Viazma, Rzhev, Likhoslav] we passed through. Everything was quiet and calm."[26] On the contrary, at the sight of Nicholas's train, gendarmes and soldiers shouted out "loud hurrahs." But the mood aboard the train changed that evening when the commanders of the imperial trains received, at the same time as thousands of other engineers and station masters across Russia, a message addressed in the name of the President of the Duma, Rodzianko. "Railroad workers! The old regime, which created chaos in all aspects of State affairs, has proved powerless," it went, urging them to remain at their posts despite news of the Petrograd disturbances, for the "State Duma has taken the formation of a new government into its own hands."[27] Nicholas's authority was now being openly usurped.

In fact, the broadcast was the first act of the newly formed "Provisional Committee of the State Duma for the Restoration of Order in Petrograd," a self-appointed group of elders from the now prorogued Duma that considered itself (as the message to Russia's railway workers made clear) Russia's government-in-waiting — the very "government of public confidence" that Nicholas had failed to give. Technically, the message itself had been made possible by the seizure of the Transport Ministry by Bublikov (the Duma deputy mentioned above). It was a shrewd and possibly crucial move. Because of it, Nicholas would ultimately end his journey not, as planned, early in the morning of March 1/14, with his wife and family at Tsarskoye Selo, but later that same evening in Pskov, the "guest" of a general, Ruzsky, who had already identified himself as being in favor of constitutional change.

The next message the imperial trains received, at two o'clock in the morning, was that the line ahead of them was blocked, its stations allegedly taken over by soldiers who, unlike the ones who had cheered the emperor throughout the day, had mutinied and gone over to the Revolution. The soldiers, they were also told, had machine guns. In fact, it was a ruse concocted by Bublikov on behalf of the Provisional Committee, to buy the latter the time it needed to make its challenge to Nicholas's authority permanent. Nonetheless, Nicholas and his staff did not know this. A discussion ensued before, at half past three in the morning, the imperial trains, not wanting to fall into the alleged mutineers' hands, changed route, zigzagging via a sideline, cross-country, eastwards again through the towns of Staraya Russa and Dno. Because it was a sideline, the trains traveled slowly. When the imperial train reached Staraya Russa, the large crowd that had assembled on the platform removed hats and bowed deeply.[28] Here, barely 170 miles from

---

[26] Cited in Hasegawa, *February Revolution*, 438.
[27] Cited in Hasegawa, *February Revolution*, 368.
[28] Hasegawa, *February Revolution*, 439.

Petrograd, Russia seemed no more inclined to rid itself of tsarism any more than the troops they had passed the previous day.

That afternoon, at four, the imperial trains arrived at Dno, on the Mogilev-Petrograd line. There a telegram from Rodzianko was waiting for Nicholas, asking him to wait at Dno so that Rodzianko could come to him from Petrograd for a face-to-face discussion; but although the trains waited, Rodzianko did not appear. Told that Rodzianko had been caught up with other matters, Nicholas and his entourage were now also misleadingly told that the stations between them and Tsarskoye Selo had now fallen into the hands of the mutiny (no evidence of the actual existence of which they had yet seen *anywhere*). So it was that Nicholas proceeded from Dno to what he and his entourage assumed to be the security of General Ruzsky's headquarters at Pskov. He arrived at eight o'clock, having spent two whole days crisscrossing the snowy Russian countryside. This was not an accident. As Hasegawa comments, "An important force was at work to nullify Nicholas's intervention in the course of events."[29] That force was Bublikov and the Provisional Committee, who, in control of the Ministry of Transport, had been telling a lie to keep the tsar at bay and isolated just long enough to be able to present him — the king on a checkmated chessboard — with a constitutional *fait accompli*.

In what turned out to be the final whole day of the Russian *teokratia*, then, Nicholas had been the victim of a ruse: no mutinous troops "with machine guns" had seized the line between Moscow and Petrograd; no revolutionary force "blocked" the way between Dno and Tsarskoye Selo. On the contrary, Ivanov reached the imperial village safely, albeit after an unusually slow journey, and spoke, that evening, to a visibly shaken empress in an audience room in the Alexander Palace. Still stricken with measles, the children were too ill to be moved, she told him; she would stay put and ask him not to do anything to arouse the enmity of the Tsarskoye Selo garrison, which had indeed mutinied the previous evening. The 1,200 soldiers guarding the palace and their commander General Groten remained loyal, but Alexandra doubted the trustworthiness of some of them. She had spent the night of February 28 dressed.[30] For its part, Ivanov's journey had been so slow because Bublikov, in control of the Transport Ministry, had directed railway workers to obstruct it. When, on that basis, one station master had refused to let Ivanov pass, Ivanov, confident of the loyalty of the troops he commanded, threatened force. The convoy proceeded. Reaching Tsarskoye Selo an hour after Nicholas had arrived in Pskov, Ivanov, fulfilling the instructions

---

[29] Ibid., 440. [30] Ibid., 466.

Nicholas had given him, announced himself dictator, vested with authority over all government ministries. Only after his conversation with representatives from the General Staff's representatives in Petrograd, who had come to Tsarskoye Selo to see him, a meeting with the empress, and the receipt of two telegrams, one from Alekseev directing him to work *with* rather than direct his forces *against* the Provisional Committee, and one from Nicholas, authorizing Alekseev's (see below, p. 351), did Ivanov withdraw his forces to the town of Vyritsa, twenty miles away. The knife of legitimate authority, though in place, had suddenly been taken away from the Revolution's throat.[31]

Nicholas, by contrast, had not reached his planned destination at all. Instead, he and his entourage found themselves pulling up at the same station, in the same weather, where I had stood watching the snow fall with Pavel. Everyone aboard noticed that the mood was different. While the governor was waiting on the platform, the customary guard of honor was not. The tokens of loyalty they had witnessed at Staraya Russa and all the previous day were missing. There was no loyal crowd. Missing also was Ruzsky, the local front commander, who, in a breach of protocol unimaginable in other circumstances, arrived a few minutes late on the station platform in day-to-day (rather than the customary dress) uniform.[32] Ruzsky had been promoted only two and a half years before by Nicholas to the rank of aide-de-camp general, an honorific title that implied the special confidence of the emperor. But Ruzsky was also a closet liberal, one of two generals to have urged Nicholas, in compliance with a request from Rodzianko, to concede a Duma ministry as early as February 26. As Hasegawa puts it, Ruszky's sympathies "lay with the liberal opposition from the very beginning of the revolution."[33]

News of the formation of the Provisional Committee under Rodzianko in the entry hall of the Tauride Palace had therefore brought Ruzsky comfort. This Provisional Committee, Rodzianko had assured Ruzsky, had matters in hand: the Petrograd garrison had pledged its loyalty to it and there was no reason for matters to go any further. If only the tsar would agree to a ministry of public confidence chosen by the Duma leaders that made up this Committee, the soldiers would return to their barracks and the war with Germany could continue with Russia being at long last what Rodzianko, Guchkov (and, in fact, also Ruzsky) had long wished it to be: a monarchy in name only. Indeed, Ruzsky had already withdrawn the troops he was required to contribute to Ivanov's force.

Crucially, Ruzsky was strengthened in his constitutional ambitions through his conversations with his boss, Alekseev, with whom, in the hours before the tsar's arrival, Ruzsky, it seems, had spoken by Hughes wireless apparatus.[34] In this conversation, Alekseev seems to have told

---

[31] Ibid., 466–67.   [32] Ibid., 492.   33 Ibid.   [34] Ibid, 491.

Ruzsky that Stavka's preference now lay with the formation of a responsible ministry, that is, of a government that was, like England's, outwardly monarchical but answerable in fact to the Duma as Russia's parliament. Responsible for confirming this preference in Alekseev were two things: first, news of the spread of the mutiny from the Petrograd to the Moscow and Kronstadt garrisons; second, Alekseev's communications with Rodzianko, who assured him of the Provisional Committee's success in having the mutineers accept this formula as a condition for ending the insurrection. If the Duma had already obtained power in practice, Alekseev seems to have reasoned, and the anarchic garrison soldiers' insurrection was already as good as over in Petrograd, what was the point in Ivanov's mission? Why risk a civil war for the sake of an anachronism ("holy tsarist authority") that the Russian war effort could just as well do without? In the hands of men such as Rodzianko, government "by popular dispensation" was entirely acceptable. Indeed, all things being equal, it was to a soldier such as Alekseev *preferable* for being more *rational* and more *efficient*: in reducing the conditions for Russian victory to secularized notions of professionalism, technical-scientific efficiency and practical utility, the Great War was accelerating the Russian elite's adoption of the conclusions of nineteenth-century philosophy.

Thus, Alekseev, without consultation with Nicholas, recognized the Provisional Committee not as a *revolutionary* body that had sought to put itself at the head of a rebellion in a bid for power, but as the *de facto* repository of Russia's legitimate governing authority. The only condition that Alekseev, being a "conservative," laid down, apparently, was that the *form* (but not the substance) of "holy tsarist authority" — a crown, a throne, court ceremony — be retained (as they had been in England) to legitimate the continued activity of Russia's existing state institutions (including the imperial manifestos creating the Duma and Stavka themselves) and the commissions of the tens of thousands of their existing agents, from commissioned officers to civil servants. Alekseev, on behalf of Russia, had made a momentous decision. Ruzsky's brief was to get Nicholas to consent to it.

His cause was aided by the ignorance in which Nicholas and his advisors, who knew nothing of the discussions going on by telegram and wireless apparatus between Ruzsky and Alekseev, had been kept. Under the impression that *he* was still supreme commander, Nicholas was operating as if the plans agreed at Stavka two days before were still valid; he assumed that Ivanov's expedition — which Nicholas, at this stage, had not called off — was still advancing towards Petrograd. Indeed, at that moment it was, but among the telegrams waiting for Nicholas at Pskov was one from Alekseev one appealing to Nicholas to order it to halt. "The suppression of the disorders by force," Alekseev's telegram warned, raising for the first time the prospect that a "disturbance in the rear" could provoke the disintegration of the frontline army, "is dangerous under the present conditions." To preserve "Russia and the army" from "ruin," Alekseev begged Nicholas for a government of public confidence headed by "a person whom Russia would believe" and entrusted with the "formation of a cabinet."[35] Also waiting for Nicholas in Pskov were telegrams from General Brusilov, his cousin Grand Duke Aleksandr Mikhailovich and his own brother, Grand Duke Mikhail. All urged him to make constitutional concessions. On the other hand, there was no telegram from Alexandra, and no information available from other sources about her safety or that of the children. Nicholas recorded his frustration: "Shame and humiliation," he wrote in his diary. "Failed to reach Tsarskoye Selo. But all my thoughts are there. How it must be painful for Alexandra to be alone in these events. Help us, Lord!"[36]

At around ten p.m. that night, Ruzsky finally talked alone with Nicholas. Ruzsky began by warning that his report would be unlike others he had given; it would concern not military affairs, but affairs of "state structure" which, he recognized, went beyond his competence.[37] Nicholas invited him to speak his mind. Ruzsky did so. Listening, Nicholas discovered that the telegram from Alekseev that he had read on his arrival was already out of date. Urged on him by Ruzsky was an outright responsible ministry. According to Ruzsky, Nicholas dismissed such a constitutional change "quietly, coolly, but with the feeling of deep conviction."[38] Ruzsky almost lost his nerve: even in view of Ruzsky's own constitutional convictions, and at this advanced stage in the revolution, the tsar possessed for Ruzsky a semi-sacred aura that he found difficult to overcome. But he steeled himself by thinking of all the grievances he had accumulated inside him against Nicholas's regime during the war. As Ruzsky later recalled, "I realized that for the first and only time in my life I had the opportunity to tell the Emperor everything that I thought of the various individuals occupying responsible posts in the country and of the great mistakes that it seemed to me had been made in the running of the country and the activities of Stavka."[39] After so many years of evident frustration, we can imagine how satisfied Ruzsky felt when he had finished. Yet if his outburst surprised Nicholas, Nicholas did not betray it.

On the contrary, it was now Nicholas's turn to surprise Ruzsky. He did so first by claiming that he agreed with Ruzsky in most of his unflattering assessments of Russia's ministers and generals. But he did so above all, it seems, by articulating a degree of political awareness

[35] Ibid., 490.   [36] Nicholas II, March 1, 1917, in Diary (2), 625.
[37] The record of the conversation can be found in S. N. Vil'chkovskii, "Prebyvanie gosudaria imperatora v Pskove, 1 i 2 marta 1917 goda," *Russkaia Lietopis'* 3 (1922): 161–87.
[38] Vil'chkovsky, "Prebyvanie," 169.   [39] Ibid.

and a sense of the meaning of his office that, for a moment, appears to have given Ruzsky pause. Recalled Ruzsky: "The Emperor's fundamental opinion was that he desired nothing for himself in terms of his own personal interests, and [was] not holding onto power for itself, but believed himself not possessed of the right (*ne v prave*) to transfer the whole matter of governing Russia into the hands of people who, being in government today, might cause the greatest harm to the Motherland (*rodina*), but tomorrow wash their hands of responsibility and resign from Cabinet."[40] As autocrat, the tsar was supposed to be possessed of unlimited powers. But here Ruzsky had heard that granting Russia a responsible ministry was something Nicholas did not have the *power* to do: he was bound by a higher authority that Ruzsky and others had not taken into account. Giving full expression to the theocratic conception of his office that he had entertained since his earliest days as tsar, Nicholas explained: "Were the ministers responsible to the Duma, it would make no difference. Seeing what the ministers are doing is not for Russia's good, I will never be able to agree with them, comforting myself with the thought that matters are not in my hands and that the responsibility is not mine. *I* am responsible before God and Russia for everything that has happened and will happen."[41] As Nicholas had, after all, asked of God at his coronation, "Let My heart be in Your hands . . . so that on the Day of Judgment *I* may give account without shame to You."[42]

Russia, then, Nicholas was saying between the lines, was still in 1917 a *teokratia*, where power — and even the regime structure itself — came from God, with the tsar as the image, on earth, of God's ruling power over the cosmos. It was not, however, that Nicholas was such a captive to the theocratic principle that he had not contemplated the possibility, in Russia, of the alternative — of authority not "by the grace of God," but by "popular dispensation." He had — and had found it wanting not only on abstract theological grounds but on more practical, moral grounds, too. That a ministry responsible to the Duma might bear the burden of public office only so long as it suited its members seemed to him a formula not for responsibility but for moral hazard, recklessness, drift. Indeed, it was as if Russia's last monarch had already been vouchsafed a vision of the weightless careerism and metaphysical confusion of modern, twenty-first-century democracy.[43]

---

[40] Ibid. My translation. Cf. Dominic Lieven's translation: "I am not entitled to give up the whole matter of governing Russia to the hands of those who, today in the government, could cause such blunders to the Fatherland and tomorrow wash their hands, and send in their resignations from the cabinet." See Lieven, *Nicholas II*, 232.

[41] Ibid. Here, however, I use Lieven's translation: *Nicholas II*, 232. Cf. Pipes, *Russian Revolution*, 310, who translates the same text somewhat differently.

[42] *Chin" deiistviia*, 33. My italics.

[43] Consider the similarity of the argument Pope Leo XIII had made in his encyclical, *Immortale Dei*, in 1885. Here Leo argues that government according to democratic

Undeterred, however, Ruzsky replied by reiterating his and Alekseev's position. They were not seeking the end of the monarchy, a republic, a regime from which the tsar would be purged, and in which there would be no room for the symbolic and ceremonial trappings of tsarism. On the contrary, with Rodzianko (and the bulk of the Duma's "conservative liberals"), they desired a "ceremonial tsarism," a constitutional monarchy of the English kind. Ruzsky even quoted the principle on which the modern British monarchy was famously founded, whereby the monarch "reigns but does not rule" (or "reigns but the government rules," as Ruzsky paraphrased).[44] If, in 1917, Ruzsky implied, such a formula had bestowed on Britain more than two centuries of constitutional stability, how could it be reasonable for Nicholas to object to the introduction of this formula into Russia?

Nicholas countered with words that reiterated how integrally a part of his very *being* the theocratic principle underlying political authority in Russia was. "Such a formula," Nicholas said, he simply "could not understand." To get his head around it, he told Ruzsky, he would have to have been not only "raised differently" but (as if paraphrasing Jesus's words in John's Gospel) "born again and formed anew" (cf. Jn 3:4–6).[45] That is, Nicholas would have had to undergo a *religious* conversion regarding the sources of power. Indeed, it says everything about the differences between not only Ruzsky and Nicholas but also Nicholas and the entire liberal opposition, that to Russia's last tsar Ruzsky's "English formula" was less a *principle* than it was a *sleight of hand* — a verbal trick that separated the name of a thing (*tsar*: the ruling authority) from its substance (the act of actually ruling). In rejecting it, Nicholas was rejecting subscription to what was, at bottom, the heretical temptation of nominalism as the price for keeping his crown. As Nicholas said, he was "not hanging onto power for himself but could not make a decision against his conscience. Even if he resigned responsibility for the course of State affairs before men [*pered" liud'mi*], he could not consider himself anything other than responsible before God (*ne mozhet schitat', chto on cam" ne otvietstven pered" Bogom"*)."[46]

The exchange is the strongest indication in the record of Nicholas's conversation with Ruzsky that Russia's last tsar intuited that the fundamental issue at stake in the events surrounding him was *theological*. After all, if the only condition that the Church had laid down when

---

maxims is "nothing more nor less than the will of the people, and the people, being under the power of itself alone, is alone its own ruler." He laments that the leaders of such a polity are, of necessity, men who have been charged with "not the *right* so much as the *business* of governing" (my italics). Beneath the name of "responsible government" there is, then, Leo insists, a purely *voluntarist* regime that leads naturally to a purely transactional (rather than a really, that is, *substantively* responsible) political order.

[44] Vil'chkovsky, "Prebyvanie," 170. My translation.
[45] Ibid.   [46] Ibid.

baptizing Constantine, centuries before, was that he, on behalf of the whole Empire, should acknowledge the truth of Christ as *the* Truth, who would continue to make that acknowledgment now, if the tsar were bound to speak only as he was bidden—not by Christ, the Truth Himself, according to conscience, but according to the passing dictates of men elected from time to time to the Duma?[47] On Ruzsky's terms, Russia could only ever *nominally* be Christian (and in the long run, of course, not at all). Indeed, if Nicholas refused the temptation of political nominalism, the argument here is that he did so it out of intuitive obedience to the metaphysical realism germane to historical, mystical-dogmatic Christianity: in the Eastern Church, the consecrated Bread and Wine are not merely nominal symbols of Christ's Body and Blood; they are the things themselves. So it was with the office of tsar. A verbal trick would not do: a tsar *rules*, responsible *before God* for his actions, *or he is not tsar at all*. Unless one were possessed of the authority of God himself, it would be unholy to subtract the substance of a thing while leaving behind, under the same name, only its appearance—a diabolical upending of the order of things as established by, and cohering in, the Logos. Not for nothing, after all, had Nicholas's coronation oath been sealed with sacramental anointing and the Eucharist: his authority as tsar had been given an anchor in the truest order of things that was; he could not unilaterally draw it up.[48] (And not unrelatedly, it seems to me, does Schmemann identify the temptation of nominalism—"the peculiar divorce of the *forms* of the Church's life from their content"—as the obstacle which more than any other blocks today "every attempt to recover the true experience of the Church.")[49]

So it was that Nicholas's words and actions in March 1917 appeared to justify Merezhkovsky's assertion, in his 1907 tract *Le Tsar et la Révolution*, that "Even if it wanted to, the Russian monarchy could not give us a constitution."[50] Although Merezhkovsky rejected it as *false*, nonetheless he understood that the historical political theology of Eastern Orthodoxy—the theocratic conception of politics of the Eastern Church—would not allow the untethering of the claims of the sacred and the political that constitutionalism required. To Merezhkovsky's friend and philosophical fellow-traveler Dmitri Filosofov, writing in the same volume, Russia's tragedy was not that it had a tsar who did not understand the nature of his office, but that she had one who did and took it seriously. For that office was only mistakenly viewed as secular;

---

[47] On this "condition," or, better, "bond of faith," see Schmemann, *Church, World, Mission*, 36.
[48] On the tsar as "sacramental anchor" of the political order, see Williams, *Sergii Bulgakov*, 60.
[49] Schmemann, *Church, World, Mission*, 23.
[50] Merezhkovsky, *Tsar et la révolution*, 73.

in its essence and origins it was sacred, religious. Russian society might change around Nicholas II, becoming secularized. But, said Filosofov as if anticipating the words of Ruzsky's exchange with Nicholas, Nicholas "does not hang on to power for the love of it, but for the religious fear of letting it go." So long as he wished to remain Orthodox, he had no choice but to remain in fact a theocrat, responsible in conscience to God: "the most powerful man in the world ... is in a position of extreme weakness and cannot advance. All he can do is stay in the same place, waiting for the collapse of his reign and his empire."[51]

Of course, Filosofov, not himself subscribing to Church Orthodoxy, deplored this. But better than many of his contemporaries, he had seen to the heart of what was at stake. Hence his ensuing affirmation, which we have already seen, that "primary responsibility for the chaos currently prevailing in Russia lies" not with liberalism or Socialism, ideas of Kantian or Marxist inspiration, but "with Orthodoxy ... it is Orthodoxy that will cause the Tsar to perish." But we can also put this more sympathetically. If, ultimately, Nicholas *was* a martyr for anything, it would not be enough to say that he was a martyr for *teokratia* or the theocratic principle in the abstract: he was also a martyr, like all the martyrs, probably, for a metaphysical realism without which authentic Christian faith is impossible. In Bulgakov's terms, Nicholas in 1917 withstood the "hot wind" of Kantianism. The following year he would pay for that resistance with his life.

But this is to anticipate. Back in Pskov, the yawning gulf in philosophical and theological principles between them having now been gestured at, Nicholas and Ruzsky turned to more pragmatic matters. Thus, apparently accepting the thought experiment of popular sovereignty, Nicholas ran through, with what Ruzsky was impressed enough to call "unusual clarity of expression," the names of all those men, in the Duma, the Progressive Bloc and the Voluntary Organizations, who would doubtless put themselves forward to govern Russia in a ministry responsible to the Duma—Guchkov, Lvov, Miliukov, Rodzianko. Nicholas did not question their patriotism. But, he said, such "civic activists" being "inexperienced in the art of government and, having obtained power, would not know how to acquit their duties."[52] Not just a matter of principle (although it was supremely that), Nicholas was saying, changing Russia's form of government in the middle of a world war, would be practically disastrous, too. Nicholas, it dawned on Ruszky, was a more astute ruler than he had imagined. Experience,

---

[51] Ibid.
[52] Vil'chkovsky, "Prebyvanie," 170. This time, I have used Pipes's translation: *Russian Revolution*, 310. Cf. Lieven, *Nicholas II*, 232: "had no administrative experience and, having been entrusted with the burden of authority, would ... prove unable to cope with their task."

rather than natural aptitude, had made him so. And, indeed, events soon enough proved him right. Despite the supreme confidence with which the men above would approach the government ministries they were about to put themselves at the head of, even the most "successful" of them, Lvov, would last barely five months in office. Guchkov and Miliukov, meanwhile, would survive but fifty-eight days.[53]

All the same, Ruzsky would not budge. To break down the tsar's resistance, he played his trump card. At eleven o'clock a second telegram arrived from Alekseev. In it, Alekseev confirmed that, in championing a responsible ministry, Ruzsky had been speaking for Alekseev, too. If Nicholas did not accept the proposed constitutional change, then what he risked was "the disorganization of the army and the impossibility of continuing the war."[54] What Alekseev did not mention was that there were no signs of disloyalty among the frontline troops, that mutinies remained restricted to the lower-quality recruits found among garrisons in the rear, and that Ivanov's force had been unmoved after its exposure to the revolutionaries: in other words, the "knife" for the insurrection's forcible suppression still existed, but Alekseev had *chosen* not to use it. And he had done this for the reasons we have already seen: the formation of the Provisional Committee and its promise, via Rodzianko, to him that it was in control of the situation, persuaded him to think no longer of events in Petrograd as an insurrectionary challenge to legitimate authority, but as an opportunity for the orderly transfer of it from a tsar in whom he had lost confidence to professionals who claimed to be able to quiet the rear. So, Nicholas should recognize, Alekseev said, "a responsible ministry, the composition of which should be entrusted to the chairman of the State Duma [i.e. Rodzianko]."[55] Alekseev had even taken the liberty of preparing the text of a manifesto for Nicholas to sign to that purpose.

"Alekseev's desertion," says Hasegawa, was, to Nicholas, a "great blow."[56] Alekseev was, after all, Nicholas's own appointee. Beyond this, by raising the prospect of the army's "disorganization" and the "impossibility" of continuing the war with Germany, Alekseev had trapped Nicholas between two loyalties. So long as he lacked the information to rebut Alekseev's assessment, Nicholas was in a conflict between his piety and his patriotism: the duties he owed to God according to the theocratic principle, and those he owed to his country and the men fighting for her. He might sacrifice himself for the sake of a Christian-realist view of his office, but would he sacrifice *them*? Would he sacrifice *Russia*? In the end, Nicholas seems to have decided that he could not, in conscience, do that. He told Ruzsky that he would sign Alekseev's manifesto establishing

---

[53] See Pipes's withering observations on the incompetence of Russia's new rulers: *Russian Revolution*, 320–23.   [54] Hasegawa, *February Revolution*, 494.
[55] Ibid.   [56] Ibid.

a responsible ministry (whereby the "tsar reigns but the government rules"). It was also at this time that he consented to a telegram in his name withdrawing Ivanov's battalion to Vyritsa (see above, p. 344). Thus, with recourse to numerous false pretenses (from Bublikov's duping of the commanders of the imperial train to Rodzianko's reassurances to Alekseev at Stavka), the Duma's Provisional Committee had apparently finally succeeded in wresting executive control of the government from the tsar; Russia would no longer be a *teokratia* (except in name only, if the "tsar" survived as a constitutional rubberstamp). In particular, Rodzianko's assurance that the Provisional Committee was in control of events in Petrograd was crucial, for it was on the grounds of that assurance that Alekseev had shifted his view of the revolution from an anarchic rebellion to an apparently orderly and bloodless transition. And as Ruzsky himself admitted, without Alekseev's intervention, his own argument with Nicholas might have amounted to nothing.[57]

Believing he had prevailed, therefore, in changing Russia's constitution, Ruzsky quit the imperial train and returned to his own headquarters, planning to communicate his victory to Alekseev and Rodzianko. But Nicholas's resistance, his commitment to *teokratia*, had not yet been vanquished. Left alone by Ruzsky, his piety apparently asserted itself. In the telegram Nicholas himself had drawn up for Rodzianko, he made no mention of a responsible ministry. When Nicholas put his signature to that document, then, Russia's form of government *would not* change. Rather, in his telegram, Nicholas merely invited Rodzianko to form a cabinet, while he himself as emperor would appoint the ministers of war, the navy, and foreign affairs. To all intents and purposes, then, the government, while many of its members would be appointed by the chairman of the Duma, would as a body still be responsible to the tsar, while Nicholas's own responsibility before God for Russia had not been abolished. But to dispatch this telegram, he relied on Ruzsky, who controlled the necessary technical apparatus. And reading the proposed text of Nicholas's telegram, Ruzsky erupted. Asking the tsar for another audience, Ruzsky appeared back at the Imperial train at midnight. Another conversation ensued, Ruzsky asking whether he had misunderstood Nicholas's earlier agreement to a responsible ministry, and Nicholas confirming, at last, that he hadn't: the tsar would grant a responsible ministry for the "good of Russia."[58] At this point, Ruzsky, "completely exhausted" and allegedly barely able to stand up, went to bed, asking to speak to Rodzianko as soon as possible by wireless apparatus to share with him the good news.

In the end, Ruzsky didn't sleep long. At three thirty in the morning, Rodzianko called via the Hughes apparatus in the General Staff

---

[57] Ibid., 495.　　　　　[58] Ibid.

building, opposite the Winter Palace, in revolutionary Petrograd. When Ruzsky had last heard from Rodzianko, Rodzianko had told Ruzsky that the Committee had matters in hand in the capital. "All measures for security of order in the capital are being taken ... the railway is maintained carefully and without interruption. There is no danger for ... food supplies.... The disorder which had erupted is being liquidated. Calm is being restored, although with great difficulty."[59] Now, however, only a few hours later, Ruzsky, who had negotiated with Nicholas on that basis, learned from Rodzianko that the situation in Petrograd was quite different. Expecting Rodzianko to react with relief and jubilation at the news of the creation of a responsible ministry, Ruzsky was shocked when Rodzianko replied to the effect that Ruzsky had misunderstood the degree of disorder that prevailed in the capital. In these circumstances, a responsible ministry was far from enough to calm the crowd; Nicholas himself would have to go. "It is obvious you and His Majesty have not taken into account what is happening here," Rodzianko scolded, patronizingly, before describing a scene completely at odds with his earlier picture. "One of the most terrible revolutions is approaching, the course of which is impossible to reverse." Far from transformed, through the Committee's ministrations, into an orderly transfer of power, a violent soldiers' insurrection was still underway. Officers were being killed in the streets, said Rodzianko, and all the ministers, except for those of war and the navy, had been locked up in the Peter and Paul Fortress. "Anarchy" and "demoralization" threatened the State with "downfall." "I consider it necessary to tell you," Rodzianko concluded, "that what you have proposed is not enough; the problem of the dynasty has been put point blank."[60]

A hundred years later, it is easy to see how this "problem" which Rodzianko claimed to have been suddenly posed "point blank" had in fact been raised and decided months before among the conspiratorial circles of which Rodzianko was part. Removing Nicholas from the throne was the whole point of a palace coup: it was not a prospect unexpectedly sprung on Rodzianko and his colleagues now. As Lyandres puts it, "contrary to the conventional view that the Duma President resisted the abdication ... or that the abdication was forced on him ... and that he only acquiesced only after much wavering and soul-searching, Rodzianko had concluded well before the Revolution that Russia could not be saved without replacing 'the obstinate tsar.'"[61] From this point of view, the insurrection, although doubtless frightening, was at the same time a godsend, so long as Rodzianko could keep one step ahead of events. Indeed, that he had deliberately misled Ruszky, Alekseev and Stavka on this matter is confirmed by the dishonesty evident in other elements

---

[59] Ibid., 496. [60] Ibid. [61] Lyandres, *Fall of Tsarism*, 285.

of Rodzianko's early morning conversation with Ruzsky. For example, Rodzianko told Ruzsky, in reference to the mutinous troops said to have blocked the path of the imperial train to Tsarskoye Selo, that he had taken immediate measures to remove this obstacle, when in fact, the Provisional Committee had all along lent its support to Bublikov's policy of blocking their progress through misinformation. Similarly, in reply to Ruzsky's question why he had not appeared at Dno to meet Nicholas, Rodzianko claimed that it was because he could not leave Petrograd, where, in the setting of the people's "rekindled passions," the people "believe only in me and carry out only my orders."[62] Of course, had this been true, and had Rodzianko really enjoyed undisputed authority in Petrograd, then there would have been no grounds for informing Ruzsky that the manifesto the latter had prevailed on Nicholas to sign was unsatisfactory to a crowd before whose demands he was powerless.

Evidently, then, Rodzianko never possessed the authority claimed. Indeed, he had hidden from Ruzsky and Alekseev the existence of a body to which he was himself beholden: the Petrograd Soviet. An *ad hoc* council made up of representatives of the companies and regiments that had taken part in the Petrograd garrison insurrection, with added workers' representatives from the factories, this Soviet had taken over the Duma's old meeting room, the grand Catherine Hall, in the Tauride Palace, when the Duma itself obeyed the tsar's order of prorogation.[63] At the very time when Ruzsky was seeking to persuade Nicholas to accept a responsible ministry, the Soviet, whose Military Commission, and not Rodzianko or the Provisional Committee, *actually* controlled the mutinous troops, imposed on the Provisional Committee a list of demands to formalize the two bodies' cooperation. The fourth point was "immediate preparations for the convocation of a Constituent Assembly, to be elected on a universal, secret, direct, and equal ballot."[64] Such a measure, and the Provisional Committee's consent to it, already represented the *de facto* abolition of the monarchy. But Rodzianko had made no mention either of the Soviet or of its demands in his conversation with Ruszky, even though it was in order to negotiate with this radical body that the President of the Duma had really been forced to miss his appointment with the tsar in Dno. It was a sign of things to come: no policy measure or legislative act by the ministers of the Provisional Government that crossed the calculations of the leaders of this body would be allowed to stand.[65]

For now, however, despite having agreed barely hours before to the Soviet's demand for a Constituent Assembly, Rodzianko, when asked

---

[62] Hasegawa, *February Revolution*, 496.
[63] Pipes, *Russian Revolution*, 289–96.
[64] Cited in Pipes, *Russian Revolution*, 298.
[65] Pipes, *Russian Revolution*, 304–7.

by Ruzsky what he meant by the "dynastic question," presented what had been his goal since the end of December: Nicholas's abdication in favor of his son, Alexei, who, under the regency of his uncle, Nicholas's younger brother, Grand Duke Mikhail, would now reign over a Russia transformed into a constitutional monarchy ruled by the Duma. Dishonestly, Rodzianko even told Ruzsky that for the continuation of the monarchy under Alexei there was a "definite, terrible demand" among "the troops everywhere . . . and the people." Revealing extraordinary vanity, Rodzianko's idea, apparently, was to outwit both the tsar *and* the Soviet to obtain, through the manipulation of Stavka, the abdication he had wanted since December. And, with that end in sight, Rodzianko dismissed the manifesto creating a responsible ministry that Ruzsky had spent most of the night wringing out of Nicholas with such difficulty. "Power is slipping from my hands," Rodzianko swooned misleadingly, for it had never really been in them. "The anarchy has reached such a degree that I am compelled tonight to announce the formation of the Provisional Government. Unfortunately, the manifesto was too late; it should have been issued immediately after my first telegram. . . . Time was wasted and there is no return."[66] It was a superb performance. It is almost possible to picture the wave of the Duma president's handkerchief.

All the same, the contradictions in Rodzianko's report weren't difficult to see. On the one hand, he was the "only person" whose orders the soldiers and people would obey, yet power was "slipping" from his hands; there was "anarchy," but a "definite and terrible demand" for the continuation of the *monarchy* through Alexei's succession. Historians have questioned why Ruzsky didn't do more to push Rodzianko on these inconsistencies, and the same questions can be posed of Alekseev's response to Ruzsky and Rodzianko's wireless conversation.[67] Even as the latter was still ongoing, Ruzsky's chief-of-station, Danilov, was sending a typed record by telegraph to Alekseev at Stavka. By six o'clock that morning, Alekseev had read the complete conversation. He then appears to have spent several hours thinking about what to do next, including by seeking other sources of information than Rodzianko's about what was going on in Petrograd. These must have confirmed Rodzianko's story. For by around nine a.m. Alekseev had made up his mind. Knowing that the transcript of the Ruzsky-Rodzianko conversation had so far been kept from the tsar, he telegrammed Pskov with instructions for Nicholas to be woken at once and shown the record. He received the reply that — a sign, surely, of the anguish in which the previous night's betrayal of *teokratia* had left him — Nicholas had only just fallen asleep. But Alekseev insisted. "All etiquette must be put aside," he underlined.

---

[66] Cited in Hasegawa, *February Revolution*, 497.
[67] Hasegawa, *February Revolution*, 499.

Ruzsky arrived with the records at the imperial train at 10.45. Nicholas read them in silence. When he had finished, he got up and walked over to the window, where he stood for a moment, motionless. Turning around to address Ruzsky, he told him that he would consider Rodzianko's recommendation. But, he added, "he thought the people would not understand such a move, that the Old Believers would not forgive him for betraying the coronation oath and the Cossacks for abandoning the front."[68] It was not that Nicholas had finished inwardly with *teokratia*. It was rather that he would cease to hold Russia hostage against its will to the theocratic principle, or to the risk of the civil war which he had been led to believe might ensue if, at this stage, an attempt was made to put down the insurrection by force. He would let himself be guided, instead, by his feelings of patriotism for Russia. "If it is necessary, for Russia's welfare, that I step aside, I am prepared to do so," Nicholas told Ruzsky, consenting, in principle, to his abdication.[69] Then, as if to seal Nicholas's decision, an officer arrived with a telegram from Stavka in which Alekseev advised Ruzsky to recommend Nicholas's abdication. Explaining that it was a circular telegram on which all front commanders had been invited to comment, Ruzsky suggested that Nicholas wait until their responses had been received before taking any further action. Nicholas went to lunch and then walked silently on the platform, the weight of Russian history and the theocratic principle on his conscience: in the middle of a world war, Russia stood on the verge of abandoning what Bulgakov called the "spontaneous feeling of the Russian people, on which the Russian Statehood had been built," and Nicholas would have to be the one to sanction it.

While Nicholas had been reading the records of Rodzianko's conversation with Ruzsky, the future of the revolution fell into Alekseev's hands. Given the revelation of Rodzianko's dishonesty during the night, Alekseev had three options before him: first, he could do nothing and await for orders from his tsar and supreme commander; second, he could rescind his order of the previous evening to Ivanov and authorize the resumption of the mission to restore order forcibly in Petrograd now that the real character of events — a disorderly soldiers' insurrection — had been revealed by Rodzianko; or third, he could comply with Rodzianko's effective demand for Nicholas's abdication in favor of Alexei. Alekseev chose the third course. Given the doubts that Alekseev entertained about Rodzianko's trustworthiness, we may wonder at his decision. But whatever untruths and inconsistencies Rodzianko had indulged in, he and the other members of the Provisional Committee (which overnight had proclaimed the establishment of a new Provisional *Government*) had decisively ranged the Duma on the side of the mutiny.

---

[68] Cited in Pipes, *Russian Revolution*, 312.   [69] Ibid.

Were Alekseev to proceed, therefore, with the earlier plan to put the garrison insurrection down, the army would be obliged to fire not only on rebel peasant soldiers and factory workers, but also on Petrograd's liberal political leadership. The thought, apparently, was unconscionable, and Alekseev decided to sacrifice the tsar and bury the theocratic principle instead.

For that reason, Alekseev then cabled the text of the Ruzsky-Rodzianko conversation to his immediate subordinates, the individual front commanders, with a covering message stating that he recommended Nicholas's abdication in favor of Alexei. "The situation does not permit other solutions, and every minute of further vacillation will only enhance these demands," he advised them.[70] The reason for this, said Alekseev, was that the railways and what he termed the "existence of the army" were already "in the hands," as he put it, of the Provisional Government. By this, Alekseev cannot have meant that there was any sign that frontline units had joined the revolution (since they had not, as frontline commanders must have known) but that the capital's munitions factories, its Transport Ministry and government bank vaults had fallen out of the existing tsarist regime's hands. It was not, therefore, burgeoning mutiny on the front with Germany, but the risk that such a mutiny of frontline troops *might* ensue if the decision were made to retake the capital by force in the face of the new Provisional Government's resistance, that informed Alekseev's recommendation. Alekseev also chose to believe Rodzianko when the latter said that the crowds wanted the continuation of the monarchy. Yes, he admitted, the Provisional Government was effectively seizing power from a lawfully constituted government. But, he argued, to oppose this "coup" (as Alekseev called it) would be to jeopardize the prosecution of the war against Germany. However distasteful it might be to betray their supreme commander, it was far better to let things in Petrograd run their course.[71]

Thus Nicholas's sojourn in Pskov reached its denouement. Knowing that the tsar would be most inclined to abdicate if it was the army, rather than the Provisional Government, that did the asking, Alekseev had concluded his circular telegram to front commanders with a request that they forward to Nicholas at Pskov their agreement or otherwise with the course of action that Alekseev had outlined (i.e. Nicholas's abdication) as the best way out of the crisis. By two p.m. the cables from the front commanders had arrived. Ruzsky presented them to Nicholas. He smoked while he read them. All recommended abdication

---

[70] Cited in Hasegawa, *February Revolution*, 500–1.
[71] "The army must fight with all its strength against the external enemy, and the decision concerning the internal affairs must spare it the temptation to take part in the coup, which will be less painfully carried out under the decision from above": Alekseev, cited in Hasegawa, *February Revolution*, 501.

(Grand Duke Nikolai Nikolaevich adding that he did so "on his knees"), although one, refreshingly, called the Provisional Government a "gang of bandits."[72] Summing up Stavka's attitude, and anticipating the twin angles of piety and patriotism from which Nicholas would approach the question, Alekseev urged Nicholas to make a decision "without delay and as God inspires you ... for the sake of the security and independence of the fatherland and for the sake of its achievement of victory."[73] Present with Ruzsky were two other generals. Both agreed that Nicholas should abdicate.[74] There was silence. Then Nicholas made the sign of the cross and agreed to renounce the throne. The generals followed Nicholas's example. Nicholas "turned to Ruzsky, thanked him for his 'valorous and faithful service' and kissed him."[75] So, it was decided at around 3 p.m. on March 2, 1917, that Russia ceased to be a *teokratia*. As "someone" in Nicholas's entourage said, in a phrase strikingly pregnant with religious echoes, "It is over" (cf. Jn 19:30).[76] Had not Bulgakov said that the tsar "bore his authority like the cross of Christ"? Not just a dynasty, but a people's moral-religious ideal, had expired—and God (whose natural image in the *oikumene* the tsar always only was) had been driven from the *polis*.

A year later, the lingering conviction of the mystical significance of events led Bulgakov to lend these words to the Refugee: "The wider the events of the War spread out, the more clearly one sees their fatal character.... Everything we need and which might rescue us arrives late, or not at all. On the other hand, everything harmful is successful.... Just consider it: at the height of the World War, Rasputin's influence grows stronger, and this leads to revolution—on the eve of a crucial offensive.... Of course, in this entire fatal chain of circumstances, one can see the sin of the authorities and the darkness of the people, and even the direct plan of the enemy. But I cannot escape the thought that what is at work here is an invisible hand ... some sort of mystical plot ... that a black Providence is at work ... the fall of a world empire, essentially in several hours, or perhaps months?"[77]

---

[72] Pipes, *Russian Revolution*, 312.   [73] Hasegawa, *February Revolution*, 504.
[74] Ibid.   [75] Ibid.   [76] Ibid., 506.
[77] Bulgakov, "At the feast of the gods," 85.

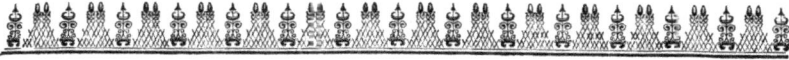

CHAPTER TWELVE
Travails of an Ex-theocrat

T PSKOV, THEN, IN MARCH 1917, THE TSARIST regime passed out of history because, to take at their word the men who claimed to speak for Russia, the theocratic conception of politics on which it had rested, and which, from the beginning, it had sought to realize (that is, of an "authority by the grace of God and not popular dispensation," whereby politics as a phenomenon is received as "always already" a gift from God, and an act, therefore, of sacred representation) was no longer comprehensible, among either those who had to execute its orders or those who had to obey, as anything more than a mere form of words to be honored at best in the breach. In terms of how such men represented the nature of the world they lived in to themselves, the source of this incomprehensibility was, we have argued, a philosophical one: after Kant, God was no longer a philosophically secure enough notion on which to build a politics. But if the theocratic ideal collapsed as a *historical regime* because it had previously collapsed in *Russian culture*, then, this collapse had not, even then, been unequivocal: as we have seen, in accounts of Nicholas's journey across the countryside on February 28–March 2, many signs of enduring loyalty to, even veneration for, the tsar appear. Perhaps, then, it would be better to say that, under pressure from developments in European philosophy, the theocratic principle in Russian culture in 1917 was in flux, but always remained as an element in Russian culture to be revived. Certainly, it also survived in Nicholas's heart. In abdicating, Nicholas had not repudiated the theocratic principle; he simply ceased to require his people to be bound by it. Instead, Nicholas took, as we shall see, the theocratic principle with him into exile, an inseparable part of that faith that was the source of the virtues for which, after his execution, he was canonized. Far from *beginning* with the abdication, then, Nicholas's orientation towards God continued, unchanged in its foundations, *despite* it. If the Canonization Committee (deaf itself, apparently, to the claims of *teokratia*) failed to see anything, it would be *that*.

Departing Pskov in the early hours of the morning on March 3, 1917, Nicholas returned by train to Stavka, where he disembarked later the same day, no longer tsar, or at least no longer emperor. Did one, could one, ever cease to be tsar? The question is disputed. According to one view, the mark left by the coronation anointing, a sacrament, was indelible. So, we have seen the Refugee cite the Eastern Church's historical "eleventh anathema" cursing those "who would think that Orthodox rulers ascend the throne not through God's blessing of them, or that in anointment the gifts of the Holy Spirit . . . do not pass to them."[1] But if the gifts of the Holy Spirit did pass to the tsar at his anointing, were they taken away if ever he gave up the throne? In Russia, the question had never arisen. Deposed emperors (Peter III, Paul I) tended to perish with or shortly after their act of removal from power. Voluntary abdication had never been envisaged. But if Nicholas's experience is any way illuminating, then certainly the mark was indelible. Even after his abdication, Nicholas, while never disputing that he had lost his power to command as *emperor*, never ceased to speak and act, on the other hand, as if he bore responsibility before God for Russia as *tsar*.

When he abdicated, Nicholas had not reckoned with becoming a prisoner. But history was leaving the Romanovs behind. The following day, the fourth, the Petrograd Soviet voted in favor of Nicholas's arrest, along with that of all the other male members of the Romanov dynasty. But it took several days for the Provisional Government to act on the Soviet's demands, and it was as a free man that, on the fifth, a Sunday, Nicholas went to his final Divine Liturgy in Mogilev. Then, on March 8/21, the Provisional Government issued a decree placing Nicholas under arrest. Before it was served, however, Nicholas was "given permission" (as his cousin Sandro, who was present, put it) to say farewell to the men who, only a few days earlier, had been bearers of an oath to serve him forever. It was a last display of the sensibilities of the now-vanished old regime. Sandro recalled:

> General Alekseev invites us to assemble in the main hall of GHQ. Nicky is to address the members of his former staff. By eleven a.m. the hall is packed. Generals, officers and persons in attendance on the Emperor are present. Nicky enters — calm, reserved, bearing the semblance of a smile on his lips. He thanks the staff and begs them to continue their work "with the same loyalty and in a spirit of self-sacrifice." He invites them to forget all feuds, to serve Russia and lead our army to victory. Then he says his adieus, in curt, soldier-like sentences, avoiding words that could suggest pathos. His modesty makes a tremendous impression. We shout "Hurray," as we never had in the last twenty-five years. Elder generals cry. A moment more, and someone is bound to step forward and implore Nicky to reconsider his decision.[2]

For Nicholas, it was an emotional moment. "My heart almost exploded," he wrote in his diary.[3] Then, Alekseev informed him that he was under arrest: accompanying him, not as aides but as keepers, on

---

[1] Bulgakov, "At the feast of the gods," III.
[2] Maylunas and Mironenko, *Lifelong Passion*, 571–72.
[3] Nicholas II, March 8, 1917, in Diary (2), 626.

the train to Tsarskoye Selo were four members of the Duma, including the Deputy Bublikov who, in seizing control of the railways during the events of the previous week, had been responsible for the two days Nicholas had spent crisscrossing the Russian countryside ineffectually while the Duma Committee strengthened its hand in Petrograd. A detachment of soldiers boarded the train to make sure nobody attempted to free the former emperor. "Heavy, painful, melancholy" was Nicholas's description of his feelings that evening.

Significantly, such feelings were not so far from those apparently felt by a great many of the men in the army Nicholas had until recently commanded. Alekseev noted that far from celebrating the downfall of tsarism, many rank-and-file troops "showed sadness and regret for the abdication of Nicholas II."[4] The civilian residents of Mogilev shared this sadness. Though the town was festooned with red bunting, Nicholas noticed as he was driven to the station that the "behavior of the crowd was in curious contrast to this exhibition": as the car in which he was being conveyed passed, those lining the street got down on their knees in one last customary show of respect for a man they evidently considered indelibly tsar, too.[5] Even more touching were the actions of some school-age girls on the platform. "When I got into the train," Nicholas recalled later, "I noticed five or six schoolgirls standing on the platform trying to attract my attention. I went to the window and when they saw me they began to cry and made signs for me to write something for them. So I signed my name on a piece of paper, and sent it to the children."[6] As the day was bitterly cold, Nicholas sought to encourage the girls to go home. But they insisted, it seems, in keeping vigil with him, during the whole two hours it took before the train departed.

The following day, March 9/22, at eleven o'clock in the morning, Nicholas disembarked at the imperial station at Tsarskoye Selo.[7] (The Russian Style station survives today, a crumbling, boarded-up shell on which the imperial arms can still just be made out, in the shadow of a 1960s Soviet apartment block.) In ordinary times, an honor guard would have met him there—and, indeed, even in the new era inaugurated by the abdication, the higher officers on duty planned to raise the customary cheer. But their plans were discovered and the task of meeting Nicholas assigned to lower-ranking officers of secure revolutionary sympathies. They were a disheveled lot, with revolutionary caps on their heads and cigarettes hanging from their mouths. Driven from there the

---

[4] McMeekin, *Russian Revolution*, 147.   [5] Dehn, *Real Tsaritsa*, 193.
[6] Ibid., 193–94.
[7] For details in this paragraph see Paul de Benkendorff, "Derniers jours du Tsar à Tsarskoie Selo 11 mars—14 aout 1917: I," *Revue des Deux Mondes* 43 (1928): 539–40; and Robert Service, *Last of the Tsars: Nicholas II and the Russian Revolution* (London: Macmillan, 2017), 36–37.

short distance to the palace, Nicholas was entering a new world. Once
the palace gates would have swung open automatically as the imperial
car approached. But on that day, the palace guard, fully aware of the
identity of the man sitting in the car, held them shut. "Who is there?"
asked the sentinel. "Nicholas Romanov," came the reply from the driver
of the car. "Let him pass!" cried the duty officer, and the guards opened
the gates. The aged Minister of the Court, Paul Benkendorff, called
the scene a "repugnant comedy." More was to follow. Walking up the
steps of the Alexander Palace, Nicholas tipped his hat to the sentry. As
a historian has noted, "For the first time in his life, no one responded
with any kind of salute."[8] And waiting inside the palace was a crowd
of spectators, both sympathetic and hostile. Nicholas shuddered and
directed his footsteps towards the family's apartments. There, in private,
Nicholas and Alexandra were reunited.[9]

੒ ੒ ੒

For her part, Alexandra had spent a harrowing week. Nursing her dangerously ill children while contemplating the possibility of the desertion
of the palace guard to the insurrection that had already conquered the
Tsarskoye Selo garrison, she discovered that her world had fallen apart
when news of Nicholas's abdication reached her. Nonetheless, she, her
husband and their children were still alive, and she ordered a liturgy
of thanksgiving that included a procession through the palace rooms
of the miraculous icon of Our Lady of the Sign, to which Alexandra
was devoted, to be served while she awaited Nicholas's expected return.
Two days before, she had been unable to stand when the news of Nicholas's abdication had been broken to her. But on this Sunday, Alexandra
herself walked behind the icon. "It was a strange sight to witness the
solemn little procession as it traversed the almost deserted splendors
of the Palace," recalled Lili Dehn, who was present. "Incense wafted
wreaths of perfume towards heaven, the solemn chant rose and fell, the
gold and blues of the Virgin's draperies glowed when the icon passed
the windows." Dehn even fancied that she saw something of the Virgin herself in Alexandra, who went everywhere veiled in her nun-like,
Red Cross nurse's uniform. In a reflection, perhaps, of the hope that
Alexandra had invested over the years in the image, "The expression in
the eyes," she said, "seemed the same."[10]
    The same impression struck the local priest, Fr Belyaev, who per-
formed the thanksgiving liturgy and led the procession. Belyaev would
reappear later in the Romanovs' story, but this was his first close contact
with the family of Russia's last monarch, and, having been exposed, like

---

[8] Service, *Last of the Tsars*, 36.   [9] Dehn, *Real Tsaritsa*, 188.
[10] Ibid., 171–72.

everyone else, to the propaganda of the liberal opposition, what he saw surprised him. "From the entranceway, we ascended to the children's wing on the second floor," Belyaev recorded in his diary: "We passed a number of brightly lit rooms, and entered a large, dimly lit room in which the sick children lay in their individual beds. The icon was placed on the table prepared for it. It was so dark... that I could barely make out who was present: the Empress, in the uniform of a Sister of Mercy, stood next to the Heir's bed.... Slender wax candles were lit before the icon."[11] A father himself, Belyaev intuitively shared Alexandra's worry as a parent. Then, playing on a linguistic parallelism clearer in Russian than in English, he drew a connection between the Virgin Mary, Queen (*tsaritsa*) of Heaven, to whom Alexandra had turned in her hour of need, and Alexandra herself, "queen" (*tsaritsa*) of Russia. "Suppressing her womanly weakness," Belyaev wrote, wanting to magnify rather than belittle Alexandra's moral feat, "and all her human ills, she heroically, selflessly, devoted herself to caring for the sick. Placing all her reliance on the Queen of Heaven, she decided that the first thing to be done was to pray before the Icon of Our Lady of the Sign.... On her knees, tearfully, the earthly queen implored the help and intercession of the heavenly queen." Belyaev sought to comfort the woman in front of him: "As I offered her the cross, I said to her: Take courage and be strong, Your Majesty.... God is merciful. In all things, rely on His will. Believe, hope, and pray without ceasing." When Belyaev left the palace, he saw that Alexandra was still by her children's side, praying "fervently." By that time, he said, "the Palace was already ringed with troops and all the people within it were under arrest."[12]

By now, not only Nicholas but the whole family and their retinue were prisoners. The day before Nicholas had returned, General Kornilov (who would later lend his name to the so-called "Kornilov Affair" of August, but who at that time commanded the Tsarskoye Selo garrison) arrived to read a warrant of arrest for the empress and the instructions, from the Provisional Government, that the palace was now to be sealed. From that moment, recalled Benkendorff, "All the doors of the palace were locked and sealed, with the except of three: that which opened onto the kitchens, that which opened onto the façade and that which opened onto the garden." Staff was to be reduced to a minimum, the family's correspondence opened and read before dispatch. The telephone lines were cut, and the new troops, hostile and querulous, who invested the palace bullied the domestic staff; at night, the palace grounds echoed with the pot shots they fired into the sky.[13] Enclosed in this sealed

[11] Marilyn Swezey, ed., *The Romanovs under house arrest: From the 1917 diary of a palace priest*, trans. Leonid Michail tschenko (Jordanville, NY: Holy Trinity Publications, 2018), 15–16.   [12] Ibid., 16.
[13] Benkendorff, "Derniers jours: I," 536–37.

world were thirteen persons in addition to Alexandra and her children.

While they were overjoyed a few days later to have Nicholas, they were shocked at what they saw. "Suddenly, I heard the sound of foot-steps," recalled Alexandra's faithful friend, Lili Dehn: "I knew to whom they belonged—but they were no longer the footsteps of a confident and happy man. They sounded as if the person who was advancing was very, very tired." Nicholas had been away for less than a fortnight. But he had aged a decade. "I now realized how greatly he had altered," continued Dehn: "The Emperor was deathly pale, his face was covered with innumerable wrinkles, his hair was grey at the temples. He looked like an old man."[14] The precariousness of their position was impossible to ignore. Dehn watched in horror from a window as Nicholas sought the simple relief of a walk in the palace park. At every turn, a soldier appeared to block him. "The Emperor made a nervous movement with his hand, but he obeyed, and retraced his steps; but the same thing occurred—another sentinel barred his passage."[15] Russia's "God-wed" tsar had become a cornered animal. Then, in the evening, a convoy of vehicles carrying a detachment of several hundred soldiers loyal to the Soviet (including a machine gun company) appeared outside the gates of the palace. Apparently fearing that the former emperor was planning to escape, they desired Nicholas's imprisonment in the Peter and Paul Fortress. But their commander, S. D. Mstislavsky, a Socialist Revolu-tionary who wore an old sheepskin jacket and carried a revolver in his pocket, nonetheless agreed to depart peacefully after he succeeded in having Nicholas (who at the time was sitting with his sick children in the nursery) presented to him in a palace corridor.[16]

The hostility of the soldiers guarding the family was a constant reminder of the change the Revolution had brought to Russia. Recalled Sophie Buxhoeveden, one of Alexandra's ladies-in-waiting who elected to remain in captivity with the former imperial family: "soldiers, who, barely a month before, had been spick and span, perfectly disciplined troops, had degenerated into an undisciplined rabble. They were slov-enly in their dress, their crushed caps were set awry on huge mops of unkempt hair, their coats were unbuttoned, and their nonchalant man-ner of performing their duties was a continual irritation to the Emperor. They lolled out of the guardroom and sat about smoking and reading papers."[17] Once, when Nicholas attempted to ride his old bicycle, a soldier stuck the tip of his bayonet through the spokes, causing Nich-olas to fall, to the guffaws of the watching guards.[18] And yet although the guardsmen refused to return his greetings, Nicholas persisted in

---

[14] Dehn, *Real Tsaritsa*, 189.   [15] Ibid., 190.
[16] Benkendorff, "Derniers jours: I," 542–43; Pipes, *Russian Revolution*, 333.
[17] Buxhoeveden, *Tragic Empress*, 289.   [18] Ibid., 304.

addressing them with a courteous and friendly *zdravstvuyite* ("hello"). When they did not answer, he pretended that they had not heard him. Among some, it became a habit to mock the former emperor for the relatively low rank of colonel he had held in his own army before making himself supreme commander. "Colonel Romanov" they called him. But it says much about Nicholas's natural humility that he thought this slight reflected worse on his detractors than it did on him. "It's very silly to think this behavior can affect my soul," he told Lili Dehn. After all, "colonel," he said, "is a very worthy appellation."[19]

Far worse were the shooting at the goats, deer, swans, and other tame animals in the palace park, the provocative commandeering of palace furniture, or the unannounced spot inspections of Alexandra, Alexei, or the grand duchesses' bedrooms. Alexandra was forced to change in a corner of her room to avoid the gaze of a provocatively positioned sentry. Moreover, the children were still ill, and two leering soldiers insisted on being present when doctors were called to the bedside of the delirious, seventeen-year-old Grand Duchess Maria. Thefts were not uncommon: a soldier entered Buxhoeveden's rooms while she slept during the night, with the aim of stealing her rings. If all this was bearable it was because Colonel Kotsbue, whom Kolybinsky, the new commander of the Tsarskoye Selo garrison, had put in charge of the palace, was sympathetic and respectful, while much of their former domestic staff (maids, cooks, footmen) insisted on staying to serve them. Thus, shielded from the worst of the Revolution by Kotsbue, and genuinely loved, it would seem, by those who continued to wait on them, the family and its closest attendants took comfort in the preservation of as many as possible of Tsarskoye Selo's old routines. True, the pot plants Alexandra loved had been confiscated, and fruit, as a luxury, was forbidden. But together they ate lunch daily at one and took tea together at four. Dinner was served at seven.[20]

Russia's new rulers took little interest in the representatives of the old regime. Guchkov, now War Minister in the Provisional Government, had called on Alexandra in the interval between his appearance at Mogilev to obtain Nicholas's abdication and the latter's return to Tsarskoye Selo five days later. But he was the last minister to make the journey there before Aleksandr Kerensky, the firebrand Trudovik who had denounced the tsarist regime as a band of killers and traitors in the Duma the previous autumn, appeared on March 21/April 3, almost ten days after Nicholas's return. Convinced that Alexandra had been involved in pro-German activities, Kerensky had all the palace's private rooms searched in his presence. Drawers were opened, cupboards searched, and Nicholas and Alexandra called to a behind-closed-doors cross-examination.[21]

---

[19] Dehn, *Real Tsaritsa*, 201.   [20] Service, *Last of the Tsars*, 56.
[21] Benkendorff, "Derniers jours: I," 545–48.

Furious to learn that Alexandra had been destroying her own and other close friends' diaries, Kerensky allowed the former empress to remain at the palace, but on his orders her two closest confidantes, Lili Dehn and Anna Vyrubova, who was still recovering from a life-threatening case of measles, were sent away to prison. The sympathetic and respectful commander of the palace, Kotsbue was replaced with Korovichenko, a soldier of more reliably revolutionary sentiments.

Kerensky believed his interview with Nicholas had allowed him to fathom the deposed emperor's character.[22] Nicholas II was an "extremely reserved man, who distrusted and utterly despised mankind," said Kerensky, revealing a complete inability to read the character of the man in front of him: " ... He did not care for anything or anyone except his son and perhaps his daughters." Indeed, a "terrible indifference to all external things" made Russia's last monarch seem barely human, "like some unnatural automaton." Consistent with the radically secular frame of thought that Kerensky, as an *intelligent*, had assimilated, Kerensky attributed Nicholas's inhumanity to his continued belief in the possibility of religion. "As I studied his face," Kerensky affirmed, "I seemed to see behind his smile and charming eyes a stiff, frozen mask of utter loneliness and desolation. I think he may have been a mystic, seeking communion with Heaven ... weary of all earthly things." Unconsciously, Kerensky was, indirectly, revealing the religious meaning of the Russian Revolution. It is manifest, in his implicit subscription to Kant's purely secular rationality, that Kerensky was a bad judge of character because he was a bad judge, in the end, of what was real.

If, in fact, while Nicholas took his faith with him into exile, it does not follow that his faith emerged from the abdication unshaken. Striking for its absence in the record Nicholas left behind in his diary of these earliest weeks of his life as "ex-theocrat" is the interior recourse to God in prayer that litters his diary elsewhere. Having referred all things to God for years, Nicholas suddenly went silent. Did this reflect a questioning of his faith in God, or a sense of shame and unworthiness connected with his ultimate failure to uphold his coronation vows? In either case, equally striking is how relatively quickly and comprehensively Nicholas's "dark night" was overcome. Although the *teokratia* was gone, Nicholas's fundamental orientation towards God, albeit perhaps shaken for a time, remained, at its core, unweakened. In due time, it reasserted itself.

A clear help to him in these early weeks was Alexandra, whose chief concern and consolation remained, as always, religion. Wheeled around the palace in the Red Cross uniform she refused to remove, she reminded onlookers of a nun, praying constantly, as she did, for her still ill and bedridden children, or embroidering prayers into pillows and bestowing

---

[22] For what follows, see Pipes, *Russian Revolution*, 334–36.

them as gifts on all around her. Her preferred occupation was to read the Bible or the mystical tracts of the Byzantine and Syrian Church fathers. "For months," recalled Sophie Buxhoeveden, "every shot fired in the garden, every heated discussion in the guard room might have been the first step towards disaster." But, she continued, Alexandra's inner fortitude "never deserted her.... She had put those she loved into the hands of the Supreme Power, feeling the hopelessness of human help, and in her constant prayers, [she] found the wonderful serenity and courage she kept to the end."[23]

The love of God, and their own love for each other, bound the family together. In the earliest days of the family's house arrest, Alexandra requested the services of a priest to say the Liturgy on Sundays and feast days in the palace's internal chapel. It took ten days for Russia's new authorities to grant the request (Benkendorff having had to plead with the arch-plotter Guchkov for this mercy).[24] But, finally, on March 11/24, a group comprising a priest, Fr Afanasy Belyaev (who had brought the icon of Mary for the procession that Alexandra earlier ordered), protodeacon, cantor and choir of four, was given permission to remain in the palace overnight from Vespers on Saturday until after the Divine Liturgy on Sunday. All the same, the guards sought to make the coming and going of the clergy as difficult as possible: Saturday evenings and Sunday mornings "were always made the occasion of long discussions, terminating in violent abuse."[25]

In this, of course, the Revolution manifested how far it was, in its inner logic, a judgment in favor of secularization. But if, with the abdication, Russia had been emancipated from the theocratic principle, it would be a mistake to imagine that Nicholas for that reason allowed his family or his retinue to withhold their prayers for the government that now ruled Russia: Russia had repudiated the governance of God; but God had not, Nicholas prayed, repudiated Russia. Thus, recalled Buxhoeveden, Nicholas "reverently made the sign of the cross when the Provisional Government was prayed for in church," and sought to "inculcate this spirit into all those around him." Indeed, when one day Nicholas noticed that the countess herself had failed to make the sign of the cross when the government was remembered in the liturgy, he took her aside and corrected her, "saying that I should not forget that it was Russia for which I was praying."[26] Indeed, it says something both of Nicholas's patriotism and of his magnanimity that he prayed that God would lavish on those who had usurped his powers the very same guidance and inspiration that his opponents had written off as unnecessary "mysticism." "The Provisional Government is Russia's government. You

---

[23] Buxhoeveden, *Tragic Empress*, 294.   [24] Benkendorff, "Derniers jours: I," 539.
[25] Buxhoeveden, *Tragic Empress*, 292.   [26] Ibid., 298.

may well not like Prince Lvov and his colleagues. But you have to pray
that Our Lord should give guidance in the matter of rule," he admon-
ished Dehn, faithful to the theocratic principle to the end.[27]

Others also struggled with the change that had come over Russia. Fr
Belyaev, celebrating the first Sunday Divine Liturgy in the Palace since
the Revolution, had not considered himself a principled adherent of
tsarist *teokratia*. As a "mitered" archpriest, Belyaev, though not a bishop,
belonged to the upper ranks of the clergy.[28] But he did not know the
imperial family well. In October 1916, he had been made rector or priest-
in-charge of Nicholas and Alexandra's Fyodorov Sovereign Cathedral,
which, as a regimental church, came with additional duties for Belyaev
as chaplain to the Tsarskoye Selo garrison. This was barely a few months
before the Revolution and prior to arriving at the Alexander Palace in
March 1917, Belyaev had never spoken to either Nicholas or Alexandra.
He brought with him only those ideas about Russia's last monarch
and his family that he had formed from a distance and from received,
popular opinion. But all the same, Belyaev, to his own surprise, found
himself choking on the changes that the church authorities had already
introduced into the liturgy. As he recalled in his diary, "When at the
great entrance I was required, for the first time in the presence of the
Sovereign, to commemorate not the 'Pious Autocrat and Emperor,' etc.,
but instead the 'Russian Authorities and the Provisional Government,'
I at first could not bring myself to do so, and barely kept from bursting
into tears."[29] He completed the liturgy with his "voice breaking and
stumbling over the words."

By the middle of March, Holy Week was approaching, and Benkendorff, foreseeing that a priest would be needed twice daily, wrote to
Guchkov asking that permission be granted Belyaev to remain in the
palace throughout Holy Week, and to hear the confessions of the staff
and offer them Holy Communion. (It was assumed that Nicholas and
Alexandra's own confessor, Fr Aleksandr Vasiliev, would arrive in time
to take theirs.) Again, for weeks, no answer came. But finally, the permission arrived, and on the Saturday before Palm Sunday, Belyaev and
his colleagues took up temporary residence in the palace. Exceeding their
original assignment for Holy Week, they were to stay with the former
imperial family for the next fortnight.[30]

≈ ≈ ≈

Given a room on the top floor of the palace, above the chapel, with
a window looking down on a small private garden, Belyaev found
himself thrust into a spiritual drama that slowly opened his eyes to

---

[27] Cited in Service, *Last of the Tsars*, 48.   [28] Swezey, *Romanovs*, 65–67.
[29] Ibid., 18.   [30] Benkendorff, "Derniers jours: I," 544.

the Revolution's religious meaning. Not consciously committed to (nor even, perhaps, *aware of*) the theocratic principle, Belyaev tells us he favored a constitution. His diary is a record of how much direct observation — and one single personal conversation — with Nicholas, Alexandra, and their children both surprised him and opened his eyes to the possibility of a sacred politics, which he appears not before to have considered. In a way, he was about to have his own vision on the Yalta Embankment. Thus, on Belyaev's first day, he served three liturgies, the traditional Holy Tuesday reading of the Gospels in the morning, and compline and matins in the evening. Nicholas attended all three, Alexandra the last two. On Holy Wednesday, Belyaev spent three hours taking the retinue's confessions, but he did not speak to Nicholas and his family. Then, the local Soviet chose the next day, Holy Thursday (the commemoration of Christ's institution of the Eucharist), for a competing funeral service for the "martyrs of the Revolution," who were to be reburied that day in the palace grounds. Intended as an affront to the Old Regime, the ceremony struck Belyaev as expressing a deeper rejection of God that he was not sure whether the participants themselves were conscious of, but which he could himself only find sacrilegious. It moved the priest to repeat the prayer of Christ for his executioners: "Truly, they know not what they do."[31]

For her part, Buxhoeveden believed that had it not been for an unexpected change in the weather, which scattered the crowd of rebellious soldiers and workers, the event might have ended with the storming of the palace and the threatening of Nicholas and Alexandra's lives. "Thousands of workmen and soldiers came to the function, carrying banners and placards on which were mottoes of every shade of socialistic and communistic thought. They made incendiary speeches in front of the red coffins, while the bands played appropriate music, varied from time to time by a funeral march."[32] Indeed, the latter funeral marches, she said, were the "only concession" to what she ironically called "old-time prejudice" (i.e. religion) for "every sign of anything reminiscent of a religious ceremony was carefully avoided." In other words, it was a mass gathering whose atheism was not accidental but deliberate. The Revolution was aware of its own religious meaning.

In such a setting, the piety of the imperial family stood out all the more clearly to Belyaev. Nicholas and Alexandra participated in the liturgies he performed not merely as acts of duty or convention, but actively, it seemed, with real faith. Stands with the Scriptures were placed in front of them so that they could follow the readings attentively.[33] Having only known the imperial family through the newspapers, Belyaev, it seems,

---

[31] Swezey, *Romanovs* 21.   [32] Buxhoeveden, *Tragic Empress*, 301.
[33] Swezey, *Romanovs*. 21.

had not previously attributed to them such authentic piety. But now he did, unreservedly. "One must really be this near to the former Royal Family, must see for oneself in order to comprehend just how fervently — often on their knees — in what an Orthodox manner, the former Royal Family prays to God. With what obedience, meekness, and humility do they stand during the divine services, giving themselves over entirely to the will of God," he wrote on Holy Thursday evening in his diary.[34]

This impression was reinforced the following day, Good Friday. Belyaev, having confessed forty-two members of the palace staff and retinue, was struck again, at the day's Vespers service, by the former imperial family's sincerity. Emphasizing God's boundless love for the repentant sinner ("that love that caused the Father to leave the Son during the moment of his unbearably difficult Passion") and concluding with a prayer to Christ ("With Thy Passion and Death . . . I profoundly sense that in all my sufferings, I am not alone. Thou, O Lord, art with me. And walking with me, I will not fear evil even in the shadow of death") from beside the *epitaphion* (the ceremonial funerary shroud of the dead Christ), Belyaev was both surprised and gratified by the visible effect it had on those listening. By the time he had finished, many were weeping. Nicholas later told him it had touched him deeply.[35] The year before, at Stavka, Nicholas and his generals had carried the *epitaphion* together.

Thence, Belyaev was called away to the nursery to confess the two youngest grand duchesses, Maria and Anastasia, as well as Alexei. (Olga was still too ill.) The nursery, Belyaev discovered when he arrived, looked more like a church than it did a suite of children's bedrooms. "In the corner of each Grand Duchess's room was a real iconostasis, filled with a multitude of icons of various sizes, bearing the images of especially venerated saints. Before the iconostasis was a folding analogion [lectern] covered with a towel, on which were prayer books, service books, and the holy Gospel and a cross. . . . In furniture and décor, the rooms presented an image of a pure and innocent childhood. . . . "[36] Then, Belyaev confessed each of the children in private separately, sitting with each child for forty minutes. Acquaintance with the children's inner worlds confirmed the impression that was forming. "Grant, O Lord," he wrote in his diary, "that all children be on as high a moral level as were the children of the former tsar! Such was their lack of hatred, their humility, their submission to the will of their parents, unquestioning dedication to the will of God, purity of thought and complete ignorance of secular filth — both passionate and sinful — that I was astounded." Indeed, such was the children's purity that he was not sure whether, if he ventured to suggest sins they had perhaps omitted, he might not have been acquainting them with things of which they had until that time been entirely ignorant.

---

[34] Ibid., 21–22.   [35] Ibid., 23.   [36] Ibid., 24.

But the strongest impressions left that day on Belyaev were left by his first exchange of words with Nicholas and Alexandra with whom he (lacking the required permission) had not yet spoken but that evening was unexpectedly called to confess. Belyaev recorded the unusual nervousness with which he was seized: he prayed before the altar in the palace chapel, venerated the *epitaphion* shroud of the dead Christ, and robed himself especially carefully. His diary also reflects his apparent surprise when introduced to the imperial couple's bedroom. First, there was the "single, wide bed," which he evidently took as a sign of a marital fidelity not always to be expected among the high-born. Second, there was the couple's bedroom chapel, where the confession was to take place, which Belyaev described as "covered from top to bottom with icons, [and] oil lamps burning before the icons. In a recess in the corner, there stands a special iconostasis, with carved columns and places for famous icons. Before it is a folding analogion, bearing a large ancient altar Gospel, a cross, and many Divine Service books."[37] Evidently expecting a more secular environment than the one he found, Belyaev had brought a cross and a Gospel with him, but they were clearly superfluous, and he didn't know where to put them.

With Nicholas and Alexandra in the bedroom was their second-oldest daughter, Tatiana. As she had not confessed earlier in the nursery, she did so now. First to confess after her was Alexandra. Respecting the confessional seal, Belyaev tells us only that she was "clearly agitated," having "fervently prayed and decided to confess before the holy cross and Gospel all the ills of her heart, according to the Orthodox rite, fully cognizant of the greatness of the Mystery." Once Alexandra had finished, Nicholas followed. It was a remarkable moment. With it, the chink of light that had, that week, opened on Nicholas's soul became for Belyaev a wide-open window. Although Belyaev's monarchism had never been unconditional, the historical and spiritual privilege he had been conceded was not lost on him. He represented it in analogical terms we have seen before. "Oh, how inexpressibly fortunate I felt to have been made worthy through the mercies of God to become intermediary between the Heavenly King (in Russian, *tsar*, i.e. Christ) and the earthly one. For next to me stood the one who was loftier than anyone else living on earth. He was even now the Anointed One given to us by God, one who for twenty-three years . . . was our reigning Russian Orthodox tsar."

Perhaps most moving for Belyaev was the discovery, both sweet and painful, that in the figure who now knelt before him, Russia's theocratic regime had not been a mere pious fiction mouthed with bored convention by a ruling dynasty more interested in power than in religion. On the contrary, Belyaev concluded, Nicholas II was a genuine

---

[37] Ibid., 25.

Orthodox Christian. Continued Belyaev: "the humble servant of God Nicholas . . . on bended knees, gazes upon the cross and the Gospel and in the presence of my unworthiness, relates to his Heavenly Father the hidden secrets of his long-suffering life, and reduced to dust before the greatness of the Heavenly King, tearfully asks forgiveness for his transgressions, voluntary and involuntary."[38] Indeed, Nicholas's very piety compounded, for Belyaev, the tragedy of 1917. "[W]ishing good for all his enemies, not harboring any offense, praying fervently for Russia's prosperity, deeply believing in her glorious future," Nicholas, it seemed to Belyaev, ought to have been the best-loved and most successful of Russian emperors. And to Belyaev's credit, he resolved to tell him so once he had administered his priestly absolution. But first Belyaev had to find the right form of words.

Being a whole generation older than Nicholas, Belyaev remembered the hope felt by educated Russian society at the time of Nicholas's accession to the throne in 1894 that the new tsar would prove more liberal than his father, Alexander III. Those hopes had been dashed. But Belyaev was now aware that Nicholas had acted not out of hunger for power but out of conviction, and, as a priest, Belyaev wanted to comfort this penitent son of the Church. And yet he was at a loss what to say. "What joy could I, through my clumsy words of comfort and calm, instill in the heart of one who was cruelly isolated from his people, who until now had been certain of the rightness of his actions as directed to the good of his beloved homeland?"[39] Finally, Belyaev blurted, revealing his political opinions: "Oh, Your Majesty! What good you would have done for Russia had you but given her a full constitution, and thereby fulfilled the wishes of the people. Everyone welcomed you as an angel of good, love, and peace." How comforting Belyaev imagined Nicholas could have found such words to be is unclear: hadn't Nicholas just heard his confessor confirm everything the liberal opposition had been saying for years? Certainly, Nicholas's faith, including in the theocratic principle, seems to have been at least momentarily shaken. "Can this possibly be true?" Belyaev records Nicholas asking in return before proceeding to a recapitulation of the events surrounding the abdication. As Nicholas spoke, Belyaev noticed that he was weeping. At this point, the confession was over, Nicholas and Belyaev emerged from the oratory. Alexandra rejoined them. Together, they chatted about shared interests: the Fyodorov Sovereign Cathedral, family life. Belyaev heard Alexandra say: "I was misunderstood. I wanted good."[40] The following days' Easter services were spent in heartfelt solemnity.

෨   ෨   ෨

---

[38] Ibid., 25–26.   [39] Ibid., 26.   [40] Ibid., 27.

According to the terms of Belyaev's original assignment, Easter Monday should have been his last day in the palace. He had come to serve the Easter liturgies, and now, he believed, he was free to go and be reunited with his own family. But Belyaev had become a victim of circumstance. Since entering the palace, the Soviet had issued a decree banning all communication between those in the palace and the outside world. And as Belyaev was in the palace, that included him. Having entered the palace a free man, Belyaev had become a prisoner. And yet it says much about Nicholas and Alexandra that when they were informed of Belyaev's predicament, their immediate instinct was an expression of solidarity. "Do you have anything to read?" asked Nicholas in a note he sent to the priest. When Belyaev replied that he would welcome some books, Nicholas sent him *The Truth of Orthodoxy*, which he had himself recently read and enjoyed. While Belyaev was the ordained priest deputed to the palace to serve the spiritual needs of the former, during this period of his *de facto* incarceration, a new dynamic had entered the relationship between the two parties. Increasingly, it was the former tsar and his family who took it upon themselves to care for the spiritual needs of Belyaev the priest. Thus, when he had finished *Truth of Orthodoxy*, Belyaev found himself the recipient of another book: *At Prayer in Calm and in the Storm*, sent to his rooms by one of Alexandra's ladies-in-waiting, Countess Hendrikova.

Finally, on April 22/May 5, Belyaev was released from the palace. But he returned every Saturday evening to say Vespers for the family. On such occasions, he lodged in his old rooms overnight, and returned to his home outside the palace after serving the Divine Liturgy the following morning. Now, he was even more alert to the imperial family's spiritual and psychological state. Returning to say Vespers a week later, Belyaev noted in the family (with whom he was still not allowed to converse) the "same sorrow and the same solitude. Joy and comfort in prayer." Intuitively, as a priest, Belyaev was entering, by proxy, into their sufferings. Indeed, in the homily he preached at the conclusion of the Divine Liturgy the following Sunday, he found himself unintentionally giving expression to thoughts and feelings that Nicholas, Alexandra, and their family could not find words for themselves. He recalled the moment. "I was speaking about enduring suffering, which faces man, abandoned by everyone, in an inexpressible, oppressive state, horrifies him, and the sole comfort he finds is in prayer." At this point, there escaped from someone, Belyaev recalled, without saying whether the voice was a man's or a woman's, "such an irrepressible, loud, and powerful, heartrending sigh, that it amazed all the listeners. And that response of spiritual torment emanated from the place where only the Imperial family was standing."[41] Was it Alexandra, releasing the inner,

---

[41] Ibid., 38.

spiritual and emotional burden of being which she had carried since the age of twenty-two, as an empress, a mother, and carer to a chronically ill child? Or was it Nicholas, releasing the weight of the *teokratia*?

∾   ∾   ∾

What can we say of Nicholas's inner life during these months? We know that he was concerned for Russia. On May 1/14, news reached Nicholas that Russia's government had taken a dramatic lurch to the left. Victims of the maelstrom that had engulfed them after it had been revealed that Miliukov, as foreign minister, and Guchkov, war minister, intended to pursue the tsarist war aim of seizing Constantinople, both men had already resigned the ministerial posts they had so long coveted. Correctly foreseeing the inexperience of those who clamored most loudly for power, Nicholas's conversation with Ruzsky had proved prophetic. Under house arrest at Tsarskoye Selo, a more spiteful soul than Nicholas's might have indulged in *Schadenfreude*. But Nicholas did not. "What does the future hold for poor Russia?" he merely asked in his diary before adding, "God's will be done!" It was Russia that mattered, not revenge.

That spring, the façade of a certain amount of continuity with pre-Revolutionary days fell away. In the cabinet, Guchkov and Miliukov's places were taken by Socialists committed to "democratizing the army" and concluding a peace "without annexations."[42] Pursued to its logical conclusion, such a strategy could only bring about the disintegration of a Russian army that, in May, was still largely at its posts against the enemy. Under the effect of the Soviet's notorious Military Order No. 1, and the spread among the troops of the Bolsheviks' relentless, German-funded defeatist propaganda, morale was wavering, especially in the north, near Petrograd.[43] The economy, too, which Russia's tsarist government had repurposed for the war, was in freefall. With the workers who now controlled the factories voting for wage rises and shorter working days, production plummeted; inflation sky-rocketed. The food shortages that had been the pretext for the general strike that gave rise to the garrison mutiny in March now became a reality. It was not without a certain symbolic significance that, at the Alexander Palace, the first items to run out were wine and bread for Holy Communion.

To keep their spirits up, Nicholas, his children, and the more robust members of the retinue did plant a vegetable garden. Nicholas and his former aide, Prince Dolgorukov, felled the necessary trees, and cut them up for firewood for the following winter.[44] They were given an hour and a half a day by their captors for this work, and they threw

---

[42] McMeekin, *Russian Revolution*, 140–46.   [43] Ibid., 148–50.
[44] Benkendorff, "Derniers jours: II," 803.

themselves into it. They would have enjoyed the work more, recalled Buxhoeveden, had they not been forced to do it under the eyes of the public (who came from Petrograd to gawk at Russia's former emperor at his daily walk under the supervision of an armed escort, through the palace fence) and the glare of the guards.[45] The soldiers guarding the family were increasingly hostile, even, at times, truculent. Reflecting the success of the Progressive Bloc's wartime insinuations of her alleged role as a German spy, Alexandra was the focus of their insults. Too weak to walk out into the garden, she was pushed in a wheelchair. Incensed, the soldiers "swore loudly at her for not being made to walk." Coarseness and the latent threat of violence pervaded the palace, its "benches and walls were scribbled over with the coarsest insults." When one considers the sexual allusions these insults were likely to have contained (a legacy, again, of the Progressive Bloc's insinuations of sexual impropriety between Alexandra and Rasputin) as well as the age and innocence of the grand duchesses, the environment must have seemed very threatening and oppressive indeed. The guards' hostility was directed towards clergy, too. When Belyaev told off a party of soldiers for lying about on the lawn beside the Fyodorov Sovereign Cathedral, they replied by calling him a "filth-eating pope."[46]

By the time summer arrived, Nicholas was deeply dismayed at Russia's condition. "It seemed to me that the Sovereign had a very pale, suffering appearance, and was very ill. Something is bothering him," Belyaev wrote in his diary on May 28, "and he is silently, patiently enduring his suffering. He prays fervently, on his knees."[47] Still forbidden to talk to the family directly for more than a few minutes, Belyaev did the best he could to comfort Nicholas, preaching a sermon on the sixteen-year-old Grand Duchess Anastasia's birthday celebrating the "joy parents experience in having children who manifest a high moral standard, sincere love, childlike faith, and wholehearted obedience."[48] Indirectly, it was praise for Nicholas and Alexandra's work as Christian parents, and Nicholas appreciated it. "Thank you, *batiushka*, for your kind and comforting words," Nicholas said simply when he approached to venerate the cross at the end of the liturgy.

Russia, however, was sliding towards anarchy. Along the front with Germany, it risked defeat and occupation. To revive Russia's flagging war effort, Kerensky, since early May Guchkov's replacement as Minister of War, embarked on a month-long tour of the front, from the Baltic to Romania, delivering morale-raising speeches to the troops as preparation for a renewed offensive against Germany and Austria-Hungary in

---

[45] Buxhoeveden, *Tragic Empress*, 305.
[46] In Russian, a "pope" is a derogatory word for a priest.
[47] Swezey, *Romanovs*, 42.   [48] Ibid., 43.

Galicia on June 16/29. It began auspiciously, with the most spectacular shell bombardment yet seen on the Eastern Front. Briefly, the Russians surged forward. When the news of the first victories was communicated to Nicholas, he, ever the Orthodox theocrat, instantly sent word to Belyaev asking him to come and celebrate a liturgy of thanksgiving.[49] But soon Russia's armies were turned back, and by early July, the offensive — and the Russian army — was to all intents and purposes finished.[50] The Provisional Government's prestige and credibility were irretrievably damaged. A Bolshevik-inspired rebellion was suppressed. But during these so-called "July Days," it was a close call. "Surely," Nicholas asked on one occasion, "Kerensky can stop this licentiousness? How is this possible? Aleksandr Fyodorovich [i.e. Kerensky] was placed there by the people. The people must obey and not run amok."[51] As Nicholas well knew, the argument he had been presented with by the opposition was that a person chosen by the people and accountable to them would better command the people's loyalties than a tsar chosen by God and accountable to him. So why, Nicholas asked, had that so quickly not proved to be the case? "Where are the people who might take events in hand and prevent strife and bloodshed?" Nicholas asked in his diary.[52] Events answered him mockingly quickly. On July 6/20, Prince Lvov, a man who, just six months before, had been supremely confident of his superior ability to govern Russia, shared the fate of Guchkov and Miliukov, and resigned as Chairman of the Provisional Government in favor of Kerensky.[53] Grotesquely, Kerensky, who had spent much of his professional life before the Revolution railing against tsarism, moved into Alexander III's suite in the Winter Palace, began using the imperial train, shed his old workers' clothes, and took a mistress.[54] But while the thirty-seven-year-old Kerensky (devoid of any sense of the theocratic principle) was playacting at being tsar, Russia — to paraphrase Bulgakov's General — was visibly disintegrating, having lost its entelechy.

෴   ෴   ෴

With the failure of Kerensky's June Offensive, and Lvov's subsequent fall, the Revolution lurched further left. As it did so, the imperial family's continuing presence at Tsarskoye Selo became untenable. On July 11/24, Kerensky informed the family that they were to be moved, for

---

[49] Ibid., 44.   [50] McMeekin, *Russian Revolution*, 163.
[51] Pipes, *Russian Revolution*, 336–37.
[52] Nicholas II, July 5, 1917, in Diary (2), 642.
[53] Although members of different political parties, Lvov and Kerensky had been co-conspirators since their mutual membership of the Freemasonry lodge assembled in 1915 and 1916 with the aim of overthrowing Nicholas's government. By resigning in favor of Kerensky, Lvov was endeavoring to ensure that power remained in the hands of one of the members of this original conspiratorial circle. See McMeekin, *Russian Revolution*, 180.
[54] Ibid.

their safety. He did not say where, and, for the rest of July, the family entertained the hope that it would be Crimea. The golden days they had once enjoyed there must have seemed impossibly remote. "Three years since Germany declared war," Nicholas noted in his diary on July 19/August 1: "It seems a whole lifetime has been lived in these three years! Lord, help me and save Russia!" He was no longer tsar, but he couldn't abandon the habits of a lifetime. The government's "first task," he noted in his diary, when informed that Kerensky had taken over the Provisional Government Chairmanship, "should be strengthening the discipline of the army and the lifting of its morale as well as the introduction of some kind of order into Russia's domestic affairs."[55]

As ever, faith in God sustained the family's morale. Unable to join Belyaev and his clergy to celebrate the feast day of St Serafim at the Fyodorov Sovereign Cathedral, they marked it instead the following Sunday at the palace. By now, Alexei was regularly serving as an acolyte, and Belyaev's diary shows that the priest was becoming increasingly aware of Alexei's apparently unexpectedly deep inner piety. "Divine Liturgy was served as usual, at its usual time, and attended by the same people [i.e. Nicholas, Alexandra, their children, remaining retinue and servants]," Belyaev recorded. "The Heir served in the altar, and towards the end of the liturgy went into the nave, where the entire Imperial Family was standing. With them, he listened to my talk on how the memory of St Serafim had been celebrated in our Fyodorov Sovereign Cathedral." Doubtless, Alexei had heard from his parents that he owed his very birth to Serafim's prayers. Fourteen years had elapsed since Serafim's canonization festival, but Nicholas and Alexandra, having lost none of their devotion to Serafim, had passed it on to their children. "Everyone listened attentively, and I sensed that the spirit of St Serafim was with those who were praying," wrote the priest.

On July 28/August 8, the family was informed that they would be sent not to Crimea, as hoped, but to a "remote provincial town three or four days distant in the East." The accompanying instruction that they should take "warm clothes" suggested their destination was somewhere in Siberia, Nicholas correctly guessing that a "remote provincial town" meant the old Cossack fort of Tobolsk.[56] Nicholas had been to Tobolsk once, as tsarevich, in 1892. But none of the others had ever been to the other side of the Urals, which marked the division between European Russia and the forests and tundra of Siberia. They would depart on August 1/14. Two days later (the second-last before their scheduled departure) Alexei turned thirteen. "May the Lord give him health, patience, fortitude of soul and body in these heavy times,"

---

[55] Nicholas II, July 25, 1917, in *Diary* (2), 645.
[56] Buxhoeveden, *Tragic Empress*, 310.

Nicholas wrote in his diary. As usual, the primary act of celebration for a birthday in the family was the Divine Liturgy, which Belyaev performed at eleven o'clock. Although it had been said that the family was being transferred east not for the sake of punishment but for their safety, Belyaev sensed, nonetheless, that they would never be back.

It says much about Nicholas and his family that they spent this whole day, the second last before exile to Siberia, at prayer. After the Divine Liturgy for Alexei's birthday, Alexandra asked Belyaev to say a prayer service (*moleben*) in honor of the Mother of God. Belyaev agreed, and for a final time Alexandra's beloved image — Our Lady of the Sign — was brought for a solemn procession through the palace, just as it had been during the terrifying days of early March five months earlier, when Alexandra had faced the mutinous Tsarskoye Selo garrison alone. Somehow evading the embargo on flowers, Alexandra had obtained a small posy of carnations which she asked Belyaev to attach to the crown on the head of the infant Jesus pictured seated on His Mother's lap in the image. The following day they would become exiles; Alexandra was placing their fate in the Virgin's hands. "How especially warm it was to pray to her holy countenance together with all our people," Nicholas would write in his diary later that evening.[57]

Certainly, everyone present was deeply moved. "We implored God with all our strength to accord Their Majesties and their children a safe journey," recalled Benkendorff, who was present: "The emotion seized us all; we were sobbing."[58] With the magnanimity and good will towards the Provisional Government we have seen before, they sang a rendition of the "Many Years," a hymn of long life and prosperity to the ruling power which for twenty-two years Nicholas had heard intoned at the end of church liturgies for himself as tsar. This time, however, he sang it in honor of the Provisional Government, for the sake of a victorious conclusion to the war with Germany. Then, the family approached Belyaev one by one for a blessing. With that, the final service of God ever to be celebrated in the Alexander Palace came to an end: the age of secularization was dawning in it, too. Then, in a moving scene that captured the parting of ways taking place, the soldiers who had carried the icon on its litter to the palace lifted it again to their shoulders and processed with it, through the semi-circular hall onto the balcony that lay just outside it, down the steps and across the park to its home church. Like people bidding farewell to an old friend, Nicholas, Alexandra, and their children followed the soldiers with the icon on their shoulders as far as the balcony steps. There they stopped, while the icon continued on its way, never to be seen by them again.

---

[57] Nicholas II, July 30, 1917, in Diary (2), 646.
[58] Benkendorff, "Derniers jours: II," 809.

As Benkendorff put it, "it was as if the past itself were departing, never to return!"[59]

That evening, Nicholas, Alexandra, and their children took leave of their servants, thanked them for their service, and returned for a final night to their private rooms. There, Alexandra went through the clothes she could not take with her to Siberia. Ever the Christian in heart, she gathered them up and had them sent to the Polish refugees who, having been driven out of their homes by the war, had taken up residence in Tsarskoye Selo.[60] The following day was the Romanovs' last in their old home. The rooms of the palace were half-empty and they spent most of the day at a loose end. Taking Benkendorff out into the kitchen garden where Nicholas and his daughters had spent the past few months cutting wood and growing vegetables, Nicholas instructed him to ensure that the timber and the garden's future harvest went to the servants who had done the work with them. At 11:30 p.m. Kerensky arrived, bringing with him an unexpected visitor: Nicholas's younger brother, the Grand Duke Mikhail Aleksandrovich. Nicholas had had no contact with him since briefly transferring the throne to him on March 3/16. Conversation did not come easily to the brothers. With the words, "God keep you," Nicholas took leave of his brother, and the two men embraced. Mikhail left the meeting in tears.[61] Ten months later, Mikhail would be shot in the back of the head in a forest outside the town of Perm in the Ural Mountains, one month and four days before his brother's own murder.[62]

ری   ری   ری

In the end, there were many false starts that night. Time and again, Nicholas, Alexandra, and their children were told it was time to leave. But either the trucks or the drivers or the train that should have been waiting for them at the station weren't ready. "The Empress and her children sat about, the poor little boy, green with fatigue, perched on a box and holding his favorite spaniel, Joy, by a leash, while the Emperor talked to his gentlemen through the long, weary night," recalled Buxhoeveden, who was present: "Once or twice they returned to their rooms to rest, but were immediately recalled by news that the cars were coming."[63] The problem was that the local soldiers' soviet did not want its members to assist in the evacuation of the former Imperial family; neither would the railway workers move the train. The closer the family remained to Petrograd, the easier it would be to bring the former emperor to justice, regular or summary, the soviet reasoned. Only

[59] Ibid.   [60] Buxhoeveden, *Tragic Empress*, 310.
[61] Benkendorff, "Derniers Jours II," 810.   [62] Service, *Last of the Tsars*, 245.
[63] Buxhoeveden, *Tragic Empress*, 311.

hours of haranguing by Kerensky overcame their resistance and secured their cooperation. Not until six in the morning, having been awake all night, did the family leave the palace. Their official status was "State Prisoners."[64]

Once on board the train, Nicholas and his family were informed their destination was such as they had guessed it: Tobolsk. The journey there took them via the provincial Russian towns of Viatka and Perm and the industrial city of Ekaterinburg. Occasionally, in the vastness of the Russian countryside, the train would stop, and the family would alight, to go for a walk and pick late summer flowers and berries. But at stations in the towns and cities *en route*, the family was strictly instructed to keep the curtains in the windows drawn. Their exile was secret; nobody was to know the identities of the occupants of the train. Edging across the Russian countryside at a snail's pace, the train reached the former Cossack fortress of Tyumen in the early hours of August 3/16. The early arrival was deliberate. The railway did not go to Tobolsk; the only way to reach the town was by river transport, and Tyumen stood on the banks of the Tura River, a tributary of the larger Tobol and still larger Irtysh on whose banks, just downriver from the confluence with the Tobol, the town of Tobolsk stood. Arriving in the middle of the night in Tyumen, Russia's former imperial family therefore quit the train, and transferred to a riverine packet steamer called the *Rus*. Indeed, the train proceeded along the rails almost as far as the jetty. As Nicholas recorded in his diary, the whole operation was designed with a maximum of secrecy in mind. So far as they knew, nobody in Tyumen knew they had been there, and nobody in Tobolsk knew they were coming.

❦ ❦ ❦

The *Rus* was a small, single-story river steamer with a main cabin below decks, and, on the roof of the main cabin, a pilot's post and a couple of white benches for passengers to enjoy the view and breeze. It would be the imperial family's home for the next week. Once the sun had risen, Nicholas and Alexandra spent much of the day here on deck. They were not just enjoying the view. They were looking for something specific. Rasputin had prophesied to Alexandra that one day she would see the village, the sleepy hamlet of Pokrovskoye, he came from. Now, on the boat from Tyumen to Tobolsk, the prophecy was fulfilled: inscrutably, out of all the possible locations in the vast expanses of Russia, Kerensky had selected for Nicholas and Alexandra's place of exile a destination that could only be reached by passing by Rasputin's village. Alexei's tutor, the Swiss Pierre Gilliard, who voluntarily followed the family

---

[64] Ibid.

into exile, recorded the moment the village came into view aboard the *Rus*: "We passed the native village of Rasputin, and the family, gathered on deck, were able to observe the house of the *starets*, which stood out clearly from among the *isbas* [peasant huts]. There was nothing to surprise them in this event, for Rasputin had foretold that it would be so, and chance once more seemed to confirm his prophetic words."[65] Least surprised of all was Alexandra, who recorded the moment in her diary. "This is where Grigori Efimovich [Rasputin] lived. It was on this river that he used to catch fish and sometimes he brought them to us in Tsarskoye Selo."[66] She can only have felt vindicated that she had for so many years put her faith in a man with such an evident gift of clairvoyance.

A day later, the *Rus* steamed into Tobolsk. Although the Romanovs were supposed to be traveling in secret, hundreds of people had lined the bank to see them: 1,700 miles from revolutionary Petrograd, the mood was anything but revolutionary. As the "Freedom House" (the name mockingly given to the old governor's mansion in which the family were to be interned) wasn't yet ready, the family spent their first week in Tobolsk aboard the *Rus* moored in the Tobolsk docks. Every day, reverent crowds came down to see them. As Nicholas noted in his diary, the crowd wasn't content to watch from the bank, but waded out into the river, returning to shore only when it began to rain.[67] Others took to boats to try to see the former tsar and his family. In the provinces, Russia retained its entelechy as a tsardom. During their time in the town, the family would repeatedly notice townsfolk bowing and making the sign of the cross beneath their rooms.

Finally, on August 13/26, Freedom House, their place of confinement, was ready for the family. Going before them, a priest went through the rooms, sprinkling them with holy water as an exorcism. At the family's disposal was the first floor. According to Gilliard, it was "a spacious and comfortable building." But Nicholas missed the opportunity for exercise. "A nuisance that in such weather it should be forbidden to go for a walk on the river or in the forest," Nicholas complained at the end of August. "Here the feeling of being under arrest is much stronger."[68] Having enjoyed a routine of daily exercise all his life, Nicholas found his mood suffering from the lack of opportunity for physical exertion. Eventually, he mentioned this to Colonel Kobylinsky, whom Kerensky had appointed commandant of the palace back in March. Ordering the delivery of some beech trunks, Kobylinsky issued Nicholas and his suite

---

[65] Gilliard, *Thirteen Years*, 124.
[66] Cited in Service, *Last of the Tsars*, 78.
[67] Nicholas II, August 7, 1917, in in Diary (2), 647.
[68] Nicholas II, August 22 and 24/25, 1917, in Diary (2), 650.

with saws and axes, and the family cut their own timber for the stoves and kitchens. Nicholas relished the exercise.[69]

Structure was given to the day through the education of the children. Lessons began at nine and continued until eleven, when the whole party, less Alexandra, who was increasingly bedridden, walked in the yard. At one, lunch was served, and, from two, games were improvised as well as they could be in the yard. Lessons resumed, after tea, at four o'clock. At seven thirty, dinner was served, followed by coffee. With all the retinue invited to sit with the former emperor and empress, the evenings were enlivened with parlor games and cards. Otherwise, Nicholas read aloud to the children, while Alexandra and the older grand duchesses occupied themselves with needlework. They staged a production of Anton Chekhov's *The Bear*. As always, however, Orthodox Christianity remained the family's fundamental source of inspiration. In this regard, the regime of house arrest caused a real privation: for the first time in their lives, Nicholas, Alexandra and their children were forbidden to attend divine services. This was doubly frustrating because barely three hundred yards away on the other side of the road was a parish church, consecrated to the Annunciation (a feast so loved by Alexandra that a representation of it hung, as we have seen, in pride of place in the Alexander Palace). An appeal for permission to leave the house for the Sunday Liturgy failed. But the authorities did allow the parish priest, assisted by four nuns from a local convent to do the singing, to come and say a truncated liturgy that excluded the Eucharist in Freedom House. In his diary, Nicholas dubbed such a service a "little Mass," and he noted every celebration such a "Mass" that the family was permitted until, finally, on September 8/21, the feast of the Virgin's Nativity, they gained permission to cross the road and attend a complete liturgy in the little parish church. On October 22, the family finally received Holy Communion for the first time since the final liturgy with Belyaev. "What spiritual comfort in these trying times!" Nicholas recorded in his diary.[70]

෨෨ ෨෨ ෨෨

The Great October Revolution was a perfunctory affair, almost an anticlimax.[71] Fanning out across Petrograd after dark on October 25/ November 7, Trotsky's Red Guards seized the reins of power, often without violence. When the Guards informed the young cadets that manned the city's checkpoints that they were being relieved, the latter often enough surrendered their posts willingly. At the Central Telegraph

[69] Gilliard, *Thirteen Years*, 126.
[70] Nicholas II, October 22, 1917, in Diary (2), 656.
[71] McMeekin, *Russian Revolution*, 207–8.

Office, Red Guardsmen simply walked in and disconnected the Winter Palace, where the cabinet of the Provisional Government was meeting, from the phone lines, while Kerensky donned a disguise and escaped in the American ambassador's car. Making it as far as Pskov, Kerensky rallied seven hundred officers before fighting a pitched battle with the Bolshevik Guardsmen on the Pulkovo Hills, just outside Tsarskoye Selo, on October 28/November 10. Defeated, Kerensky went into hiding, making it, ultimately, to exile in France, and then in the United States. Meanwhile, back in Petrograd on October 25, the Red Guards took government installations one by one: the telegraph office, Moscow Station, Mariinsky Palace, and Peter and Paul Fortress. At 2 p.m., 5,000 sailors from Kronstadt arrived, and, later that afternoon, the famous battleship *Aurora*. Defending the Provisional Government ministers inside the Winter Palace were a few hundred cadets and the Women's Death Battalion. Lenin warned the ministers that if they did not surrender, the *Aurora* would open fire with its guns at 6:30 p.m. but the ministers, giving no answer to Lenin's ultimatum, merely continued their discussion of government business in the White Drawing Room (where Nicholas and Alexandra had once been accustomed to have breakfast). At 9 p.m., the *Aurora* fired two blanks. (There was no live ammunition available: Lenin's ultimatum had been a bluff.) And the so-called "storming" of the Winter Palace began. By the early hours of October 26/November 8, it was all over. Resistance to Bolshevik rule would survive longer in some centers, notably Moscow, where a week-long battle for the Kremlin raged until the surrender of government forces on November 2. Then, when, beginning in Petrograd itself, a general strike of railway and telegraph workers, schoolteachers and bank tellers, spread across the country, Lenin founded the Cheka, an instrument of terror empowered to carry out extrajudicial killings that would terrorize Soviet citizens for decades.[72] By Christmas 1917, European Russia, west of the Urals, was in Bolshevik hands. In distant Tobolsk, by contrast, Nicholas and his retinue followed the confusing swirl of events as best they could. But they were often in the dark as to what was happening, and the ignorance weighed on them. All the same, they learnt of Kornilov's bid to march on Petrograd in August and were bitterly disappointed when it failed. Haunting Nicholas "more and more," said Alexei's Swiss tutor Pierre Gilliard, was a "grave moral anxiety" about the responsibility he himself might have borne for Russia's state.[73]

ஐ   ஐ   ஐ

---

[72] As Sean McMeekin has commented, the irony of what would come to be known as "the Great Socialist Revolution" of 1917 was that "the world's first proletarian government was forced to devote its primary energies to strikebreaking." McMeekin, *Russian Revolution*, 219.   [73] Gilliard, *Thirteen Years*, 127.

News of the Bolshevik takeover arrived in Tobolsk months before concrete signs of Bolshevik authority. Although the Provisional Government no longer existed, the regime in Freedom House, where Nicholas, Alexandra, and their children were imprisoned, ticked over after October 25 as it had done before. Indeed, in contrast to the struggle for power playing itself out in the capital, a growing sense of mutual understanding, perhaps even camaraderie, was developing between the members of Russia's former imperial family and the guardsmen who were their imprisoners. Helping break the wall of resentment was the presence of the imperial children. To the guards, the young and often invalid Alexei was still referred to, affectionately, as "the Heir," while the gentle and innocent grand duchesses demonstrated thoughtfulness and real human interest by asking the men about their villages and families. It wasn't long before the circle of their affection extended from the children to their father, the former emperor himself. Although such fraternizing was forbidden, Nicholas and his children would slip quietly into the guardhouse and talk or play draughts with the soldiers. When a physical task needed completing, he and the men worked together on it, and, increasingly, the men joined the family for religious services, too.[74] While Lenin, in Petrograd, was installing the world's first expressly atheist regime, in distant Tobolsk Russia's former tsar and his family were inspiring the soldiers guarding them to acts of faith radically out of touch with the spirit of the Revolution.

Religious services and amateur theater remained the family's primary source of refreshment. But the isolation and steady drip of bad news from Russia's war effort fed a mounting sense of demoralization, which was reflected in Nicholas's diary. "Both these days were exactly the same," he wrote, taking the unprecedented step of combining two days together at the beginning of December.[75] But by the beginning of December, it was so cold (minus sixteen degrees) that Alexei, who could not afford the risk of a nosebleed on account of the cold, dry air, and Alexandra could not come with them to Mass. On December 10/23, the first letter from Nicholas's mother reached them. A week later, they gathered firewood from the yard to heat their first bath in weeks. The most difficult stage of the Romanovs' period of house arrest was approaching. Of course, the family did not know that, and the great feast of Christ's Nativity seemed to refresh Alexandra's spirits, particularly. "A joyful Xmas might sound like a mockery," she wrote in her idiosyncratic English to Buxhoeveden on Christmas Eve 1917, "but it means joy over the New-Born King, who died to save us all, and does not that renew one's trust and faith in God's infinite mercy? He is far above all, is All in all; He will

---

[74] See Nicholas II, October 27 and 28, 1917, in Diary (2), 656.
[75] Nicholas II, December 1 and 2, 1917, in Diary (2), 660.

show mercy, when the right time comes, and we must patiently and resignedly await His good will."[76] For his part, Nicholas ended the year with the same prayer we have seen him repeat in so many years past: "Lord, save Russia!" The following morning, the family did as it always did on the first day of the year (the Feast of the Lord's Circumcision) and went to Mass.

On January 13/26, however, they attended the little Church of the Annunciation on the other side of the road for the last time until the end of March; as part of the increasingly strict regime of supervision to which they were now subjected, church visits were being curtailed. Instead, a priest would call on Sundays to celebrate the truncated form of the Liturgy (an *obednitsa*) in Freedom House drawing room. In a letter to a friend, Alexandra made a point of noting the religious illiteracy that this revealed among their captors: "They do not understand there can be no celebration of Mass without a field chapel in one's home."[77] Alexandra resented the indifference that lay behind this ignorance, but, as she vowed in a letter to a friend, "so be it, I won't grumble. I remember that the Lord hears our prayers everywhere."

Finally, on January 26/February 11, the "Great Socialist Revolution" arrived in Tobolsk when the soldiers' committee voted to dismiss Freedom House's existing commanders, and replace them with ones loyal to the Bolsheviks. The same day, news reached Nicholas that Lenin (who had, of course, been brought to Russia by Germany for just this purpose) had sought an "immediate cessation of hostilities" with the Germans.[78] When the Bolsheviks then began parceling out land in Russia's villages, hundreds of thousands of soldiers melted away from the front, back into Russia's vast interior, to stake their claims in the handout. All that Nicholas had worked (and prayed) for since the outbreak of the War was going up in smoke. With no army in existence to stop the German advance, by February 6/20, Revel (Tallinn) and Rovno had fallen. In distant Siberia, as Gilliard observed, "the Tsar was deeply affected."[79] "The Germans are at Pskov," wrote Alexandra in dismay a few weeks later. "Peace will be concluded on the most horrible, disgraceful and ruinous terms for Russia. One's hair stands on end, but God will save.... I'm constantly longing to go to church, and pour out my heart there," confided a woman, the hated "Nemka," whose alleged espionage on behalf of Imperial Germany had served as a pretext for the Duma opposition's attack on the monarchy.[80] And although it would have been easy to do

[76] Buxhoeveden, *Tragic Empress*. 321.
[77] Cited in Vladimir Kozlov, Vladimir Khrustalev, and Alexandra Raskina, eds., *The Last Diary of Tsaritsa Alexandra*, trans. Laura E. Wolfson (New Haven, CT: Yale University Press, 1997), 14.
[78] McMeekin, *Russian Revolution*, 227. [79] Gilliard, *Thirteen Years*, 131.
[80] Kozlov et al., *Last Diary*, 50

so, Alexandra did not make the mistake of imagining that she, her family and friends were the only people suffering in Russia. "Don't lose heart, my dear," she wrote to Rita Khitrova, a former helper at Alexandra's Tsarskoye Selo hospital and a friend of Olga's, who had been refused permission to join the family in exile, despite traveling on her own all the way from Petrograd to do so, "the worse it gets, the nearer is God with His spiritual Help. Believe in Him firmly and steadfastly. He will save our precious, long-suffering homeland.... It's horrible, what is taking place everywhere, one's soul grieves for all of these innocent victims, but He knows best what is necessary."[81]

Nicholas, too, was feeling the strain of captivity. On March 15 (New Style), the anniversary of his abdication brought all these misfortunes home to him. Officially nothing more than a private citizen under house arrest in a remote, provincial center, Nicholas retained in his own self-perception that inseparable responsibility for Russia he had borne as tsar. "How much longer will our unfortunate Russia be tormented and torn apart by her internal and external enemies?" he asked: "It sometimes seems that no strength is left to bear any more, and you don't even know what to hope for, what is to be wished for. And yet there is none like God!" he confessed, tsar and theocrat to the end. "May His holy will be done!"[82] To Nicholas and Bulgakov alike, Russia would be saved from the abyss through Orthodoxy.

And in those days, at the start of March 1918, nothing summed up Russia's desperate straits more than the Treaty of Brest-Litovsk. Signed, coincidentally, by Bolshevik negotiators on March 3, a year and one day after Nicholas signed his act of abdication, the treaty established German domination over Western Eurasia. The news, which was so electric that it arrived almost instantly even in distant Tobolsk, represented the worst possible outcome to the war Nicholas could have hoped for. "The Tsar was very depressed," Gilliard recorded. In Nicholas's eyes, Brest-Litovsk was a "disgrace," a "suicide." But, he predicted (correctly), his cousin, the German Kaiser, would "get no gain from it." "It won't save them from ruin!" he said, agreeing in this, it turned out, with Lenin, who was also gambling on Germany's succumbing to revolution before Brest-Litovsk could become permanent.

Alexandra, too, execrated Brest-Litovsk as an "utterly disgraceful peace," one she found impossible to believe God would allow to stand for long. "Being under the German yoke, you know, is worse than the Tatars. No, the Lord won't permit such an injustice."[83] When it was reported that they themselves, Nicholas, Alexandra, and their children, had become bargaining chips, Alexandra was heard to swear under her

---

[81] Ibid., 27.   [82] Nicholas II, March 15, 1918, in Diary (2), 669.
[83] Ibid., 71.

breath that she "would rather die in Russia than be saved by the Germans."[84] No matter how threatening conditions around them might become, such words would forever sum up her and Nicholas's attitude to rescue by their German cousin. They disdained the idea that it might be the conquering German army that would deliver Russia from Bolshevism. "What a nightmare, that the Germans are supposed to save everyone and establish order. What could be worse and more degrading than that? . . . God save and help Russia!" wrote Alexandra to Vyrubova. So much for the alleged treachery of the "Nemka."

怘 怘 怘

When Lent arrived, Nicholas, Alexandra, and their children approached the fast with all their accustomed piety. By now, Alexei and the grand duchesses were helping sing the Sunday liturgy, performed in truncated form as it was in the drawing room by a priest who was not permitted to talk to them. Ritually, the commencement of Lent is marked by the institution on weekdays of a "Liturgy of Presanctified Gits," a Mass distinguished by its own more somber Lenten chants, in which no new elements (the bread and wine) are consecrated as Christ's Body and Blood, but only those previously consecrated are received. Nicholas recorded his joy on March 20, when, in an act of generosity, the soldiers' committee gave them permission to return to the little church of the Annunciation on the other side of the street for the first time since January. "Finally, after a break of two months," wrote Nicholas, "we made it back to the church for the Liturgy of the Presanctified . . . the usual singers sang our beloved melodies." It was a welcome source of refreshment. For two days later, Nicholas noted it had been a year since their detention as a family had started. "It is unpleasant to recall the past year," he reflected, his mind turning again to God. "What awaits us in the future? Everything is in God's hands! All our trust is in Him!" The following day the whole family received the Holy Mysteries.

Of course, Nicholas was not alone in deriving comfort from religion. Far from it. Alexandra's diary in 1918, though reduced to little more than a skeletal outline of her day, radiates the spiritual and religious intensity with which the former empress met life in Tobolsk. Responsible for the children's spiritual instruction, every day she noted the readings from the Bible and other spiritual authors she set the children. For Alexei, in January, it was the Gospel of St Mark and Gogol's *Meditations on the Divine Liturgy*; for Tatiana and Maria, it was the Wisdom books of the Old Testament and Fr Grigory Diachenko's *Spiritual Readings: Complete yearly cycle of brief homilies for each day of the year*, supplemented with extracts from the writings of the Church

---

[84] Gilliard, *Thirteen Years*, 134.

Fathers (St Euthymius of Palestine, St John Chrysostom); for Anastasia, it was the Prophet Isaiah. In addition, Alexei was studying the life of King David, while the girls were reading a history of the Orthodox Church, and practicing their German by studying hymns from the hymnal of the Evangelical Lutheran Church, in which Alexandra had been baptized and grown up. For Alexei, this study of King David, which began in January with David eating the sacred shewbread, continued throughout February, Alexandra making special note of the days when the lesson concerned David's anointing by the prophet Samuel as king of Israel, his wars against the Philistines, plans for the Temple, and death, forty years later. As Samuel's anointing of David was the model for the Orthodox coronation ceremony, these readings cannot have been anything other than a specially constructed course in what amounts to the origins of *teokratia*.

To this tight-knit family, religion was quite simply everything. In the evenings at the start of March, Nicholas read aloud to the family the *Life of St Nicholas*, the fourth-century Greek bishop after whom he was named, one of Russia's unofficial patrons. On the feast of the Fyodorov Icon of the Mother God in the second week of Lent, Tatiana read for her mother the feast's akathist. "Don't know anything new," Alexandra wrote in the third week of March to her friend Anna Vyrubova, "my heart is troubled, but there is a brightness in my soul, I feel the closeness of the Heavenly Creator, Who in His mercy never abandons His own. But the things happening in Moscow!! God help us!"[85] Understandably, in this frame of mind, Alexandra was as thrilled and grateful as Nicholas to have received permission to return to church for the beginning of Lent. "We've been permitted to be in church on Wednesday, Friday, and Saturday mornings (we're taking communion after two months), this will be such a joy and a consolation," she wrote to a friend: "One feels so strongly drawn there during such a difficult time. Praying at home is not the same thing at all—in the room where we sit, where the piano is and where we've put on plays."[86] Finally, in the little church building, surrounded by the icons and in the low, flickering light of the candles, Alexandra could pour out her heart as she had long wished to. Nonetheless, the family had so internalized the rite that when, two weeks later, on March 25, the Feast of the Annunciation arrived, and the family were forbidden either to go to church or to receive a priest in the house to celebrate the liturgy, Alexandra and her daughters self-reliantly sang the chants ("without any rehearsal," Nicholas recorded in his diary) for the rest of the family and retinue.

Indeed, in marked contrast to the expressions of suspicion, fear, and exasperation that filled her letters to Nicholas in 1915 and 1916,

---

[85] Kozlov et al., *Last Diary*, 70.   [86] Ibid., 72.

Alexandra's letters from captivity in Tobolsk reveal the portrait of a remarkably peaceful and trusting Christian soul. It was as if the collapse of Russian *teokratia* had, for Alexandra, been a release, even a rebirth, into an altogether more carefree and childlike faith. "When will it all end?" she asked, in a letter to Vyrubova.[87] But, in a sense, it didn't matter. The trial itself was a blessing. It had taught her to love things as they were rather than withholding that love until she had succeeded in bending them, by her will, into that ideal shape she thought they should be. "How I love my country [Russia], with all its faults! It grows dearer and dearer to me, and I thank God daily that He has allowed us to remain here and did not send us further away," she wrote. And this was despite all the invective she had been the object of. "Believe in the people, darling," she wrote, rather improbably in view of her circumstances as the people's prisoner to Vyrubova: "Just now it is in bad hands, and darkness, and anarchy reigns. But the King of Glory will come, and will save, strengthen, and give wisdom to the people who are now deceived." She had traded a half dozen palaces as empress of Russia for a worn room in a faded provincial governor's mansion, and yet she was happy. "Soon spring is coming to rejoice our hearts. The way of the cross first, then joy and gladness."[88] Time was yielding before timelessness. "It will soon be a year since we parted," she observed, writing to Vyrubova, "but what is time? Life here is nothing—Eternity is everything, and what we are doing is preparing our souls for the Kingdom of Heaven." Others sensed it, too. "The Empress's deep religious faith had come to her aid and helped her to bear her trials with fortitude and be hopeful to the end. In Tobolsk," wrote Buxhoeveden, reviewing the same letters we are considering here, "she gained that unearthly calm that sometimes comes to those who feel the great Shadow before them, without perhaps entirely realizing how near it lurks."[89]

Indeed, in her letters to Vyrubova, Alexandra gave evidence of having attained real sainthood: resignation to the Divine Will, joy in suffering, a desire only to see the good in others. "All is in God's will," she wrote that March from her room in frozen Tobolsk. "The deeper you look, the more you understand that this is so. All our sorrows are sent us to free us from our sins or as a test of our faith, an example to others. It requires good food to make plants grow properly and the gardener, walking through His garden, wants to be pleased with His flowers. If they do not grow properly, He takes His pruning knife, and cuts, waiting for the sunshine to coax them into growth again. I should like to paint a picture of this beautiful garden and all that grows in it. I remember English gardens and at Livadia you saw an illustrated book I had, so you will understand." And when the agents of her

---

[87] Buxhoeveden, *Tragic Empress*, 323.   [88] Ibid., 324.   [89] Ibid.

oppression — wild and battle-hardened decommissioned soldiers-cum-revolutionaries — passed beneath her window, in her heart she blessed them. "Sometimes we see men with the most awful faces," she reflected. "I would not include them in my garden picture. The only place for them would be outside, where the merciful sunshine could reach them and make them clean from all [the] dirt and evil [...] with which they are covered."[90] By excluding them from her garden, she did not wish for their damnation; on the contrary, she desired for them that purification by the grace and love of God that would make them capable at last of entering into it. For such ill-used young men, she wanted what she felt she had found: the Kingdom of Heaven.

In the last week of March, the first detachment of Bolshevik guards arrived in Tobolsk. From these newcomers, the family was clearly expecting the worst. "The Bolsheviks have come," Alexandra wrote to the daughter of the old Minister of the Court, Count Frederiks, in distant Petrograd, "but nothing has happened."[91] The family understood the danger for them inherent in the guards' arrival, but put their trust in God. "We have Bolsheviks in town [but] it's all right, don't worry. The Lord is everywhere and will work a miracle," Alexandra wrote the same day to Vyrubova.[92] And with the Bolshevik attack on the Church growing apace, they were more and more inclined to attribute a religious meaning to the Revolution, too.[93] "We shall share [Christ's sufferings] with Him," Alexandra wrote to Vyrubova, apparently in reference not only to herself and her friend but all historical, Orthodox Russia, "enduring without protest all the sufferings God has sent down us. Why ought we not to suffer, if He, innocent and sinless, freely suffered? We are atoning for all our age-old sins; we are washing away in blood all the blemishes that have polluted our souls."[94] And perhaps because she could see this higher, purificatory meaning in their sufferings, no matter what she and her family went through, she had evidently resolved not to be afraid. "The Almighty overshadows us everywhere. Wherever we go, always and everywhere, we shall meet the love of God," she wrote in her recently published spiritual notebooks from 1917.[95]

Looking for the deeper explanation of what they and Russia were going through, Nicholas and Alexandra were also, therefore, predisposed to welcome such explanations as they hit upon. Barely a week before the Bolshevik guards detachment, two very different visitors had arrived

---

[90] Ibid., 325.   [91] Kozlov et al., *Last Diary*, 85.   [92] Ibid.
[93] By a decree of Lenin's on January 23, 1918, Church and State were separated, and all religious instruction outside the home was banned. The Church's lands had been confiscated as part of the original decrees establishing Bolshevik power. See Pospielovsky, *Russian Church*, 1:31–32.   [94] Kozlov et al., *Last Diary*, 78.
[95] HM The Empress Alexandra Fyodorovna Romanova, *Garden of the Heart: A spiritual diary* (New York: Concept, 2016), 14.

in Tobolsk: Vladimir Stein, whom Nicholas knew by sight as a former deputy vice-governor of Mogilev, with money (250,000 rubles), books and tea, as gifts "from good people" in Moscow; and Sergei Markov, an officer in the Crimean Cavalry Regiment of which Alexandra was colonel, who had come to Tobolsk with letters from Petrograd to try to arrange the family's escape. Communicating with the family through those members of the retinue still able to pass in and out of Freedom House, Markov was the conduit for Alexandra's letters to the outside world. One of the men was also, apparently, the conduit for some fresh reading material. "Yesterday I started to read aloud [for the family] Nilus's book on the Antichrist, to which have been added the 'protocols' of the Jews and Masons," Nicholas recorded in his diary two days after Annunciation.[96]

We have met Nilus before in Nicholas and Alexandra's biography, as the Orthodox priest and publicist who helped coordinate the campaign for the canonization of St Serafim of Sarov that left such a deep imprint on the couple back in 1903, drawing them away from the temptation of occultism represented in the figure of Monsieur Philippe and back towards the harbor of historical mystical-dogmatic Orthodoxy. But Nilus was also a vehement anti-Semite, convinced that modern civilization ("science, technological progress, democracy, even the application of reason to religious and philosophical questions") was a work of the Antichrist, which the latter sought to realize through a worldwide conspiracy of Jews and Freemasons for world domination.[97] The work (part autobiography, part tract) in which Nilus publicized this theory was known as *The Great in the Small: Antichrist considered as an imminent political possibility*. First published in 1901 and again in 1903, it was published a third time in 1905 with the *Protocols of the Elders of Zion* inserted this time into its pages, in a bid to attract Nicholas himself to his cause.[98] It is not clear that *Great in the Small* made any impression on Nicholas when first presented to him at this time. But the *Protocols*, which he took at face value, did. Nonetheless, Nicholas later approved an investigation into their authenticity, commissioned by Stolypin, which ultimately ruled that the *Protocols* were a fabrication, indeed, one produced by the Okhrana itself. "Drop the *Protocols*," Nicholas, to his credit, immediately instructed government officials.[99]

But in the setting of 1918, with the Russian *teokratia* visibly subverted but the reasons for and agents of its subversion still a matter of dispute,

---

[96] Nicholas II, March 27, 1918, in Diary (2), 672.

[97] The quotation describing Nilus's beliefs is from Cohn, *Warrant*, 90. For an illustrative excerpt of Nilus's writings, see ibid., 288.

[98] Ibid., 67. But cf. ibid., 87, where Cohn rather confusingly describes the 1905 edition as the *second*, not third, edition of *Great in the Small*.

[99] See Cohn, *Warrant*, 115.

Nicholas was prepared to give Nilus's text another hearing. (Indeed, *The Great in the Small* had only recently been published for the *sixth* time, in 1917.[100]) "Very timely reading matter," Nicholas commented. Alexandra, who doubtless shared the opinion, noted the new reading matter (*The Great in the Small*) in her diary, too.

ᐔᑌ ᐔᑌ ᐔᑌ

The arrival of the Bolshevik guards in Tobolsk heralded the approach of the end of Nicholas and Alexandra's lives. Sovnarkom began discussing the desirability of trying Nicholas for his crimes as head of State in January. In February, it charged the People's Commissariat for Justice with preparing a case; on April 1, the Presidium of the Communist Party's All-Russian Central Executive Committee adopted, in secret, a resolution for the transferal of the entire former imperial family from house arrest in Tobolsk to Moscow. Five days later, the Presidium amended that resolution so that now the Romanovs would be transferred not to Moscow, but to the Urals transport hub and mining town, Ekaterinburg.

This change had to do with the arrival in Tobolsk of the Bolshevik guards, as recorded by Alexandra. For those guards, while nominally taking their orders from Lenin, were not acting on Sovnarkom's authority at all. Rather, the Bolshevik guards on the streets of Tobolsk at the end of March 1918 were the armed representatives of the local Bolshevik soviet at Omsk, an old Cossack fortress-cum-railway hub on the Irtysh River, five hundred miles southeast of Tobolsk. Since the Bolsheviks' suppression of the Constituent Assembly in January 1918, Russia had been in a civil war, with "White" (anti-Bolshevik) and "Green" (anti-Bolshevik but pro-Socialist) armies opposing Trotsky's Red Army ("the Reds").[101] In such a civil war, the Romanovs were valuable, and the Omsk Soviet wanted the former tsar under its control before the Urals Soviet at Ekaterinburg, their chief rivals in this "race for the tsar," got to them first. In 1918, the Bolsheviks were not yet the terror-ridden, centrally micromanaged Party of Stalin, and by the beginning of April, the guards of both Soviets had installed themselves in town. It was up to the Presidium in Moscow to manage this "race for the Tsar" as best it could.

At Freedom House itself, conditions were becoming more and more hostile. An order arrived from Moscow (where Lenin had moved the capital in March) for the guards to be much stricter with the prisoners. Meanwhile, the members of the retinue still residing across the road at the Kornilov Mansion, and at liberty to come and go from

---

[100] Cohn, *Warrant*, 67; also, Service, *Last of the Tsars*, 116.

[101] See Smith, *Russia in Revolution*, 161–63; McMeekin, *Russian Revolution*, 281 ff.; and, on the "Greens," Jonathan D. Smele, *The "Russian" Civil Wars, 1916–1926: Ten years that shook the world* (London: Hurst & Co., 2016), 138–39.

Freedom House, were now forcibly interned with the other prisoners in the house itself. Already cramped living quarters had to be rearranged to accommodate the presence of four new adult bodies, two men and two women. Alexandra's diary records "great fuss changing rooms," and the hanging of a partition in one of the halls to create a semblance of privacy.

Compounding the discomfort was the sudden return, as if by malign coincidence, of Alexei's illness. Having been mostly well since Christmas, on April 12 he suffered a hemorrhage in his abdomen as the result of a coughing fit. The following day, he was vomiting and, now in agony, was unable to sleep for more than twenty minutes in twenty-four hours. It was the worst case of his hemophilia since the incident at Spała, when the doctors, but not his mother or Rasputin, had given him up for dead. Rasputin, of course, was now dead himself. But there is no hint in Alexandra's diaries or letters of panic or nervous breakdown. Clearly, she suffered with Alexei, sitting by his side all day and all night, and recording the frequency of his pains ("every half-hour very strong cramp . . . for three minutes") and occasional improvements ("towards the evening better"). But her anchor, it seems, held firm. "Yesterday, he finally began to eat a little," Alexandra wrote to Vyrubova a week later, on April 19: "He is very thin . . . he can move around a little, his back hurts and he is tired of lying on it, his bones hurt. I sit with him all day long, and usually hold his leg, so I have become like his shadow." But, she said, summing up the situation, "The Lord is merciful." [102]

As the Bolshevik authorities in Moscow lacked independent forces of their own in Siberia, the only real way to resolve the impasse between the Omsk and Ekaterinburg soviets was by choosing to support one of them over the other. And, in the event, the Presidium chose Ekaterinburg. It lay, after all, six hundred miles closer to Moscow on the railway, and Sovnarkom's plan remained a public trial for Nicholas in the capital. But probably even more decisive was the fact that many of the members of the Bolshevik Central Committee had their roots in the mining town. This included Yakov Sverdlov, Lenin's confidant and the Committee's powerful secretary, and Nikolai Krestinskii, a founding member of the future Politburo. Indeed, the authorities in Moscow had made this decision as early as April 9, when Sverdlov wrote to his former provincial colleagues in Ekaterinburg, instructing them to appoint one of their number, Vasily Yakovlev (a thirty-two-year-old factory worker turned professional revolutionary, armed robber, and street fighter), extraordinary commissar, with powers from Moscow to take custody of the former imperial family, and to transfer them to custody in Ekaterinburg. [103] But such were the difficulties involved in assembling

---

[102] Kozlov et al., *Last Diary*, 102.   [103] Service, *Last of the Tsars*, 158.

men for the task that it wasn't until another two weeks later that Yakovlev, at the head of a new Ekaterinburg detachment, first knocked on the
door of Freedom House. It was April 23, 1918 (New Style).

∾   ∾   ∾

Of Yakovlev's arrival, the family expected the worst. The grand duchesses
burned their letters, while the younger two, Maria and Anastasia, soon
to turn nineteen and seventeen respectively, went further and burned
their diaries, too. But in the end, Yakovlev appeared to be thoroughly
civil, decent, even charming.[104] "We expected him at eleven o'clock, so
Alix was not yet ready," Nicholas recorded: "He came in clean-shaven,
smiling and embarrassed, and asked whether I were pleased with the
guard and the accommodations. Then he went into Alexei's room almost
at a run, without stopping, inspected the remaining rooms and, apologizing for the disturbance, went downstairs."[105] About half an hour
later, when Alexandra was ready to receive him, Yakovlev returned, this
time with a doctor, who verified the gravity of Alexei's illness. Yakovlev addressed Nicholas as "Your Majesty," and the Swiss Gilliard with
a "Bonjour, Monsieur."[106] It was a sterling performance in winning a
victim's trust. Nicholas and Alexandra, it seems, were completely taken
in. In her diary, Alexandra said Yakovlev gave the "impression of an
inteligent [sic] highly nervous workman, engeneer [sic]."[107] But Gilliard, who heard Yakovlev ask Kobylinsky on his way out of the house
whether the family had much luggage, correctly guessed the purpose of
the visit: the family was to be moved, doubtless to somewhere under
stricter Bolshevik control. In fact, just two days after Yakovlev's arrival,
he was proved right: the family was to leave Tobolsk.

---

[104] Robert Massie, "Introduction," in Kozlov et al., *Last Diary,* xxxii.
[105] Nicholas II, April 10 (Old Style), 1918, in Diary (2), 674.
[106] Ibid., xxxii.
[107] Kozlov et al., *Last Diary,* 106.

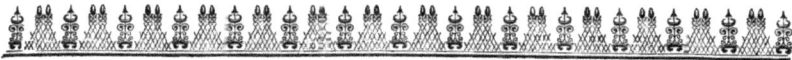

CHAPTER THIRTEEN

Ekaterinburg

THE "RUSSIAN GOLGOTHA"

RIGINALLY, YAKOVLEV'S INSTRUCTIONS WERE to remove the whole family to Ekaterinburg. But having informed Moscow of the impossibility of moving the suffering Alexei, he received revised orders to take Nicholas alone, and any who wished to accompany him. It left Alexandra in an impossible situation. She had never before in her life abandoned her child during a fit of hemophilia but she did not want to be separated from her husband, either—to strengthen him, if the Bolsheviks sought to force him to sign the Treaty of Brest-Litovsk, or subjected him to a trial. After much agonizing, Alexandra decided that she would go with Nicholas, as would Maria. The other girls—Olga, Tatiana, and Anastasia—would remain with Alexei, and the family would be reunited when the latter was well enough to travel. Also to go with Nicholas and Alexandra were five others from the remaining domestic staff and retinue: Prince Dolgoruky (Nicholas's valet), Dr Botkin (the imperial physician), Anna Demidova (Alexandra's maid) and Ivan Sednyov (a footman to the grand duchesses). They left at 4 a.m. the following morning. Lending the whole turn of events an unintended symbolism, Holy Week was due to start in a few days. Bolshevik authorities had determined that the beginning of the final stage of the family's lives should coincide with the Orthodox Church's week-long memorial of Christ's sufferings and crucifixion.[1] Certainly, the family were about to commence their own passion.

The journey itself was an ordeal. Waiting for Nicholas, Alexandra, Maria, and the five members of staff and retinue traveling with them, in the darkness of the following morning, was Yakovlev, with eight riflemen and a mounted escort of ten. The nearest railhead was at Tyumen, 150 miles away. To get them there, Yakovlev had commandeered three tarantasses. A peasant vehicle, better used for transporting loads than people (though the peasants used it for both), a tarantass consisted of two long poles hung parallel across the front and rear axle with a basket made of wicker strapped to the poles by way of a tray or cabin. There was no suspension, seating, or even hard sides for the travelers to wedge themselves against. Rather, they lay, prone on their backs or propping themselves up the best they could on their luggage. Gilliard and others

---

[1] Alexandra, Diary, April 12/25, 1918: Kozlov et al., *Last Diary*, 108.

searched the yard at Freedom House for straw to lay on the bottom of the tarantass Nicholas was traveling in. For Alexandra and Maria, they managed to get Yakovlev to agree to the laying of a mattress.

Early spring was an arduous time to travel. Rain fell alternately with snow. Beyond the town stretched a bleak, half-frozen world in which the rivers were already swelling with meltwater. "Road perfectly atrocious, frozen ground, wind, snow, water up to the horses' stomachs, fearfully shaken, pain all over," wrote Alexandra in her diary at the end of the day.[2] They changed horses every four hours. After the fourth change (when they had already been jolting and swinging across the countryside for twelve hours), Alexandra and Maria's tarantass popped a lynchpin, and mother and daughter were forced to crawl over into another basket: Nicholas and Alexandra had chosen Maria precisely because of all their daughters, she was the stoutest-hearted. Finally, at 8 p.m. that evening, after fourteen hours rocking to and fro above the mud, the journey was suspended. Lodging for the night was in an old shop in the village of Ievlevo.

Woken at four, they began the following day's travel by crossing the swollen River Tobol on foot on duckboards as far as the main channel, where a ferry took them to the other side. There, they were delayed for hours before Yakovlev ordered the convoy to proceed at 7.15 a.m. He was visibly agitated ("fidgety, running about, telegraphing," as Alexandra put it). What Nicholas and Alexandra did not know was that, distrusting Moscow and wanting to make sure Nicholas got his just deserts, a faction within the Ekaterinburg Bolsheviks were plotting behind Yakovlev's back to overpower the convoy and take custody of its human cargo.[3] The purpose of Yakovlev's frantic telegraphing had been to expose his knowledge of the plot to the Ekaterinburg soviet leadership and order them to bring the men into line. Also telegraphed were the leaders of the soviet at Tyumen, whom Yakovlev ordered to come and meet him on the road with an armed escort.

Otherwise, the second day of travel was easier than the first. Spring had forced the long arm of winter; the air was warm and the sky blue. ("Lovely weather, road atrocious," Alexandra recorded, matter-of-factly.) Nicholas, seated beside Yakovlev in the leading tarantass, disarmed him (metaphorically) with conversation. When it turned, inevitably, to religion, the former monarch surprised Yakovlev by the strength of his commitment to the principle of freedom of conscience.[4] But the identity of the convoy's cargo had got out. Changing horses at a village on

---

[2] Alexandra, April 13/26, 1918: Kozlov et al., *Last Diary*, 109. "The rain was cold, with an unpleasant wind," wrote Nicholas: "The road was difficult and terribly jolting from the frozen surface. Crossed the Irtysh in quite deep water." Nicholas II, April 13/26, 1918, in Diary (2), 674.   [3] Service, *Last of the Tsars*, 170.
[4] Ibid., 171.

the route, a guard recalled being approached by a local peasant. "Young fellow, would you kindly tell me where in God's name you are taking our little-father tsar [*tsar-batiushka*]?" "To Moscow, grandpa, to Moscow!" was the guardsman's triumphant reply.[5]

Nothing short of extraordinary was the place chosen for another change of horses that day. Nervous of an ambush, Yakovlev typically arranged for these to be accomplished in a few minutes. But in the early afternoon of the second day, the party found itself stopped for longer than usual; Nicholas described the stop as *dolgo* ("long"). Outwardly, the village looked no different from others they had stopped in. But gazing out from the baskets of the tarantass, Nicholas and Alexandra were amazed to find themselves staring into the eyes of people they recognized: it was Rasputin's wife and children, whom they had met and sat with on several occasions at Vyrubova's house in Tsarskoye Selo. Rasputin had told Alexandra that she and Nicholas would see where he came from; now, when control of their own lives was out of their own hands, they had done so, not just once, but twice.

Finally, Nicholas and Alexandra's journey was completed later that night, when, by the light (as Alexandra recorded in her diary) of a "lovely sunset and moon," Yakovlev's party, escorted by an advance cavalry detachment sent to meet him by Bolshevik authorities, rode into Tyumen. Taken immediately to the train station, Nicholas, Alexandra, Maria, and their few retainers were bundled into a dirty railway car. Still, Nicholas and Alexandra did not know where they going. In glorious spring weather, they spent most of the following day—Palm Sunday—guessing. At first, Alexandra thought that they were traveling west, towards Moscow. But Nicholas, recognizing the names of the towns they pulled into, saw that they were traveling east, towards the Siberian town of Omsk. But this did not resolve the question. For, as Nicholas knew, Omsk was a hub for railways that extended not only east across Siberia to Vladivostok and the Pacific Ocean, but also, by a southerly route through Chelyabinsk, back to Moscow. They hoped they would continue east. But if they didn't, the southerly route across the Urals was preferable to the alternative route to Moscow, via "Red" Ekaterinburg, where they knew their lives would be in danger. The following day the uncertainty was resolved. Having failed to reach Omsk, they could see that the possibility of exile had been snatched from them. Instead of traveling east towards Vladivostok, they were traveling west again, to probable trial in Moscow, via Ekaterinburg. It was Passion Monday, and, ordinarily, they would have gone to church. Without a

[5] Ibid.

priest, they ministered to each other as best they could. "Nicholas read to me the Gospels for today," wrote Alexandra in her diary, ever marking the time liturgically.

Nicholas and Alexandra did not know it, but going on behind the scenes was a battle for custody of them. Yakovlev, their captor, was under orders from Yakov Sverdlov, chairman of the Bolshevik's Central Executive Committee (and Lenin's right-hand man), to get Nicholas from Tobolsk to Moscow. He was to do this via Ekaterinburg, Sverdlov instructed, so as to satisfy the demands of the local Urals Soviet there, fearful as they were of "losing" the tsar. By the time he had reached Tyumen, however, Yakovlev had formed the opinion that the two parts of his instructions were incompatible: he could take the Romanovs to Ekaterinburg, but if he did so, he believed, they would likely never reach Moscow, as the Urals Soviet would never let Nicholas leave alive. But Sverdlov, under pressure from the Urals Soviet, insisted: they were to go to Ekaterinburg first. Yakovlev ordered the train to turn around. "I would go anywhere at all, only not to the Urals," Nicholas replied when informed of the change of direction.

The night between the Monday and Tuesday of Holy Week, then, Nicholas and Alexandra's train rolled back through Tyumen. At 8.30 a.m. the following morning, it came to a halt in Ekaterinburg. To meet the imperial couple, a hostile crowd had gathered at the station, chanting slogans that looked forward to the deaths of the "bloodsuckers." Fearing a lynching, Yakovlev set up a protective cordon of machine gunners around the train. For three hours, a standoff ensued. Eventually, Yakovlev ordered the train to quit the station for a quieter freight terminal, a mile and a half from the city center. There, Yakovlev released his prisoners into the hands of the Romanovs' new captors: twenty-seven-year-old Aleksandr Beloborodov, a factory worker and Chairman of the Urals Soviet; Boris Didkovsky, Beloborodov's deputy, and Filipp Goloshchyokin, a forty-two-year-old dentist and Urals Soviet executive committee member who managed the negotiations for custody of the Romanovs by telegraph with Moscow. Seated in two cars with a truck "filled with soldiers armed to their teeth" (as Alexandra recalled) following, Nicholas, Alexandra, and Maria, along with the family doctor Evgeni Botkin, the valet, Terenty Chemodurov, and a footman, Leonid Sednyov, were transported through the backstreets of a city much larger and more industrial than Tobolsk. Not going any further with them, however, were Nicholas's aides-de-camp, Prince Vasily Dolgorukov and Count Ilya Tatishchev. Accused of planning an escape, the two men were separated from the party and driven to the municipal prison. Their incarceration ended two months and ten days later when, a week before the Romanovs themselves, they were taken from their cells and shot.

The family's new captors gave them every reason to miss Tobolsk. "Drove through bystreets til reached a small house, around wh[ich] high wooden palings have been placed," wrote Alexandra in her diary. A small crowd had gathered. But the Soviet leaders ordered them away. Papers were signed, and Nicholas and Alexandra's luggage brusquely searched. When a soldier wrenched Alexandra's purse from her hand, Nicholas protested that "until now" he and his family had been dealing with "decent and honest people." The comment only earned Nicholas a reminder from Deputy Urals Soviet leader Didkovsky that he, Alexandra and their retinue were now "prisoners," in the full sense of the word. The party of seven was then shown inside. They did not know that they would never leave the house they were entering alive. At their disposal were four rooms on the upper floor: a corner bedroom, which Nicholas, Alexandra, and Maria took for themselves; a toilet and bathroom; a dining room occupied by a large mahogany table, at the end of which Botkin, Chemodurov and Sednyov slept; and a drawing room, without doors. In two rooms beside the dining room guards were posted. Nicholas tried to look at things in the best light. Their new lodgings, he said in his diary, were "good" and "clean." But humiliations were everywhere, especially the bell on a string which they had to ring if ever they needed to bathe or use the toilet. Alexandra simply refused to use it. A high fence blocked their view through the window. Underlining the sense of powerlessness, spring had now indisputably arrived, and above the fence palings, the sky was blue, the weather "glorious." It was also Wednesday of Holy Week, and, as Alexandra noted, the day ended with Nicholas reading the Bible to the group.

   ඏ ඏ ඏ

Named after the wife of Peter the Great, Russian Empress Catherine (Ekaterina) I, Ekaterinburg was founded in 1723 to tap the wealth of some of the world's richest deposits of minerals and precious and semi-precious stones.[6] By 1800, the Ural Mountains, with the smelting works at Ekaterinburg at their center, was the largest iron-producing area in the world. In 1814, gold was discovered, and in 1819, platinum. When the Revolution struck in 1917, ninety percent of the world's platinum was being produced in Ekaterinburg, and recently discovered deposits of chromite, copper, manganese, and asbestos were beginning to be exploited. Also abundant were diamonds, amethysts and emeralds, as well as the jasper, porphyry and lapis lazuli used to such dazzling and extravagant effect in the decoration of St Petersburg's fabulous palaces and cathedrals. While factories and workers' slums ringed the city, at

---

[6] Helen Rappaport, *The Last Days of the Romanovs: Tragedy at Ekaterinburg* (New York: St Martin's, 2008), 3.

its center the River Iset had been dammed, and a row of neoclassical mansions constructed on the grand flag-stoned embankments laid beside the man-made lake thus created.

In this important but sharply divided city, the Romanovs' last home was a two-story stone mansion known as the Ipatiev House. Set on the side of a low hill that ran down to the edge of the man-made lake at the center of the city, it had been the property of the prosperous mining engineer and merchant Nikolai Ipatiev before being seized by the Urals Soviet, two days before Nicholas and Alexandra arrived, and transformed into a prison.[7] A high double fence had been erected around the property and a detachment of fifty guardsmen recruited on wages of four hundred rubles a month (a third more than the doctors working in the city's hospitals under the new Bolshevik pay scales) from among workers at the city's iron and metal works. Set over the prisoners was the house commandant, Aleksandr Avdeev, a lathe-turner in his twenties from the same metal works.[8] Short, slovenly, and corrupt, Avdeev, who liked to throw parties and often appeared to be drunk, would later be replaced. But he was the authority that ruled over Nicholas and Alexandra now, and it was he who had snatched Alexandra's purse from her on their arrival.

⇛ ⇛ ⇛

During the two and a half months they were behind the walls and double fences of the Ipatiev House, Nicholas, Alexandra and their children led the lives of captives. The Bolshevik Central Executive Committee (headed by Sverdlov) in Moscow cabled the leaders of the Urals Soviet instructions that the family was to be held "in the strictest fashion." They hardly needed the encouragement. As word filtered out that Russia's last tsar and his family were being held in Ekaterinburg, a number of their supporters made the journey to the Urals and requested permission to see them. None was ever admitted. Neither was the local British consul (whose residence stood only a short walk from the Ipatiev House), nor any of the other Allied or Central Powers' consular representatives. The only person other than the guards allowed to enter and leave the Ipatiev House and the outside world was Dr Vladimir Derevenko, a specialist surgeon, a year younger than Nicholas, who had been treating Alexei since 1912. But as Derevenko's visits were personally supervised by Avdeev, the house commandant, only the most strictly necessary conversations about medical matters were conducted. As for food, Beloborodov put the family on prisoners' rations. During the first weeks, their meals were delivered to the house direct from the local Soviet workers' canteen. But after a while, the simple ingredients were

---

[7] Service, *Last of the Tsars*, 184–85.　　[8] Rappaport, *Last Days*, 21.

delivered to the Romanovs' cook, Ivan Kharitanov, who prepared the family's meals in the upper-floor kitchen behind the family's rooms, in which he also slept. The girls helped him with the baking. Faithful to the end, Kharitanov perished in the same cloud of cordite that ended his masters' lives in July, and has now also been sainted. To supplement the family's meager rations, the abbess of a local Orthodox monastery sent cream, radishes, fish soup, gherkins, sausages, and bread to the house.[9] Taking custody of the provisions, Avdeev kept the choicest foodstuffs for himself and the guards and passed on what was left to the prisoners.

Outwardly, the most oppressive features of life were the lodgings themselves. The family was allowed out of their upper floor rooms for an hour of exercise only once a day. Their exercise yard was a plot of ground forty yards long between the house and the fence that surrounded it. As he had done in Tobolsk, Nicholas asked for timber to split. But this time the request was denied, and Nicholas, who had always been active, suffered greatly for the want of physical exertion. Frustration, restlessness, and insomnia set in. Making conditions even worse was the order on May 2/15 to seal the upper-story windows and paint over them from the outside with white paint. Once the old man assigned the task had finished, Nicholas recorded in his diary that even though it was a beautiful spring day, looking out of the window was like "looking into a fog."[10] Eventually, when it became obvious that the heat would become oppressive, one of the windows was unsealed and lowered a few inches; a small shaft of light and blue sky could be seen from one of the rooms. Nonetheless, their quarters soon became damp, stale, and airless. The guards were ordered not to talk to them.

The other thing denied to them was the regular services of a priest. On only four occasions, in the two and a half months they were in Ekaterinburg, were clergy permitted to enter the Ipatiev House. The first was on Easter Saturday, four days after their arrival, on April 21/ May 4, when Nicholas and Alexandra made their confessions. The liturgy celebrated was that of Matins for Easter Sunday, the celebration of Christ's Resurrection. "Great indeed was the comfort of praying in such circumstances and of hearing 'Christ is risen!'" wrote Nicholas in his diary.[11] Despite the limitations imposed on them, these services brought Nicholas, Alexandra, and their children great comfort. But if their faith sustained them, it was because, assiduously observing the fasts and holy days of the Church calendar, and improvising as best they could the liturgies they were denied attendance at, they took responsibility for their own spiritual lives.

---

[9] Rappaport, *Last Days*, 24.
[10] Nicholas II, May 2, 1918, in Diary (2), 678.
[11] Nicholas II, April 21, 1918, in Diary (2), 676.

Indeed, they had begun doing this almost as soon as they had been installed in the house. As we have seen, Nicholas and Alexandra arrived in Ekaterinburg in the Wednesday of Holy Week, the week before Easter. The following day, "Great and Holy Thursday," being the day when Jesus's Last Supper with His disciples, His institution of the Eucharist, and betrayal by Judas are commemorated, is among the holiest days in the Orthodox year. In 1917, Fr Belyaev had served the day's liturgy in the palace at Tsarskoye Selo. A year later, in Ekaterinburg, Nicholas, Alexandra, Maria, and their retainers improvised for themselves, with Nicholas reading the day's Gospel readings for the group shortly after they had woken in the morning. Then, at six o'clock that evening, Nicholas read for Alexandra a part of the Old Testament Book of Job, before constructing a makeshift oratory by laying out the icons they had brought with them on a table in the drawing room. After supper, at nine p.m., Nicholas and Botkin together read for the group the so-called Liturgy of the Twelve Gospels, the anticipated service of Matins for Good Friday, consisting of twelve separate readings of the Passion of Christ, as narrated in the New Testament, interspersed with hymns based on the Psalms and Old Testament prophecies.[12] The service's final reading is the sealing of Christ's body in the tomb. The following day, Good Friday, began with Nicholas reading the Gospel reading for Vespers on Good Friday, and another passage, from Job, for Alexandra. But it was the Gospels only that Nicholas recorded in his diary. "In the morning and evening, as on all these days [of Passion Week], I read the corresponding Gospels aloud in the bedroom."[13]

In the evening, the whole group gathered, and Nicholas read (as noted by Alexandra) both an excerpt from Nilus's anti-Semitic *Great in the Small* and the Church's appointed Gospels for the Matins of Easter Saturday. In their minds, Bolshevism and Judaism were evidently connected and an analogy between the sufferings of Christ at the hands of "the Jews" (as the Gospel of St John describes it) and their own at the hands of the Urals Soviet seems to have suggested itself. Indeed, Nicholas continued to pair readings of the day's appointed Gospel with that of a passage from *Great in the Small* until the following Wednesday of Easter Week. Thereafter, the reading from the *Great in the Small* appears to have been dropped, and the family's day began with Nicholas reading the day's Gospel and lesson (i.e. the appointed New Testament epistle or Acts of the Apostles) alone. In addition, Alexandra always had Nicholas or one of her daughters read to her the day's homily found in the *Complete Yearly Cycle of Brief Homilies for Each Day of the Year*, by the Orthodox priest Fr Grigory Diachenko.

Otherwise, Nicholas and Alexandra spent their days reading books borrowed from the Ipatievs' private library (indeed, Nicholas appears

---

[12] Ibid.					[13] Ibid.

to have read Tolstoy's *War and Peace* for the first time in his life in Ekaterinburg), preparing for the commandant's daily inspection, playing cards, and writing to the four children, whom they had left behind in Tobolsk. By now, Alexandra had written twelve unanswered letters. Then, after nearly two weeks of silence, on April 25/May 8, a wire from Olga brought, in Nicholas's words, "refreshment" to the inmates of the Ipatiev House.[14] A week later, a parcel containing coffee and chocolate arrived from Alexandra's elder sister, Ella.[15] She, too, had by now been arrested. As Ella's note to her sister with the parcel had not included information about where she was being held, Alexandra assumed, from what she had been able to gather from the papers, that she was being held in Perm. But, in fact, the parcel had likely been let through because Ella was herself at that time being held in Ekaterinburg: later, she with a party of five other members of the dynasty, was sent ninety miles north to the village of Alapaevsk.[16]

After no further news from the children, Nicholas and Alexandra were abruptly informed on May 4/17 that their three other daughters and invalid son had left Tobolsk, and were on their way to meet them. In fact, it wasn't for another three days that the children, in the company of their tutors Pierre Gilliard and Sidney Gibbs and other retainers, finally left the town, once again aboard the packet steamer *Rus*. Two days later, they landed, presumably at the same wharf in Tyumen where they had transferred the previous year, and were embarked on a train for Ekaterinburg. The retinue had misgivings about the wisdom of bringing the children to this place. But Olga, Tatiana, Anastasia, and Alexei insisted on rejoining their parents. Of their progress, Nicholas and Alexandra received no information. "We still don't know where the children are or when they will arrive," wrote Nicholas on May 9/22 before being suddenly informed the next day that the children were a few hours away.[17] "Towards 11 the girls suddenly turned up with Alexei — thank God — such a joy to have them," Alexandra recorded.[18] "What an enormous joy it was to see them again and to embrace them after the four-week separation and the uncertainty," Nicholas echoed in his diary, vividly depicting the stream of questions each party poured out upon reunion with each other. "There was no end to the questions and answers. They had, poor things, suffered much moral distress both in Tobolsk and during the three-day trip." Alexei, meanwhile, was still in pain and could not walk. He had to be carried from room to room. Neither were Gilliard and Gibbs, nor any other members of the retinue from

[14] Nicholas II, April 25, 1918, in Diary (2), 677.
[15] Nicholas II, May 3, 1918, in Diary (2), 679.
[16] Service, *Last of the Tsars*, 243.
[17] Nicholas II, May 9, 1918, in Diary (2), 679.
[18] Nicholas II, May 10, 1918, in Diary (2), 680.

Tobolsk, admitted to the house. The family was united, but powerless, and its youngest member suffering. (Indeed, he would never walk again.)

By the end of May, Nicholas and Alexandra had been in Ekaterinburg for more than three weeks. Finally, on May 20/June 2, a priest, Fr John Storozhov, was allowed to visit.[19] With the assistance of his deacon, Storozhov celebrated the Divine Liturgy (as he would be allowed to do on two further occasions). But he was not allowed to communicate with the family, or deliver a homily. Guards watched his every movement, and he was unsure whether he should hold out the cross for the family to kiss as is customary at the end of the service. Using only his eyes to communicate with the priest, Nicholas indicated to Storozhov his desire for the priest to conclude the service as usual, and Storozhov, not detecting an objection from the guards present, consented.[20] Alexei, still unable to walk, observed the whole thing from his bed in the half-gloom created by the painted-over windows. Despite this concession, and the refreshment brought about by the children's arrival, the captivity was beginning to weigh on their moods.

The onset of summer was compounded Nicholas's frustration. "It is unbearable to sit locked up inside and be unable to go out into the garden when you wish and to pass good weather indoors." He had pain in his lower legs and back and was sleeping badly. He had arthritis, hemorrhoids, and his teeth were rotting.[21] On May 25/June 7, he was so exhausted from the pain and lack of sleep that he could not get out of bed for Alexandra's birthday.[22] Monitoring Nicholas's health and Alexei's, Alexandra, meanwhile, continued to suffer the migraines, heart palpitations and sciatica she had suffered for years. Sometimes, she went outside during their exercise breaks and sat with Alexei, who himself sat in her wheelchair. But though she continued to note and appreciate the "glorious weather," often she remained inside in bed. Also suffering was Nicholas and Alexandra's eldest daughter, Olga. The Revolution and imprisonment had made an already naturally quiet and reflective young woman withdrawn. Rather than joining her father and sisters during their permitted walks in the yard, she retreated into herself in silence.[23]

The family took refuge in routine. They rose at eight, washed, dressed, and said their prayers. The commandant Avdeev arrived for his inspection at nine, the guards bringing tea and black bread in his wake. Lunch was at one, though it was frequently delayed, a light evening meal at eight. The mornings were filled with reading, washing and mending clothes, letter-writing, and a half-hour walk in the yard.

---

[19] Nicholas II, May 20, 1918, in Diary (2), 681.
[20] Service, Last of the Tsars, 206.
[21] Slater, Many Deaths, 39, 156.
[22] Nicholas II, May 25, 1918, in Diary (2), 682.
[23] Rappaport, Last Days, 25, 78.

Another half-hour walk in the yard was permitted in the afternoons, and evenings were taken up with endless games of cards, hymn-singing, Bible-reading, and prayers again before bed. Of the songs they sang, the Liturgy's Cherubic Hymn, which had long been their favorite, doubtless took on added significance in Ekaterinburg. "Let us put away all earthly care that we may receive the King of All," it exhorted them. Three of the children had brought dogs with them, which they played with during their exercise breaks. Eventually, some of the guards built the young women a swing.[24] But that this was a prison they were very unlikely ever to escape cannot have been lost on them. "Are putting up yet higher planks before all our windows, so that not even the tops of the trees can be seen," noted Alexandra on May 23/June 5.[25]

Around this time, the Czechoslovak Legion mutinied, and threw its weight behind the overthrow of Bolshevik power.[26] Russia descended ever further into civil war. The Romanovs noted the mood of skittishness and increased hostility towards them that this produced in their guards, but were ignorant of its cause. The Czechoslovak advance towards Ekaterinburg provoked the intensification in the Bolsheviks' reign of terror. On June 10, Nicholas's former aides-de-camp, Prince Dolgorukov and Count Tatishchev were led out of their cells in Ekaterinburg's municipal prison and executed. Three days later, Ascension Day, the forty-year-old Grand Duke Mikhail Aleksandrovich, Nicholas's younger brother, to whom the Russian throne had briefly been passed the year before, was driven out of the city of Perm in the northern Urals, where he was being held, and shot in the head. At the end of the same month, nineteen randomly chosen representatives of Ekaterinburg's non-laboring class — priests, doctors, merchants, shop-owners, lawyers, and factory managers — were shot and buried in a mass grave at a sewage dump outside the city.[27] Clergy were especially hated. In all, forty-five priests were murdered in Ekaterinburg in the summer of 1918, "shot, drowned, bayoneted, their eyes gouged out, tongues and ears hacked off and their mangled bodies thrown in the river."[28]

Nicholas and Alexandra were informed of none of these killings, but felt the insecurity of the local Bolshevik regime in Ekaterinburg in other ways. The day Mikhail was shot, Nicholas received an order from Avdeev telling him to prepare his family for rapid departure, apparently, for Moscow. "Anarchists," Nicholas said Avdeev had told him, were threatening order in town. Obediently, the family packed their bags, only for Avdeev to return later that night, and say that they would remain a few more days in Ekaterinburg. The following day, the whole

---

[24] For this routine, see Rappaport, *Last Days*, 23–24.
[25] Alexandra, May 23, 1918: Kozlov et al., *Last Diary*, 157.
[26] Smele, *"Russian" Civil Wars*, 67–71.   [27] Rappaport, *Last Days*, 38.
[28] Ibid., 37.

plan was called off. Then, towards the end of the month, the Cheka hit upon the idea of testing the family's openness to any possible rescue attempted by monarchist groups, and arranged for the delivery to the family of four forged letters in French. Allegedly addressed to them by an anonymous loyal officer of the old imperial army, the letters invited the family to confirm their willingness to participate in a rescue attempt despite the risks involved and to describe, if so, the internal layout of the Ipatiev House. The family fell for the trick; and Olga, it seems, in a letter written on behalf of her father (whose handwriting would have been easily recognized) dutifully obliged with a verbal description of the house. Naturally, the family's rescuers never came. "The days passed and passed and nothing happened — the expectation and uncertainty were tormenting," Nicholas recorded in his diary.[29] Kept on file by the Urals Soviet, Olga's letter and the four forgeries later became evidence "justifying" the family's murder.

By the end of June 1918, it must have seemed to the Romanovs that the most likely thing they would die of was the heat. At the beginning of the month, Alexandra had hoped that the raising of the perimeter fences would allow for the opening of the windows sealed and white-washed back in May. It didn't. It was high summer and outside the weather was beautiful and sunny. In the family's dark, airless rooms, however, the heat and smell were becoming unbearable. "Worked, very hot, stuffy as no windows open & smells strong of kitchen everywhere," wrote Alexandra.[30] The other thing it undoubtedly smelt of was the nearby toilet and unwashed adult bodies living in cramped proximity.

Finally, relief, both physical and spiritual, came on Trinity Sunday. First, two guards came and opened one of the windows. "Such joy, deli-cious air at last & one window no longer whitewashed," noted Alexan-dra.[31] "The air in the rooms became fresh and in the evening even cool," Nicholas echoed. Second, their priest arrived equally unexpectedly to celebrate what Nicholas called "a real Mass and Vespers."[32] This meant that, in contrast to the previous two occasions on which a priest had been permitted into the house, when a Divine Liturgy without commu-nion had been performed, this time the sacrifice of the Lord's Body and Blood would be offered, "simply," as Alexandra put it, "on the table with all our images and lots of birch tree branches."[33] It was "the first since 3 months," Alexandra said, and she was right: the last time the family had been present at a Mass was at the parish church in Tobolsk on March 23. How their lives had changed since then, they must have thought.

[29] Nicholas II, June 14, 1918, in Diary (2), 683.
[30] Alexandra June 4, 1918: Kozlov et al., Last Diary, 169.
[31] Alexandra, June 10, 1918: Kozlov et al., Last Diary, 175.
[32] Nicholas II, June 10, 1918, in Diary (2), 683.
[33] Alexandra June 10, 1918: Kozlov et al., Last Diary, 175.

Revived, Alexandra and Alexei (who, it seems, often ate alone) managed
to eat lunch with the rest of the family at the dining table, and, in a concession to the spectacular weather, the family were, extraordinarily, given
two hours' exercise in the yard. But it was but a brief respite. Summer
temperatures rose higher. Despite the open window, the heat inside was
"colossal." And the open window, together with the family's favorable
response to the spurious rescue attempt, had made the guards jittery. On
June 27, a guard almost shot the seventeen-year-old Anastasia in the head
when she dared to poke her nose for a moment out of the window.[34]

As Helen Rappaport points out, these were trying circumstances for
any family. Living cheek-by-jowl in the five rooms available to them
were four menstruating young women between the ages of seventeen
and twenty-two, and their ill, probably menopausal, mother. Their
younger brother was unable to walk — unable, indeed, even to straighten
his leg — while their father was often incapacitated from the insomnia and other illnesses we have seen. In the same cramped space there
lived the family doctor (Botkin), the cook, a maid, a footman, and the
scullery boy Sednyov, Alexei's cherished playmate. Around them were
rough men, who talked dirty and scrawled obscenities and lewd pictures
depicting their mother's alleged relations with Rasputin on the walls
of the bathroom, hallway, and toilet. The family had been ordered not
to fraternize with the guards, but some of the young grand duchesses
had been drawn, it seems, to the coarse, but, nonetheless — by comparison with their father — vigorous men who formed the backdrop of
their days. Nineteen-year-old Maria, in particular, it seems, flirted with
her captors. "The men of the Special Detachment at the Ipatiev House
clearly liked Maria best of the family: she had natural openness and a
lovely smile . . . she even showed the guards her photo albums."[35] Some
time at the end of June, apparently, she was caught in a compromising
situation with one of the guards. Her family was shocked at what they
regarded as immorality. The "details are very sketchy," writes Rappaport,
"but it is clear that in the final weeks at Ekaterinburg her mother and
elder sister froze her out for her behavior."[36]

Whatever its exact nature, the event was a jolt to Beloborodov and
the rest of the Urals Soviet leaders: allowed to go too far, friendly relations between the guards and grand duchesses threatened to destroy
the entire house's security regime. There was also increasing evidence
of theft, unauthorized plundering by the guards under Avdeev of the
Romanovs' many boxes of property in storage in the house. Blame fell
on the house commandant, the young lathe-turner Avdeev. On July
4/17, he was dismissed, and the Romanovs were presented during lunch

---

[34] Service, *Last of the Tsars*, 230.   [35] Rappaport, *Last Days*, 81.
[36] Ibid., 82.

in their hot, airless rooms with their new, and final, commandant, the former medical orderly, Yakov Yurovsky. A "big, beetroot-cheeked man with a personality to match," in the words of historian Robert Service, Yurovksy had been born to an exiled Jewish family in Siberia in 1878.[37] Having been convicted of murder in 1898, he somehow ended up in Ekaterinburg, where, sometime around 1900, he converted to Lutheranism (to escape the tsarist-era legal penalties against Jews) and began working in a jewelry shop. In 1905, he joined the Bolshevik Party, before leaving Russia shortly afterwards for Berlin, where for seven years he worked as a watchmaker, and trained as a photographer. Returning to Russia in 1912 with his wife and three children, Yurovsky and his family lived first in Baku, before setting up a photographer's studio in Ekaterinburg. Yurovsky did well out of this business. Before long, his family had an apartment in the city center, and a dacha on the city outskirts. When war broke out in 1914, ill health and physical infirmity saw him drafted as a medical orderly. In 1917, he deserted, and, still a Bolshevik, began to play a part in local politics. A year later, Yurovsky was working for the Cheka.[38] Within less than a fortnight of his appointment, he would be charged with the task of carrying out the family's physical elimination.

Yurovsky moved fast to "professionalize" the Ipatiev House security regime. Suspecting Russians of being inherently more prone to fraternize, he restricted the service of ethnic Russian guards to the house perimeter. Inside, he employed foreign, in the event mainly Latvian, guards, whose Russian was less good, and who, not being Orthodox, were presumed to be free from any lingering mystical reverence for a man who remained in the minds of many simply the "little father-tsar." On the very day he took over command of the house, Yurovsky ordered the Romanovs to make a complete inventory of all their jewels, rings and other valuables, ordering them to remove and surrender all jewelry they were wearing. Forced to comply, Alexandra was left with two bracelets she could not get off and Nicholas with his engagement ring, which likewise, he could no longer remove from his finger. Yurovsky was not yet preparing to murder the family in his custody, as neither Sovnarkom in Moscow nor the leaders of the local Urals Soviet had agreed on the family's final fate. But like every good Chekist, Yurovsky knew the importance of trying to win his captives' and future victims' trust. Thus, having taken the family's jewelry during his inventory, he returned it to them in a sealed bag for their own safekeeping, along with a watch of Nicholas's that he said had been stolen from the Romanovs' luggage by one of the former guards. Suddenly, too, all the food that the nuns had been sending for months started reaching the intended

---

[37] Service, *Last of the Tsars*, 228. For Yurovsky's biography, see Rappaport, *Last Days*, 31–32.   [38] Service, *Last of the Tsars*, 228.

recipients. For a moment, there was a brief improvement in the family's conditions. "We have only learnt about this now, after the change [in commandants]," Nicholas wrote in disbelief in his diary, "because the whole amount of provisions has begun reaching the kitchen."[39] But before long the family had nicknamed Yurovsky "the Ox," and he was increasingly domineering. On June 28/July 11, the family noticed mid-morning that workmen had arrived to affix iron bars to the family's single unsealed window. "We are starting to like this character less and less!" wrote Nicholas in his diary's second-last entry.[40]

ʕ ʕ ʕ

Precisely when and, crucially, *by whom*, the decision was made to liquidate Nicholas, Alexandra, and their children is still a matter of conjecture, to be pieced together from a mass of incomplete evidence. Did the order come from Lenin and the Sovnarkom in Moscow? Or did the leaders of the local Urals Soviet — Beloborodov, Goloshchyokin — take the initiative? Certainly, at the start of July 1918, Lenin's official policy was still to bring Nicholas to Moscow for public trial. But Bolshevik rule across Russia was increasingly shaky. In the Urals, the Czechs and Whites were advancing daily, and the Urals Soviet wanted Moscow's permission to finish the Romanovs off locally if the danger of the family falling into liberators' hands arose. The leader of the Urals Soviet, Goloshchyokin, raised the subject with Lenin and Sverdlov in Moscow when he arrived there on June 21/July 4 (the day Yurovsky took up his post as Ipatiev House commandant) for the summer's scheduled All-Russian Congress of Soviets.[41] While Lenin was alive to the risks of the imperial family falling into enemy hands, it seems he did not give Goloshchyokin the blanket permission to kill the Romanovs that the Urals Soviet was looking for. Perhaps Lenin told him that Sovnarkom had abandoned the idea of a public trial of Nicholas in Moscow. Perhaps Lenin gave the Urals Soviet tacit permission to eliminate Nicholas and his family if the advance of the Czechs necessitated it. We don't know. What we do know is that Goloshchyokin left Moscow on June 24/July 7 with the Sovnarkom still asserting its right to determine the Romanovs' fate: the Urals Soviet were to remain in close and constant contact by telegraph with Moscow. Five days later, Goloshchyokin was back in Red Ekaterinburg. By that stage, the Czechs were not much more than twenty miles from the city; every other city they had attacked had fallen and there was no reason, local Red Army commanders told the leaders of the Urals Soviet, why Ekaterinburg should be any different. They could hold out for another week or so, at best. The sounds of

---

[39] Nicholas II, June 23, 1918, in Diary (2), 684.   [40] Ibid.
[41] Service, *Last of the Tsars*, 238–42.

the Czech guns could be heard from the streets in the middle of the city. Alexandra made frequent note of them in her diary. "Constantly hear artillery passing, infantry & twice cavalry during the course of this week.... Wounded daily arrive in town," she wrote on June 29/July 12, the day Goloshchyokin arrived back in town.[42]

Things now began moving quickly. On July 1/14, a Sunday, the Romanovs were permitted their final Orthodox liturgy. "Had the joy of an *obednitsa* — the young Priest for the 2nd time," Alexandra noted in her diary.[43] By this, she meant Fr Ioann Storozhov, who had celebrated the liturgy for the family exactly three weeks before, on Trinity Sunday. This Sunday, however, was the first religious service the Romanovs had been permitted since the Chekist Yurovsky had taken command of the house, and we know quite a lot about it thanks to the record that Storozhov, who had been a public prosecutor before taking holy orders, later took of it, having realized the event's significance.[44]

Storozhov had not intended to celebrate a liturgy for Russia's last tsar and his family that day. On the contrary, he was preparing to celebrate in his own parish, when one of Yurovsky's agents from the Ipatiev House knocked at the door and instructed him to come and perform a service for the house's inmates. All the same, Storozhov naturally complied, and his parishioners were served by someone else. With him to the Ipatiev House Storozhov took his deacon, Vasily Buimirov. The two men arrived at the house at ten o'clock. Immediately, they noticed the house's changed appearance. It was much more obviously a prison than it had been before, with telephone wires now running everywhere. Introduced first to Yurovsky, Storozhov, somehow sensing that this liturgy he had been called to perform would function as the family's last rites, asked the house commandant whether he had permission to serve the family a full Mass (*obednya*), with the offering of the Body and Blood of the Lord as Eucharist, or merely the shorter liturgy of the Word (*obednitsa*) with hymns, prayers, and Bible readings only. When Yurovsky answered, predictably, that only the short service was to be offered, Storozhov was downcast; his deacon murmured in protest. But again both men complied.

The family and remaining retinue and servants were waiting for the churchmen in the drawing room. When Storozhov, now in his vestments, entered, Alexei was sitting in his mother's wheelchair, with Alexandra beside him. The grand duchesses, in identical dark skirts and white blouses, were gathered by their father. Mother and son, thought

---

[42] Alexandra, June 29, 1918: Kozlov et al., *Last Diary*, 194.
[43] Alexandra, July 1, 1918: Kozlov et al., *Last Diary*, 196. In fact, Alexandra was mistaken; this was the *third* time Storozhov had celebrated for them: Rappaport, *Last Days*, 160.
[44] For Storozhov's record, see Nikolai Ross, *Gibel' tsarskoi sem'i: Materialy sledstviia po delu ob ubiistve Tsarkoi sem'i (avgust 1918–fevral' 1920)* (Frankfurt am Main: Possev, 1987). My discussion, however, is dependent on Rappaport, *Last Days*, 159–63.

Storozhov, looked well; Nicholas and his daughters seemed weary, subdued. In the middle of the room was the table that the family had lovingly arranged with their icons that would serve as a makeshift ambo (lectern) and resting place for Storozhov's field altar. Yurovsky watched from a corner. The liturgy began.

Before being called upon to minister to them in captivity in Ekaterinburg, Storozhov had known nothing of Russia's last tsar and his family, other than what had been printed in the newspapers. For years, little of that had been flattering. When he had served the liturgy for them, he had therefore (like Belyaev before him) been surprised at the depth and sincerity of their piety, and the profound and humble respect they showed him as a priest. In the past, the family, bowing to Storozhov when he had entered, had recited the prayers of the liturgy fervently, while Nicholas had sung all the responses by heart. But this time, on July 1/14, it was different. Again the family bowed, and showed him every respect. But during the prayers they were silent; Nicholas did not sing the responses. When his deacon Buimirov intoned the prayer for the dead that was a conventional part of every liturgy, this time, for the first time, and in a way that was not normally required, the family dropped in silence to their knees. Did they, too, know, Storozhov wondered, that death was approaching, and that this service he was performing for them was their last rites? Reciting the great prayer in which the Mother of God is implored to give to all those who sorrow "strength and dignity to carry the cross of suffering," Storozhov sensed instinctively that the somber and silent family was praying it together with him inwardly. Although not permitted to offer a full Mass with Eucharist, Storozhov had nonetheless with him particles of the *prosphoron* or dedicated bread from which his own parish's Eucharist would be consecrated later that day. With Yurovsky's permission, he gave these, at the end of the service, to Nicholas and Alexandra. Coming forward with tears in their eyes to kiss the cross in Storozhov's hands, the grand duchesses whispered an all but inaudible *spasibo* ("thank you").

Not allowed to converse with the family, Storozhov was led away as soon as the service ended; he never saw them again. But before he left the Ipatiev House, Storozhov did spend a few moments talking in private with Yurovsky. "Well, they've said their prayers and unburdened themselves," said the house commandant, who had been raised a Jew in a family exiled to Siberia by power of the tsar.[45] Now, of course, Yurovsky was a Bolshevik, a Chekist, and an atheist. But "I have never discounted the power of religion," he told the Orthodox priest in front of him. Neither, of course, had Lenin. That was why, already in 1918, its practice had, wherever possible, to be destroyed. Under Russia's new, soon-to-be-proclaimed

---

[45] Rappaport, *Last Days*, 162.

Soviet constitution, priests like Storozhov would no longer be citizens. "You know, father, something has happened to them in there," said the deacon, Buimirov, to Storozhov as they walked back past the mansions by the lake to St Catherine's.[46] Indeed, this final liturgy that Storozhov and Buimorov had just celebrated was among the only religious services in his life that Nicholas made no record of in his diary. His simple entry the day before would be his last: "We have no news from anywhere."[47]

∾ ∾ ∾

The formal decision was taken two days later by the Urals Soviet Executive Committee on July 3/16.[48] Hearing Goloshchyokin's report of his trip to Moscow, the committee was disappointed to learn that Lenin had not given them the blanket permission to kill the Romanovs they had wanted. But that they believed that Lenin had given Goloshchyokin tacit, *conditional* permission to kill the family is suggested by the fact that the conversation turned immediately to the approaching Czechs, and the tenability of Bolshevik power itself in Ekaterinburg. The consensus that the family had to be killed already existed; all that had to be discussed was where and how, and whether Ekaterinburg's current circumstances satisfied the conditions that Lenin, in distant Moscow, had laid down. Having apparently satisfied themselves that those conditions had been met, the members of the Committee then found themselves confronted with a choice between two broad plans for the killing. Beloborodov favored transporting the family alive to the outskirts of town, staging an escape attempt, and shooting them in the forest. Goloshchyokin, the Military Commissar and liaison with Moscow, argued instead for killing them where they were in the house: nobody would believe the story of an escape attempt, and, protected by the high fences that now surrounded it, the Ipatiev House offered even greater secrecy than the forest. Voting with Goloshchyokin, the Committee ordered Yurovsky to put the plan into effect that evening. In their mercy, the Committee agreed that one member of the family and retinue might be withdrawn from the house before the killing: the fourteen-year-old servant boy and apprentice cook, Leonid Sednyov, Alexei's friend and playmate.

∾ ∾ ∾

We know from Alexandra's diary that her primary occupation during these last days was Bible-reading, specifically the Old Testament. The minor Jewish prophets — Hosea, Joel, Amos, Obadiah — were being read to her by her daughters, as well as the Wisdom of Ben-Sirach. Of that latter, we know Maria read chapters twenty-six to thirty-one on July 2/15, and we can only imagine what Alexandra thought as her daughter's voice

<hr/>

[46] Ibid., 163.   [47] Nicholas II, June 30, 1918, in Diary (2), 684.
[48] Service, *Last of the Tsars*, 251.

intoned the following verses.[49] "The necessities of life are water, bread, and clothing, and also a house to assure privacy. Better is the life of the poor under their own crude roof than sumptuous food in the house of others" (Sir. 29:21–2). Perhaps she took heart in a verse she might have recalled from the beginning of the same book: "Those who fear the Lord will have a happy end; on the day of their death, they will be blessed" (Sir. 1:13). Or, perhaps, attaining to the meaning we have proposed to discern in the events that had befallen her and her family, she thought of a passage from the Prophet Hosea that Tatiana had read to her the day before: "They made kings, but not through me; they set up princes, but without my knowledge" (Hos. 8:4). Even in Alexandra's *lectio divina*, there could be detected, ringing through time from Ancient Israel, a certain suggestion of the theological meaning of Russia's present.

The following day, July 3/16, Alexandra and her eldest daughter Olga continued sewing hidden diamonds into the corsets they had brought with them. Alexandra called the activity "arranging our medicines."[50] It was dull and overcast, and Alexei, who, thanks to Yurovsky's ostensible solicitude for his health, had had the luxury of eggs sent from the nuns at the convent for breakfast, had come down with a cold. Later, Nicholas and others went out into the yard for the morning's allotted half-hour of exercise, and Tatiana read aloud the Books of the Prophets Amos and Obadiah. If Tatiana managed to finish the last Book, as Alexandra's diary implies, then the last words of Scripture heard by Russia's last empress were, providentially perhaps, a promise: "those who have been saved shall go up to Mount Zion [...], and the kingdom [Russian: *tsarstvo*, "tsardom"] shall be the Lord's" (Obad. 1:21). Then, at eight o'clock that evening, supper was served, the servant boy Sednyov suddenly plucked from their company "to go and see his Uncle," as Alexandra put it in her diary, recording the pretext Yurovsky had come up with to spare the boy death in the scene of horror he was even then preparing. "Wonder whether it's true & we shall see the boy back again!" wrote Alexandra, evidently sensing that something was amiss.[51] Then she and Nicholas played bezique, said their prayers, and at 10.30 went to bed. Possessed now, it would seem, of an unshakeable inner calm, Alexandra was herself perhaps becoming an example of a mystery she had once contemplated abstractly. As she wrote in her last spiritual notebook, "Some of the best Christians that the world has ever known were its greatest sufferers, but at the same time, nothing could shatter the peace of their souls."[52] As for what prayer meant to her, she left us with a definition of that, too. "What is prayer?" she asked: "It is when we are close to Christ."[53]

---

[49] Alexandra, July 2, 1918: Kozlov et al., *Last Diary*, 197.
[50] Alexandra, July 3, 1918: Kozlov et al., *Last Diary*, 198.
[51] Ibid.
[52] HM Empress Alexandra, *Garden of the Heart*, 18.
[53] Ibid., 10.

To do the killing, Yurovsky chose eleven men in addition to himself: one for each of the eleven victims and one extra. Half of them were trusted Russian and Chekists like himself, such as his deputy Grigory Nikulin and Petr Ermakov, a Bolshevik military commissar. The other half were the supposedly more dispassionate and professional Latvians to whom Yurovsky had confided interior guard duties in the house. But when, late that evening, he informed the group of the task to which he was appointing them ("Today, we're going to shoot the entire family"), two of the Latvians refused to shoot on the girls and had to be replaced by others.[54] Collecting all the weapons available in the Ipatiev House, Yurovsky gave to each man his weapon or weapons. The twelve men would kill the family of seven and the four retainers with fourteen handguns: two Brownings, two Colts, two Mausers, a Smith & Wesson and seven Nagants. But before they could do so, Yurovsky had to wait for permission from Moscow. For though the immediate decision to arrange for the family's slaying had been made in Ekaterinburg, they would not put their plans into action until they had received the party leader's blessing. But time was growing short. The Czechs were only twenty miles away, and the sound of their artillery boomed across the city. Moreover, summer nights in the Urals are short. From three or four in the morning, it would already be light, and by then they had to have finished the grisly business not only of killing the family, but of disposing of their bodies so that nobody ever found them again.

The telegram sent from Ekaterinburg, asking for the Sovnarkom to bless the Urals Soviet's decision, arrived in Moscow at 9.22 p.m., 11.22 p.m. in Ekaterinburg. It was not presented for discussion to the Sovnarkom; Lenin and Sverdlov arrogated the decision to themselves. How long it took for Lenin to reach his decision and cable a reply we do not know. But before at the latest eleven o'clock that evening (and probably much earlier), Lenin had reached his decision, and Sverdlov, putting his party leader's decision into effect, dispatched a bodyguard on motorbike from the Kremlin to the Central Telegraph Office with a reply. Precisely what that reply said we do not know, for, intentionally, no copy of Lenin's response to the Urals Soviet request was preserved: Sverdlov ordered the bodyguard tasked with the mission to bring back to him at the Kremlin both the copy and the tape of the telegram. When the telegraphist had refused, the guard pulled his revolver and all record of Lenin's telegram (and evidence of his guilt for the Romanovs' killing) was destroyed. But that Lenin consented to the murder is clear enough. A little before 1.30 a.m. on July 17, a messenger arrived from the Urals

---

[54] Service, *Last of the Tsars*, 252.

Executive Committee with the codeword to be spoken in case of a positive reply from Moscow: "chimneysweep."[55] The killing could begin.

          ᵔ   ᵔ   ᵔ

It was the family's physician, Dr Botkin, who responded to the banging on the door in the middle of the night.[56] The Czech guns were getting closer, Botkin was told, and for their own safety, the family had to go down into the basement. They were not to panic but do this calmly. The action was a precaution, not an emergency. Taking their time to wash and dress properly, it was two o'clock before the family was ready. Nicholas went first, carrying in his arms Alexei, who could not walk. After him came Alexandra, leaning on her eldest daughter Olga's arm, and, behind them, the three other grand duchesses, in order of precedence. Then down the stairs went Botkin, the servant Trupp, the maid Demidova, carrying two cushions for Alexandra to sit on, and the cook Kharitonov last. In answer to their enquiries, they were told to leave their belongings behind in their rooms. There would be time enough to come back for them. Also locked into the place of confinement behind them were two of the three pet dogs the family had with them. At the bottom of the narrow staircase, on the lower floor of the house that had been dug into the hillside facing the lake at the center of the city, they were shown into an empty and almost windowless storage room. (The one window there was had been nailed shut.) Light was provided by a single bulb hanging by a wire from the ceiling. The doors at the back of the room, leading into a further walk-in cupboard, were locked. When Alexandra complained about the lack of chairs, two were provided, one for her and one for Alexei. Yurovsky assigned the group their places. Nicholas he put at the front and center of the group, opposite the doorway. Seated on a chair to his left was Alexei, and, to the left of the boy, his mother, Alexandra. By the wall, behind their mother's chair stood the grand duchesses. Behind Nicholas stood the physician Botkin and behind him were the footman Trupp and cook Kharitonov. At the back of the room, in front of the locked cupboard doors, was the maid Demidova. The party murmured with chit-chat. Even at this late stage, they were not, it seems, afraid, but curious, and hopeful of possible deliverance, at least from the confines of the Ipatiev House. They might remain in Bolshevik custody, but just to be taken somewhere else would be an improvement on the months of monotony they had endured upstairs. They remained in these positions for half an hour, Yurovsky having explained that a truck would be along presently to take them somewhere

---

[55] Ibid., 253. Certainly, it is Service's view that Lenin ordered the killings.
[56] The following paragraphs depend on Rappaport, *Last Days*, 184–96; Service, *Last of the Tsars*, 254–57; and a first-person narrative, reconstructed on the basis of a number of often conflicting memoirs and recollections, in Slater, *Many Deaths*, 1–15.

safer. At length, they heard it arrive; its motor remained running.

During those thirty minutes, Yurovsky, who had locked the double doors to the room holding the Romanovs behind him, went to call the truck up to the house and see to it that its driver did not kill the engine after he had arrived: the aim was to conceal, as far as possible, the sound of the bullets that would soon start flying. Returning with this errand completed, he assembled his chosen gunmen by the door, undid the locks and entered. "Well, here we all are," Nicholas, stepping forward, is believed to have said to him. "What are you going to do now?" Clearing his throat, Yurovsky asked the family to stand and began reading the decree drafted earlier that day by the Executive Committee of the Urals Soviet. "In view of the fact that your relatives in Europe continue their assault on Soviet Russia, the presidium of the Urals Regional Soviet has sentenced you to be shot," said Yurovsky, reading from the piece of paper in his hands. "What? What?" asked Nicholas in reply, but turning around so that his questions were in fact addressed not to Yurovsky but to his family. While Botkin echoed Nicholas's incredulity ("So you're not taking us anywhere?"), Yurovsky continued reading the decree: as the Czechoslovak Legion was approaching, and the "crowned executioner . . . guilty of countless crimes against the people" was at risk of escaping the people's judgment, the decision had been taken that the "former Tsar Nicholas Romanov" was to be shot.

A moment of dumbfounded silence fell upon the room. Then Yurovsky, drawing his pistol from his trouser pocket, shot Nicholas at point-blank range in the chest. According to the plans agreed beforehand, at this first shot, every gunman behind was to fire directly on the designated victim who had been assigned him. But the discipline such plans depended on did not outlast the blast of Yurovsky's pistol. While Nicholas stood already dying, three other gunmen stepped forward and emptied their pistols into his chest. Allegedly lifted off his feet by the volley of bullets fired at him, Nicholas thudded to the floor, his blood spraying over Alexei. Thus what was supposed to have been a clinical operation descended into a confused and panic-stricken hunt at close quarters. With Nicholas dead, the men opened fire on his wife, her skull torn open by a bullet striking the left of her head while she made the sign of the cross. While she slumped to the floor, brain tissue splattered over her daughters behind her, who were screaming. According to some reports, the girls ran about in terror; according to others, they got down on their hands and knees on the floor, desperately trying to escape the horror and stray bullets flying around and over them. Perhaps they did both. Many of those in the room, of course, had already been struck, and probably all had soiled themselves in terror. Certainly, it seems, Alexei, shaking in his chair, had done so, the pool of his urine merging with that of blood from his mother dead on the floor beside him. The air was filled with smoke. Killed along with Nicholas and Alexandra in the initial shooting were Trupp and Kharitonov. But the flaws of Yurovsky's plan were amply revealed. Visibility was so low, the noise so deafening, and the gunmen themselves choking so badly on the smoke, that Yurovsky was forced to call a halt to the killing so that the killers could take a step outside to revive themselves. Some of them vomited; the moans of the wounded and terrified survivors emanated from the room behind them.

His men revived, and the smoke now having lessened, Yurovsky returned to the room. The grand duchesses were still alive, as were Alexei, Botkin, and Demidova. Closest to the door was Botkin, sprawled on the floor with two wounds to the abdomen. Walking over to him, Yurovsky shot him in the temple. Nobody who reads an account of the night of July 16/17 can do so without being moved to their very core for the sake of the grand duchesses especially. We think of them as girls, but they were young adults, really: twenty, nineteen, seventeen, and sixteen years old, respectively. Utterly innocent of any crime, real or imagined, they had been engulfed in a horror that no human soul should ever have to endure. Their mother and father had been killed before their eyes. Alone, now, in the world, for the first time in their lives, they were quarry for their parents' killers. Shot in the thigh, Maria had exhausted herself pounding on the locked doors of the cupboard at the back of the room and now lay moaning. Feet away from her in the shadows of the room's far corner, Olga and Tatiana, the two eldest, found comfort in a sister's embrace. They were clutching each other when Ermakov, one of Yurovsky's men, began lunging into them with an eight-inch bayonet. But he was drunk, and the girls' vital organs were protected by corsets inlaid with pearls and diamonds. Seeing what was happening, Yurovsky walked over and shot Tatiana in the back of the head. Recovering a degree of composure, the killer with the bayonet drew his pistol and shot Olga through the jaw. One might have thought that this horrifying experience might have alerted the men to the uselessness and inhumanity of their bayonets. But inexplicably, with Olga and Tatiana now lying dead, slumped on top of each other, the scene repeated itself just feet away with Maria. Bayoneted without success by the same man, Ermakov, who had failed the first time to kill her elder sisters, she, too, was shot in the head by Yurovsky. By that time, Ermakov had taken his bayonet to the youngest grand duchess, Anastasia. But after the first blows failed to fell her, he shot her in the head himself, without waiting for Yurovsky.

Incredibly, the last of the family to die was its physically weakest member, fourteen-year-old Alexei.[57] Somehow, it seems, one of the gunmen

---

[57] Rappaport, *Last Days*, 191. But Slater believes that Alexei died before his sisters:

emptied a whole clip of his bullets into the teenage boy's body without killing him. Seeing the boy still alive, Ermakov stabbed at him, too, with his bayonet before, once again, Yurovsky, this time needing to find another weapon, shot him through the temple. Of the victims, the only one alive now in the room was the maid, Demidova. Wounded in the thigh, she had fainted, but now came to, screaming, "Thank God, I'm saved!" Of course, she had spoken too soon. Walking over to her, Ermakov swung at her with his bayonet while the maid did her best to protect herself, using two pillows secretly stuffed with jewels as a makeshift shield. Eventually, they were taken from her and Ermakov stabbed her through the chest. Walking the room to check pulses, Yurovsky established that all the victims were dead. The whole thing had taken twenty minutes. Slipping and sliding on the blood- and tissue-covered floor, the gunmen stripped the bodies of valuables. Anastasia, it seems, was still not dead: rolled onto a stretcher, she moaned and quivered. Ermakov shot her in the head a second time and she went silent.[58] Some of the men vomited. Withdrawing to his office to rest, Yurovsky handed over command to Ermakov, whose job it was, despite being drunk, to get the bodies loaded onto the truck. Hovering in the background while the men did this, unable to gain a sure foothold in the blood despite the sheets they tried to wrap the eleven bodies in, were Goloshchyokin and, probably, Beloborodov. A Cheka agent, Aleksandr Lisistyn, who was present, prepared a report for Moscow. With the bodies heaped haphazardly on top of each other on a layer of sawdust, Ermakov climbed in beside the driver, and ordered the vehicle to depart. Originally, it had been Yurovsky's plan to allow Ermakov to drive the bodies to the forest, and dispose of them at the agreed site there. But having recovered his strength, and concluding that Ermakov was too drunk to be trusted, Yurovsky followed behind in a motor car with Goloshchyokin. Overloaded, the truck traveled slowly; it was now almost daylight.

೧೪ ೧೪ ೧೪

The site, an old mineshaft nine miles away in a forest to the north and west of the city, had been chosen the day before. The plan was to dump the bodies in the pool of water that filled the bottom of the shaft. But almost nothing went as planned. The road through the forest was wet and rutted; when the truck got stuck, the bodies had to be loaded off and put onto carts provided by workmen comrades of Ermakov's whom he had enlisted to help eliminate the family. Drunk, these men had been expecting to find the Romanovs alive and rape the women. Yurovsky almost lost control of them when the men realized the girls

---

Many Deaths, 7.
[58] Slater, *Many Deaths*, 8.

were already dead. All the same, the men's carts proved indispensable for getting the corpses further into the forest. When they reached the agreed mineshaft, they found a party of peasants sitting by a fire a few hundred feet away, having come out to cut the summer hay that grew by the road. They were sent away, but the sun was now high, and the bodies several hours old when they were finally unloaded and stripped of their clothes, revealing the diamonds, pearls, sapphires, and rubies that had been sewn into the family's undergarments, or hidden inside the coverings of their outer clothing's buttons. On her upper arm, Alexandra was found wearing a spiral of thick gold wire. Allegedly, a sixteen-pound sack of jewels and other valuables was collected. Making a pile of the blood-soaked clothes, Yurovsky ordered it doused with petrol and set ablaze, while Ermakov, with his rifle butt, tried to smash in the family's faces. Then, taking the stiff and naked corpses by the arms and legs, the men swung them one-by-one into the shaft. Unfortunately, however, nobody had checked exactly how deep the shaft was and soon the bodies were piling on top of each other, unsubmerged. Someone suggested tossing in a hand grenade. But the idea was dismissed, and branches were cut instead and laid across the mouth of the pit. Everybody knew it was a temporary solution, at best. With the sun now high, Yurovsky and Ermakon returned to Ekaterinburg to fetch the tools and equipment needed to dispose properly of the bodies. Taking the jewels with him, he left the men to guard the bodies.

It was not until dawn on July 18 that Yurovsky returned to the mineshaft. With him this time were fresh men, a unit of professional Chekists, and a cart loaded with ropes and spades. Then he ordered the men to get the bodies out of the shafts using the ropes. To do this, someone had to climb down into the pool and fasten the knots around the family's ankles. Coming out feet first, washed clean from the night they had spent in the pool of water, the corpses were laid under a tarpaulin. But the question still hadn't been answered: what to do with them? Waiting for nightfall, the men not on sentry duty dozed by the bodies. At 9.30 p.m., Yurovsky gave orders for the bodies to be loaded back on to the carts they had used to drag them through the forest the night before, and to reload them on the truck that had been stuck, but was now free again. By now, the bodies were putrefying, and the men had to tie rags over their mouths and noses. With the bodies back in the truck, the plan was to drive south to the Moscow Highway, in the forest, off to the side of which were deeper mines, where the bodies could be hidden. But the ground in the forest was wet and the truck struggled just as much this second night as it had done the night before. Halfway back to Ekaterinburg, it got stuck again, where the road crossed a muddy rut. Once again, the bodies were unloaded and someone found some railway sleepers to lay across the rut to get the wheels spinning again. They could carry on with the task, but did they have to? It was now after midnight and the men were exhausted and hungry. Then someone had an idea. What if they buried the bodies there, in the soft mud of the rut in the bend of the road, and laid the railway sleepers back over them? Yurovsky consented. But not all the bodies would be buried there, to complicate the task of identifying them by any who later chanced to find them. Two would be cremated.

Thus, a pyre of brushwood was made one hundred and fifty yards down the road, and Maria and Alexei's bodies were thrown on to it and doused with kerosene. Despite the intense heat, which could be felt by the men digging in the road some distance away, it took most of the night to reduce the bodies to charred bones and ash. They were dug into the ground on the spot. Meanwhile, a hole, six by four-and-a-half by three feet deep, was dug where the truck had been bogged. Just before dawn, the nine remaining bodies were thrown, in a jumble, into it. Unloading jugs of acid from the supplies he brought with him from Ekaterinburg, Yurovsky had them doused. The faces and hair dissolved instantly. Then the men filled the pit, and the heavy timber beams were laid over the top. "We hid them so well the world will never find them," boasted Petr Voikov, Bolshevik Commissar of Food Supplies for the Urals, as he surveyed what looked like nothing more than a boggy patch in a forest track overlaid with a little bridge of railway sleepers.[59] Russia's last imperial family had vanished. As Del Noce would later put it, to Lenin, "Kerensky's escape was not very important, but the destruction of the imperial family was essential" — in order, that is, that the "revealed truths" of Marxism-Leninism's dialectical materialism might not only supplant but also offer a secularized, "scientific" substitute for the theocratic principle, and that "red tsars" such as Lenin and Stalin should receive the "right" to rule — their "anointment" — from the force of history itself.[60] Symbolically, too, only through the destruction not only of the life, but also the *face* and *body* of one who remained indelibly tsar — and, hence, the "face of God" in the polis — could the Bolsheviks demonstrate to the world that of all the heirs to the atheist conclusions of nineteenth-century philosophy *they* were the most consistent (and, for precisely this reason, that of all the new ideological and scientific regimes sprung from the Great War, their new Soviet order was necessarily the *most modern* and the *most rational*).

---

[59] Slater, *Many Deaths*, 14.
[60] Del Noce, "Right and left," in *Crisis of Modernity*, 257. See also Del Noce, "Latent metaphysics within contemporary politics," and "Notes on secularization and religious thought," in *Crisis of Modernity*, 67, 274.

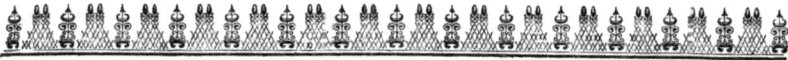

CHAPTER FOURTEEN

Teokratia Regenerate

UT IF IT IS TRUE THAT THE UNDERLYING cause of the Russian Revolution was ideational—the collapse in Russian culture (at least among the elite and the workers) of the theocratic principle—then striking about Russia today would be that same principle's *revival*. Twenty-five years after the collapse of the regime that put Nicholas, Alexandra and their children to death, and hid their desecrated bodies in the earth, Russia is dotted with churches, shrines and other memorials erected in honor of the last representative of the Russian *teokratia* and his family. Through the icons, moreover, of these Royal Passion-bearers, the once-unknown faces of the last Romanovs have become familiar, the hostility and oblivion directed towards them in Soviet times having been replaced with incitements to affection, intentional commemoration, mimesis, and prayer. Far from forgetting or cursing the last tsar, the modern believing Russian is supposed to remember his sufferings, imitate his faith, and seek his help from beyond the grave. We have seen evidence aplenty of this already, from Petersburg to Crimea and Belarus. I discovered more, and perhaps the most significant, when, the summer after my late winter pilgrimage to Pskov, I retraced Nicholas and Alexandra's journey into exile and death in Tobolsk and the Urals.

My first destination was Tobolsk. Founded by Cossack adventurers and fur traders in 1586, Tobolsk is one of Siberia's oldest Russian settlements.[1] Set on a bluff carved out of the landscape by the vigorous River Irtysh (a tributary of the Ob, Russia's longest river and the world's seventh, in whose torrents meltwater from the Altai drains away to the Arctic) it is perhaps also one of its loveliest: on a table of grass, on the other side of which (backed, the morning I arrived after two days on the Trans-Siberian from Moscow, by the yellow-blue haze of the morning) stands Siberia's best-preserved Cossack fortress, an easily defensible square of stout, whitewashed walls, guarded at the corners by four towers topped with the distinctive upside-down cones of Russian kremlin architecture. According to the local woman — a journalist who knew everybody — who had volunteered to be my guide, only twenty years before the place had been neglected, run-down, dirty, and dangerous, the haunt of drunks. The transformation was due to Putin, on a visit

---

[1] For a history of Siberia, see James Forsyth, *A History of the Peoples of Siberia: Russia's North Asian Colony, 1581–1990* (Cambridge: Cambridge University Press, 1992).

in the early 2000s. Shocked at the fort's dereliction, he ordered the local authorities to clean it up. Today, however, rising above the walls, two golden onion domes, surrounded by four smaller bright blue onions spangled with golden stars, lent the citadel an authentic air of Holy Rus.

We entered inside the fortress gates. In the soft morning light, garden beds, a path, and cast-iron streetlamps bordered the grassy yard in the middle of the fort. After decades of neglect, the Tobolsk Kremlin is today a working Orthodox seminary, and the only building open to visitors in the complex is its largest and most impressive: the 1686 Cathedral of the Holy Wisdom, a triple-apsed cathedral with the five onion domes I had seen from a distance. Stripped and used as a granary in the 1930s, and repurposed as a history museum under Khrushchev, it was returned to the Orthodox Church in 1993, and beautifully restored. Every niche, from the columns to the window bays and the undersides of the stone arches supporting the roof, bears the image of an angel or a saint. And on the northern wall, I spotted them, six familiar faces in the front row of a full-length depiction of Russia's New Martyrs: Nicholas, Alexandra and their children wearing Muscovite kaftans and headdresses, clutching crosses and a New Testament scroll.

Exiting into the square on the other side of the fort, we entered the tsarist-era administrative building that now serves as the Tobolsk Regional Museum. Here, the rehabilitation of the family's reputation continued, and two large exhibition rooms displayed artefacts connected to Nicholas and his family. In the first, a gold-trimmed red velvet throne sat on a triple-stepped dais beneath a canopy hung with the imperial crown, apparently rescued from the pre-revolutionary governor's mansion. On the wall directly opposite hung Nicholas and Alexandra's portraits, and, in prominent capitals, "GOD SAVE THE TSAR!." Glass cabinets filled with late imperial memorabilia made up the rest of the room's exhibits. In one was the mammoth ivory fountain pen presented to Nicholas when, in 1892, while still tsarevich, he had called in Tobolsk on his overland journey back to St Petersburg from Vladivostok. In another was a commemorative pillow slip brought by Nicholas and Alexandra to Tobolsk in their baggage in 1917. Forbidden as they were for public display only a little more than a generation ago, such objects, insignificant in themselves, bear witness to the change in attitude we have seen before.

The second of the two rooms, which recreated the décor of the suite in the local governor's mansion during the Romanovs' Tobolsk exile, suggested this impression especially. To the left of the entrance, a roped-off area featured a square, dark wooden dining table with seating for six, while a samovar, screen partition, potted palm tree and sideboard with *stil modern* finishes completed the tableau. On the other side of the room, a sofa and armchair, gathered around a small coffee table with a grandfather clock, sidled up to a writing desk in front of a wall hung with a mass of old icons. Apparently, everything on display was original.[2] One cabinet displayed a long white shawl knitted by the empress herself, probably during one of her pregnancies, and recognizable in numerous later photographs of her, while, on the adjacent wall, a perspex plaque presented an extract from Nicholas's diary in Alexandra's hand, originally written on their 1894 wedding day: *When this life ends, we will meet again in another world to be together forever.* A nearby cabinet showed a New Testament opened at the title page with Alexandra's ornate signature, and the year, "1914." Dominating the whole room was the Tercentenary Romanov family portrait that had been blown up and affixed to one of the walls. On the small table standing in front of this portrait was a faux period photo album with Romanov family photographs.

"We wanted the exhibition to be *interaktivniy*," said the museum director whom my guide had arranged to show me through the exhibition, inviting me to leaf through the album with her.

She then pointed to a listening post where visitors could listen to an audio recording of a poem called "A Prayer," composed for the Grand Duchesses Olga and Tatiana in October 1917 by Sergei Bakhteev (a monarchist poet devoted to Nicholas and his family), conveyed to them in exile by their friend, Countess Hendrikov, and subsequently found among the Grand Duchesses' papers after their deaths.

"With all that we know these days, it's very difficult to be objective about their deaths," she added. "Killing the tsar was Russia's original sin; all this country's troubles in the twentieth century flowed from it. Our task here at the museum is to enlighten those who do not understand this."

ை ை ை

Leaving the museum, I followed my guide down the path to the lower town, on the floodplain of the Irtysh below. Flat, and crisscrossed by drainage canals, the lower town was the kind of place where cattle still wandered in the street, grazing the grass that grew along the wide verges in the milky light of the hazy Siberian summer. From the bottom of the escarpment, we walked two blocks to "Freedom House," where the Romanovs had been held. For a governor's residence, it was surprisingly small: a nondescript double story building constructed as an oblong, with the narrow end towards the street. From the street, a flight of three or four shallow steps led up to the main door, framed by a modern-looking portico, its white paint having peeled away to reveal

---

[2] The memorabilia is now on display in a new, permanent museum and memorial to the Romanovs' Tobolsk captivity, opened after my visit in the governor's mansion in the lower town where the family was imprisoned.

the brickwork. The Romanovs' quarters had been on the upper floor. The much larger merchants' mansion next door, a neoclassical building with pilasters, balustrade, oculus and an elegant cast iron balcony, where the members of the Romanovs' retinue lodged, was far more impressive. Opposite the house, an expanse of grass formed a park that was the setting for the small, white Church of the Annunciation, whose small onion dome the Romanovs must have been able to see from their windows, and where they were occasionally granted permission, as we have seen, to attend services. When "Freedom House," currently in a state of disrepair, has been restored, the Romanov exhibits currently on display in the museum will be moved here, to be displayed, as it were, in situ.

෨ ෨ ෨

The next morning, I boarded a clapped-out local bus for the village of Pokrovskoye, a two-and-a-half-hour journey over a hundred or so miles of flat and shrubby Siberian pastureland. As a rule, Western Siberia is a wet, low-slung land of myriad winding rivers, coniferous forest, fens, water meadows and oxbow lakes interconnected, if they're connected at all, by the twisting golden threads of slow-flowing rivers. In Siberia, the rivers drain south to north, towards the Arctic Ocean. In spring, meltwater traveling downstream from the slopes of the high Altai Mountains in the south is blocked at its entrance to the sea by an immense stopper of ice in the sub-Arctic Gulf of Ob, where the thaw arrives much later. For a few weeks, the bursting rivers cause the whole land to become a shallow inland sea. The first Cossacks crossed this vast landlocked territory by boat, as had Nicholas and Alexandra in 1917. Even today, the single-lane highway that the bus trundled along clung to the ribbon of dry land between the absurdly meandering bed of the Tobol (which constantly doubled back on itself) and the patchwork of lakes.

This was the same difficult country that Nicholas and Alexandra had covered by tarantass in 1918. A journey that took them a day and a half, I completed in a morning. After a couple of hours on the bus, a small green bench made of prefabricated concrete and a road sign, "Pokrovskoye," marked Rasputin's village, where Yurovsky had changed horses in 1918. I hauled my pack off the bus and was left alone beside the highway. Nothing but the same featureless, over-exposed landscape stretched away into the distance. Some cattle grazed where an unsealed road met the highway. In the distance, glowing lozenges on the green horizon indicated the existence of farmsteads, their tin roofs glinting painfully in the midday sun. All was silent. I had come to see Rasputin's house for myself.

A couple of hundred yards down the unsealed road, I reached the houses on the edge of the village, a distended assemblage of simple dwellings, consisting of a square of horizontally laid wooden beams, roofed with corrugated iron. The newer examples were laid over a concrete slab. With the sun at its zenith, it was hot, and, with a pack on my back, I was sweating profusely. Where the village center lay, I did not know; no signage showed the whereabouts of Rasputin's house. I needed a guide, and found a man spreading a tarpaulin over a slab of concrete, executing extensions to his house. A large, silver SUV sat parked on the driveway.

I asked whether he knew where I could find a taxi.

"A taxi?" he replied. "There is no taxi. Where do you want to go?" I explained.

"I'll take you myself. I'll just have to duck in and tell my wife where I'm going. Come in and meet her."

He turned to go inside, then swung back and offered me a muscular hand: "Mikhail."

I needed a guide and had found one.

Mikhail's wife was a tall, slim woman with dark hair pulled back in a sporty-looking ponytail. She was wearing a grey tracksuit, as if she had intentions of going to the gym.

"*Dobro pozhalovat*. Welcome to our home," she said, introducing herself as Lyuba.

The television was playing. Watching it together were Mikhail's mother and his sister, Elena, with a five-month-old baby perched on her lap. Gesturing towards a brown-upholstered armchair, Lyuba invited me to sit. As I did so, Mikhail and Lyuba's own daughter, Maria, entered the room. She was eight years old. "How are you?" she asked boldly in English, suppressing a cheeky smile.

As Mikhail's mother made tea in the linoleum-floored kitchen opposite, we made the kind of conversation typical among strangers. Mikhail worked as an electrician, Lyuba in a beauty parlor. They had only one child so far but wanted more, hence the extensions to the family home I had found Mikhail working on. His mother already lived with them, as did Elena, who appeared to be unmarried. As a couple, Mikhail and Lyuba struck me as prosperous in local terms, and optimistic about the future. I detected no embarrassment in living in Pokrovskoye, nor a longing to leave a village in the Siberian countryside for life in the city.

Tea, with jam not milk, was presented, as well as cake and home-made *kvass* (a sweet, slightly fizzy drink of fermented ryebread). At length, the conversation turned to the purpose of my visit to Pokrovskoye.

"You're writing a book on Nicholas II?" Mikhail asked energetically. "I did the *khrestnyi khod* in his honor at Ekaterinburg last year. I'm a believer, Orthodox. To me, he is a saint and a martyr. It was a terrible sin for the Russian people to kill their tsar. But what do they say about him in the West?"

I replied that most historians faulted him for not handing over more power to the Duma, and considered that, ultimately, the Revolution was his fault for frustrating Russia's transition to democracy.

"Ah — democracy!," Mikhail snorted, waving his hand in the air — amused more than impatient: "That's the West's answer to everything: always more democracy. But this is Russia. We are an Orthodox people, and this country is so big. Democracy is not our path. We need a strong leader, a tsar."

I cannot remember how convinced I looked. But it was Mikhail who broke the short silence that descended.

"Come on. Get in the car. Let's go to Rasputin's house!"

ᖇᖇ   ᖇᖇ   ᖇᖇ

Mikhail's vehicle was a ten year old SUV, decked in the usual symbols of Russian patriotism: a white, red and blue Russian flag, with a double-headed eagle super-imposed on its surface, hanging from the central rear-vision mirror. It took only a few minutes to reach Rasputin's house, a large, wooden, two-and-a-half story building larger than many of the modern ones in the village today, but relatively low to the ground, as the lower story was half underground, and the uppermost story was apparently a windowed attic. A modest, colonnaded portico, and intricately carved windows, suggested prosperity and an appreciation for comfort; a high fence surrounded the property. And yet, remarkable in itself, all this is a reconstruction. Still standing as late as 1979, the original had been bulldozed by Soviet authorities fearing foreign interest in the site during the 1980 Moscow Olympics. The building that stands on the site today dates from 1990 (its peeling pale green paint makes it look older than it really is), when the collapsing Communist regime made it possible to acknowledge public interest in Pokrovskoye's most famous son for the first time since the Revolution.

When we arrived, however, the house-museum was shut. On the other side of the fence, someone, a caretaker, was cutting the grass, but Mikhail failed to persuade him to open the house. A granite plinth inscribed with Nicholas's diary entry from April 14/27, 1918 (when he and Alexandra had unexpectedly pulled up in front of the house) had been erected beside the gate. Evidently, someone had wanted to remind visitors that Russia's last tsar had stood where we were standing now.

Not to be deterred, Mikhail suggested that we drive to the other side of town where one of his friends, a teacher in the local school, had assembled a collection of Rasputin-related memorabilia which he planned to display in the private museum he was about to open. I agreed, and a few minutes later we had met his friend.

Ilya was a tall, taciturn man, with thinning, brown hair, and a half-distracted mien. He and Mikhail had been friends since childhood, when they had attended the same village school where Ilya now taught. Having studied history at university, Ilya had also written the only history of Pokrovskoye that existed. He led us upstairs, where several rows of identical veneer display cabinets displayed a carefully arranged collection of photographs, drawings, souvenir postcards, posters, medals and plates. Most of the black and white photographs of the Romanovs were copies of those already publicly available. But each had nonetheless been mounted (at some expense) behind glass on a separate stainless-steel photo frame. There were no labels yet, but the overall meaning was obvious enough to infer from the combination of dignified state portraits of Nicholas as emperor, and shots of the Romanovs at home in Tsarskoye Selo, with modern icons of the family as "Royal Passion-Bearers." In the following room, similar rows of the same veneered display cabinets were filled with a collection of what might as well have been a collection of every book-length publication on Rasputin, in any language, over the past fifty years — Russian, English, French, Spanish, Dutch. Even if Ilya had read only the Russian titles, they represented a considerable investment of time and money in the Siberian "holy man."

The Russian Orthodox Church does not recognize Rasputin as a saint, but a movement exists to promote his case. I asked Ilya whether he thought Rasputin was deserving of such a title: "It is a good question. A mystery. Certainly, it seems he had healing powers that science today cannot explain. But the Russian Orthodox Church has not glorified him as a saint, and I respect that. That's why you see no so-called 'icons' of Rasputin here. The Church forbids them. They are not icons at all. Just pictures that some people venerate on their own private initiative. But, who knows, perhaps one day the Church will change its mind." Ilya's own motives seemed simpler. Rasputin was, after all, the most famous person Pokrovskoye had ever produced, and, it seems, Ilya believed he had spotted a commercial opportunity: "My intention is to open the museum to tourists. In the summer, busloads of Americans, French, Germans, Chinese come to Pokrovskoye now and they all want to know about Rasputin. The house-museum that you tried to visit this morning can't accommodate them all at once, and as that place is a reconstruction, there's nothing there that we can't show them here." I had not seen much evidence of a bustling tourist industry in Pokrovskoye. Rather, Ilya had the look of an enthusiast. At heart, it seemed to me, Ilya was a collector and he wanted to show the world his collection.

At this point, a telephone call interrupted my visit. Olga, a woman I had once met on the bus to Kronstadt, was waiting for me at the bus stop in Tyumen. She was expecting me now. The problem was that Tyumen was fifty miles away, and, chatting away with Ilya and Mikhail, I was about to miss the afternoon bus.

I explained the situation.

"*Spokoino*. Don't worry," Mikhail told me for the second time that day. "Forget about the bus. I'll go home and get Lyuba and we'll drive you to Tyumen."

I protested that being personally chauffeured a distance like that was more than anyone could reasonably ask of a new acquaintance, and that in any case there was no need: I didn't mind catching the bus, and if we hurried, and left for the bus stop straight away, I'd make it in time. But Mikhail dismissed the thought with a wave of his hand.

"How would you have time to say goodbye to the family?" Mikhail replied.

Returning to the house, I was ushered back into the sitting room and presented with another cup of tea and another plate of cake, while Mikhail made preparations for the journey. Lyuba would come too, and, together, she and Mikhail would make the most of the trip to stock up on some hardware Mikhail needed for the renovations.

Half an hour later, we were all in the SUV, Mikhail and Lyuba in the front, and I in the back. On the flat and open highway, Mikhail evidently had no intention of observing the speed limit, and the journey passed quickly. At that time, the war in Eastern Ukraine still dominated the Russian news, and we spent the journey discussing it. Mikhail and his wife were unapologetic about their support for the rebels in the Donbass, and the assistance the Russian government lent them. They scoffed when I told them that the rest of the world thought Russia was a police state and Putin a war criminal. They were young, patriotic, and hopeful about their country's future. They dismissed bad press about Russia as American propaganda. And both young people were in their own ways studies in a certain kind of Russian-ness: Mikhail by being — in a way that contradicted a Western tendency to view religion as gentle, consoling, and feminine — the adherent of an overtly "masculine" and patriotic form of Orthodoxy that didn't shy away from conflict, and which was unapologetically inseparable from the simple fact of being Russian; Lyuba in being outwardly "Western" in her short-sleeved t-shirt, tight jeans and carefully styled hair, and yet inwardly Russian, inasmuch as she lent her support to every one of her husband's religious-nationalist opinions, not, it appeared, as part of a bid to please him, but independently, with a snicker and a glint of the eye at Western (mis)representations of her country all her own.

We pulled up at the petrol station that was the agreed rendezvous with my host in Tyumen.

"I have friends in Vladivostok," Mikhail said, enthusiastically thrusting a piece of paper with their phone number on it as I gathered my pack. (I had told them during our journey that after Tyumen our plan was to double back to Ekaterinburg and then proceed from there across Siberia to the Pacific.) "Don't be afraid to get in touch with them when you get there if you need anything."

Having befriended me only earlier that day, Mikhail had driven me back and forth across Pokrovskoye, arranged entry to his friend's museum, and driven me fifty miles to Tyumen. Now he was proposing to anticipate a need for help 4,000 miles away.

Waiting for me on the curb in Tyumen was Liudmila. A retired doctor and amateur historian, Liudmila was an older, sturdy-looking woman with brown hair and a kind face, whom I had sat next to by chance on the bus between St Petersburg and Kronstadt. While we were crossing the frozen waters of the Gulf of Finland, she had pulled out of her handbag the icon of Rasputin that her father had given her in her youth, and, interested in the project I was researching, she had given me her email address. We had remained in touch ever since. It had been more than a year since we had last seen each other, and I was expecting a friendly greeting. Instead, a stiff look and the tone in her voice betrayed her irritation with the foreigner that she believed had taken her for granted. Having expected me to arrive from Pokrovskoye much earlier, she had arranged, she explained, a half-day's program (pronounced in Russian "pragram," with the "r" trilled and equal stress on each syllable) of meetings and visits in Tyumen. (In Russian, program is a word that implies a certain amount of inflexibility: once agreed between the parties involved, a program cannot be lightly changed or deviated from.) I was both touched and irritated. On one hand, she had not told me about her program; on the other, its mere existence once again reflected a degree of hospitality I had never expected. I apologized, explaining the situation in Pokrovskoye. Her stiff expression softened, the smile returned to her face, and I could see we were friends again. We had to hurry, she said, her sense of duty having revived: Tyumen had a lot to offer someone interested in the Romanovs and she didn't want me to miss it.

Founded in 1587 by the Cossacks, Tyumen is, after Tobolsk, the oldest Russian settlement east of the Urals, spread on the low, flat banks of the Tura River, a sluggish ribbon of water, 1,250 miles from Moscow. Today, Tyumen is the regional hub of Western Siberia's oil and gas industries, and a sizeable city of two million people. A couple of modern towers rise above the low-rise jumble of nineteenth-century timber houses and concrete 1960s apartment blocks.

The first stop on the program of visits that Liudmila had arranged for me in Tyumen was the "Museum on the Wharf," a private museum installed on the upper floor of one of the nineteenth-century timber houses that lined the banks of the Tura, and once the head office of the West Siberian Steamship Company. As we have seen, Nicholas and

Alexandra had passed through Tyumen twice during their exile in Siberia, once in 1917, to board the packet steamer which took them by boat to Tobolsk, and a second time in 1918, when they arrived, shaken, by tarantass. The Museum on the Wharf was connected to the first of these events, located as it was at the spot on the river where Nicholas, Alexandra and their children had transferred, in the middle of the night in August 1917, from the train that had brought them from Tsarskoye Selo to the *Rus*.[3]

In the Romanovs' day, the railway ran all the way down to the river. Today, it no longer does, and the museum stands instead in an overgrown garden, where a billboard-sized image of Nicholas, Alexandra, and their children, faded from its exposure to the elements, welcomes the visitor. Waiting in the garden to receive us was the nervous, bird-like Polina. A slight, raven-haired woman with dark eyes and thin lips, wearing a blue singlet underneath a sleeveless denim jacket with a short denim mini skirt, she didn't at all resemble the heavy-set, kerchiefed woman I had become used to seeing at Romanov shrines. But she was the museum's curator, and, explaining the museum's history, she beckoned us into the house. Inside, on the upper floor, a bric-a-brac of mounted newspaper clippings, historical photographs, cargo nets, anchors, logbooks, and lading certificates from the turn of the last century recalled the history of the Western Siberian Steam Ship Company.

Downstairs, the ground-floor room was dedicated to the Romanovs. On one wall, a row of portraits printed from Wikipedia showed every Russian ruler from Vladimir of Kiev to Nicholas II, while, on the opposite side of the room, a heavy wooden desk had been spread with dark green felt, in imitation, apparently, of Nicholas II's writing desk in the Alexander Palace. On this desk, Romanov family albums (filled, again, with photographs found on the internet) stood open for the public to leaf through in homage to the same naïve, *interaktivnyi* spirit I had seen in the museum in Tobolsk. Nearby, display cabinets presented more commonly available photographs of Nicholas, Alexandra, and their children alongside more recent icons of the family together, as the sainted Royal Passion-bearers and objects of veneration. Many of these appeared to be the gifts of Orthodox pilgrims, not only from Russia, who had come to venerate the memory of the family's brief presence on the property. One had left a Serbian flag behind. Nothing, but for the modern icons, was original but everything, it seemed, was well-loved.

Of course, seen through the critical lens of Western museology, the ensemble, like most private museums in Russia, laughably lacked any museological value. But as a testament to its own time and place, it was eloquent: in Russia, the fabric of local and national memory that had been torn up and shredded in the Revolution was now being sewn

---

[3] See Nicholas II, August 4, 1917, in Diary (2), 647.

back together (whether according to its original pattern, or to one that more properly reflected the needs and concerns of its restorers), and private museums like this one, and Ilya's in Pokrovskoye, represented an amateur's bid to stitch some of it back together. That bid was to be applauded, not mocked or despised.

Then there was Polina, our guide herself. As the museum's unpaid curator, she had been given the use of a corner of the large ground floor for a display of artefacts connected to the woman who was without doubt her personal heroine: Grand Duchess Olga Aleksandrovna, Nicholas II's youngest sister, who, in 1916, divorced the imperial cousin to whom she had been unhappily married, and, shortly later, wed the commoner, Peter Kulikovsky. After the Revolution, the couple and their two children went into exile, first in Denmark, and then in Canada. Olga was a watercolorist, and Polina had hung a wall in the museum with copies of her work: a garden with flowers, a child eating breakfast, Copenhagen's Amelienborg Palace, scenes from the modest farm she and Kulikovsky worked for a while after the Revolution in the Danish countryside. Despite Olga's lost station in life, she and Kulikovsky remained faithful to each other to the end.

The story clearly spoke to the romantic Polina. "Love is the most important thing in life," she breathed airily, gazing at the wall of Olga's watercolors. A few years earlier, her heroine's now aged daughter (also named Olga after mother) had visited the Museum on the Wharf, and Polina proudly showed me pictures taken at this semi-royal visit.

Having now seen all there was to see in the museum, we inspected the monuments in the garden. The first of these was a slab of grey granite, topped with a triple-barred Orthodox cross, and mounted with the modern Russian coat-of-arms and a lithograph engraving of an icon of the Romanovs as Royal Passion-Bearers. "Pray for us, Royal Martyrs!" it read. Nearby, a plaque mounted on a second slab of granite lying, grave-stone-like, on the ground at the foot of the cross recorded the particulars of the Romanovs' brief sojourn on the property. The Romanovs had only been in Tyumen for a few hours at the most. But just as in Tobolsk and Pokrovskoye, their passing presence has been recorded and memorialized.

໑ ໑ ໑

From the Museum on the Wharf, we drove back into town, where, in a narrow office in a 1970s steel and concrete building, Liudmila introduced me to a middle-aged man of medium height who was ataman of the Tyumen district Cossack host.[4] As loyal to the monarchy as his Cossack

---

[4] The Cossacks, conquerors of Siberia, lived for centuries as a caste of hereditary light cavalry, proud of their horsemanship and jealous of the honor of the Tsar, in self-governing Cossack villages under the headship of elected local, district and provincial atamans, and

ancestors, the ataman, named Boris, was evidently devoted to the Royal Passion-bearers, and pulled books, icons, and other objects connected to their veneration off the shelves around us. Among these was a photograph of the icon of Nicholas II, which the local Cossacks revered: the so-called "Wonder-working Royal Cossack Icon of Nadym" (a Cossack town in the northern Urals). Painted with a narrow, angular face, and wearing his 1896 coronation regalia, Russia's last monarch looked out at the viewer from underneath the miter-like imperial crown, the imperial orb and scepter in either hand. Over an ermine-lined cape, embroidered with the Russian double-headed eagle of the Imperial coat of arms, he wore the diamond-studded collar of the Order of St Andrew the First-Called. It was an icon less, perhaps, of Nicholas II, than of the *idea of the tsar* we have been tracing.

Then, Boris pointed to what looked like a dark, tear-shaped effusion, beneath Nicholas's left eye.

"You see, there, the icon is weeping. How, I don't know. It was a miracle. I saw it with my own eyes!"

The miracle, he said, was a token of the tears that Nicholas was shedding for Russia in heaven. Nicholas's crown and orb, too, he said, also occasionally emitted a myrrh-like substance.

The icon was the Urals' Cossacks' most sacred possession, and Boris and his band of Cossacks had made it their mission to carry the image across Russia. He showed me photographs of himself and his men in military-style khakis, carrying the icon in procession across Red Square and down Nevsky Prospekt in St Petersburg, as well as in the main public squares and streets of provincial Russian towns.

During some of these processions, further miracles had taken place, Boris said. For example, in 2003, Boris and his Cossacks had been carrying it in procession for the centenary of the canonization of St Serafim of Sarov, at the monastery at Diveyevo (the same monastery to which Nicholas, Alexandra and the rest of the court had traveled for

---

valuable to the imperial government as a largely self-sustaining border force: Hosking, *People and Empire*, 11–12. Liable at any time to be called for war service, the Cossacks fed themselves off their own lands in peacetime, and rode into war on their own horses. In the Far East, new "hosts" (as a Cossack band was called) were still being founded along the Chinese border in the 1890s. The Cossacks were traditionally seen as one of the pillars of the tsarist regime, and in the aftermath of their victory in the Civil War of 1918–21, the Bolsheviks implemented a program of "de-Cossackization" that attempted to wipe out Cossack identity, by clearing Cossack villages and depriving families of their lands and horses. Those who resisted were shot. During the Second World War, some of the taboo against Cossack identity was lifted for the sake of tapping the Cossacks' skills as horsemen. But still penalties remained. See Peter Holquist, "'Conduct merciless mass terror': Decossackization on the Don in 1919," *Cahiers du monde russe* 38 (1997): 127–62. Only since the fall of Communism has being a Cossack become something that it is no longer necessary to hide. On the contrary, the rehabilitation of the traditionally pious and patriotic Cossacks goes hand-in-hand with the revival of Orthodoxy and other broadly conservative and right-wing movements in Putin's Russia.

the original canonization festivities in 1903), when, suddenly, St Serafim himself appeared among the marchers. An onlooker having captured the miracle on her camera, Boris showed me the photographic record of the apparition: a blaze of light in what might have been the vague form of an old man hovered just above the ground, as a procession of Boris's Cossacks held the three-meter-high icon of Nicholas aloft on their shoulders. Without wanting, as I didn't, to dismiss the possibility of a miracle, it seemed to me that none of the men themselves wore expressions that suggested they had noticed the apparition, which might also have been a simple over-exposure of the lens.

Then, Boris said, describing another alleged miracle, a parish priest in the village of Golovshchino saw an apparition of Nicholas II above the altar, holding a Cross, and with his heart pierced with six arrows, while celebrating the Divine Liturgy on the Royal Passion-bearers' feast day. The priest painted an icon depicting the scene, and Boris and his men later visited the village to venerate it.

Boris continued leafing through his albums. Photographs of Boris's men alongside bearded hierarchs — bishops, archimandrites, patriarchs — in flowing black clerical robes revealed his Cossacks' close relationship with the Russian Orthodox Church. A mixed bag of veterans, volunteers and amateurs, Boris's Cossacks also enjoyed close relations with Russia's professional armed forces. One picture showed them in the breakaway republic of Abkhazia, having mounted an icon of Alexei on a Russian tank. Another showed regular Russian soldiers standing to attention in front of a tank mounted with the icons of Alexei, Serafim of Sarov and Sergei of Radonezh, while two Cossacks in dress uniform and a Russian priest stood alongside, and a Russian flag fluttered in the breeze behind them.

I asked Boris why icons of Alexei, a sick and apparently gentle boy of only thirteen when he was shot, figured so prominently in his album. He explained that among the Cossacks, the cult of Alexei had a special place.

"In Imperial Russia, the Tsar's eldest son was by tradition Supreme Ataman of All the Cossack Host," said Boris, taking a laminated cardboard image of Alexei off the bookshelf to his left and placing it in my hands to look at. With his round face and dark hair and eyes, Alexei always resembled his Anglo-German mother more than his father, and the icon captures this element of his historical likeness. Dressed in the white, gold-trimmed uniform of the Supreme Ataman, the teenage boy holds a Cross in his right hand, looking at a point beyond the view, with the golden disc of a halo behind his head, and the white-handled hilt of a ceremonial dagger protruding from his belt.

"Through our allegiance to him, all the different regional Cossack hosts were united. That's why, alongside his father, we venerate Alexei especially: he was the last one who united us all. He is a symbol of Holy Rus — sovereign, Orthodox, powerful — that we Cossacks have pledged to die for."

Turning the icon over, I found a prayer to Alexei printed on the reverse:

> *Holy branch of the Root of the Romanovs,*
> *O Passion-bearing Tsesarevich Aleksei!*
> *On earth you were crowned with illness and tears,*
> *and, behold, even your own blood!*
> *Now standing in heaven before Christ the Tsar [i.e. "Christ the King"]*
> *pray that He would establish a Lawgiver in the Russian land*
> *and that we would understand how to be men.*

"Take it," he said, pushing the image of Alexei into my hands. "I want you to keep it."

🙙 🙙 🙙

With all the two meetings in our appointed program completed, Liudmila took me to the waterfront. In mid-summer, the spring melt was a distant memory and the Tura's flow was sluggish and muddy. But receipts for the sale of Western Siberian oil and gas had recently paid for the construction of a landscaped promenade and foreshore embankment.

"Just a few years ago the place was a dump. In fact, where we're standing now used to look exactly the way it still does on the other side," Liudmila said, pointing first to the new paving beneath our feet and then to the grubby beach backed by a tangle of scrub on the opposite bank.

"I used to go swimming here as a girl. People still do that. But until they built the embankment, nobody would have dreamt of walking here at night. It was too dangerous, too unpleasant," she said, choosing her words carefully to convey more than she wished to say directly.

I looked around. It was close to nine o'clock. The sun was a golden disk slowly descending towards the horizon. It had been a hot day, and the evening was warm, the sky burnt pink. Couples strolled arm in arm past us, enjoying the cool of the embankment's lower terrace. Children weaved through the crowd on rollerblades while their parents followed behind.

"I wanted to bring you here to show you that our town is civilized," Liudmila said.

Elsewhere in town, critics of the government could doubtless be found who would dismiss the sums of money invested in the amenities around us as a cynical gesture designed to buy off local citizens while Putin and his friends in Moscow stole Siberia's birthright. Politics in Russia was like that. But Liudmila was proud of the new embankment. It struck me as a sign to her of how life was improving, approaching that standard of amenity she and other Russians increasingly knew first-hand, from weekends in Paris and Milan and winter vacations in Turkey, Egypt, and Thailand.

"And it's good that they haven't allowed bars and cafes," Liudmila added, as if in reference to scenes she had witnessed on holiday in Western Europe. "This is an area for being active, not eating and drinking. Besides, if there were café tables everywhere, where would the rollerbladers go?"

Of course, on a practical level, she was right. But on another I couldn't help but think that she was missing the point, and that a certain naïve and distinctly Russian distrust of open-ended signs of sociability was reasserting itself. If people gathered, it was only right that they do so for the sake of a common defined purpose (a church, a Cossack host, a ballet school, a chess or football club), not for idle talk and aimless distraction. Like many Russians, Liudmila, it seems, wanted the reassurance of knowing that the people in her town looked as though they were living the same way as everyone else in the world, but in her heart of hearts didn't want them to stop being themselves: Russians.

As we strolled on the warm summer evening, she told me about her life. She had six children — four girls, two boys — spread around the country. A daughter was in St Petersburg, married to a prosperous businessman, another in Moscow. One son was in the army, another studying to be an engineer. Only the youngest, a daughter, was still at home. She herself was retired after a career as a doctor. She had grown up in Tyumen in Soviet times, but her family was originally from a village not far from Pokrovskoye. Peasant farmers like Rasputin, her grandparents had been moderately prosperous before the Revolution. The family had a horse, a few cattle, a two-story house, and an electric sewing machine. Accused of being kulaks, they lost it all in the dekulakization campaigns first introduced by Stalin in 1929. As a priest, one of her grandfathers was a double target for repression. They lost the cattle, the horses, and the house, but the sewing machine they buried in the yard. It was with a sense of personal triumph that Liudmila said that when Communism finally collapsed, she and her mother (who had been a girl when they buried it) went back to the village and dug it back up again. It was ruined, of course, but nonetheless a victory of sorts against the system that had upended their lives. To this day, she remained opposed to Communism — to its censorship, its atheism, and desire to control everything — and was surprised to learn that people outside Russia might imagine that Russians would want that system back again. She greeted my description of the re-Stalinization thesis popular among Western pundits with disbelief.

Certainly, what I had done and seen over the past few days in Tobolsk, Pokrovskoye, and Tyumen would have been impossible in Soviet times. Memory of the exile of Russia's imperial family was suppressed, and anyone who had tried to do then what I had in the past few weeks ran the real risk of arrest. Outwardly, for two or three generations, Trotsky had been right: Russia had vomited up the monarchy so that, ostensibly, it could never again crawl back down people's throats. But time had proved Trotsky wrong. Russia was not a monarchy, and it may never, formally, be one again. But it seems the ideal of the tsar could not be expunged from Russian culture, and where that culture, nourished by the Orthodox Church, had survived, the theocratic principle, the ideal of the tsar as God's regent, had revived. And Liudmila, for whatever reason, had helped me plot some of the compass points of its local revival.

I arrived by train in Ekaterinburg at the same station ("Ekaterinburg 1"), where, a hundred years before, the crowd had bayed for Nicholas and Alexandra to be turned over to them. Renamed "Sverdlovsk," after Sverdlov, the local boy who, having risen to become chairman of the Bolshevik Central Executive Committee, had conveyed Lenin's tacit approval for Nicholas's murder to the Urals Soviet, Ekaterinburg-Sverdlovsk possessed in early Soviet times a certain cachet, as the city that had put Russia's last tsar to death. In the 1920s and 1930s, visiting Soviet dignitaries were given triumphant tours of the (still standing) Ipatiev House. In 1979, however, the worrying arrival of the Orthodox pilgrims at the site led the local Communist Party boss (a big, gung-ho man called Boris Yeltsin) to order the house's demolition. Now, with a population of 2.4 million, and rechristened Ekaterinburg, the city is the fourth-largest in Russia, and the undisputed capital of the Urals. But the surrounding district is still called Sverdlovsk, a compromise that allows the multiple Russias — tsarist, Soviet, and post-Soviet — to limp along together.

It was July 16, the eve of the Royal Passion-bearers' feast day. Although it was the middle of summer, the city had just been drenched by a violent downpour. As I crossed the city in a cab, the rain eased to a cold and steady drizzle that remained for much of the next three days. Not only my first but virtually my *only* views of Ekaterinburg, were of a morose and somber city under permanently leaden skies, where everything seemed to be a different shade of gunmetal. As mentioned earlier, the River Iset that runs through the city was turned into a lake in the nineteenth century, around which, by the time of the Revolution, rows of impressive mansions had been built for the city's rich. The old Ipatiev House had not been in the first of these rows, however, and to reach the site where it once stood, I walked uphill across a park along a path between beds of red, white and cream-colored pansies doing their best to look cheerful as the rain set back in, and I pulled the hood of my raincoat back over my head.

Today, on the hillside site once occupied by the Ipatiev House, there stands the *Khram-na-krovi* (the "Church on the Blood"), a neo-Russian Style church, consisting of white concrete slabs, with a tall central helmet dome topped with an Orthodox cross, and four smaller helmet domes, with similar crosses, surrounding. In front of the building, a temporary stage with a tented roof had been erected on a lawn laid with beds of pansies, while, to either side of it, metal frames the size of roadside billboards had been hung with large sheets of canvas emblazoned with huge photographs of the Romanovs. From where I stood, the two elder daughters, Olga and Tatiana, looked down on the street, while beside them was a canvas with a picture of all four grand duchesses, and another with a photograph showing their young parents admiring one of them as an infant on Alexandra's lap. Directly beside the stage was a similar canvas screen, this time showing an icon of the family as Royal Passion-Bearers, while another, some distance away, provided a daily guide to the events of Ekaterinburg's "Royal [Russian: *tsarist*] Days" festival, held annually to mark the anniversary of the Royal Passionbearers' murder, which was approaching.

On the street in front of the stage, a queue of mud-spattered tourist coaches disgorged pious women in the standard garb of Orthodox pilgrims: plain ankle-length (or, at least, below the knee) skirt, boots, zipped jacket, anorak, or parka, handbag, and (usually floral) scarf covering the hair. A handful of men in tracksuits, denim jackets and army surplus gear were sprinkled among them. One wore an icon around his neck with webbing tape, the same way Vasily had in Mogilev. But mostly the crowd was female, and, I assumed, from out of town. Not only the condition of the buses they had arrived in, but the air of provincial simplicity, not to say poverty, that surrounded them suggested that they did not live in the high-rise apartments from the early 2000s that stood beyond them at the end of the street in front of me.

I followed the pilgrims as they made their way past the tented stage on to a terrace at the foot of the church building. Here were more canvas billboards of the Romanovs: Nicholas in military outfit at an army review, Alexei as a boy in his sailor suit with playmates, Alexandra and the grand duchesses in nursing uniforms, Nicholas and Alexandra together at a state ceremony in the Kremlin. Sometimes these canvases quoted their letters and diaries, too. The most moving of these was a passage from a letter written by the eldest grand duchess, Olga, on her father's behalf, during their house arrest in Tobolsk in early 1918, and sent from there to the family's friends and supporters.

> *Father asks that it be made known to all those who have remained loyal to him that they are not to take revenge for him, for he has forgiven all and prays for all and [he also asks] that they remember*

that the evil that is now in the world will become stronger. But evil will not conquer evil, only love.[5]

If the letter is authentic, it is the most beautiful Nicholas ever wrote (or, as the case seems to have been, dictated). In 1996, the Canonization Commission cited it to support its recommendation that Nicholas be canonized as a saint for the Christian virtue he had achieved in captivity after the abdication.

Consecrated in 2010, the *Khram-na-krovi* ("Church on the Blood") consists of an upper church and lower (crypt) church stacked one on top of the other. By the entrance, a monumental bronze sculpture depicts Nicholas, Alexandra and their children descending from the upper to the lower floors of the Ipatiev House a few moments before the massacre. Clustered around a giant Cross positioned symbolically in the center of the stairwell, Nicholas, in military uniform, holds Alexei in his arms (the boy's head resting on his father's left shoulder) while, either side of Nicholas, the two elder girls, Olga and Tatiana, face their future murderers. At the top of the staircase, Alexandra and the couple's two younger daughters, Maria and Anastasia, face the modern church, their backs to the viewer. The art critic might fault the sculpture for sentimentality or melodrama. But, *in situ*, this bronze of a family moments before its annihilation is powerful and, again, I found myself moved. Then, following the example of the people around me, I entered the lower church. Incorporating the floor of the basement room in which the family was shot into its fabric, this lower church really is, quite literally, "on the blood." Above the door, a notice in large golden lettering appealed to the family: *"Royal Passion-Bearers, pray to God for us!"*

       ᴘᴏ̃   ᴘᴏ̃   ᴘᴏ̃

Inside, the air was dense with the heat and smell of burning candles, warm bodies, and overclothes still damp from the earlier rain. Just inside the door, a queue started. I joined it, not knowing what lay at the end of it: the ceiling was low, and the glow from the bronze chandeliers was mostly thrown upwards to the painted ceiling above, leaving us below to stand in a tunnel of dim light. Around me was a sea of kerchiefs and plastic anoraks. A few of their wearers spoke quietly, checking the details of the festival's events with pilgrims around them, relating to one another correctly but without airs and graces, like distant members of a single extended family that meets only so often. The atmosphere was pious, respectful, and even affectionate, solemn but not grave. No priest or clergyman was present to direct events because

---

[5] The typed text of the letter can be found, in Russian, in the Romanov-related materials gathered in A. V. Syroboiarskii, *Skorbnaia Pamiatka* (unnamed publisher, 1928). But it appears there without authenticating archival information.

none, it seemed, was needed. In answer to a question that I had asked myself at the very beginning of this long journey, it seems to me that the veneration of the sainted Romanovs belongs at least as much to the people as it does to the Church's priests and bishops. Nobody was forcing these people to be there; the family they had come to venerate were *theirs*; they loved them. If this was so, then, remarkably, the proverbial "wall" that separated Nicholas and Alexandra from the Russian people during their lifetimes has dissolved — and the "truth" manifest in the veneration of Nicholas II would be that the quintessentially Russian, but fashionably disparaged, "myth" of a mystical communion between the tsar and people was never the "fabrication" alleged, almost without exception, by the opponents of tsarism, but a real aspiration pursued in good faith in Russian history by ruler and people after all.[6]

The lower church was shaped like a T with the left-hand top bar removed. Thus, directly in front of us, an iconostasis indicated the presence of the sanctuary and the altar within for celebrating the Divine Liturgy. Only two rows high, on account of the low ceiling, the iconostasis seemed to have been made from wood overlaid with plaster, and then inlaid with bright white tiles. Shiny white stucco pilasters with gold highlights served as frames for eight icons on the lower tier, and eight on the tier above. The warm, flickering light from the mass of candles in the candlestands in front of them danced on their gold-leaf background, while winged seraphim and cherubim painted on the ceiling gazed down from above. In the center of the lower tier of icons, the Royal Doors, through which the priests come and go from the sanctuary, showed the traditional themes of the Annunciation and four Evangelists, while, to either side, traditional images of Christ as Pantokrator, and Mary as the Mother of God, with Christ on her lap, guarded the way to the altar. But to either side of them, six further icons showed the sainted figures the pilgrims had come to venerate: to the left of the Virgin, Alexandra, Tatiana, and Maria had an icon of their own, while to the right of Christ were Nicholas and Alexei (sitting on his father's lap) together, Olga, and Anastasia. Each was dressed in seventeenth-century Muscovite-style robes, and each wore a martyr's crown and halo. Instead of the martyr's crown, the icon of Nicholas had him wearing the Cap of Monomakh, and Alexei, as tsarevich, a diadem. The tier of eight icons above them shows the very events of Holy Week and Pascha (Easter), from the Raising of Lazarus to Christ's Crucifixion, Descent from the Cross, and Resurrection that were being commemorated during the very days when Nicholas, Alexandra, and Maria were first interned in the Ipatiev House.

---

[6] On this famous subject, see Michael Cherniavsky, *Tsar and People: Studies in Russian Myths* (New Haven, CT: Yale University Press, 1961).

In front of this icon stood a dozen or so women in kerchiefs, who lit candles and bowed, saying their prayers. But the slow-moving queue of pilgrims that I was part of did not stop here, but snaked into a large alcove to the right. There, more full-length icons of the Romanovs in medieval robes had been erected in niches carved into white and grey marble. In front of them were wooden showcases containing curios. These included the small, laminated icon of the Royal Passion-Bearers that had orbited the Earth 240 times during the fifteen days it spent among the handful of items taken into space by a Russian cosmonaut aboard the International Space Station in 2007, and the hand-drawn stencil of Nicholas in a navy cap and uniform, dating from the first legal celebration of the Romanovs' feast in Ekaterinburg in 1989. To a different category belonged the reliquary, decked with flowers, that contained a portion of the remains of St Serafim of Sarov. Pilgrims bowed before this reliquary, while others circulated behind the relics, crossing themselves in front of the icons in the marble niches.

By now, we were very close to our goal. Ahead of me, in the candle-lit half-light, I saw three steps leading up to a platform. From there, there was a view into a small room screened off from the platform by a low, bronze rail, with an opening in the middle in the shape of a miniature Royal Doors, topped with a Russian imperial crown. Framing the walls and archway of this room was a mass of flowers, and, on the far wall, an icon showing two angels in triumph beside an empty cross. This was the floor of the basement room of the Ipatiev House where the Romanovs and four remaining staff were murdered, amid scenes of appalling horror, on the night of July 16/17, 1918.

෴   ෴   ෴

In silence, in single file, by candlelight in the far corner of the crypt church beneath Ekaterinburg's *Khram-na-krovi*, I and the pilgrims behind me approached the massacre scene. Having ascended the steps leading up to the platform, the pilgrims dropped to their knees. Crossing themselves, and bowing their necks to kiss the floor, which, having been soaked in the saints' blood, is itself a first-order relic, they shuffled sideways on their knees until they had reached the other end of the platform, then rose and descended the three steps down on foot. Every available space—above the platform, on the columns to its sides, and across the top of the nearby icons—was hung with red, pink, and white flowers, while a mass of beeswax candles released their sweet, honey smell into the air and threw warm, flickering light on the walls. Those who hadn't finished their devotions continued in the space at the bottom of the steps, kneeling with heads bent in the direction of the platform, praying. Before long, it was my turn, too.

Although they are clearly the central object of veneration, the former imperial family are not the only ones either to have died in the Ipatiev House basement or to be venerated as saints there today. On the wall on the other side of the lower church, there were black and white photographic portraits of the four "faithful companions" (as they're called) who perished with the imperial family in the room on the other side of the chamber I was now in: the maid Anna Demidova (1878–1918), the valet Aleksei Trupp (1856–1918), the cook Ivan Kharitonov (1870–1918), and the family physician, the now sainted Dr Evgeny Botkin (1865–1918). This was their *podvig* ("feat") too.

In this corner of the building, a spiral staircase connected the upper and lower churches. In a detail that struck me as touching, twenty or so mainly older women lay resting, in the cavity created by the staircase, on rubber sleeping rolls they had spread on the floor. On the other side of them were trestle tables with large plastic drums of water and thin plastic bags of *pirozhki* (pastries stuffed with cabbage and egg or fish). Wherever these pilgrims were from, home was not near enough for them to return to and rest there; neither, unlike me, did they have a hotel to retire to. Instead, like pilgrims for centuries, they looked to the Church to provide everything; and because they had not asked for comfort, only a pilgrimage's essentials, the Church did so. For many in modern Russia, Orthodoxy isn't just the warm light of a candle in front of a gold-leafed icon: it is also lying side-by-side with one's fellow pilgrims, amid all the odors of warm human bodies, on a cheap sleeping roll on a church floor.

⁘ ⁘ ⁘

Exiting the lower church, I returned to the terrace overlooking the skyline of the modern city, and followed a flight of steps to the entrance of the upper church. Inside, perhaps a hundred people were milling about in groups of two or three, while a queue of pilgrims, thirty or forty-strong, waited patiently to kiss the festal icon of the Romanovs erected on a stand in front of the iconostasis. In the corners of the building, smaller queues had also formed behind the black-robed priests hearing confessions: people were preparing for that evening's Holy Communion. The upper church's dimensions were completely different from those of the lower, crypt church. Here, the ceiling was high, a funnel-effect of inverted domes and half domes meeting the viewer's eye when he or she looked up. The surfaces of the inverted archways thus created had been painted with scenes from the Gospels, primarily in shades of white, brown and blue backed with gold leaf: the Nativity, the Crucifixion, various miracles. And at the highest point, underneath the helmet dome that externally crowned the building, the stern countenance of Christ the Pantokrator, King of the Universe, his brows furrowed, his mouth set and his eyes locked in a piercing glare, stared down over the scene below. The floor, meanwhile, was laid with patterns of different-colored marble — white, dark green, dark red — of which material, too, authentic or faux, the gleaming white iconostasis had also been made. It was inlaid with a stunning array of full-length icons backed by gold: Christ, the Virgin, two archangels, and, in another touching detail, in honor of the city we found ourselves in, St Catherine ("holy Ekaterina").

At first sight, the presence of the Romanovs in this iconostasis was muted: none of the personal icons I had seen downstairs were visible. But there was another, perhaps more interesting. It is a rule of thumb in an Orthodox church that the icon of the building's patron (the saint or sacred event after which the church takes its name) can be found to the right of the Royal Doors as the viewer faces the icon screen. In the *Khram-na-krovi*, this icon showed hundreds of tiny, almost cartoon-like figures in serried rows, stacked one on top of each other, beneath a figure of Christ flanked by the Virgin and St John the Baptist in intercession at the top. Beginning on the line immediately below this with images of the Kievan princes Sts Boris and Gleb, this catalogue of holy figures is a symbolic representation of Russian history as sacred history, the history of its saints: the formal dedication of the *Khram-na-krovi* is to "all the saints resplendent in the land of Rus." This icon served as their collective image.

And from *this* icon the Romanovs were far from excluded. On the contrary, towards the center, seven rows down from the top and five up from the bottom, at approximate eye-level to the viewer, clothed in white, and wearing the golden crowns of martyrdom, stood Russia's Royal Passion-bearers. And in view of their central position in Russian history as sacred history, if such an icon tells us anything it is perhaps that — *contra* Marx and a whole modern school of history that has followed him — we misread history (*all* history, not only Russia's) if we fail to perceive its providential theo-centricity. What, after all, was the theocratic principle at the heart of tsarism but, to paraphrase Del Noce, the "affirmation of the divine governance of the world," the sign and secondary agent of that Providence that always was, as Lenin well knew, the "opposite of the idea of revolution, aimed at achieving complete human governance"?[7] The regime — the Russian *teokratia* — that gave political form to that affirmation may have collapsed. The icon reminds us, nonetheless, that the revolutionary logic of atheism that would both *vindicate* and *be vindicated by* that collapse does not, in fact, stand vindicated. The Ipatiev House, where Russia's last theocratic

---

[7] The thought regarding Providence is from Del Noce, "Latent metaphysics within contemporary politics," in *Crisis of Modernity*, 63.

ruler was murdered, is now a church; the family whose bodies disappeared in the forest has not been erased, but glorified. Despite the Bolsheviks' best efforts, Providence has not been unseated. And there, by the door, in the last bay of the iconostasis in the upper church, I found an icon of the Romanovs: on a backdrop of shimmering gold leaf, full-length figures of Nicholas, Alexandra and Alexei, crowned and dressed in the robes of medieval Muscovy, stand surrounded by the similarly crowned and robed grand duchesses. Significantly for our theme, on the wall adjacent frescoed images of the Emperor (St) Constantine and his mother, St Helen, looked out with the sainted Romanovs on the interior of the church—the first Christian theocrat and the last, the commissioners of the *Khram-na-krovi* having apparently drawn the same connection between them, the period they framed, and the ideal they represented, as had Bulgakov.

Leaving the upper church, I found myself again outside. Gusts of wind whipped around the building, but the rain had stopped. Following the stairs down to the lower terrace, I passed a tall, white-haired man standing lonely guard with the Romanov imperial standard that he had tied to a black plastic rod and slashed to the shaft of a shopping trolley. The standard's white, yellow and black horizontal bands flapped wildly in the wind. On the next terrace, half a dozen people venerated an icon of the Romanovs erected on a stand decorated with flowers, despite the inhospitable weather. A young man knelt and touched his head to the ground. A little further along, two women posed for a photograph in front of a screen playing a digital slideshow of black and white Romanov photographs.

~ ~ ~

It was close to eleven o'clock at night when I set out to return to the *Khram-na-krovi*. The gusty wind that had whipped the city during the day had gone, but the drizzle had returned, and the Ekaterinburg night was cold. In an hour or so, the Divine Liturgy in honor of the Romanovs' feast day would commence. Yet as I made my way back on foot to the *Khram-na-krovi*, few citizens of the modern city seemed to take any notice of the event. The streets were dark and quiet. Not only that, but "Red" Ekaterinburg still seemed hale and hearty: at a curbside kiosk on the corner where Lenin Avenue met the similarly Bolshevik-named 1905 Street, *The Urals Worker*, the newspaper of the still-active regional Communist Party, was still being sold, while, opposite the 1950s Stalinist Gothic House of Soviets, Lenin still stood on his plinth. What, then, I asked myself, was I returning now in the middle of the night to see at the *Khram-na-krovi*—the same few hundred people I had seen at the shrine earlier that afternoon, gathered now for a commemorative Mass? Was that really worth this effort, in the dark, in the rain, and in the cold? Unable to let Trotsky win so easily, however, I packed an umbrella and drinking bottle into a rucksack, and stepped out into the night.

I caught my first sight of the church's floodlit profile against the black of the night while still a few blocks away. Then I heard the amplified sound of the liturgy as broadcast by loudspeakers, followed by the voice of a man speaking into a microphone. It was the voice of the Bishop of Ekaterinburg, saying festal Mass for the crowd of people gathered in the street in front of the stage erected in front of the *Khram-na-krovi*. Whereas, earlier in the day, I had had no trouble reaching the church directly, now the whole six-laned street in front of it was densely packed with onlookers, watching the bishop and accompanying clergy perform the liturgy on the stage itself, or on the large screens erected either side of it. Some carried Russian flags, others the old white, yellow and black imperial standard I had seen earlier. *Za Veru, Za Tsarya, Za Otyechestvo* ("For the Faith, Tsar, and Fatherland") read the words superimposed on top of one of these standards. Others held triple-barred Orthodox crosses in their hands. From the boards erected all along the terrace, halfway up the slope the church sat on, the Romanovs looked out over a throng of perhaps two or three thousand people. Meanwhile, to the right of the stage, a cluster of scarlet processional icons — of Christ, the Virgin, the sainted Nicholas II, the whole family of "Royal Passion-Bearers" — rose over the heads of the crowd, trimmed in golden tassels, while a posse of young, athletic-looking men in tracksuits and puffer jackets took turns lending a shoulder to a litter-shaped construction: two long parallel beams of wood (for resting on the shoulder) threshed together with two shorter horizontal beams, mounted with a triangular shaped "bed" for two large icons placed back-to-back. The forward-facing image was a historical portrait of Nicholas in dress uniform; that on the rear was Alexandra, in gown and jewels. Together with the processional icons, this "litter" would indicate the head of the procession about to begin. The people I had seen at the *Khram-na-krovi* earlier in the day had been mostly old, poor, and female; the midnight hour and physicality of the procession, it seems, had added to their number the young, the male, and the middle class.

Towards two o'clock in the morning, the time when, almost a hundred years before, the gunmen had opened fire on the Romanovs, the Liturgy reached its climax, and the Bloodless Sacrifice was offered. Then, when the rite had concluded, the bishop, resplendent in a black robe embroidered in gold, and wearing a golden miter, gave a homily. Notwithstanding the macabre events of which the recently concluded Liturgy was a commemoration, he was in a jubilant mood. He reminded

those gathered to regard July 17 not as the moment of the Romanovs'
death, but as the moment of their birth into eternal life. "Nicholas II
not only *was* Russia's tsar," he told the crowd: "He *is* Russia's tsar still.
He is still with us, watching us, praying for Russia in heaven." When
he had finished, music began playing from the loudspeakers; as if taking the bishop at his word, the crowd sang the old imperial anthem,
Bozhye, Tsarya khrani ("God Save the Tsar"). A few minutes later, we
were moving. Just as their executioners loaded the Romanovs' bodies
on to trucks and transported them in the early hours of the morning
to the forest on Ekaterinburg's outskirts, so, in the same early hours
of the morning, we, as pilgrims, would retrace that route. The only
difference was that we would do so on foot. Russians call this kind
of penitential procession a *krestnyi khod*, or "way of the Cross," an
act of faith and penitence for sins committed and forgiveness sought.
The changing peloton of young men bearing Nicholas and Alexandra's
images on the timber litter went first.

At the conclusion of the Liturgy, the crowd was still a couple of
thousand strong. All gathered in one place in the middle of the night,
this felt like a numerous enough crowd if one was part of it, but it
only represented a tiny fraction of Ekaterinburg's inhabitants. But like
the Pied Piper in Bremen, this initial two or three thousand attracted
more and more people to it the further it processed through the city.
By the time we had reached the eight-laned *Prospekt Lenina* on the site
of the demolished Cathedral of St Catherine, our numbers had easily
doubled. The streets empty of traffic, we walked down the middle of
the road — or more accurately, we *marched* according to the pace set by
the young men carrying the litter at the front of the procession — and
their aim, it seemed, was to reach the mineshaft as quickly as possible,
as if it were a test of strength, endurance, manhood. Everybody else
struggled to keep up as best they could. To my left, a young mother
in cheap plastic sandals pushed an equally cheap plastic stroller across
a tarmac showing the wear of its heavy load of daytime traffic, while,
elsewhere around me, groups of four, five or six pilgrims had formed.
Marching, head down, to see where they were going, they chanted a
responsory. *Prosti nas, Gospodi!* ("Forgive us, Lord!"), one of the group
would begin. *Yesu Khriste sie Bozhe* ("Jesus Christ is God"), the rest of
the group would reply in unison. As if to sustain their momentum,
they chanted it over and over, cyclically. Still others recited a litany of
the names of the Passion-Bearers one by one: *Svitoy Nikolai, Svitaya
Aleksandra, Svitoy Alexei, Svitaya Olga*, etc., etc. "Pray for us!"

Beyond the lake, the *Prospekt Lenina* opened out into Ekaterinburg's
central square. Named after the 1905 Revolution, this was the location
of the old Stalinist Gothic House of Soviets, which serves today as the

seat of the city's municipal administration. Facing it was the monument to Lenin I had seen earlier in the day. On a weathered, grey stone plinth, a bronze Vladimir Ilich wore a greatcoat, holding its lapel with his left hand reaching towards the sky, fingers upturned, with his right. An inscription read: "Everything that we have achieved shows that we have based ourselves on the most wondrous strength in the world — the strength of the workers and peasants." I wondered how the crowd would react to it. But Ekaterinburg's modern-day pilgrims seemed far more preoccupied with their own sins than they were with Lenin's. The crowd surged around the plinth, stranding it in a sea of chanting pilgrims. But the Bolshevik revolutionary, who had ordered the Romanovs' murder, was ignored, as if either the crowd had not seen the monument, or, if they had, there existed no connection at all between it and the action they were engaged in.

By now it was 3:30 a.m. in the morning. The sun would rise soon, but for now it was still dark, and we walked by the light of the streetlamps. As we entered the streets of apartment blocks on the other side of the city center, people opened their windows or came out on the balconies, if they had them, to wave us their support. Our numbers kept growing, but our pace didn't slacken. Our movement was like that of a collectivity rather than an assembly of individuals. Like a game herd, we trampled what was in our path, thinking more of the destination the group was trying to reach than of our personal safety. Where there were roadworks, we walked across, not around them. Where there was a railway line, we surged over it. Still, around me, the chanting continued. Feeling conscious of being a non-Russian, I kept my mouth shut. Endeavoring to keep towards the front of the march, I was invited on the outskirts of town to lend a shoulder to the carrying of the litter. I declined with a shake of the head, doing my best to avoid a second invitation by melting back into the crowd. At length we reached the edge of the city. Here, we turned on to the elevated motorway ringing the city. By now we had a police escort: they had closed one half of the motorway for us and, walking shoulder to shoulder, I could see that we filled all three lanes, median strip and verge. After walking about two thirds of a mile down the motorway, I climbed the median strip and looked behind me. The moving sea of pilgrims snaked down the motorway as far as I could see. I estimated a crowd of between 16,000 and 20,000 now, and took a moment to gather my breath (and senses) as the stream of pilgrims continued to pass me. Men in jeans and shaved heads who looked as though they had lived tough lives, pious Orthodox girls the same age as the Romanov grand duchesses, in delicate shoes and neat dresses. Older women in thin beige blouses and brown cardigans, covered with thin, almost transparent, plastic raincoats. The better-off among the crowd had stuffed a few belongings in the canvas packs they wore on their backs; the humbler toted plastic bags. Many carried sleeping rolls. Some walked arm-in-arm with friends, others kept to themselves. And still the unending chorus rang out. *Prosti nas, Gospodi!* And its reply, *Yesu Khriste sie Bozhe.* (Surely, Trotsky must have been turning in his grave: the monarchy had not only climbed back down people's throats; it was exuding from the pores of their skin.)

The sun had risen by the time we entered the forest. The unpaved trail was narrower than the highway, and we now walked in a long snaking line through the conifers, six or seven abreast, at the same brisk pace as when we had started. It was raining again. After four hours of walking my feet were tired; as blisters developed in my wet shoes, every step became a kind of small agony. Beneath my plastic raincoat I sweated profusely. I had reached the end of the inadequate supply of water I had brought with me and wondered about the young woman with the stroller and plastic sandals I had seen earlier in the night. Had she really managed to walk so far? We marched like this, along a train line, for probably no more than an hour and a half, but it felt longer. Everyone was tired. Though a few still chanted, most now walked in silence.

As we have seen, Yurovsky and his men initially tried to dispose of the Romanovs' corpses in a mineshaft to the north-west of the city, beyond the modern ring road, some ten or eleven miles from the central square. Exactly a week after they had done so, on July 25/August 7, the Czechoslovak legion entered Ekaterinburg.[8] By this stage, Ekaterinburg's Bolsheviks had fled. (The final guards had departed the Ipatiev House five days before the Czechs arrived, on July 21/August 3.) Before they had left, however, the story they had put to the Ekaterinburg public was that Nicholas had been executed, but Alexandra and their family had been taken away for safekeeping to an unknown location, probably Perm, the town to which Ekaterinburg's Bolsheviks were now retreating. But as soon as the Czechs inspected the Ipatiev House and found the basement room with its bloodstains in the floor and bullet holes in the walls, the hunt began for the victims' corpses. A few days later, they found the clearing in the forest where Yurovsky and his men had stripped the bodies and burned their clothes. There was ash, but no bodies. Neither did they have time to complete their investigations. In the summer of 1919, the Reds retook Ekaterinburg, Bolshevik rule was restored, and the investigation into the Romanovs' murder could continue only from abroad. But in view of the evidence of a large and powerful fire beside the mineshaft, Nikolai Sokolov, the last officially-appointed White investigator, concluded in 1924 that the Romanovs' bodies had been incinerated and their ashes disposed of in the neighboring mineshaft pit. Until the rediscovery

---

[8] Service, *Last of the Tsars*, 253–62.

of the remains under the by now buried sleepers in the depression in the road — first, by a group of amateurs in 1979, and a second time, officially, in 1991 — this is how it was believed the Romanovs met their end.[9] For this reason, the mineshaft, known as Ganina Yama, where the Romanovs' bodies were first unsatisfactorily dumped, but from which they were later exhumed and buried elsewhere, remains the official site of the Church's commemoration of them as Royal Passion-Bearers. In the cold hours either side of dawn, this mineshaft was our destination.

Today, the Ganina Yama mineshaft is a green-roofed monastery. A little after eight o'clock in the morning, its walls broke the monotony of the conifer forest. The sight revived everyone's spirits. Despite the gruesome events that took place here, which we had come to remember, we poured through the wooden, onion-domed gates in a festive mood. To the right, a cozy-looking pilgrim's canteen offered tea, bread, and other modest refreshments, but only relatively few of my companions turned aside to take advantage of the opportunity. Most continued along the paved path that led, through trees that added a landscaped appearance to the monastery, to "Mineshaft No. 7" at the other end of the compound, where, in the early hours of July 17, 1918, the Orthodox Church believes Russia's Royal Passion-Bearers' remains were incinerated and cast into the earth.

As far as Russian monasteries go, Ganina Yama is new. Its barely twenty-five years of existence pale in comparison to the centuries of operations that others can boast. In late Soviet times, the site on which the monastery now stands was nothing but a damp and dreary conifer forest, littered with the overgrown mouths of abandoned mineshafts. The shaft in which the Bolsheviks attempted to destroy the family's bodies was a state secret. Only berry and mushroom pickers came here — and the handful of private Romanov investigators disguised as such. The Orthodox faithful did not, for fear of attracting the suspicion of Soviet authorities. (The first to do so, back in the 1970s, were allegedly guided to the pit by an old man from a neighboring village, who, as a young boy, seventy-three years previously, had secretly observed the Bolsheviks at work in their attempt to obliterate the family's remains.) A generation later, by contrast, Ganina Yama is something the Church is proud of, and on a day such as the one I visited, in the company of 16,000 other pilgrims, the Ekaterinburg Church's intention to transform the complex into one of the country's premier pilgrimage destinations is evident. The original plan, formed in the 1990s, was for a single church on the site. Today, however, there are seven — one each for Nicholas, Alexandra, and their five children — built in wood in the style of the medieval Russian north, and each presenting the sky above with a nest

---

[9] For the full story, see Slater, *Many Deaths*, 16–45.

of onion domes. (One church alone sports twelve.) The largest church is in stone, in tented Muscovite style. A working monastery, it is a big and sophisticated facility that combines the monastic atmosphere of the shrine with something of the feel and appearance of a medieval-themed holiday lodge in the forest. Thus, the pilgrim's canteen by the gate was in fact only the lower part of a modern, three-story, honey-colored brick building (complete with wheelchair ramp) that can sleep 180 people with Wi-Fi, secure parking, and conference facilities for 200. Opposite are a well-stocked library and icon shop. The monks, by contrast, live at the other end of the complex, shielded from the distraction to their lives presented by the pilgrims by the numerous intervening church buildings. Standing watch over the whole is a tall timber bell tower, whose verticality sets off the straight, naked trunks of the surrounding conifers. The tower is topped, of course, with another onion dome.

A thoughtfully laid-out network of neat, paved paths links the whole complex together. Traditionally, the Orthodox frowned on three-dimensional images; unlike the Catholic Church, the Orthodox rules for sacred art traditionally placed a ban on sculpture. Today, however, that ban seems to have been relaxed. Carefully placed at prominent points along this network, bronze busts of Nicholas, Alexandra, and their children, greeted the pilgrims. As the guidebook I picked up put it, "the August family seems to accompany the pilgrims throughout the monastery. Emperor Nicholas II meets them near the entrance to the monastery, Empress Alexandra Feodorovna points the way to the Tsarist temple [i.e. that one specifically dedicated to the family's canonization], and Tsarevich Alexei and the Grand Duchesses call upon us to bow to the feat of the Tsarist Passion-Bearers at Mine Number 7." Certainly, plenty of people seemed willing to take up that invitation. When I passed Nicholas's bust, on the morning of the procession, a queue thirty-people long had formed to cross themselves and bow before it. The sight repeated itself at Alexandra's bust a little further along. Shouldering my way to the front of the crowd, in front of the sculpture of Alexei and his sisters, I noticed that it included an inscription with the words of Fr Belyaev, their confessor in captivity at Tsarskoye Selo, which we have seen before: "The royal children were extremely pure morally. God grant that all children should be as morally high as the children of the Tsar!"

The focal point of the monastery was a grassy depression in the earth, towards the rear left corner of the complex. The depression was the mouth of the now-filled mine pit. As we have seen, the Russian Orthodox Church continues to believe, on the basis of Sokolov's report into the family's murder, that the Romanovs' corpses were turned into dust here, and it venerates the mineshaft like a holy relic. A church building, dedicated to the Tsarist Passion-Bearers, abutted the shaft from one side, while a covered, timber gallery had been constructed, extending in a semi-circle around the grassy depression, allowing pilgrims the chance to perambulate around the shaft, and to view it from every angle.

On the day I visited, its low railing was hung with a canvas banner showing Nicholas II's image and the words, "Forgive us, O Sovereign of ours [*Gosudar' nash*]!" in a way that reiterated the bishop's message earlier in the night, whereby Nicholas remained Russia's tsar from beyond the grave. Meanwhile, the hole itself had been planted with birches and lilies, and the slender white stems of the latter lent an air of genuine pathos to the scene. On a paved platform at the closest point to the shaft, a weathered, wooden Orthodox cross (made from an oak tree felled at the site of a Nazi-Soviet tank battle in 1943) stood beside a granite memorial stone. Recorded in the inscription on the stone was a quotation from the book of the Prophet Amos that Alexandra had been reading in the days before the murder: *I will not spare him, for he burned the bones of the king of Edom into lime* (Amos 2.1). Thus, a curious historical antinomy arises. While the cross associates Nicholas and Alexandra's death with those of the Soviet war dead, in what is to be understood, doubtless, as a common act of self-sacrifice for Holy Russia, the stone pointedly refuses to extend that association to the Soviet Union's earliest leadership. Not just Yurovsky himself, but Lenin and, indeed, his whole revolutionary project fall under God's curse for desecrating the body of the tsar/king. As I stood watching, a queue formed for the pilgrims to kiss this cross (which both affirms and repudiates different, entangled elements of Russian history) and to venerate the Royal Passion-bearers by touching their foreheads to the ground on the platform in front of the mineshaft. This was the nearest the pilgrims would get to the ground which the Church continues to believe is sown with the Royal Passion-Bearers' incinerated relics.

Meanwhile, over beyond the church, on the other side of the depression, a curious gathering was taking place. There, on the pavement, the young litter-bearers who had borne the trellis, with the icons of Nicholas and Alexandra in state costume, at the head of the procession, all the way from the *Khram-na-krovi*, had raised the litter again to their shoulders. A large group of pilgrims was gathered in a semi-circle round them, taking it in turns to approach the litter, venerate the images of Russia's last tsar and empress on it, and then crawl underneath it to the other side. I did the same, before the activity was interrupted by the arrival of the black- and gold-robed and mitered bishop, accompanied by the head (*igoumen*) of the monastery and a dozen other clerics. He was in high spirits, and smiled warmly from behind his dark beard at the crowd of pilgrims around him, who pressed forward to kiss his hand.

Moving to the platform by the Cross, he addressed a few words to the crowd, thanking them for coming, before giving a short address to the crowd from beside the cross at the mouth of the mineshaft. "Last night, at the *Khram-na-krovi*, we recalled the deaths of the Tsarist Passion-Bearers at the hands of their cruel executioners. Today, we celebrate the fact that they are in heaven, where they do not feel the cold, and where there is no fear or suffering," he reiterated.

What is the meaning of this place, other than its being perhaps the most striking sign of the survival, or spontaneous regeneration, in Russian culture, of the theocratic principle? Visiting the mineshaft in the immediate wake of the Romanovs' canonization as Passion-Bearers in 2000, the former Patriarch, Aleksei II of Moscow, described the Ganina Yama mineshaft as "a living antimension, permeated with particles of burned holy relics."[10] In the Orthodox Church, an altar is only fit for the celebration of the Eucharist if it is laid at the beginning of the Divine Liturgy with a rectangular cloth into which small particles of the saints' relics have been sewn, known as an "antimension." But if Ganina Yama is an antimension, does this make all Russia an altar fit, symbolically, for the celebration of the Eucharist?

By now, however, sheer exhaustion was starting to get the better of the crowd. On the grass, beneath the conifers, spread a patchwork of brightly colored squares and rectangles. They were the sleeping rolls I had seen people carrying with them through the night. The pilgrims, exhausted from their march, were sprawled out supine upon them under the trees, unbothered by the dampness left by the morning's rain. It was a picture of simplicity, of the kind of which Russians alone, among the peoples of modern Europe, seem capable. And, indeed, we were not in Europe. Technically, there, on the eastern watershed of the Urals, we were in Asia.

After the bishop had finished his address, I moved off to explore the rest of the complex. One by one, inside each of the monastery's churches, I discovered where the rest of the previous night's 16,000-strong crowd had gone. Not in the center of the narthex, but on mats unrolled along the side walls, or behind the screen created by a conveniently placed icon, were more dozing pilgrims. Strangers all to one another, they nonetheless behaved like family, not embarrassed by their neighbor's body lying next to them on the floor, nor inhibited by any sense that the satisfaction of this basic human need to sleep was out of place in a church. Truly, the Russian's church is also his home. Unlike the Russians, however, I had no sleeping roll; even had I had one, self-consciousness (and a fear of elephantiasis from the forest's ticks) would have prevented me spreading

---

[10] See the history of the monastery on the Ganina Yama website: https://ganinayama. ru/o-monastyre/istoriya-monastyrya/. Accessed September 28, 2024.

it alongside theirs on the grass. Making the most of a fleet of old buses provided later in the day, free of charge, by the diocese, I returned to Ekaterinburg, regained the comfort of my hotel, and slept.

ಠಠ ಠಠ ಠಠ

Since the logic, whatever its nature, that demanded the liquidation of Nicholas, Alexandra, and their children and retainers also demanded the killing and liquidation of their relatives, the commemoration the following day, July 18, of the so-called "Alapaevsk murders" was the final element of Ekaterinburg's "Royal (lit: *Tsarist*) Days" festivities. It marked the gruesome murder at Bolshevik hands of Alexandra's sister, Ella, and her cell attendant Varvara (glorified as saints in the Russian Orthodox Church Outside Russia in 1981 and in the Russian Orthodox Church, Moscow Patriarchate, in 1992), along with half a dozen other members of the former imperial family, in the dark conifer forests one hundred or so miles to the north of Ekaterinburg, two days after the murders of Nicholas, Alexandra, and their children.[11] To return to the clearing in the forest, outside the village of Alapaevsk, where the murders took place, Royal Days organizers were offering places on a full-day excursion by minibus from Ekaterinburg. I made a booking, and, the following morning, the scheduled minibus called to collect me under the leadership of a middle-aged woman in a beige parka named Marina. Eight or so other pilgrims of either sex were already in the minibus. The rain had returned, and a fine, misty drizzle fell on and off as we drove through Ekaterinburg's wet streets and north along the highway to Alapaevsk. As we did so, Marina read aloud to us the official Life (or *Zhitye*) of St Elizabeth the New Martyr, concluding her reading with the recitation, in a high-pitched voice, of the personal hymn the Church had written in Ella's honor.

> It is beyond human words to praise the strength of thy love in the days of troubles and misfortunes that befell our motherland, when thou didst refuse to leave Russia and the monastery founded by thee, and when thou didst strengthen thy nuns to stand up for the Orthodox faith even in the face of death.... Rejoice, O thou who didst fall in love with our land! Rejoice, O thou who art glorified by the Russian people! Rejoice, O thou who didst teach us to protect ourselves with a shield of faith when attacked by enemies...![12]

ಠಠ ಠಠ ಠಠ

Ella took the veil as an Orthodox nun after the assassination of her husband, Nicholas's youngest uncle, Grand Duke Sergei Aleksandrovich,

---

[11] Service, *Last of the Tsars*, 263–64.
[12] For the English translation, see: http://www.orthodox.cn/liturgical/akathist/princess_elizabeth_en.htm. Accessed January 22, 2025.

in the grounds of the Kremlin in February 1905. In 1909, she founded
her own Order of Mary and Martha, Sisters of Mercy, dedicating her
life to the practical service of the poor.[13] Having been arrested at her
convent in Moscow on Lenin's orders—along with her cell attendant,
Varvara, a commoner who insisted on coming with her—and sent to
the remote Urals village of Alapaevsk, with five other (mostly minor)
members of the old ruling dynasty, she was murdered in 1918. The same
Czech advance that had necessitated the killing of Nicholas, Alexandra
and their children in Ekaterinburg also necessitated the killing of Ella
and the other Romanovs with her. So it was that on July 18, the dark
conifer forests of the Urals provided the backdrop for another murder
scene.[14] Although many of the facts remain confused, their outlines are
clear, and the story, once again, is gruesome.[15]

What seems clear is that at noon on July 17/30, 1918 (when, a hundred
miles to the south, Yurovsky and his men were haplessly trying a second time to dispose of Nicholas, Alexandra and their children's already
decomposing bodies), Ella and the other Alapaevsk captives were told
that, with a Czech army closing in on the town, they had to depart that
evening, for their own protection, to the village of Sinyaichikha, fifteen
miles away. According to some accounts, the party was rushed through
dinner for a departure in the early evening; according to others, they
retired as usual, only to be woken shortly after midnight. Either way,
the various versions of events agree that they were bundled into horse-
drawn carts and driven the two hours to Sinyaichikha. Rather than
being taken into the village, however, the prisoners were driven into
the forest, unloaded from the wagons in a clearing, and made to walk
to the rim of an abandoned mine deeper in the forest.

What happened next is not clear. According to the only eye-witness
account (by one of the killers themselves, Vasily Ryabov) the Bolshevik
guards, rather than shooting the party, sought to procure their deaths

---

[13] On this remarkable woman, see Christopher Warwick, *Ella: Princess, Saint and
Martyr* (Chichester: Wiley, 2006) and, from an Orthodox point of view, Lubov Millar,
Grand Duchess Elizabeth of Russia: New Martyr of the Communist Yoke (Richfield
Springs, NY: Nikodemos Orthodox Publication Society, 1991).
[14] With Ella in captivity were Grand Duke Sergei Mikhailovich (a cousin of Nicholas II's
father), his secretary, Feodor Remez, and four "Princes of the Imperial Blood"—John,
Constantine and Igor Konstantinovich, and Vladimir Paley. Aged between 24 and 32,
the first three of these latter "princes of the imperial blood" were sons of Grand Duke
Constantine Konstantinovich, another cousin of Nicholas's father (and the last member
of the dynasty to be buried, in 1916, in the Imperial Mausoleum, while the Russian
Empire still existed). As officers in the Russian Army, all three princes had seen active
combat during the Great War; indeed, their brother, Oleg, was the only Romanov to
die in military service for Russia during the Great War. The last, "Prince Paley," was
the twenty-one-year-old son of Nicholas's uncle, Grand Duke Paul Aleksandrovich and
his mistress (later wife), Olga von Pistolkhors ("Princess Paley").
[15] My reconstruction here follows Warwick, *Ella*, 303–9.

only indirectly, by pushing the party one by one into the shaft and trusting to the drop to kill them. They threw Ella first, followed by Varvara and then the men. When Grand Duke Sergei tried to resist, he was shot in the back of the head. As for Ella, Varvara and the others, however, the drop failed to have its intended effect, for the guards heard splashing and the sound of voices singing the Orthodox prayer *Lord, Save your People*: apparently, a rock ledge covered by water at the bottom of the mineshaft had broken the prisoners' fall. Allegedly, the guards then threw two hand grenades down the shaft. And yet even after these explosions, the singing continued, so the guards stuffed the shaft mouth with brush and built a built fire to suck the oxygen out of the cavity. Extraordinarily, even after this fire had burned down, a local peasant, who claimed he had been secretly watching from the bushes, later testified that he heard voices singing the *Cherubic Hymn* rising from the pit. Other versions of the account have Ella binding the brow of her cousin, Prince John, with a rag torn from her veil in the watery darkness.

But did Ryabov invent his account to disguise the brutality of what really happened? When, after the Czechs had conquered the area, the White authorities exhumed the bodies, all showed evidence that the victim had been subjected to severe, even fatal, beatings *before* being cast down the shaft. Ella and Varvara, for example, both had bruising about the head, and Varvara also to her breasts. The men's injuries were worse. Grand Duke Sergei's aide showed bleeding in the chest, lungs, neck and head, while the young princes had sustained not only bruising, but long gashes across the skull and bleeding *inside* the cranium. Savagely beaten by rifle butt, to such an extent that his brain had been left "a red mass," young Prince Paley was likely dead before his body reached the lip of the pit. Ryabov's story of hapless executioners faced with victims who simply would not die appears to have been concocted, then, to cover up the wanton violence and calculated acts of disfigurement that really occurred. The men, it seems, took the opportunity to enjoy the power that circumstances, and a rifle each, had given them.

అ అ అ

Beyond the Ekaterinburg's grey and mournful silhouette, the countryside became bucolic, even picturesque. Dark green conifer forests alternated with wet, hay-colored fields of crops, watched over by simple but cozy-looking homesteads. Stands of birches stood as windbreaks along the borders of quiet, lonely paddocks, and occasionally we passed through a town or a village; at least once, we crossed a river. At a remote, backwoods filling station, we stopped to use the amenities, if we wished, and drink black tea or instant coffee from small white plastic cups. (Presumably because smoking is considered a sin among the Orthodox, I noticed that although the ground was littered with cigarette butts, nobody in our party lit up.) Finally, at around 11 o'clock, we saw the first signs for Alapaevsk. Passing the town, we continued north along the route that Ella, Varvara, and the rest of their party were taken by horse-drawn cart on their way to their deaths. At length the minibus drew to a halt on what any other day of the year would have been a quiet back road through the surrounding forest. But a convoy of vehicles, including four or five large tourist buses, had already arrived at the church and chapel complex constructed around the mouth of the mineshaft.

Today, the mineshaft down which Ella, Varvara and the already broken bodies of the princes had been cast sits not in remote forest, but directly adjacent to the nearby road, separated from the tarmac by a white-washed brick wall. An onion-domed gate fitted with a bell tower pierces this wall, and by either side of the entrance icons of Ella and Varvara, in the distinctive grey woolen habits of Ella's order, had been hung. Like the mineshaft at Ganina Yama, the scene at Alapaevsk's Lower Selimskaya pit was peaceful: grass had grown over the mouth of the filled hole, and the resulting depression in the earth was planted with white lilies. Around the pit, the slender-trunked conifers had been left standing, preserving the memory of the dark conifer forest where Ella and her companions lived their final earthly moments.

To the left of the pit, a neat, white, single-domed chapel had been dedicated to "St Elizabeth, the Neo-Martyr" (i.e. Ella). The chapel's narthex opened directly on to the hole. Inside, a hundred pinpricks of light, from the candles that pilgrims before me had lit, flickered before icons of Ella, Varvara, the Virgin, the Royal Passion-bearers, Serafim, and the rest of the panoply of Orthodox saints. (One particularly evocative image of Elizabeth and Varvara showed them standing either side of an abyss that was the icon painter's interpretation of the mineshaft, outside the door of the chapel, that had been the instrument of the women's passion.) Near the entrance, information panels explained to the visitor the significance of the "Alapaevsk Martyrs" through quotations from Ella's diary and letters: "Striving to make those near us happy... we must do good to everybody"; "Happiness doesn't lie in living in palaces and being rich. All of this it is possible to leave behind. True happiness is that which neither people nor events can steal. You will find it in the life of the soul and the giving away of self. Strive to make those around you happy, and you will be happy." Like her sister the Empress, Ella's faith was a composite mixture of an authentically "mystical" Orthodox piety and the very practical sense of earthly duty characteristic of the Victorian morality both girls had received from their English mother and grandmother (who was, after all, none other than Queen Victoria herself). A hundred years later, after Russia has begun its return to

Orthodoxy, but Britain itself has long since abandoned any allegiance to the Victorian values that Ella and Alexandra knew, the example of St Elizabeth the New Martyr and her sister, the Royal Passion-bearer St Alexandra, is instilling the combination that defined the royal sisters' faith in a new generation of Russians. Indeed, the works clearly going on while I was there to build a much bigger, tetraconch (four-apsed) church on the other side of the shaft appeared to testify that a major new pilgrimage site was under construction.

ಌ   ಌ   ಌ

Marina left us to wander through the crowd. Perhaps a thousand people were at the Alapaevsk complex that day, together constituting a scene — austere, chaste, and pious — that was becoming increasingly familiar. Bearded, black-robed priests roamed the site with busy, serious expressions, in preparation for the approaching arrival of the bishop who was coming to celebrate the liturgy, while nuns in almost identical black robes and the fez-like *kolubka* did their best to assist. Behind a row of trestle tables, women in long, floral dresses, dark-colored cardigans, and kerchiefs tied under their chin sold devotional literature (Ella's Life or *Zhitye*, Akathist, inspirational collections of sayings) beside icons and cheap commemorative bells and plates. The ground floor of one of the rectangular buildings had been opened as a canteen, serving steaming borscht (made with vegetable stock, not beef) in white plastic bowls, and the same egg-, cabbage- and fish-filled *pirozhki* that I had seen at Ganina Yama. Among the faithful (as at every religious festival in late imperial Russia) wandered the poor — mostly hunched, older women, or ragged-bearded war veterans missing a leg and hopping around on crutches — while a middle-aged mother or father stood beside a deformed or crippled adult child. All begged for alms from those who passed, though hardly any even of the able-bodied pilgrims looked wealthy. The sky, meanwhile, was the same brooding, leaden grey it had been all day. Drizzle was again falling, and, where gravel had not been lain, the ground underneath had turned to mud. And, yet, away from the stalls, under the trees separating the makeshift pilgrims' "fair" from the mineshaft, was spread a multi-colored patchwork of the same blue, pink, and green plastic sleeping rolls the pilgrims had carried strapped to their packs two nights before. Untroubled by the mud and the rain, their owners lay on them, awaiting the bishop and the liturgy with the same hardy simplicity I had seen at the conclusion of the previous night's pilgrimage in Ekaterinburg.

A little after 12 o'clock, the Bishop of Ekaterinburg, the same prelate who had preached at the *Khram-na-krovi* and Ganina Yama, arrived. The priests formed an escort through the crowd, while the pilgrims crowded forward to catch a glimpse of him, and, if they got close enough, to bow and kiss the bishop's hand. Once he had reached Ella's small chapel, the liturgy began, and immediately the inadequacy of the current amenities became apparent. Scarcely more than a hundred standing could squeeze behind the clergy and into the narthex. The rest, including me, stood outside, shoulder to shoulder, in a semi-circle around the mouth of the mineshaft, listening as best we could to the muffled echo of the chants. Even with the Russian pilgrim's store of patience and tolerance for discomfort, keeping this up for almost two hours was a challenge, doubly so in the rain. But clad in raincoats or thin plastic ponchos, most kept to their post.

At length, the liturgy ended, and the bishop came back outside to deliver his feast-day homily from the doorstep of the white, onion-domed chapel on the edge of the shaft. The rain had lifted, and the sky was clearing. The bishop began with the recitation of Ella's early life, her German and English ancestry, her Lutheran upbringing, and the education she had received in Germany as a princess — an education, the bishop noted, that included (as it did for her younger sister, Russia's future empress) philosophy and theology.

"For all of this privileged early life," the bishop said, "only in Orthodoxy, in the believing Russian people, did St Elizaveta find true faith. Depth of feeling. Warmth. Love. Spiritual understanding. These are Russian virtues, the fruits of our Russian Orthodox faith. Everyone knows that the West does not have these things, does not know these virtues."

The bishop concluded his homily by connecting the Alapaevsk pilgrimage to the wider "Royal Days" celebrations.

"There are many," he said, "who still speak with ignorance about our Tsar, who spread lies and prejudice. That's why this Royal Days festival is so important. It reminds us of the great feat [*podvig*] of the Royal [lit: *tsarist*] Passion-bearers, their faithfulness to our holy Orthodox faith and their sacrifice [*otdaniye*] for Russia. You have come from the four corners of our land. Go home and tell your friends and neighbors the truth about our tsar and his right-believing family!"

෴ ෴ ෴

Lunch that day was in a small, family-run canteen set, almost picturesquely, beside a rococo green, eighteenth-century church (its paint peeling off in patches), above a broad bend in a local river on the way into Alapaevsk. Fields of rye ran down to the river, a cluster of ramshackle cottages on its bank. But for the tarmac of the highway, and its garnish of signage and power lines, the scene appeared timeless. Marina led our party inside an establishment that was less a specialized commercial operation than a large dining room in a family home. The eleven of us were seated at one long table that was already set when we arrived with pickled carrots, cabbage and gherkins, the harvest, doubtless, of the carefully tended beds of tomatoes, cucumbers, and lettuces visible behind the house. Outside the big cities, Russians are a people who still live close to the earth.

I sat at lunch beside some of the younger members of our party. Attractive women in their mid-thirties, Anya and Irina wore the pious floral kerchiefs of the older women pilgrims, but being a pilgrim was only one of many roles each played in life. With glossy chestnut hair tucked under her kerchief, and natural, manicured nails, Anya had worked as a secondary school English teacher until the birth, seven years before, of her first child, a son. Her husband was a Ekaterinburg businessman, and together the family evidently belonged to Russia's relatively prosperous new middle class. "We are not poor," she explained, describing previous holidays in Greece and Jerusalem, which combined rest [*otdykh*] with pilgrimages to Orthodox religious sites. "But we can't afford to take our holidays [*otdykhat'*] abroad the way we used to, either," she said in reference to the sanctions imposed on Russia after events in Ukraine. She and her friend, the cheerful, effervescent Irina, had studied together at university. The carefree Irina, who was unmarried, was still working as a teacher, and couldn't wait to "digitize" the fact of our acquaintance. Within minutes we were "friends" on vKontakte, the Russian version of Facebook. Both women had come to Orthodoxy as adults in their twenties, and had been at the *Khram-na-krovi* and Ganina Yama earlier in the week. They hadn't done the night-long march through the streets of Ekaterinburg, but were very impressed that I had.

I commented on how radically Russians' attitudes towards the last tsar and his family seemed to have changed since Communist days. They told me that they had only been children when Communism had collapsed, and had only the foggiest memories of the Soviet system. But they sought to dispel any idea I might have had that either the Orthodox piety, or the enthusiasm for Nicholas II and his family, that I had witnessed over the previous three days was universal. There were plenty of Russians, they said, especially among the older generation, who still had an unfavorable view of the Romanovs, and of the tsarist era, in general. Many such people called themselves Orthodox and got their children baptized, but they weren't interested in cultivating a deeper faith. For Anya and Irina themselves, however, the Church was, with their families, *vsyo* ("everything").

Lunch was served while we talked — more borscht, a modest helping of beef Stroganoff, and, for dessert, black tea and a bowl each of tinned peaches. I asked them what the Royal Passion-bearers meant to them, and why they had taken three days away from their families to spend it in churches and monasteries. Anya answered first: "To me, it is about repentance [*pokayaniye*]. The Russian people committed a terrible crime, a sin, in killing the Tsar. To this day, I cannot understand how God allowed such a beautiful, believing, Orthodox family to suffer such a brutal death. We, all the Russian people, need to repent of the spiritual sickness that came over us at that time and made that tragedy possible." She especially loved St Elizaveta's example. "She was a beautiful, Orthodox woman, don't you think? A model of love and humility." She paused to gather her thoughts before continuing, reflectively: "Of course, Russia is very different from the way it was a hundred years ago. But I don't think the sickness that led us to betray the Tsar and Imperial Family has wholly gone away, either. Politically, economically, spiritually — we have so many problems. For that reason, when I go on a pilgrimage, I ask the Blessed and Right-Believing Tsar Nicholas not only for forgiveness for what happened in the past but also for his help for Russia today." Marina clapped her hands. It was time for us to resume our places in the bus.

෴ ෴ ෴

Alapaevsk's Cathedral of the Holy Trinity was the last destination of our pilgrimage. Unlike the remains of Nicholas, Alexandra and their children, the bodies of Ella and her companions were found. Exhumed, they were taken in September 1918 to Alapaevsk's Holy Trinity Cathedral, for the performance of a solemn Orthodox requiem. In Ella's case, they were already looked on as the holy relics of a saint. Eight months later, when the Reds threatened to restore Bolshevik rule to Alapaevsk, a monk smuggled Ella's body across Siberia, out of Russia and into China. In 1920, Ella's surviving sisters (including the grandmother of the future Prince Philip, Duke of Edinburgh, consort of the late Queen Elizabeth II) and brother paid for her and Varvara's remains to be transported by ship to the Holy Land, where, today, they are buried in the Russian Orthodox Church of St Mary Magdalene on the Mount of Olives.[16] In 2010, some of her relics returned to Russia, including to Alapaevsk, where they are offered to the faithful for veneration annually during the Royal Days festival.

On the cathedral doors, a hand-written note in large letters asking "Brothers and Sisters" (the standard Orthodox word for one's fellow believers) for donations of food stuffs, toilet paper and other household items, bore witness to the local church's expectations regarding the number of pilgrims who would need to be fed and cared for. We went inside the building. During Stalin's anti-religion campaign in 1931, the Cathedral was closed. Gutted, stripped, and with its bell towers torn

---

[16] Warwick, *Ella*, 309–12.

down, it was used as a bread factory until 1988. Reconsecrated in 1998, it still offers reminders of its fate in Soviet times: while a serviceable iconostasis has been reinstalled, and reproduction icons hung wherever possible on the bare white walls, the floor — exposed, cracked concrete — remains that of the factory it once was. For the pilgrims I was traveling with, however, the humility of the surroundings took nothing away from what this simple building offered. Sitting on a low table spread with a red and gold cloth in front of the iconostasis was a silver casket, the lid lifted to reveal a reliquary in the shape of a hand and forearm beneath the glass. Before it stood a queue of twenty or thirty people waiting to kiss it.

Indeed, the whole scene was a powerful reminder of the simplicity the Russian believer is capable of, the cathedral's twin aisles repeating, on a greater scale, a practice I had seen before at the *Khram-na-krovi* and Ganina Yama. Russian churches, as we have seen, have no pews, and, to the right of me, between the central nave and southern wall, and from the steps of the iconostasis to the narthex, the floor of the Cathedral was entirely covered with gymnastics mats, borrowed from the local high schools and sporting clubs, and repurposed for pilgrims to sleep on. The mats stacked in the corner of the building suggested that, at night, the central nave was slept on, too. Meanwhile, the left aisle had been partitioned off by a thin plyboard screen, open at the end nearest the iconostasis, behind which stood a makeshift kitchen and dining hall: tables set with bread and dry biscuits were flanked by long, wooden benches, while beneath the icons hanging on what was ordinarily the Cathedral's northern wall pots of soup rested on serving tables. In its own humble way, this, too, was an image of the sacred city — the transcendent cosmic ideal of ordered unity — of which Russian culture as a whole remains so implicitly conscious.

CHAPTER FIFTEEN

Moscow

THE RETURN OF THE KING

N MAY 15, 1913 (FIVE YEARS BEFORE THE TRAG-
edy at Ekaterinburg), Nicholas, Alexandra and their children left
Tsarskoye Selo for a pilgrimage to the ancient Rus lands north of
Moscow. The year marked the three-hundredth anniversary of the
election of Nicholas's ancestor, Mikhail, as the first Romanov tsar.
As part of the dynasty's Tercentenary celebrations, Nicholas and his family
were returning to their roots. When they arrived in Vladimir, a day later,
all the city's church bells rang, as the royal party were driven from the
station to attend a prayer service in the white limestone Cathedral of the
Dormition. Built by Prince (St) Andrey Bogoliubsky ("the God-loving")
in 1189, to house the sacred icon of the Virgin he had plundered from
a relative in Kiev, the cathedral subsequently became the resting place
of no fewer than three slain and subsequently sainted Russian princes—
Andrey himself, Andrey's son Prince Gleb (who was distinguished by
his "gentleness, simplicity, humility, and charity"), and Prince George
of Rostov (slain in battle against the Tatars in 1238). The Tercentenary
pilgrimage's official court chronicler, E. V. Bogdanovich, recorded that
Nicholas venerated the relics of them all.[1] Could anyone have imagined
that, just five years later, Nicholas himself would have been slain, or that,
just under a hundred years later still, he, too, would have been sainted?

Apparently, large crowds lined the road as Nicholas and Alexandra
were then driven to the pretty, nearby town of Suzdal to tour its homely
churches and monasteries. Ordinarily peaceful, the town, which even
today retains a medieval appearance on account of never having been
connected to the railway, throbbed with townsfolk and peasants from
the surrounding village, who spontaneously broke out in patriotic songs
wherever Nicholas and Alexandra went. In the afternoon, the Tsar and
his family returned to Vladimir, to conclude the day with a liturgy of
thanksgiving in the cathedral constructed on the site of Andrey Bogoliubsky's medieval palace, where the sainted prince had been murdered
by his retinue. Met at the cathedral by the bishop, Nicholas, Alexandra and their children venerated Andrew's relics, before going with the
bishop to the spot where Nicholas's twelfth-century predecessor had been
murdered. Here, Bogdanovich pointedly noted that Nicholas "crossed

---

[1] E. V. Bogdanovich, *Istoricheskoe Palomnichestvo Nashego Tsarya v 1913 g.* (Moscow:
Russian Orthodox Church-Moscow Patriarchate, 2017), 28.

himself," naturally unaware that only five years later he himself — Russia's last princely ruler — would also be murdered.[2] (Indeed, the visitor to the same cathedral today finds icons of Nicholas paired with those of Andrey, his medieval predecessor, while a nun from the convent in the grounds relates tales of the sainted tsar-martyr's local apparitions.)

Sleeping on the train, the Imperial Family arrived the following morning in Nizhny Novgorod, the market town on the upper reaches of the Volga that, in medieval times, constituted the northeastern limit of Rus. In Russia, Nizhny Novgorod is closely associated with the names of a peasant, Minin, and a prince, Pozharsky, who liberated Russia from the Poles in 1612, clearing the way for the election of a new dynasty, the Romanovs, a year later. When they arrived, Nicholas and Alexandra attended an open-air liturgy of thanksgiving for the event, before Nicholas dedicated the foundation of a monument to the peasant-patriot, Minin. According to Bogdanovich, wherever the Tsar and his family went, a deafening roar received them. "Possible to hear, but not to describe in words was the hurrah of terrible force that spread through the crowds like a wave, and stopped only when Their Majesties returned to their carriage," he wrote.[3] The day came to an end when the Imperial Family boarded the steamer, the SS *Mezhen*, that would take them up the Volga to Kostroma. All through the night, according to Bogdanovich, villagers from the riverside settlements the steamer passed shouted hurrahs while, aboard, the Imperial Family slept.

The two days that the Imperial Family passed in their next stop, Kostroma, were the first of the pilgrimage's crescendos (the other being its climax in Moscow). Nicholas and Alexandra's first visit here was to the Ipatiev Monastery, on the banks of the Volga River, where the young Mikhail Romanov had been at his prayers when messengers arrived from Moscow to announce that he had been elected Russia's new ruler. In one of the mysterious coincidences of Russian history, Nicholas II would be executed, five years later, in a house bearing the same name as the monastery in which the first Romanov tsar began his reign. In 1913, however, even the more skeptical observers of Nicholas and Alexandra's Tercentenary pilgrimage conceded that this leg of the tour was a success. Thousands had crossed the Volga earlier in the morning to shout hurrah when Nicholas arrived.[4] Driven immediately after disembarkation from their steamer to the Ipatiev Monastery, they arrived there at the same time as a *krestnyi khod* or cross procession carrying one of Russia's holiest icons, the Fyodorov Mother of God (after whom Alexandra had received her patronymic, "Fyodorovna," and Nicholas and

---

[2] Ibid., 48.   [3] Ibid., 61.
[4] Nicholas II was not the first Tsar to visit Kostroma. The last one to do so had been his father, Alexander III, thirty-four years before, in 1881. Nicholas himself accompanied his father on that visit.

Alexandra together had named their favorite Tsarskoye Selo cathedral).[5] At this point, the bishop and clergy performed the Divine Liturgy in the Ipatiev Monastery Cathedral, along with a special service of prayers to the Savior and Mother of God. Thus, in 1913, not only the Tsar but Russia's entire ruling estate prayed together on the very stones where Mikhail had knelt in 1613, seeking to avoid the office to which fate had appointed him. After the liturgy, Nicholas and Alexandra toured the rooms in the monastery in which Mikhail had lodged.

Another enormous crowd followed, the next day, as Nicholas and Alexandra returned to Kostroma, to venerate the Fyodorov Mother of God in the Epiphany Convent that was its home. A further service of prayers was performed. Then, as if to underline their intention of rededicating Russia to Mary, the Tsar and Empress venerated the holy image again in the ornate shrine where, for centuries, generations of pilgrims had prostrated themselves for the sake of obtaining the Virgin's benefactions. "May the veil of her gracious, all-powerful intercessions stretch unceasingly also over you, our most pious Sovereign, Empress, Heir, and all the ruling house," said the dean of the cathedral at the conclusion of his address.[6] Nicholas and Alexandra almost certainly took this as seriously as it was meant. Indeed, we have already seen how Nicholas sent to army headquarters at Mogilev for the icon of Our Lady of Vladimir at the beginning of the 1916 Brusilov offensive, while, during the anxious days of February 1917, Alexandra constantly sought the Virgin's aid in the form of another Marian image, Our Lady of the Sign.

From the cathedral, the royal party made another *krestnyi khod* or procession of the Cross, to Kostroma's town square. Here, they laid the foundation of Russia's national Tercentenary monument, which, of all the Empire's thousands of towns and villages, Kostroma had been given the honor of hosting. After lunch, the Imperial Family visited the local Red Cross hospital. Alexandra had not yet taken the Red Cross nurses' training she would take after the outbreak of war in 1914, but her interest was, perhaps, already piqued. Finally, it was time to leave. According to Bogdanovich, the "tsar's departure formed a wondrous scene.... All Kostroma was there [by the river pier]. As one the crowd breathed love towards the Tsar, and when these thousands of people saw the Sovereign, every voice rose into a joyful cry. Hats and scarves were thrown into the air ... the church bells rang. The people cried 'hurrah,'

---

[5] According to legend, the Marian image had appeared, as if from heaven, on three occasions, to the town's prince and its people between 1259 and 1262. It was called "Fyodorov" because, on the third and final occasion of the icon's appearance, it bore the face of the revered warrior saint St Theodore or, in Russian, *Fyodor*. A few years later, it saved Kostroma from an attack by the Mongols. To it, therefore, Mikhail had naturally turned in 1613, when the messengers arrived from Moscow announcing his election as Tsar; and to it he entrusted his Throne, and the dynasty that would proceed, in time, from his loins. Ever since, the image had been considered the Romanovs' dynastic palladium.

[6] Bogdanovich, *Istoricheskoe*, 98.

sang 'God Save the Tsar,' and, accompanied by the people's love, the Tsar boarded the steamer...."[7]

From Kostroma, Nicholas and Alexandra sailed further up the Volga to the ancient city of Yaroslavl. After a day in Yaroslavl filled with commemorative activities like those elsewhere, the Imperial Family departed by train for Rostov, Pereyeslav-Zalessky, and the great Sergei-Trinity Lavra at Sergiev Posad. This was the route that Mikhail himself had taken to claim his throne in Moscow in 1613, and, in retracing it, Nicholas, Alexandra, and their children spent a day each in these medieval towns, with their onion-domed churches and picturesque, high-walled monasteries. Finally, on May 24, nine days after having departed St Petersburg, the Imperial Family arrived by train in Moscow.

Nicholas's arrival in Moscow was the climax of the Romanovs' 1913 Tercentenary, and the local population responded accordingly. From the station, Nicholas II, again re-enacting Mikhail's movements, rode a golden-saddled mare into the city, preceded only by the Cossacks of his personal convoy. Behind him followed the rest of the grand dukes, and the senior members of the armed forces, on horseback. Alexandra and the children were drawn in a single carriage, the carriages of the rest of the dynasty's grand duchesses following the Empress's. Cheering crowds lined the streets, and from the steps of the city's churches (all of whose bells were pealing at once) the clergy, in full ceremonial vestments, blessed Nicholas and his family with the holy icons as they passed. At the entrance to Red Square, the procession halted. Nicholas, dismounting from his horse, was received here by one of Moscow's auxiliary bishops, who blessed him, before, in the company of the clergy, Nicholas, Alexandr and their children entered the little chapel—of the Iverskaya Mother of God, another Marian icon—that guarded the entrance to the great square, to pray. From there, the Imperial Family proceeded on foot to Red Square, where, says Bogdanovich, a crowd stretching all the way to the banks of the river greeted them with a "mighty hurrah." "It was as if this mighty outburst of popular feeling... stirred even the clouds in the stormy sky, tore them open, and, opening the sky's blue vault, let the sunbeams light up a beautiful picture of the Tsar... entering the ancient, ruling Kremlin," he continued. Less than ten years after the Revolution of 1905, he seemed to be saying, the challenge hurled at tsarism had been surmounted. Met by the Metropolitan of Moscow at the Kremlin's Savior Gate (opposite the polychromatic domes of St Basil's), Nicholas was then led away to a further round of prayers in the Kremlin's cathedrals, to the cheers of a massive crowd.

Also present that day was the British diplomat and secret agent, R. H. Bruce Lockhart. In his estimate, too, "the mass emotion engendered

---

[7] Ibid., 107.

by this visit was overwhelming." Reflecting on the event, he identified something more in it too. The crowds' enthusiasm, he believed, was inspired "partly but not wholly by patriotism and by pageantry. Something in it too there was of religious mysticism, and dominating every other impression in my mind was the feeling that, so far from being the 'little father' of the official propagandists, the small figure in the center of the procession was *more like a sacred icon* than a human being."[8] An icon, then, but of what? Surely, of the ideal of *teokratia*, the theocratic principle, of an authority, to quote Bulgakov, "not on account of its own name, but God's."

Two days later, after many more visits, liturgies and presentations, the Tercentenary celebrations concluded at Moscow's white-walled Novospassky Monastery, three miles downriver of the Kremlin, where, before their election to the Russian throne, the Romanov family of *boyars* (noblemen) had maintained a family mausoleum. There, under the eyes of another great crowd, the Metropolitan of Moscow, accompanied, this time, by the brothers of the monastery, proceeded — in the presence of Nicholas, Alexandra, and their children, government ministers, court and military officials, and thousands of ordinary Russians with their own children — to celebrate a final liturgy of thanksgiving for the tsar, the dynasty, the Orthodox faith and Russia. To Bogdanovich, it amounted to a kind of sacred vision: "The Metropolitan celebrated the Divine Liturgy solemnly, the charming voices of the synodal choir alternating with those of the choir of the Novospassky brotherhood, and together with the incense the warm prayers of the Tsar and his loyal subjects rose to the sky.... Praise be to God...! In their future working and everyday life," he continued, reflecting on the impression left on all the children present, "let this one beautiful memory remain. Let them remember the bright and glorious vision of the Tsar among his beloved people that struck them in their childhood."[9] Five years later, of course, it was all gone.

இ இ இ

Today, in Moscow, the monuments, and with them the memory, of the old monarchy are more visible and prominent than they have been since 1917. Indeed, even in Soviet times, more of the built legacy of tsarism survived than was sometimes immediately appreciated in casual Western representations of the capital of world Communism.[10] The redbrick mass of the neo-Russian National Historical Museum that guards the northern entrance to Red Square, for example, was originally opened

---

[8] See Bruce Lockhart's preface in Bing, *Letters of Tsar*, 8. Italics mine.
[9] Bogdanovich, *Istoricheskoe*, 209–10.
[10] A valuable guide to the history of the Moscow cityscape is Caroline Brooke, *Moscow: A cultural history* (Oxford: Oxford University Press, 2006). With all the alterations (many of which I list below) to the Soviet appearance of the city that have since been made, however, the gazetteer section of the book is already beginning to feel its age.

in 1886 as the "Alexander III Museum." Diagonally adjacent to it, the elegant façade of GUM (*Gosudarstvennyi Universal'nyi Magazin*: State Department Store), beautifying the entire eastern boundary of the Square, was opened in 1893. A stone's throw away, on what still goes by its Soviet name ("Revolution Square"), but was named, until 1917, after the Resurrection, rises the sprawling modernist profile of the 1903 Metropole Hotel that served as Lenin's first headquarters in the city. In Soviet days, with its dream-like mosaic murals by Silver-Age artist Mikhail Vrubel on the exterior walls three stories above the pavement, it was often obscured by the mass of red bunting that hung in the Moscow streets, urging the comrades it daily harangued to work harder, fulfil the Plan and realize Socialism. But, today, with the bunting gone, the Metropole is once again a top-end hotel, and Vrubel's mosaic murals once again lend a last tsarist feel to this corner of the Moscow cityscape. At breakfast, a harpist serenades guests beneath the vast, glass-domed atrium. Across the street, the famous porticoed façade of the Bolshoi Theater predated the Revolution by almost a century. As the largest meeting room in the city, the Bolshoi was the standard venue of Soviet congresses, including the one Goloshchyokin attended in July 1918, hoping to obtain from Lenin permission to eliminate the former imperial family. The Soviet Union itself was proclaimed here in 1922. And yet anyone who attends an evening at the ballet here can see that he does so now in interiors restored to their appearance in 1913, with Nicholas and Alexandra's entwined "N&A" monogram reinstalled above the doors.

Of course, for all the continuity in Moscow's imposing urban fabric between late tsarist and high Soviet days, there was great destruction, too, and it says much about the way in which the fundamental coordinates of Soviet life have been abolished, or reconfigured, in the new Russia that many of the monuments that the Communist regime destroyed to uproot Muscovites' memory of both the tsar and Orthodoxy have been reconstructed or restored. Demolished by Stalin in the 1930s, to provide unobstructed access to Red Square for the tanks and massed formations of his military parades, for example, the little gate Chapel of the Iverskaya Mother of God, where Nicholas and Alexandra stopped to pray before proceeding to the Kremlin in 1913, has been restored, as has the beautiful galleried Church of the Kazan Mother of God just on the other side, which Stalin also destroyed. Indeed, while great red stars still rise above the Kremlin towers, and Lenin, for now, remains in his mausoleum (with Stalin buried in a more modest grave behind), the Red Square the visitor beholds now is, in its overall articulation, much more that of Nicholas II than of his Soviet successors. Once again, glinting double-headed eagles survey the whole from their perches as weathervanes on the tented, Neo-Russian towers of the National History

Museum; the holy icons have returned to the central place above each of the Kremlin's gates that they had in 1913; and, of course, the flag flying from the Kremlin is the white, blue and red tricolor proclaimed the flag of the Russian Empire by Nicholas II in 1896.

The observant visitor will discover other evidence of the once execrated monarchy's return, too. By the walls of the Kremlin, new gardens have been laid out. The column erected in honor of the Romanov Tercentenary of 1913 — reinscribed only five years later in 1918 in honor of Marx, Engels and a host of other revolutionaries — has been recut *again* in its original appearance in honor of the Romanovs. On the four-hundredth anniversary of the dynasty in 2013, it was rededicated in memory of Russia's former ruling house. A year later, for the bicentenary of Russia's defeat of Napoleon in 1814, a statue of Nicholas's ancestor Alexander I (1801–25), who led Russia to victory, was opened by Putin at a point further along in the garden. In 2017, the large stone cross which (the herself subsequently martyred) Ella had had erected in memory of her assassinated husband (Nicholas's authoritarian uncle the Grand Duke Sergei) in 1905 was restored to a place of honor inside the grounds of the Kremlin.

On that occasion, Putin made a speech, in which he noted his satisfaction that, a hundred years after the Revolution, "churches are rebuilt, monasteries open anew, and holy places that were lost are returned. Russia's history is regaining its unity. We treasure each page in this history, no matter how difficult. These are our national spiritual roots."[11] Ella herself Putin praised as a "remarkable woman" who "did not leave the country even during the darkest days and to her death remained true to the ideals of Christian forgiveness and love." (Indeed, so powerful have Russians found Ella's example that her Order has been revived, and the Sisters of Charity once again feed the poor and house the orphaned in the same convent of Mary and Martha that Ella opened on Moscow's south bank in 1909.) Further along the Kremlin walls, meanwhile, at the traffic junction that cuts the Kremlin off from the bank of the river, a colossal bronze statue of St Vladimir the Great, Equal-to-the Apostles, the first baptized grand prince of Kiev holds out a huge Orthodox cross as the founder of the Russian State. Surely, Trotsky would be horrified: in the restoration and erection of monuments such as those named above, not only the historical monarchy but also, perhaps, the age-old Russian yearning for a ruler who rules "not on account of his own name, but God's," which Trotsky believed the Revolution had torn up from the roots of the Russian soul, can be observed slowly but surely "climbing

---

[11] Russian President Vladimir Putin, "Unveiling of monument to Grand Duke Sergei Alexandrovich," March 4th 2017: http://www.en.special.kremlin.ru/events/president/transcripts/54447. Accessed September 30, 2024.

back down people's throats" — not as a regime, certainly, but as an ideal and a symbol. Three miles downriver, central Moscow's only statue of Nicholas II now stands in the grounds of the Novospassky, where the 1913 Tercentenary celebrations concluded.

But perhaps the most potent symbol of Soviet atheism's reversal is the restored bronze dome of the neo-Byzantine Christ the Savior Cathedral. Opened by Alexander III in 1881 to the sounds of Tchaikovsky's *1812 Overture* (which was specially written for the occasion), the Cathedral was the largest place of Orthodox worship in the Russian Empire. It was also blown up on Stalin's orders in 1934, in perhaps the most strikingly symbolic instance of the Revolution as event in the history of secularization. Ripped from the walls beforehand, the Cathedral's interior marble cladding was repurposed to decorate the walls of the stations of the new, and famously lavish, metro system. For sixty years, the riverside site on which the Cathedral had stood was the world's largest open-air swimming pool. The 130-story "Palace of Soviets," with its projected 330-foot high statue of Lenin on top, that Stalin planned to build on the site, was never constructed, victim as it was of the Second World War and post-War de-Stalinization. But with the fall of Communism, the swimming pool was filled in, and, in 1997, the imperial-era Cathedral that Stalin had demolished was reconstructed. Today, a statue of Emperor Alexander II, the Tsar-Liberator, who emancipated the peasantry, stands on a plinth in the neighboring garden.

As it was before the Revolution, then, Moscow's Cathedral of Christ the Savior is again Russia's largest Orthodox place of worship, its vast interior re-clad in plates of cool, polychromatic marble. From the dome at the center of the building, an image of Christ the *Pantokrator*, King of All, once again looks down symbolically over all Russia, while the Cathedral's restored iconostasis presents a thirty-foot-high wall of images of Christ, the Virgin, and Byzantine and Russian saints. Beneath it, the Liturgy of St John Chrysostom, with all its royal imagery, is again celebrated. On a supporting column opposite the royal doors, at the center of the high iconostasis, the outline of a throne indicates the place where the tsar himself would once have prayed. Mounted over it is an icon of the holy King (lit. "tsar") David, the Bible's first anointed king and prototype of all Orthodox-Christian representations of *teokratia*.

It was for their impromptu performance on the steps in front of the icon screen here in 2011, that the members of the all-female punk band Pussy Riot received their prison sentences under the new Russia's new blasphemy laws forbidding the "offending of religious feelings." Calling on the Virgin Mary to "banish Putin" and "become a feminist," the young women presented their protest as against the close and (in their view) corrupt relationship that has developed since the fall of Communism between the government and the Russian Orthodox Church.[12] ("Patriarch Gundyaev believes in Putin. Better believe in God, you vermin! Fight for rights, forget the rite—Join our protest, Holy Virgin!") But however pure or impure that relationship, the mere fact of it is another sign in its own way of the perdurance in Russian culture of the ideal of *teokratia*. Notable, too, are the cultural transformations that the band's members fault this relationship for frustrating. "Congregations genuflect. Black robes brag, golden epaulettes. Freedom's phantom's gone to heaven. Gay Pride's chained and in detention." As it is for most liberal observers of Russia, Russian and foreign, the close relationship between the Church and the authorities is seen in lyrics such as these as being motivated only by cynicism. Perhaps it is. But what they fail to see is that it is accepted—even *expected*—by Russians because it approximates an age-old ideal: that of *teokratia*, according to which the act of ruling is itself an act of sacred representation inseparable from the business of religion.

Nearby, on a stand of its own in front of the iconostasis, an icon as high as I am tall, and two arm spans wide, demands the visitor's attention. A visually stunning kaleidoscope of robes and faces, heavy in the greens, reds and ochres of the medieval northern Russian iconographical tradition, this "Assembly of the New Russian Martyrs" presents for veneration the images of the several thousand bishops, monks, priests, nuns, and Orthodox laymen and women shot or otherwise murdered in the aftermath of what Russians of a certain generation year after year celebrated as the "Great Socialist Revolution" of October 1917, the founding event of the Soviet Union.[13] We have noted copies of this icon elsewhere in our travel, but this image, here in Moscow, is the prototype. It is worth decoding.

Thus, in a large center panel, the beards, capes, and veils of martyred Orthodox clergy stand in serried rows in front of a representation of the very building I was standing in: Moscow's Christ the Savior Cathedral itself. After all, having been demolished by Stalin, the cathedral may itself be considered a "martyr." Meanwhile, in the front rank of this army of martyrs and confessors, a space had been cleared among the clerics. There, on a tiny dais, slightly below the center of the panel, stands a family in Muscovite garb and regalia—those martyrs for the theocratic principle, the Royal Passion-Bearers. Meanwhile, a border of smaller images framing the central panel represents what we might call the *religious meaning* of the Russian Revolution in a manner reminiscent of a cartoon reel. Little

---

[12] Pussy Riot, "Punk Prayer": https://genius.com/Pussy-riot-punk-prayer-english-translation-lyrics. Accessed September 30, 2024.

[13] On these martyrs and the place of their commemoration in the contemporary Russian Orthodox Church, see (albeit from a critical, "Kantian" perspective) Zuzanna Bogumil, "Between history and religion: the New Russian Martyrdom as an invented tradition," *East European Politics, Societies and Cultures* 32:4 (2018): 936–63.

khaki men with rifles expel monks from monasteries, break open the sarcophagi of the saints, and desecrate their relics. Others cast bishops into rivers with stones tied around their legs, or dump them in the desert to die of thirst. Above each frame, a label names the martyr depicted, while the Bolshevik soldiers who act as their executioners are simply designated as *bezbozhiye*: the "godless ones." Notable, for our purposes, are two panels of this serious cartoon reel halfway up the border on the right-hand side. In one, a pair of women lie at the bottom of a mineshaft while the "godless ones" toss grenades in on top of them: it is Ella and her cell attendant, Varvara. In another, a family huddles together in a basement while a phalanx of the godless point bristling rifles at them, "'the Royal Passion-Bearers,' Nicholas, Alexandra, and their children in Ekaterinburg."[14] It is sometimes alleged that "Putin's Russia" is but a continuation in another guise of the Soviet Union. But if this is true, then it is one in which, as this icon makes clear, that regime's genesis is held up as, effectively, the work of the Evil One.

     

If it is right that this book should end, then, in Moscow, where it began, it is because the re-evaluation of the monarchy evident in Russia's capital today began there, too. Indeed, what modern Moscow presents to the visitor is the triumph of a re-evaluation that began as early as 1918, when the intellectual circle of which Bulgakov was a member, that, in 1909, had published the famous essay collection, *Vekhi* ("Signposts"), published a sequel: *Out of the Depths*. Full of regret for the vanished tsarist regime, whose flaws its contributors nonetheless always recognized, *Out of the Depths* was the first probing of the sources and meaning of a revolution which, all agreed, was a catastrophe that shed, in a way, new light on the merits of the old regime. "For the first time, the country became truly free to fulfil its cherished ideals: the best Russian people came to power, and even better, more energetic and ardent people prodded them towards the realization of desired goals. And suddenly, somehow, all this caved in, and we woke up at a broken basin, worse than that, without any basin, and even without the old ramshackle hut that, despite everything, had been dear to our heart," ironized the philosopher and Orthodox convert from Judaism, Semyon Frank.[15] Where before the Revolution there was only blame to apportion, suddenly there was virtue to recognize. "For

---

[14] This is not the only image of Nicholas, Alexandra, and their children presented for veneration in the cathedral. On the contrary, on a stand by the northern wall, a large and striking icon of the Royal Passion-Bearers shows Russia's last imperial family not in the conventional, stylized garb of martyrs' robes or medieval kaftans, but in the elegant, early twentieth-century attire they actually wore, as if the painter intended the image as a window not only on heaven or an idealized Holy Rus, but on the Old Russia as it actually existed before the Revolution with both its *teokratia* and its debt to Western Europe. It is the only icon of its kind I have seen anywhere in Russia.

[15] Semyon Frank, "De Profundis," in Woehrlin, *Out of the Depths*, 221.

all the errors of the old regime, one must admit that up to the last day it remained at its post, and did what it considered possible to save the remnants of the spiritual heritage bequeathed to it by the past," added the former diplomat, V. N. Muravyov.[16] "At the present time, when we live under the authority of the Soviet bureaucracy and under the heel of the Red Guard, we begin to understand what the bureaucracy and police of the overthrown monarchy were, and what cultural role they fulfilled," agreed Petr Struve (with Bulgakov and Nikolay Berdyaev, probably the collection's best-known contributor).[17] Unremittingly critical of Russia's new Bolshevik rulers, and immediately suppressed by the Soviet censors, *Out of the Depths* remained impossible to read legally in Russia until Gorbachev's *perestroika* in the 1980s.

A former Marxist who found his way, via Solovyov's Christian idealism, to Orthodoxy, and shared with Bulgakov, Frank, and Merezhkovsky in the religious-philosophical revival of Russia's Silver Age, Struve had already before the Revolution gone from being the founder of the Union of Liberation in 1904, to being late-imperial Russia's best-known voice of liberal conservatism. Certainly, Struve continued to blame the monarchy for not agreeing earlier to share power with the representatives of the nobility and Russia's responsible classes. The "revolution was created from two ends: the historical monarchy with its jealous refusal to admit cultured and educated groups to authoritative participation in the structure of the state; and the intelligentsia of the country with its short-sighted struggle against the state," he wrote.[18] And yet Struve now credited the tsarist system with a wisdom he had not previously perceived. One of the "most noteworthy lessons of the Russian Revolution," said Struve, was the discovery of the "degree to which the overthrown monarchical regime was technically satisfactory." Indeed, he now believed that he had been wrong to identify it as the source rather than the mere symptom of the problem that afflicted Russia. After all, he reasoned, the "very inadequacies of this regime were rooted, not in its systems and institutions, not in the 'bureaucracy,' the 'police,' and the 'autocracy' . . . but in the temper of the people . . . the entire social environment. To some extent, the latter were even held in check by those same [previously criticized, monarchical] systems and institutions."[19] Basically, the monarchy had represented as benign a regime as was realistically possible at that time.

To read *Out of the Depths* today, then, is both to be taken back to Moscow in 1918, when the dizzying magnitude of Russia's downfall had become shockingly impossible to ignore, and to be provided with an

---

[16] V. N. Murav'ev, "The roar of the tribe," in Woehrlin, *Out of the Depths*, 164.
[17] Petr Struve, "The historical meaning of the Russian Revolution and national tasks," in Woehrlin, *Out of the Depths*, 205.
[18] Struve, "Historical meaning," in Woehrlin, *Out of the Depths*, 210.
[19] Ibid., 204.

insight into the conservative, anti-revolutionary rationale that animates much Russian political culture under Putin today. For, in 1918, Struve's remedy for Russia's revolutionary catastrophe was a species of national spiritual-patriotic renewal, inspired by the best of Russian history that is as good a description as any of the temper of government-sponsored cultural policy in Russia today. Precisely because the Revolution "broke the old links in the Russian people that united persons — national, state, and religious links; and it did not create any new ones in their place," Struve believed, the only antidote to it, if Russia was to nourish her own people again spiritually and contribute positively to world history, was to repair those links, and the means for doing so was love for Russia itself, for its past, its Orthodox religion, and its culture (all of which, in 1918, lay in ruins).[20] As Struve has it in *Out of the Depths*, "Before the countenance of the profaned Kremlin and destroyed . . . cathedrals, I say to every Russian youth: it doesn't matter to Russia whether you believe in socialism, the republic, or the commune; but it is important to Russia that you respect the greatness of its past, that you hope for and demand greatness for its future. . . . Russia's past and only its past, is the guarantee of the future. On that heap of ashes into which the fanaticism of socialist leaders and the raging of the masses they deceived have transformed a great country, only the national idea in conjunction with national passion will give birth to vital forces."[21]

Today, Putin's public pronouncements often seem inspired by the same spirit. As he put it in a speech praising Alexander III in 2017, a week after the centenary of the Great October Revolution (which Putin pointedly declined to mark publicly), "a strong, sovereign and independent state should rely not only on its economy and military power but also on its traditions; that it is crucial for a great nation to preserve its identity whereas any movement forward is impossible without respect for one's own history, culture and spiritual values." Indeed, when Putin has declared that Russia has "no national idea but patriotism," he could just as easily have been echoing the liberal-conservative Struve.[22] As for Putin's view of the Revolution itself, in his longest and most carefully worded commentary on what he called the "result of an accountability deficit in both those who would like to conserve, to freeze in place the outdated order of things that clearly needs to be changed, and those who aspire to speed change up, resorting to civil conflict and destructive resistance," Putin pleaded the cause of moderate, gradual reform in distinctly Struvian terms: "Today, as we turn to the lessons of a century ago, namely, the Russian Revolution of 1917, we see how ambiguous its

---

[20] Ibid., 215.   [21] Ibid., 217.
[22] "Putin Declares Patriotism Russia's Only National Idea," *Moscow Times*, February 4, 2016: https://www.themoscowtimes.com/2016/02/04/putin-declares-patriotism-russias-only-national-idea-a51705. Accessed September 30, 2024.

results were.... Let us ask ourselves: was it not possible to follow an evolutionary path rather than go through a revolution? Could we not have evolved by way of gradual and consistent forward movement rather than at a cost of destroying our statehood and the ruthless fracturing of millions of human lives?"[23]

When, then, history finally renders its verdict on Putin's regime, perhaps Struve's goals for a future restored Russia should be taken as the stick by which to measure it. Indeed, this seems to be the measure suggested by the best of Russia's contemporary "young conservative" intellectuals.[24] As one of them has put it: "The most complicated task of conservative ideology today is to create the image of the successful, educated citizen of his or her own country, living in dignified conditions and enjoying all the benefits of progress, but for all this preserving his or her own (traditional) values—and not just the 'image,' one might add, of such a citizen but the actual substance."[25]

$$\infty \quad \infty \quad \infty$$

Of course, Struve's re-evaluation of the monarchy does not amount to an articulation of the theocratic principle more than Putin's does. But Bulgakov's "At the feast of the gods," from which we have quoted extensively, appeared in the same volume of *Out of the Depths*. And if it is fitting that I should conclude my journey in search of the Romanovs in Moscow, this is, above all, because it was also in Moscow that Bulgakov—a deeper thinker than most of his contemporaries—completed his journey, from the Marxist atheist he was at the beginning of his intellectual career to the idealist, Orthodox Christian, and Orthodox-Christian "tsarist" that he tells us, in his posthumously published *Autobiographical Fragments*, he had become by its end. This last identity may not conform to the image of Bulgakov, the Orthodox "liberal" and Christian Socialist, which has become fashionable in some circles. And there *is*, to be sure, a tension between Bulgakov's apparently ongoing private commitment to the theocratic principle in its traditional tsarist form, and the embedding of it in a new and frankly liberal and democratic framework he promoted in exile in Western Europe in his published works.[26] If then, the question is whether "the tsarist ideal" that, as

[23] Russian President Vladimir Putin, "Meeting of the Valdai International Discussion Club," October 19, 2017: http://en.kremlin.ru/events/president/news/55882. Accessed October 9, 2024. For commentary, see Alexei Miller, "The Russian Revolution of 1917: History, Memory, and Politics," *Russia in Global Affairs*, February 26, 2018: https://eng.globalaffairs.ru/articles/the-russian-revolution-of-1917-history-memory-and-politics/. Accessed October 9, 2024.
[24] On these, see Marlene Laruelle, "The Emergence of the Russian Young Conservatives," in A. James McAdams and Alejandro Castrillon, *Contemporary Far-Right Thinkers and the Future of Liberal Democracy* (London: Routledge, 2022), 149–66.
[25] Mikhail Remizov et al., *Konservatizm kak faktor 'miakoi sily' Rossii* (Institute of National Strategy, undated), 49.
[26] For example, as Bulgakov put it, writing in France in the 1930s, the "Christian Empires were only a symbol of what ought to be, and it would certainly be a grave error to identify

Williams observed, "for a time wholly overshadowed any commitment to democracy as a self-evident good," overshadowed Bulgakov's commitment to democracy forever, then the answer is no—so long as democracy is seen only as a mechanism for effecting the good of human liberty, not an end in itself. [27]

In fact, Bulgakov never renounced his loyalty to the tsarist ideal, because his understanding of what political order fundamentally *was*—an act of sacred representation—remained, to the end, inseparably rooted in God: theocratic. Moreover, Bulgakov himself, I think, would tell us, as he must have told himself, not to seek to abolish but to accept such tensions and paradoxes. [28] As he puts it in *Autobiographical Fragments*, "Life is only given once to a man.... The important, spiritual, and terrible things to which it was determined that our generation should be witnesses were lived and experienced by each participant in his or her own way." [29] Not every published comment can be brought, perhaps, into conformity with the yearnings of the heart, any more than a theologian's deepest intuitions can be made on every occasion to conform with the demands of what passes in any given age for received opinion. Part of the mystery of human personhood is the complexity of every human personality.

So, Bulgakov took no active part in the Revolution, he tells us. But that does not mean that he was indifferent to it; he participated in it inwardly, he "felt it and meditated upon it," and "what takes place in people's souls has just the same right to our attention as external events." Indeed, Bulgakov implies, insofar as our interest lies not in the *what* of history's events, or in an immediate, proximate sense of their *why*, but in their profoundest *meaning* and ultimate, determining spiritual and philosophical sources, then this "witness of the soul" might even be superior. And as far as that witness was concerned, Bulgakov participated in the Revolution as in a terrible private agony. "I experienced the Revolution tragically," Bulgakov wrote, in words that show how faithful

---

the symbol or the dream with reality. Christian emperors lead [*sic*] their peoples towards the Christ as far as such an orientation was possible. But this time is past, for life itself has put an end to any real representation of the people of the Church in the person of the prince, a representation which was the basis for the Emperor's authority in the Church. In this representation, the power of the prince has become a fiction.... The people have begun their own life, apart from such representation.... And now if the State can be penetrated by the spirit of the Church, it must be from within, not from without, not from above but from below." See Sergius Bulgakov, *The Orthodox Church*, rev. ed., trans. Lydia Kesich (Crestwood, NY: St Vladimir's Seminary Press, 1988), 159.

[27] Williams, *Sergii Bulgakov*, 60.

[28] Certainly, Williams, discussing to what extent Bulgakov in the 1930s could still be described as a "Christian Socialist" does not feel compelled to reconcile Bulgakov's largely favorable writings on democracy at this time with the enduring commitment to the theocratic principle—and, indeed, to the person of Nicholas II—that he reveals in private in his later *Autobiographical Fragments*.

[29] Bulgakov, *Avtobiograficheskie*, 73.

he remained to the truths revealed to him on the Yalta Embankment, "as the death of all that had been to me the dearest, sweetest, and most joyful in Russian life — as the death of love. Yes, for me, the Revolution was a catastrophe of love, of a love that had taken its object out of the world, emptied her soul and despoiled it. [...] I loved the Tsar, wanted Russia only with the Tsar and without the Tsar Russia to me was not Russia."[30] This does not mean that Bulgakov's love for the tsar, while effectively unconditional and experienced by him as an integral element of Orthodoxy, was ever uncritical. He loved the tsar as the embodiment of the ideal of what he took to be the authentic Orthodox ideal of *teokratia*, the government of the nation by the tsar not on his own behalf but on that of God, and the resultant coordinating, by way of the tsar's consecrated conscience, of the political order — the affairs of nation and State — with an order of truth lodged not in the emancipated human will (whether that of a Roman or Peter-the-Great-style emperor or that, collectively, of the people) but in the divinely ordered cosmos.

Bulgakov was never an advocate, therefore, of either royal absolutism *per se* or charismatic dictatorship; if he was for the autocracy, it was for a paradoxically self-effacing autocracy that existed to give effect, not to the ruler's own self-aggrandizing rights, but to God's, and for that reason he constantly found himself internally conflicted, angry both with the monarchy's opponents and angry with the tsar himself. As he put it, "I was not a monarchist in the party-political sense, as there are and were in Russia, and in general I did not know with whom to share these sentiments of mystical love [for the tsar]. But I had it in my soul the way it is when the nearest, most precious being dies after a long and hopeless illness.... In reality, the agony of tsarist autocracy extended through the whole reign of Nicholas II, a continuous and unbroken suicide of the autocracy."[31]

Indeed, if Bulgakov blamed anyone for the Revolution, it was Nicholas II, it would seem. So, in *Autobiographical Fragments*, he could even disagree with the views of his colleagues, cited above, in *Out of the Depths*. "Unfortunately, far and above any revolutionary, the Revolution was accomplished by the tsar himself, who was attracted by irresistible evil forces — via the Yalu, Port Arthur and Tsushima, via the countless zigzags of his policies and the final marasmus of the war — to suicide." Russia's history was like a Greek tragedy, thought Bulgakov, "without personal fault but with tragic fate." Thus, Nicholas II was a "theocratic tsar, as he truly and deeply understood in his own tsar's heart," and more praiseworthy still, he was this "in spite of all those who surrounded him, who wanted to see in him only a political monarch, the autocratic emperor"; yet all the same, the Russian *teokratia*'s "political distortion

---

[30] Ibid.   [31] Ibid., 73–74.

into capricious despotism, combined with mystical aberrations to do with Rasputin and even the domestic psychology of the empress" was so complete that the intelligentsia's (secularizing) revolution prevailed and the ideal and institution of *teokratia* passed out of history. Nicholas II, "with such strengths of mind and will as he was endowed with could not have been a better monarch than he was," Bulgakov concluded. That, *too*, was Russia's tragedy and the cause of the twentieth-century Russian catastrophe.

The Revolution itself Bulgakov lived through in Moscow. By 1914, Bulgakov, having resigned his post as Professor of Political Economy at the University of Moscow in protest over government interference, was, apparently, not formally employed.[32] Understandably, then, the outbreak of the Great War caught him wrestling with the opposing feelings generated by the tragedy sketched above: for Bulgakov a "hidden, mystical love for the tsar" sat uncomfortably inside him alongside the "constantly irritated wound in his heart" brought about by the actual autocracy's "repeated violation of this feeling."[33] Unexpectedly, the first few weeks and months of the war saw this inner torment resolved. In an upsurge of patriotism, the country rallied behind the dynasty, and, as Bulgakov put it, the "streets of the capital [St Petersburg] witnessed the historically unheard-of sight of student demonstrations with the tsar's portrait and singing the national anthem."[34] Nicholas II returned the students' demonstration of loyalty with warmth and respect, and Bulgakov's heart, he said, "swelled with joy." All Russia, he dared believe for a moment, was on the verge of making his vision on the Yalta Embankment its own. But quickly disaster and disillusionment set in. Russia's early victories (in Galicia) turned into defeats (in Poland). Nicholas dismissed his cousin Grand Duke Nikolai Nikolaevich (a figure, says Bulgakov, who "had somehow made himself popular") and appointed himself Supreme Commander. ("I recall that I experienced this like the death of the country and dynasty, which it proved to be: I simply sobbed with the sheaf of newspaper in my hands.") The Duma assumed a revolutionary posture, and some sort of "mystical hand" seemed to lay hold of tsarist authority itself, driving it towards destruction. "The monthly change of ministers, impermissible in peace time, became like the temperature of the patient of a consumptive illness. I was exhausted from the torment, I died and was completely paralyzed. I was assisting at the death throes of a beloved being: the Russian tsardom in the person of the tsar."[35] The ministerial appointments of Khvostov and Protopopov Bulgakov experienced, in common with the opinion of most members of educated Russian society at the time, as "abominations."

---

[32] Louth, *Orthodox Theologians*, 43; Williams, *Sergii Bulgakov*, 124.
[33] Bulgakov, *Avtobiograficheskie*, 86.   [34] Ibid.   [35] Ibid., 87.

When the first blow for the Revolution, the assassination of Rasputin, was struck in December 1916, Bulgakov was at a small monastic house outside Moscow. "The five o'clock Vespers service was prayed as usual, people made their confessions and received Holy Communion after the Liturgy.... And then when Mass had finished, from room to room the astonishing news spread: Rasputin was dead."[36] The news had a profound effect on Bulgakov. With it, he realized how far apart he stood from the majority of his contemporaries, especially those closest to him among the intellectual elite, who were his friends. "My first, unmediated feeling was not at all of joy, as it was for most, but shock and bewilderment."[37] Everyone rejoiced, even the monks. The bishop who had celebrated Mass made the sign of the cross in gratitude. "I remember how much it struck me," recalled Bulgakov, himself seized, apparently alone, with evil premonition.[38] In this mood, Bulgakov returned to Moscow, where he met even more effusive rejoicing than at the monastery. Finding "hardly a single like-minded person" as himself, he became convinced that Rasputin's murder had "unleashed the Revolution."[39] Every last inhibition vanished. "People became open about and began speaking and even writing — true, not about killing the tsar — but about a palace coup."[40] Inspired by Maklakov's notorious (Bulgakov called it "vile") article likening Russia to a careening vehicle, and appealing desperately for the simple act of a change of chauffeur, his friends and acquaintances in the Duma began discussing whether so-and-so would be suitable for a given role in a given ministry as "naturally," said Bulgakov, "everything had been decided down to the last detail. I felt as if I was the only sane person in an epidemic of involuntary madness; it was not possible to understand the general blindness any other way."[41]

Particularly bitter to him were the speeches and actions, at this time, of the future head of the Provisional Government, Prince Lvov. He and Bulgakov had served together in the Second Duma of 1906, and, having known Lvov then as a "loyal servant of the Tsar," Bulgakov was shocked at the transformation when, from December 1916, Lvov began to adopt an openly revolutionary position.[42] Bulgakov also fell out with his friends, including Nikolai Berdyaev and Prince E. Trubetskoy and the other members of the Moscow religious-philosophical set that Solovyov had founded. In their own writings and activities, they contributed to increasing the revolutionary feeling; for defending the tsar, people Bulgakov had known for years looked on him as an idealist and a utopian. "And yet I repeat," he said, "I felt as though I was the only sober man among drunks, the only realist among so many illusionists, and my realism was Orthodoxy, the source of my sobriety love for the reigning emperor."[43]

[36] Ibid.   [37] Ibid.   [38] Ibid., 88.   [39] Ibid.
[40] Ibid.   [41] Ibid.   [42] Ibid.   [43] Ibid., 89.

As Bulgakov put it, capturing in a striking metaphor his perception of the roots of the looming Russian catastrophe, "I saw utterly clearly, I knew as a sixth sense, that the tsar is not a chauffeur that it is possible to change at a moment's notice, but the rock on which the hooves of the charging Russian steed are proved."[44]

A soirée at a private apartment in Moscow's Nikolsky Pereulok, today a fashionable shopping street a stone's throw from the Kremlin, in December 1916, especially stayed with him. To it had been invited I. D. Demidov, a Kadet deputy recently returned from an inspection tour of the front, whom, until this point, Bulgakov had respected for his sobriety and good sense:

> His report was rich in content, full of the wonderful and touching deeds of the Russian soldier and gave complete hope for victory. But it was also a total indictment of the tsar as Supreme Commander and his irresponsible and harmful changing of commanders of the various divisions and armies. The report was angry, passionate, and, in its own way, convincing, making us believe that Russia's cause was in unfaithful hands [i.e. Nicholas's] and that these hands had to be removed for the sake of victory, for the salvation of the Motherland.[45]

At the same time, however, Bulgakov was struck by the obvious contradictions in Davidov's claims. The allegations didn't add up. On the one hand, morale in the army was strong and victory to be hoped for; on the other, the man at the top under whom this hope of victory had become possible was a threat to the survival of Russia? To Bulgakov, Demidov revealed how far the spirit of revolution had infiltrated the army and captured the hearts and minds of the upper command. "I felt that evening as if death entered my soul," he recalled.[46] A discussion as to what was to be done ensued. In a packed room, speaker after speaker lauded the cause of revolution. Yet, of all those gathered there that evening, and suffering the taunts of his friend from *Vekhi*, Nikolai Berdyaev, who threw his voice behind Nicholas's removal, Bulgakov alone warned against the idea. Even if limited to a palace coup, a change of regime could not be without consequence for Russia's war effort, but would almost certainly provoke a collapse of the front. "Of them all, I was the only one who spoke against, that is expressed the simple thought that revolution, be it only a palace coup, cannot take place in a vacuum.... Oh, how often I have recalled that December evening with hopeless anguish!" he exclaimed.[47] After this, during the first weeks and months of 1917, "meetings took place all over Moscow," says Bulgakov, "at which a palace coup was openly discussed, as if it were an event that might happen tomorrow."[48] Arriving from Petrograd to animate them,

---

[44] Ibid.   [45] Ibid.   [46] Ibid., 90.   [47] Ibid.
[48] Ibid.

Bulgakov recalls, was Guchkov himself, the Octobrist and organizer of the most advanced plot to remove Nicholas, who would later travel to Pskov to obtain Nicholas's abdication manifesto, and become revolutionary Russia's first (albeit short-lived) War Minister.

The decisive day arrived with the demonstrations that broke out in Petrograd on February 26, 1917. The day happened to be Bulgakov's wife's birthday and, as usual, they spent the day in prayer at the Trinity-Sergius Monastery. Heavy snow lay on the ground. "How good it was to wander . . . among the sketes [i.e. the cells of the monastic elders] and the surrounding village."[49] When they got home to Moscow that evening, the news reached them. Their world had changed in an instant. Days such as the one they had just enjoyed were numbered, never to return. Such idylls of "Holy Rus" would not survive the collapse of the *teokratia*. Over the following days, news of the worsening situation in the capital reached them with what Bulgakov called "discouraging swiftness and certainty," and very quickly the revolution spread to Moscow. So-called "revolutionary bulletins" (which "as a rule were terrible to read from the beginning") began appearing.[50] Next, the police disappeared, and the crowds took justice into their hands, hunting down disguised constables and subjecting them to public humiliations. Vigilante groups, "sinister, long-haired types with revolvers in their hands," filled the vacuum left by the collapse of the old order. Finally, the Kremlin fell "almost without a shot," and the crowds began singing "their hideous revolutionary songs at their hideous demonstrations."[51] "Everybody celebrated, everybody rejoiced . . . everything was in red, and hideous red rags covered everything"; immediately, Bolshevik agitators appeared demanding an end to the war.[52]

Bulgakov was horrified at both its speed and its ugliness. "The Revolution was to me hateful and disgusting."[53] He "languished in anxiety for the Imperial Family."[54] And, yet so powerful was the Revolution as a phenomenon of collective conscience, says Bulgakov, that the desire to conform himself to the prevailing spirit almost mastered him, too. Thus, he recalled a "moment of cowardice" that reads like a repetition of his soon-regretted rejoicing with the students of the Polytechnic Institute on the streets of Kiev in 1905, only engaged in this time with even less conviction:

> I, too, wanted to force some rejoicing and join the crowd in celebration of "freedom." But I lacked the character to see it through to the end. I walked with the crowd on Ostozhenka Street on the day of the parade and got drunk. But it only lasted half an hour and nothing came of it, other than my own disgust. I saw and felt that

---

[49] Ibid., 90–91.   [50] Ibid., 91.   [51] Ibid.   [52] Ibid.
[53] Ibid.   [54] Ibid.

the Revolution was a big red lout, that life was becoming vulgar and low, and that already Russia was no more.[55]

At this stage, Nicholas still had not yet renounced the throne. But already Bulgakov watched as everyone around him in Moscow lost their heads with joy and celebration. Unable to stay away, he listened as his fellow-professors and students gave rousing speeches and swore oaths to "seize freedom." And all the while Bulgakov, like Hamlet, watched but never expressed publicly his own bitter disappointment. Neither did his sense of evil premonition leave him. "It was Cross Veneration week in Lent. Everyone had forgotten this, of course," recalled Bulgakov, "but I had the heaviest presentiment of the significance of this symbolic coincidence. Indeed, every one of my thoughts and anxieties — vain and powerless that they were, alas! — was with him, God's Anointed. How was it with him? Would he hang on to the throne?"[56] Then, from Petrograd, rumors of Nicholas's abdication began to arrive, and Bulgakov "knew in [his] heart that they were true because the people at the center of the Revolution hated the tsar. They didn't want a constitution, just the tsar's downfall as the Yids told them to," Bulgakov said in an anti-Semitic comment that shows how far the over-representation of secularized (former) Jews in the revolutionary movement had gone in pushing disposing Bulgakov, who always rejected "Black Hundredism," to an anti-Semitism that he would have surely rejected in relation to (religious) Jews not involved in the revolutionary movement.[57]

In any case, from that moment, says Bulgakov, he foresaw everything up to and including the tsar's murder, "for this great wickedness could not be anything other than tsaricide, that "black Mass of the Revolution."[58] For a while, the press reported regularly on the fate of the former imperial family. That the empress had been ill, and that so also had been Alexei, was suddenly discovered. "When I read about it, the final, impotent tears flowed from my eyes," recalled Bulgakov.[59] Then, the news arrived that Nicholas II had been arrested and imprisoned in Tsarskoye Selo. From then on, only intermittent news arrived about Nicholas II. "And yet it was amazing that in the middle of this sea of lies, accusations and profanities, he (i.e. Nicholas II) remained noble, spotless. Not a single unworthy, thankless, un-tsar-like act did he commit. Such dignity, such resignation, such humility. My thoughts were with them: what is going on with them? How are they?"[60] Easter 1917 came. "Evidence appeared," Bulgakov recalled, "that they made their confessions, took Holy Communion, and that they were allowed a priest. It was said that the emperor worked in the garden to the insults of the

[55] Ibid., 91–92.   [56] Ibid., 92.
[57] Ibid. On Bulgakov and anti-Semitism, see Williams, *Sergii Bulgakov*, 293–303.
[58] Bulgakov, *Avtobiograficheskie*, 92.   [59] Ibid.   [60] Ibid., 92–93.

representatives of the new thug-ocracy."[61] The news became less frequent. And then, Bulgakov said, addressing himself, "the deafening flow of events gushed forth so impetuously that you were forced to forget about the imperial prisoners until new rumors began to arrive."[62] The content of those rumors was, of course, that Nicholas and his family had been shot. So painful was the thought that Bulgakov, apparently, couldn't even write of it. At this point, his whole autobiography breaks off abruptly. Far from shaking his love of Nicholas or his belief in the tsar's holy authority, then, the experience of the Revolution had only confirmed Bulgakov in the sublime vision of Nicholas as embodiment of the theocratic ideal that Bulgakov had been given on the Yalta Embankment. Indeed, so completely had Bulgakov internalized that epiphany that, imperceptibly, Nicholas's story had become *Bulgakov's* story: after Nicholas's implied murder, Bulgakov's own autobiography peters out into broken episodes and vignettes, only to be resumed, years later, in the very different circumstances of flight and exile.

---

[61] Ibid., 93.

[62] Ibid.

The Symbol of Politics, Russia & West

ID THE THEOCRATIC PRINCIPLE COLLAPSE IN 1917, and subsequently revive? Or did it never in fact go away? Certainly, it seems that for all its conscious goal of abolishing *teokratia*, in conformity with the atheistic conclusions of nine-teenth-century philosophy which it sought to realize historically, Russian Communism always sublimated that Eastern Orthodox ideal more than it abolished it. As Nikolai Berdyaev, Bulgakov's Silver-Age friend and colleague, famously quipped in 1948, the Moscow of the Third Rome gave way in 1917 to the Moscow of the Third International: if the goal of the Russian *teokratia* had been, as Bulgakov put it, to construct the "City of God on earth," as far as was possible, then in its dream of a proletarian utopia the Soviet Union existed to realize a certain, secularized version of the same with a man-god (the proletar-iat) in the place of the God-Man (Christ).[1] Indeed, if, as early as 1918, Bulgakov, more far-sighted than most of his contemporaries, believed that Bolshevism appeared likely to survive in Russia where the liberal-ism of the Provisional Government failed, it was because Marxism was "authentically" pseudo-theocratic (and earlier still, Merezhkovsky, too, had foreseen this requirement). Though heading the world's first athe-ist state, Lenin had consigned *teokratia* to the dustbin of history less than he had naively secularized it. To be sure, Marxism denied that any world beyond the material existed, and yet, all the same, in Marxism, there was a *spirit* seeking to take form in history. As the General in Bulgakov's 1918 dialogue put it, the Bolshevik regime was at least carried out in bracing *russky stil* ("Russian style"), that is, it was based on a *myth*, a supra-historical idea that realized itself in history: "Bolshevism, after all, desires an Orthodox kingdom, only one according to a Socialist creed. For us, there is Holy Russia and an Orthodox people, for them, a Socialist homeland and a Socialist pseudo-theocracy.... Even their persecution of the Church is...from Socialistic piety and zeal in the faith, and, surely, it is better than atheistic 'tolerance.'"[2] If Marxism had any saving graces at all, then, it was that its own (albeit confused and mistaken) goal of utopia and the (almost personalized) determin-ism that it allotted to history quietly pointed beyond its own official materialistic nihilism.

---

[1] Nikolai Berdiaev, *The Russian Idea* (London: Macmillan, 1948), 9.
[2] Bulgakov, "At the feast of the gods," 81–82.

That, too, was the judgment of the Catholic Italian philosopher of history, Augusto Del Noce. Surveying the world in 1970, when an avowedly atheist Communist Party of the Soviet Union still ruled Russia from the Kremlin, Del Noce satirized the intellectual consensus that prevailed in the West's by now thoroughly secularized universities. "Every intellectual keeps saying," he wrote, "that by now we have entered the age of *homo progressivus*, and that demythologization is a sign of our maturity. Supposedly, Russia's historical delay is due to the fact of being, in part, still under the spell of myth." And yet, he noted, citing a colleague's recent work on myth and symbol, that "mythical consciousness is not just a residue of the original [i.e. primitive] consciousness that survived the advent of rational thought, but rather something necessary to human beings, in order to meet each other and find their way." For this reason, Del Noce opined, the "greatest paradox of contemporary history" was that "Russia's official atheism 'guards' an explicitly sacral myth" while the, officially, "non-atheist West . . . can stand against it only as a democracy 'devoid of the sacred.' Who, in the West still thinks about the unity of the religious and political spheres?"[3] To Del Noce, the answer was precisely: no one. Rather, by 1970, the Western sexual revolution had produced a form of secularization more radical than the one on display in the Soviet Union because the "critical," sublated Marxism of the West (which had, far more profoundly than the "dogmatic" Marxism of the Soviet Union, assimilated the conclusions of Kant's philosophy), no longer pointed, even despite itself, to any "spirit" beyond history. On the contrary, truth in the West had been so radically immanentized in the individual that the foundations of an official nihilism more profound than the Soviet Union's had been established. Paradoxically, then, it was "unquestionably true" to Del Noce that Russia, even with Marxists in the Kremlin, represented the "last bastion of the sacral mindset in the field of politics."[4] Of course, we would call it the last bastion of the theocratic principle. All the same, Del Noce thought, Russia would need "its own revision process, but of the opposite kind with respect to the Western process I have described," that is, *reversing* rather than radicalizing its historical judgment in favor of secularization. But he wondered: ". . . where will such process lead it?"[5] Today, I think we know the answer: to the visible resurgence of a theocratic principle that, while shaken and even in the minds of the intelligentsia discredited definitively, had never in fact died in Russian culture.

---

[3] Del Noce, "The Death of the Sacred," in id., *Crisis of Modernity*, 119.
[4] Del Noce wondered whether this underlying commitment, even under Communism, to the theocratic principle was 'the reason why in Russia religiosity has made a comeback . . . ? Is this why the Orthodox Church has been affected the least (or not at all) by the new Modernism, the theology of secularization and of the death of God . . . ?" Ibid.
[5] Del Noce, "The Death of the Sacred," 135.

৵৹   ৵৹   ৵৹

In the end, it was not only the theocratic principle that was revealed to Bulgakov on the Yalta Embankment. Revealed to him *through it* also that day was Russia. The theocratic principle was Russia's "entelechy." And wasn't this the meaning, and the tragedy, for Bulgakov of Nicholas II's murder? With it, Russian history, having lost its organizing principle, ended. In establishing the world's first atheist State, Russia, having become Marxist, ceased to be *Russia*. Unlike Bulgakov, however, who died in Paris in 1944, we know that the story did not end there, with the triumph of atheism. On the contrary, like Bulgakov himself at an earlier stage in his life, Russia has woken up from its flirtation with Marxism, renounced that theory's essential atheism, and returned, outwardly at least, on the level of much of its culture, to its ancestral Orthodoxy. In that sense, Bulgakov's story *is* Russia's story, and Nicholas's canonization in 2000 can be regarded as Russia's own "vision on the Yalta Embankment." The images of Nicholas as tsar that were removed and destroyed a hundred years ago have been restored as images of Nicholas the Royal Passion-bearer. Nicholas II, a man Russia had to "unsee," has not only been restored to view, but is offered now a man in whom God in a real sense is visible (inasmuch as God — grace, the energies, the divine life — is visible in all the saints through the Holy Spirit Who dwells in them and thereby makes them all icons of God's glory).[6] But what, more than the regeneration of the apparently discredited theocratic principle in Russian culture, does this fact point to? To answer that question, we need to reflect on the nature of the symbolic form of reasoning here implied.

In an essay on the theology of history, one of the great Catholic theologians of the twentieth century noted the difficulties sometimes faced by modern persons in making the movement, natural to ancient and medieval man, from an appreciation of the *fact* of reality to its higher meaning or cause. "It is a fact of experience that symbols have an important function in all religious life and thinking. Theological expression draws largely, in the normal course, upon images taken from sensory perception, in order to deal with spiritual realities: this is equally true of Biblical theology, and of the theology of the sacraments, as of mystical theology. Yet we have to recognize that there is something disturbing for the modern mind in this mode of intellectual activity. People conditioned to think in terms of efficient causes are inclined to

---

[6] For if God is visible, according to the Psalmist, in "Zion" (Ps 48:14), He is visible in its citizens, the saints. On the saints as "imaging" the divine life and glory, in both their bodies and their icons, see Ouspensky, *Theology of the Icon*, 1:166. Indeed, we could cite the Royal Passion-bearer (St) Alexandra, too: "Christ puts His own divine life into those who follow Him. He becomes embodied in them." See HM Empress Alexandra, *Garden of the Heart*, 8.

feel that the notion of exemplary causality must imply a lower standard of comprehension, better suited perhaps to poetry than to scientific knowledge, and falling short, at all events, of the strict criteria needed for full conviction. This line of criticism must be taken seriously, for it involves a kind of rebellion against the symbolic element in all theological teaching."[7]

Indeed, as the same theologian goes on to show, not only must this dismissal of symbolic reasoning be taken seriously; it must also be corrected. By dismissing the language and logic of symbols, modern man's ability to understand the world around him has been impoverished. Not merely arbitrary "emblems" or "logos" (as the plural of the term "logo"), as we especially in the post-nominalist and post-Kantian West are constantly tempted to regard them as being, symbols have a constant, real significance, as the result of the "effort of mind to extract the intelligible meaning contained within physical reality. This is not something purely subjective; the mind does not merely project its own pattern upon the world of things but discovers a real content through symbolic experience: that which is revealed from without."[8]

Indeed, symbolic reasoning is inseparable from any theology worthy of the name. As the same theologian continues, precisely because the function of symbols "is to afford us access through the visible into a higher, transcendent plane of being," symbols are a "hierophany, a manifestation of the holy, so that one aspect or another of the divine being and activity is revealed in all of them. There is an objective validity in religious symbolism which is rooted in the real nature of things.... Symbolism is no survival from a past, pre-logical mentality of man, but depends on the functioning of laws which never cease to govern realities of mind and of nature. It is directed towards the discovery of analogies between the visible and invisible worlds, and towards the formulation of their meaning. It is a genuine mode of apprehension of the things of God."[9] And how deeply the indispensability of symbols and symbolic theology is appreciated in the Eastern Church—visibly manifest in the central place of the holy icons—scarcely needs affirming.[10] As the great early Byzantine Christian writer known as Dionysius the Areopagite puts it, "We have therefore to run counter to mass prejudice and ... make the holy journey to the heart of the sacred symbols. And we must certainly not disdain them, for they are the descendants and bear the mark of the divine stamps. They are the manifest images of unspeakable and marvelous sights."[11]

---

[7] Daniélou, *Lord of History*, 130.   [8] Ibid., 135.

[9] Daniélou borrows the term "hierophany" from Mircéa Eliade.

[10] Among many, see Ware, *Orthodox Way*, 14.

[11] Pseudo-Dionysius the Areopagite, *Letter* 9.2 in Luibheid and Rorem, *Pseudo-Dionysius*, 284.

And yet how can we make this "sacred journey" if the very notion of the symbol is destroyed?[12] Indeed, if our theologian and Dionysius are correct in regarding the existence of an intrinsic relationship between belief in God and the symbolic form of reasoning, then the death of the capacity for symbolic reasoning would be another symptom of the imaginative impoverishment that pervades any society that adopts atheism as "its truth." This is the reason why, although the residue of the symbolic reasoning of previous generations remains, the modern secularized West has no need of—indeed, can barely conceive—such symbols. What can Nicholas II ever be *there* but a misguided individual human being? What is a "tsar" but the name given the office he held to mystify the mundane facts of absolute power?

And yet are we not the ones who cannot see? For among the elements of the world which human beings have almost universally credited with a symbolic meaning is surely the figure of the king: the consecrated ruler who unites in his person the cosmic order of which he is the sacred representative or delegate and the human political regime of which is ruler, judge, or head. Such a figure has recurred in apparently all human cultures: the Egyptian pharaoh, the Chinese Son of Heaven, the Incan emperor, the kings of Persia and ancient Israel, the Byzantine *basileus* and tsars of Muscovy; the Holy Roman Emperor and the Christian kings of the west. To be sure, Christianity does not endorse humanity's reception of the world's natural symbols unconditionally. To the extent that they reveal something true, it takes them up, purifies them, and turn them into types, hierophanies *of Christ*. And yet for all that Christ (from being born in a manger to dying on the Cross) also serves as a stumbling block to merely human conceptions of kingship, nonetheless, Christ, the Son of David, is for the Church King of Kings ("Lord of the Serafim," "King of Israel," and "King of All"). Rightly, then, does the Areopagite consider kingship to be one of the Divine Names, a power (or energy) in the world that proceeds from the superessential divine nature to make the otherwise unknowable God known.[13]

Beginning with the French Revolution, however, the movement of history, it seems, has been towards the *nullification* of this symbol: as a symbol of the due bond between the human and terrestrial and the divine and cosmic, the king is something, it seems, the world no longer wants, has a use for, or will tolerate. In a special sense, modernity finds a particular feature of its distinctiveness in its kinglessness. After all, as the symbol of God's ruling power over the universe, the king stood

---

[12] Schmemann, in *Church, World, Mission*, 24, laments the spiritual impoverishment that flows from the degradation of precisely the Church's symbols.
[13] Pseudo-Dionysius the Areopagite, Divine Names 12, in Luibheid and Rorem, *Pseudo-Dionysius*, 126–27.

for the claims of a *cosmic order* or *higher spiritual form* — a form to which it was, in the end, the king's job to see to it that the political community he was responsible for con-*formed* — over the otherwise always potentially formless human matter of this world. For it is part of man's special dignity that he should have been given the freedom to participate, *or not*, in his own conforming — a dignity, which, it seems, has also become for modern man an intolerable burden that he would be free of. Indeed, form is something that modernity defines itself by denying. As Hans Urs von Balthasar puts it in the prolegomena to his vast masterpiece:

> There have been ages of representation when it has been natural to experience the *kalokagathon* (the beautiful-and-the-good), so much so that the temptation was always at hand to slide back from the primal form into the derived forms — so rich was the abundance of forms offered. When these secondary forms come to decay and are regarded with suspicion as belonging to an ideology, then it is both easier and more difficult to find one's way back to the origins of form . . . our eyes lose their acumen for form and we become accustomed to read things by starting from the bottom and working our way up, rather than by working from the whole to the parts. Our multi-faceted glance is indeed suited to the fragmentary and the quantitative . . . we no longer credit man with the ability to achieve form whether metaphysically or ethically.[14]

Clearly, Balthasar considers our own time one of those ages that "no longer credits man with the ability to achieve form . . . metaphysically or ethically." Although evidence of this could be found all around us (from politics to art, architecture, and popular culture) for Balthasar, the supreme testimony to modernity's defining loss of attention to the "indissolubility of form" is the crisis in marriage.[15] By this measure (i.e. divorce rates), Russia may not be much better off than we are. But to the extent that the idea of the king is the age-old form of the *polis* (and the reason why the Heavenly City, the new Jerusalem, is precisely the Kingdom of God in the Person of His Son, the divine King of Kings), then Russia at least, in the canonization of Nicholas II, can be to seen to have retrieved — because perhaps it never entirely lost — the eyes to see *this* form, and with it, perhaps, the eyes, eventually, to see the rest.

In Russian culture, then, we might say, by contrast with that of Western Europe or North America, that the king has returned — and the image of that return is the Royal Passion-bearer Nicholas II (who suffers, we might add, precisely for the theocratic principle, conceived as a mechanism for realizing God's authority in the world). To put it

---

[14] Hans Urs von Balthasar, *The Glory of the Lord: A theological aesthetics*, vol. 1: *Seeing the form*, trans. Erasmo Leiva-Merikakis (San Francisco: Ignatius Press, 2009), 24–25.
[15] Ibid., 26, 27.

another way, in the canonization of the last tsar, Russian culture has rediscovered for itself precisely that symbol of God's ruling power in the universe that Western civilization has sought to abolish: that of the king. Can the world be indifferent to the rediscovery of this symbol, or does it not concern the rest of the world, too?

For does it follow that a civilization, such as the modern West, that has abolished kingship, has abolished with it a certain natural, symbolic witness to God? If so, then perhaps the value to *us in the West* of Russian culture's retrieval of the king-as-symbol lies in the opportunity it provides, by observation from outside, for re-engagement with the (half-forgotten) claims over the kings of this world of the one King of All (Christ, the King of Kings) to whom that symbol points. And if those claims are important, it is because on the acknowledgment of them hangs, more than we might care to admit, the reality of the whole order of the sacred. Indeed, we might say that a given society's recognition of *that* symbol — the symbol of the king — is directly proportional to its ability to recognize that "higher, transcendent plane of being" on which the reality of every other symbol depends. As Bulgakov put it in 1932, in a famous work on the Eucharist, "All prophecy relates to a theocracy (more precisely, Christocracy), which is revealed on earth and accomplished in history, as the revelation of its inner meaning and the end of its path. The king who has been pierced is the subject of contemplation, or rather, worship and veneration, by all peoples, and the god-fighting Christomachians" (one thinks of the Bolshevik guards persecuting the saints in the border of the icon of the New Russian Martyrs) will "bow down before the King of Jerusalem in His royal city."[16]

Of course, qualifications are also necessary. Today, Russia is not a monarchy, and most Russians, it seems, do not want it to be one. But to insist on the failure of political monarchism in Russia may be to miss the point. As Bulgakov put it in his contribution to *Out of the Depths*, it would be "too great an absurdity, a failure of history, if everything were simply restored."[17] And yet, Nicholas's canonization, the implicit recognition by the Church and by (*elements*, at least, of) Russian culture, that Nicholas was, in the end, as Merezhkovsky and friends foresaw ten years in advance of the Revolution, a martyr for the theocratic principle, and such devotion as the Royal Passion-Bearers have attracted — taken together, all these suggest that in the depths of what Bulgakov might call the "Church consciousness" of the Russian people, the theocratic principle only *appeared* to have been rejected in 1917. In fact, it lay dormant or was sublated during the Soviet era (hence, the

---

[16] Sergii Bulgakov, *The Eucharistic Sacrifice*, trans. Mark Roosien (Notre Dame, IN: Notre Dame University Press, 2021), 51–52.
[17] Bulgakov, "At the feast of the gods," 116.

semi-sacred aura that surrounded the embalmed Lenin or, still more, the "Red Tsar," Stalin), but now, with the collapse of Communism and the revival of Orthodoxy, the theocratic principle has spontaneously revived or come out of the shadows of the Russian subconsciousness and has, as an ideal, attached itself to its original, manifesting symbol: the Orthodox tsar, God's anointed, the representative and symbol of the authority of the God-Man Christ (literally, *the* Anointed One) over all the earth. This intuition does not mean that the Constantinian era of the Church (and, therefore, also the Constantinian era of the *world*) does not remain, as Bulgakov saw, over, in Russia as elsewhere: twenty-first century Moscow is *not* the capital of a revived Orthodox monarchy, with the anointed tsar Vladimir Putin at its head. But once again the Russian Church, and the culture it leads and infuses, *does* yearn for its "bridegroom," for a ruler wed to God on behalf of his people by the Church and to his people for God's sake in it. And precisely because this theocratic ideal no longer can be embraced constitutionally (for history, as Bulgakov saw, cannot fail, and Russia's 1917 judgment in favor of secularization cannot wholly be reversed), that yearning has taken the form of a saint's cult that is less significant than the underlying ideality of power that it symbolizes.

Albeit in part rather than *in toto*, Russia has reversed the judgment in favor of secularization it made in 1917. Whatever is formally stated in Russia's secular 1993 constitution, in Russian culture, at its deepest level, political authority does not arise from the people, democratically; it descends, as it always has done, once again from God, theocratically. To repeat: twenty-first-century Russia is not a *teokratia*. But all the same, Russians' unconscious conception of political order might with justice be described as sub-theocratic: residually aware of God's claims over it — that is to say, of the existence of a cosmic order of right and wrong over and above its lawmakers — but unable (and, indeed, unwilling, because of the lingering wounds of the twentieth century) to rouse itself to the consummation of a new *teokratia* constitutionally. And from this fact would flow not just a certain, eye-catching cynicism whose extremes attract the attention of shocked Western observers of Russian culture's often unflattering contemporary *surface*, but many of the salient differences that prevail between Russia and the West, respectively.[18]

In Putin's Russia, we might say, the "truth" of the theocratic

---

[18] For the cynicism of contemporary Russian culture, see, for example, Peter Pomerantsev, *Nothing is True but Everything is Possible* (New York: Public Affairs, 2015). We might say that such Western observers find in a kind of secular moralism, as the philosopher Semyon Frank might have predicted they would, the psychologically necessary internal defense against their own still greater nihilism. For Frank, see "The ethic of nihilism: a characterization of the Russian intelligentsia's moral outlook," in Schatz and Zimmerman, *Vekhi*, 131–55.

mystery of power has not been revived constitutionally. But the political consequences of that mystery's regeneration in Russian culture are felt. Once again, as the proliferating icons of Russia's last monarch would seem to testify, the "bride" of Russian Church-society calls for the "bridegroom" of the Russian State, and, naturally enough, in Bulgakov's schema, the would-be bridegroom hears it. Hence the references, in the Kremlin's rhetoric, to Russia's traditional religions (above all, Orthodoxy), Russian history, and Russian high culture as objects of respect and veneration and sources of unity. All these are things that may properly *be loved*, and in their presence, it would seem, the would-be bridegroom would expect Russians to submit freely and, as it were, loyally limit their demands for "freedom." Here, appeals to religion, culture, and history are not redundant, but an effective way of pointing to "values" — if not exactly, for all Russians, to a *living* tradition — that underlie Russia's claim to existence as an "imagined community" (or the fact of its really being a moral one, depending on how you look at it).[19] In either case, for the reasons we have seen, the claims of authority are accepted as normal and the mark of its *proper use* lies precisely *not* in the open-ended (because secular) task of ethical-legal conflict resolution, but in the "romancing" of the bride through the promised careful stewardship of her dowry. That dowry is the transmission, from one generation to the next, of what is assumed to be the more or less closed and stable body of moral and religious ideals that incorporate Russia's population as a subject of history, the people known as the *Russians*, united and defined in some important but difficult to define way by Orthodoxy (which, nonetheless, only a handful of the population practices consequentially every Sunday).

And yet, for all the reversal of the logic of secularization that this represents vis-à-vis the Soviet regime, the regime that emerges in Russia today is not *teokratia* as such. On the contrary, precisely that part of the process of secularization that Bulgakov recognized as irreversible reveals itself in the fact that the "bride" in today's Russia is not continuous with the Russian Church, as it could be imagined as being in Bulgakov's day, but a moral community not quite coterminous with it; while the "bridegroom" is not, of course, "by the grace of God," a hereditary monarch and anointed son of the Church, but, formally, an elected president, a people's tribune, "by popular dispensation."

---

[19] Benedict Anderson, *Imagined Communities: Reflections on the origin and spread of nationalism*, rev. ed. (London: Verso, 2006). Unsurprisingly, Anderson's fundamental logic is secular and Marxist. Presumably, because real metaphysical goods don't exist, the only way to explain people's belief in their existence is through the childish activity of "imagination." To say this is not to deprecate imagination; it is to say that any account of imagination that denies that the act of imagining can intuit the real is in itself a deprecation of the imagination.

Obviously, in the presence of two such secularized parties, the bond between the bride and bridegroom cannot be elevated to the Church's liturgy, as it was before 1917. Like the cohabiting parties to a common-law marriage, the union is *de facto*, not *de jure*, pragmatic rather than sacramental. There is eros, but of a guarded kind. Both would-be bride and would-be bridegroom reserve the right to take a certain independence from the objects of their love. Perhaps this or that element of the order exterior to modern Russian society will no longer be found congenial: the trick is to ensure that both parties evolve their attitudes at more or less the same pace.

But all the same, as we have suggested, perhaps we may well call Russian democracy "sub-theocratic," inasmuch as it responds to the same "theocratic" impulse but is unable to rouse itself to the transcendence of the tension between the two through the bond of the Church (where precisely in the Eucharist order and freedom are united) that sealed the old *teokratia*.

Hence the tendency on the part of the modern, secular Russian state to lapse, as would-be "bridegroom," into a relationship not only of naked coercion vis-à-vis its common-law spouse (visible, of course, also in tsarism) but also of an apparently instinctive cynicism, reminiscent of Marxism-Leninism, where, truly, politics *was* the cosmic order and no moral or metaphysical reality existed outside it. Here, the temptation, for a modern and secular Russian state that considers itself an icon of nothing but itself, merely to instrumentalize the Church for the sake of securing obedience to itself is clear enough (and a direct function of contemporary Russia's being not excessively but *insufficiently* theocratic). But hence also the dilemma of the Russian Church and the culture she has formed before the secular, authoritarian regime of the current kind and the secular Western "legal state" that it is invited to consider its alternative. To adopt *it* in frustration with the Kremlin's alleged cynicism would be to invite an intensified secularization that would destroy (as it has in the West) even the memory of *teokratia*, if not the practice of religion itself. Such, it seems, would be the religious logic of the current Russian regime as well as the character of Russian society's dilemma before it.

And what of the West? What would Bulgakov make of *it*? To be sure, the Western, liberal-democratic "legal State" was far from all bad, Bulgakov believed. "Precisely thanks to this utilitarianism," Bulgakov wrote, "the mechanism of power, its technique, is being perfected. [...] Guarantees of all kinds of 'freedoms' are established. Something that absolutism neither knew how nor wished to arrange [...] is being done." But to disguise this void of *right*, and hence of authority, at the heart of the modern Western polity, Bulgakov believed, the Western legal state, in its moments of crisis, can do nothing but fall back on the *myth* of democracy as a regime that mystically mediates the secular people's emancipated will. Indeed, he says, democracy, considered in these terms, is its own kind of theocracy, only with the people having taken the place of God, and without the existence of anything at all beyond it. "Even secularized power," he writes, "cannot hold on utilitarianism alone — even it needs a distinctive religious consecration, which it finds in the mystical deification of the people, [...] a variant of the deified humanity. Overthrowing the thrones that rested upon divine right, the revolution itself rests on the 'popular will' which only comes to light through voting but represents a self-subsisting mystical reality"; a "type of humanistic theocracy arises which sees its task in faithfully defining and realizing the true 'will of the people.' But how is this to be achieved, and where is one to seek it?" Foreseeing, it seems, not only the crisis of Western liberalism in the 1920s and 1930s, but also in our own time today, Bulgakov answered his own question: "The awareness of the clear insufficiency of 'ballot boxes' and voting papers for this purpose, fit only for deciding separate practical questions, elicits a lengthy 'crisis of the sense of justice' (as Athenian democracy endured in the epoch of Plato, under completely analogous circumstances). The question of the 'law of the law' becomes for thoughtful jurists their own form of squaring the circle.... *Legality* proves to be the highest form of human relations." [20] In short, the question is whether mere legality is enough to hold a complex community together. Isn't love (if not of the tsar then of *something*) and the duality required to summon it, which had been banished from the modern polity, precisely needed?

Even before the Bolsheviks had seized power, then, Bulgakov predicted that, eventually, liberalism in Russia would give way to a popular dictatorship, when the "statehood of the deified people" will "obtain a personal head who with all his being will accommodate the claims of a kingdom from this world" and "the mysticism of deified humanity will be maximally manifested in conscious opposition to Christianity." [21] In short, in 1916, Bulgakov had not only foreseen that in Russia, liberalism must give way to Leninism and Leninism to Stalinism; he had foreseen that in the West, too, a merely Kantian, legal, liberal-democratic politics (proceeding, as it did, from a denial of the reality of God's existence) must eventually become anti-Christian. To be sure, Bulgakov conceded, "the external victory of 'secularization,' of the 'legal State,' was prepared with its human integrity sincerely guarding the 'good of the people' and its freedom." [22] But nonetheless, he shuddered and recoiled at the secular, democratic regime that was coming, not only in Russia, but in all the world. "Precisely this atmosphere of

---

[20] Bulgakov, *Unfading Light*, 414.   [21] Ibid.   [22] Ibid., 415.

militant deification of the people, of the kingdom of this world, forces the spiritual suffocation of those who cherish in their soul a religious ideal of power and who do not want to worship 'the beast' or receive its 'mark,'" he wrote, speaking of himself: "One can and must preserve one's loyalty and endure even a hated state system, even highly value its practical achievements, by seeing in it a relative everyday good or just a lesser evil than the antiquated and inveterately lying power of the old style. But to love this power, to feel a religious eros for it, is possible only by taking part in the cult of a democratic Caliban, 'offering sacrifices to the beast.'"[23] This was hardly inspiring; by denying the sacred mystery of power as theocracy, the Western legal state had become as good as demonic. He could think of his accommodation with it only in terms of a penance or a purification. "One ought to accept a state system that is reduced to political utilitarianism just as one would the burden of economic concerns: acknowledging the integrity of this labor, to bear it ascetically as a vital 'obedience.'"[24] But as a religious man, Bulgakov knew he would never be at home it: "the integrity, the correctness, is only a religious-moral minimum whereas religion in all of its affairs wants the maximum."[25]

In the end, then, Bulgakov's attachment to tsarism was theological. Kings had been given to the world as symbols of God on Earth, reminders to men of the ineffable sovereign and almighty divine power that had created them. Of these kings, the anointed, Orthodox tsar had been given to Russia as a special grace, a more exact, luminous, and transparent icon of the mystery of power than, in God's wisdom, other peoples had been blessed with. If, therefore, anointed tsars, and kings generally, had been abolished by the secular turn in human history that reached a certain culmination in the Russian Revolution, it was for his fellow man's knowledge of God that Bulgakov regretted it. Men had lost a symbol or a form that had served to direct them to the world of the spirit, in which the meaning and end of the mystery of power in Christ, the crucified king, was hidden. For this reason, then, while Bulgakov believed that the secular Western legal state had a certain additional value as a "negative revelation of power" (inasmuch as, through the void which Bulgakov believed lay at the heart of secular democratic politics, man might be encouraged again to embark on the search for the theocratic mystery), nonetheless the "expanded and differentiated body of power" that was the Western legal State was also "'the land of the curse,' cracked and dried out [...] it longs for heavenly water." Even in view of all the egregious flaws of the modern Russian State, Bulgakov might perhaps agree that it was the special calling of Russian culture to bear witness even (or perhaps even *especially*) to the

---

[23] Ibid.   [24] Ibid.   [25] Ibid.

more "rational," lawful, and secularized peoples of the West that, for all
Western democracy's achievements and advantages, nonetheless, to cite
Bulgakov a final time, "the legal state, with its legal guarantees and all
its earthly wisdom and human-relative truth, does not extinguish the
yearning for *a different* kingdom, not only of cold law but of love, for
a different power — the theocratic."[26]

---

[26] Ibid. He continues: "But, of course, this question has meaning only in the Church,
and it is a question here not of politics in the usual sense of the word, but precisely
of the religious overcoming of politics."

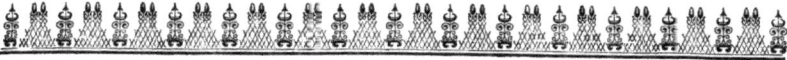

BIBLIOGRAPHY

PRIMARY SOURCES (HISTORICAL AND CONTEMPORARY)

"10 Years Since Bolotnaya, the Biggest Protests of the Putin Era," *Moscow Times*, December 9, 2021: https://www.themoscowtimes.com/2021/12/09/10-years-since-bolotnaya-the-biggest-protests-of-the-putin-era-a75739.

"Declaration on the Russian World Teaching," *Public Orthodoxy*, Eastern Orthodox Christian Studies Center at Fordham University, on March 13, 2022: https://publicorthodoxy.org/2022/03/13/a-declaration-on-the-russian-world-russkii-mir-teaching/.

"Putin Declares Patriotism Russia's Only National Idea," *Moscow Times*, February 4, 2016: https://www.themoscowtimes.com/2016/02/04/putin-declares-patriotism-russias-only-national-idea-a51705. Accessed September 30, 2024.

"Russia Builds 3 New Churches a Day, Orthodox Leader Says," *Moscow Times*, May 27, 2019: https://www.themoscowtimes.com/2019/05/27/russia-builds-3-new-churches-a-day-orthodox-leader-says-a65755.

Alexandra Fyodorovna Romanova, *Garden of the Heart: Spiritual Diary* (New York: Concept, 2016).

Balthasar, Hans Urs von, *The Glory of the Lord: A theological aesthetics*, vol. 1: *Seeing the form*, trans. Erasmo Leiva-Merikakis (San Francisco: Ignatius Press, 2009).

Benkendorff, Paul de, "Derniers jours du Tsar à Tsarskoie Selo 11 mars — 14 août 1917: I," *Revue des Deux Mondes* 43 (1928): 523–48.

Bing, Edward J., ed., *The Letters of Tsar Nicholas and Empress Marie: being the confidential correspondence between Nicholas II, last of the tsars, and his mother, Dowager Empress Maria Feodorovna* (London: Nicholson and Watson, 1937).

Bogdanovich, E. V., *Istoricheskoe Palomnichestvo Nashego Tsarya v 1913 g.* (Nizhnii Novgorod: Russian Orthodox Church-Moscow Patriarchate, 2017).

Bulgakov, Sergei, "At the feast of the gods," in William F. Woehrlin, ed. and trans., *Out of the Depths [Iz glubiny]: A Collection of Articles on the Russian Revolution* (Irvine, CA: Charles Schlacks Jr., 1986): 65–118.

——, "Heroism and asceticism: reflections on the religious nature of the Russian intelligentsia," in Schatz, Marshall S., and Zimmerman, Judith E., ed. and trans., *Vekhi. Landmarks: A collection of articles about the Russian intelligentsia* (London: M. E. Sharpe, 1994): 17–49.

——, "Under the Walls of Chersonesos" = Serge Boulgakov, *Sous les remparts de Chersonèse*, ed. and trans. Barnard Marchadier (Geneva: Ad Solem, 1999).

——, *Karl Marx as a religious type: His relation to the religion of anthropotheism of L. Feuerbach*, ed. Donald W. Treadgold, trans. Virgil R. Lang (Belmont, MA: Nordland Pub. Co., 1979).

——, *The Eucharistic Sacrifice*, trans. Mark Roosien (Notre Dame, IN: Notre Dame University Press, 2021).

——, *Avtobiograficheskie Zametki*, 2nd ed. (Paris: YMCA Press, 1991).

——, *A Bulgakov Anthology*, ed. Nicholas Zernov and James Pain (London: SPCK, 1976).

——, *The Orthodox Church*, rev. ed., trans. Lydia Kesich (Crestwood, NY: St Vladimir's Seminary Press, 1988).

——, *Unfading Light: Contemplations and speculations*, trans. Thomas Allen Smith (Grand Rapids, MI: Eerdmans, 2012).

Dehn, Lili, *The Real Tsaritsa* (Boston: Little, Brown and Co., 1922).

Dionysius the Areopagite, *Pseudo-Dionysius: The complete works*, trans. Colm Luibheid and Paul Rorem (New York: Paulist Press, 1987).

Edel, Anastasia, "The remains of the Romanovs," *New York Times*, 10 July 2017: https://www.nytimes.com/2017/07/10/opinion/red-century-russia-romanov.html

Elkhaninov, Andrei Georgievich, *Tsarstvovanie Gosudaria Imperatora Nikolaia Aleksandrovicha* (C.PB [Sankt-Peterburg"]: Sel'skago Viestnika, 1913).

Ern, Vladimir, "Ot Kanta k Kruppu," in id., *Mech i Krest: Stati o sovremennikh sobytiiakh* (Moscow: I. D. Sytina, 1915), 20–34.

Fabritsky, Semion S., *Of Bygone Days: The memoirs of an aide-de-camp to the Emperor Nicholas II*, trans. William Lee (Bowmanville, Ontario: Gilbert's Book, 2016).

Feodorovskii Gosudariev Sobor v Tsarskom Sele (St Petersburg: St Petersburg Eparchy, Russian Orthodox Church-Moscow Patriarchate, undated).

Fuhrmann, Joseph T., ed., *The Complete Wartime Correspondence of Tsar Nicholas II and the Empress Alexandra, April 1914–March 1917* (Westport, CT: Greenwood Press, 1999).

Ganina Yama Monastery website: https://ganinayama.ru/o-monastyre/istoriya-monastyrya/.

Gapon, Georgii, *Story of My Life* (New York: E. P. Dutton and Co., 1906).

Gilliard, Pierre, *Thirteen Years at the Russian Court* (unnamed publisher, 2016).

Golder, Frank Alfred, ed., *Documents of Russian History*, trans. Emanuel Armstrong (New York: Century Co., 1927).

Holy Synod of the Russian Empire, *Chin" deiistviia kakim" obrazom" sovershit'sia imeiet' sviashcheneiishee koronovanie ego imperatorskago velichestva gosudaria imperatora Nikolaia Aleksandrovicha* (St Petersburg: Holy Synod Press, 1896).

Izwolsky, Alexandre, "Souvenirs de mon ministère, II: Après la dissolution de la Douma," *Revue des Deux Mondes* 52:1 (July 1919): 100–31.

——, "Souvenirs de mon ministère, IV: Nicholas II," *Revue des deux mondes* 55:1 (January 1920): 46–77.

John of Damascus, St, *Three Treatises on the Divine Images*, trans. Andrew Louth (Crestwood, NY: St Vladimir's Seminary Press, 2003).

Kirill, patriarch of Moscow and All Rus', "Pastoral Message," May 9, 2013: http://www.patriarchia.ru/db/text/2836965.html.

Kokovtsov, Vladimir, *Out of My Past: The memoirs of Count Kokovtsov*, ed. Harold Henry Fisher, trans. Laura Matveev (Stanford, CA: Stanford University Press, 1935).

Kozlov, Vladimir, Khrustalev, Vladimir, and Raskina, Alexandra, eds., *The Last Diary of Tsaritsa Alexandra*, trans. Laura E. Wolfson (New Haven, CT: Yale University Press, 1997).

Leo XIII, pope, *Immortale Dei* (1885): https://www.vatican.va/content/leo-xiii/en/encyclicals/documents/hf_l-xiii_enc_01111885_immortale-dei.html.

Luhn, Alec, "'Finally!': pope and Russian patriarch meet for first time in 1,000 years," *The Guardian*, February 13, 2016: https://www.theguardian.com/

world/2016/feb/12/pope-francis-russian-orthodox-patriarch-kirill-make-history-cuba-first-meeting-in-1000-years.

Magoulias, Fr Jon, *The Divine Liturgy of St John Chrysostom* (n.p.: Petersen Books, 2021).

Maylunas, Andrei, and Mironenko, Sergei, eds., *A Lifelong Passion: Nicholas and Alexandra, their own story*, trans. Darya Galy (London: Phoenix Giant, 1996).

Merezhkovsky, Dmitry, Gippius, Zinaida, and Filosofov, Dmitry, *Le Tsar et la révolution* (Paris: Société du Mercure, 1907).

Nicholas II, Diary (1) = *Dnevnik Imperatora Nikolaia II* (Berlin: Slovo, 1923).

Nicholas II, Diary (2) = *Dnevniki Imperatora Nikolaia II* (Moscow: Orbita, 1991).

Paley, Princess, *Memories of Russia, 1916–1919* (London: Herbert Jenkins, 1924).

Pew Research Center, "Being Christian in Western Europe," May 29, 2018: https://www.pewresearch.org/religion/2018/05/29/being-christian-in-western-europe/.

Pew Research Center, "Russians Return to Religion, But Not to Church," February 10, 2014: https://www.pewresearch.org/religion/2014/02/10/russians-return-to-religion-but-not-to-church/.

Pussy Riot, "Punk Prayer": https://genius.com/Pussy-riot-punk-prayer-english-translation-lyrics.

Putin, Vladimir, "Meeting of the Valdai International Discussion Club," October 19, 2017: http://en.kremlin.ru/events/president/news/55882.

——, "Presidential Address to the Federal Assembly," December 4, 2014: http://en.kremlin.ru/events/president/news/47173.

——, "Unveiling of monument to Grand Duke Sergei Alexandrovich," March 4th 2017: http://www.en.special.kremlin.ru/events/president/transcripts/54447.

——, "70th Session of the United Nations General Assembly," 28 September 2015: http://en.kremlin.ru/events/president/news/50385.

——, "Unveiling of monument to Alexander III," 18 November 2017: http://en.kremlin.ru/events/president/news/56125.

Remizov Mikhail, et al., *Konservatizm kak faktor 'miakoi sily' Roccii* (Institute of National Strategy, undated).

Russian Orthodox Church-Moscow Patriarchate, *Basis of the Social Concept of the Russian Orthodox Church*: https://old.mospat.ru/en/documents/social-concepts/.

——, *Report of the Holy Synod Commission on the Canonization of Saints with Respect to the Martyrdom of the Royal Family* (1996). The text can be found in English translation at: https://www.holy-trinity.org/feasts/nicholas.html.

Shargunov, Prot. Aleksandr, *Tsar* (Zlatoust: Arvato, 2013).

Schatz, Marshall S., and Zimmerman, Judith E., ed. and trans., *Vekhi. Landmarks: A collection of articles about the Russian intelligentsia* (London: M. E. Sharpe, 1994).

Shavel'skii, Georgii, *Vospominaniia: poslednego protopresvitera russkoj armii i flota*, 2 vols. (New York: Chekhov Publishing, 1954).

Solov'ev, Vladimir, *La Russie et l'Église universelle* (Paris: A. Savine, 1889).

Spiridovitch, Alexandre, *Dernières Années de la Cour de Tsarkoïe-Selo*, 2 vols. (Paris: Payot, 1928).

Swezey, Marilyn, ed., *The Romanovs under house arrest: From the 1917 diary of a palace priest*, trans. Leonid Michailitschenko (Jordanville, NY: Holy Trinity Publications, 2018).

Syroboiarskii, A. V., *Skorbnaia Pamiatka* (unnamed publisher, 1928).

Tikhomirov, Lev, *Monarkhicheskaia Gosudarstvennost'* (Moskva: Universal, 1905).

Vil'chkovskii, S. N., "Prebyvanie gosudaria imperatora v Pskove, 1 i 2 marta 1917 goda," *Russkaia Lietopis'* 3 (1922): 161–87.

Voeikov, V. N., *S Tsarem i bez Tsaria: vospominaniia posliedniago Dvortsovago Komendanta Gosudaria Imperatora Nikolaia II* (Helsinki: publisher not identified, 1936).

Vyrubova, Anna, *Memories of the Russian Court* (London: Macmillan, 1923).

Woehrlin, William F., ed. and trans., *Out of the Depths [Iz glubiny]: A Collection of Articles on the Russian Revolution* (Irvine, CA: Charles Schlacks Jr., 1986).

World Bank, National Accounts Data: https://data.worldbank.org/indicator/ NY.GDP.MKTP.CD?locations=RU.

SECONDARY LITERATURE

Aliev, Rostislav, *The Siege of Brest, 1941: A legend of Red Army resistance on the Eastern Front*, trans. Stuart Britton (Barnsley: Pen and Sword Military, 2013).

Anderson, Benedict, *Imagined Communities: Reflections on the origin and spread of nationalism*, rev. ed. (London: Verso, 2006).

Andreeva, T. S., et al. *Tsarskoe Selo, 1917: Nakanunie...* (St Petersburg: Russkaia Kollektsiia, 2017).

Aron, Leon, *Roads to the Temple: Truth, memory, ideas and ideals in the making of the Russian Revolution, 1987–1991* (New Haven, CT: Yale University Press, 2012).

Ascher, Abraham, *The Revolution of 1905*, vol. 1: *Russia in Disarray* (Stanford, CA: Stanford University Press, 1988).

Barker, Sir Ernest, *Social and Political Thought in Byzantium* (Oxford: Oxford University Press, 1961).

Baynes, Norman H., *Byzantine Studies and Other Essays* (London: Athlone Press, 1955).

Berdiaev, Nikolai, *The Russian Idea* (London: Macmillan, 1948).

Billington, James H., *The Icon and the Axe: An interpretive history of Russian culture* (New York: Vintage Books, 1970).

Bogumil, Zuzanna, "Between history and religion: the New Russian Martyrdom as an invented tradition," *East European Politics, Societies and Cultures* 32:4 (2018): 936–63.

Bowlt, John E., *Moscow and St Petersburg, 1900–1920: Art, life and culture* (New York: Vendome, 2008).

Brooke, Caroline, *Moscow: A cultural history* (Oxford: Oxford University Press, 2006).

Burgess, John P., *Holy Rus': The rebirth of Orthodoxy in the New Russia* (New Haven, CT: Yale University Press, 2017).

Buxhoeveden, Sophie, *The Tragic Empress: The authorized biography of Alexandra Romanov* (n.p.: Taylor Street Books, 2016).

Byrnes, Robert F., *Pobedonostsev: His life and thought* (Bloomington, IN: Indiana University Press, 1968).

Caillet, Serge, *Monsieur Philippe, l'ami de Dieu* (Paris: Dervy, 2013).

Charles Taylor, *A Secular Age* (Cambridge, MA: Harvard University Press, 2007).

Cherniavsky, Michael, *Tsar and People: Studies in Russian myths* (New Haven, CT: Yale University Press, 1961).

Cohn, Norman, *Warrant for Genocide: The myth of the Jewish World-Conspiracy and the Protocols of the Elders of Zion* (New York: Harper & Row, 1967).

Dal Santo, Matthew J., "From Kant to Krupp—and Kiev: Vladimir Ern on Kantianism as a Source of War, 1914 and Today," *Telos* 205 (Winter, 2023): 128–49.

——, "Russia, the Ukraine War, and the West's Empire of Secularization," *Telos* 201 (Winter 2022): 146–64.

——, "The analogy of kingship: a mystagogy of the coronation of Charles III," *New Polity: A journal of post-liberal thought* (2023): 35–42.

——, "Theopolitics of Ukraine," *First Things*, August 2023.

Daniélou, Jean, "The conception of history in the Christian Tradition," *Journal of Religion* 30 (1950): 171–79.

——, *The Lord of History: Reflections on the inner meaning of history*, trans. Nigel Abercrombie (London: Longmans, 1958).

Davis, Nathaniel, *A Long Walk to Church: A contemporary history of Russian Orthodoxy* (Boulder, CO: Westview Press, 2003).

Del Noce, Augusto, *Age of Secularization*, trans. Carlo Lancellotti (Montreal: McGill-Queen's University Press, 2017).

——, *The Crisis of Modernity*, ed. and trans. Carlo Lancelotti (Montreal: McGill-Queen's University Press, 2014).

Dickinson, Anna, "Quantifying religious oppression: Russian Orthodox Church closures and repression of priests, 1917–41," *Religion, State & Society* 28:4 (2000): 327–35.

Dowler, Wayne, *Russia in 1913* (DeKalb, IL: Northern Illinois University Press, 2010).

Dvornik, Francis, *Early Christian and Byzantine Political Philosophy*, 2 vols. (Washington, DC: Dumbarton Oaks Center for Byzantine Studies, 1966).

Engelstein, Laura, *Slavophile Empire: Imperial Russia's illiberal path* (Ithaca, NY: Cornell University Press, 2009).

Ermichev, A. A., *V. F. Ern: Pro et Contra: Lichnost' i tvorchestvo Vladimira Erna v otsenke russkikh myslitelei i issledovatelei* (St Petersburg: Izd-vo Russkoi khristianskoi gumanitarnoi akademii, 2006).

Evtuhov, Catherine, *The Cross and the Sickle: Sergei Bulgakov and the Fate of Russian Religious Philosophy, 1890–1920* (Ithaca, NY: Cornell University Press, 1997).

Fedotov, G. P., *The Russian Religious Mind. Kievan Christianity: the 10th to the 13th centuries* (New York: Harper and Row, 1960).

Fennell, John, *A History of the Russian Church* (Longman, 1995).

Figes, Orlando, *A People's Tragedy: The Russian Revolution, 1891–1924* (London: Pimlico, 1997).

——, and Kolonitskii, Boris, *Interpreting the Russian Revolution: The Language and Symbols of 1917* (New Haven, CT: Yale University Press, 1999).

——, *Crimea: The last crusade* (Harmondsworth: Penguin, 2011).

Fisher, Alan W., *The Russian Annexation of the Crimea, 1772–1783* (Cambridge: Cambridge University Press, 1970).

Fitzpatrick, Sheila, *Everyday Stalinism. Ordinary life in extraordinary times: Russia in the 1930s* (Oxford: Oxford University Press, 2000).

Florovsky, Georges, *Ways of Russian Theology* = vols. 5 and 6 in idem, *Collected Works of Georges Florovsky*, ed. Richard S. Haugh, trans. Robert L. Nichols (Belmont, CA: Nordland Publishing Co., 1979).

Forczyk, Robert, *Where the Iron Crosses Grow: The Crimea, 1941–44* (Oxford: Osprey, 2014).

Forsyth, James, *A History of the Peoples of Siberia: Russia's North Asian Colony, 1581–1990* (Cambridge: Cambridge University Press, 1992).

Freeze, Gregory L., "A pious folk? Religious observance in Vladimir diocese, 1900–1914," *Jahrbücher für Geschichte Osteuropas* 52 (2004): 323–40.

——, "Religion and political crisis in late imperial Russia," *Journal of Modern History* 68 (1996): 308–50.

——, ed., *Russia: A history*, 3rd ed. (Oxford: Oxford University Press, 2009).

Fuller, William C., *The Foe Within: Fantasies of treason and the end of Imperial Russia* (Ithaca, NY: Cornell University Press, 2006).

Ganzer, Christian, "German and Soviet losses as an indicator of the length and intensity of the Battle for the Brest Fortress," *Journal of Slavic Military Studies* 27 (2014): 449–66.

Gatrell, Peter, *A Whole Empire Walking: Refugees in Russia during World War I* (Bloomington, IN: Indiana University Press, 2005).

——, *Government, Industry and Rearmament in Russia, 1900–14: The last argument of tsarism* (Cambridge: Cambridge University Press, 2010).

——, *Russia's First World War: A social and economic history* (London: Pearson, 2005).

——, *The Tsarist Economy, 1850–1917* (London: St Martin's Press, 1986).

Gaut, Greg, "Christian politics: Vladimir Solovyov's Social Gospel theology," *Modern Greek Studies Yearbook* 10/11 (1994/1995): 653–74.

Geifman, Anna, *Thou Shalt Kill: Revolutionary terrorism in Russia, 1894–1917* (Princeton, NJ: Princeton University Press, 1993).

Grover, Stuart, "The World of Art Movement in Russia," *Russian Review* 32 (1973): 28–42.

Guroian, Vigen, "Constantine and Christendom," in Guroian, *The Orthodox Reality: Culture, theology and ethics in the modern world* (Grand Rapids, MI: Baker Academic, 2018), 23–35.

Halperin, Charles, *Russia and the Golden Horde: The Mongol impact on medieval Russian history* (Bloomington, IN: Indiana University Press, 1985).

Hasegawa, Tsuyoshi, *The February Revolution: Petrograd, 1917* (Seattle, WA: University of Washington Press, 1981).

Heretz, Leonid, *Russia on the eve of modernity: Popular religion and traditional culture under the last tsars* (Cambridge: Cambridge University Press, 2008).

Holquist, Peter, "'Conduct merciless mass terror': Decossackization on the Don in 1919," *Cahiers du monde russe* 38 (1997): 127–62.

Horujy (Khoruzhii), Sergei S., "Vladimir Solov'ev's legacy after a hundred years," *Russian Studies in Philosophy* 46 (2007): 5–34.

Hosking, Geoffrey, *Russia and the Russians: A history*, 2nd ed. (Harmondsworth: Penguin, 2012).

——, *Russia: People and empire, 1552–1917* (London: Fontana Press, 1998).

——, *The Russian Constitutional Experiment: Government and Duma, 1907–1914* (Cambridge: Cambridge University Press, 1973).

Ioffe, Grigory, *Understanding Belarus and Why Western Foreign Policy Misses the Mark* (Lanham, MD: Rowman and Littlefield, 2008).

Jedin, Hubert, ed., *History of the Church*, vol. 3, trans. John Patrick Dolan (New York: Seabury Press, 1980).

Kalinin, N. N., and Zemlianichenko, M. A., *Romanovy i Krym. 'U vsekh nas ostalas' toska po Krymu...'* (Simferopol': Biznes-Inform, 2021).

Kantor, V. K., "Vladimir Solov'ev: The imperial problems of world theocracy," *Russian Studies in Philosophy* 46 (2007): 76–102.

Kantorowicz, Ernst H., *The King's Two Bodies: A study in medieval political theology* (Princeton, NJ: Princeton University Press, 2016).

Katkov, George, *Russia, 1917: The February Revolution* (New York: Harper & Row, 1967).

Kee, Alistair, *Constantine versus Christ: The triumph of ideology* (London: SCM Press, 1982).

King, Greg, *The Last Empress: The life and times of Alexandra Feodorovna Tsarina of Russia* (New York: Carol Publishing, 1994).

Kizenko, Nadieszda, *A Prodigal Saint: Father John of Kronstadt and the Russian people* (University Park, PA: State University of Pennsylvania Press, 2000).

Kontzevich, Helen, *Saint Seraphim, Wonderworker of Sarov and His Spiritual Inheritance* (Saint Xenia Skete, 2004).

Kozelsky, Mara, *Christianizing Crimea: Shaping sacred space in the Russian Empire and beyond* (DeKalb, IL: Northern Illinois University Press, 2010).

Kruse, Simon, "Prins Romanoff og det symbolske besøg," Berlingske, September 12, 2015: https://www.b.dk/globalt/prins-romanoff-og-det-symbolske-besoeg.

Laruelle, Marlene, "The Emergence of the Russian Young Conservatives," in A. James McAdams and Alejandro Castrillon, eds., *Contemporary Far-Right Thinkers and the Future of Liberal Democracy* (London: Routledge, 2022), 149–66.

Leithart, Peter, *Defending Constantine: The twilight of an empire and the dawn of Christendom* (Downers Grove, IL: IVP Academic, 2010).

Lewis, Simon, "The 'Partisan Republic': Colonial myths and memory wars in Belarus," in Julie Fedor, Markku Kangaspuro, Jussi Lassila, Tatiana Zhurhenko, eds., *War and Memory in Russia, Ukraine and Belarus* (London: Palgrave Macmillan, 2017), 371–95.

Lieven, Anatol, *Russia and Ukraine: A fraternal rivalry* (Washington, DC: United States Institute of Peace Press, 1999).

Lieven, Dominic, *Nicholas II: Emperor of All the Russias* (London: Pimlico, 1993).

——, *Empire: The Russian Empire and its rivals* (London: John Murray, 2000).

——, *Towards the Flame: Empire, war and the end of Tsarist Russia* (Harmondsworth: Penguin, 2015).

Lossky, Vladimir, *In the Image and Likeness of God*, John H. Erickson and Thomas E. Bird, eds. (Crestwood, NY: St Vladimir's Seminary Press, 1974).

——, *The Mystical Theology of the Eastern Church* (Crestwood, NY: St Vladimir's Seminary Press, 1976).

Louth, Andrew, "The place of theosis in Orthodox theology," in Michael J. Christensen and Jeffrey A. Wittung, eds., *Partakers of the Divine Nature: The history and development of deification in the Christian traditions* (Grand Rapids, MI: Baker Academic, 2007), 23–31.

——, *Modern Orthodox Theologians: From the Philokalia to the present* (Downers Grove, IL: IVP Academic, 2015).

Lyandres, Semion, "Progressive Bloc politics on the eve of the Revolution: Revisiting P. N. Miliukov's 'Stupidity or Treason' Speech of November 1, 1916," *Russian History* 31 (2004): 447–64.

——, *Fall of Tsarism: Untold stories of the February 1917 Revolution* (Oxford: Oxford University Press, 2013).

Mack, Glen, and Coleman Carter, Joseph, eds., *Crimean Chersonesos: City, chora, museum and environs* (Austin, TX: Institute of Classical Archaeology of The University of Texas, 2003).

Mack, John, "Nicholas II and the 'Rescript for Peace' of 1898: Apostle of peace or shrewd politician?" *Russian History* 31 (2004): 83–103.

Magoulias, Harry J., *Byzantine Christianity: Emperor, Church, and the West* (Chicago: Rand McNally and Co., 1970).

Marples, David, "History, memory and the Second World War in Belarus," *Australian Journal of Politics and History* 58 (2012): 437–48.

——, *Belarus: A denationalized country* (London: Routledge, 2012).

Martin, Janet, *Medieval Russia, 980–1584*, 2nd ed. (Cambridge: Cambridge University Press, 2007).

Massie, Robert, *Nicholas and Alexandra* (New York: Atheneum, 1967).

Matich, Olga, *Petersburg/Petersburg: Novel and city, 1900–1921* (Madison, WI: University of Wisconsin Press, 2010).

McCool, Gerald A., *Nineteenth-century scholasticism: The search for a unitary method* (New York: Fordham University Press, 1977).

McGuckin, John, "The legacy of the 13th apostle: origins of the East Christian conceptions of Church and State relation," *St Vladimir's Theological Quarterly* 47. 3–4 (2003): 251–88.

McMeekin, Sean, *The Russian Origins of the First World War* (Cambridge, MA: Harvard University Press, 2011).

——, *The Russian Revolution: A new history* (London: Profile Books, 2021).

Melvin, Mungo, *Sevastopol's Wars: Crimea from Potemkin to Putin* (Oxford: Osprey, 2017).

Mendel, Arthur, "On interpreting the fate of Imperial Russia," in Theofanis George Stavrou, ed., *Russia under the Last Tsar* (Minneapolis, MN: University of Minnesota Press, 1969), 13–41.

Meyendorff, John, *A Study of Gregory Palamas*, trans. George Lawrence (Crestwood, NY: St Vladimir's Seminary Press, 1964).

——, *Byzantine Theology: Historical trends and doctrinal themes* (New York: Fordham University Press, 1979).

Mihailova, Natalya, "Russian, Serbian patriarchs sanctify monument to Nicholas II in Belgrade," *Pravmir*, November 17, 2014: http://www.pravmir.com/russian-serbian-patriarchs-sanctify-monument-nicholas-ii-belgrade/.

Millar, Lubov, *Grand Duchess Elizabeth of Russia: New Martyr of the Communist Yoke* (Richfield Springs, NY: Nikodemos Orthodox Publication Society, 1991).

Miller, Alexei, "The Russian Revolution of 1917: History, Memory, and Politics," *Russia in Global Affairs*, February 26, 2018: https://eng.globalaffairs.ru/articles/the-russian-revolution-of-1917-history-memory-and-politics/.

Miller, David J. D., and Sarris, Peter, eds., *The Novels of Justinian: A complete annotated English translation* (Cambridge: Cambridge University Press, 2018).

Miner, Steven Merritt, *Stalin's Holy War: Religion, nationalism, and alliance politics, 1941–1945* (Chapel Hill, NC: University of North Carolina Press, 2003).

Mochul'skii, K. V., *Vladimir Solov'ev* (Paris: YMCA Press, 1951).

Morgan, Christopher, and Orlova, Irina, *Saving the Tsars' Palaces* (New York: Polperro Heritage, 2005).

Morson, Gary Saul, "Suicide of the Liberals," *First Things*, October, 2020: https://www.firstthings.com/article/2020/10/suicide-of-the-liberals.

Mossolov, A. A., *At the Court of the Last Tsar: Being the memoirs of A. A. Mossolov, head of the court chancellery, 1900–1916*, trans. E. W. Dickes (London: Methuen & Co. 1935).

Nikolai Ross, *Gibel' tsarskoi sem'i: Materialy sledstviia po delu ob ubiistve Tsarkoi sem'i (avgust 1918–fevral' 1920)* (Frankfurt am Main: Possev, 1987).

O'Donovan, Oliver, *The Desire of the Nations: Rediscovering the roots of political theology* (Cambridge: Cambridge University Press, 1996).

——, *Ways of Judgement* (Grand Rapids, MI: Eerdmans, 2008).

Obolensky, Dmitri, *The Byzantine Commonwealth: Eastern Europe, 500–1453* (London: Weidenfeld and Nicholson, 1971).

Oldenburg, S. S., *The Last Tsar: Nicholas II, his reign and his Russia*, 4 vols. (Gulf Breeze, FL: Academic International Press, 1975–1978).

Ostrogorsky, George, *History of the Byzantine State*, rev. ed. (New Brunswick, NJ: Rutgers University Press, 1969).

Ouspensky, Leonid, *The Theology of the Icon*, trans. Anthony Gythiel, 2 vols. (Crestwood, NY: St Vladimir's Seminary Press, 1992).

Perabo, Betsy C., *Russian Orthodoxy and the Russo-Japanese War* (London: Bloomsbury, 2017).

——, "Russia's Unfinished Symphony of Church and State," *Political Theology Network*, July 2, 2018: https://politicaltheology.com/russias-unfinished-symphony-of-church-and-state/.

Petro, Nicolai, "The Gospel According to Poroshenko: Politics, Religion, and the New Church of Ukraine," *Yale Journal of International Affairs*, April 4, 2019: https://www.yalejournal.org/publications/the-gospel-according-to-poroshenko-politics-religion-and-the-new-church-of-ukraine.

——, "The Russian Orthodox Church," in Andrei Tsygankov, ed., *The Routledge Handbook of Russian Foreign Policy* (London: Routledge, 2018).

Pipes, Richard, *Russia under the Old Regime*, 2nd ed. (Harmondsworth: Penguin Books, 1995).

——, *The Russian Revolution* (New York: Vintage Books, 1991).

Plokhy, Serhii, *The Cossack Myth: History and nationhood in the age of empires* (Cambridge: Cambridge University Press, 2012).

——, *The Last Empire: The final days of the Soviet Union* (London: One World, 2015).

——, *Yalta: The Price of Peace* (New York: Viking, 2010).

Pomerantsev, Peter, *Nothing is True but Everything is Possible* (New York: Public Affairs, 2015).

Porter, Tom, "Thousands gather for rival pro-Ukrainian and pro-Russian rallies in Crimea," *International Business Times*, March 9, 2014: http://www.ibtimes.co.uk/thousands-gather-rival-pro-ukrainian-pro-russian-rallies-1439538.

Pospielovsky, Dmitry, *The Russian Church Under the Soviet Regime, 1917–1982*, 2 vols. (Crestwood, NY: St Vladimir's Seminary Press, 1984).

Price, Richard, "The canonization of Serafim of Sarov: piety, prophecy and politics in late imperial Russia," in Andrew Louth, ed., *Studies in Church History*, vol. 47: *Saints and Sanctity* (Cambridge: Cambridge University Press, 2011), 346–64.

Proffer, Carl, and Proffer, Ellendea, eds., *The Silver Age of Russian Culture: An anthology* (Ann Arbor, MI: Ardis, 1971)

Radzinsky, Edvard, *The Last Tsar: The Life and Death of Nicholas II*, trans. Marian Schwartz (New York: Anchor Books, 1993).

Rappaport, Helen, *The Last Days of the Romanovs: Tragedy at Ekaterinburg* (London: St Martin's, 2008).

——, *The Romanov Sisters: The lost lives of the daughters of Nicholas and Alexandra* (London: St Martin's, 2014).

Romanovsky-Krassinsky, HSH Princess, *Dancing in Petersburg: The memoirs of Kschessinska*, trans. Arnold Haskell (London: Victor Gollanz, 1960).

Ruble, Blair A., *Leningrad: Shaping a Soviet City* (Berkeley, CA: University of California Press, 1990).

Sakwa, Richard, *Frontline Ukraine: Crisis in the borderlands* (London: I. B. Tauris, 2015).

Sanborn, Joshua A., *Imperial Apocalypse: The Great War and the destruction of the Russian Empire* (Oxford: Oxford University Press, 2014).

Sarris, Peter, *Empires of Faith: The fall of Rome to the rise of Islam* (Oxford: Oxford University Press, 2011).

Sasse, Gwendolyn, *The Crimea Question: Identity, transition, conflict* (Cambridge, MA: Harvard University Press, 2007).

Savchenko, Andrew, *Belarus: A perpetual borderland* (Leiden: Brill, 2009).

Schindler, David, "What is liberalism?" *New Polity: A journal of post-liberal thought* 1:1 (May, 2020): https://newpolity.com/blog/what-is-liberalism.

Schmemann, Alexander, *Church, World, Mission: Reflections on Orthodoxy in the West* (Crestwood, NY: St Vladimir's Seminary Press, 1979).

——, *For the Life of the World: Sacraments and Orthodoxy* (Crestwood, NY: St Vladimir's Seminary Press, 1973).

——, *The Historical Road of Eastern Orthodoxy* (New York: Holt, Rinehart and Winston, 1963).

Schulz, Hans-Joachim, *The Byzantine Liturgy: Symbolic structure and faith expression*, trans. Matthew J. O'Connell (New York: Pueblo, 1986).

Service, Robert, *Last of the Tsars: Nicholas II and the Russian Revolution* (London: Macmillan, 2017).

——, *Lenin: A biography* (London: Pan Books, 2000).

——, *Penguin Modern History of Russia: From tsarism to the twenty-first century*, 3rd ed. (Harmondsworth: Penguin Books, 2009).

Slater, Wendy, *The Many Deaths of Tsar Nicholas II: Relics, remains and the Romanovs* (London: Routledge, 2007).

Smith, Douglas, *Rasputin* (London: Macmillan, 2016).

Smith, S. A., *Russia in Revolution: An empire in crisis, 1890–1928* (Oxford: Oxford University Press, 2018).

Somov, Sergei, *Pravoslavnye Monastyri Belarusi* (Minsk : Chetyri Chetverti, 2003).

Sophia Kishkovsky, "In Russian Chill, Waiting Hours for Touch of the Holy," *New York Times*, November 23, 2011: https://www.nytimes.com/2011/11/24/world/europe/virgin-mary-belt-relic-draws-crowds-in-moscow.html.

Steinberg, Mark, *Fall of the Romanovs: Politics and personal dreams in a time of revolution* (New Haven, CT: Yale University Press, 1995).

Stone, Norman, *Eastern Front, 1914–1917* (Harmondsworth: Penguin, 1998).

Strickland, John, *The Making of Holy Russia: The Orthodox Church and Russian nationalism before the Revolution* (Jordanville, NY: Holy Trinity Publications, 2013).

Tikhon (Agrikov), Archimandrite, "A Sermon on a church candle," *Pravmir*, August 25, 2012: http://www.pravmir.com/a-sermon-on-a-church-candle/.

Valliere, Paul, *Modern Russian Theology: Bukharev, Soloviev, Bulgakov: Orthodox Theology in a New Key* (Grand Rapids, MI: Eerdmans, 2001).

Verner, Andrew M., *The Crisis of the Russian Autocracy: Nicholas II and the 1905 Revolution* (Princeton, NJ: Princeton University Press, 1990).

Waldron, Peter, "State Finances," in Dominic Lieven, ed., *Cambridge History of Russia*, vol. 2: *Imperial Russia (1689–1917)* (Cambridge: Cambridge University Press, 2008), 468–86.

Walicki, Andrei, *A History of Russian Thought: From the Enlightenment to Marxism*, trans. Hilda Andrews-Rusiecka (Stanford, CA: Stanford University Press, 1979).

Ware, Timothy (Kallistos), *The Orthodox Way*, rev. ed. (Crestwood, NY: St Vladimir's Seminary Press, 1995).

——, *The Orthodox Church*, rev. ed. (Harmondsworth: Penguin Books, 1997).

Warwick, Christopher, *Ella: Princess, Saint and Martyr* (London: Wiley, 2006).

Watson, Alexander, *Ring of Steel: Germany and Austria-Hungary at War, 1914–1918* (London: Allen Lane, 2014).

Williams, Rowan, *Sergii Bulgakov: Towards a Russian Political Theology* (Edinburgh: T&T Clark, 2001).

Wortman, Richard S., *Scenarios of Power: Myth and ceremony in Russian Monarchy from Peter the Great to the abdication of Nicholas II*, rev. ed. (Princeton, NJ: Princeton University Press, 2006).

——, *Russian Monarchy: Representation and rule* (Brighton, MA: Academic Studies Press, 2013).

Wybrew, Hugh, *The Orthodox Liturgy: The development of the Eucharistic Liturgy in the Byzantine rite* (Crestwood, NY: St Vladimir's Seminary Press, 1990).

Yusupov, Felix, prince, *Lost Splendour* (London: Jonathan Cape, 1953).

Zernov, Nicholas, *The Russians and Their Church*, 3rd ed. (Crestwood, NY: St Vladimir's Seminary Press, 1978).

Zwahlen, Regula M., "Sergii Bulgakov's Reinvention of Theocracy for a Democratic Age," *Journal of Orthodox Christian Studies* 3:2 (2020): 175–94.

Zygar, Mikhail, *All the Kremlin's Men: Inside the court of Vladimir Putin* (New York: Public Affairs, 2016).

INDEX

ABOUT THE AUTHOR

MATTHEW DAL SANTO is Professor of Dogmatics
(Church History) at St Patrick's Seminary and University,
Menlo Park, California. Educated at the Universities of
Sydney and Cambridge, he is a former Lightfoot Scholar
in Ecclesiastical History and former Fellow of Trinity
College, Cambridge. He has held research fellowships in
Russian history, politics, and religious culture at the Saxo
Institute, University of Copenhagen; the Center for the
Study of Statesmanship, Catholic University of Amer-
ica; and the Kennan Institute for Russian and Eastern
European Studies at the Woodrow Wilson International
Center for Scholars, Washington, D. C.

9 798892 801171